The
OXFORD

Primary School Thesaurus

The

OXFORD

Primary
School
Thesaurus

The OXFORD

Primary School Thesaurus

Compiled by
Alan Spooner

OXFORD UNIVERSITY PRESS

Oxford University Press, Walton Street, Oxford, OX2 6DP

Oxford New York
Athens Auckland Bangkok Bogotá Buenos Aires
Calcutta Cape Town Chennai Dar es Salaam Delhi Florence
Hong Kong Istanbul Karachi Kuala Lumpur Madrid
Melbourne Mexico City Mumbai Nairobi Paris
São Paulo Singapore Taipei Tokyo Toronto Warsaw

and associated companies in
Berlin Ibadan

Oxford is a trade mark of Oxford University Press

© Oxford University Press 1998
1 3 5 7 9 10 8 6 4 2

A CIP catalogue record for this book is available
from the British Library

ISBN 0 19 910428 X (educational edition)
ISBN 0 19 910429 8 (trade edition)

Typeset by Pentacor PLC, High Wycombe

Printed in Great Britain by Clays Ltd, St Ives plc

Preface for teachers and parents

The function of a thesaurus

The function of a thesaurus is to jog the memory about words we know but which don't spring to mind, and to introduce new words to us. In these ways it can help us avoid overuse of a narrow repertory of words, and to express ourselves with greater sophistication and precision. However, young thesaurus users should not be led to assume that unearthing unfamiliar words will necessarily make their writing 'better' than using familiar ones. It would be unfortunate if 'looking it up in the thesaurus' were regarded as a kind of verbal lucky-dip. If children are to develop a proper awareness of subtle distinctions of meaning and usage, their use of a thesaurus must be complementary to – not a substitute for – their sharing of language experience with mature users of English in real situations.

The features of this thesaurus

In this thesaurus headwords are arranged in a single alphabetical sequence. Each headword is followed by an example sentence illustrating how the headword might be used. When a headword has more than one meaning, the entry is divided into numbered senses with an example sentence for each sense (see **accident**). The example sentence is then followed by a list of synonyms arranged alphabetically (for example,

at **allegation** we have given the synonyms *accusation, charge,* and *claim*).

Where it seems useful to do so, we give a usage warning, either in the form of a brief note (e.g. under **mad**), or as a single word (e.g. *informal*) in italics and within brackets immediately before the word.

Where appropriate, an antonym – a word which is opposite in meaning to the headword – is given. If the antonym is relevant to a particular sense it is placed at the end of that numbered sense (e.g. at **broad** we have given the antonym *narrow* for sense 1 and the antonym *specific* for sense 2). If the antonym is relevant to all senses it is placed at the end of the entry (e.g. at **brave** we give the antonym *cowardly*).

Some entries include a boxed section of related words. These are words that belong to the same 'word family' as the headword. For example, at the entry **cup** we have given a list of related words that includes *beaker, glass, mug,* and *tumbler*. These are not synonyms of the headword, but they all have a common relationship to the word **cup**. These should provide useful material for word study and wider discussion about language.

Alan Spooner

Using this thesaurus ...

A thesaurus can help you to use language more interestingly and more clearly by reminding you of a variety of words you might use. In this thesaurus, you will find synonyms (words which are similar in meaning to the word you thought of); antonyms (words which mean the opposite); and useful lists of words that are related in other ways.

A thesaurus does not give you definitions of words. If you want a definition of a word, you will need to track it down in a dictionary such as *The Oxford Primary School Dictionary*.

Remember that although synonyms are similar to each other in meaning, it is very rare that two words are used in exactly the same way. For example, beautiful, pretty, and good-looking are similar in meaning, and we might talk about *beautiful weather*, or *pretty flowers*, or *good-looking men*; but we don't talk about *pretty weather* or *good-looking flowers*. So, when we come across a new word, we need to find out how people use it.

In this thesaurus you will find ...

Parts of speech
After the headword, we show the job that the word usually does when you use it in a sentence. This job is called the part of speech. The important parts of speech are: *noun, verb, adjective, adverb, pronoun, preposition, conjunction.*

Headwords
These are the words you look up. They are printed in bold type so that you can find them easily.

Related words
Words that are not necessarily synonyms but are related to the headword in other ways are enclosed in a box.

Cross-references
Sometimes we suggest that you look up another entry to find more useful words. This is called a cross-reference.

brass *noun*
FOR OTHER METALS, SEE **metal**

MUSICAL INSTRUMENTS OFTEN MADE OF BRASS ARE: bugle, cornet, euphonium, flugelhorn, horn, trombone, trumpet, tuba

bravery *noun*
Everyone praised the firemen's bravery boldness, courage, determination, fearlessness, gallantry, grit, [*informal*] guts, heroism, pluck, valour
AN OPPOSITE IS cowardice

break *verb*
1 *Don't lend him anything, because he's bound to break it* burst, chip, crack, crumple, crush, damage, demolish, destroy, fracture, ruin, shatter, smash, snap, splinter, split, squash, wreck
2 *If you break the law, you can expect to be punished* disobey, disregard, violate
3 *Our relay team broke the school record* beat, better, do better than, exceed, go beyond, surpass
to break down *The car broke down on the motorway* fail, go wrong, stop working

Opposites
If the word you look up has a useful opposite (or antonym), it appears after the synonyms.

Warnings
When you need to be specially careful how you use a word (for example, because it is informal) we put a warning in brackets just before the word or sentence concerned.

Numbers
When a headword can be used in more than one way, we number the different uses.

Example sentences
Sentences showing how you might use a word are printed in italics.

Synonyms
These are words which are similar in meaning to the headword.

Phrases
If a headword is often used in a phrase, the phrase appears at the end of the entry, with an example sentence and a list of synonyms, just as for the headword itself.

Aa

abandon verb
1 *He abandoned his family and went off to Australia.* desert, forsake, leave.
2 *The sailors abandoned the damaged ship.* evacuate, quit, withdraw from.
3 *The weather was so bad that we abandoned our plan.* abort, cancel, discard, drop, give up, scrap.

abbreviate verb
The word 'Doctor' can be abbreviated to 'Dr'. cut, reduce, shorten.

abide verb
I can't abide cigarette smoke. bear, endure, put up with, stand, tolerate.
to abide by *You must abide by the rules.* accept, carry out, follow, keep to, obey, stick to, submit to.

ability noun
She has the ability to do well. aptitude, brains, competence, expertise, gift, intelligence, potential, power, skill, talent.

ablaze adjective
The whole house was ablaze before the firemen arrived. alight, blazing, burning, on fire.

able adjective
1 *She's an able tennis player.* accomplished, capable, clever, competent, effective, expert, gifted, skilful, skilled, talented, useful.
AN OPPOSITE IS incompetent.
2 *I'm able to stay until teatime.* allowed, free, permitted, ready, willing.
AN OPPOSITE IS unable.

abnormal adjective
We had abnormal weather last winter. exceptional, extraordinary, freak, funny, odd, peculiar, queer, strange, uncharacteristic, unexpected, unnatural, unusual, weird.
AN OPPOSITE IS normal.

abolish verb
Some people would like to abolish homework. [*informal*] do away with, eliminate, end, get rid of, put an end to.
AN OPPOSITE IS create.

abominable adjective
Everyone was shocked by the abominable crime. appalling, awful, beastly, brutal, contemptible, cruel, despicable, detestable, disgusting, dreadful, foul, hateful, horrible, horrifying, loathsome, repulsive, revolting, terrible, vile.

aboriginal adjective
The aboriginal inhabitants were badly treated by the settlers. earliest, first, native, original.

abort verb
The control tower told the pilot to abort take-off. abandon, call off, cancel, halt, stop, terminate.

abound verb
Fish abound in this river. be plentiful, teem.

about preposition
1 *We heard a story about space travellers.* concerning, connected with, involving.
2 *There are about two hundred children in the school.* approximately, around, close to, roughly.

abrasive adjective
Don't use anything abrasive when you clean the bath. gritty, harsh, rough, scratchy, sharp.

abroad adverb
I enjoy travelling abroad. in foreign countries, overseas.

abrupt adjective
1 *I was surprised when the film came to an abrupt end.* hasty, hurried, quick, sudden, unexpected.
AN OPPOSITE IS gradual.
2 *We didn't like his abrupt manner.* blunt, gruff, impolite, rude, tactless, unfriendly.
AN OPPOSITE IS polite.

absent *adjective*
Why were you absent from school?
away, missing.
Being absent from school without a
good reason is **playing truant**.
AN OPPOSITE IS present.

absent-minded *adjective*
*He's so absent-minded that he forgot his
bus money twice last week.* careless,
forgetful, inattentive, vague.
AN OPPOSITE IS alert.

absolute *adjective*
1 *The teacher asked for absolute silence.*
complete, perfect, total, utter.
2 *The king had absolute power.*
dictatorial, tyrannical, unrestricted.

absorb *verb*
A sponge absorbs water. fill up with,
hold, retain, soak up, suck up, take in.

absorbed *adjective*
to be absorbed in something *I was
absorbed in my book.* be engrossed in,
be interested in, be preoccupied with,
concentrate on, think about.

absorbent *adjective*
Absorbent substances soak up liquids.
porous, spongy.

abstract *adjective*
*I prefer dealing with practical things
rather than abstract ideas.* academic,
intellectual, philosophical, theoretical.
AN OPPOSITE IS concrete.

absurd *adjective*
1 *I can't believe his absurd explanation.*
illogical, irrational, nonsensical,
senseless, silly, stupid, unreasonable.
AN OPPOSITE IS sensible.
2 *That dress makes her look absurd.*
laughable, ludicrous, ridiculous, silly.
AN OPPOSITE IS serious.

abundant *adjective*
*The birds have an abundant supply of
food in the summer.* ample, generous,
lavish, liberal, plentiful, profuse.
AN OPPOSITE IS meagre.

abuse *verb*
1 *If you don't abuse your possessions,
they will last a lot longer.* damage,
harm, misuse, spoil, treat roughly.

2 *The referee was abused by players
from both teams.* be rude to, [*informal*]
call someone names, insult, swear at.
3 *People who abuse animals should be
prosecuted.* hurt, ill-treat, injure,
torment.

abuse *noun*
They yelled abuse at us. curses, insults,
obscenities, swear words.

abusive *adjective*
*We were upset by their abusive
language.* cruel, hostile, hurtful,
impolite, insulting, obscene, offensive,
rude, unpleasant.
AN OPPOSITE IS polite.

abysmal *adjective*
[*informal*] *The film was so abysmal
that I fell asleep.* appalling, awful, bad,
dreadful, terrible, worthless.

abyss *noun*
*The explorers stared down into the dark
abyss.* chasm, crater, gap, hole,
opening, pit, rift.

academic *adjective*
1 *She's a very academic student.*
[*informal*] brainy, clever, intelligent,
scholarly, studious.
2 *Philosophy is a very academic
subject.* abstract, intellectual,
theoretical.
AN OPPOSITE IS practical.

accelerate *verb*
The bus accelerated. go faster, increase
speed, pick up speed, speed up.

accent *noun*
1 *She speaks English with a Welsh
accent.* intonation, pronunciation, tone.
2 *She told me to play the first note of
each bar with a strong accent.* beat,
emphasis, pulse, rhythm, stress.

accept *verb*
1 *I accepted her gift.* receive, take,
welcome.
AN OPPOSITE IS reject.
2 *The club accepted my application for
membership.* agree to, approve,
consent to.
AN OPPOSITE IS reject.
3 *She accepts that she is guilty.*
acknowledge, admit, agree, confess,
recognize.

AN OPPOSITE IS deny.
4 *You have to accept the referee's decision.* put up with, resign yourself to, tolerate.

acceptable *adjective*
1 *I think money is always an acceptable birthday present.* appreciated, pleasant, pleasing, useful, welcome, worthwhile.
2 *Our teacher complained that our behaviour was not acceptable.* adequate, appropriate, passable, permissible, satisfactory, suitable, tolerable.
AN OPPOSITE IS unacceptable.

accepted *adjective*
It's accepted that she is our best player. acknowledged, agreed, recognized, undeniable, unquestioned.

access *noun*
The access to the playing field is through the iron gates. approach, entrance, way in.

access *verb*
She showed us how to access the data we stored in the computer. get at, make use of, obtain, reach.

accessible *adjective*
Make sure the first aid box is accessible. at hand, available, convenient, handy, within reach.
AN OPPOSITE IS inaccessible.

accident *noun*
1 *Several people were injured in the accident.* calamity, catastrophe, collision, crash, disaster, misfortune, mishap.
An accident involving a lot of vehicles is a *pile-up*.
A railway accident may involve a *derailment*.
2 *I met her in town by accident.* chance, coincidence, fluke, luck.

accidental *adjective*
1 *The damage may have been accidental.* unfortunate, unintentional, unlucky.
2 *He made an accidental discovery.* casual, fortunate, lucky, unexpected, unforeseen, unplanned.
AN OPPOSITE IS deliberate.

acclaim *verb*
The crowd acclaimed the arrival of the famous actor. celebrate, honour, praise.

accommodate *verb*
1 *The hostel can accommodate thirty guests.* cater for, hold, house, provide for, put up, take in.
2 *If you need anything, we'll try to accommodate you.* aid, assist, help, oblige, please, serve, supply.

accommodation *noun*
After the fire, the family was given temporary accommodation. housing, lodgings, shelter.

KINDS OF HOLIDAY
ACCOMMODATION: apartment, bed and breakfast, boarding house, guest house, hotel, motel, self-catering, timeshare, youth hostel.

ACCOMMODATION FOR STUDENTS: [*informal*] digs, hall of residence.

ACCOMMODATION FOR THE ARMED SERVICES: barracks, billet, married quarters.

PLACES WHERE PEOPLE NORMALLY LIVE: bedsitter, flat, house.
SEE ALSO **house**.

accompany *verb*
A friend accompanied me. escort, go with, tag along with, travel with.

accomplish *verb*
We accomplished the task she gave us. achieve, carry out, complete, do successfully, execute, finish, perform, succeed in.

accomplished *adjective*
My sister is an accomplished pianist. expert, gifted, skilful, skilled, talented.

accomplishment *noun*
Playing the piano is one of her many accomplishments. ability, gift, skill, talent.

accord *noun*
of your own accord *Mum was amazed when I washed up of my own accord.* spontaneously, unasked, voluntarily, willingly.

accordingly *adverb*
1 *It rained, and accordingly sports day was postponed.* consequently, so, therefore.
2 *You're the leader of the group, and you must behave accordingly.* appropriately, suitably.

account *noun*
1 *I wrote an account of my trip.* chronicle, description, diary, history, log, narrative, record, report, story.
2 *Money is of little account compared with your health.* concern, consideration, importance, interest, significance, use, value.

account *verb*
to account for *Can you account for your odd behaviour?* explain, give reasons for, justify, make excuses for.

accumulate *verb*
1 *Why do I accumulate so much rubbish?* collect, gather, heap up, hoard, pile up, store up.
AN OPPOSITE IS scatter.
2 *Your savings accumulate if you put a regular amount in the bank.* build up, grow, increase, multiply.
AN OPPOSITE IS decrease.

accumulation *noun*
There's an accumulation of odds and ends in my cupboard. collection, heap, hoard, mass, pile.

accurate *adjective*
1 *We took accurate measurements of the room.* careful, correct, exact, meticulous, minute, precise.
2 *I don't think that's an accurate description of him.* factual, faithful, perfect, reliable, true, truthful.
AN OPPOSITE IS inaccurate.

accusation *noun*
She denied the accusation completely. allegation, charge, complaint.

accuse *verb*
I think it was unfair to accuse her. charge, inform against, make allegations against.
AN OPPOSITE IS defend.

accustomed *adjective*
accustomed to *We are not accustomed to this hot weather.* acclimatized to, familiar with, used to.

ache *noun*
The ache in my tooth got worse. discomfort, pain, soreness, throbbing.
SEE ALSO **pain**.

ache *verb*
My legs ached from the previous day's exercise. be painful, hurt, throb.

achieve *verb*
1 *Will she ever achieve her ambition to play at Wimbledon?* accomplish, attain, carry out, fulfil, succeed in.
2 *The new group achieved success with their first CD.* acquire, earn, get, score, win.

achievement *noun*
I congratulate you on your achievement. accomplishment, attainment, success, triumph.

aching *adjective*
I slipped off my shoes to ease my aching feet. hurting, inflamed, painful, sore, tender, throbbing.

acid *adjective*
Lemons have an acid taste. bitter, sharp, sour, tart.

acknowledge *verb*
1 *I acknowledge that you are right.* accept, admit, agree, confess, grant.
AN OPPOSITE IS deny.
2 *Please acknowledge my letter.* answer, reply to, respond to.

acquaint *verb*
to acquaint someone with *Please acquaint me with the facts.* advise of, inform of, reveal, tell about.
to be acquainted with *Are you acquainted with the area?* be familiar with, know.

acquire *verb*
Where can I acquire a copy of this book? get, get hold of, obtain.
To acquire something by paying for it is to **buy** or **purchase** it.

acquisition *noun*
His latest acquisition is a motorbike. possession, property, purchase.

acquit *verb*
Both defendants were acquitted by the magistrate. clear, declare innocent, discharge, dismiss, free, let off, release, set free.
AN OPPOSITE IS convict *verb*.

across *preposition*
My friend lives across the river. beyond, on the other side of, over.

act *noun*
1 Rescuing the baby from the burning house was a brave act. action, deed, exploit, feat, operation.
2 The best act at the circus involved three clowns. item, performance, sketch, turn.
to put on an act Don't take any notice of him: he's only putting on an act. fool about, pose, pretend, show off.

act *verb*
1 We must act straight away. do something, take action.
2 Give the medicine time to act. function, have an effect, take effect, work.
3 He acted like a baby. behave, carry on.
4 I acted the part of a shepherd in our play. appear as, perform, play, portray, represent.

action *noun*
1 The driver's prompt action prevented an accident. act, deed, effort, feat, measure.
2 The film was packed with action. activity, drama, energy, excitement, liveliness, movement, vigour, vitality.
3 His father was killed in action in the Second World War. battle, fighting.
4 The action of our clock needs repairing. mechanism, works.

activate *verb*
Who activated the fire alarm? set off, start, switch on, trigger off.

active *adjective*
1 Although he's quite old, he's still very active. busy, dynamic, energetic, enterprising, enthusiastic, lively, vigorous.
2 I'm an active supporter of our club. committed, dedicated, devoted, enthusiastic, hard-working, industrious, involved, zealous.
AN OPPOSITE IS inactive.

activity *noun*
1 The market place was full of activity. action, animation, excitement, life, liveliness, movement.
2 Gardening is Dad's favourite spare-time activity. hobby, interest, job, occupation, pastime, pursuit, task.

actor, actress *nouns*
A company of actors performed a play in the school hall. performer, player.
The most important actor in a play is the **lead** or the **star**.
The other actors are the **supporting actors**.
All the actors in a play are the **cast** or the **company**.
FOR OTHER PERFORMERS, SEE **entertainer**.

actual *adjective*
Those were the Prime Minister's actual words. authentic, factual, genuine, real, true.
AN OPPOSITE IS imaginary.

actually *adverb*
Is this where it actually happened? certainly, definitely, genuinely, in fact, really, truly.

acute *adjective*
1 I had an acute pain. intense, piercing, severe, sharp, sudden, violent.
AN OPPOSITE IS slight.
2 The explorers suffered from an acute shortage of food. crucial, important, serious, urgent, vital.
AN OPPOSITE IS unimportant.
3 She's too acute to be deceived by that trick. alert, clever, intelligent, keen, observant, perceptive, quick, sharp, shrewd, smart.
AN OPPOSITE IS stupid.

adapt *verb*
1 *Dad adapted the car so that we can safely put the dogs in the back.* alter, change, convert, modify, reorganize, transform.
2 *They adapted to life in the country very quickly.* acclimatize, become accustomed, adjust.

adaptable *adjective*
He's an adaptable player who plays well in any position. cooperative, flexible, versatile.

add *verb*
to add to 1 *I have some things to add to what you've already got.* attach to, combine with, integrate with, join on to, put together with, tack on to, unite with.
2 *I think mint sauce adds to the flavour of lamb.* enhance, improve, increase.
to add up 1 *He added up the figures.* calculate, count up, find the sum of, find the total of, reckon up, work out.
2 [*informal*] *Her story doesn't add up.* be convincing, make sense.
to add up to *What do the figures add up to?* amount to, come to, make, total.

added *adjective*
The heavy rain was an added nuisance on our long journey. additional, extra, further.

addiction *noun*
It is dangerous when smoking becomes an addiction. compulsion, craving, habit, obsession.
An addiction to alcohol is ***alcoholism***.

additional *adjective*
They have opened additional facilities at the leisure centre. added, extra, further, increased, more, new, supplementary.

address *noun*
1 *I wrote the address on the envelope.* directions.
2 *The Queen gave a televised address to the nation.* speech, talk.
An address in church is a ***sermon***.

address *verb*
The head addressed us in assembly. lecture to, make a speech to, speak to, talk to.

adequate *adjective*
1 *A sandwich will be adequate, thank you.* ample, enough, sufficient.
2 *Your work is adequate, but I'm sure you can do better.* acceptable, competent, passable, respectable, satisfactory, tolerable.
AN OPPOSITE IS inadequate.

adhere *verb*
I tried to make the stamp adhere to the envelope. cling, stick.

adhesive *noun*

SUBSTANCES USED TO STICK THINGS: adhesive tape, cement, glue, gum, paste, [*trademark*] Sellotape, wallpaper paste.

adjacent *adjective*
adjacent to *They have a house adjacent to the park.* beside, neighbouring, next to.

adjourn *verb*
We adjourned the meeting for a cup of tea. break off, interrupt, stop, suspend.

adjust *verb*
1 *I tried to adjust the TV picture.* correct, improve, modify, put right, tune.
2 *I adjusted the central heating thermostat.* alter, change, regulate, set, vary.
to adjust to *At first it was hard to adjust to my new school.* adapt to, become acclimatized to, get accustomed to, get used to, settle in to.

ad lib *adjective*
Instead of making a proper speech, he made a lot of ad lib remarks. impromptu, improvised, made-up, spontaneous, unprepared, unrehearsed.

ad lib *verb*
I had to ad lib when I lost my notes. improvise, make it up.

administer *verb*
1 *The head administers the school.*
administrate, control, direct, govern,
lead, look after, manage, organize,
preside over, run, supervise.
2 *A nurse administered vitamin pills to
all the children.* deal out, dispense,
distribute, give out, hand out.

admirable *adjective*
She has many admirable qualities.
commendable, excellent, fine, good,
likeable, lovable, praiseworthy, worthy.
AN OPPOSITE IS contemptible.

admire *verb*
1 *I admire her skill.* applaud, approve
of, esteem, have a high opinion of, look
up to, respect, think highly of, value.
AN OPPOSITE IS despise.
2 *We stopped to admire the view.*
appreciate, be delighted by, enjoy.

admission *noun*
1 *We were surprised by his admission
that he was guilty.* acceptance,
acknowledgement, confession,
declaration.
AN OPPOSITE IS denial.
2 *Admission to the castle is by ticket
only.* access, admittance, entrance,
entry.

admit *verb*
1 *The hospital admitted all the victims
of the accident.* accept, allow in, let in,
receive, take in.
AN OPPOSITE IS exclude.
2 *He admits that he is guilty.* accept,
acknowledge, agree, confess, grant,
own up.
AN OPPOSITE IS deny.

adolescence *noun*
*She spent her childhood and
adolescence in France.* puberty, your
teens, your youth.

adopt *verb*
1 *We adopted a stray cat.* befriend,
foster, take in, [*informal*] take under
your wing.
2 *I adopted her suggestion.* accept,
choose, embrace, follow, take up.

adorable *adjective*
I have four adorable Siamese cats.
attractive, charming, darling, dear,
delightful, lovable, lovely, sweet.

adore *verb*
1 *She adores her grandad.* idolize, love,
worship.
2 [*informal*] *I adore toffee!* enjoy, like,
love.
AN OPPOSITE IS hate.

adorn *verb*
*Before the party we adorned the room
with streamers and balloons.* decorate,
festoon.

adult *adjective*
An adult tiger needs a large territory.
full-size, fully grown, grown-up,
mature.
AN OPPOSITE IS immature.

advance *noun*
1 *You can't stop the advance of science.*
development, evolution, growth,
progress.
2 *Our new computer is a great advance
on the old one.* improvement.

advance *verb*
1 *As the army advanced, the enemy
fled.* approach, come near, forge ahead,
gain ground, go forward, make
headway, make progress, move
forward, press on, proceed, progress.
AN OPPOSITE IS retreat.
2 *Computer technology has advanced
in our lifetime.* develop, evolve, grow,
improve.

advanced *adjective*
1 *The new car has advanced safety
features.* the latest, modern,
sophisticated, up to date.
AN OPPOSITE IS obsolete.
2 *Some people are shocked by his
advanced ideas.* forward-looking,
innovative, new, novel, progressive,
revolutionary, [*informal*] trendy,
unconventional.
AN OPPOSITE IS old-fashioned.
3 *She is advanced for her age.* grown-
up, mature, well-developed.
AN OPPOSITE IS backward.
4 *This maths is too advanced for me.*
complex, complicated, difficult, hard.
AN OPPOSITE IS elementary.

advantage *noun*
We had the advantage of the wind behind us. aid, assistance, benefit, help, use.
to take advantage of It was unfair to take advantage of him while he was ill. exploit, impose on, make use of, use.

adventure *noun*
1 They set out on a dangerous adventure. enterprise, exploit, venture.
2 She travelled the world in search of adventure. danger, excitement, risk, thrills.

adventurous *adjective*
1 The adventurous explorers took many risks. bold, daring, enterprising, heroic, intrepid.
2 She gets a great thrill out of her adventurous voyages. challenging, dangerous, eventful, exciting, perilous, risky.
AN OPPOSITE IS unadventurous.

adverse *adjective*
Unfortunately, the medicine had an adverse effect on me. contrary, harmful, negative, unfavourable.
AN OPPOSITE IS favourable.

advertise *verb*
We made posters to advertise our concert. announce, make known, [informal] plug, promote, publicize.

advertisement *noun*

ADVERTISEMENTS IN GENERAL: advertising, promotion, publicity.

AN ADVERTISEMENT ON TELEVISION: [informal] advert, [informal] break, commercial.

AN ADVERTISEMENT ON A HOARDING OR NOTICEBOARD: bill, notice, placard, poster.

AN ADVERTISEMENT IN A NEWSPAPER: classified advertisement, [informal] small ad.

AN ADVERTISEMENT THROUGH THE POST OR GIVEN OUT IN THE STREET: circular, handout, leaflet.

advice *noun*
I was glad to have his advice. counsel, guidance, help, opinion, recommendation, suggestion, tip.

advisable *adjective*
The doctor said it would be advisable to stay in bed. desirable, prudent, sensible, wise.
AN OPPOSITE IS unwise.

advise *verb*
1 What did the doctor advise? advocate, prescribe, recommend, suggest.
2 He advised me to rest. counsel, encourage, urge.

aeroplane *noun* SEE **aircraft**

affair *noun*
1 The crash was a mysterious affair. event, happening, incident, occasion, occurrence, thing.
2 She's been having an affair with an older man. love affair, relationship, romance.
affairs Dad won't discuss his business affairs with strangers. business, concerns, matters, questions, subjects, topics.

affect *verb*
1 Acid rain affects trees. act on, attack, harm, have an effect or impact on.
2 The bad news affected us deeply. concern, disturb, grieve, trouble, upset, worry.

affected *adjective*
He gave an affected smile. assumed, false, insincere, pretended, unnatural.
AN OPPOSITE IS genuine.

affection *noun*
He felt great affection for his sister. attachment, devotion, fondness, friendliness, love, tenderness.
AN OPPOSITE IS hatred.

affectionate *adjective*
She gave him an affectionate kiss. caring, devoted, fond, loving, tender.
AN OPPOSITE IS unfriendly.

afflict *verb*
He was afflicted with a skin disease. bother, distress, harass, plague, torment, trouble.

affluent *adjective*
 The owners of the big house must be
 very affluent. prosperous, rich,
 successful, wealthy, well off.
 AN OPPOSITE IS poor.

afford *verb*
 Can you afford £10 for the school trip?
 manage, pay, spare.

afloat *adjective*
 I don't enjoy life afloat because I get
 seasick. aboard ship, at sea, on board
 ship.

afraid *adjective*
 He didn't let them see that he was
 afraid. alarmed, anxious,
 apprehensive, cowardly, fearful,
 frightened, intimidated, nervous,
 scared, terrified, timid.
 AN OPPOSITE IS brave.
 to be afraid I'm afraid of huge spiders.
 dread, fear, worry about.

age *noun*
 We are studying what life was like in
 the Victorian age. days, epoch, era,
 period, time.

age *verb*
 1 He's aged since we last saw him.
 become older, look older.
 2 Wine needs to age. develop, mature.

agenda *noun*
 What is on your agenda for today? list,
 plan, programme, schedule, timetable.

aggravate *verb*
 Some people think that the informal
 use of aggravate to mean annoy is
 incorrect
 1 The medicine only aggravated the
 pain. add to, increase, intensify, make
 more serious, make worse, worsen.
 AN OPPOSITE IS lessen.
 2 [informal] Their continual teasing
 aggravated us. annoy, bother, irritate,
 provoke, trouble, vex.

aggravating *adjective*
 [informal] I wish they'd stop making
 that aggravating noise. annoying,
 irritating, maddening, tiresome,
 trying, vexing.

aggression *noun*
 The aggression shown by our opponents
 was completely unjustified.
 aggressiveness, bullying, hostility,
 provocation, violence.

aggressive *adjective*
 We weren't frightened by their
 aggressive behaviour. attacking,
 bullying, hostile, provocative,
 quarrelsome, violent, warlike.
 AN OPPOSITE IS friendly.

agile *adjective*
 Mountain goats are extremely agile.
 acrobatic, lively, mobile, nimble, quick-
 moving, sprightly, supple, swift.
 AN OPPOSITE IS clumsy or slow.

agitate *verb*
 1 The thunderstorm agitated the
 animals. alarm, disturb, trouble,
 unsettle, upset, worry.
 AN OPPOSITE IS calm.
 2 We agitated for a proper road crossing
 outside the school. campaign, make a
 fuss, press, push.
 3 The wind agitated the surface of the
 water. beat, churn, ruffle, stir.

agitated *adjective*
 He was very agitated before the exam
 started. anxious, disturbed, edgy,
 excited, fidgety, flustered, nervous,
 restless, ruffled, unsettled, upset.
 AN OPPOSITE IS calm.

agitator *noun*
 A person who makes a fuss to get good
 things done is a **campaigner**.
 A person who makes a fuss to cause
 trouble is a **troublemaker**.

agonizing *adjective*
 I had agonizing toothache. painful,
 severe.

agony *noun*
 I could hardly bear the agony. anguish,
 distress, pain, suffering, torment,
 torture.

agree *verb*
 1 I'm glad that we agree. be united,
 think the same.
 AN OPPOSITE IS disagree.
 2 I agree that you are right. accept,
 acknowledge, admit, allow, grant.
 AN OPPOSITE IS disagree.

3 *I agree to pay my share.* be willing, consent, promise.
AN OPPOSITE IS refuse.
to agree on *We agreed on a price.* choose, decide, establish, fix, settle.
to agree with 1 *I don't agree with capital punishment.* advocate, argue for, defend, support.
2 *Onions don't agree with me.* suit.

agreement *noun*
1 *There's a large measure of agreement between us.* conformity, consensus, consent, harmony, sympathy, unanimity, unity.
AN OPPOSITE IS disagreement.
2 *The two sides signed an agreement.* alliance, treaty.
An agreement to end fighting is an **armistice** or **truce**.
A business agreement is a **bargain**, **contract**, or **deal**.

aground *adjective*
The ship was aground. beached, marooned, stranded, stuck.

ahead *adverb*
1 *Dad went on ahead to get things ready.* before, in advance, in front.
2 *I stared ahead, trying to see through the mist.* forwards, to the front.

aid *noun*
1 *With your aid, I can do it.* assistance, backing, cooperation, help, support.
2 *I think we could send more aid to the poorer countries.* contributions, donations, subsidies.

aid *verb*
The local people aided the police in their investigation. assist, back, collaborate with, cooperate with, contribute to, encourage, further, help, lend a hand to, promote, subsidize, support.

ailment *noun*
She's suffering from some ailment. complaint, disease, illness, sickness.
SEE ALSO **illness**.

aim *noun*
What's your main aim in life? ambition, desire, dream, goal, hope, intention, objective, purpose, target, wish.

aim *verb*
1 *I aim to be a musician.* intend, mean, plan, propose, want, wish.
2 *She aimed the gun at the target.* line up, point, take aim with, train.
3 *She aimed the ball at the stumps.* direct, send.

aimless *adjective*
He leads an aimless life. meaningless, pointless, purposeless.

air *noun*
1 *We shouldn't pollute the air we breathe.* atmosphere.
2 *This room needs some air.* fresh air, ventilation.
3 *She was singing a traditional air.* melody, song, tune.
4 *There was an air of mystery about the place.* appearance, feeling, look, mood, sense.

air *verb*
1 *He opened the window to air the room.* freshen, refresh, ventilate.
2 *I have a right to air my opinions.* express, make known, make public, reveal, show off, voice.

aircraft *noun*

AIRCRAFT WHICH ARE HEAVIER THAN AIR: aeroplane, airliner, biplane, bomber, delta wing, fighter, gunship, helicopter, jet, jumbo jet, jump jet.

SMALL AIRCRAFT USUALLY FLOWN AS A SPORT: glider, hang-glider, microlight.

AIRCRAFT WHICH CAN LAND ON WATER: flying boat, seaplane.

AIRCRAFT WHICH ARE LIGHTER THAN AIR: airship, balloon, hot-air balloon.

PARTS OF AIRCRAFT: aileron, cabin, cargo hold, cockpit, elevator, engine, fin, flap, fuselage, joystick, passenger cabin, propeller, rotor, rudder, tail, tailplane, undercarriage, wing.

PEOPLE WHO FLY AIRCRAFT: airman, aviator, flier, pilot. ➡

PLACES WHERE AIRCRAFT TAKE OFF AND LAND: aerodrome, airfield, airport, airstrip, heliport, landing strip, runway.

TRAVELLING IN AIRCRAFT: aviation, flying.

airy *adjective*
1 *We sat and talked in a pleasant airy room.* fresh, open, ventilated.
AN OPPOSITE IS stuffy.
2 *He made some rather airy promises.* imprecise, indefinite, vague.

ajar *adjective*
I left the door ajar and my hamster escaped. open, unlatched.

alarm *verb*
The barking dog alarmed the sheep. agitate, distress, frighten, panic, scare, shock, startle, surprise, upset, worry.
AN OPPOSITE IS reassure.

alarm *noun*
1 *Did you hear the alarm?* alarm signal, alert, warning.

THINGS THAT ACT AS AN ALARM: alarm clock, bell, fire alarm, hooter, gong, siren, whistle.

2 *The sudden noise filled me with alarm.* anxiety, apprehension, distress, fear, fright, nervousness, panic, terror, uneasiness.

alcohol *noun*

SOME ALCOHOLIC DRINKS: ale, beer, lager, spirits, wine.

SOME SPIRITS: brandy, gin, rum, vodka, whisky.

alert *adjective*
A sentry must be alert at all times. attentive, awake, careful, observant, on the alert, on the lookout, ready, sharp-eyed, vigilant, wary, watchful, wide awake.
AN OPPOSITE IS inattentive.

alert *verb*
We alerted them to the danger. inform, make aware, notify, signal, tip off, warn.

alien *noun*
She felt like an alien in her new school. foreigner, immigrant, newcomer, stranger.

alien *adjective*
1 *When I was abroad, everything was so alien.* different, exotic, foreign, strange, unfamiliar.
AN OPPOSITE IS familiar.
2 *I read a story about alien beings and their spaceship.* extraterrestrial.

alienate *verb*
I think I alienated him when I said I didn't like his cat. antagonize, make an enemy of, offend, provoke, upset.

alight *adjective*
1 *Is the fire alight yet?* burning, ignited, on fire.
2 *The sky was alight with fireworks.* ablaze, bright, illuminated, lit up, shining.

alike *adjective*
1 *The twins are alike.* identical, indistinguishable.
2 *The people's reactions to our exhibition were alike.* comparable, the same, similar, uniform.

alive *adjective*
Is your goldfish still alive? breathing, existing, flourishing, in existence, live, living, surviving.
Living creatures in general are ***animate*** things.
AN OPPOSITE IS dead.

allegation *noun*
The allegation against him was never proved. accusation, charge, claim.

allege *verb*
She alleged that he was a thief. assert, claim, contend, declare, maintain, make an accusation.

allegiance *noun*
The king did not doubt the allegiance of his knights. devotion, duty, faithfulness, fidelity, loyalty, obedience.

alliance *noun*
The two sides formed an alliance. association, federation, league, partnership, union.
An alliance between political parties is a **coalition**.

allot *verb*
We allotted a fair share to every member of the group. assign, deal out, dispense, distribute, divide out, give out, grant, ration out, share out.

allow *verb*
1 Dad won't allow smoking in the house. agree to, approve of, authorize, consent to, give permission for, license, permit, put up with, stand, support, tolerate.
AN OPPOSITE IS forbid.
2 We allowed £5 each for food. budget, earmark, give, grant, set aside.

allowance *noun*
1 Our cats have a daily allowance of food. amount, measure, portion, quota, ration, share.
2 Mum gives me my allowance on Saturdays. pocket money.
3 They offered us an allowance for our old cooker. deduction, discount, reduction.

ally *noun*
The two countries work together as allies. friend, partner.
AN OPPOSITE IS enemy.

almost *adverb*
1 I have almost finished. all but, as good as, just about, nearly, not quite, practically, virtually.
2 Almost a hundred people came to our concert. about, approximately, around.

alone *adjective, adverb*
1 Did you go to the party alone? on your own, separately, unaccompanied.
2 It's sad to be alone when everyone else is enjoying themselves. desolate, friendless, isolated, lonely, solitary.

also *adverb*
We also need some bread. additionally, besides, furthermore, in addition, moreover, too.

alter *verb*
I got confused because they altered their plans. adjust, amend, change, make different, modify, revise, transform, vary.

alteration *noun*
She advised me to make some alterations to my work. adjustment, amendment, change, improvement, modification.

alternate *verb*
My brother and I alternate on washing up. rotate, take turns.

alternative *noun*
1 I lost my bus money, so I had no alternative but to walk home. choice, option.
2 I don't like this book, so can I have an alternative? replacement, substitute.

altogether *adverb*
1 I'm not altogether satisfied. absolutely, completely, entirely, fully, perfectly, thoroughly, totally, utterly, wholly.
2 Altogether, it wasn't a bad holiday. generally, in general, on the whole.

always *adverb*
1 The sea is always in motion. constantly, continuously, endlessly, eternally, for ever, perpetually, unceasingly.
2 This bus is always late. consistently, continually, invariably, persistently, regularly, repeatedly.

amalgamate *verb*
1 The two teams amalgamated. combine, come together, join forces, link up, merge, unite.
2 We amalgamated the two teams. combine, fuse, integrate, join, merge, mix together, put together.
AN OPPOSITE IS separate.

amateur *noun*
All the players in this team are unpaid amateurs.
AN OPPOSITE IS professional.

amateurish *adjective*
She complained that it was amateurish work. clumsy, crude, incompetent, poor, rough, shoddy, unprofessional, unskilful.
AN OPPOSITE IS skilled.

amaze *verb*
He amazed me when he said I had won first prize. astonish, astound, shock, stagger, startle, stun, surprise.

amazed *adjective*
I was amazed by the unexpected news. astonished, astounded, dumbfounded, [*informal*] flabbergasted, speechless, staggered, stunned, surprised.

amazing *adjective*
Flying over the North Pole was an amazing experience. astonishing, breathtaking, extraordinary, incredible, phenomenal, remarkable, sensational, staggering, stupendous, tremendous, wonderful.

ambiguous *adjective*
I'm still not sure what he believes because his reply was ambiguous. confusing, puzzling, uncertain, unclear, vague, woolly.
AN OPPOSITE IS definite.

ambition *noun*
1 She has talent and ambition. drive, enterprise, enthusiasm, zeal.
2 Her ambition is to run in the Olympics. aim, desire, dream, goal, hope, intention, objective, target, wish.

ambitious *adjective*
If you are ambitious, you will probably succeed. committed, enterprising, enthusiastic, go-ahead, keen.
AN OPPOSITE IS apathetic.

ambush *noun*
The soldiers set up an ambush for the enemy patrol. attack, surprise attack, trap.

ambush *verb*
They ambushed the enemy patrol. attack, intercept, pounce on, surprise, swoop on, trap.

amend *verb*
I amended the poster to make its message clearer. alter, change, modify, revise.

amiable *adjective*
I don't know him well, but he seems quite amiable. agreeable, amicable, approachable, friendly, genial, good-natured, good-tempered, kind-hearted, likeable, pleasant, well-disposed.

ammunition *noun*

KINDS OF AMMUNITION: bullet, cartridge, grenade, missile, round, shell, shrapnel.

amnesty *noun*
The government granted an amnesty to political prisoners. pardon, reprieve.

among *preposition*
I hid among the bushes. amid, between, in, in the middle of, surrounded by.

amount *noun*
1 Dad wrote a cheque for the correct amount. sum, total, whole.
2 There's a large amount of food in the cupboard. bulk, mass, measure, quantity, supply, volume.

amount *verb*
to amount to What does the bill amount to? add up to, come to, equal, make, total.

ample *adjective*
1 The car has an ample boot. big, large, roomy, spacious.
AN OPPOSITE IS small.
2 We had an ample supply of food. abundant, considerable, generous, lavish, liberal, plentiful, profuse, substantial.
AN OPPOSITE IS meagre.
3 No more, thanks—that's ample. [*informal*] heaps, lots, [*informal*] masses, more than enough, plenty, [*informal*] stacks, sufficient.
AN OPPOSITE IS insufficient.

amplify *verb*
1 She used a megaphone to amplify her voice. boost, increase, make louder.
AN OPPOSITE IS muffle.
2 Could you amplify your earlier statement? add to, develop, elaborate, expand, fill out, lengthen, make fuller.
AN OPPOSITE IS reduce.

amputate *verb*
After the accident, they thought they might have to amputate the victim's leg. cut off, remove, sever.

amuse *verb*
I think this joke will amuse you. cheer up, divert, entertain, make you laugh, [*informal*] tickle.
to amuse yourself *How do you like to amuse yourself?* be entertained, occupy your time, pass the time.

amusement *noun*
1 *What's your favourite amusement?* diversion, enjoyment, entertainment, fun, game, hobby, interest, leisure activity, pastime, pleasure, recreation, sport.
2 *We tried not to show our amusement.* hilarity, laughter, merriment, mirth.

amusing *adjective*
I didn't find his jokes very amusing. comic, diverting, entertaining, funny, hilarious, humorous, witty.
AN OPPOSITE IS boring or serious.

analogy *noun*
To explain the circulation of the blood she used the analogy of a central heating system. comparison, metaphor, parallel, simile.

analyse *verb*
We analysed the results of our experiment. examine, investigate, scrutinize, study.

analysis *noun*
What did your analysis of the data show? breakdown, examination, investigation, scrutiny, study.

analytical *adjective*
We took an analytical look at the information we collected. methodical, scientific, systematic.
AN OPPOSITE IS superficial.

anarchy *noun*
There would be anarchy if we had no police. chaos, confusion, disorder, lawlessness, mutiny, pandemonium, riot.

ancestor *noun*
Our family's ancestors came from France. forefather, predecessor.
AN OPPOSITE IS descendant.

ancestry *noun*
She was proud of her Scottish ancestry. blood, descent, extraction, heredity, origins, pedigree, stock.

ancient *adjective*
1 *Does that ancient car still go?* antiquated, obsolete, old, old-fashioned, out of date.
2 *In ancient times, our ancestors were hunters.* early, past, primitive, remote.
Valuable ancient furniture is ***antique***.
Remains of ancient animals and plants are ***fossilized*** remains.
The times before written records were kept are ***prehistoric*** times.
The ancient Greeks and Romans lived in ***classical*** times.
AN OPPOSITE IS modern.

angelic *adjective*
1 *After his naughtiness yesterday, she was amazed by his angelic behaviour today.* good, innocent, saintly, virtuous.
2 *We listened to the angelic singing of the choir.* beautiful, heavenly, serene.
AN OPPOSITE IS devilish.

anger *noun*
I was filled with anger when I heard how cruel they had been. bitterness, fury, indignation, rage, [*old use*] wrath.
An outburst of anger is a ***tantrum*** or a ***temper***.

anger *verb*
His abrupt manner angered her. [*informal*] aggravate, annoy, antagonize, enrage, exasperate, incense, infuriate, irritate, madden, provoke.
AN OPPOSITE IS pacify.

angle *noun*
1 *We planted the tree in the angle between two walls.* corner, space.
2 *The lecturer took an interesting angle on the topic.* approach, outlook, point of view, slant, view.

angry *adjective*
You'd better stay away from her if she's angry! annoyed, bad-tempered, bitter, cross, enraged, exasperated, fuming, furious, hostile, ill-tempered, incensed, indignant, infuriated, livid, [*informal*] mad, raging, seething, [*old use*] wrathful.
AN OPPOSITE IS calm.

anguish *noun*
He groaned in anguish. agony, anxiety, distress, grief, heartache, misery, pain, sorrow, suffering, torment, torture, woe.

animal *noun*
We saw some strange animals in the zoo. beast, brute, creature.
A large or frightening animal in stories is a *monster*.
A word for wild animals in general is *wildlife*.
A scientific word for animals is *fauna*.

DIFFERENT KINDS OF ANIMAL: amphibian, arachnid, bird, fish, insect, invertebrate, mammal, marsupial, mollusc, reptile, rodent, vertebrate.
An animal that eats meat is a *carnivore*.
An animal that eats plants is a *herbivore*.
An animal that eats many things is an *omnivore*.
Animals that sleep most of the winter are *hibernating animals*.
Animals that are active at night are *nocturnal animals*.

SOME EXTINCT ANIMALS: brontosaurus, dinosaur, dodo, mastodon, pterodactyl, pterosaur, quagga.

SOME MAMMALS FOUND WILD IN BRITAIN: badger, bat, coypu, deer, dormouse, fox, hare, hedgehog, mink, mouse, otter, pine marten, polecat, rabbit, rat, shrew, squirrel, stoat, vole, weasel.

MAMMALS THAT LIVE IN THE SEA: dolphin, porpoise, seal, sea lion, walrus, whale. ➡

MAMMALS YOU MIGHT SEE IN A ZOO: aardvark, antelope, ape, armadillo, baboon, bear, beaver, bison, buffalo, camel, cheetah, chimpanzee, chipmunk, dromedary, elephant, elk, gazelle, gibbon, giraffe, gnu, gorilla, grizzly bear, hippopotamus, hyena, jackal, jaguar, kangaroo, koala, lemming, lemur, leopard, lion, llama, lynx, marmoset, marmot, mongoose, monkey, moose, musquash, ocelot, opossum, orang-utan, panda, panther, platypus, polar bear, porcupine, reindeer, rhinoceros, skunk, tapir, tiger, wallaby, wildebeest, wolf, wolverine, wombat, yak, zebra.

MAMMALS SOMETIMES KEPT AS PETS: cat, dog, donkey, ferret, gerbil, goat, guinea pig, hamster, horse, mouse, rabbit, rat.

MAMMALS SOMETIMES KEPT BY FARMERS: [*plural*] cattle, cow, goat, horse, pig, sheep.
SEE ALSO **bird, fish, insect, reptile**.

FEMALE ANIMALS:
Female dog or wolf: *bitch*.
Female cattle, elephant, or whale: *cow*.
Female deer, hare, or rabbit: *doe*.
Female sheep: *ewe*.
Female deer: *hind*.
Female lion: *lioness*.
Female horse: *mare*.
Female goat: *nanny goat*.
Female pig: *sow*.
Female tiger: *tigress*.
Female fox: *vixen*.

MALE ANIMALS:
Male goat: *billy goat*.
Male hare or rabbit: *buck*.
Male deer: *buck*, *hart*, or *stag*.
Male elephant or whale: *bull*.
Male cattle: *bull* or *steer*.
Male fox or wolf: *dog*.
Male sheep: *ram*.
Male horse: *stallion*.
Male cat: *tom*.

YOUNG ANIMALS:
Young cattle: *calf*.
Young male horse: *colt*.
Young fox or lion: *cub*. ➡

Young deer: **fawn**.
Young female horse: **filly**.
Young horse: **foal**.
Young cow: **heifer**.
Young goat: **kid**.
Young cat: **kitten**.
Young sheep: **lamb**.
Young hare: **leveret**.
Young pig: **piglet**.
Young dog: **pup**, **puppy**, or **whelp**.
Young seal: **pup**.

GROUPS OF ANIMALS:
A **flock** of sheep.
A **herd** of cattle or elephants.
A **leap** of leopards.
A **litter** of puppies or kittens.
A **pack** of wolves.
A **pride** of lions.
A **school** of porpoises or whales.

animated *adjective*
I could hear animated chatter from the next room. bright, brisk, bubbling, busy, cheerful, eager, enthusiastic, excited, exuberant, lively, spirited, sprightly, vivacious.
AN OPPOSITE IS lethargic.

animosity *noun*
It's obvious that there's a lot of animosity between them. antagonism, dislike, enmity, hate, hatred, hostility, ill will, malice, resentment, spite, unfriendliness.
AN OPPOSITE IS friendliness.

annexe *noun*
We slept in the annexe to the hotel. extension, wing.

annihilate *verb*
Nuclear weapons could annihilate the human race. destroy, exterminate, [*informal*] finish off, kill off, wipe out.

anniversary *noun*
The anniversary of the day you were born is your **birthday**.
The anniversary of the day someone

was married is their **wedding anniversary**.

SOME SPECIAL ANNIVERSARIES:
bicentenary, centenary, coming-of-age, jubilee, silver wedding, golden wedding, diamond wedding, ruby wedding.

announce *verb*
1 *The head announced that sports day was cancelled.* declare, proclaim, report, reveal, state.
2 *The DJ announced the next record.* introduce, lead into, present.

announcement *noun*
1 *The head reads the announcements in assembly.* notice.
2 *An official issued an announcement.* declaration, proclamation, pronouncement, statement.
3 *I heard the announcement on TV.* bulletin, news flash, report.

announcer *noun*

VARIOUS PEOPLE WHO ANNOUNCE THINGS: broadcaster, commentator, compère, herald, master of ceremonies, messenger, newscaster, newsreader, presenter, reporter, town crier.

annoy *verb*
1 *Did my sudden change of plans annoy you?* [*informal*] aggravate, anger, displease, exasperate, irritate, make you cross, upset, vex, worry.
AN OPPOSITE IS please.
2 *Please don't annoy me while I'm working.* badger, bother, harass, nag, pester, plague, provoke, trouble, try, worry.

annoyance *noun*
1 *Her annoyance was obvious.* anger, exasperation, irritation, vexation.
2 *Is the dog an annoyance to you?* bother, nuisance, trouble, worry.

annoyed *adjective*
Annoyed customers queued up to get their money back. angry, cross, displeased, exasperated, irritated, offended, sore, upset, vexed.
AN OPPOSITE IS pleased.

annoying *adjective*
He's got a lot of very annoying habits.
[informal] aggravating, exasperating,
irritating, maddening, provoking,
tiresome, troublesome, trying, vexing,
worrying.

anonymous *adjective*
1 An anonymous benefactor paid for
our trip. nameless, unidentified,
unknown, unnamed.
2 I received an anonymous letter.
unsigned.

answer *noun*
1 Did you get an answer to your letter?
acknowledgement, reaction, reply,
response.
A quick or angry answer is a **retort**.
2 This could be the answer to all our
problems. explanation, solution.

answer *verb*
1 I answered her question.
acknowledge, give an answer to, react
to, reply to, respond to.
2 'I'm quite well,' I answered. reply,
respond, retort, return.
To answer quickly or angrily is to
retort.
to answer back She doesn't like it when
I answer back. argue, object, protest.

antagonize *verb*
Don't antagonize the neighbours by
making a noise. alienate, anger, annoy,
make an enemy of, offend, provoke,
upset.
AN OPPOSITE IS please.

anthology *noun*
We put together an anthology of our
favourite poems. collection,
compilation, miscellany, selection.

anticipate *verb*
I anticipate that the result will be a
draw. expect, forecast, foretell, hope,
predict.

anticlimax *noun*
It was an anticlimax when they
abandoned the game. disappointment.

antiquated *adjective*
I was surprised that he used such an
antiquated computer. aged, ancient,
obsolete, old-fashioned, out of date,
primitive.
AN OPPOSITE IS new.

antique *adjective*
The palace was full of antique
furniture. old, old-fashioned.
Antique cars are **veteran** or **vintage**
cars.

antiseptic *adjective*
The nurse put an antiseptic dressing on
the wound. disinfected, germ-free,
hygienic, sterile, sterilized.

anxiety *noun*
1 We waited for news with a growing
sense of anxiety. apprehension,
concern, doubt, dread, fear,
nervousness, strain, stress, tension,
uncertainty, worry.
AN OPPOSITE IS calmness.
2 In his anxiety to win, he started before
the gun went off. desire, eagerness,
enthusiasm, impatience, keenness.

anxious *adjective*
1 Are you anxious about your exams?
apprehensive, concerned, edgy, fearful,
fraught, nervous, tense, troubled,
uneasy, worried.
AN OPPOSITE IS calm.
2 I'm anxious to do my best. eager,
enthusiastic, impatient, keen, willing.

apathetic *adjective*
You won't succeed if you are so
apathetic. indifferent, listless, passive,
unambitious, uncommitted,
unemotional, unenthusiastic,
uninterested, unmotivated.
AN OPPOSITE IS enthusiastic.

apologetic *adjective*
He was apologetic about his mistake.
penitent, remorseful, repentant, sorry.
AN OPPOSITE IS unrepentant.

apologize *verb*
He apologized for being rude. be
penitent, express regret, make an
apology, repent, say sorry.

appal *verb*
The violence of the film appalled us.
disgust, distress, horrify, revolt, shock,
sicken.

appalling *adjective*
1 He suffered appalling injuries in the
accident. distressing, dreadful,
frightful, gruesome, horrible, horrific,
horrifying, shocking, sickening.
2 My work was so appalling that I had
to do it again. [informal] abysmal,
atrocious, awful, bad, disgraceful,
terrible, unsatisfactory, worthless.

apparatus *noun*
The firemen were wearing breathing
apparatus. appliances, devices,
equipment, gear, instruments,
machines, mechanisms, set-up,
systems, tools.

apparent *adjective*
There was no apparent reason for the
crash. clear, conspicuous, detectable,
evident, noticeable, obvious,
perceptible, recognizable, visible.
AN OPPOSITE IS concealed.

appeal *verb*
to appeal for They appealed for our
help. ask earnestly for, beg for, cry out
for, entreat, plead for, pray for, request.
to appeal to That kind of music doesn't
appeal to me. attract, fascinate,
interest, tempt.

appeal *noun*
1 Did you hear their appeal for help?
call, cry, entreaty, request.
An appeal signed by a lot of people is a
petition.
2 Baby animals always have great
appeal. attractiveness, charm,
fascination, interest.

appear *verb*
1 Snowdrops appear in the spring.
become visible, come into view, come
out, crop up, develop, emerge, occur,
show, spring up, surface.
2 Our visitors didn't appear until
midnight. arrive, come, [informal]
show up, turn up.
3 It appears that he's asleep. look,
seem.
4 I once appeared in a play. act,
feature, perform, take part.

appearance *noun*
1 I was startled by her sudden
appearance. approach, arrival,
entrance, entry.
2 He had a military appearance. air,
aspect, bearing, look.

appease *verb*
They offered a sacrifice to appease the
gods. calm, humour, pacify, satisfy,
soothe, win over.
AN OPPOSITE IS anger.

appetite *noun*
1 When I was ill, I completely lost my
appetite. hunger.
2 Round-the-world sailors have a great
appetite for adventure. craving, desire,
eagerness, enthusiasm, keenness,
longing, lust, passion, taste, thirst,
urge, wish, yearning, zest.

appetizing *adjective*
The appetizing smell of sizzling bacon
filled the room. delicious, tasty,
tempting.

applaud *verb*
The audience laughed and applauded.
cheer, clap.
AN OPPOSITE IS boo.

applause *noun*
At the end, the applause lasted for
several minutes. cheering, clapping,
congratulations.

appliance *noun*
These days they make appliances to do
most jobs. apparatus, device,
equipment, gadget, instrument, tool.

> VARIOUS DOMESTIC APPLIANCES:
> carpet sweeper, cooker, dishwasher,
> freezer, fridge, microwave, vacuum
> cleaner, washing machine.

application *noun*
1 We sent an application for a refund.
claim, request.
2 The job needs a lot of patience and
application. commitment, dedication,
devotion, effort, perseverance,
persistence.

apply *verb*
1 The nurse told me to apply the
ointment generously. administer, lay
on, put on, spread.

2 *My brother applied for a new job.* ask for, make an application for.
3 *The rules apply to everyone.* be relevant, refer, relate.
4 *I applied all my skill.* bring into use, employ, exercise, use, utilize.

appoint *verb*
  1 *The school governors appointed a new teacher.* choose, elect, select, settle on, vote for.
  2 *We appointed a time for our meeting.* arrange, decide on, determine, fix, settle.

appointment *noun*
  1 *I had an appointment to meet him in town.* arrangement, date, engagement.
  2 *We had to be tactful about the appointment of a new captain.* choice, choosing, election, naming, selection.
  3 *My brother got a new appointment.* job, position, post, situation.

appreciate *verb*
  1 *He appreciates good music.* enjoy, like, love.
  2 *I appreciate her good qualities.* admire, approve of, esteem, regard highly, respect, value.
  AN OPPOSITE IS despise.
  3 *I appreciate that you can't afford much.* comprehend, know, realize, recognize, see, understand.
  4 *Dad hopes that the value of our house will appreciate.* go up, grow, increase, mount, rise.

appreciative *adjective*
I enjoy playing to an appreciative audience. admiring, enthusiastic, grateful.

apprehensive *adjective*
Are you apprehensive about your exams? anxious, edgy, fearful, frightened, nervous, tense, troubled, uneasy, worried.

approach *verb*
  1 *The lion approached its prey.* advance on, come near to, draw near to, move towards.

2 *I approached the head to ask if we could have a party.* contact, go to, speak to.
3 *We approached the job cheerfully.* begin, embark on, set about, undertake.

approach *noun*
  1 *Footsteps signalled their approach.* advance, arrival, coming.
  2 *Dad made an approach to the bank manager for a loan.* appeal, application, proposal.
  3 *I like her positive approach.* attitude, manner, style, way.
  4 *The easiest approach to the castle is from the west.* access, entrance, entry, way in.

approachable *adjective*
We found him very approachable and easy to talk to. amiable, friendly, informal, kind, sympathetic, well-disposed.
AN OPPOSITE IS unsympathetic.

appropriate *adjective*
It's not appropriate to wear jeans to a wedding. apt, fitting, proper, right, suitable, tactful, tasteful, well-judged.
AN OPPOSITE IS inappropriate.

approval *noun*
  1 *We cheered to show our approval.* acclaim, admiration, appreciation, high regard, praise, respect, support.
  AN OPPOSITE IS disapproval.
  2 *The head gave her approval to our plan.* agreement, assent, authorization, [*informal*] blessing, consent, go-ahead, permission, support.
  AN OPPOSITE IS refusal.

approve *verb*
The head approved my request for a day off school. accept, agree to, allow, authorize, back, consent to, pass, permit, support.
AN OPPOSITE IS refuse.
to approve of *She approved of what I did.* admire, applaud, appreciate, commend, esteem, favour, like, praise, respect, value, welcome.
AN OPPOSITE IS condemn.

approximate *adjective*
I gave Mum an approximate number of people coming to my party. estimated, inexact, near, rough.
AN OPPOSITE IS exact.

approximately *adverb*
Approximately twelve people are coming to my party. about, around, close to, more or less, nearly, roughly, round about.

apt *adjective*
1 *He's apt to be careless.* inclined, liable, likely, prone.
2 *I need an apt quotation to put on the cover of my project.* appropriate, fitting, proper, right, suitable, well-judged.
3 *She turned out to be a very apt pupil.* clever, quick, sharp.

aptitude *noun*
He has a remarkable aptitude for music. ability, bent, expertise, gift, potential, skill, talent.

arbitrary *adjective*
He made an arbitrary decision to drop three of the best players. illogical, irrational, random, subjective.
AN OPPOSITE IS rational.

arbitrate *verb*
We couldn't settle our argument, so we asked Mum to arbitrate. act as referee, adjudicate, decide the outcome, make peace, pass judgement.

arch *verb*
The cat arched its back. bend, bow, curve.

area *noun*
1 *From the plane we saw a big area of desert.* expanse, stretch, tract.
A small area is a ***patch***.
An area of water or ice is a ***sheet***.
2 *I live in an urban area.* district, locality, neighbourhood, part, region, vicinity, zone.

arena *noun*

PLACES WHERE SPORT TAKES PLACE: amphitheatre, field, ground, park, pitch, ring, rink, stadium.

argue *verb*
1 *Whenever you two meet, you argue!* differ, disagree, fall out, fight, have an argument, quarrel, squabble.
AN OPPOSITE IS agree.
2 *He argued over the price.* bargain, haggle.
3 *The lawyer argued that the accused was innocent.* assert, claim, maintain, reason, suggest, try to prove.
to argue about something *We argue about politics.* debate, discuss.

argument *noun*
1 *There was an argument about how much they should pay.* clash, controversy, debate, difference, discussion, disagreement, dispute, fight, quarrel, row, squabble.
2 *Did you follow her argument?* line of reasoning, outline, theme.

arid *adjective*
No flowers were growing in the arid soil. barren, dry, infertile, lifeless, parched, sterile, unproductive, waterless.
AN OPPOSITE IS fruitful.

arise *verb*
Perhaps the problem won't arise. appear, come into existence, come up, crop up, emerge, happen, occur.

aristocrat *noun*
noble, nobleman or noblewoman, peer.

aristocratic *adjective*
The castle belonged to an old aristocratic family. lordly, noble, titled, upper-class.

arm *verb*
They armed themselves with sticks. equip, provide, supply.

armed services *plural noun*

THE PRINCIPAL ARMED SERVICES:
air force, army, navy.
Men and women in the services are ***troops***.
People who fight on horses are ***cavalry***.
People who fight on foot are ***infantry***. ➡

VARIOUS GROUPS IN THE ARMED
SERVICES: battalion, brigade,
company, corps, fleet, garrison,
legion, patrol, platoon, regiment,
reinforcements, squad, squadron,
task force, vanguard.

SERVICEMEN AND SERVICEWOMEN
INCLUDE: aircraftman,
aircraftwoman, cavalryman,
commando, infantryman, marine,
paratrooper, recruit, sailor, soldier.
A soldier paid to fight for a foreign
country is a **mercenary**.
SEE ALSO **fighter, officer, rank**.

armistice *noun*
An armistice ended the fighting.
ceasefire, peace, truce.

armour *noun*

PARTS OF A MEDIEVAL KNIGHT'S
ARMOUR: breastplate, gauntlet,
greave, habergeon, helmet, visor.
Armour made of linked rings was
chain armour or **chain mail**.

army *noun* SEE **armed services**

arouse *verb*
*The plan to build a bypass aroused
strong feelings.* cause, generate, lead
to, produce, provoke, set off, stimulate,
stir up, whip up.
AN OPPOSITE IS calm.

arrange *verb*
1 *I tried to arrange everything logically.*
categorize, classify, collate, display, lay
out, line up, organize, set out, sort, sort
out, tidy up.
2 *Who will help me to arrange the
party?* organize, plan, prepare, see to,
set up.

arrangement *noun*
1 *We improved the arrangement of the
library.* design, layout, organization,
planning, setting out.
2 *I changed the arrangement of the
books.* display, distribution, grouping,
order, spacing.
3 *We have an arrangement to pay for
our TV by instalments.* agreement,
bargain, contract, deal, scheme.

array *noun*
*We looked round the gleaming array of
vintage cars.* collection, display,
exhibition, show.

arrest *verb*
1 *The police arrested the suspect.*
capture, catch, detain, [*informal*] nick,
seize, take into custody, take prisoner.
2 *The doctors tried to arrest the spread
of the disease.* check, delay, halt,
hinder, prevent, stop.

arrive *verb*
When is the train due to arrive? appear,
approach, come, get in, show up, turn
up.
*When a plane arrives it **lands** or
touches down.*
to arrive at *We arrived at the station.*
get to, reach.

arrogant *adjective*
His arrogant manner annoys me.
boastful, [*informal*] cocky, conceited,
haughty, insolent, pompous,
presumptuous, proud, scornful,
snobbish, [*informal*] stuck-up,
superior, vain.
AN OPPOSITE IS modest.

art *noun*
*The art of writing letters is
disappearing fast.* craft, knack, skill,
talent, technique, trick.

VARIOUS ARTS AND CRAFTS
INCLUDE: carpentry, carving,
collage, crochet, drawing,
embroidery, enamelling, engraving,
etching, graphics, handicraft,
illustration, jewellery, knitting,
metalwork, modelling, needlework,
origami, painting, patchwork,
photography, pottery, printing,
sculpture, sewing, sketching, weaving,
wickerwork, woodwork.
FOR VARIOUS ARTISTS AND
CRAFTSMEN, SEE **artist**.

artful *adjective*
[*usually uncomplimentary*] *That was
an artful trick!* clever, crafty, cunning,
deceitful, devious, scheming, skilful,
sly, smart, tricky, wily.
AN OPPOSITE IS straightforward.

article *noun*
1 *Have you any articles for the jumble sale?* item, object, thing.
2 *Did you read my article in the magazine?* essay, piece of writing, report.

articulate *adjective*
She's a very articulate speaker. clear, eloquent, fluent, lucid.
AN OPPOSITE IS inarticulate.

artificial *adjective*
1 *Organic gardeners don't use artificial fertilizers.* man-made, manufactured, synthetic, unnatural.
2 *She had an artificial flower in her buttonhole.* bogus, counterfeit, fake, false, imitation.
AN OPPOSITE IS genuine.
3 *He gave an artificial smile.* affected, [*informal*] put on, pretended, sham, simulated.
AN OPPOSITE IS genuine or natural.

artist *noun*

ARTISTS AND CRAFTSMEN INCLUDE:
blacksmith, carpenter, cartoonist, draughtsman, draughtswoman, engraver, goldsmith, graphic designer, illustrator, mason, painter, photographer, potter, printer, sculptor, silversmith, smith, weaver.
FOR VARIOUS ARTS AND CRAFTS, SEE **art**.
FOR PERFORMING ARTISTS, SEE **entertainer**.

artistic *adjective*
Mum's flower arrangements are very artistic. aesthetic, attractive, beautiful, creative, imaginative, tasteful.
AN OPPOSITE IS ugly.

ascend *verb*
1 *It took the rescuers a long time to ascend the mountain.* climb, go up, mount, move up, scale.
2 *The plane began to ascend.* lift off, take off.
3 *The eagle ascended into the air.* fly up, rise, soar.
AN OPPOSITE IS descend.

ascent *noun*
The ancient car only just managed the steep ascent. climb, gradient, hill, incline, ramp, rise, slope.
AN OPPOSITE IS descent.

ashamed *adjective*
He was ashamed because of what he had done. apologetic, penitent, [*informal*] red-faced, remorseful, repentant, sorry.
AN OPPOSITE IS unrepentant.

ashes *plural noun*
Next morning, the ashes of the bonfire were still glowing. cinders, embers.

ask *verb*
1 *I asked him to help me.* appeal to, beg, entreat, implore, plead with.
2 *'Are you ready?' I asked.* demand, enquire, inquire.
3 *I'm going to ask you to my party.* invite, [*formal*] request the pleasure of your company.
to ask for 1 *He asked for silence.* appeal for, call for, demand, request, seek.
2 *He was asking for trouble!* attract, cause, encourage, provoke, stir up.

asleep *adjective*
I didn't hear the phone because I was asleep. dozing, having a nap, [*informal*] nodding off, sleeping, unconscious.
A patient asleep for an operation is **anaesthetized** or **under sedation**.
An animal asleep for the winter is **hibernating**.
AN OPPOSITE IS awake.

aspect *noun*
1 *There's an aspect of this affair I don't understand.* angle, detail, feature, side.
2 *He had an unfriendly aspect.* air, appearance, countenance, expression, face, look, manner.
3 *The front room has a southern aspect.* outlook, prospect, view.

assassinate *verb*
The rebels assassinated the President. kill, murder.

assault *noun*
The old lady was the victim of a serious assault. attack, beating, mugging.

assault *verb*
It's a serious crime to assault a policeman. attack, beat up, hit, mug, punch, strike.

assemble *verb*
1 *We assembled our luggage so that we were ready to leave.* bring together, collect, gather, pile up, put together.
2 *The general assembled his troops.* muster, rally, round up.
3 *A crowd assembled to watch the rescue.* accumulate, come together, converge, crowd together, flock together, gather, meet.
AN OPPOSITE IS disperse.

assembly *noun*
There was a large assembly of people in the market square. crowd, gathering, meeting, throng.
An assembly for worship is a **service**.
A large assembly to show support for something, often out of doors, is a **rally**.
An assembly to discuss political matters is a **council** or **parliament**.
An assembly to discuss and learn about a particular topic is a **conference** or **congress**.

assent *noun*
She gave her assent to the plan. agreement, approval, consent, go-ahead, permission.
AN OPPOSITE IS refusal.

assert *verb*
The accused man asserted that he was innocent. argue, claim, declare, insist, maintain, proclaim, protest, state, swear, testify.

assertive *adjective*
We need a leader who is assertive. bold, confident, decided, decisive, firm, forceful, insistent, positive, self-confident.
AN OPPOSITE IS submissive.

assess *verb*
We have tests to assess our progress. appraise, determine, estimate, evaluate, gauge, judge, measure, value, weigh up.

asset *noun*
Good health is a great asset. advantage, benefit, blessing, help.
assets *It's a big company with enormous assets.* capital, funds, possessions, property, savings, wealth.

assign *verb*
He assigned the difficult jobs to the older children. allot, consign, distribute, give, hand over, share out.

assignment *noun*
He gave me a hard assignment. duty, job, mission, piece of work, project, responsibility, task.

assist *verb*
She asked us to assist the caretaker by tidying the room. aid, collaborate with, cooperate with, help.
AN OPPOSITE IS hinder.

assistance *noun*
1 *That little boy needs some assistance with his shoelaces.* aid, encouragement, help.
2 *We bought new sports equipment with the assistance of a local firm.* backing, collaboration, cooperation, sponsorship, subsidy, support.

assistant *noun*
Can you manage on your own, or do you need an assistant? associate, colleague, helper, partner, supporter.

associate *verb*
to associate one thing with another *I associate Christmas with ice and snow.* connect with, link with, relate to.
to associate with someone *I don't think you should associate with those people!* be friends with, go about with, mix with.

association *noun*
1 *The people interested in chess formed an association.* alliance, club, fellowship, group, league, partnership, society, union.
A political association is a **party**.
A business association is a **company** or **organization**.
2 *The association between us has lasted many years.* closeness, friendship, link, partnership, relationship.

assorted *adjective*
I bought a bag of sweets with assorted
flavours. different, miscellaneous,
mixed, several, various.

assortment *noun*
There was an assortment of sandwiches
to choose from. array, choice, diversity,
mixture, selection, variety.

assume *verb*
1 I assume you'd like some tea. expect,
guess, have a hunch, imagine,
presume, suppose, suspect, think.
2 She assumed a disguise. adopt, dress
up in, put on, wear.

assumed *adjective*
She spoke with an assumed accent.
bogus, counterfeit, faked, false,
pretended.
AN OPPOSITE IS genuine.
an assumed name alias, pseudonym.

assumption *noun*
My assumption is that we can average
40 miles an hour. belief, expectation,
guess, hypothesis, supposition, theory.

assure *verb*
I assure you that I will help. promise.

astonish *verb*
My discovery will astonish you. amaze,
astound, leave speechless, shock,
stagger, startle, stun, surprise, take
aback, take by surprise, [*informal*]
take your breath away.
To be astonished is also to be
dumbfounded or **flabbergasted**.

astronomy *noun*

SOME ASTRONOMICAL TERMS:
asteroid, black hole, comet,
constellation, cosmos, eclipse,
galaxy, meteor, meteorite, moon,
nebula, nova, planet, pulsar, quasar,
satellite, shooting star, space, sun,
supernova, universe, world.

athlete *noun*
FOR VARIOUS EVENTS ATHLETES TAKE
PART IN, SEE **athletics**.

athletic *adjective*
He looks an athletic sort of person.
active, energetic, fit, muscular,
powerful, robust, sporting, strong,
sturdy, vigorous, well-built.
AN OPPOSITE IS feeble.

athletics *noun*

VARIOUS ATHLETICS EVENTS: cross-
country, decathlon, discus, high
jump, hurdles, javelin, long jump,
marathon, pentathlon, pole vault,
relay race, running, shot, sprinting,
triple jump.
FOR OTHER SPORTS, SEE **sport**.

atmosphere *noun*
1 We shouldn't pollute the atmosphere
we breathe. air.
2 There was a happy atmosphere at the
party. feeling, mood, spirit.

atrocious *adjective*
We were shocked by the atrocious crime.
abominable, barbaric, bloodthirsty,
brutal, callous, cruel, diabolical,
dreadful, evil, fiendish, horrifying,
merciless, outrageous, sadistic, savage,
terrible, vicious, villainous, wicked.

atrocity *noun*
The TV report of the atrocity shocked
us. crime, horror, outrage.

attach *verb*
Attach the trailer to the back of the car.
connect, couple, fasten, fix, join, link,
secure.

DIFFERENT WAYS TO ATTACH
THINGS TO EACH OTHER: bind, bolt,
chain, clamp, clip, glue, hook, nail,
peg, pin, screw, solder, staple, stick,
tack, tie, weld, zip.
AN OPPOSITE IS detach.

attached *adjective*
The twins are very attached to each
other. affectionate, close, dear, devoted,
fond (of), friendly, loving, loyal.
AN OPPOSITE IS hostile.

attack *noun*
1 The enemy's attack took them by
surprise. aggression, ambush, assault,
charge, invasion, raid, strike.

An attack with big guns or bombs is a
blitz or *bombardment*.
An attack by planes is an *air raid*.
2 *She was upset by his attack on her
character.* abuse, criticism, outburst.
3 *It was embarrassing when I had a
coughing attack in assembly.* bout, fit,
[*informal*] turn.

attack *verb*
1 *The criminals attacked him in the
street.* assail, assault, beat up, mug,
[*informal*] set about, set on.
To attack someone else's territory is to
invade or *raid* it.
To attack someone from a hidden place
is to *ambush* them.
To attack the enemy with bombs or
heavy guns is to *bombard* them.
To attack by rushing at the enemy is to
charge.
To attack a place suddenly is to *storm*
it.
If an animal attacks you, it might
savage you.
2 *He attacked her reputation.* abuse,
criticize, denounce.
AN OPPOSITE IS defend.

attain *verb*
I attained Grade 3 on the violin.
accomplish, achieve, arrive at,
complete, gain, get, obtain, reach.

attempt *verb*
We attempted to beat the record. aim,
endeavour, exert yourself, make an
effort, strive, try.

attempt *noun*
I did it at the first attempt. effort, try.

attend *verb*
*Are you going to attend the end-of-term
concert?* appear at, be present at, go to.
to attend to 1 *Please attend to what I
say.* concentrate on, follow carefully,
heed, listen to, mark, mind, note,
notice, observe, pay attention to, think
about.
2 *Are you going to attend to the
washing up?* deal with, see to.
3 *The nurses attended to the wounded.*
care for, help, look after, mind, take
care of, tend.

attention *noun*
1 *It looks as if you did this without
giving it proper attention.* care,
concentration, consideration, thought.
2 *Thank you for your attention.*
courtesy, good manners, kindness,
politeness, thoughtfulness.

attentive *adjective*
Drivers must be attentive at all times.
alert, careful, listening, observant, on
the alert, on the lookout, paying
attention, sharp-eyed, vigilant, wary,
watchful, wide awake.

attitude *noun*
1 *Our teacher says we need a more
serious attitude in class.* approach,
behaviour, disposition, frame of mind,
manner, mood.
2 *I think smoking is wrong, but what's
your attitude?* belief, feeling, opinion,
outlook, position, thought, view.

attract *verb*
1 *Do you think our exhibition will
attract people?* appeal to, fascinate,
interest, tempt.
2 *Baby animals attract big crowds at
the zoo.* draw, pull in.
AN OPPOSITE IS repel.

attractive *adjective*
Things can be attractive in many
different ways. We give just some
examples of ways we use the word here
1 *Aren't those puppies attractive?*
adorable, appealing, captivating,
charming, [*informal*] cute, delightful,
enchanting, fascinating, lovable.
2 *The bride and groom were an
attractive couple.* beautiful, good-
looking, handsome, pretty, striking.
3 *There was an attractive picture over
the fireplace.* artistic, beautiful,
colourful.
4 *Last holiday we stayed in an
attractive country cottage.* picturesque,
pretty, quaint.
5 *The shop has some attractive special
offers at present.* desirable, interesting,
irresistible, tempting.
AN OPPOSITE IS repulsive or
unattractive.

audible *adjective*
She didn't think her rude comments
were audible. clear, distinct.
AN OPPOSITE IS inaudible.

audience *noun*
The audience for a TV programme is
the *viewers*.
The audience for a radio programme is
the *listeners*.
The audience for a sporting event is
the *spectators*.

audio-visual *adjective*

KINDS OF AUDIO-VISUAL
EQUIPMENT USED IN SCHOOLS:
cassette player, film-projector,
interactive video, language
laboratory, microfilm reader,
overhead projector or OHP, slide
projector, tape-slide equipment,
television, video cassette recorder or
VCR, videodisc equipment.

VARIOUS KINDS OF EQUIPMENT YOU
MIGHT HAVE AT HOME: amplifier,
camcorder, earphones, headphones,
hi-fi, loudspeaker, music centre,
personal stereo, radio, record player,
stereo, tape recorder, television,
tuner, turntable, video cassette
recorder or VCR, [*trademark*]
Walkman.

austere *adjective*
1 The monks led an austere kind of life.
comfortless, frugal, plain, puritanical,
simple, sober, thrifty.
AN OPPOSITE IS lavish.
2 She seemed rather an unfriendly and
austere person. cold, formal, hard,
harsh, serious, severe, stern, strict.
AN OPPOSITE IS genial.

authentic *adjective*
1 If it's an authentic antique, it could be
valuable. actual, genuine, real.
AN OPPOSITE IS counterfeit.
2 He gave an authentic account of his
adventure. accurate, dependable,
factual, honest, reliable, true, truthful.
AN OPPOSITE IS false.

author *noun*
An author who writes novels is a
novelist.
The author of a play is a *dramatist* or
playwright.
An author who writes for films or TV is
a *scriptwriter*.
An author who writes poetry is a *poet*.
A person who writes music is a
composer.
FOR OTHER WRITERS, SEE **writer**.

authority *noun*
1 I have the head's authority to go home
early. approval, consent, permission.
2 Our teacher has the authority to tell
us what to do. influence, power, right.
3 He's an authority on steam trains.
expert, specialist.

authorize *verb*
The head authorized the purchase of a
computer. agree to, approve, consent
to, give permission for, permit, sign the
order for.

automatic *adjective*
1 We took our car through the
automatic car wash. automated,
computerized, programmed.
2 When the lights come on, blinking is
an automatic reaction. impulsive,
instinctive, involuntary, natural,
reflex, spontaneous, unconscious,
unthinking.

auxiliary *adjective*
The boat had an auxiliary engine.
additional, emergency, extra, reserve,
supplementary, supporting.

available *adjective*
Make sure the extinguisher is always
available, in case there is a fire.
accessible, at hand, convenient, handy,
ready, usable, within reach.

average *adjective*
1 She said that our work was above the
average standard. normal, ordinary,
regular, usual.
2 It was an average kind of day at
school. commonplace, everyday,
familiar, typical.
AN OPPOSITE IS extraordinary.

avert *verb*
1 *I saw he was going to hit me, and I tried to avert the blow.* deflect, fend off, turn aside, ward off.
2 *The firemen did all they could to avert disaster.* avoid, prevent, stave off.

avid *adjective*
She's an avid reader. eager, enthusiastic, fervent, keen.
AN OPPOSITE IS apathetic.

avoid *verb*
1 *I tried hard to avoid the collision.* avert, dodge, fend off, get out of the way of, keep clear of, steer clear of.
2 *The criminal avoided capture for months.* elude, escape from, evade, run away from.
3 *Why does he always avoid the washing up?* get out of, shirk.

await *verb*
I await your reply. be ready for, expect, hope for, look out for, wait for.

awake *adjective*
I was awake all night. conscious, restless, sleepless, wide awake.
Not being able to sleep is to be suffering from *insomnia*.
AN OPPOSITE IS asleep.

awaken *verb*
1 *I awakened at dawn.* become conscious, stir, wake up.
2 *Mum awakened us at seven.* alert, arouse, call, rouse, wake, waken.

award *noun*

THINGS GIVEN TO PEOPLE WHO HAVE DONE SOMETHING SUCCESSFUL: badge, cap, cup, decoration, medal, prize, reward, scholarship, trophy.

award *verb*
They awarded first prize to my friend. confer (on), give, grant, present.

aware *adjective*
aware of *Are you aware of the rules?* acquainted with, conscious of, familiar with, informed about.
AN OPPOSITE IS ignorant of.

awe *noun*
We watched in awe as the volcano erupted. admiration, amazement, dread, fear, respect, reverence, terror, wonder.

awful *adjective*
The adjective *awful* can be used in many ways. It is usually vague in meaning. We give here just some of the other words you could use
1 *The teacher complained about my awful handwriting.* [*informal*] abysmal, appalling, bad, dreadful, terrible.
2 *She also complained about our awful behaviour.* disgraceful, disobedient, naughty, shameful.
3 *I think he's an awful man.* detestable, disagreeable, horrid, nasty, unfriendly, unkind, unpleasant.
4 *We need an awful lot of rain after this drought.* big, enormous, great, huge, large, massive.
5 *We were shocked by the awful crime.* abominable, atrocious, callous, cruel, evil, horrifying, outrageous, shocking, villainous, wicked.
6 *The erupting volcano was an awful sight.* awe-inspiring, dramatic, fearful.

awfully *adverb*
It's been awfully hot today. dreadfully, exceptionally, extraordinarily, extremely, terribly, very.

awkward *adjective*
1 *The box was an awkward shape.* bulky, inconvenient, unmanageable.
AN OPPOSITE IS convenient.
2 *He was awkward with his hands.* clumsy, unskilful.
AN OPPOSITE IS skilful.
3 *I didn't know how to deal with such an awkward problem.* difficult, perplexing, thorny, [*informal*] ticklish, troublesome, trying.
AN OPPOSITE IS straightforward.
4 *I think the donkey was trying to be awkward.* exasperating, obstinate, stubborn, uncooperative, unhelpful.
AN OPPOSITE IS cooperative.
5 *He felt awkward in the smart hotel.* edgy, embarrassed, out of place, uncomfortable, uneasy.
AN OPPOSITE IS comfortable.

axe *noun*

> VARIOUS TOOLS OR WEAPONS USED
> FOR CHOPPING: battleaxe, chopper,
> cleaver, hatchet, tomahawk.

axe *verb*
[*informal*] *They axed our bus service.*
abolish, cancel, cut, end, get rid of,
terminate, withdraw.

Bb

baby *noun*
infant.
A baby just learning to walk is a
toddler.
FOR BABY ANIMALS, SEE **young**
adjective.

babyish *adjective*
*Mum got annoyed and said I was being
babyish.* childish, immature, infantile.
AN OPPOSITE IS grown-up.

back *noun*
*The people at the front of the queue told
us to go to the back.* end, rear.
The back of a ship is the ***stern***.
The back end of an animal is the
hindquarters, ***rear***, or ***rump***.
The back of a piece of paper is the
reverse.
AN OPPOSITE IS front.

back *adjective*
We sat on the back seat. end, rear.
The back legs of an animal are its ***hind***
legs.
AN OPPOSITE IS front.

back *verb*
1 *I watched Mum back into the drive.*
drive backwards, reverse.
2 *Who do you back to win?* bet on,
gamble on.
3 *A local business agreed to back our
team.* sponsor, subsidize, support.
to back away *When the dog growled,
we backed away.* back off, give way,
recoil, retire, retreat.
AN OPPOSITE IS approach.

to back out of something *I hurt my
foot, so I had to back out of Saturday's
game.* drop out of, withdraw from.
to back someone up *Will you back me
up if I need help?* help, support.

background *noun*
1 *I drew a picture of Mum with our
house in the background.*
AN OPPOSITE IS foreground.
2 *We had a lesson about the
background to the Gunpowder Plot.*
The background to an event is the
circumstances surrounding it or the
history of it.
3 *My uncle's family has a military
background.* tradition, upbringing.

backing *noun*
1 *We can have a swimming competition
if we get the head's backing.* approval,
encouragement, help, support.
2 *We got financial backing from a local
firm.* aid, assistance, sponsorship, a
subsidy.

backwards *adverb*
1 *He drove backwards into the gatepost.*
in reverse.
AN OPPOSITE IS forwards.
2 *You've got your pullover on
backwards.* back to front.

bad *adjective*
We use the word *bad* to describe
almost anything we don't like.
Therefore there are a lot of possible
synonyms, and the best ones to use will
depend on what you are talking about.
Here are some common ways we use
bad and some of the synonyms we
might use
1 *He was a bad man.* beastly, corrupt,
criminal, cruel, dangerous, deplorable,
detestable, evil, immoral, infamous,
malevolent, malicious, mean, nasty,
shameful, sinful, vicious, villainous,
wicked.
2 *I saw a bad accident on the
motorway.* appalling, awful,
calamitous, disastrous, dreadful,
frightful, ghastly, hair-raising,
hideous, horrible, shocking, terrible.
3 *She went to hospital with a bad
illness.* distressing, grave, painful,
serious, severe, unpleasant.

4 *He was punished for his bad behaviour.* abominable, [*informal*] diabolical, disgraceful, dreadful, mischievous, naughty, wrong.
5 *I had to do the work again because it was so bad.* [*informal*] abysmal, awful, [*informal*] hopeless, inadequate, incompetent, inefficient, inferior, poor, shoddy, unsatisfactory, useless, weak, worthless.
6 *We abandoned the journey because of the bad weather.* adverse, discouraging, harsh, hostile, unfavourable, unhelpful.
7 *When the fridge went wrong we threw away a lot of bad food.* decayed, decomposing, foul, mouldy, rotten, smelly, sour, spoiled.
8 *The bad smell comes from the drains.* disgusting, foul, loathsome, objectionable, offensive, repulsive, revolting, sickening, vile.
9 *Smoking is bad for your health.* damaging, dangerous, harmful, injurious.
10 *I felt too bad to go to school today.* ill, poorly, sick, unwell.
11 *I feel bad that I haven't written to Granny.* ashamed, guilty, remorseful, sorry.
AN OPPOSITE IS good.

badge *noun*

THINGS YOU WEAR OR DISPLAY TO SHOW WHO YOU ARE, WHICH ORGANIZATION YOU BELONG TO, ETC.: crest, emblem, flag, logo, medal, rosette, sign, symbol, trademark.

badger *verb*
Don't badger me while I'm busy. annoy, bother, harass, nag, pester, trouble, worry.

bad-tempered *adjective*
What made you so bad-tempered today? angry, annoyed, cross, grumpy, ill-tempered, irritable, moody, quarrelsome, rude, short-tempered, sullen.
AN OPPOSITE IS good-tempered.

baffle *verb*
The problem baffled us. bewilder, confuse, defeat, foil, fox, frustrate, mystify, outwit, perplex, puzzle, stump.

baffling *adjective*
No one could explain the baffling mystery. bewildering, confusing, frustrating, inexplicable, insoluble, mysterious, mystifying, perplexing, puzzling.
AN OPPOSITE IS straightforward.

bag *noun*

VARIOUS CONTAINERS USED TO CARRY THINGS IN ARE: basket, briefcase, carrier bag, case, handbag, holdall, sack, satchel, shopping bag, shoulder bag, suitcase.

baggage *noun*
We loaded our baggage onto a trolley. bags, belongings, cases, gear, luggage, paraphernalia, suitcases, trunks.

bake *verb*
FOR VARIOUS WAYS TO COOK THINGS, SEE **cook** *verb*.

balance *noun*
to lose your balance *I lost my balance and fell off the branch.* totter, wobble.

bald *adjective*
He has a bald patch on the back of his head. bare, hairless.

bale *verb*
to bale out *The aircraft crashed, but the pilot had managed to bale out.* eject, escape, jump out, parachute down.

ball *noun*
The Earth is the shape of a ball. globe, globule, orb, sphere.

ban *verb*
1 *They banned smoking on the buses.* forbid, make illegal, outlaw, prohibit, stop.
2 *They banned him from swimming because he annoyed the younger children.* bar, exclude.
AN OPPOSITE IS allow.

band *noun*
1 *A band of devoted followers sat round him.* company, gang, group.
2 *I play the recorder in the school band.* ensemble, group, orchestra.
3 *The team's new strip has a band of red round the white shirt.* belt, hoop, line, ring, stripe.

bandage *noun*

THINGS USED TO DRESS A WOUND ARE: dressing, gauze, lint, plaster.

bandit *noun*
Buses travelling through the mountains have been attacked by bandits. brigand, gangster, gunman, outlaw, robber, thief.

bang *noun*
1 *I heard a loud bang just before the crash.* blast, boom, crash, explosion, pop, report, thud, thump.
FOR VARIOUS WAYS TO MAKE SOUNDS, SEE **sound** *verb*.
2 *I've got a bruise where I had that bang on the head.* blow, bump, hit, knock, punch, smack, thump, [*slang*] wallop, whack.

bang *verb*
1 *You could tell she was angry by the way she banged the saucepan on the table.* hit, slam, thump.
2 *The cat hates it when the fireworks bang.* crack, explode, go off.

banish *verb*
He was banished from his native land for ever. deport, eject, exile, expel, send away.

bank *noun*
1 *I put half my pocket money in the bank.*

OTHER PLACES WHERE YOUR MONEY CAN BE LOOKED AFTER: building society, post office, savings bank.

2 *There were fishermen all along the river bank.* brink, edge, margin, shore, side.
3 *I sat and rested on a grassy bank.* embankment, mound, ridge, slope.
4 *The pilot had to keep his eye on the bank of instruments.* array, collection, rank, row, series.

bank *verb*
1 *I banked half of my pocket money.* deposit, pay in, save.
2 *The plane banked as it came in to land.* lean over, tilt, tip.

banner *noun*
Colourful banners fluttered in the wind. flag, pennant, standard, streamer.

banquet *noun*
They held a banquet in honour of the visiting President. dinner, feast.

bar *noun*

LONG PIECES OF METAL OR WOOD USED FOR VARIOUS PURPOSES ARE: beam, girder, joist, pole, rail, railing, rod, shaft, stake, stick, strut.
A bar of chocolate can be called a **block** or **slab**.
A bar of soap can be called a **cake**.

bar *verb*
1 *The club barred her because she didn't pay her subscription.* ban, exclude, keep out, prohibit.
2 *A fallen tree barred our way.* block, check, hinder, impede, obstruct, stop.

barbaric *adjective*
Many were killed in the barbaric attack. barbarous, brutal, cold-blooded, cruel, inhuman, ruthless, savage.
AN OPPOSITE IS humane.

bare *adjective*
1 *He was bare from the waist up.* exposed, naked, nude, unclothed, undressed.
2 *Dad's got a bare patch on top of his head.* bald, hairless.

3 *There was no shelter on the bare hill.* barren, bleak, treeless.
4 *The bare room looked cold and cheerless.* empty, unfurnished.
5 *Shall we put some pictures on that bare wall?* blank, plain.
6 *They didn't even have enough money for the bare necessities.* basic, essential, minimum.

bargain *noun*
1 *I'll make a bargain with you.* agreement, deal, pact.
2 *The coat I bought was a bargain.* good buy, special offer.

bargain *verb*
Mum bargained with the salesman about the price. argue, do a deal, haggle, negotiate.

bark *verb*
The dog barked fiercely. growl, yap.

barracks *noun*

OTHER KINDS OF ACCOMMODATION FOR SOLDIERS: billet, camp, garrison, quarters.

barrage *noun*
1 *The soldiers were attacked with a barrage of gunfire.* bombardment, volley.
2 *They built a barrage to control the flow of the river.* barrier, dam, weir.

barrel *noun*

VARIOUS KINDS OF BARREL ARE: butt, cask, drum, keg, oil drum, tub, water-butt.
FOR OTHER THINGS TO KEEP LIQUIDS IN, SEE **container**.

barren *adjective*
The camel train had to cross miles of barren desert. arid, bare, dried-up, infertile, lifeless, sterile, uncultivated.
AN OPPOSITE IS fertile.

barricade *noun*
The protesters built a barricade across the road. barrier, obstacle, obstruction.
SEE ALSO **fence** *noun*.

barrier *noun*
1 *They asked the spectators to stay behind the barrier.* barricade, fence, railing, wall.
SEE ALSO **fence** *noun*.
2 *I'd like to be friends with the French visitors, but my ignorance of their language is a barrier.* drawback, handicap, hindrance, obstacle.

barter *verb*
I bartered my comic for his sweets. exchange, swap, trade.

base *noun*
1 *Little flowers were growing near the base of the wall.* bottom, foot.
The base of a statue is a ***pedestal***.
2 *Dad laid some paving slabs to make a base for his new shed.* basis, foundation, support.
3 *The explorers returned to their base.* camp, depot, headquarters.

basement *noun*

OTHER PARTS OF A BUILDING BELOW GROUND ARE: cellar, crypt, dungeon, undercroft, vault.

bashful *adjective*
Don't be bashful—speak up for yourself. coy, embarrassed, modest, nervous, reserved, retiring, sheepish, shy, timid.
AN OPPOSITE IS assertive.

basic *adjective*
1 *I learned the basic moves in chess.* chief, crucial, essential, fundamental, important, key, main, principal, vital.
2 *My knowledge of French is very basic.* elementary, simple.
AN OPPOSITE IS advanced.

basin *noun*
I filled the basin with hot water. bowl, dish, sink.
FOR OTHER THINGS TO PUT LIQUIDS IN, SEE **container**.

basis *noun*
1 *Our experienced players formed the basis of the team.* base, core, foundation.
2 *On what basis did you decide to be a vegetarian?* principle.

bask *verb*
> Are you going to stay basking in the sun all afternoon? enjoy yourself, lie, lounge, relax.

basket *noun*

> VARIOUS KINDS OF BASKET ARE: hamper, laundry basket, pannier, punnet, shopping-basket, trug.
> FOR OTHER CONTAINERS, SEE **container**.

bat *noun*
> In golf, you hit the ball with a *club*.
> In tennis, you hit it with a *racket*.
> In snooker, you hit it with a *cue*.

bath *noun*
> To wash all over you can also have a *shower*.
> Special kinds of bath are *jacuzzi*, *sauna*, and *Turkish bath*.

bathe *verb*
> **1** On hot days we often bathe in the river. go swimming, splash about, swim, take a dip.
> To walk about in shallow water is to *paddle*.
> To walk through deep water is to *wade*.
> **2** The nurse gently bathed the wound. clean, cleanse, rinse, wash.

bathroom *noun*

> FITTINGS YOU MAY FIND IN A BATHROOM: bath, bidet, extractor fan, jacuzzi, lavatory, medicine cabinet, mirror, shaver point, shower, shower curtain, taps, tiles, toilet, towel rail, ventilator, washbasin.
>
> THINGS PEOPLE USE IN A BATHROOM: bath mat, bath salts, comb, cosmetics, curlers, flannel, foam bath, gel, hairbrush, loofah, make-up, nail brush, nail scissors, pumice stone, razor, scales, shampoo, shaver, soap, sponge, toiletries, toilet roll, toothbrush, towel, tweezers.

batter *verb*
> We battered on the door for ages, but no one came. beat, keep hitting, pound.
> FOR OTHER WAYS OF HITTING, SEE **hit** *verb*.

battle *noun*
> Both armies lost many soldiers in the battle. action, clash, conflict, engagement, hostilities, struggle.
> A series of battles is a *campaign* or *war*.
> SEE ALSO **fight** *noun*.

bay *noun*

> VARIOUS PLACES WHERE THE SEA SHORE CURVES INWARD: cove, creek, estuary, fjord, gulf, harbour, inlet, sound.

be *verb*
> **1** I'll be here until lunchtime. continue, remain, stay, survive.
> **2** The concert will be in November. come about, happen, occur, take place.
> **3** She wants to be a writer. become, develop into.

beach *noun*
> We played all day on the beach. sands, seashore, shore.

bead *noun*
> **1** She wore a string of pretty beads.
> FOR OTHER WORDS, SEE **jewellery**.
> **2** Beads of sweat stood out on his forehead. blob, drip, drop, droplet, pearl.

beam *noun*
> **1** The old house was full of wooden beams.

> OTHER LONG PIECES OF WOOD USED FOR VARIOUS PURPOSES: bar, boom, joist, mast, plank, pole, post, rafter, rail, railing, rod, shaft, spar, stake, stick, strut, support, timber.

> **2** The lighthouse sent out a strong beam of light. gleam, ray, shaft, stream.

beam *verb*

1 *Everyone in the photo was beaming happily.* grin, laugh, smile.
AN OPPOSITE IS frown.
2 *The radio waves were beamed towards a satellite.* aim, broadcast, direct, radiate, send out, transmit.

bean *noun*

SOME KINDS OF BEAN ARE: broad bean, butter-bean, French bean, haricot bean, kidney bean, runner bean, soya bean.
Beans, peas, lentils, etc., are *legumes* or *pulses*.

bear *verb*

1 *The rope won't bear my weight.* carry, hold, support, take.
2 *They bore the injured player off the field on a stretcher.* bring, carry, fetch, take, transfer.
3 *The gravestone bears an inscription.* display, have, show.
4 *I can't bear this toothache.* abide, endure, put up with, stand, suffer, tolerate.
5 *She has borne three children.* give birth to.

bear *noun*

VARIOUS KINDS OF BEAR ARE: black bear, brown bear, grizzly bear, polar bear.
Popular animals rather like bears are the *koala* and *giant panda*.
A toy bear is a *teddy bear*.
FOR OTHER ANIMALS, SEE **animal**.

bearable *adjective*
The pain is bad, but it is bearable. acceptable, endurable, tolerable.
AN OPPOSITE IS unbearable.

bearing *noun*
He was an elderly man with a military bearing. appearance, look, manner, posture.
bearings *I lost my bearings in the fog.* direction, position, sense of direction.

beast *noun*
At one time many wild beasts lived in the jungle. animal, creature.
You might call a large or frightening beast a *brute* or *monster*.
FOR OTHER WORDS, SEE **animal**.

beastly *adjective*
I hated him for playing that beastly trick. cruel, horrid, nasty, spiteful, unkind, unpleasant.
AN OPPOSITE IS kind.

beat *verb*
1 *He beat the dog with a stick.* batter, cane, flog, hit, lash, strike, thrash, whack, whip.
FOR OTHER WAYS TO HIT, SEE **hit** *verb*.
2 *I'm sorry to say that our opponents beat us.* conquer, defeat, get the better of, overcome, overwhelm, rout, thrash, vanquish, win against.
3 *I beat some eggs to make an omelette.* mix up, stir briskly, whip, whisk.
4 *My heart beat faster.* pound, thump.
to beat someone up *The bully threatened to beat me up.* assault, attack, [*informal*] knock about, [*informal*] set about.

beat *noun*
1 *After you've been running, you feel the beat of your heart.* pulse, throb.
2 *I like music with a strong beat.* accent, rhythm.

beautiful *adjective*
1 *The bride looked very beautiful.* attractive, charming, [*informal*] cute, good-looking, glamorous, gorgeous, lovely, pretty, radiant.
A man who is pleasing to look at is *good-looking* or *handsome*.
2 *I enjoyed the beautiful views as we drove through the mountains.* delightful, glorious, magnificent, picturesque, scenic, spectacular, splendid.
3 *We had beautiful weather on our holiday.* brilliant, excellent, fine, glorious, marvellous, sunny, superb, wonderful.
AN OPPOSITE IS nasty or ugly.

beauty *noun*
1 *The film star was famous for her beauty.* attractiveness, glamour, grace, loveliness.
2 *We admired the beauty of the surrounding countryside.* appeal, glory, magnificence, radiance, splendour.
AN OPPOSITE IS ugliness.

beckon *verb*
When he beckoned to me, I ran to see what he wanted. gesticulate, make a sign, signal.

become *verb*
1 *I hope you won't become angry if I tell the truth.* begin to be, turn.
2 *If you buy a pet, remember that little puppies become big dogs!* change into, develop into, grow into, turn into.
3 *That colour becomes you.* look good on, suit.

bed *noun*
1 *This bed isn't very comfortable.*

VARIOUS KINDS OF BED: air-bed, divan, double bed, four-poster, single bed, water-bed.
A bed for a baby is a *cot*, *cradle*, or *crib*.
Two single beds one above the other are *bunk beds*.
A bed on a ship or train is a *berth*.
A bed made of net or cloth hung up above the ground is a *hammock*.

PARTS OF A BED: base, bedpost, bedstead, headboard, mattress.

THINGS YOU USE TO MAKE A BED WARM AND COMFORTABLE: bed linen, bedspread, blanket, bolster, continental quilt, counterpane, coverlet, duvet, eiderdown, electric blanket, mattress, pillow, pillowcase, pillowslip, quilt, sheet, sleeping bag.

2 *Mum filled the flower bed with geraniums.* border, patch, plot.
3 *The wreck settled on the bed of the sea.* bottom.
4 *Dad erected his shed on a bed of concrete.* base, foundation, layer.

bedclothes *plural noun*
bedding, sheets and blankets.

bedraggled *adjective*
The dog came in out of the rain looking very bedraggled. dirty, dishevelled, messy, scruffy, untidy, wet.
AN OPPOSITE IS smart.

beer *noun*
FOR VARIOUS DRINKS, SEE **drink** *noun*.

beetle *noun*

SOME OF THE MANY KINDS OF BEETLE ARE: cockchafer, cockroach, Colorado beetle, deathwatch beetle, dung-beetle, furniture beetle, ladybird, stag beetle.
FOR OTHER INSECTS AND CRAWLING CREATURES, SEE **insect**.

before *adverb*
1 *Have you been here before?* already, in the past.
2 *If you want to come with me, you should have told me before.* earlier, in advance, previously, sooner.

beg *verb*
1 *The next-door cat comes round to beg for food.* cadge, [*informal*] scrounge.
2 *He begged me not to tell the teacher.* ask, entreat, implore, plead with.

begin *verb*
1 *We began the journey at breakfast time.* commence, embark on, set out on, start.
2 *We plan to begin a chess club next term.* found, initiate, introduce, launch, set up.
3 *When did the trouble begin?* arise, break out, come into existence, crop up, emerge, happen, originate, spring up.
AN OPPOSITE IS end or stop.

beginner *noun*
I'm only a beginner. learner, novice, starter.
A beginner in a trade or a job is an *apprentice* or *trainee*.
A beginner in the police or armed services is a *cadet* or *recruit*.

beginning *noun*
The beginning of the new rail service should mean fewer traffic jams. commencement, establishment, foundation, initiation, introduction, launch, opening, start.

The beginning of life on earth was *creation* or *genesis*.
The beginning of your life was your *birth*.
The beginning of the day is *dawn* or *daybreak*.
The beginning of a journey is the *starting point*.
The beginning of a stream or river is the *origin* or *source*.
A piece of writing at the beginning of a book is an *introduction*, *preface*, or *prologue*.
A piece of music at the beginning of a musical or opera is a *prelude* or *overture*.
AN OPPOSITE IS end.

behave *verb*
1 *The car behaves better since it was serviced.* act, perform, run, work.
2 *I wish you would behave!* be good, be on your best behaviour.

behaviour *noun*
She congratulated us on our good behaviour. actions, attitude, conduct, manners.

being *noun*
They looked like beings from another planet. animal, creature, individual, person.

belch *verb*
1 *The chimney belched smoke.* discharge, emit, send out.
2 *Smoke belched out of the chimney.* erupt, gush.

belief *noun*
1 *Some people are persecuted because of their religious belief.* creed, doctrine, faith, religion.
2 *My belief is that he stole the money.* conviction, feeling, notion, opinion, theory, view.
3 *His belief in fairies made everyone laugh at him.* believing, confidence, faith, trust.

believe *verb*
1 *I believe what he says.* accept, have faith in, rely on, trust.
AN OPPOSITE IS disbelieve.
2 *I believe that she cheated.* assume, feel, know, presume, reckon, suppose, think.

bell *noun*

VARIOUS KINDS OF BELL: alarm bell, carillon, chimes, church bells, doorbell, knell, peal of bells, tubular bells, warning bell.

VERBS EXPRESSING DIFFERENT WAYS BELLS SOUND: chime, clang, clink, jangle, jingle, peal, ping, resonate, reverberate, ring, sound the knell, strike, tinkle, toll.

belong *verb*
1 *This book belongs to me.* be owned by.
2 *Would you like to belong to the squash club?* be a member of, be connected with.
3 *I belong here with my friends.* be at home, be welcome, have a place.

belongings *plural noun*
Make sure you take your belongings with you when you get off the train. goods, possessions, property, things.

below *preposition*
1 *We saw goldfish swimming below the surface.* beneath, under, underneath.
2 *The temperature never fell below 20 degrees.* less than, lower than.

belt *noun*
We walked through a belt of woodland. band, line, stretch, strip.

bench *noun*
1 *We sat down on a bench in the park.* form, seat.
A long seat in a church is a *pew*.
2 *The carpenter laid his tools out on the bench.* table, workbench, work table.

bend *verb*
The metal was bent into strange shapes. arch, buckle, coil, curl, curve, distort, flex, fold, loop, turn, twist, warp, wind.
A word for things which bend easily is *flexible*.
AN OPPOSITE IS straighten.
to bend down *I bent down behind the wall so that they couldn't see me.* bow, crouch, duck, kneel, stoop.

bend *noun*
Watch out for the dangerous bend in the road. angle, corner, curve, turn, twist, zigzag.

benefactor *noun*
An anonymous benefactor paid for our trip. backer, donor, patron, promoter, sponsor, supporter, well-wisher.

benefit *noun*
1 One benefit of living in the country is that the air is cleaner. advantage, convenience, gain, good thing.
AN OPPOSITE IS handicap.
2 Since he lost his job he's been living on benefit. [informal] dole.
Other terms for benefit people get from the government include **income support**, **social security**, and **welfare**.

benevolent *adjective*
A benevolent sponsor gave us money for sports equipment. charitable, friendly, generous, helpful, kind, liberal, sympathetic, warm-hearted.
AN OPPOSITE IS malevolent.

bent *adjective*
1 After the accident, the car was a mass of bent metal. arched, buckled, coiled, contorted, crooked, curved, distorted, folded, twisted, warped.
AN OPPOSITE IS straight.
2 [slang] The bent politician was dismissed from the government. corrupt, dishonest, untrustworthy.
AN OPPOSITE IS honest.

bequeath *verb*
In her will, she bequeathed her money to her grandchildren. hand down, leave, pass on.

bereaved *adjective*
Someone whose husband or wife dies is **widowed**.
A child whose parents die is **orphaned**.

bereavement *noun*
They wore black because there was a bereavement in the family. death, loss.

berserk *adjective*
to go berserk The dog went berserk when a wasp stung him. [informal] be beside yourself, become frantic, become frenzied, go crazy, lose control of yourself, go mad, rampage, riot.

berth *noun*

PLACES WHERE SHIPS TIE UP:
anchorage, dock, harbour, haven, landing stage, moorings, pier, port, quay, slipway, wharf.

beside *preposition*
They parked their car beside ours. alongside, by, close to, near, next to.
beside the point The fact that it is raining is beside the point. irrelevant, neither here nor there, unimportant.
to be beside yourself He was beside himself when he found out they had cheated him. become frantic, be upset, go berserk, lose control of yourself.

besides *adverb*
I don't really want to go, and besides, I haven't got any money. additionally, also, furthermore, in addition, moreover.

besiege *verb*
1 The Greeks besieged Troy for 10 long years. blockade, cut off, isolate.
2 The superstar was besieged by reporters. encircle, surround.

best *adjective*
1 She is our best player. finest, leading, outstanding, supreme, unequalled, unrivalled.
2 Our shop only sells vegetables of the best quality. excellent, first-class, top.
AN OPPOSITE IS worst.

bet *noun*
I had a bet that she would win. gamble, wager.

bet *verb*
He bet everything he had on a horse race. gamble, risk.

betray *verb*
1 He betrayed us by revealing our plans to our opponents. be a traitor to, cheat, conspire against, double-cross.
2 He betrayed his friend to the police. inform against, [informal] tell tales about.
3 I thought I could trust her, but she betrayed my secret. disclose, give away, let out, reveal, tell.

better *adjective*
  1 *Which of these dresses do you think is better?* preferable, superior.
  2 *I had flu, but I'm better now.* cured, healed, healthier, improved, recovering, well.

beware *verb*
  Beware! There are thieves about. be careful! be on your guard! look out! take care! watch out!
  beware of *Beware of the bull.* avoid, guard against, heed, keep clear of, look out for, mind, watch out for.

bewilder *verb*
  I was bewildered by the misleading instructions on the packet. baffle, confuse, fox, mystify, perplex, puzzle.

beyond *preposition*
  You'll find the post office just beyond the butchers. after, past, the other side of.

bias *noun*
  1 *She has a bias towards science.* bent, inclination, leaning, liking, preference, tendency.
  2 *The referee was guilty of bias.* favouritism, one-sidedness, prejudice, unfairness.
  A bias against people of one particular race is **racism**.
  A bias against one sex is **sexism**.

biased *adjective*
  The crowd thought that the referee's decision was biased. one-sided, prejudiced, unfair.
  AN OPPOSITE IS impartial.

bicycle *noun*

> DIFFERENT KINDS OF CYCLE: bicycle or [*informal*] bike, moped, motor bike or motor cycle, mountain bike, [*old use*] penny-farthing, racer or racing bike, scooter, tandem, tricycle.

bid *noun*
  1 *I made a bid at the auction for a rare stamp.* offer.
  2 *His bid to beat the world record failed.* attempt, effort, go, try.

big *adjective*
  The adjective *big* can refer to anything that is more than the normal size or importance. Therefore there are a lot of possible synonyms, and the best ones to use will depend on what we are talking about. Here are some common ways we use *big* and some of the synonyms we might use
  1 *I need a big box to put my things in.* large, roomy, sizeable, spacious.
  2 *She gave us big helpings of food.* ample, considerable, enormous, great, huge, substantial, [*informal*] tremendous.
  3 *The weightlifter was a big man.* burly, colossal, enormous, gigantic, huge, hulking, mighty.
  4 *He eats so much that he's getting big.* fat, overweight, plump, stout.
  5 *Space exploration involves travelling big distances.* immense, infinite, vast.
  6 *During the storm, we were terrified by the big waves.* high, mountainous, tall, towering.
  7 *It's awkward carrying big parcels on the bus.* bulky, heavy, hefty, weighty.
  8 *We gave the winners a big round of applause.* deafening, enthusiastic, loud, thunderous.
  9 *I have some big decisions to make.* grave, important, serious, significant.
  10 *She's a big name in the music business.* famous, influential, leading, notable, powerful, prominent.
  AN OPPOSITE IS small or unimportant.

bill *noun*
  Dad went pale when he saw the bill for repairs to the car. account, invoice, statement.

bin *noun*
  FOR VARIOUS CONTAINERS, SEE **container**.

bind *verb*
  1 *I bound two sticks together with some string.* attach, connect, fasten, join, lash, rope, secure, tie.
  2 *The nurse started to bind the wound with a bandage.* cover, dress, wrap.

bird *noun*

> The study of birds is **ornithology**.
> A female bird is a **hen**.
> A male bird is a **cock**. ➡

A group of birds is a *flock*.
A young bird is a *chick* or *fledgling*.
A young bird in a nest is a *nestling*.
A family of chicks is a *brood*.
FOR SPECIAL NAMES FOR YOUNG
BIRDS, SEE **young** *adjective*.

SOME DIFFERENT KINDS OF BIRDS
ARE: birds of prey, game birds, sea
birds, songbirds, waders, waterfowl,
wildfowl.

BIRDS SOMETIMES KEPT AS PETS
ARE: budgerigar, canary, cockatoo,
macaw, mynah bird, parakeet,
parrot, peacock.

BIRDS WHICH FARMERS KEEP FOR
THEIR EGGS OR MEAT ARE: chicken,
duck, goose, ostrich, turkey.
Birds kept by farmers are *poultry*.

BIRDS YOU MAY SEE IN BRITISH
GARDENS OR COUNTRYSIDE:
blackbird, blackcap, bullfinch,
bunting, chaffinch, chiffchaff,
corncrake, crow, cuckoo, curlew,
dove, dunnock, fieldfare, finch,
flycatcher, goldcrest, goldfinch,
greenfinch, hedge sparrow, jackdaw,
jay, lapwing, lark, linnet, magpie,
martin, nightingale, nightjar,
nuthatch, ousel, peewit, pigeon,
pipit, plover, raven, redbreast,
redstart, robin, rook, shrike, skylark,
sparrow, sparrowhawk, starling,
stonechat, swallow, swift, thrush, tit,
treecreeper, warbler, waxwing,
wheatear, whitethroat, woodpecker,
wren, yellowhammer.

SOME BIRDS YOU MIGHT SEE IN
OTHER COUNTRIES OR IN A ZOO:
cassowary, crane, emu, flamingo,
humming bird, ibis, kiwi,
kookaburra, ostrich, pelican,
penguin, stork, toucan, vulture.

BIRDS WHICH LIVE ON OR NEAR
LAKES, STREAMS, OR MARSHES:
avocet, bittern, coot, dabchick,
dipper, diver, duck, egret, goose,
grebe, heron, kingfisher, mallard,
moorhen, sandpiper, snipe,
spoonbill, swan, teal, wagtail,
wigeon. ➡

BIRDS WHICH LIVE ON OR NEAR THE
SEA: albatross, auk, chough,
cormorant, dunlin, fulmar, gannet,
guillemot, gull, kittiwake,
oystercatcher, petrel, puffin,
razorbill, redshank, seagull, shag,
shearwater, shelduck, skua, tern,
turnstone.

SOME BIRDS OF PREY: buzzard,
eagle, falcon, hawk, hen harrier,
kestrel, kite, merlin, osprey, owl,
peregrine, sparrowhawk.

GAME BIRDS WHICH PEOPLE HUNT,
OR USED TO HUNT: grouse,
partridge, pheasant, ptarmigan,
quail, woodcock.

PARTS OF A BIRD ARE: beak, bill,
claw, crest, down, feathers, plumage,
tail, talon, wing.

PLACES WHERE BIRDS LIVE OR
BRING UP THEIR YOUNG: aviary,
cage, nest, nesting box.

birth *noun*
The movements of a woman's womb
when a baby is born is *labour*.
A medical specialist in childbirth is an
obstetrician.
The birth of Jesus is called the
Nativity.

biscuit *noun*

SOME DIFFERENT KINDS OF
BISCUIT ARE: chocolate biscuit,
cracker, crispbread, digestive biscuit,
ginger-nut, macaroon, oatcake,
pretzel, rusk, shortbread, wafer.

bisect *verb*
The lines bisect each other. cross,
divide, intersect.

bit *noun*
1 *We divided the chocolate so that we
each had a bit.* chunk, fraction, hunk,
lump, piece, portion, section, segment,
share.

2 *I swept up the bits off the floor.* chip, fragment, scrap.
A small bit of food is a **morsel**.
A bit broken off a cake or loaf is a **crumb**.
A bit of dust is a **particle** or **speck**.

bite *verb*
To bite at something hard is to **gnaw** it.
To bite and crush something hard is to **crunch** it.
To bite off very small bits at a time is to **nibble**.
When a fierce animal bites you it **savages** you.
When a dog tries to bite you it **snaps** at you.
When an insect bites you it **stings** you.
FOR OTHER WORDS, SEE **eat**.

bitter *adjective*
1 *The unripe plums had a bitter taste.* acid, harsh, sharp, sour, unpleasant.
AN OPPOSITE IS sweet.
2 *He was very bitter when I got the prize instead of him.* envious, jealous, malicious, resentful, sore, spiteful, unkind, unpleasant, vicious.
AN OPPOSITE IS pleased.
3 *I wore my anorak to keep out the bitter wind.* biting, cold, freezing, icy, [*informal*] perishing, piercing, raw, wintry.
AN OPPOSITE IS mild.

black *adjective, noun*

WORDS TO DESCRIBE THINGS THAT ARE BLACK OR NEARLY BLACK:
blackish, coal-black, dark, dirty, dusky, ebony, gloomy, inky, jet-black, murky, pitch-black, pitch-dark, raven, sooty.

blade *noun*

VARIOUS WEAPONS AND IMPLEMENTS THAT HAVE A BLADE:
axe, chopper, cutlass, dagger, knife, razor, sabre, scalpel, scissors, sword.

blame *verb*
It was unfair to blame the driver for the accident. accuse, condemn, criticize, reproach, scold.

blank *adjective*
1 *We need something to fill in that blank space.* bare, clean, empty, plain, unmarked, unused.
2 *He gave me a blank look.* absent-minded, baffled, expressionless, mindless, vacant.

blank *noun*
Fill in the blanks. break, gap, space.

blasphemous *adjective*
I was shocked to hear such blasphemous language in church. irreverent, wicked.
AN OPPOSITE IS reverent.

blast *noun*
1 *When he opened the door, I felt a blast of air.* burst, gale, gust, rush.
2 *We heard the blast of a trumpet.* blare, noise, roar.
3 *Windows were broken by the blast.* explosion.

blaze *noun*
Firemen fought the blaze for hours. fire, flames, inferno.

blaze *verb*
Within a few minutes the dry timber was blazing. burn brightly, flare up.

bleak *adjective*
1 *They got lost and had to spend the night on a bleak hillside.* bare, barren, cheerless, cold, comfortless, exposed, wintry.
AN OPPOSITE IS comfortable.
2 *After losing so many matches, our team's future looks bleak.* depressing, dismal, gloomy, grim, hopeless, miserable.
AN OPPOSITE IS promising.

blemish *noun*
Dad noticed a blemish on the paintwork of our car. defect, fault, flaw, imperfection, mark, stain.

VARIOUS KINDS OF BLEMISH YOU CAN HAVE ON YOUR SKIN ARE:
birthmark, blackhead, blister, corn, freckle, mole, pimple, scar, spot, verruca, wart, whitlow, [*slang*] zit.

blend *verb*
Blend the flour with a tablespoon of water. beat together, mix, stir together, whip, whisk.
to blend with *Many birds are camouflaged so that they blend with the background.* become part of, disappear into, match, merge with, tone in with.

blessing *noun*
1 *The priest pronounced a blessing.* grace, prayer.
AN OPPOSITE IS curse.
2 *He gave the plan his blessing.* approval, backing, consent, permission, support.
AN OPPOSITE IS disapproval.
3 *Central heating is a blessing in the winter.* advantage, asset, benefit, comfort.
AN OPPOSITE IS evil *noun*.

blight *noun*
The problem of drugs is a blight on society. affliction, curse, evil, plague.

blind *adjective*

WORDS TO DESCRIBE PEOPLE WITH IMPAIRED VISION: astigmatic, colour-blind, long-sighted, near-sighted or short-sighted, visually handicapped.

DISEASES CAUSING IMPAIRED VISION INCLUDE: cataract, glaucoma.

blind to *She's blind to his faults.* ignorant of, unaware of.
AN OPPOSITE IS aware of.

bliss *noun*
She gave a sigh of bliss. delight, ecstasy, happiness, joy, pleasure.
AN OPPOSITE IS misery.

blissful *adjective*
We spent a blissful week together. delightful, ecstatic, happy, heavenly, joyful.
AN OPPOSITE IS miserable.

blob *noun*
You've got a blob of ice cream on your chin. drop, lump, spot.

block *noun*
1 *A block of stone fell from the lorry.* chunk, hunk, lump, piece.
We also talk about
a *bar* of chocolate.
a *brick* of ice cream.
a *cake* of soap.
an *ingot* of metal.
a *slab* of concrete.
2 *The basin overflowed because there's a block in the drainpipe.* blockage, jam, obstacle, obstruction.

block *verb*
1 *A tall building blocked our view.* hamper, hinder, interfere with, obstruct.
2 *A mass of leaves had blocked the drain.* [slang] bung up, clog, fill, stop up.
To block a hole is to *plug* it.
To block the street with traffic is to *jam* it.
3 *The demonstrators blocked the street.* barricade, close, shut off.

blockage *noun*
Dad spent ages clearing the blockage in the drain. block, obstacle, obstruction.
A blockage caused by traffic is *congestion* or a *traffic jam*.
A place where a blockage is likely to happen is a *bottleneck*.

bloodshed *noun*
The battlefield was a scene of appalling bloodshed. butchery, killing, massacre, murder, slaughter, slaying.

bloodthirsty *adjective*
The bloodthirsty soldiers committed many atrocities. barbaric, brutal, cruel, ferocious, fierce, inhuman, murderous, pitiless, ruthless, sadistic, savage, vicious, violent, warlike.

bloody *adjective*
1 *Why is your handkerchief all bloody?* blood-soaked, blood-stained.
2 *Many soldiers died in the bloody battle.* gory, gruesome, horrific.

bloom *noun*
The branches were covered in white blooms. flower.

bloom *verb*
> The daffodils bloomed early this year.
> blossom, flourish, flower, open.
> AN OPPOSITE IS fade.

blossom *noun*
> *Blossom usually refers to a mass of
> flowers rather than a single flower*
> *I love to see the cherry blossom in
> spring.* blooms, buds, flowers.

blot *noun*
> *The paper was covered with ink blots.*
> blob, blotch, mark, smear, smudge,
> spot, stain.

blot *verb*
> *I accidentally blotted the page with ink.*
> mark, smudge, spoil, spot, stain.
> **to blot something out** *Fog blotted out
> the view.* conceal, cover, hide, mask.

blow *noun*
> **1** *The batsman gave the ball a hefty
> blow.* bang, [*informal*] bash, hit, knock,
> stroke, swipe, thump, [*informal*]
> wallop, whack.
> A blow with your fist is a ***punch***.
> A blow with the palm of your hand is a
> ***slap*** or ***smack***.
> An accidental blow is a ***bump***.
> **2** *The loss of her purse was a terrible
> blow.* calamity, disaster, misfortune,
> shock, surprise, upset.

blow *verb*
> *The heater blows out hot air.* blast,
> puff.
> To make a shrill sound by blowing is to
> ***whistle***.
> **to blow up 1** *I need to blow up the tyres
> on my bike.* fill, inflate, pump up.
> **2** *We heard the bomb blow up.* detonate,
> explode, go off.
> **3** *The soldiers tried to blow up the
> enemy hideout.* blast, bomb, destroy.
> **4** *Do you think they could blow up this
> photograph?* enlarge.

blue *adjective, noun*

> VARIOUS SHADES OF BLUE ARE:
> azure, cobalt, indigo, navy blue,
> sapphire, sky-blue, turquoise.

blueprint *noun*
> *The blueprint for the new car was kept
> very secret.* design, pattern, plan,
> proposal.
> The first example of an invention is a
> ***prototype***.

bluff *verb*
> *You'll never bluff them into letting you
> go.* [*slang*] con, deceive, fool, trick.

blunder *noun*
> *I made a terrible blunder.* error, fault,
> [*informal*] howler, mistake, slip, slip-
> up.

blunt *adjective*
> **1** *This blunt knife is useless.*
> AN OPPOSITE IS sharp.
> **2** *I was upset by his blunt remarks
> about my work.* abrupt, direct, frank,
> honest, outspoken, plain, rude,
> straightforward, tactless.
> AN OPPOSITE IS tactful.

blur *verb*
> **1** *The steamy windows blurred the
> view.* cloud, darken, obscure, smear.
> **2** *The accident blurred her memory.*
> confuse, muddle.

blurred *adjective*
> **1** *I couldn't make out the faces in the
> blurred photo.* foggy, fuzzy, hazy, out of
> focus, unclear, unfocused.
> **2** *She had only a blurred memory of
> how the accident happened.* confused,
> dim, faint, indistinct, vague.
> AN OPPOSITE IS clear.

blush *verb*
> *He blushed when they accused him of
> lying.* colour, flush, go red.

blustery *adjective*
> *I don't like this blustery weather.* gusty,
> squally, windy.
> AN OPPOSITE IS calm.

board *noun*

> VARIOUS KINDS OF WOODEN BOARD
> ARE: blockboard, chipboard, panels,
> planks, plywood, timber,
> weatherboards.

board *verb*
1 *We boarded the plane for Paris.* enter, get on, go on board.
To board a ship is to **embark**.
2 *The victims of the fire were boarded in a hotel.* accommodate, house, lodge, put up.

boast *verb*
I hate the way he boasts about the pocket money he gets. bluster, brag, crow, gloat, show off, [*informal*] swank.

boastful *adjective*
There's no reason to be boastful because you have rich parents. arrogant, [*informal*] big-headed, [*informal*] cocky, conceited, vain.
AN OPPOSITE IS modest.

boat *noun*
FOR VARIOUS KINDS OF BOAT, SEE **vessel**.

bob *verb*
Something bobbed up and down in the water. bounce, dance, move, toss.

body *noun*

> The study of the human body is *anatomy*.
> The main part of your body except your head, arms, and legs is your *trunk* or *torso*.
> The shape of your body is your *build* or *figure* or *physique*.
> A person's dead body is a *corpse*.
> The dead body of an animal is a *carcass*.
>
> VISIBLE PARTS OF THE HUMAN BODY ARE: abdomen, ankle, arm, armpit, breast, buttocks, calf, cheek, chest, chin, ear, elbow, eye, finger, foot, forehead, genitals, groin, hand, head, heel, hip, instep, jaw, knee, kneecap, knuckle, leg, lip, mouth, navel, neck, nipple, nose, pores, shin, shoulder, skin, stomach, temple, thigh, throat, waist, wrist.
>
> INNER PARTS OF THE BODY ARE: arteries, bladder, bowels, brain, eardrum, glands, gullet, gums, guts, heart, intestines, kidneys, larynx, liver, lung, muscles, nerves, ovaries, pancreas, prostate, sinews, ➡

> stomach, tendons, tongue, tonsil, tooth, uterus, veins, windpipe, womb.
>
> PARTS OF YOUR SKELETON ARE: backbone or spine, collar bone, cranium or skull, pelvis, ribs, shoulder blade, vertebrae.
>
> SOME FLUIDS IN YOUR BODY ARE: bile, blood, hormones, saliva.

bog *noun*
Take care not to sink into the bog! fen, mud, peat bog, quagmire, quicksands, swamp.

bogus *adjective*
Dad's sick of getting bogus phone calls. counterfeit, fake, false.
AN OPPOSITE IS genuine.

boil *verb*
1 *I boiled the potatoes.*
FOR OTHER WAYS TO COOK THINGS, SEE **cook** *verb*.
2 *Is the water boiling yet?* bubble, seethe, steam.

boil *noun*

> VARIOUS KINDS OF INFLAMED PLACE ON THE SKIN ARE: abscess, blister, carbuncle, chilblain, gumboil, inflammation, pimple, sore, spot, ulcer, [*slang*] zit.

boisterous *adjective*
We are always rather boisterous on the last day of term. disorderly, lively, noisy, rowdy, unruly, wild.
AN OPPOSITE IS well-behaved.

bold *adjective*
1 *Be bold and take a risk!* adventurous, assertive, brave, confident, courageous, daring, enterprising, fearless, heroic, intrepid, valiant.
AN OPPOSITE IS cowardly.
2 *I put a bold heading at the top of the poster.* big, bright, clear, conspicuous, large, noticeable, obvious, prominent, striking.
AN OPPOSITE IS inconspicuous.

bolt *verb*
   1 *Did you remember to bolt the door?*
   bar, fasten, lock, secure.
   2 *The animals bolted when they heard
   the clap of thunder.* dash away, escape,
   flee, panic, run away, rush off,
   stampede.
   3 *Don't bolt your food.* eat hastily,
   gobble, gulp, guzzle.

bomb *noun*
   FOR OTHER WEAPONS, SEE **weapon**.

bombard *verb*
   *The city was bombarded by enemy
   forces.* assail, assault, attack, blast,
   bomb, fire at, pound, shell, shoot at.

bombardment *noun*
   *The city was in ruins after the enemy
   bombardment.* attack, barrage, blitz.

bond *noun*
   1 *The prisoner tried to escape from his
   bonds.* chains, fetters, handcuffs,
   ropes.
   2 *Their interest in music makes a bond
   between them.* attachment, connection,
   link, relationship, tie.

bone *noun*
   The bones of your body are your
   skeleton.
   SEE ALSO **body**.

bonus *noun*
   *When we went on holiday, Mum gave
   me a bonus on top of my normal pocket
   money.* extra, supplement.

book *noun*
   *How many books are there in the
   library?* volume.

The particular volume which you
own is your *copy* of the book.
A book issued by a particular
publisher at a particular time is an
edition of the book.
A book with hard covers is a
hardback edition.
A book with soft covers is a
paperback edition.
A book which is typed or
handwritten but not printed is a
manuscript. ➡

THIN BOOKS IN PAPER COVERS:
booklet, brochure, leaflet, pamphlet.

VARIOUS KINDS OF PRINTED BOOK:
album, annual, anthology, atlas,
dictionary, directory, encyclopedia,
guidebook, hymnal or hymn book,
manual, missal, picture book, prayer
book, reading book, reference book,
story book, textbook, thesaurus.

THINGS A BOOK MAY CONTAIN:
appendix, bibliography, chapters,
contents page, foreword,
illustrations, index, introduction,
preface, prologue, title page.

BOOKS YOU CAN WRITE OR DRAW IN
ARE: account book, diary, exercise
book, jotter, notebook, scrapbook,
sketchbook.
FOR VARIOUS KINDS OF WRITING,
SEE **writing**.

book *verb*
   1 *We booked tickets for the play.* order,
   reserve.
   2 *I've booked the disco for the party.*
   arrange, engage, organize.

boom *verb*
   1 *The guns boomed.*
   FOR VARIOUS WAYS TO MAKE SOUNDS,
   SEE **sound** *verb*.
   2 *Business is booming, I'm happy to
   say.* be successful, do well, expand,
   flourish, grow, prosper, thrive.

boost *verb*
   The aim of advertising is to boost sales.
   aid, assist, bolster, build up, encourage,
   expand, help, improve, increase,
   promote.
   AN OPPOSITE IS deter.

border *noun*
   1 *The runaways were safe once they
   had crossed the border.* boundary,
   frontier.
   2 *We did a pretty design round the
   border of our poster.* edge, margin.
   A border round the top of a wall is a
   frieze.
   A border round the bottom of a dress is
   a *hem*.

A decorative border at the bottom of a curtain is a *frill* or *fringe*.
3 *Mum filled the border with geraniums.* flower bed.

bore *verb*
1 *We bored holes for the screws.* drill, pierce.
2 *You can see little holes where woodworm have bored into the antique chair.* burrow, penetrate, tunnel.

boring *adjective*
1 *The film was so boring I fell asleep.* dry, dull, repetitive, tedious, tiresome, unexciting, uninteresting.
2 *She's got a very boring voice.* dreary, flat, monotonous, uninspiring.
AN OPPOSITE IS interesting.

borrow *verb*
1 *I borrowed her pen and forgot to give it back.* cadge, [*informal*] scrounge.
AN OPPOSITE IS lend.
2 *We asked if we were allowed to borrow someone else's ideas.* copy, crib, make use of, take, use.

boss *noun*
FOR WORDS FOR PEOPLE IN CHARGE OF SOMETHING, SEE **chief** *noun*.

bossy *adjective*
We resented her bossy manner. assertive, bullying, dictatorial, officious, tyrannical.

bother *verb*
1 *Does the noise bother you?* annoy, exasperate, irritate, upset, vex, worry.
2 *Please don't bother me while I'm busy.* disturb, harass, nag, pester, plague, trouble.
3 *Don't bother to wash up.* make an effort, take trouble.

bother *noun*
1 *There was some bother in the youth club last night.* difficulty, disturbance, fuss, [*informal*] misbehaviour, problem, trouble.
2 *Is the dog being a bother to you?* annoyance, inconvenience, irritation, nuisance, pest, worry.

bottle *noun*

> DIFFERENT KINDS OF BOTTLE:
> carafe, decanter, flagon, flask, jar, pitcher, wine bottle.
> FOR OTHER THINGS YOU CAN PUT LIQUIDS IN, SEE **container**.

bottle *verb*
to bottle something up *She was disappointed, but she bottled up her feelings and carried on.* conceal, cover up, repress, suppress.

bottom *noun*
1 *The mountaineers set up camp at the bottom of the mountain.* base, foot.
AN OPPOSITE IS top.
2 *The wreck sank to the bottom of the sea.* bed, depths, floor.
AN OPPOSITE IS surface.
3 *A wasp stung me on the bottom.* [*informal*] backside, behind, buttocks, rear, rump, seat.

bottom *adjective*
Who got bottom marks? least, lowest.
AN OPPOSITE IS top.

bough *noun*
The robin perched on a bough of the tree. branch, limb.

bounce *verb*
I missed the ball because it bounced at an awkward angle. rebound, ricochet.

bound *adjective*
1 *Our friends are bound to arrive by teatime.* certain, sure.
2 *She felt bound to warn him of the risk.* committed, compelled, forced, obliged, pledged, required.
3 *The accident was bound to happen.* destined, doomed, fated.
to be bound for *The rocket was bound for the moon.* be aimed at, be directed towards, go towards, head for, make for, travel towards.

bound *verb*
1 *He bounded over the fence.* jump, leap, spring, vault.
2 *Two puppies bounded across the lawn.* bounce, caper, frisk, frolic, skip.

boundary *noun*
> *The fence marks the boundary of the school property.* border, edge, end, frontier, limit, perimeter.

bouquet *noun*
> *The bride carried a lovely bouquet of flowers.* arrangement, bunch.
> A small arrangement of flowers is a *posy* or *spray*.
> Flowers bound together to make a circle are a *garland* or *wreath*.
> A flower you wear on your lapel is a *buttonhole*.

bout *noun*
> **1** *I had an embarrassing bout of coughing during the concert.* attack, fit, period, [*informal*] turn.
> **2** *The referee ended the bout after twenty minutes.* combat, contest, fight, match.

bow *noun*
> *As we entered the harbour, we watched from the bow of the ship.* front, prow.

bow *verb*
> *The men bowed respectfully in front of the queen.*
> The corresponding movement of a woman is to *curtsy*.

bowl *noun*
> *Don't spill the soup when you put the bowl on the table!* basin, dish.

bowl *verb*
> *He bowled a faster ball at the nervous batsman.* fling, hurl, pitch, throw.

box *noun*
> *I put my toys away in a box.* carton, case, chest, crate, tea chest, trunk.
> A small box to keep jewellery in is a *casket*.
> A box a dead person is buried in is a *coffin*.
> FOR OTHER CONTAINERS, SEE **container**.

boy *noun*
> lad, schoolboy, youngster, youth.

boycott *verb*
> *We boycotted the local farm shop when we heard how badly they treated their animals.* avoid, stay away from.

brag *verb*
> *I don't think you should brag about winning.* boast, crow, gloat, show off, [*informal*] swank.

brain *noun*
> *Use your brain!* intellect, intelligence, mind, reason, sense.

brainy *adjective* [*informal*]
> *I'm good at games, but my brother is the brainy one.* bright, clever, intellectual, intelligent, wise.
> AN OPPOSITE IS stupid.

branch *noun*
> **1** *A robin perched on a branch of the tree.* bough, limb.
> **2** *He works in a branch of the armed services.* department, division, part, section.

branch *verb*
> *Follow the track until it branches into two.* divide, fork.
> **to branch out** *I decided to branch out and take up water-skiing.* diversify, do something new.

brand *noun*
> *Which brand of baked beans do you prefer?* kind, make, sort, type, variety.
> The sign of a particular brand of goods is a *trademark*.

brandish *verb*
> *He brandished his gleaming sword.* flourish, shake, wave.

brass *noun*
> FOR OTHER METALS, SEE **metal**.

> MUSICAL INSTRUMENTS OFTEN MADE OF BRASS ARE: bugle, cornet, euphonium, flugelhorn, horn, trombone, trumpet, tuba.

brave *adjective*
> **1** *It was very brave of you to go on your own.* bold, courageous, daring, fearless, gallant, heroic, intrepid, plucky, valiant.
> **2** *The defenders put up a brave resistance.* determined, resolute, stout.
> AN OPPOSITE IS cowardly.

bravery *noun*
  Everyone praised the firemen's bravery.
boldness, courage, determination,
fearlessness, gallantry, grit, [*informal*]
guts, heroism, pluck, valour.
AN OPPOSITE IS cowardice.

brawl *noun*
  *After the match, there was a brawl
between opposing supporters.* fight,
quarrel, [*informal*] scrap, scuffle,
tussle.

brazen *adjective*
  *I don't know how he expected us to
believe such a brazen lie.* cheeky,
impertinent, impudent, insolent,
obvious, shameless, undisguised.

breach *noun*
  1 *He was disqualified because he was
guilty of a breach of the rules.* breaking,
violation.
  You can also talk about an **offence**
against the rules.
  2 *Engineers worked all night to repair a
breach in the sea wall.* crack, gap, hole,
opening, split.

bread *noun*

FORMS IN WHICH YOU BUY BREAD:
bagel, baguette, bap, chappati, cob,
French stick, loaf, nan, roll, sliced
loaf, stick.

KINDS OF BREAD ARE: brown bread,
fruit loaf, granary bread, rye bread,
unleavened bread, white bread,
wholemeal bread.

---

break *verb*
  1 *Don't lend him anything, because he's
bound to break it.* burst, chip, crack,
crumple, crush, damage, demolish,
destroy, fracture, ruin, shatter, smash,
snap, splinter, split, squash, wreck.
  2 *If you break the law, you can expect to
be punished.* disobey, disregard,
violate.
  3 *Our relay team broke the school
record.* beat, better, do better than,
exceed, go beyond, surpass.
  to break down *The car broke down on
the motorway.* fail, go wrong, stop
working.

to break off *We'll break off for lunch at
one o'clock.* finish, have a rest, pause,
stop.
to break out *A flu epidemic broke out
just after Christmas.* begin, spread,
start.
to break out of *The prisoner tried to
break out of gaol.* escape from, get
away from.
to break up *After six months, the group
broke up.* disintegrate, fall apart,
separate, split up.

break *noun*
  1 *They repaired a break in the pipe.*
breach, crack, hole, leak, opening,
puncture, rift, split, tear.
  2 *We'll have a break now if you are
tired.* [*informal*] breather, interval, lull,
pause, rest.

breakable *adjective*
  *Be careful with that box—there are
breakable things in it.* brittle, delicate,
fragile, frail.

breakdown *noun*
  1 *We had a breakdown on the
motorway.* engine failure, stoppage.
  2 *I saw a breakdown of the season's
football results in the newspaper.*
analysis.

breakthrough *noun*
  *Doctors believe there has been a
breakthrough in cancer research.*
development, discovery, leap forward,
progress, revolution.

breath *noun*
  There wasn't a breath of wind. breeze,
pant, puff, sigh, waft, whisper.

breathe *verb*
  To breathe in is to **inhale**.
  To breathe out is to **exhale**.
  To breathe heavily when you have been
running, etc., is to **pant** or **puff**.
  The formal word for breathing is
respiration.

breathless *adjective*
  *I was breathless after running home
from school.* exhausted, gasping, out of
breath, panting, puffing, tired out,
wheezing.

breed *verb*
  1 *Frogs usually breed in any convenient pond.* have young ones, increase, multiply, produce young, reproduce.
  2 *Bad hygiene breeds disease.* cause, cultivate, encourage, generate, promote.

breed *noun*
  What breed of dog is that? kind, sort, type, variety.
  The evidence of how a dog has been bred is its *pedigree*.

breezy *adjective*
  It was a bright, breezy day. fresh, windy.
  FOR VARIOUS KINDS OF WIND, SEE **wind** *noun*.

brevity *noun*
  Owing to the brevity of the speeches, we finished early. briefness, conciseness, shortness.

brew *verb*
  1 *I'm just going to brew some tea.* make.
  When you brew beer it *ferments*.
  2 *I think a storm is brewing.* develop, form, loom, on the way, threatening.

bribe *verb*
  They tried to bribe the referee with a large sum of money. influence, pervert, tempt.

brick *noun*

> VARIOUS KINDS OF BRICK OR BLOCK USED IN BUILDING: block, breeze-block, building block, flagstone, paving block, paving stone, set or sett, stone.

bridge *noun*

> VARIOUS KINDS OF BRIDGE: aqueduct, cantilever bridge, drawbridge, flyover, footbridge, overpass, pontoon bridge, suspension bridge, swing bridge, viaduct.
> A structure like a bridge is an *arch* or *archway*.

brief *adjective*
  1 *We paid a brief visit to Granny.* hasty, fleeting, quick, short, temporary.
  2 *Give me a brief account of what happened.* abbreviated, concise, condensed, shortened.
  AN OPPOSITE IS long.

brief *noun*
  Our teacher gave us the brief for our project. directions, guidelines, information, instructions, outline, plan.

brief *verb*
  Please sit down while I brief you on our plan for the match. advise, give instructions, inform, instruct, prepare, put you in the picture.

bright *adjective*
  1 *I blinked in the bright sunshine.* blazing, brilliant, dazzling, glaring, intense.
  2 *The brass rail was bright and shiny.* gleaming, glittering, lustrous, polished.
  3 *We used bright colours to make an attractive poster.* glowing, showy, strong, vivid.
  Colours that shine in the dark are *luminous* colours.
  4 *He's a bright lad!* alert, clever, intelligent, sharp, wise.
  5 *She gave me a bright smile.* cheerful, good-humoured, happy, radiant, sunny.
  AN OPPOSITE IS dull or gloomy.

brighten *verb*
  1 *Getting a letter from you brightened my day.* cheer, gladden, light up.
  2 *It was a cloudy morning, but it brightened after lunch.* become sunny, clear up, lighten.

brilliant *adjective*
  1 *The fireworks gave off a brilliant light.* blazing, bright, dazzling, glaring, gleaming, glittering, glorious, shining, splendid, vivid.
  AN OPPOSITE IS dim.
  2 *Brunel was a brilliant engineer.* clever, exceptional, intelligent, talented.
  AN OPPOSITE IS incompetent or stupid.

3 [*informal*] *I saw a brilliant film last week.* enjoyable, excellent, [*informal*] fabulous, [*informal*] fantastic, marvellous, outstanding, wonderful.

brim *noun*
I filled my glass to the brim. brink, edge, rim, top.

bring *verb*
1 *Did you bring the shopping home?* carry, deliver, fetch, transport.
2 *Bring your friends in.* conduct, escort, guide, invite, lead.
3 *Their performance brought great applause.* attract, draw, earn, generate, lead to, result in.
to bring something about *The new head brought about many changes.* arrange, be responsible for, cause, create, introduce, organize.
to bring something off *Our team brought off a convincing win.* accomplish, achieve, succeed in.
to bring someone up *She was brought up by her grandparents.* care for, educate, foster, look after, raise, rear, teach, train.

brink *noun*
I stood on the brink of a deep crater. edge, lip, rim.

brisk *adjective*
1 *The doctor says I should take a brisk walk every day.* energetic, fast, invigorating, quick, rapid, vigorous.
2 *He has a very brisk manner.* animated, bright, businesslike, lively, snappy, sprightly.
AN OPPOSITE IS slow.

brittle *adjective*
These wafer biscuits are very brittle. breakable, crisp, delicate, easily broken, fragile, frail.
AN OPPOSITE IS flexible.

broad *adjective*
1 *There was a broad square in front of the palace.* extensive, great, large, open, roomy, spacious, vast, wide.
AN OPPOSITE IS narrow.
2 *He just gave me a broad outline of what happened.* general, imprecise, indefinite, vague.
AN OPPOSITE IS specific.

broadcast *noun*
There is going to be a TV broadcast from our local church. programme, relay, transmission.

broadcast *verb*
They will broadcast the concert on TV. relay, send out, televise, transmit.

broadcaster *noun*

SOME PEOPLE WHO BROADCAST ON RADIO OR TV: actor, announcer, comedian, commentator, compère, disc jockey or DJ, musician, newsreader, presenter, singer.
FOR OTHER WORDS, SEE **entertainer**.

broaden *verb*
Try to broaden your interests instead of watching TV all day. develop, diversify, enlarge, expand, extend, increase, widen.

broad-minded *adjective*
She likes both pop and classical music, and has a broad-minded outlook on most things. liberal, tolerant, unbiased, unprejudiced.
AN OPPOSITE IS narrow-minded.

brochure *noun*
We got some holiday brochures from the travel agent's. booklet, catalogue, leaflet, pamphlet.

brood *verb*
1 *The hen was brooding her clutch of eggs.* incubate, sit on.
2 *Don't brood about mistakes you made in the past.* fret, mope, worry.

brown *adjective, noun*

VARIOUS SHADES OF BROWN ARE: beige, bronze, buff, chestnut, chocolate, dun, fawn, khaki, russet, sepia, tan, tawny.

browse *verb*
1 *I wasn't reading carefully—I was just browsing.* dip in, look through, scan, skim.
2 *The cattle were browsing in the meadow.* feed, graze.

bruise *verb*
I fell and bruised my leg. hurt, injure, mark.
FOR OTHERS KINDS OF WOUND, SEE **wound** *verb.*

brush *noun*

VARIOUS KINDS OF BRUSH: broom, hairbrush, paintbrush, scrubbing brush, toothbrush.

brush *verb*
He spent ages brushing his hair. groom, tidy.
to brush up *Are you going to brush up your French before we go abroad?* improve, refresh your memory of, revise, [*informal*] swot up.

brutal *adjective*
The brutal murder was reported in all the newspapers. atrocious, barbarous, beastly, bestial, bloodthirsty, callous, cold-blooded, cruel, ferocious, heartless, inhuman, merciless, pitiless, ruthless, sadistic, savage, vicious, violent, wild.
AN OPPOSITE IS gentle or humane.

brute *noun*
1 *He was a cold-blooded brute.* barbarian, monster, sadist, savage.
2 *During the storm, we were sorry for the poor brutes out in the fields.* animal, beast, creature.
FOR OTHER WORDS, SEE **animal**.

bubble *noun*
A word for bubbles in fizzy lemonade is *effervescence.*
The bubbles made by soap or detergent are *lather* or *suds.*
Bubbles on top of a liquid are *foam* or *froth.*
The bubbles on top of beer are the *head.*

bubble *verb*
A pot of coffee bubbled on the stove. fizz, foam, froth, seethe.

bubbly *adjective*
1 *I don't like bubbly drinks because they get up my nose.* effervescent, fizzy, sparkling.
2 *She had a bright and bubbly personality.* animated, cheerful, lively.

buck *verb*
to buck up [*informal*] *Buck up—we're late!* be quick, hurry, make haste.

bucket *noun*
He filled a bucket with water to wash the car. can, pail.

buckle *noun*
She wore a belt with a large silver buckle. clasp, fastener, fastening.

buckle *verb*
1 *Buckle your safety belts.* clasp, clip, do up, fasten, hook up, secure.
2 *The framework buckled under our weight.* bend, cave in, collapse, crumple, fold up, twist, warp.

budding *adjective*
My sister is a budding actor. potential, promising.
AN OPPOSITE IS experienced.

budge *verb*
1 *The stubborn donkey wouldn't budge.* change position, give way, move, shift.
2 *We kept pushing, but we couldn't budge him.* dislodge, move, shift.

budget *verb*
to budget for *Have you budgeted for a holiday this year?* allow for, plan your spending for, provide for.

buffet *noun*
1 *We went to the buffet for a snack.* bar, café, cafeteria, snack bar.
2 *Mum prepared a buffet for our party.* FOR VARIOUS KINDS OF MEAL, SEE **meal**.

bug *noun*
1 *Birds help to control bugs in the garden.* insect, pest.
2 [*informal*] *I had a stomach bug.* germ, infection, virus.
3 *A bug in the computer program meant that we couldn't run it.* error, fault, mistake, virus.

bug *verb*
Spies bugged their telephone conversations. intercept, listen in to, tap.

build verb

Dad is going to build a shed in the garden. assemble, construct, erect, make, put together, put up, raise, set up.

to build up 1 *I'm beginning to build up a collection of CDs.* accumulate, assemble, collect, put together.
2 *Gloomily, we watched the opposition's excitement build up.* escalate, grow, increase, intensify, rise.

builder noun

VARIOUS PEOPLE WHO WORK ON BUILDINGS: bricklayer, construction worker, contractor, joiner, labourer, mason, plasterer, plumber, surveyor.
A person who designs buildings is an **architect**.
A person who works on very high buildings is a **steeplejack**.

building noun

construction, structure.

VARIOUS BUILDINGS: arcade, barn, barracks, bungalow, castle, cathedral, chapel, church, cinema, college, cottage, factory, farmhouse, filling station, flats, fortress, garage, grandstand, gymnasium, hall, hangar, hotel, house, inn, library, lighthouse, mansion, mill, monastery, mosque, museum, pagoda, palace, pavilion, police station, post office, power station, prison, pub or public house, restaurant, school, shed, shop, skyscraper, stable, synagogue, temple, theatre, tower, warehouse, windmill.

VARIOUS PARTS OF A BUILDING: balcony, basement, cellar, corridor, courtyard, crypt, dungeon, foyer, gallery, lobby, porch, quadrangle, room, staircase, veranda.
SEE ALSO **room**.

VARIOUS ARCHITECTURAL FEATURES OF BUILDINGS: arch, balustrade, banister, bay window, bow window, brickwork, buttress, capital, ceiling, chimney, colonnade, column, dome, door, ➡

dormer window, eaves, floor, foundations, gable, gutter, joist, masonry, parapet, pediment, pillar, pinnacle, portal, rafter, roof, tower, turret, vault, wall, window, windowsill.
SEE ALSO **castle, church**.

SOME BUILDING MATERIALS: asphalt, bricks, cement, concrete, fibreglass, glass, hardboard, metal, mortar, paint, perspex, pipes, plaster, plasterboard, plastic, plywood, putty, rubber, slates, stone, tar, tiles, timber, wood.

bulb noun

We planted some daffodil bulbs last autumn.

SOME FLOWERS THAT GROW FROM BULBS: amaryllis, bluebell, crocus, daffodil, freesia, hyacinth, lily, snowdrop, tulip.
Things rather like bulbs are **corms** and **tubers**.

bulge noun

What's that bulge in your shopping bag? bump, hump, knob, lump, swelling.

bulge verb

His pockets bulged with all sorts of odds and ends. stick out, swell.

bulk noun

1 *The great bulk of the jumbo jet amazed us.* dimensions, magnitude, size.
2 *We spent the bulk of our time practising for the big match.* best part, greater part, majority.

bulletin noun

We waited for an official bulletin about the President's health. announcement, communication, message, newsflash, report, statement.

bully verb

The head said that if he continued to bully younger children he would be severely punished. frighten, intimidate, persecute, terrorize, threaten, torment.

bump *verb*
1 *He bumped us deliberately.* bang into, collide with, crash into, knock, ram, slam into, smash into, strike, thump, wallop.
2 *We bumped up and down on the rough road.* bounce, jerk, jolt, shake.
to bump into someone *I didn't expect to bump into you today!* come across, meet.
to bump someone off [*slang*] *He tried to bump off the rest of the gang when they double-crossed him.* [*informal*] do away with, [*informal*] finish off, kill, murder.

bump *noun*
1 *We heard a slight bump as the ship hit the quay.* bang, blow, knock, thud, thump.
2 *Dad had a bump in the car.* collision, crash, smash.
3 *How did you get that bump on your head?* bulge, hump, lump, swelling.

bumpy *adjective*
1 *My bottom was sore after the bumpy ride.* bouncy, jerky, jolting, rough.
2 *The car jolted up and down on the bumpy road.* irregular, knobbly, lumpy, uneven.

bunch *noun*
1 *A bunch of keys was dangling from the hook.* cluster, collection, set.
FOR OTHER WORDS FOR THINGS YOU KEEP TOGETHER, SEE **collection**.
2 *a bunch of flowers.* bouquet, spray.
3 [*informal*] *I got a bunch of friends to help me tidy the garden.* band, crowd, gang, group, mob, party, team.

bunch *verb*
Our opponents' supporters bunched together on the other side of the field. assemble, cluster, collect, crowd, gather, group, herd, huddle.
AN OPPOSITE IS scatter.

bundle *noun*
I carried a bundle of jumble down to the church hall. bale, collection, pack, package, parcel.

bundle *verb*
1 *I bundled together some old clothes for the jumble sale.* bind, fasten, pack, tie.
2 *They bundled him into the car.* move hurriedly, push, remove.

bungle *verb*
If you bungle a job, you must do it again! make a mess of, mess up, ruin, spoil.

buoyant *adjective*
1 *Lifebelts are made of buoyant material.* floating, light.
2 *We were in a buoyant mood after winning our match.* cheerful, happy, lively, optimistic.

burden *noun*
1 *They moved slowly, as if carrying a heavy burden.* cargo, load, weight.
2 *The captain has the burden of organizing the players.* anxiety, duty, obligation, responsibility, trouble, worry.

burglar *noun*
The burglars made a terrible mess of the house. intruder, robber, thief.

burglary *noun*
FOR OTHER WORDS, SEE **stealing**.

burly *adjective*
The weightlifter had a burly figure. [*informal*] beefy, brawny, hefty, husky, muscular, powerful, stocky, stout, strong, sturdy, tough, well-built.
AN OPPOSITE IS thin.

burn *verb*
1 *The bonfire burned all day.* be ablaze, be alight, be on fire, blaze, flame, flare, flicker.
To burn without flames is to *glow* or *smoulder*.
2 *The furnace will burn anything you put in it.* consume, incinerate, reduce to ashes.
To start something burning is to *ignite*, *kindle*, or *light* it.
To burn something slightly is to *char*, *scorch*, or *singe* it.
To hurt someone with boiling liquid or steam is to *scald* them.
To burn a dead body is to *cremate* it.
To burn a mark on an animal is to *brand* it.

burning *adjective*
I had a burning desire to tell them my secret. acute, eager, fervent, intense, passionate, strong.

burrow *noun*
The bank was full of rabbit burrows. hole, tunnel.
A piece of ground with many burrows is a *warren*.
A fox's hole is an *earth*.
A badger's hole is an *earth* or *set*.

burrow *verb*
The rabbits burrow under our fence. dig, excavate, tunnel.

burst *verb*
We had so much shopping that I expected the bag to burst. break, give way, split, tear.
to burst out laughing *I burst out laughing when I saw her surprise.* laugh loudly, roar with laughter, start laughing.

bury *verb*
The dog buried his bone in the garden. conceal, cover, hide, secrete.

bus *noun*

> VARIOUS KINDS OF BUS: coach, double-decker, minibus.
> Old-fashioned words for bus are *charabanc* and *omnibus*.
> A bus which gets its power from overhead electric wires is a *trolleybus*.
> A *tram* is like a bus that runs on rails set in the road.

bush *noun*
Dad planted some bushes to hide the compost heap. shrub.

bushy *adjective*
He had big bushy eyebrows. hairy, shaggy, thick, untidy.

business *noun*
1 *She runs a catering business.* company, firm, organization.
2 *The new shop does a lot of business.* buying and selling, commerce, deals, trade, trading.

3 *What sort of business do you want to go into?* career, employment, industry, job, occupation, profession, trade, work.
4 *I have urgent business to see to.* affairs, duties, matters, problems, responsibilities, tasks, work.

businesslike *adjective*
If you are businesslike, the job won't take long. efficient, methodical, orderly, practical, systematic, well-organized.

bustle *verb*
He bustled about the kitchen preparing dinner. dash, hurry, move busily, rush, scurry, scuttle.

busy *adjective*
1 *Everyone was busy getting ready for the parents' evening.* active, bustling about, employed, [*informal*] hard at it, industrious, involved, occupied, slaving, working hard.
AN OPPOSITE IS idle.
2 *It's busy in town on Saturdays.* bustling, frantic, hectic, lively.
AN OPPOSITE IS peaceful.

butt *verb*
The goat butted him in the stomach. hit, knock, push, ram, shove.
to butt in *Please don't butt in when I'm talking.* interrupt.

buttocks *plural noun*
[*informal*] backside, behind, bottom, [*slang*] bum, rear, rump, seat.

buy *verb*
Dad is saving up until he can buy a new TV set. acquire, get, pay for, purchase.
AN OPPOSITE IS sell.

bystander *noun*
The police asked bystanders to describe the accident. eyewitness, observer, onlooker, passer-by, spectator, witness.

Cc

cabin *noun*
1 *The climbers took refuge in a cabin in the hills.* hut, shack, shanty, shed, shelter.
2 *We slept in a cabin on the cross-Channel ferry.*
A sleeping place on a ship is also called a ***berth***.

cable *noun*
1 *The ship was moored to the quay by strong cables.* chain, cord, line, rope.
2 *Don't trip over the electric cable.* flex, lead, wire.
3 *They sent a message by cable.* telegram.

cadet *noun*
My cousin is a cadet in the police force. beginner, learner, recruit, trainee.

cadge *verb*
The cat from next door comes round to cadge food. ask for, beg for, [*informal*] scrounge.

café *noun*

VARIOUS PLACES WHERE YOU CAN HAVE FOOD AND DRINK: bar, bistro, buffet, cafeteria, canteen, coffee bar, restaurant, snack bar, takeaway, tearoom.

cage *noun*
A large cage or enclosure for birds is an ***aviary***.
A cage or enclosure for poultry is a ***coop***.
A cage or enclosure for animals is a ***pen***.
A cage or box for a pet rabbit is a ***hutch***.

cake *noun*

SOME KINDS OF CAKE: angel cake, birthday cake, bun, Christmas cake, doughnut, éclair, flan, fruit cake, gateau, gingerbread, macaroon, Madeira cake, meringue, muffin, parkin, sandwich cake, scone, shortbread, simnel cake, sponge, Swiss roll, teacake, wedding cake.

caked *adjective*
Our shoes were caked with mud. clogged, coated, covered, dirty.

calamity *noun*
The earthquake was the worst calamity in the country's history. accident, catastrophe, disaster, misfortune, mishap, tragedy

calculate *verb*
I calculated how long it would take us to drive from London to Oxford. add up, compute, count, determine, figure out, reckon, total, work out.
To calculate something roughly is to ***estimate***.

call *noun*
1 *I thought I heard a call for help.* cry, exclamation, scream, shout, yell.
2 *Grandad made an unexpected call.* stay, stop, visit.
3 *There's not much call for suntan oil in winter.* demand, need.

call *verb*
1 *He called in a loud voice.* cry out, exclaim, shout, yell.
2 *I wanted to call you, but the line was out of order.* phone, ring, telephone.
3 *The head called me to his office.* invite, summon.
4 *In case I overslept, I asked Mum to call me at eight.* arouse, awaken, rouse, wake, waken.
5 *Grandad called on his way home from the shops.* drop in, pay a visit.
6 *What did they call the baby?* baptize, christen, name.
to call something off *The weather was so bad that we called the game off.* abandon, cancel, postpone.
to call someone names *She thinks it's funny to call people names.* insult, make fun of, mock.

calling *noun*
> He is a gifted surgeon, totally dedicated to his calling. business, career, employment, job, occupation, profession, trade, work.

callous *adjective*
> The mugging of the elderly couple was a callous crime. cold, cold-blooded, cruel, hard-hearted, heartless, inhuman, merciless, pitiless, ruthless, uncaring, unfeeling, unsympathetic.
> AN OPPOSITE IS kind.

calm *adjective*
> **1** It's a lot easier to put up a tent in calm weather. peaceful, quiet, serene, still, tranquil, windless.
> AN OPPOSITE IS stormy or windy.
> **2** The sea was calm, and we had a pleasant voyage. flat, motionless, placid, smooth.
> AN OPPOSITE IS stormy.
> **3** He remained calm while everyone else panicked. cool, level-headed, patient, relaxed, sedate, unemotional, unexcitable, untroubled.
> AN OPPOSITE IS anxious or excitable.

camera *noun*

> SOME TYPES OF CAMERA: [*old use*] box camera, cine-camera, Polaroid camera, SLR or single lens reflex camera, video camera.

camouflage *noun*
> We used leafy branches as camouflage for our hideout. cover, disguise, mask, screen.

camp *noun*
> From the hill we saw a camp in the field below us. camping ground, campsite.
> A military camp is an **encampment**.

campaign *noun*
> **1** Will you join our campaign to save the whale? action, crusade, movement, struggle.
> **2** The army launched a campaign to recapture the city. operation, war.

cancel *verb*
> We had to cancel the game because of the weather. abandon, give up, scrap, [*slang*] scrub.
> To cancel something after it has already begun is to **abort** it.
> To put something off until later is to **postpone** it.
> To cancel items on a list is to **cross out** or **delete** or **erase** them.
> **to cancel something out** The points we won today cancel out the points they won last week. compensate for, make up for, neutralize, wipe out.

candidate *noun*
> A candidate for a job is an **applicant**.
> A candidate in an examination is an **entrant**.
> A person competing with others in a contest is a **competitor**, **contender**, or **contestant**.

canopy *noun*
> We sheltered from the rain under a canopy. awning, cover, shade.

cap *noun*
> **1** When he plays cricket, he wears his team cap.
> FOR DIFFERENT KINDS OF HAT, SEE **hat**.
> **2** Who left the cap off the ketchup bottle? cover, lid, top.

cap *verb*
> The highest mountains are always capped by snow. cover, top.

capable *adjective*
> She's a capable tennis player. able, accomplished, clever, competent, efficient, expert, gifted, proficient, skilful, skilled, talented.
> AN OPPOSITE IS incompetent.
> **to be capable of** She's capable of doing something silly.
> You could also say that she is **liable** or **likely** or **prone** to do it.
> AN OPPOSITE IS incapable of.

capacity *noun*
1 *He has a great capacity for hard work.* ability, capability, competence, potential, power, talent.
2 *What's the capacity of this oil tank?* size, volume.
3 *In his capacity as captain, he has a right to tell us what to do.* function, job, position, post.

cape *noun*
1 *We could see the island from the cape.* headland, peninsula, promontory.
2 *The soldier wrapped his cape around him and tried to keep dry.* cloak, [*old use*] mantle.

caper *verb*
I watched the lambs caper about in the sunshine. bound, dance, frisk, frolic, hop, jump, leap, play, prance, romp, skip, spring.

capital *noun*
1 *Paris is the capital of France.* chief city, centre of government.
2 *Dad has enough capital to start a new business.* assets, cash, finance, funds, money, property, resources, riches, savings, wealth.
capital letter *Start a new sentence with a capital letter.* block capital, block letter, initial letter.

capsize *verb*
The boat capsized in the storm. keel over, overturn, tip over, turn over, turn turtle, turn upside down.

capsule *noun*
1 *The doctor gave her some capsules.* lozenge, pill, tablet.
2 *The world's most powerful rocket launched the space capsule.*
FOR WORDS TO DO WITH TRAVEL IN SPACE, SEE **space**.

captain *noun*
The captain brought his ship safely into harbour. commander, master, skipper.
FOR PEOPLE IN CHARGE OF VARIOUS THINGS, SEE **chief** *noun*.

captivating *adjective*
She was a lively and captivating girl. appealing, attractive, charming, [*informal*] cute, delightful, enchanting, fascinating, lovable.
AN OPPOSITE IS repulsive.

captive *noun*
The captives were chained to their beds. convict, prisoner.
A person who is held captive until some demand is met is a **hostage**.

captive *adjective*
The captive rebels were put in prison. arrested, captured, detained.

PEOPLE AND ANIMALS CAN BE HELD CAPTIVE IN DIFFERENT WAYS: caged, chained, enslaved, gaoled or jailed, imprisoned, in custody, in detention, in fetters, [*old use*] in the stocks, interned, on remand, trapped.

AN OPPOSITE IS free.

captivity *noun*
No one enjoys captivity. confinement, detention, gaol, imprisonment, prison, slavery.
AN OPPOSITE IS freedom.

capture *verb*
1 *After a chase, the police captured the suspect.* arrest, catch, corner, [*informal*] nab, overpower, secure, seize, take prisoner, trap.
2 *In spite of the long siege, the enemy were not able to capture the castle.* conquer, occupy, take, take over, win.

car *noun*
There are too many cars on the city streets. [*American*] automobile, motor, motor car.

KINDS OF CAR: convertible, coupé, [*trademark*] Dormobile, estate, fastback, four-wheel drive, hatchback, [*trademark*] Jeep, [*trademark*] Land Rover, limousine, [*trademark*] Mini, patrol car or police car, saloon, [*old use*] shooting brake, sports car, tourer.
Very early cars are **veteran** or **vintage** cars.

SOME PRINCIPAL PARTS OF A CAR: battery, body, bonnet, boot, brakes, chassis, clutch, engine, exhaust pipe, fuel tank, gearbox, lights, radiator, silencer, starter, steering, suspension, transmission, wheels, windscreen. ➡

PRINCIPAL CONTROLS IN A CAR:
accelerator, brake, choke, clutch,
gear lever, handbrake, ignition key,
indicators, steering wheel,
windscreen wipers.
FOR OTHER VEHICLES, SEE **vehicle**.

carcass noun
*The carcass of the animal was hidden
by the bushes.* body, corpse, remains.

card noun

CARDS WE SEND ON VARIOUS
SPECIAL OCCASIONS: birthday card,
Christmas card, Easter card, get
well card, greetings card, invitation,
notelet, picture postcard, sympathy
card, Valentine.

CARDS WE PLAY GAMES WITH:
playing cards.
A complete set of playing cards is a
pack.
All the cards with the same sign on
them are a *suit*.

THE SUITS IN A PACK OF CARDS:
clubs, diamonds, hearts, spades.

CARDS OF DIFFERENT VALUE: king,
queen, jack or knave, numbers from
10 down to 2, ace, joker.
The king, queen, and jack are the
court cards.

SOME CARD GAMES: beggar-my-
neighbour, brag, bridge, canasta,
cribbage, old maid, patience, poker,
pontoon, rummy, snap, solo, whist.

care noun
1 *He doesn't have a care in the world!*
anxiety, burden, difficulty, problem,
responsibility, sorrow, stress, trouble,
worry.
2 *He did the job with great care.*
attention, caution, concentration,
thoroughness, thought, vigilance,
watchfulness.
AN OPPOSITE IS carelessness.
3 *She left the baby in my care.* charge,
control, keeping, protection, safe
keeping.

to take care *Please take care not to spill
paint on the carpet.* be careful, be on
your guard, look out, watch out.
to take care of someone or something
*She had to take care of her sick mother
last week.* attend to, care for, look after,
mind, nurse, tend, watch over.

care verb
She doesn't seem to care what happens.
be interested, be troubled, bother,
mind, worry.
to care for someone or something
1 *She had to care for her sick mother
last week.* attend to, look after, mind,
nurse, take care of, tend, watch over.
2 *Do you care for me?* be fond of, love.

career noun
*What sort of career do you want when
you grow up?* business, calling,
employment, job, occupation,
profession, trade, work.
FOR VARIOUS CAREERS, SEE **job**.

career verb
*She careered down the hill into the
village.* dash, hurtle, race, rush, shoot,
speed, zoom.

carefree adjective
*The carefree days of the summer
holidays were over.* casual, cheerful,
easygoing, happy, happy-go-lucky,
light-hearted, peaceful, relaxed,
restful, untroubled.
AN OPPOSITE IS anxious or tense.

careful adjective
1 *She congratulated us on our careful
work.* accurate, conscientious,
methodical, meticulous, neat, orderly,
organized, painstaking, precise,
systematic, thorough, thoughtful.
2 *Dad kept a careful watch on the
bonfire.* alert, attentive, cautious,
responsible, vigilant, wary, watchful.
AN OPPOSITE IS careless.
to be careful *Please be careful when
you cross the road.* be on your guard,
look out, take care, watch out.

careless adjective
1 *This is a very careless piece of work.*
inaccurate, messy, shoddy, slipshod,
sloppy, slovenly, thoughtless, untidy.

2 *I was careless and cut my finger.*
absent-minded, inattentive,
incautious, irresponsible, negligent,
rash, reckless, thoughtless.
AN OPPOSITE IS careful.

caress *noun*
He gave her a loving caress. embrace,
hug, kiss, pat, stroke, touch.

caress *verb*
He caressed her hair gently. smooth,
stroke, touch.

cargo *noun*
*Some planes carry cargo instead of
passengers.* freight, goods,
merchandise.

carnival *noun*
*The whole village comes out for the
annual carnival.* celebration, fair,
festival, fête, gala, pageant, parade,
procession, show.

carpentry *noun*
*You need saws and other tools for
carpentry.* joinery, woodwork.

carriage *noun*
FOR VARIOUS MEANS OF TRANSPORT,
SEE **vehicle**.

carry *verb*
1 *I helped Mum to carry the shopping to
the car.* bring, fetch, lift, lug, take,
transfer.
2 *Aircraft carry passengers and goods.*
convey, transport.
3 *The rear axle carries the greatest
weight.* bear, hold up, support.
to carry on *We carried on in spite of the
rain.* continue, go on, keep on,
persevere, persist, remain, stay,
survive.
to carry something out *We carried out
her orders.* accomplish, achieve,
complete, do, execute, finish, perform.

cart *noun*
FOR VARIOUS MEANS OF TRANSPORT,
SEE **vehicle**.

carton *noun*
He opened a new carton of cereal. box,
pack, package, packet.

cartoon *noun*
1 *There's always a political cartoon on
the front page of our newspaper.*
caricature, drawing, sketch.
2 *My baby brother likes cartoons on TV.*
animated film.

carve *verb*
1 *The statue was carved out of stone.*
chisel.
2 *Mum carved the chicken for Sunday
dinner.* cut, slice.

cascade *noun*
*The stream poured over the rock in a
cascade.* torrent, waterfall.

case *noun*
1 *What's in those cases in the attic?* box,
cabinet, carton, casket, chest, crate.
FOR OTHER CONTAINERS, SEE
container.
2 *I loaded my case into the boot of the
car.* suitcase, trunk.
A collection of cases that you take
when you travel is your ***baggage*** or
luggage.
3 *It was an obvious case of favouritism.*
example, illustration, instance,
occurrence.
4 *The judge said he'd never known a
case like this one.* inquiry,
investigation, lawsuit.
5 *She presented a good case for
abolishing hunting.* argument, line of
reasoning.

cash *noun*

VARIOUS WORDS FOR MONEY IN THE
FORM OF CASH: bank notes, change,
coins, coppers, currency, loose
change, notes, ready money, silver.

cast *verb*
1 *He cast a penny into the wishing-well.*
drop, fling, lob, sling, throw, toss.
2 *The statue was cast in bronze.* form,
mould, shape.

castle *noun*

VARIOUS KINDS OF FORTIFIED
BUILDING: château, citadel, fort,
fortress, motte and bailey, palace,
stronghold, tower. ➡

PARTS OF A CASTLE: bailey, barbican,
battlement, buttress, courtyard,
donjon, drawbridge, dungeon, gate,
gateway, keep, magazine, moat,
motte, parapet, portcullis, postern,
rampart, tower, turret, wall,
watchtower.

casual *adjective*

1 *It was just a casual remark, so don't
take it too seriously.* accidental, chance,
unexpected, unintentional, unplanned.
AN OPPOSITE IS deliberate.
2 *The restaurant had a casual
atmosphere.* easy-going, informal,
relaxed.
AN OPPOSITE IS formal.
3 *The teacher complained about our
casual attitude.* apathetic, careless,
slack, unenthusiastic.
AN OPPOSITE IS enthusiastic.

casualty *noun*

*It was a nasty accident, but there was
only one casualty.* death, fatality,
injury, loss, victim.

cat *noun*

An informal word for a cat is ***moggy***
or ***pussy***.
A baby's word for a cat is ***pussy***.
A young cat is a ***kitten***.
A male cat is a ***tom***.
A cat with streaks in its fur is a
tabby.

VARIOUS WILD ANIMALS OF THE CAT
FAMILY: jaguar, leopard, lion, lynx,
puma, tiger, wild cat.

catalogue *noun*

*Mum chose some curtains from a
shopping catalogue.* brochure.

catastrophe *noun*

*The drought is a catastrophe for the
farmers.* calamity, disaster, misfortune,
mishap, tragedy.

catch *verb*

1 *They yelled at me to catch the ball.*
clutch, grab, grasp, grip, hang on to,
hold, seize, snatch, take.
2 *One of the anglers caught a fish.*
hook, net, trap.

3 *The police hoped to catch the thief
red-handed.* arrest, capture, corner,
[*informal*] nab.
4 *I hope you don't catch my cold.*
become infected by, contract, get,
[*informal*] go down with.
5 *You must hurry if you want to catch
the bus.* be in time for, get on.
to catch on *Their latest record didn't
catch on.* become popular, do well,
[*informal*] make it, succeed.
to catch up with someone *If we run
we'll catch up with them.* gain on,
overtake.

catch *noun*

1 *They got a large catch of fish.* haul.
2 *The car is so cheap that there must be
a catch.* difficulty, disadvantage,
drawback, obstacle, problem, snag,
trap, trick.
3 *The window was fitted with a safety
catch.* bolt, fastening, hook, latch, lock.

catching *adjective*

Chickenpox is catching. contagious,
infectious.

category *noun*

*I entered the competition in the under-
twelves category.* class, division, group,
section, set.

cater *verb*

to cater for *The hotel catered for fifty
people at my cousin's wedding.* cook for,
provide food for, serve, supply.

cattle *plural noun*

VARIOUS KINDS OF CATTLE: bulls,
bullocks, calves, cows, heifers, oxen,
steers.
Farm animals in general are
livestock.

cause *noun*

1 *What was the cause of the trouble?*
origin, source.
You can also talk about the ***reasons*** for
the trouble.
2 *You've got no cause to complain.*
basis, grounds, motive.
3 *Who was the cause of the trouble?*
creator, originator.
4 *We are collecting for a good cause.*
object, purpose.

cause *verb*
It'll cause trouble if you don't share things. arouse, bring about, create, generate, give rise to, lead to, provoke, result in.

caution *noun*
1 *Proceed with caution.* attention, care, vigilance, wariness, watchfulness.
2 *They let me off with a caution.* reprimand, telling-off, [*informal*] ticking-off, warning.

cautious *adjective*
Dad is a cautious driver. attentive, careful, hesitant, vigilant, wary, watchful.
AN OPPOSITE IS reckless.

cave *noun*

> VARIOUS KINDS OF HOLE UNDER THE GROUND: cavern, grotto, mine, pothole, underground chamber. People who lived in caves were *cavemen* or *troglodytes*.

cave *verb*
to cave in *The miners had a lucky escape when the roof caved in.* collapse, fall in.

cavity *noun*
The dentist filled a cavity in my tooth. hole, hollow.

cease *verb*
The fighting ceased at midnight. come to an end, end, finish, halt, stop.
AN OPPOSITE IS begin.

ceaseless *adjective*
Our ceaseless noise annoyed the neighbours. constant, continual, continuous, endless, everlasting, incessant, interminable, never-ending, non-stop, perpetual, persistent, relentless, unending.
AN OPPOSITE IS brief.

celebrate *verb*
1 *Let's celebrate!* be happy, have a good time, rejoice.
2 *What shall we do to celebrate Granny's birthday?* commemorate, keep, observe.

celebrated *adjective*
She's one of the most celebrated poets in the country. distinguished, eminent, famous, notable, outstanding, popular, prominent, renowned, respected, well-known.
AN OPPOSITE IS unknown.

celebration *noun*

> DIFFERENT KINDS OF CELEBRATION: anniversary, banquet, birthday, carnival, commemoration, feast, festival, festivity, fête, gala, jamboree, jubilee, party, reunion, wedding.

celebrity *noun*
The head asked a TV celebrity to open our new sports centre. famous person, idol, personality, public figure, star, VIP.

cellar *noun*

> VARIOUS UNDERGROUND ROOMS: basement, crypt, dungeon, undercroft, vault, wine cellar.

cemetery *noun*
Several famous people are buried in the local cemetery. burial ground, churchyard, graveyard.
A place where dead people are cremated is a *crematorium*.
SEE ALSO **tomb**.

censor *verb*
Dad says they were right to censor the violence in that film. cut out, delete, edit, remove.

censure *noun*
He deserved the referee's censure for that foul. condemnation, criticism, disapproval, reprimand, reproach, telling-off.

census *noun*
They did a traffic census to find out exactly how busy the road is. count, survey.

central *adjective*
1 *The traffic is very heavy in the central part of town.* inner, interior, middle.
AN OPPOSITE IS outer.

2 *He gave us the central facts.* chief, crucial, essential, fundamental, important, main, major, principal, vital.
AN OPPOSITE IS unimportant.

centre *noun*
We got to the centre of the maze easily, but getting outside again was more difficult. heart, inside, interior, middle.
The centre of the earth or of an apple is the **core**.
The centre of an atom or a living cell is the **nucleus**.
The centre of a wheel is the **hub**.
The point at the centre of a see-saw is the **pivot**.
The eatable part in the centre of a nut is the **kernel**.
AN OPPOSITE IS edge, outside, or surface.

cereal *noun*
Many farmers grow cereals. corn, grain.

DIFFERENT CEREALS: barley, corn on the cob or maize or sweetcorn, millet, oats, rice, rye, wheat.

ceremonial *adjective*
The opening of Parliament is a ceremonial occasion. dignified, formal, majestic, official, solemn, stately.
AN OPPOSITE IS informal.

ceremony *noun*
1 *We watched the ceremony of the opening of Parliament.* rite, ritual.
A plural word is **formalities**.

A ceremony where someone is given a prize is a **presentation**.
A ceremony where someone is given a special honour is an **investiture**.
A ceremony to celebrate something new is an **inauguration** or **opening**.
A ceremony where someone becomes a member of a society is an **initiation**.
A ceremony to make a church or other building sacred is a **dedication**.
A ceremony to remember a dead person or a past event is a **commemoration**. ➡

A ceremony held in church is a **service**.

VARIOUS CHURCH CEREMONIES: baptism, confirmation, funeral, wedding.

2 *My sister had a quiet wedding without a lot of ceremony.* formality, pageantry, pomp, spectacle.

certain *adjective*
1 *I was certain I would win.* confident, convinced, determined, positive, sure.
AN OPPOSITE IS uncertain.
2 *We have certain proof that she is guilty.* absolute, clear, convincing, definite, genuine, infallible, reliable, trustworthy, undeniable, unquestionable, valid.
AN OPPOSITE IS unreliable.
3 *The damaged plane faced certain disaster.* inevitable, unavoidable.
AN OPPOSITE IS possible.
4 *If your new watch doesn't go, the shop is certain to give your money back.* bound.
for certain *I'll give you the money tomorrow for certain.* certainly, definitely, for sure, without doubt.
to make certain *Please make certain that you lock the doors before you go out.* ensure, make sure.

certainty *noun*
1 *It was a certainty that we'd quarrel sooner or later.* foregone conclusion, [*informal*] sure thing.
AN OPPOSITE IS impossibility.
2 *I saw it happen, so I can speak with certainty.* assurance, confidence, conviction, knowledge.

certificate *noun*

VARIOUS KINDS OF CERTIFICATE: birth certificate, death certificate, degree certificate, diploma, driver's licence, guarantee, insurance certificate, licence, marriage certificate, pass, permit, warrant.

certify *verb*
The doctor certified that I was fit to go back to school. confirm, declare, guarantee, testify, verify.

chain *noun*
1 *The prisoners were kept in chains.*

> CHAINS, ETC., USED TO SECURE
> PRISONERS: fetters, handcuffs, irons,
> manacles, shackles.
> One ring in a chain is a **link**.
> A chain used to link railway wagons
> together is a **coupling**.

2 *The police formed a chain to keep the crowd back.* cordon, line, row.
3 *The police described the chain of events that led to the murder.* sequence, series, string, succession.

chair *noun*
FOR FURNITURE YOU SIT IN, SEE **seat**.

challenge *verb*
I challenged my friend to beat me in the 100 metres race. dare, defy.

champion *noun*
1 *The final game decides who is the champion.* conqueror, hero, medallist, prizewinner, victor, winner.
2 *Martin Luther King was a great champion of civil rights.* backer, defender, supporter, upholder.

championship *noun*
Teams from the local schools took part in a chess championship. competition, contest, tournament.

chance *noun*
1 *They say there's a chance of rain tomorrow.* danger, possibility, probability, prospect, risk.
2 *Tomorrow is our only chance for a picnic.* occasion, opportunity, time.
3 *We took a chance and hoped it wouldn't rain.* gamble, risk.
4 *I met him quite by chance.* accident, coincidence.
An unfortunate chance is **bad luck** or a **misfortune**.
A fortunate chance is **good luck** or a **fluke**.

change *verb*
1 *They changed the batting order for today's game.* adapt, adjust, alter, rearrange, reorganize, switch, vary.
2 *Granny said I had changed since she last saw me.* alter, become different, develop, grow.
3 *If I take these jeans back to the shop, will they change them?* exchange, replace, substitute, [*informal*] swap.
to change into *Tadpoles change into frogs.* become, be transformed into, turn into.

change *noun*
There has been no change in the weather. alteration, break, difference, variation.
A change to something worse is a **deterioration**.
A change to something better is an **improvement** or a **reform**.
A very big change is a **revolution** or **transformation** or **U-turn**.
A change which involves replacing one person or thing by another is a **substitution**.

changeable *adjective*
The weather has been changeable. erratic, inconsistent, unpredictable, unreliable, unstable, variable.
If your loyalty is changeable you are **fickle**.
AN OPPOSITE IS steady.

channel *noun*

> KINDS OF CHANNEL FOR WATER TO
> FLOW ALONG: culvert, dike, ditch,
> duct, gully, gutter, overflow, pipe,
> stream, trough, watercourse.
>
> KINDS OF CHANNEL WHICH SHIPS
> CAN SAIL ALONG: canal, sound,
> strait, waterway.

chaos *noun*
1 *Mum said I had better tidy up the chaos in my room.* confusion, disorder, muddle, shambles.
2 *There was chaos in the next class when their teacher was away.* anarchy, bedlam, pandemonium, tumult, uproar.
AN OPPOSITE IS order.

chaotic *adjective*
1 *I have to admit that my room is in a chaotic state.* confused, messy, muddled, topsy-turvy, untidy, upside-down.
AN OPPOSITE IS neat.
2 *During the famine, the country was in a chaotic state.* anarchic, lawless, rebellious, riotous, unruly.
AN OPPOSITE IS organized.

chapter *noun*
I read one chapter of my book each evening. part, section.
One section of a play is an *act* or *scene*.
One part of a serial is an *episode* or *instalment*.

char *verb*
The fire charred the woodwork. blacken, scorch, singe.
SEE ALSO **burn**.

character *noun*
1 *His character is quite different from his brother's.* attitude, disposition, make-up, manner, nature, personality.
2 *Our neighbour is a well-known character in our street.* figure, individual, person, personality.
3 *Which character do you want to be in the play?* part, role.

characteristic *noun*
He has some strange physical characteristics. distinguishing feature, feature, peculiarity, point.

characteristic *adjective*
Windmills are a characteristic feature of this area. distinctive, individual, recognizable, special, unique.

characterize *verb*
1 *His paintings are characterized by bright, primary colours.* distinguish.
2 *The play characterizes Richard III as a villain.* depict, describe, portray, present.

charge *noun*
1 *The admission charge is £2.50.* price, rate.
The charge made for a ride on public transport is the *fare*.
The charge made to post a letter or parcel is the *postage*.
A charge made to join a club is a *fee* or *subscription*.

A charge made for certain things by the government is a *duty* or a *tax*.
A charge made to use a private road, bridge, or tunnel is a *toll*.
2 *A policeman read out the charge against the suspect.* accusation, allegation.
3 *Many soldiers were killed in the charge.* assault, attack, raid.
4 *They left the dog in my charge.* care, control, keeping, protection.
to be in charge of something *An experienced mountaineer was in charge of the expedition.* command, direct, lead, look after, manage, supervise.

charge *verb*
1 *What do they charge for a coffee?* ask for, make you pay.
2 *The cavalry charged the enemy line.* assault, attack, storm.

charitable *adjective*
You should try to be more charitable to people. benevolent, compassionate, generous, helpful, kind, unselfish.
AN OPPOSITE IS selfish.

charity *noun*
1 *The whole world was impressed by the charity she showed towards the poor.* benevolence, compassion, generosity, helpfulness, humanity, kindness, love, mercy, sympathy, unselfishness.
AN OPPOSITE IS selfishness.
2 *The animals' hospital depends on our charity.* donations, financial support, gifts, offerings.

charm *noun*
1 *He was captivated by her youthful charm.* appeal, attractiveness.
2 *The sorcerer recited a magic charm.* spell.

charm *verb*
The books have charmed children all over the world. bewitch, captivate, delight, enchant, entrance, fascinate, please.

charming *adjective*
1 *We drove through some charming scenery.* attractive, beautiful, delightful, enchanting, fascinating, lovely.
2 *Our neighbour's dog gave birth to four charming puppies.* adorable, appealing, captivating, [*informal*] cute, irresistible, lovable.

chart *noun*
1 *The ship's captain consulted his chart.* map.
2 *We made a chart to show differences in temperature for each month of the year.* diagram, graph, table.

charter *verb*
We chartered a coach to take us on our trip. engage, hire.

chase *verb*
The dog chased a rabbit. follow, hound, hunt, pursue, track, trail.

chasm *noun*

VARIOUS KINDS OF DEEP HOLE: abyss, canyon, crater, crevasse, gorge, gulf, opening, pit, ravine, rift.

chat, chatter *verbs*
FOR DIFFERENT WAYS WE TALK, SEE **talk** *verb*.

chatty *adjective*
Usually he doesn't say much, but today he's quite chatty. communicative, talkative.
AN OPPOSITE IS silent.

cheap *adjective*
1 *I got my anorak at a cheap price in the market.* bargain, cut-price, discount, reasonable, reduced.
2 *Beans on toast is a cheap meal.* economical, inexpensive.
AN OPPOSITE IS expensive.
3 *That cheap watch of mine didn't last long.* inferior, shoddy, [*informal*] tacky, trashy, worthless.
AN OPPOSITE IS superior.

cheat *verb*
1 *He cheated me by selling me a watch that doesn't go.* [*slang*] con, deceive, [*informal*] diddle, double-cross, [*informal*] fleece, [*slang*] fool, hoax, [*slang*] rip off, swindle, trick.
2 *Anyone who cheats in a test is severely punished.* copy, crib.

cheat *noun*
Don't trust him—he's a cheat. cheater, fraud, hoaxer, impostor, swindler.

check *verb*
1 *You must check your work carefully.* examine, inspect, scrutinize.
2 *The heavy traffic checked our progress.* block, delay, halt, hamper, hinder, hold back, obstruct, slow, slow down, stop.

check *noun*
Dad took the car to the garage for a check. check-up, examination, inspection, test.

cheeky *adjective*
Don't be so cheeky! disrespectful, facetious, flippant, impertinent, impolite, impudent, insolent, insulting, irreverent, mocking, rude, saucy, shameless.
AN OPPOSITE IS respectful.

cheer *verb*
1 *We cheered when our side won.* applaud, clap, shout, yell.
AN OPPOSITE IS jeer.
2 *The good news cheered us.* comfort, console, delight, encourage, gladden, please.
AN OPPOSITE IS sadden.
to cheer up *The weather cheered up.* become more cheerful, brighten.

cheerful *adjective*
The sun was shining, and we set out in a cheerful mood. animated, bright, buoyant, delighted, elated, festive, glad, gleeful, good-humoured, happy, jolly, jovial, joyful, light-hearted, lively, merry, optimistic, pleased, radiant.
AN OPPOSITE IS sad.

chemist *noun*
An old-fashioned word is ***apothecary***.
A chemist's shop is a ***dispensary*** or ***pharmacy***.

chequered *adjective*
The tablecloth had a chequered pattern.
check, criss-cross.
Scottish cloth with a chequered
pattern is ***tartan***.

cherish *verb*
I cherish the gifts she gave me. adore,
be fond of, keep safe, look after, love,
prize, treasure, value.

chess *noun*

> THE PIECES USED IN PLAYING
> CHESS: bishop, castle or rook, king,
> knight, pawn, queen.
>
> SOME TERMS USED IN PLAYING
> CHESS: castle, check, checkmate,
> mate, move, stalemate, take.

chest *noun*
*I found some old books in a chest in the
attic.* box, case, crate, trunk.

chew *verb*
The dog was still chewing his bone.
crunch up, gnaw, grind up, munch.

chicken *noun*

> KINDS OF CHICKEN: bantam, broiler,
> chick, cockerel, fowl, hen, pullet,
> rooster.

chief *noun*
*BBC chiefs announced that the
programme would be axed.* boss,
leader.

> PEOPLE IN CHARGE OF VARIOUS
> EVENTS, ORGANIZATIONS, OR
> GROUPS: administrator, captain,
> chairperson, chieftain, commander,
> commanding officer, controller,
> director, employer, executive,
> foreman, governor, head, manager,
> master, mistress, officer, overseer,
> owner, president, principal,
> proprietor, [*uncomplimentary*]
> ringleader, superintendent,
> supervisor.
> SEE ALSO **ruler**.

chief *adjective*
1 *Leave out the details, and just give me
the chief facts.* basic, central, crucial,
dominant, essential, foremost,
fundamental, important,
indispensable, key, main, major,
necessary, predominant, primary,
principal, prominent, significant, vital.
AN OPPOSITE IS unimportant.
2 *He's the Queen's chief minister.* head,
senior.

chiefly *adverb*
The snow falls chiefly in the north.
especially, generally, mainly, mostly,
predominantly, primarily, principally.

child *noun*

> VARIOUS WORDS FOR PEOPLE WHO
> ARE NOT YET GROWN UP:
> adolescent, baby, boy, girl, infant,
> juvenile, [*informal*] kid, lad, lass,
> toddler, youngster, youth.
>
> VARIOUS WORDS FOR SOMEONE'S
> CHILD: daughter, descendant,
> offspring, son.
> A child who expects to inherit a title
> or fortune from parents is an ***heir*** or
> ***heiress***.
> A child whose parents are dead is an
> ***orphan***.
> A child looked after by a guardian is
> a ***ward***.
>
> WORDS FOR VARIOUS TIMES OF
> YOUR LIFE BEFORE YOU ARE
> GROWN UP: adolescence, babyhood,
> boyhood, childhood, girlhood,
> infancy, schooldays, your teens,
> youth.

childish *adjective*
It's childish to make rude noises.
babyish, immature, infantile, juvenile.
AN OPPOSITE IS mature.

chill *verb*
1 *The wind chilled us to the bone.* cool,
freeze, make cold.
AN OPPOSITE IS warm.
2 *Chill the soup before serving it.* keep
cold, refrigerate.

chilly *adjective*
1 *It's a chilly evening, so wrap up warm.* cold, cool, crisp, fresh, frosty, icy, [*informal*] nippy, raw, wintry.
AN OPPOSITE IS warm *adjective.*
2 *She gave me a very chilly look.* distant, hostile, unfriendly, unsympathetic.
AN OPPOSITE IS friendly.

chime *noun*
The church clock chimed at midnight. ring, strike.
FOR VARIOUS WAYS BELLS SOUND, SEE **bell**.

chimney *noun*
A chimney on a ship or steam engine is a *funnel*.
A pipe to take away smoke and fumes is a *flue*.

china *noun*
You can wash up while I put the china away. crockery, cups and saucers, porcelain.
SEE ALSO **pottery**.

chink *noun*
1 *He peeped through a chink in the fence.* crack, crevice, cut, gap, opening, rift, slit, slot, split.
2 *I heard the chink of coins.* clink, ping, ring.
FOR VARIOUS WAYS TO MAKE SOUNDS, SEE **sound** *verb.*

chip *noun*
1 *I swept up the chips of wood.* bit, flake, fragment, piece, sliver, splinter, wedge.
2 *This mug's got a chip in it.* crack, flaw, nick, notch.

chip *verb*
I chipped a cup while I was washing up. crack, damage, nick, notch, scratch, splinter.

chivalrous *adjective*
He's a very chivalrous man. bold, brave, courageous, heroic, valiant, worthy.
AN OPPOSITE IS cowardly.

choice *noun*
1 *We ran out of petrol, so we had no choice but to walk.* alternative, option.
2 *She wouldn't be my choice as team captain.* pick, preference, vote.
3 *The greengrocer has a good choice of vegetables.* array, assortment, diversity, mixture, range, selection, variety.

choke *verb*
1 *My collar is choking me.* stifle, strangle, suffocate, throttle.
2 *Thick fumes made the fireman choke.* cough, gasp.
choked *The main roads are choked in the rush hour.* blocked, [*informal*] bunged up, clogged, congested, impassable, jammed, obstructed.

choose *verb*
1 *We had a show of hands to choose a new captain.* appoint, elect, select, vote for.
2 *I chose the green anorak.* decide on, opt for, pick out, plump for, select, settle on, single out.
3 *I chose to buy the green anorak.* decide, make a decision, prefer, resolve.

choosy *adjective* [*informal*]
My baby brother is very choosy about his food. finicky, fussy, hard to please.

chop *verb*
1 *He chopped the log into thin pieces.* cut, split.
2 *We chopped down the undergrowth to make a path.* hack, slash.
To chop down a tree is to *fell* it.
To chop off an arm or leg is to *amputate* it.
To chop a branch off a tree is to *lop* it.
To chop food into small pieces is to *dice* or *mince* it.

chorus *noun*
1 *Mum sings in the chorus of the local operatic society.* choir.
2 *Our teacher sang the verses, and we joined in the chorus.* refrain.
in chorus *It was such an easy question that we answered in chorus.* all at once, simultaneously, together.

chronic *adjective*
1 *She has chronic pain from her rheumatism.* constant, continual, continuous, incessant, incurable, permanent, persistent.
AN OPPOSITE IS acute or temporary.
2 [*informal*] *He's a chronic driver!* awful, bad, dire, dreadful, terrible.

chronicle *noun*
He wrote a chronicle of his life during the war years. account, diary, history, journal, narrative, record, story.

chunk *noun*
I cut myself a chunk of cheese. block, hunk, lump, piece, portion, slab, wedge.

church *noun*

> THE MAIN TRADITIONS OF THE CHRISTIAN CHURCH: Orthodox, Protestant, Roman Catholic.
>
> VARIOUS PLACES WHERE CHRISTIANS WORSHIP: abbey, basilica, cathedral, chapel, convent, minster, monastery, nunnery, parish church, priory, tabernacle.
> FOR PLACES WHERE PEOPLE OF OTHER RELIGIONS WORSHIP, SEE **worship**.
>
> PARTS OF A CHURCH: aisle, belfry, chancel, chapel, cloister, crypt, dome, nave, porch, sanctuary, spire, steeple, tower, transept, vestry.
>
> THINGS YOU MAY FIND IN A CHURCH: altar, Bible, candles, communion table, crucifix, font, hymn books, lectern, memorials, pews, prayer books, pulpit.
>
> SOME FESTIVALS AND EVENTS CELEBRATED IN CHURCH: Advent, Ascension Day, Ash Wednesday, baptism or christening, Christmas, communion, confirmation, Easter, Good Friday, Lent, mass, the Nativity, Palm Sunday, Pentecost, Whitsun.
>
> THINGS THAT MAY BE PART OF WORSHIP IN CHURCH: benediction or blessing, communion, hymn, prayer, psalm, readings from the Bible or scripture, sermon. ➡

> PEOPLE CONNECTED WITH A CHURCH: archbishop, bishop, cardinal, chaplain, choirboy, choirgirl, churchwarden, clergyman or clergywoman, the congregation, curate, deacon, deaconess, elder, lay reader, minister, parson, pastor, the Pope, preacher, priest, rector, sexton, sidesman, verger, vicar.

churchyard *noun*
burial ground, cemetery, graveyard.

cinders *plural noun*
The cinders from the fire were still glowing. ashes, embers.

circle *noun*

> THINGS WITH A CIRCULAR SHAPE: disc, hoop, ring, wheel.
>
> THREE-DIMENSIONAL ROUND SHAPES: ball, globe, orb, sphere.
> The distance round a circle is the *circumference*.
> The distance across a circle is the *diameter*.
> The distance from the centre to the circumference is the *radius*.
>
> THINGS WITH A CURVED OR NEARLY CIRCULAR SHAPE: band, belt, coil, cordon, curl, ellipse, loop, oval, spiral.
>
> VARIOUS CIRCULAR MOVEMENTS: circulation, cycle, revolution, rotation, turn, whirl.
> A circular race track is a *circuit*.
> Once round a circuit is a *lap*.
> A circular trip which ends where you began is a *tour*.
> A circular trip round the world is a *circumnavigation*.
> A circular trip of a satellite round a planet is an *orbit*.

circle *verb*
The vultures circled overhead. turn, twist, wheel.

circular *adjective*
The pond was circular in shape. round.

circular *noun*
I wonder if people read these circulars the postman brings? advertisement, leaflet, notice, pamphlet.

circulate *verb*
1 *Blood circulates in the body.* go round, move round.
2 *I asked friends to circulate notices about our sale.* distribute, issue, send round.

circulation *noun*
1 *We had a lesson explaining the circulation of blood round the body.* flow, movement, transmission.
2 *The local newspaper has a big circulation.* distribution, sales figures.

circumference *noun*
We raced round the circumference of the playing field. border, boundary, edge, fringe, perimeter.

circumstances *plural noun*
On the news they explained the circumstances which led to the tragedy. background, causes, conditions, context, details, facts, particulars, situation.

circus *noun*

SOME PEOPLE WHO PERFORM IN A CIRCUS: acrobat, animal trainer, clown, conjuror, contortionist, equestrian artist or horse rider, juggler, lion-tamer, ringmaster, tightrope walker, trapeze-artist, trick cyclist.

citizen *noun*
All adult citizens can vote in a general election. inhabitant, native, resident, subject, taxpayer, voter.

citrus fruit *noun*

VARIOUS CITRUS FRUITS: clementine, grapefruit, lemon, lime, mandarin, orange, satsuma, tangerine.

city *noun* SEE **town**.

civil *adjective*
I know you're angry, but please try to be civil. civilized, considerate, courteous, obliging, polite, respectful.
AN OPPOSITE IS rude.

civilization *noun*
We have been studying the civilization of ancient Egypt. achievements, attainments, culture, society.

civilized *adjective*
Civilized people shouldn't need to use violence. cultivated, cultured, democratic, educated, polite, sophisticated, well-behaved, well-mannered.
AN OPPOSITE IS uncivilized.

claim *verb*
1 *When you hand in the purse you found, are you going to claim a reward?* ask for, collect, demand, insist on, request.
2 *He claims that he's an expert.* allege, argue, assert, declare, insist, maintain.

clamber *verb*
We clambered over the rocks. climb, crawl, move awkwardly, scramble.

clammy *adjective*
The walls of the cellar were unpleasantly clammy. damp, moist, slimy, sticky.

clamp *verb*
FOR VARIOUS WAYS TO FASTEN THINGS, SEE **fasten**.

clang, clank *verbs*
FOR VARIOUS WAYS TO MAKE SOUNDS, SEE **sound** *verb*.

clap *verb*
1 *We clapped her performance.* applaud.
2 *He clapped me on the shoulder.* hit, pat, slap, smack.

clarify *verb*
We asked the teacher to clarify what he wanted us to do. explain, make clear, simplify, throw light on.
AN OPPOSITE IS confuse.

clash *noun*
1 *The clash of cymbals made me jump.* crash.
2 *There was a clash between rival supporters at the match.* argument, conflict, confrontation, fight, [*informal*] scrap, scuffle.

clash *verb*
1 *The cymbals clashed.* crash.
FOR OTHER WAYS TO MAKE SOUNDS, SEE **sound** *verb*.
2 *My favourite TV programmes clash at 8 o'clock tonight.* coincide, happen at the same time.
3 *Demonstrators clashed with the police.* argue, fight, get into conflict, quarrel, squabble.

clasp *verb*
1 *I clasped her hand.* cling to, grasp, grip, hold, squeeze.
2 *She clasped him in her arms.* embrace, hug.

clasp *noun*
The cloak was held in place by a gold clasp. brooch, buckle, clip, fastener, fastening, hook, pin.

class *noun*
1 *There are 32 children in our class.* form, set, stream.
2 *There are many different classes of plants.* category, classification, division, group, kind, set, sort, species, type.
3 *He came from a different social class.* level, rank, status.

TERMS SOMETIMES USED TO LABEL SOCIAL CLASSES: aristocracy or nobility, commoners, middle class, ruling class, upper class, working class.

classic *noun*
This book is a classic! masterpiece, model.

classic *adjective*
Notice that *classic* means *excellent of its kind*, while *classical* means either *to do with the ancient Greeks and Romans*, or *to do with serious music written in the past Did you see him score that classic goal on Saturday?* admirable, excellent, exceptional, fine, first-class, first-rate, great, masterly, model, perfect.
AN OPPOSITE IS ordinary.

classified *adjective*
The spy gave classified information to the enemy. confidential, private, secret, top secret.

classify *verb*
We classified the plants according to the shape of their leaves. class, grade, group, organize, put into sets, sort.

claw *verb*
The cat clawed his leg. savage, scratch, tear.

clean *adjective*
1 *We took care to leave the place clean after our party.* spotless, tidy.
Clean clothes are **laundered** or **washed** clothes.
A clean piece of paper is **blank** or **unused** paper.
A clean car is a **polished** or **shiny** car.
A clean lavatory is **hygienic** or **sanitary**.
A clean bandage is a **sterile** bandage.
Clean water is **clear**, **fresh**, **pure**, or **unpolluted** water.
AN OPPOSITE IS dirty *adjective*.
2 *He's always led a good clean life.* decent, respectable.
AN OPPOSITE IS indecent.
3 *The referee said he wanted the boxers to have a clean fight.* fair, honest, honourable, sporting, sportsmanlike.
AN OPPOSITE IS dishonourable.

clean *verb*

WAYS TO CLEAN THE HOUSE: dust, hoover, mop, polish, scrub, spring-clean, sweep, vacuum.

WAYS TO CLEAN YOURSELF: bath, shampoo your hair, shower, soap yourself, sponge yourself, spruce yourself up, wash. ➡

WAYS TO CLEAN CLOTHES: dry-clean, launder, rinse, wash, wring out.

WAYS TO CLEAN A CAR: buff up, polish, shampoo, sponge down, wax.

WAYS TO CLEAN THE PANS AND DISHES: rinse, scour, scrape, sponge, swill, wipe.

WAYS TO CLEAN WATER: distil, filter, purify, sterilize.

WAYS TO CLEAN THE LAVATORY: cleanse, disinfect, flush, sanitize, scrub out.
AN OPPOSITE IS contaminate or dirty.

clear *adjective*
The adjective *clear* can be used in many ways. We illustrate some common ways here, and some of the synonyms you could use.
1 *I saw fish swimming in the clear water.* clean, colourless, pure, transparent.
AN OPPOSITE IS opaque.
2 *It was a beautiful clear day.* bright, cloudless, sunny, unclouded.
A clear night is a **moonlit** or **starlit** night.
AN OPPOSITE IS cloudy.
3 *She gave a clear signal.* bold, plain, unambiguous, unmistakable, visible.
AN OPPOSITE IS ambiguous.
4 *Her voice was clear, although she was phoning from America.* audible, distinct.
AN OPPOSITE IS muffled.
5 *The signature on this letter is not clear.* legible, recognizable.
AN OPPOSITE IS illegible.
6 *My camera takes nice clear pictures.* focused, sharp, well defined.
AN OPPOSITE IS unfocused.
7 *Are you sure that your conscience is clear?* blameless, innocent, untroubled.
AN OPPOSITE IS guilty.
8 *After hearing her clear explanation, I knew what to do.* intelligible, lucid, understandable.
AN OPPOSITE IS confusing.
9 *There's a clear difference between a male blackbird and a female.* conspicuous, definite, noticeable, obvious, perceptible, pronounced.
AN OPPOSITE IS imperceptible.
10 *The police made sure the road was clear for the ambulance.* empty, free, open, passable, uncrowded, unobstructed.
AN OPPOSITE IS congested.

clear *verb*
The verb *clear* can be used in many ways. We illustrate some common ways here, and some of the synonyms you could use.
1 *I cleared the weeds from the flower bed.* eliminate, get rid of, remove, strip.
2 *She cleared the blocked drainpipe.* clean out, open up, unblock, unclog.
To clear a channel is to **dredge** it.
3 *I cleared the misty windows.* clean, polish, wipe.
4 *If the fire alarm goes, clear the building.* empty, evacuate.
5 *The fog cleared.* disappear, evaporate, melt away, vanish.
6 *The forecast said that the weather will clear.* become clear, brighten, lighten.
7 *The court cleared him of all blame.* acquit, free, release.
8 *The horse cleared the fence.* bound over, get over, jump, leap over, pass over, spring over, vault.
to clear off [*informal*] *Clear off and leave me alone!* get out, go away, leave.
to clear up *Please clear up this mess before you go.* clean up, remove, put right, put straight, tidy up.

clench *verb*
1 *He clenched his teeth.* close tightly, grit, squeeze together.
2 *She clenched the coin tightly in her hand.* clasp, grasp, grip, hold.

clergyman, clergywoman *nouns*

VARIOUS MEMBERS OF THE CLERGY: archbishop, bishop, canon, cardinal, chaplain, curate, deacon, deaconess, dean, minister, parson, pastor, preacher, priest, rector, vicar.

clerical *adjective*
> My job involves a lot of clerical work.
> office, secretarial.

VARIOUS PEOPLE DOING CLERICAL
WORK IN AN OFFICE: bookkeeper,
clerk, computer operator, filing clerk,
office boy, office girl, receptionist,
secretary, shorthand typist, typist,
word processor operator.

clever *adjective*
> **1** *My brother is very clever and always
> passes his exams.* able, academic,
> [*informal*] brainy, bright, intelligent,
> knowledgeable.
> AN OPPOSITE IS unintelligent.
> **2** *She's very clever with her fingers.*
> accomplished, capable, gifted, skilful,
> talented.
> If you are clever at a lot of things, you
> are **versatile**.
> AN OPPOSITE IS unskilful.
> **3** *They are clever enough to get away
> with it.* quick, sharp, shrewd, smart.
> Uncomplimentary synonyms are
> **artful**, **crafty**, **cunning**, **wily**.
> AN OPPOSITE IS stupid.

cliff *noun*
> The car rolled over the edge of a cliff.
> crag, precipice, rock face.

climate *noun*
> FOR WORDS TO DO WITH CLIMATE, SEE
> **weather**.

climax *noun*
> The excitement built up to a climax.
> crisis, high point, peak.
> AN OPPOSITE IS anticlimax.

climb *verb*
> **1** *It took us several hours to climb the
> mountain.* ascend, clamber up, go up,
> scale.
> To reach the top of a mountain is to
> **conquer** it.
> **2** *The plane climbed into the clouds.* lift
> off, soar, take off.
> **3** *The road climbs steeply up to the
> castle.* rise, slope.

to climb down 1 *It's harder to climb
> down the rock than to get up it.*
> descend, get down from.
> **2** *We all told him he was wrong, so he
> had to climb down.* admit defeat, give
> in, surrender.

climb *noun*
> It's a steep climb up to the castle.
> ascent, gradient, hill, incline, rise,
> slope.

climber *noun*
> The climbers were all roped together.
> mountaineer, rock-climber.

cling *verb*
> **to cling to someone or something**
> **1** *The child clung to her mother.* clasp,
> clutch, embrace, grasp, hug.
> **2** *Ivy clings to the wall.* adhere to,
> fasten on to, stick to.

clinic *noun*

PLACES WHERE YOU CAN GO TO
CONSULT DOCTORS OR NURSES:
health centre, hospital, infirmary,
medical centre, sanatorium, sickbay,
surgery.

clip *verb*
> **1** *I clipped my papers together.* pin,
> staple.
> FOR VARIOUS WAYS TO FASTEN
> THINGS TOGETHER, SEE **fasten**.
> **2** *Dad was clipping the hedges in the
> back garden.* cut, trim.
> To cut unwanted twigs off a tree or
> bush is to **prune** it.

cloak *noun*
> She wrapped a cloak around her. cape,
> coat, [*old use*] mantle, wrap.

clock *noun*

INSTRUMENTS USED TO MEASURE
TIME: alarm clock, chronometer,
digital clock, grandfather clock,
hourglass, pendulum clock,
stopwatch, sundial, timer, watch,
wristwatch.

clog *verb*
> In the autumn, dead leaves clog the
> drain. block, bung up, choke, congest,
> fill, jam, obstruct, stop up.

close *adjective*
1 *Our house is close to the shops.*
adjacent, handy (for), near.
To be actually by the side of something
is to be **adjacent** or **neighbouring**.
To fire a gun at close range is to fire at
point-blank range.
AN OPPOSITE IS distant.
2 *The twins are very close.* affectionate,
attached, devoted, fond of each other,
friendly, intimate, loving.
AN OPPOSITE IS unfriendly.
3 *The police made a close examination
of the stolen car.* careful, detailed,
minute, painstaking, searching,
thorough.
AN OPPOSITE IS casual.
4 *It was an exciting race because it was
so close.* equal, even, level, well-
matched.
AN OPPOSITE IS one-sided.
5 *Open the window—it's very close in
here.* airless, [*informal*] fuggy, humid,
muggy, stifling, stuffy, suffocating.
AN OPPOSITE IS airy.

close *verb*
1 *Don't forget to close the lid.* fasten,
seal, secure, shut.
2 *The rioters tried to close the road.*
barricade, block, obstruct, stop up.
3 *He closed the meeting by thanking the
chairman.* complete, conclude, end,
finish, stop, terminate, [*informal*] wind
up.

closely *adverb*
Please listen closely. attentively,
carefully, conscientiously.

clot *verb*
*If you cut yourself, the blood will clot
and form a scab.* solidify, thicken.

cloth *noun*
*The curtains were made of striped
cotton cloth.* fabric, material, stuff.
A word for cloth in general is **textiles**.

SOME KINDS OF CLOTH: calico,
canvas, cashmere, chiffon, chintz,
corduroy, cotton, denim, felt, flannel,
flannelette, gabardine, gauze,
hessian, lace, linen, lint, mohair,
muslin, nylon, oilcloth, plaid,
polyester, poplin, rayon, sacking,
satin, silk, taffeta, tartan, tweed,
velvet, wool, worsted.

clothe *verb*
to be clothed in *They were clothed in
white.* be dressed in, be wearing.

clothes *plural noun*
*What clothes are you taking away on
holiday?* clothing, garments.

A set of clothes to wear is a **costume**,
outfit, or **suit**.
A soldier wears a **uniform**.
A uniform worn by servants is a
livery.
A priest may wear a **cassock**, a
surplice, or **vestments**.
A nun or monk wears a **habit**.

VARIOUS GARMENTS: blazer, blouse,
caftan, cardigan, chador or chuddar,
coat, dhoti, dress, dungarees, frock,
gown, gymslip, jacket, jeans, jerkin,
jersey, jumper, kilt, kimono, lounge
suit, miniskirt, parka, pullover, robe,
sari, sarong, shirt, shorts, singlet,
skirt, slacks, smock, sweater,
sweatshirt, trousers, trunks, T-shirt,
tunic, waistcoat.

THINGS YOU WEAR ON TOP OF
OTHER CLOTHES: anorak, apron,
cagoule, cape, cloak, duffel coat,
greatcoat, mackintosh, oilskins,
overalls, overcoat, pinafore, poncho,
raincoat, shawl, stole, track suit,
windcheater.

VARIOUS UNDERCLOTHES: bra,
briefs, drawers, girdle, knickers,
[*informal*] panties, pants, petticoat,
slip, underpants, vest.

THINGS YOU WEAR AT NIGHT OR
WHEN GETTING DRESSED: dressing
gown, housecoat, négligée,
nightclothes, nightdress, [*informal*]
nightie, pyjamas.

THINGS YOU WEAR ON YOUR
HANDS: gauntlets, gloves, mittens.

THINGS YOU WEAR ON YOUR LEGS:
garters, leggings, leg warmers,
socks, stockings, tights.

THINGS YOU WEAR ROUND YOUR
NECK: collar, cravat, muffler,
necktie, scarf, tie.
FOR THINGS YOU WEAR ON YOUR
HEAD AND FEET, SEE **hat, shoe**. ➡

> PARTS OF A GARMENT: belt, bodice, button, buttonhole, collar, cuff, hem, lapel, pocket, seam, sleeve, waistband, zip.

cloud *noun*
A cloud of steam rose from the kettle. billow, haze, mist, puff.

cloud *verb*
to cloud over *The sky clouded over.* become cloudy, become dull, darken.

cloudless *adjective*
The forecast promised that it would be a cloudless day. bright, clear, sunny, unclouded.
A cloudless night is a ***moonlit*** or ***starry*** night.
AN OPPOSITE IS cloudy.

cloudy *adjective*
1 *The day was cold and cloudy.* dark, dismal, dull, gloomy, grey, overcast, sunless.
AN OPPOSITE IS cloudless.
2 *We couldn't see any fish in the cloudy water.* hazy, milky, muddy, murky.
AN OPPOSITE IS clear or transparent.

clown *noun*
My friend likes being a clown and making us laugh. comedian, comic, fool, jester, joker.

club *noun*
1 *The intruder threatened him with a club.* baton, stick, truncheon.
2 *Would you like to join our club?* association, circle, group, organization, society, union.

club *verb*
The intruder clubbed him on the head. [*informal*] bash, batter, hit, strike, thump, whack.
FOR OTHER WAYS OF HITTING, SEE **hit** *verb*.
to club together *My sister and I clubbed together and bought a new CD.* combine, join up, share the cost.

clue *noun*
I don't know the answer—give me a clue. hint, idea, indication, lead, pointer, suggestion, tip.

clump *noun*
We walked towards a clump of trees on the hill. cluster, collection, group, thicket.
A clump of grass, hair, etc., is a ***tuft***.

clumsy *adjective*
He's so clumsy—he's always breaking things. awkward, careless, inept, ungainly.
AN OPPOSITE IS graceful.
An informal word for a clumsy person is a ***butterfingers***.

cluster *noun*
A cluster of people waited outside the theatre. assembly, bunch, collection, crowd, gathering, knot.
SEE ALSO **group** *noun*.

clutch *verb*
He clutched the rope. catch, clasp, cling to, grab, grasp, grip, hang on to, hold on to, seize, snatch.

clutches *plural noun*
He had her in his clutches. control, grasp, power.

clutter *verb*
to clutter up *My brother's belongings are cluttering up my bedroom!* lie about, litter, make untidy, mess up.

clutter *noun*
We'll have to clear up all this clutter. junk, litter, mess, muddle, odds and ends, rubbish.

coach *noun*
1 *We went to London by coach.* bus.
FOR OTHER VEHICLES, SEE **vehicle**.
2 *Their football team has a new coach.* instructor, trainer.

coach *verb*
He was coached by a former champion. instruct, teach, train.

coarse *adjective*
1 *The blanket was made of coarse woollen material.* bristly, hairy, harsh, rough, scratchy.
AN OPPOSITE IS soft.
2 *He objected to her coarse remarks.* crude, impolite, improper, indecent, offensive, rude, smutty, vulgar.
AN OPPOSITE IS polite.

coast noun

After the disaster, oil was washed up along the coast. coastline, shore.
SEE ALSO **seaside**.

coast verb

I coasted down the hill on my bike. cruise, freewheel, glide.

coat noun

1 *Put on your coat if you are going out.*

KINDS OF COAT YOU CAN WEAR: anorak, blazer, cagoule, cardigan, dinner jacket, [*old use*] doublet, duffel coat, greatcoat, jacket, [*old use*] jerkin, mackintosh, overcoat, raincoat, waistcoat, windcheater.

WORDS FOR AN ANIMAL'S COAT: fleece, fur, hair, hide, pelt, skin.
FOR OTHER GARMENTS, SEE **clothes**.

2 *The cupboard door needs a coat of paint.* coating, covering, layer.

coax verb

We coaxed the animal back into its cage. persuade, tempt.

cocky adjective [informal]

I didn't like him because he was so cocky. arrogant, boastful, cheeky, conceited, pleased with yourself, vain.
AN OPPOSITE IS modest.

code noun

Everyone in the club must behave according to our code of conduct. laws, regulations, rules.

coil noun

VARIOUS COILED SHAPES OR MOVEMENTS: corkscrew, curl, screw, spiral, twirl, twist, whirl, whorl.

coil verb

The snake coiled itself round a branch. curl, loop, roll, spiral, turn, twist, wind, writhe.

coin noun

Have you got a 10p coin for the slot machine? bit, piece.
coins *I keep come coins handy to pay my bus fare.* change, coppers, loose change, silver, small change.

coin verb

We coined a new name for our group. create, devise, invent, make up, produce, think up.

coincide verb

My birthday coincides with a bank holiday. clash, fall together, happen together.

coincidence noun

We met by coincidence. accident, chance, fluke, luck.

cold adjective

1 *Wrap up warm in this cold weather.* arctic, bitter, chilly, cool, crisp, freezing, frosty, icy, raw, snowy, wintry.
2 *I tried to shelter from the cold wind.* biting, fresh, keen, penetrating, piercing.
3 *I was cold in spite of my thick anorak.* frozen, numb, [*informal*] perished, shivering, shivery.
4 *The room was cold and dark.* bleak, draughty, unheated.
AN OPPOSITE IS hot.
to be cold *You'll be cold without a coat on.* freeze, shiver, tremble.
To be ill with a low temperature because of the cold is to suffer from **hypothermia**.
5 *He gave me a cold stare.* cool, distant, heartless, indifferent, reserved, stony, uncaring, unemotional, unfeeling, unfriendly, unkind, unsympathetic.
AN OPPOSITE IS kind.

cold-blooded adjective

Cold-blooded properly refers to animals with blood that changes temperature according to the surroundings, but it is often used to describe cruel behaviour or a cruel person
We were horrified to read about the cold-blooded murder. barbaric, brutal, callous, cold, cruel, hard-hearted, heartless, inhuman, merciless, pitiless, ruthless, savage.
AN OPPOSITE IS humane.

collaborate verb

She and her sister collaborated on the project. cooperate, work together.

collaboration *noun*
The book is the result of several years of collaboration between the two men. association, cooperation, partnership, teamwork.

collapse *verb*
1 *Many buildings collapsed in the earthquake.* buckle, cave in, crumple, disintegrate, fall in, fold up, tumble down.
2 *Some people collapsed in the heat.* faint, fall down.

colleague *noun*
He discussed the project with his colleagues. associate, partner.

collect *verb*
1 *Squirrels collect nuts.* accumulate, gather, hoard, pile up, save, store up.
2 *A crowd collected to watch the fire.* assemble, come together, converge.
AN OPPOSITE IS scatter.
3 *We collected a large sum for charity.* raise, take.
4 *I collected the bread from the baker's.* bring, fetch, get, obtain.

collection *noun*
Dad has an interesting collection of old records. accumulation, array, assortment, hoard, pile, set.
A collection of books is a *library*.
A collection of various items in a book is a *compendium* or *omnibus*.
A collection of poems is an *anthology*.
A collection of weapons is an *arsenal* or *stockpile*.

collective *adjective*
If it affects us all, it ought to be a collective decision. combined, democratic, joint, shared, united.
AN OPPOSITE IS individual.

college *noun*
FOR PLACES WHERE PEOPLE STUDY, SEE **education**.

collide *verb*
to collide with *The car collided with a man on a bike.* bump into, hit, run into, smash into, strike.

collision *noun*
The collision dented the front wing of the car. accident, bump, crash, impact, knock, smash.
A collision involving a lot of vehicles is a *pile-up*.

colloquial *adjective*
We taught our French visitor some colloquial English phrases. conversational, everyday, informal, slangy.
AN OPPOSITE IS formal.

colony *noun*
1 *At one time Britain had colonies all over the world.* possession, settlement, territory.
2 *I found a colony of ants in the garden.* FOR WORDS FOR VARIOUS GROUPS, SEE **group** *noun*.

colossal *adjective*
A colossal statue towered above us. enormous, gigantic, huge, immense, massive, monstrous, monumental, towering, [*informal*] tremendous, vast.
AN OPPOSITE IS small.

colour *noun*
What do you call that colour? hue, shade, tinge, tint, tone.

NAMES OF VARIOUS COLOURS:
amber, auburn, azure, beige, black, blue, bronze, brown, buff, chestnut, chocolate, cobalt, cream, crimson, emerald, fawn, gilt, ginger, gold, golden, green, grey, indigo, ivory, jet-black, khaki, lavender, maroon, mauve, navy blue, olive, orange, pink, puce, purple, red, rosy, russet, salmon pink, sandy, scarlet, silver, tan, tawny, turquoise, vermilion, violet, white, yellow.

SUBSTANCES WHICH GIVE THINGS THEIR COLOUR: colouring, cosmetics, dye, make-up, paint, pigment or pigmentation, stain.

colours *The colours of the regiment fluttered in the breeze.* banner, flag, standard.

colour *verb*
1 *The teacher said we could colour the models we made.* dye, paint, tint.
2 *His fair skin colours easily.* blush, burn, flush, redden.

colourful *adjective*
1 *The garden was ablaze with colourful flowers.* bright, brilliant, gaudy, showy.
AN OPPOSITE IS colourless.
2 *The book gave a colourful description of life in the Middle Ages.* exciting, lively, picturesque, striking, vivid.
AN OPPOSITE IS dull.

colourless *adjective*
Everything looked colourless until the sun came out. drab, dull, grey, neutral, pale.
Something which has lost its colour is **bleached** or **faded**.
AN OPPOSITE IS colourful.

column *noun*
1 *A lot of classical buildings have columns supporting the roof.* pillar, post, shaft, support.
2 *A column of soldiers wound its way across the desert.* file, line, procession, row, string.
3 *She writes a column in the local newspaper.* article, feature, leader, piece.

comb *verb*
1 *I had a wash and combed my hair before going out.* arrange, groom, tidy, untangle.
2 *I combed the house in search of my pen.* hunt through, ransack, rummage through, scour, search thoroughly.

combat *noun*
FOR VARIOUS KINDS OF FIGHTING, SEE **fight** *noun*.

combat *verb*
There's a campaign to combat vandalism in our district. battle against, fight, grapple with, oppose, reduce, resist, stand up to, tackle.

combination *noun*

A combination of parts or things into one whole thing is a **synthesis** or **unification**.
A combination of two businesses is an **amalgamation** or a **merger**.
A combination of substances is a **compound** or **fusion**. ➡

A combination of metals is an **alloy**.
A combination of ingredients for a cake is a **blend** or a **mixture**.
When two people combine together, it is a **marriage** or **partnership**.
When friends combine to help each other, it is an **alliance** or **association**.
When criminals combine to do something bad, it is a **conspiracy**.

combine *verb*
1 *Let's all combine our resources.* add together, amalgamate, integrate, join, put together.
2 *I combined the cake ingredients in a bowl.* blend, mingle, mix, stir together.
3 *The local schools combined to organize a charity concert.* band together, cooperate, get together, unite

come *verb*
1 *We expect our guests to come at dinner time.* appear, arrive, visit.
AN OPPOSITE IS go.
2 *When you hear a cuckoo, you know that summer is coming.* advance, draw near.
to come about *Can you tell me how the accident came about?* happen, occur, result, take place.
to come across *I came across the pen you lost.* discover, find.
to come round, to come to *How long did it take me to come round after the operation?* become conscious, revive.
to come to 1 *Tell me when we come to my station.* approach, arrive at, get close to, near, reach.
2 *What did the bill for repairs to the car come to?* add up to, amount to, total.

comedy *noun*

VARIOUS KINDS OF COMEDY: clowning, farce, humour, jokes, satire, situation comedy or [*informal*] sitcom, slapstick, wit.

PEOPLE WHO TRY TO MAKE OTHER PEOPLE LAUGH: clown, comic, entertainer, humorist, [*old use*] jester, joker, satirist.

comfort noun
1 *The news brought comfort to us all.*
consolation, encouragement,
reassurance, relief.
2 *If I had a million pounds, I could live
in comfort.* affluence, contentment,
ease, luxury.

comfort verb
*He was upset, so we tried to comfort
him.* calm, cheer up, console,
encourage, reassure, soothe,
sympathize with.

comfortable adjective
1 *I sat in a comfortable chair and fell
asleep.* cosy, easy, padded, relaxing,
snug, soft, upholstered, warm.
2 *On holiday you need comfortable
clothes.* casual, informal, loose-fitting.
3 *Our cat leads a comfortable life.*
agreeable, contented, happy, luxurious,
pleasant, relaxed, restful, serene.
AN OPPOSITE IS uncomfortable.

comic, comical adjectives
We laughed at his comic remarks.
amusing, diverting, funny, hilarious,
humorous, witty.
To be comical in a cheeky way is to be
facetious.
To be comical in a silly way is to be
absurd, **farcical**, **ludicrous**, or
ridiculous.
To be comical in a hurtful way is to be
sarcastic or **satirical**.

command noun
1 *You can start when I give the
command.* instruction, order.
A sacred command is a
commandment.
2 *She has command of the whole
expedition.* authority (over), charge,
control, management, power (over),
supervision.
3 *She has a good command of Spanish.*
ability (in), knowledge, mastery, skill
(in).

command verb
1 *The officer commanded his troops to
fire.* bid, direct, instruct, order, tell.
2 *The captain commands the ship.*
administer, be in charge of, control,
direct, govern, head, lead, manage,
supervise.

commander noun
*The commander of the expedition
decided that it was too dangerous to
continue.* head, leader, officer-in-
charge.
SEE ALSO **chief** noun.

commemorate verb
*They held a ceremony to commemorate
those who died in war.* be a memorial
to, be a reminder of, celebrate, honour,
pay tribute to, remember.

commence verb
*You may commence work when I give
the order.* begin, embark on, start.

commend verb
The head commended us on our work.
applaud, compliment, congratulate,
praise.
AN OPPOSITE IS criticize.

commendable adjective
*She said that my effort was very
commendable.* admirable, good,
praiseworthy, useful, worthwhile.
AN OPPOSITE IS worthless.

comment noun
*Was there any comment in the
newspaper about the way we played?*
mention, observation, opinion,
reference, remark, statement.
A hostile comment is a **criticism**.

commentary noun
*I couldn't go to the match, but I heard
the commentary on the radio.* account,
analysis, broadcast, description,
report, review.

commerce noun
*A lot of people in the city work in
commerce.* business, buying and
selling, trade, trading.

commercial adjective
1 *Do you think the new sports centre
will be a commercial success?* economic,
financial.
2 *Her novels are both well written and
commercial.* money-making, profitable,
profit-making.

commercial noun
*We watched the new commercial for the
breakfast cereal.* [informal] advert,
advertisement, [informal] plug.

commit *verb*
The police intercepted the burglar before he could commit another crime. carry out, do, execute, perform.
to commit yourself to something *I committed myself to help with the jumble sale.* be determined, promise, resolve, undertake, vow.

commitment *noun*
1 *Every player has the commitment to win.* dedication, determination, enthusiasm, keenness, passion, resolution.
2 *Dad has a commitment from the builder that he'll finish the job this week.* guarantee, pledge, promise, undertaking, vow.

committee *noun*

VARIOUS GROUPS OF PEOPLE WHICH DISCUSS AND ORGANIZE THINGS:
A group appointed to discuss or decide something is a ***panel***.
A group which runs a business organization is a ***board***.
A group which decides whether someone is guilty or not is a ***jury***.
A group elected to run a town is a ***council***.
A group elected to govern a country is an ***assembly*** or ***parliament***.
The group of ministers who control the government is the ***cabinet***.

common *adjective*
1 *Colds are a common complaint in winter.* commonplace, daily, everyday, familiar, frequent, normal, ordinary, prevalent, unsurprising, well known, widespread.
AN OPPOSITE IS rare.
2 *'Good morning' is a common way to greet people.* conventional, customary, habitual, regular, routine, standard, traditional, typical, usual.
AN OPPOSITE IS uncommon.
3 *After it appeared in the paper, the story was common knowledge.* communal, general, public, universal.
AN OPPOSITE IS private.
4 *Mum says it's common to pick your nose.* coarse, crude, rude, vulgar.
AN OPPOSITE IS refined.

commonplace *adjective*
1 *The lecturer made a lot of commonplace remarks.* boring, obvious, ordinary, predictable, routine, trivial, unexciting.
SEE ALSO **common**.
AN OPPOSITE IS memorable.
2 *Foreign travel is commonplace these days.* common, frequent, normal, ordinary, routine, usual.

commotion *noun*
Police had to stop the commotion when gangs of rival supporters met each other. bedlam, chaos, confusion, disorder, disturbance, excitement, fuss, hullabaloo, pandemonium, [*informal*] racket, riot, row, trouble, turbulence, turmoil, unrest, upheaval, uproar.

communal *adjective*
I didn't like the communal washing facilities at the campsite. common, public, shared.
AN OPPOSITE IS private.

communicate *verb*
The head communicated her decision in a letter to our parents. announce, convey, disclose, express, indicate, make known, pass on, proclaim, publish, report.
To communicate in writing is to ***correspond***.
To communicate face to face is to ***confer***, ***converse***, or ***discuss things***.
to communicate with *The police communicated with each other by radio.* get in touch with, make contact with, speak to, talk to.

communication *noun*
Human beings have various methods of communication. communicating, contacting one another, understanding one another.

VARIOUS KINDS OF SPOKEN COMMUNICATION: chatting, conversation, dialogue, gossip, message, rumour, telephone conversation.

VARIOUS KINDS OF WRITTEN COMMUNICATION: cable, correspondence, greetings card, letter, note, postcard, telegram. ➡

VARIOUS OFFICIAL
COMMUNICATIONS: announcement,
bulletin, communiqué, dispatch,
memo or memorandum, news flash,
notice, proclamation, statement.

VARIOUS ELECTRONIC
COMMUNICATIONS: computer
network, e-mail, fax, satellite,
telecommunications.

THE MEDIA OR MASS MEDIA:
advertising, broadcasting, cable
television, newspapers, the press,
radio, television.

communicative *adjective*
*He's not very communicative, so it's
hard to know what he's thinking.*
chatty, frank, open, talkative.
AN OPPOSITE IS secretive.

community *noun*
A community sharing a home and way
of life is a *commune*.
A community sharing a home in Israel
is a *kibbutz*.

compact *adjective*
The computer is light and compact.
portable, small.
AN OPPOSITE IS large.

companion *noun*
*I'm glad I had a companion on the long
journey to London.* comrade, friend,
[*informal*] mate, partner.

company *noun*
1 *We enjoy other people's company.*
companionship, fellowship, friendship,
society.
2 *My cousin works for a clothing
company.* business, concern,
establishment, firm, organization.

comparable *adjective*
I think your work is comparable to hers.
equivalent, similar.
AN OPPOSITE IS different (from).

compare *verb*
Compare these sets of figures. match
up, relate, set side by side.
When you compare things which are
obviously different, you **contrast**
them.
to compare with *We can't expect our
young team to compare with theirs.*
compete with, equal, match, resemble,
rival.

comparison *noun*
1 *That's an unfair comparison—we are
amateurs and they are professionals.*
analogy, parallel.
2 *There's no comparison between their
team and ours.* likeness, match,
resemblance, similarity.

compartment *noun*
*Dad's toolbox has compartments for
different tools.* division, section, space.

compassion *noun*
*He was filled with compassion when he
saw the famine victims.* feeling, love,
pity, sympathy, tenderness.

compatible *adjective*
1 *They discovered they weren't really
compatible.* well suited.
2 *We bought a new computer and a
compatible printer.* matching.
AN OPPOSITE IS incompatible.

compel *verb*
You can't compel me to come with you.
force, make.

compensate *verb*
*When I broke our neighbours' window, I
had to compensate them for the
damage.* pay back, pay compensation
to, repay.

compensation *noun*
*How much compensation did she get for
the accident?* damages, payment,
repayment.

compère *noun*
The compère introduced the next act.
announcer, presenter.
A compère on a pop music programme
is a *disc jockey* or *DJ*.

compete *verb*
I'm competing in the next event. be a contestant, enter, participate, perform, take part.
to compete against *We have to compete against a strong team this week.* contend with, oppose, play against.

competent *adjective*
1 *Dad wants a competent builder to build our extension.* able, accomplished, capable, efficient, experienced, expert, proficient, qualified, skilful, skilled, trained.
2 *She said that my work was competent, but not brilliant.* acceptable, adequate, satisfactory.
AN OPPOSITE IS incompetent.

competition *noun*

VARIOUS KINDS OF COMPETITION: championship, contest, game, knock-out competition, match, quiz, race, rally, series, tournament, trial.
SEE ALSO **sport**.

competitive *adjective*
We played in a competitive spirit. keen, lively, sporting.
AN OPPOSITE IS cooperative.

competitor *noun*
All the competitors paraded round the stadium. challenger, contender, contestant, opponent, participant, rival.
People who take part in an exam are **candidates** or **entrants**.

compile *verb*
I compiled an anthology of poems about animals. assemble, collect, edit, gather together, put together.

complacent *adjective*
You can't be complacent until the job is finished. contented, pleased with yourself, self-satisfied, smug.
AN OPPOSITE IS anxious.

complain *verb*
Don't take any notice of her—she always complains. find fault, fuss, grouse, grumble, moan, protest.
to complain about *In the café, she started to complain about the food.* criticize, find fault with, object to.
AN OPPOSITE IS praise.

complaint *noun*
1 *If you have a complaint about the food, tell the manager.* criticism, grievance, objection.
2 *Sore throats are a common complaint in winter.* ailment, disease, illness, infection, sickness, [*informal*] upset.

complete *adjective*
1 *Is this the complete set?* comprehensive, entire, full, intact, whole.
AN OPPOSITE IS incomplete.
2 *I can sit down now that my jobs are complete.* accomplished, completed, concluded, ended, finished.
AN OPPOSITE IS unfinished.
3 *My attempt to bake a cake was complete disaster.* absolute, downright, perfect, [*informal*] proper, pure, sheer, thorough, total, utter.

complete *verb*
She's just completed her first novel. carry out, conclude, end, finish.

complex *adjective*
Servicing an aircraft is a complex task. complicated, detailed, difficult, elaborate, [*informal*] fiddly, intricate, involved.
AN OPPOSITE IS simple.

complexion *noun*
A healthy diet is the secret of a good complexion. skin.

WORDS TO DESCRIBE DIFFERENT KINDS OF COMPLEXION: clear, dark, fair, freckled, pale, pasty, ruddy, sickly, spotty, swarthy, tanned, weather-beaten.

complicated *adjective*
His ideas were too complicated for me to understand. complex, detailed, difficult, elaborate, intricate, involved, sophisticated.
AN OPPOSITE IS simple.

complication noun
I thought the job would be easy, but there was a complication. difficulty, problem, snag.

complimentary adjective
It's nice to get complimentary remarks. admiring, appreciative, approving, favourable.
If complimentary remarks are not deserved, they are **flattering**.
AN OPPOSITE IS critical or insulting.

compliments plural noun
It was nice to get compliments about my cooking. appreciation, approval, congratulations, praise, tribute.
Compliments which you don't deserve are **flattery**.
AN OPPOSITE IS insults.

component noun
The factory made components for cars. bit, part, piece, spare, spare part.

compose verb
Beethoven composed nine symphonies. create, devise, make up, produce, think up, write.
to be composed of *Mosaic is composed of small bits of stone and glass.* be made of, comprise, consist of.

composition noun
We played a composition written by our teacher. piece, work.
FOR VARIOUS KINDS OF COMPOSITION, SEE **music**.

compound noun
A compound of substances is a **blend**, **fusion**, or **synthesis**.
A compound of metals is an **alloy**.

comprehend verb
She just couldn't comprehend what had happened. appreciate, figure out, follow, grasp, perceive, realize, understand.

comprehensive adjective
She gave us a comprehensive account of her travels. complete, detailed, encyclopedic, extensive, full, inclusive, thorough.
AN OPPOSITE IS selective.

compress verb
I tried to compress all my clothes into one bag. cram, crush, flatten, jam, press, squash, squeeze, stuff.

comprise verb
The class comprised children from many different backgrounds. be composed of, consist of, contain, include.

compromise verb
The two sides agreed to compromise. make concessions, meet halfway, strike a balance.

compulsory adjective
The wearing of seat belts is compulsory. necessary, obligatory, required.
AN OPPOSITE IS optional.

compute verb
I computed how much the project would cost. calculate, estimate, figure out, reckon, work out.

computer noun

SOME KINDS OF COMPUTER: laptop, mainframe, micro or microcomputer, minicomputer, palmtop, PC or personal computer, word processor.

THINGS YOU CAN DO ON A COMPUTER: calculating, data processing, desktop publishing, formatting, information retrieval, playing games, printing, producing spreadsheets, programming, storing information, word processing.

SOME PARTS OF A COMPUTER SYSTEM: CD ROM drive, chip, disk drive, hard disk, interface, joystick, keyboard, microchip, microprocessor, modem, monitor, mouse, printer, processor, silicon chip, terminal, VDU.

OTHER TERMS USED IN COMPUTING: bit, bug, byte, cursor, data, database, digital, diskette, floppy disk, hard copy, hardware, memory, menu, network, peripheral, printout, program, software, virus, window.

comrade *noun*
The soldiers carried their injured comrades to safety. companion, friend, mate, partner.

concave *adjective*
AN OPPOSITE IS convex.

conceal *verb*
1 The dog tried to conceal its bone. bury, cover up, hide.
2 We tried to conceal our hiding place. camouflage, disguise, make invisible, mask, screen.
3 Don't conceal the truth. hush up, keep quiet about, keep secret, suppress.

conceit *noun*
The conceit of that woman is ridiculous. arrogance, pride, vanity.

conceited *adjective*
He was so conceited when he won first prize! arrogant, [informal] big-headed, boastful, [informal] cocky, proud, self-satisfied, vain.
AN OPPOSITE IS modest.

conceive *verb*
1 Who conceived this silly plan? devise, [informal] dream up, invent, make up, originate, plan, produce, think up, work out.
2 I could not conceive how the plan would work. imagine, see.

concentrate *verb*
1 Please try to concentrate and avoid mistakes. apply yourself, be attentive, think hard, work hard.
2 The crowds concentrated in the middle of town. collect, converge, gather.

concentrated *adjective*
This bottle contains concentrated fruit juice. condensed, strong, undiluted.
AN OPPOSITE IS diluted.

concept *noun*
I find the concept of aliens invading Earth hard to believe. idea, notion, thought.

conception *noun*
1 She has no conception of how difficult it is. comprehension, concept, idea, inkling, notion, understanding.
2 It takes nine months from the conception of a baby to its birth. conceiving.

concern *verb*
1 Road safety concerns us all. affect, be important to, be relevant to, involve, matter to, relate to.
2 It concerns me that we are destroying the rain forests. bother, distress, trouble, upset, worry.

concern *noun*
1 My private life is no concern of theirs. affair, business.
2 Global warming is a great concern to us all. anxiety, fear, worry.
3 She's the head of a business concern. company, enterprise, establishment, firm.

concerning *preposition*
The head spoke to me concerning my future. about, regarding, relating to, relevant to, with reference to.

concert *noun*
FOR VARIOUS ENTERTAINMENTS, SEE **entertainment**.

concession *noun*
If you are under 16, you get a concession on bus fares. allowance, reduction.

concise *adjective*
I gave the police a concise account of what happened. brief, condensed, short.
A concise account of something is a **précis** or **summary**.
AN OPPOSITE IS long.

conclude *verb*
1 We concluded the Christmas concert with carols. complete, end, finish, round off, wind up.
2 Our concert concluded with some carols. close, culminate, terminate.
3 They concluded that he was guilty. assume, decide, deduce, gather, infer, suppose.

conclusion *noun*
  1 *At the conclusion of the concert, everyone joined in the carols.* close, completion, culmination, end, finale, finish.
  2 *Now that you've heard the evidence, what is your conclusion?* decision, deduction, judgement, opinion, verdict.

concrete *adjective*
  We need some concrete evidence. actual, definite, factual, firm, objective, physical, real, solid, substantial.
  AN OPPOSITE IS abstract.

condemn *verb*
  1 *We condemn people who behave violently.* criticize, denounce, deplore, disapprove of, reproach.
  AN OPPOSITE IS praise.
  2 *The judge condemned him to death.* sentence.
  AN OPPOSITE IS acquit.

condensation *noun*
  I wiped the condensation off the windows. mist, steam.

condense *verb*
  1 *Can you condense your story so that it fits on one page?* compress, reduce, shorten, summarize.
  AN OPPOSITE IS expand.
  2 *Steam condenses on a cold window.* become liquid, form condensation.
  AN OPPOSITE IS evaporate.

condition *noun*
  1 *Is your bike in good condition?* order, state.
  2 *A dog needs exercise to stay in good condition.* fitness, health, shape.
  3 *It's a condition of membership that you pay a subscription.* obligation, requirement, term.
  on condition that *You can come on condition that you pay your own fare.* only if, provided or providing that.

conduct *verb*
  1 *A guide conducted us round the museum.* accompany, escort, guide, lead, take.
  2 *We asked the head to conduct our meeting.* administer, control, handle, lead, manage, organize, preside over, run, supervise.
  To conduct an orchestra is to **direct** it.
  to conduct yourself *Didn't we conduct ourselves well!* act, behave, carry on.

conduct *noun*
  Our teacher congratulated us on our good conduct. attitude, behaviour, manners.

confer *verb*
  1 *The mayor conferred the freedom of the city on the victorious team.* award (to), give (to), grant (to), present (to).
  2 *He conferred with his advisors before making a decision.* compare notes, consult, converse, discuss things, exchange ideas, have a discussion, talk things over.

conference *noun*
  The firm's managers had to go to a conference. consultation, discussion, meeting.
  SEE ALSO **meeting**.

confess *verb*
  She confessed her guilt to the police. acknowledge, admit, own up to, reveal.

confession *noun*
  I was surprised by his confession that he was guilty. acknowledgement, admission, disclosure.

confide *verb*
  to confide in *If you confide in me, I won't tell anyone.* open your heart to, tell secrets to.

confidence *noun*
  1 *We can face the future with confidence.* faith, hope, optimism.
  AN OPPOSITE IS doubt.
  2 *I wish I had her confidence.* assurance, boldness, conviction, firmness, self-confidence.
  confidence trick *He got the money with a confidence trick.* deception, fraud, hoax, swindle, trick.
  to have confidence in *I have confidence in her ability to succeed.* believe in, rely on, trust.

confident *adjective*
1 *I am confident that we will win.*
certain, optimistic, positive, sure.
AN OPPOSITE IS doubtful.
2 *She is a confident sort of person.*
assertive, bold, fearless, self-confident,
unafraid.

confidential *adjective*
The details of the plan are confidential.
private, secret.
AN OPPOSITE IS public.

confine *verb*
1 *They confined their discussion to
official matters.* limit, restrict.
2 *The police confined our supporters at
one end of the ground.* coop up, enclose,
fence in, hem in, isolate, shut in,
surround.

confirm *verb*
1 *The strange events confirmed his
belief in ghosts.* back up, justify, prove,
reinforce, support.
AN OPPOSITE IS disprove.
2 *I wrote to confirm my order.* make
official, verify.
AN OPPOSITE IS cancel.

confiscate *verb*
The police confiscated his air gun.
seize, take away, take possession of.

conflict *noun*
There's a lot of conflict in their family.
antagonism, disagreement, fighting,
friction, hostility, opposition,
quarrelling, strife, unrest.
SEE ALSO **fight** *noun*.

conflict *verb*
to conflict with *Her account of what
happened conflicts with mine.* clash
with, contradict, contrast with, differ
from, disagree with.
conflicting *You and I hold conflicting
opinions on the subject.* contradictory,
contrasting, different, incompatible,
opposite.

conform *verb*
to conform to or **with** *The club expels
anyone who doesn't conform with the
rules.* abide by, agree with, fit in with,
follow, keep to, obey, submit to.
AN OPPOSITE IS disobey.

confront *verb*
*I decided to confront her and ask her
why she insulted me.* challenge, face up
to, stand up to.
AN OPPOSITE IS avoid.

confuse *verb*
1 *Complicated rules confuse people.*
baffle, bewilder, mystify, perplex,
puzzle.
2 *You must be confusing me with
someone else.* mix up, muddle.

confusion *noun*
1 *There was great confusion when the
lights went out.* bedlam, chaos,
commotion, fuss, hullabaloo,
pandemonium, turmoil, uproar.
2 *I saw the confusion on their faces.*
bewilderment, perplexity, puzzlement.

congested *adjective*
*The roads are congested during the
rush hour.* blocked, clogged, crowded,
full, jammed, obstructed, [*informal*]
snarled up.
AN OPPOSITE IS clear.

congratulate *verb*
We congratulated the winners. applaud,
compliment, praise.
AN OPPOSITE IS criticize.

connect *verb*
1 *What's the best way to connect these
wires?* attach, couple, fasten, fix
together, join, link, tie together.
AN OPPOSITE IS separate.
2 *There was evidence connecting him
with the crime.* associate, make a
connection between, relate.

connection *noun*
*There is definitely a connection between
smoking and cancer.* association, link,
relationship.

conquer *verb*
1 *They thought they could conquer their
enemies if they fought one more battle.*
beat, crush, defeat, get the better of,
overcome, overwhelm, rout, thrash,
vanquish.
2 *Gaul was conquered by Julius
Caesar.* capture, occupy, possess, seize,
take, win.
3 *Hillary conquered Everest in 1953.*
climb, reach the top of.

conqueror *noun*
Cheering crowds greeted the
conquerors. victor.

conquest *noun*
The book gave an account of the
Norman conquest of Britain. invasion,
occupation.

conscience *noun*
Would your conscience allow you to
kill? morals, principles, sense of right
and wrong.

conscientious *adjective*
He's a conscientious worker. attentive,
careful, dependable, dutiful, hard
working, meticulous, painstaking,
reliable, responsible, thorough.
AN OPPOSITE IS careless.

conscious *adjective*
1 In spite of the knock on his head, he
remained conscious. alert, awake,
aware.
AN OPPOSITE IS unconscious.
2 She made a conscious effort to
improve her work. deliberate,
intentional, planned.
AN OPPOSITE IS accidental.

consecutive *adjective*
She was away for three consecutive
days. continuous, running (say three
days running), successive.

consent *verb*
to consent to She consented to my
request. agree to, approve of, authorize,
grant.
AN OPPOSITE IS refuse.

consequence *noun*
1 She did it without thinking of the
consequences. effect, outcome, result,
sequel, upshot.
2 The loss of one penny is of no
consequence. importance, significance.

conservation *noun*
The conservation of the environment is
important to us all. maintenance,
preservation, protection.
AN OPPOSITE IS destruction.

conservative *adjective*
1 He's conservative about what he eats.
conventional, narrow-minded, old-
fashioned, reactionary, traditional,
unadventurous.
AN OPPOSITE IS progressive.
2 At a conservative estimate, the repairs
will cost £100. cautious, moderate,
reasonable.
AN OPPOSITE IS extreme.

conserve *verb*
We should conserve natural resources.
be economical with, look after,
preserve, protect, save, use wisely.
AN OPPOSITE IS waste.

consider *verb*
1 I considered the problem carefully.
contemplate, examine, meditate about,
ponder on, reflect on, study, think
about, weigh up.
2 I consider this to be very important.
believe, judge, reckon.

considerable *adjective*
We need a considerable amount of rain
to fill the reservoirs. big, large,
respectable, significant, sizeable,
substantial.
AN OPPOSITE IS negligible.

considerate *adjective*
It was considerate of you to lend her
your umbrella. caring, charitable,
helpful, kind, kind-hearted,
neighbourly, obliging, sympathetic,
thoughtful, unselfish.
AN OPPOSITE IS selfish.

consideration *noun*
1 Thank you for your consideration.
help, kindness, sympathy,
thoughtfulness, unselfishness.
2 After careful consideration, I decided
not to go on the trip. reflection, thought.

consist *verb*
to consist of 1 The country consists
largely of mountains. be composed of,
be made of, comprise, contain, include,
incorporate.
2 Her job consists mostly of meeting
people. involve.

consistent *adjective*
1 *These plants need to be kept at a consistent temperature.* constant, regular, stable, steady, unchanging.
2 *Fortunately, our goalkeeper is a consistent player.* dependable, predictable, reliable.
AN OPPOSITE IS inconsistent.

consolation *noun*
When you're depressed, you need some consolation. comfort, relief, support, sympathy.

console *verb*
He did his best to console me when my dog died. comfort, soothe, support, sympathize with.

conspicuous *adjective*
1 *The church spire is a conspicuous landmark.* eye-catching, notable, obvious, prominent, unmistakable, visible.
2 *I had made some conspicuous mistakes.* clear, evident, glaring, noticeable, obvious.
AN OPPOSITE IS inconspicuous.

conspiracy *noun*
Guy Fawkes was involved in a conspiracy to blow up Parliament. plot, scheme.

conspire *verb*
The men conspired to cheat their employer. intrigue, plot, scheme.

constant *adjective*
1 *There is a constant noise of traffic on the motorway.* ceaseless, continual, continuous, endless, incessant, never-ending, non-stop, permanent, perpetual, persistent, relentless, steady, unending, uninterrupted.
AN OPPOSITE IS changeable.
2 *He has been my constant friend for many years.* dependable, devoted, faithful, firm, loyal, reliable, true, trustworthy.
AN OPPOSITE IS unreliable.

constitute *verb*
In soccer, eleven players constitute a team. compose, comprise, form, make up.

construct *verb*
We constructed a shelter in the back garden. assemble, build, erect, fit together, make, put together, put up, set up.
AN OPPOSITE IS demolish.

construction *noun*
1 *The construction of the shelter took an hour.* assembly, building, erecting, erection, setting-up.
2 *The shelter was a flimsy construction.* building, structure.

constructive *adjective*
Does anyone have any constructive suggestions? creative, helpful, positive, practical, useful, valuable, worthwhile.
AN OPPOSITE IS useless.

consult *verb*
1 *If you are ill, consult the doctor.* ask, confer with, discuss things with, get advice from, speak to.
2 *If you don't know how to spell a word, consult your dictionary.* refer to.

consume *verb*
1 *Our guests consumed all the food in ten minutes!* devour, gobble up, guzzle.
SEE ALSO **drink, eat.**
2 *The ship consumed a great deal of fuel.* use up.
3 *The building was consumed by fire.* destroy.

consumer *noun*
Shops try to give consumers what they want. buyer, customer, shopper.

contact *verb*
I'll contact you when I have some news. call, call on, communicate with, correspond with, get in touch with, notify, phone, ring, speak to, talk to, write to.

contagious *adjective*
Mumps is a very contagious disease. catching, infectious.

contain *verb*
1 *This box contains various odds and ends.* hold.
2 *A dictionary contains words and definitions.* comprise, consist of, include, incorporate.

container *noun*

SOME CONTAINERS FOR DRINKS:
beaker, bottle, can, cup, decanter,
flask, glass, goblet, mug, tankard,
teapot, thermos, tumbler, urn,
vacuum flask, wineglass.

SOME CONTAINERS USED IN
COOKING: billycan, bowl, casserole,
cauldron, dish, jug, kettle, pan, pot,
saucepan, teapot.

OTHER CONTAINERS FOR LIQUIDS:
barrel, basin, bath, bucket, butt,
cask, churn, cistern, decanter, dish,
drum, jar, keg, pail, pitcher, tank,
test tube, tin, trough, tub, vase, vat,
vessel, water-butt, watering can.

CONTAINERS FOR NON-LIQUIDS:
bag, basket, bin, box, briefcase,
caddy, canister, carton, cartridge,
case, casket, chest, coffer, coffin,
crate, drum, dustbin, envelope,
hamper, handbag, haversack, hod,
holdall, knapsack, money box,
pannier, pocket, pouch, punnet,
purse, receptacle, rucksack, sachet,
sack, satchel, scuttle, skip, suitcase,
tea chest, tin, trunk, wallet.

contaminate *verb*
Chemicals contaminated the water.
infect, poison, pollute.
AN OPPOSITE IS purify.

contemplate *verb*
1 *She sat on the bed, contemplating
herself in the mirror.* gaze at, look at,
observe, stare at, survey, view, watch.
2 *We contemplated what to do next.*
consider, meditate about, ponder,
reflect on, study, think about, weigh
up.
3 *I contemplate taking a holiday soon.*
intend, plan, propose.

contemporary *adjective*
The two senses of *contemporary* are
very different. Sense 1 describes things
that belong to the same time as each
other, whereas sense 2 describes things
belonging to our own time

1 *The coronation of Elizabeth II and the
first conquest of Mount Everest were
contemporary events.* simultaneous.
2 *Do you like contemporary music?*
current, fashionable, the latest,
modern, the newest, [*informal*] trendy,
up-to-date.

contempt *noun*
His contempt for her was quite obvious.
disgust, dislike (of), hatred (of),
loathing, low opinion (of), scorn.
AN OPPOSITE IS admiration.

contemptible *adjective*
Mugging is a contemptible crime.
despicable, detestable, disgraceful,
hateful, loathsome, mean, shameful,
wretched.
AN OPPOSITE IS admirable.

contemptuous *adjective*
He gave a contemptuous sneer.
arrogant, disrespectful, haughty,
insolent, insulting, jeering, scornful,
sneering.
AN OPPOSITE IS admiring.

contend *verb*
I contend that I was right. argue,
assert, claim, declare, maintain.
to contend with 1 *They had to contend
with strong opposition.* compete with,
fight against, grapple with, oppose,
strive against, struggle against.
2 *Among other things, we had bad
weather to contend with.* cope with,
deal with, face, put up with.

content *noun*
Skimmed milk has a low fat content.
element, ingredient, part.

content *adjective*
Are you content to let me do it? happy,
willing.
AN OPPOSITE IS unwilling.
SEE ALSO **contented**.

contented *adjective*
*After a big dinner, he looked very
contented.* comfortable,
[*uncomplimentary*] complacent,
content, fulfilled, happy, peaceful,
pleased, relaxed, satisfied, serene,
tranquil, untroubled, well fed.
AN OPPOSITE IS discontented.

contentment *noun*
There was a smile of contentment on his
face. comfort, contentedness,
happiness, relaxation, satisfaction,
serenity, tranquillity, well-being.
AN OPPOSITE IS discontent.

contest *noun*
It was an exciting contest between two
excellent players. bout, challenge,
competition, encounter, fight, game,
match, struggle, tournament.

contest *verb*
Several players contested the referee's
decision. argue against, challenge,
disagree with, oppose, quarrel with,
question.

contestant *noun*
The contestants in the competition were
evenly matched. competitor, contender,
participant, player.

continual *adjective*
I get sick of their continual arguing.
constant, eternal, frequent, perpetual,
persistent, recurrent, repeated,
unending.
AN OPPOSITE IS occasional.
SEE ALSO **continuous**.

continue *verb*
1 They continued the search until it got
dark. keep up, persevere with, prolong,
pursue, [informal] stick at, sustain.
2 This rain can't continue for long.
carry on, go on, keep on, last, linger,
persist.
3 We'll continue our work after lunch.
proceed with, resume.

continuous *adjective*
We had continuous rain all through our
holiday. ceaseless, everlasting,
incessant, never-ending, non-stop,
unbroken, unceasing, uninterrupted.
SEE ALSO **continual**.
An illness which continues for a long
time is a **chronic** illness.
AN OPPOSITE IS intermittent or
occasional.

contract *noun*
The builder's contract says that they
will finish the work this month.
agreement, deal, undertaking.
A contract to rent a house is a **lease**.
A contract between two countries is an
alliance or **treaty**.
A contract to end a dispute about
money is a **settlement**.

contract *verb*
1 Most substances contract when they
get colder. become smaller, reduce,
shrink.
AN OPPOSITE IS expand.
2 A local firm contracted to build our
extension. agree, arrange, sign an
agreement, undertake.
3 She contracted a mysterious illness.
become infected by, catch, develop, get.

contradict *verb*
I didn't dare to contradict her.
challenge, disagree with, speak
against.

contradictory *adjective*
My brother and I have contradictory
opinions about eating meat. conflicting,
contrary, converse, different,
incompatible, opposite.
AN OPPOSITE IS similar.

contraption *noun*
Dad's got a weird contraption for
sweeping up dead leaves. apparatus,
contrivance, device, gadget, invention,
machine, mechanism.

contrary *adjective*
1 During the discussion, two contrary
views were expressed. contradictory,
conflicting, converse, different,
opposite.
AN OPPOSITE IS similar.
2 She's a sulky, contrary child.
awkward, defiant, difficult,
disobedient, obstinate, perverse,
rebellious, stubborn, uncooperative,
unhelpful, wilful.
AN OPPOSITE IS cooperative.

contrast *verb*
  1 *The teacher contrasted the work of the two students.* compare, emphasize differences between, make a distinction between.
  2 *His painting contrasts with mine.* clash, differ (from).

contrast *noun*
  She pointed out the contrast between my work and his. difference, distinction, opposition.
  AN OPPOSITE IS similarity.

contribute *verb*
  Will you contribute something to our charity collection? donate, give, provide.
  If you contribute regularly to something, you **subscribe** to it.
  to contribute to *Good weather contributed to our enjoyment.* add to, encourage, help.

contribution *noun*
  I gave a contribution to the local animal shelter. donation, gift.
  A regular contribution to something is a **subscription**.
  An official contribution to the work of a charity is a **grant**.
  A contribution to a collection in church is an **offering**.

contributor *noun*
  1 *We have some generous contributors to our fund.* benefactor, donor, patron, supporter.
  A business which contributes to a charity is a **sponsor**.
  A person who contributes regularly is a **subscriber**.
  2 *She is a regular contributor in the local paper.* correspondent, journalist, reporter, writer.

contrive *verb*
  He contrived a way to do it. create, invent, make up, plan, think up.

control *noun*
  1 *A teacher needs to have control in the classroom.* authority, discipline, power.

2 *Control of what happens in school is the job of the head teacher.* administration, command, direction, government, management, organization, supervision.
  to be in control of
  SEE **control** *verb*.

control *verb*
  1 *The government controls the country's affairs.* administer, be in charge of, be in control of, command, conduct, deal with, direct, govern, guide, look after, regulate, rule, run, superintend, supervise.
  2 *Can't you control that dog?* handle, manage, restrain.
  3 *They built a dam to control the floods.* check, contain, curb, hold back.

controversial *adjective*
  The referee's decision to award a penalty was controversial. debatable, questionable.

controversy *noun*
  There is much controversy about the building of a bypass. argument, debate, disagreement, dispute, quarrelling.

convalescent *adjective*
  My aunt is convalescent after an operation. getting better, improving, making progress, [*informal*] on the mend, recovering.

convenient *adjective*
  1 *Is there a convenient place to put my umbrella?* accessible, appropriate, available, nearby, suitable.
  AN OPPOSITE IS inconvenient.
  2 *Dad has a convenient tool for tightening screws.* handy, helpful, labour-saving, neat, useful.

convention *noun*
  Shaking hands is a social convention. custom, tradition.

conventional *adjective*
  He taught me the conventional way to say hullo in French. accepted, common, customary, everyday, habitual, normal, ordinary, orthodox, regular, routine, standard, traditional, usual.
  AN OPPOSITE IS unconventional.

converge *verb*
Motorways converge in one mile.
coincide, combine, come together, join,
meet, merge.
AN OPPOSITE IS divide.

conversation *noun*
An informal conversation is a *chat* or
gossip.
A more formal conversation is a
discussion.
A very formal conversation is a
conference.
Conversation in a play or novel is
dialogue.

converse *verb*
We conversed happily for several
minutes. chat, engage in conversation,
have a conversation, talk.
FOR DIFFERENT WAYS TO TALK, SEE
talk *verb*.

converse *noun*
I thought she hated me, but apparently
the converse is true. opposite, reverse.

conversion
The conversion of the house into flats
has created extra accommodation for
students. adaptation, alteration,
changing, converting, transformation.

convert *verb*
1 We are going to convert our attic into
a games room. adapt, alter, change,
transform.
2 I never used to like football, but my
cousin converted me. change someone's
mind, convince, persuade, reform, win
over.

convex *adjective*
AN OPPOSITE IS concave.

convey *verb*
1 The breakdown truck conveyed our
car to a garage. bear, bring, carry,
deliver, move, take, transfer, transport.
To convey something by sea is to *ferry*
or *ship* it.
2 What does his message convey to you?
communicate, indicate, mean, reveal,
signify, tell.

convict *noun*
Two escaped convicts kidnapped them
at gunpoint. criminal, prisoner.

convict *verb*
The burglar was convicted and sent to
prison. condemn, declare guilty, prove
guilty, sentence.
AN OPPOSITE IS acquit.

conviction *noun*
1 He spoke with conviction. assurance,
certainty, confidence, firmness.
2 She has strong religious convictions.
belief, faith, opinion, principle, view.

convince *verb*
He convinced them that he was
innocent. persuade, prove to someone,
satisfy.

convoy *noun*
A convoy of ships passed along the
horizon. armada, fleet, group.

cook *verb*

To cook food for guests or customers
is to *cater* for them.
Cooking as a business is *catering*.
The art or skill of cooking is *cookery*.

VARIOUS WAYS TO COOK FOOD: bake,
barbecue, boil, braise, brew, broil,
casserole, fry, grill, poach, roast,
sauté, simmer, steam, stew, toast.

OTHER THINGS YOU DO WHEN YOU
ARE COOKING: baste, blend, chop,
grate, freeze, infuse, knead,
liquidize, marinade, mix, peel, sieve,
sift, stir, whisk.

THINGS YOU MIGHT USE WHEN YOU
ARE COOKING: baking tin, barbecue,
basin, blender, bowl, breadboard,
breadknife, carving knife, casserole,
cauldron, chip pan, chopping board,
colander, deep fat fryer, dish, food
processor, frying pan, grill, hotplate,
jug, kettle, ladle, liquidizer,
microwave, mincer, mixer, oven, pan,
pepper mill, plate, pot, pressure
cooker, rolling pin, rôtisserie, salt
cellar, saucepan, scales, skewer,
spatula, spit, strainer, timer, tin
opener, toaster, whisk, wok, wooden
spoon.
SEE ALSO **crockery, cutlery, kitchen**.

cook *noun*
> The chief cook in a restaurant or hotel is the **chef**.
> A person who cooks food as a business is a **caterer**.

cool *adjective*
> **1** *The weather is cool for the time of year.* chilly, coldish.
> AN OPPOSITE IS hot.
> **2** *Would you like a cool drink?* chilled, iced, refreshing.
> AN OPPOSITE IS hot.
> **3** *She remained cool when everyone else panicked.* calm, level-headed, patient, relaxed, sensible, unexcitable, unflustered.
> AN OPPOSITE IS frantic.
> **4** *I was rather cool when she asked me to go out with her.* cold, distant, half-hearted, indifferent, lukewarm, unenthusiastic.
> AN OPPOSITE IS enthusiastic.
> **5** *[informal] He thinks it's cool to wear sunglasses.* chic, fashionable, smart, *[informal]* trendy.

cooperate *verb*
> *We need everyone to cooperate on this job.* assist each other, collaborate, combine, get together, help each other, join forces, support each other, work as a team, work together.

cooperation *noun*
> **1** *The teacher was impressed by our cooperation.* collaboration, teamwork.
> **2** *I could do this job quicker if I had your cooperation.* assistance, help, support.

cooperative *adjective*
> *As everyone was cooperative, we finished early.* constructive, friendly, helpful, obliging, supportive, united, working as a team.
> AN OPPOSITE IS uncooperative.

cope *verb*
> *Shall I help you, or can you cope on your own?* carry on, get by, make do, manage, survive.
> **to cope with** *She coped with her problems cheerfully.* deal with, handle, manage.

copy *noun*
> **1** *She asked me to make a copy of the article.* carbon copy, duplicate, photocopy.
> **2** *That isn't the original painting—it's a copy.* replica, reproduction.
> A copy made to deceive someone is a **fake** or a **forgery**.
> A person who looks almost the same as a brother or sister born at the same time is a **twin**.
> A living organism which is identical to another is a **clone**.

copy *verb*
> **1** *I copied the article for you.* duplicate, photocopy, reproduce, write out.
> **2** *It's illegal to copy banknotes.* fake, forge.
> **3** *She copied my ideas!* crib, make use of.
> **4** *My parrot can copy my voice.* imitate, impersonate, mimic.

core *noun*
> *It's very hot in the core of the earth.* centre, heart, inside, middle.

corn *noun*
> *Corn is one of the most important crops farmers grow.* grain.

> VARIOUS KINDS OF CORN: barley, corn on the cob or maize or sweetcorn, oats, rye, wheat.

corner *noun*
> **1** *I'll meet you at the corner of the road.* crossroads, intersection, junction, turn, turning.
> The place where two lines meet is an **angle**.
> **2** *I sat in a quiet corner and read her letter.* alcove, hiding place, recess.

corner *verb*
> *After a chase, the police cornered him.* capture, catch, trap.

corpse *noun*
> *The corpse of the badger was hidden by the bushes.* body, carcass, remains.

correct *adjective*
1 *Your answers are all correct.*
accurate, exact, faultless, right.
2 *I hope he has given us correct information.* authentic, factual, genuine, precise, reliable, true.
3 *What's the correct procedure?*
acceptable, appropriate, proper, regular, suitable.
AN OPPOSITE IS wrong.

correct *verb*
1 *Shall I correct my mistakes?* alter, put right.
2 *The optician says glasses will correct my eyesight.* cure, improve, make better.
3 *He spent the day correcting exam papers.* mark.

correspond *verb*
to correspond with 1 *I didn't expect her version of the story to correspond with mine.* agree with, be consistent with, be similar to, coincide with, match, tally with.
2 *I correspond with a girl in Paris.* communicate with, send letters to, write to.

correspondence *noun*

> VARIOUS KINDS OF CORRESPONDENCE: e-mail, fax, letter, memorandum or memo, message, note, postcard.

corrode *verb*
Some acids may corrode metal. eat away, rot, rust.

corrupt *adjective*
1 *His corrupt behaviour disgusted everyone.* evil, immoral, improper, perverted, sinful, wicked.
2 *Corrupt officials had accepted millions of pounds in bribes.* criminal, crooked, dishonest, untrustworthy.
AN OPPOSITE IS honest.

cosmetics *plural noun*
make-up.

> SOME COSMETICS: blusher, body lotion, cleanser, deodorant, eyeliner, eyeshadow, face cream, lipstick, mascara, moisturizer, nail varnish, perfume, powder, scent, talc or talcum powder, toner.

cost *verb*
How much would this watch cost? be worth, go for, sell for.

cost *noun*
The bill shows the total cost. amount, charge, expenditure, expense, payment, price.
The cost of travelling on public transport is the *fare*.

costly *adjective*
It would be too costly to repair the car. dear, expensive.
AN OPPOSITE IS cheap.

costume *noun*
The Chinese women were wearing national costumes. outfit, set of clothes, set of garments, suit.
A costume you dress up in for a party is *fancy dress*.
A set of clothes worn by soldiers, members of an organization, etc., is a *uniform*.
SEE ALSO **clothes**.

cosy *adjective*
It's nice to feel cosy in bed when it's cold and wet outside. comfortable, relaxed, secure, snug, soft, warm.
AN OPPOSITE IS uncomfortable.

couch *noun*
He lay on the couch watching TV all afternoon. settee, sofa.
SEE ALSO **bed, seat**.

counsel *verb*
He was in so much trouble that they asked a social worker to counsel him. advise, give help to, guide.

count *verb*
1 *I began to count the cost of our holiday.* add up, calculate, compute, estimate, figure out, reckon, total, work out.
2 *It's playing well that counts, not winning.* be important, matter.
to count on *You can count on me to support you.* bank on, believe in, depend on, have faith in, rely on, trust.

countenance *noun*
The clown had a sad countenance. appearance, expression, face, features, look.

counterfeit *adjective*
The police are on the lookout for counterfeit works of art. bogus, copied, fake, false, forged, imitation, sham.
AN OPPOSITE IS genuine.

countless *adjective*
There's a countless number of stars in the sky. endless, infinite, innumerable, numerous, untold.
AN OPPOSITE IS finite.

country *noun*
1 *Delegates from all the European countries came to the conference.* land, nation, people, state, territory.

A country ruled by a king or queen is a **kingdom**, **monarchy**, or **realm**.
A country governed by leaders elected by the people is a **democracy**.
A democratic country with a President is a **republic**.
A country governed by one person with unlimited power is a **dictatorship**.
A group of countries ruled by one person is an **empire**.
A group of countries cooperating together is a **commonwealth**.

2 *There is some very mountainous country in Norway.* countryside, landscape, scenery.

couple *verb*
The two train carriages were coupled together. connect, fasten, hitch, join, link.

coupling *noun*
We made sure that the coupling was secure. connection, fastening, link.

coupon *noun*
If you save ten coupons you get a free mug. ticket, token, voucher.

courage *noun*
You need courage to be a firefighter. boldness, bravery, determination, fearlessness, grit, [*informal*] guts, heroism, nerve, pluck, valour.
AN OPPOSITE IS cowardice.

courageous *adjective*
Although it was a frightening experience they were very courageous. bold, brave, daring, determined, fearless, gallant, heroic, intrepid, plucky, resolute, unafraid, valiant.
AN OPPOSITE IS cowardly.

courier *noun*
1 *A courier delivered the package.* carrier, messenger.
2 *The courier showed us to our hotel.* guide.

course *noun*
1 *The ship's course was to the west.* direction, passage, path, progress, route, way.
2 *In the normal course of events we have lunch at one o'clock.* development, programme, progression, sequence, succession.
of course *Of course you can come with us.* certainly, definitely, naturally, undoubtedly.

court *noun*
If you commit a crime, you are taken to court.
A court which deals with minor cases is a **magistrate's court**.
A court which deals with important cases is the **High Court**.
A court which tries members of the armed services is a **court martial**.
An inquiry into the cause of someone's death is an **inquest**.
An inquest is held at a **coroner's court**.

courteous *adjective*
I received a courteous reply to my letter. civil, considerate, friendly, helpful, polite, respectful, well-mannered.
AN OPPOSITE IS rude.

cover *verb*
1 *A coat of paint will cover the graffiti.*
blot out, camouflage, conceal, disguise,
hide, mask, obscure.
2 *She covered her face with her hands.*
protect, screen, shade, shield, veil.
3 *The hikers are hoping to cover twenty-
five miles a day.* progress, travel.
4 *An encyclopedia covers many
subjects.* contain, deal with, include,
incorporate.
5 *Will £10 cover your expenses?* be
enough for, pay for.

cover *noun*
1 *The cover of the book was torn.*
wrapper.
A cover for a letter is an *envelope*.
A cover to keep papers in is a *file* or
folder.
2 *On the bare hillside, there was no
cover from the storm.* hiding place,
refuge, sanctuary, shelter.
3 *A helicopter gave them cover from the
air.* protection, support.

covering *noun*
*There was a light covering of snow on
the hills.* blanket, cap, carpet, coating,
film, layer, sheet, skin, veil.

cowardly *adjective*
It was cowardly to run away. faint-
hearted, timid, unheroic, [*informal*]
yellow.
SEE ALSO **afraid**.
AN OPPOSITE IS brave.

coy *adjective*
She gave him a coy smile. bashful,
modest, reserved, self-conscious, shy,
timid.
AN OPPOSITE IS bold.

crack *noun*
1 *There's a crack in this cup.* break,
chink, chip, flaw, fracture, split.
2 *He climbed into a crack between two
rocks.* cranny, crevice, gap, opening,
rift.
3 *They heard the crack of a pistol shot.*
FOR VARIOUS WAYS TO MAKE SOUNDS,
SEE **sound** *verb*.
4 *She gave him a crack on the head.*
blow, knock, whack.
FOR OTHER WAYS OF HITTING, SEE **hit**
verb.

crack *verb*
He cracked a bone in his foot. chip,
fracture.
FOR OTHER WAYS TO DAMAGE THINGS,
SEE **damage**.

craft *noun*
1 *I admire the carpenter's craft.* art,
expertise, handicraft, skill, technique.
FOR VARIOUS ARTS AND CRAFTS, SEE
art.
2 *All sorts of craft were in the harbour.*
boats, ships, vessels.
FOR VARIOUS BOATS AND SAILING
CRAFT, SEE **vessel**.
3 *He got his own way by craft rather
than by honest means.* cunning, deceit,
deviousness, trickery.

crafty *adjective*
A crafty look came into his eyes. artful,
cunning, deceitful, devious, scheming,
sly, sneaky, tricky, wily.
AN OPPOSITE IS straightforward.

cram *verb*
1 *We can't cram any more people
in—the car is full.* compress, crush,
force, jam, pack, squeeze.
2 *She's cramming for a biology exam.*
revise, study, [*informal*] swot.

cramped *adjective*
The classroom is very cramped.
crowded, restricted, tight,
uncomfortable.
AN OPPOSITE IS roomy.

cranky *adjective*
*I thought he was a bit cranky until I got
to know him.* abnormal, crazy,
eccentric, odd, peculiar, strange, weird.
AN OPPOSITE IS normal.

cranny *noun*
*The spider crawled into a cranny in the
wall.* crack, crevice, gap, hole, opening,
rift, split.

crash *noun*
1 *I heard a loud crash from the kitchen.*
bang, smash.
FOR OTHER WAYS TO MAKE SOUNDS,
SEE **sound** *verb*.

2 *We saw a nasty crash on the motorway.* accident, bump, collision, smash.
A crash involving a lot of vehicles is a *pile-up*.
A train crash may involve a *derailment*.

crash *verb*
1 *The car crashed into the barrier.* bump, collide, knock, smash.
2 *The dishes crashed to the floor.* fall, plunge, topple.

crate *noun*
We packed our belongings in crates. box, case, chest, packing case.

crater *noun*
The explosion left a crater in the ground. abyss, cavity, chasm, hole, opening, pit.

crawl *verb*
I had to crawl along a narrow ledge. creep, edge, move slowly.

craze *noun*
It's the latest teenage dance craze. cult, enthusiasm, fad, fashion, obsession, passion, trend.

crazy *adjective*
1 *The dog went crazy when it was stung by a wasp.* berserk, delirious, frantic, frenzied, hysterical, insane, mad, wild.
2 *That was a crazy idea!* absurd, daft, eccentric, farcical, idiotic, ludicrous, ridiculous, senseless, silly, stupid.
AN OPPOSITE IS sensible.

creamy *adjective*
Mix the ingredients together until they form a creamy liquid. rich, smooth, thick, velvety.

crease *noun*
I need to iron the creases out of this shirt. fold, furrow, groove, line, wrinkle.
A crease made deliberately in a skirt, etc., is a *pleat*.

crease *verb*
Pack the clothes carefully, so you don't crease them. crinkle, crumple, crush, wrinkle.

create *verb*
1 *We were creating a dreadful noise.* cause, make, produce.
2 *The government plans to create more jobs for young people.* bring about, bring into existence, make, originate, set up, start up.

> YOU CREATE THINGS IN VARIOUS WAYS:
> You **write** a poem or story.
> You **compose** music.
> You **draw** or **paint** a picture.
> You **carve** a statue.
> You **invent** or **think up** a new idea.
> You **design** a new product.
> You **devise** a plan.
> You **found** a new club or organization.
> You **manufacture** goods.
> You **generate** electricity.
> You **build** or **construct** a model or a building.
> AN OPPOSITE IS destroy.

creation *noun*
1 *We don't know much about the creation of life on earth.* beginning, birth, generation, initiation, origin.
2 *Our class helped with the creation of a nature reserve.* building, construction, establishing, foundation.
3 *This recipe for ice cream is my own creation.* concept, invention.

creative *adjective*
She's a very creative person. artistic, imaginative, inspired, inventive, original.
AN OPPOSITE IS unimaginative.

creator *noun*
Disney was the creator of the Mickey Mouse films. deviser, inventor, maker, originator, producer.

> The creator of a design is an *architect* or *designer*.
> The creator of a novel or story is an *author* or *writer*.
> The creator of a piece of music is a *composer*.
> The creator of a work of art is an *artist*.
> The creator of a picture is a *painter* or *photographer*. ➡

The creator of a statue is a *sculptor*.
The creator of beautiful furniture,
etc., is a *craftsman* or
craftswoman.
The creator of goods for sale, etc., is a
manufacturer.

creature *noun*
We should treat all living creatures
with respect. animal, beast, being.
SEE ALSO **animal, bird, fish, insect,
reptile.**

credible *adjective*
I didn't find his story credible.
believable, convincing, likely,
persuasive, possible, reasonable,
trustworthy.
AN OPPOSITE IS incredible.

credit *noun*
Her success brought credit to the school.
approval, distinction, fame, glory, good
reputation, honour, praise.
AN OPPOSITE IS dishonour.

credit *verb*
1 You won't credit her far-fetched story.
accept, believe, have faith in, trust.
AN OPPOSITE IS doubt.
2 The bank credited £10 to my account.
add.

creditable *adjective*
The head said that we gave a creditable
performance. admirable,
commendable, excellent, good,
praiseworthy, respectable, worthy.
AN OPPOSITE IS worthless.

creed *noun*
Students of all races and creeds attend
the college. doctrine, faith, religion, set
of beliefs.

creep *verb*
1 I watched the lizard creep back into
its hiding place. crawl, edge, move
slowly, slither, wriggle.
2 I had to creep out without waking the
others. move quietly, slink, slip, sneak,
steal, tiptoe.

creepy *adjective*
The creepy noises made me a bit
nervous. eerie, ghostly, [*informal*]
scary, sinister, [*informal*] spooky,
uncanny, unearthly, weird.

crest *noun*
1 The bird had a large red crest on its
head. comb, plume, tuft.
2 When we got to the crest of the hill,
there was a wonderful view. brow,
crown, head, peak, summit, top.

crevice *noun*
Plants grew in the crevices in the rock.
crack, cranny, gap, opening, rift, split.
A deep crack in a glacier is a *crevasse*.

crew *noun*
FOR WORDS FOR GROUPS OF PEOPLE,
SEE **group** *noun*.

crib *verb*
He was caught cribbing in a test. cheat,
copy.

cricket *noun*

WORDS FOR PEOPLE PLAYING
CRICKET: batsman, bowler, cricketer,
fielder or fieldsman, wicketkeeper.
A person who makes sure players
keep to the rules in cricket is an
umpire.

SOME POSITIONS OF FIELDERS IN
CRICKET: cover, fine leg, gulley, long-
off, long-on, mid-off, mid-on, mid-
wicket, point, slip, square leg, third
man.

SOME OTHER TERMS USED IN
CRICKET: bail, boundary, crease,
innings, maiden over, over, pad, run,
stump, wicket.

crime *noun*
1 Crime is a big problem in modern
society. delinquency, dishonesty,
lawbreaking, wrongdoing.
2 The law punishes anyone who
commits a crime. offence.

VARIOUS CRIMES: abduction, arson,
blackmail, burglary, extortion,
hijacking, kidnapping,
manslaughter, mugging, murder,
pilfering, poaching, rape, robbery,
shoplifting, smuggling, stealing,
theft, vandalism.

PEOPLE WHO COMMIT VARIOUS
CRIMES: assassin, bandit,
blackmailer, brigand, burglar,
gangster, gunman, highwayman,
hijacker, hooligan, ➡

kidnapper, mugger, murderer,
outlaw, pickpocket, pirate, poacher,
rapist, robber, shoplifter, smuggler,
swindler, terrorist, thief, thug,
vandal.

criminal *noun*
These men are dangerous criminals.
[*informal*] crook, delinquent,
lawbreaker, offender, wrongdoer.
A criminal who has been sent to prison
is a *convict*.
SEE ALSO **crime**.

criminal *adjective*
*He was involved in criminal activities
for years before he was caught.*
[*informal*] bent, corrupt, [*informal*]
crooked, dishonest, illegal, unlawful,
wrong.
AN OPPOSITE IS honest.

cripple *verb*
1 *Will the accident cripple him
permanently?* disable, handicap, maim.
If you are crippled, you may be *lame* or
handicapped.
2 *The ship was crippled in the storm.*
damage, immobilize, put out of action.
To cripple a machine or vehicle
deliberately is to *sabotage* it.

crisis *noun*
*We had a crisis when we found a gas
leak.* dangerous situation, emergency,
problem.

crisp *adjective*
1 *Fry the bacon until it's crisp.* brittle,
crunchy.
AN OPPOSITE IS soft.
2 *It was a crisp winter morning.* cold,
fresh, frosty.

critical *adjective*
1 *The head made some critical
comments about our behaviour.*
negative, uncomplimentary,
unfavourable.
AN OPPOSITE IS complimentary.
2 *Tomorrow's game will be critical in
deciding whether the team stays in the
league.* crucial, decisive, important,
serious, vital.
AN OPPOSITE IS unimportant.

criticism *noun*
1 *I think his criticism was unfair.*
attack, disapproval, reprimand,
reproach.
2 *We had to write a criticism of a
favourite TV programme.* analysis,
assessment, review.

criticize *verb*
She criticized us for being so careless.
blame, condemn, disapprove of, find
fault with, reprimand, reproach, scold.
AN OPPOSITE IS praise.

crockery *noun*
Please put the crockery away. china,
dishes.

VARIOUS ITEMS OF CROCKERY:
basin, bowl, coffee cup, coffee pot,
cup, dinner plate, dish, jug, milk jug,
mug, plate, pot, sauceboat, saucer,
serving dish, side plate, soup bowl,
sugar bowl, teacup, teapot, tureen.

crook *noun* [*informal*]
The crooks got away with the money.
criminal, delinquent, lawbreaker,
offender, wrongdoer.

crooked *adjective*
1 *I wonder why this tree grew into that
crooked shape?* bent, deformed,
twisted, zigzag.
AN OPPOSITE IS straight.
2 [*informal*] *He ran a crooked business,
but the police caught him.* [*informal*]
bent, corrupt, criminal, dishonest,
illegal, unlawful.
AN OPPOSITE IS honest.

crop *noun*
We had a good crop of apples this year.
harvest, yield.

crop *verb*
1 *The sheep were cropping the grass.*
bite off, browse on, eat, graze on, nibble
at.
2 *I asked the hairdresser to crop my
hair short.* clip, cut, snip, trim.
to crop up *Several problems have
cropped up.* appear, arise, come up,
emerge, happen, occur, turn up.

cross *verb*
1 *Can you see the place on the map where two roads cross?* criss-cross, intersect.
2 *Look out for the place where the road crosses the river.* go across, pass over, span.

VARIOUS PLACES WHERE YOU CAN CROSS: bridge, causeway, flyover, ford, level crossing, overpass, pedestrian crossing, pelican crossing, subway, stepping stones, underpass, viaduct, zebra crossing.

to cross something out *I crossed out my name because I can't play this week.* cancel, delete.

cross *adjective*
She's often cross when she comes in from work. angry, annoyed, bad-tempered, grumpy, ill-tempered, irritable, short-tempered, vexed.
AN OPPOSITE IS even-tempered.

cross-examine *verb*
The lawyer began to cross-examine the witness. examine, interrogate, question.

crossroads *noun*
Take great care at the crossroads. intersection, junction.
A junction of two motorways is an **interchange**.

crouch *verb*
We crouched in the bushes. bend down, duck, squat, stoop.

crowd *noun*
1 *A crowd of people waited outside the theatre.* assembly, bunch, cluster, company, crush, gathering, group, horde, mob, multitude, swarm, throng.
SEE ALSO **group** *noun*.
2 *The crowd at Saturday's game beat all attendance records.* audience, gate, spectators.

crowd *verb*
1 *People crowded on the pavement to watch the procession go past.* assemble, flock, gather, muster.
2 *They crowded us into a small room.* bundle, cram, crush, herd, jam, pack, pile, push, squeeze.

crowded *adjective*
The shops are crowded at Christmas time. congested, full, jammed, overflowing, packed, swarming, teeming.
AN OPPOSITE IS empty.

crucial *adjective*
The negotiations were at a crucial stage. critical, decisive, important, momentous, serious.
AN OPPOSITE IS unimportant.

crude *adjective*
1 *Crude oil is taken to a refinery for processing.* natural, raw, unprocessed, unrefined.
AN OPPOSITE IS refined.
2 *I nailed together some planks to make a crude table.* clumsy, makeshift, primitive, rough.
AN OPPOSITE IS skilful.
3 *The teacher told them to stop using crude language.* coarse, dirty, foul, impolite, indecent, obscene, rude, smutty, vulgar.
AN OPPOSITE IS polite.

cruel *adjective*
1 *I think hunting is a cruel way to kill animals.* atrocious, barbaric, barbarous, beastly, bloodthirsty, brutal, callous, heartless, inhuman, sadistic, savage, uncivilized.
2 *He's a very cruel man.* diabolical, fiendish, fierce, hard, harsh, malevolent, merciless, pitiless, remorseless, ruthless, sadistic, stern, tyrannical, unjust, unkind, vicious, violent.
AN OPPOSITE IS kind.

crumb *noun*
I put out some crumbs of bread for the birds. bit, fragment, morsel, scrap.

crumble *verb*
1 *He crumbled the cake onto his plate.* break up, crush.
2 *The rotten wood began crumble.* decay, decompose, disintegrate.
When rubber decays, it **perishes**.

crumpled *adjective*
Your shirt is crumpled. creased, crinkled, crushed, wrinkled.

crunch *verb*
The dog crunched up a bone. chew, crush, grind, munch, smash.

crusade *noun*
The local health centre started a crusade against drugs. campaign, movement, war.

crush *verb*
1 I crushed my finger in the door. bruise, crunch, damage, injure, mangle, squeeze.
To crush something into a soft mess is to **mash**, **pulp**, or **squash** it.
To crush something into a powder is to **grind** or **pulverize** it.
To crush something out of shape is to **crumple** or **smash** it.
2 We crushed our opponents. conquer, defeat, humiliate, overcome, overwhelm, rout, [informal] thrash, vanquish.

crush *noun*
I couldn't fight my way through the crush. congestion, crowd, jam, throng.

cry *verb*
1 She cried out for help. bawl, bellow, call, exclaim, roar, scream, screech, shout, shriek, yell, yelp.
2 It was so sad I began to cry. shed tears, snivel, sob, weep.

cry *noun*
I heard a cry of pain. bellow, call, exclamation, howl, roar, scream, screech, shout, shriek, yell, yelp.

cuddle *verb*
She cuddled the baby. caress, clasp, embrace, hold closely, hug, nestle against, snuggle against.

cue *noun*
Don't miss your cue to speak. reminder, sign, signal.

culminate *verb*
The gala culminated in a firework display. build up (to), finish, reach a climax, terminate.

culprit *noun*
Police are searching for the culprits. criminal, delinquent, offender, troublemaker, wrongdoer.

cult *noun*
1 They were members of a religious cult. group, sect.
2 The series has become a bit of a cult in Britain. craze, fad, fashion, obsession.

cultivate *verb*
1 They cleared more forests so they could cultivate the land.

VARIOUS THINGS YOU DO TO CULTIVATE LAND: dig, fertilize, hoe, irrigate, manure, mulch, plough, prepare, rake, till, turn, work.

THINGS YOU DO TO CULTIVATE PLANTS: feed, plant out, sow, take cuttings, tend, water.

VARIOUS ASPECTS OF WORKING ON THE LAND: agriculture, farming, forestry, gardening, horticulture.

2 We want to cultivate good relations with our neighbours. develop, encourage, further, improve, promote, try to achieve.

cultivated *adjective*
She has a cultivated way of speaking. civilized, cultured, educated, polite, [informal] posh, well educated.
AN OPPOSITE IS vulgar.

cultural *adjective*
The festival included sporting and cultural events. artistic, educational, intellectual.

culture *noun*
I watched a programme about the culture of ancient Greece. art, civilization, customs, learning, traditions.

cultured *adjective*
He's a cultured man with many interests. artistic, civilized, cultivated, knowledgeable, scholarly, sophisticated, well educated, well read.
AN OPPOSITE IS ignorant.

cunning *adjective*
She worked out a cunning plan to get her own way. artful, clever, crafty, deceitful, devious, [informal] dodgy, ingenious, scheming, sly, [informal] sneaky, tricky, wily.

cup

cup *noun*

> VARIOUS THINGS TO DRINK FROM:
> beaker, bowl, chalice, glass, goblet,
> mug, tankard, teacup, tumbler,
> wineglass.
> A cup awarded as a prize is a ***trophy***.

cupboard *noun*
Put the crockery in the cupboard.
cabinet, dresser, sideboard.
A cupboard for food is a ***larder***.
SEE ALSO **furniture**.

curb *verb*
You must try to curb your anger. check,
control, hold back, limit, moderate,
repress, restrain, restrict, suppress.
AN OPPOSITE IS encourage.

cure *verb*
1 *These pills will cure your headache.*
ease, heal, help, improve, make better,
relieve.
AN OPPOSITE IS aggravate.
2 *The mechanics cured the problem
with the car's steering.* correct,
[*informal*] fix, mend, put an end to, put
right, repair, stop.

cure *noun*
I wish they could find a cure for colds.
antidote, medicine, remedy, therapy,
treatment.

curiosity *noun*
I couldn't restrain my curiosity.
inquisitiveness, interest, [*informal*]
nosiness, prying.

curious *adjective*
1 *He's always curious about other
people's private affairs.* inquiring,
inquisitive, interested (in), [*informal*]
nosy.
2 *What is that curious smell?*
abnormal, extraordinary, funny,
mysterious, odd, peculiar, puzzling,
queer, strange, unusual, weird.

curl *verb*
The snake curled itself round a branch.
coil, loop, turn, twist, wind.
FOR VARIOUS CURLED SHAPES, SEE
curve.

curly *adjective*
My hair's straight, but Mum's is curly.
curled, curling, frizzy, kinky, permed,
wavy.
AN OPPOSITE IS straight.

current *noun*
The boat drifted along with the current.
flow, stream, tide.
A current of air is a ***draught*** or ***wind***.

current *adjective*
1 *My brother knows all about the
current fashions in music.*
contemporary, modern, prevailing,
prevalent, [*informal*] trendy, up-to-
date.
AN OPPOSITE IS old-fashioned.
2 *Have you got a current passport?*
usable, valid.
AN OPPOSITE IS out-of-date.
3 *Who is the current prime minister?*
existing, present.

curriculum *noun*
*Our teacher explained the curriculum
which we have to study.* course,
programme of study, syllabus.

curse *noun*
*When he hit his finger, he let out a
curse.* oath, swearword.
Curses which use sacred words are
blasphemy.
A curse which uses rude words is an
obscenity.

curse *verb*
He cursed when he hit his finger.
blaspheme, swear, utter curses.

curve *noun*

> VARIOUS CURVED SHAPES: arc, arch,
> bend, bow, bulge, camber, circle, coil,
> corkscrew, crescent, curl, loop,
> meander, scroll, spiral, swirl, turn,
> twist, wave.
>
> ADJECTIVES TO DESCRIBE VARIOUS
> CURVED SHAPES: arched, bent,
> bowed, bulging, cambered, coiled,
> concave, convex, crescent, crooked,
> curled, curving, curvy, looped,
> meandering, rounded, serpentine,
> snaking, spiral, twisted, undulating,
> winding.

cushion *verb*
They put mattresses on the ground to cushion his fall. protect you from, reduce the effect of, soften.

custom *noun*
1 *It's our custom to give presents at Christmas.* convention, fashion, habit, routine, tradition, way.
2 *The shop offers a discount to attract custom.* business, buyers, customers, trade.

customary *adjective*
It's the customary thing to shake hands when you meet someone. common, conventional, everyday, expected, habitual, normal, ordinary, prevailing, prevalent, regular, routine, traditional, usual.
AN OPPOSITE IS unusual.

customer *noun*
There was a queue of customers at the checkout. buyer, shopper.

cut *verb*
1 *She cut the apple in half.*

> VARIOUS WAYS TO CUT THINGS: axe, carve, chip, chisel, chop, cleave, clip, gash, hack, hew, nick, notch, saw, slash, slice, slit, snick, snip, split, stab.
> To cut off a limb is to **amputate** or **sever** it.
> To cut down a tree is to **fell** it.
> To cut branches off a tree is to **lop** them.
> To cut twigs off a growing plant is to **prune** it.
> To cut hair off your face or head is to **shave** it.
> To cut wool off a sheep is to **shear** it.
> To cut grass is to **mow** it.
> To cut corn is to **harvest** or **reap** it.
> To cut unwanted bits off something is to **trim** it.
> If you trim paper with a special machine you **guillotine** it.
> To cut food into small pieces is to **grate**, **mince**, or **shred** it.
> To cut something up to examine it is to **dissect** it.
> To cut stone, etc., to make a statue is to **carve** it.
> To cut an inscription in stone, etc., is to **engrave** it. ➡

> TOOLS YOU CAN USE TO CUT THINGS: axe, carving knife, chisel, chopper, cleaver, clippers, grater, guillotine, knife, mincer, mower, razor, saw, scalpel, scissors, scythe, secateurs, shears.

2 *You need to cut your essay—it's too long.* condense, edit, shorten.
To cut parts out of a story or film because they offend people is to **censor** it.
3 *His salary was cut by 10%.* decrease, lower, reduce.
If you cut something by half, you **halve** it.

cut *noun*
1 *The nurse tried to stop the cut from bleeding.* gash, graze, injury, nick, slash, wound.
2 *There's often a cut in the price of fruit in summer.* decrease, fall, reduction.

cutlery *noun*

> VARIOUS ITEMS OF CUTLERY: breadknife, butter knife, carving knife, cheese knife, dessert spoon, fish fork, fish knife, fork, knife, ladle, salad server, spoon, steak knife, tablespoon, teaspoon.

cycle *noun* SEE **bicycle**

cynical *adjective*
She's cynical about whether the volunteers really intend to help. doubtful, negative, pessimistic, sceptical.
AN OPPOSITE IS optimistic.

Dd

daily *adjective*
Sadly, road accidents are a daily occurrence. everyday, regular.
AN OPPOSITE IS infrequent or irregular.

dainty *adjective*
The baby was wearing dainty little shoes. charming, delicate, exquisite, fine.
AN OPPOSITE IS clumsy.

dam *noun*
The dam across the river controls the flow of water. barrage, barrier, dike, weir.

dam *verb*
They plan to dam the river and create a new reservoir. block, check, hold back.

damage *verb*
I trust you not to damage the things you borrowed. harm, spoil.

VARIOUS WAYS TO DAMAGE THINGS: break, buckle, burst, chip, crack, crumple, deface, fracture, mark, scar, scratch, smash, strain, weaken. To damage something beyond repair is to ***destroy***, ***ruin***, or ***wreck*** it. To damage something deliberately is to ***sabotage*** or ***vandalize*** it.

damp *adjective*
1 *Don't wear those clothes if they are damp.* clammy, moist.
2 *I don't like this damp weather.* drizzly, foggy, misty, rainy, wet.
Weather which is both damp and warm is ***humid*** or ***muggy*** weather.
AN OPPOSITE IS dry.

dampen *verb*
1 *Just dampen the flap of the envelope and seal it.* moisten, wet.
2 *Nothing could dampen her enthusiasm.* make less, reduce.

dance *verb*
I could have danced for joy. caper, cavort, frisk, frolic, gambol, hop about, jig about, jump about, leap, prance, skip, whirl.

DIFFERENT KINDS OF DANCING: ballet, ballroom dancing, barn dancing, break-dancing, country dancing, disco dancing, folk dancing, Latin American dancing, line dancing, old-time dancing, tap-dancing. ➡

SOME BALLROOM DANCES: foxtrot, minuet, polka, quickstep, tango, waltz.

SOME TRADITIONAL DANCES: hornpipe, Highland fling, jig, morris dancing, quadrille, reel, square dancing.

SOME DANCES ASSOCIATED WITH PARTICULAR NATIONS: bolero, cancan, flamenco, limbo dancing, mazurka, polonaise, rumba, tarantella.

GATHERINGS WHERE PEOPLE DANCE: ball, [*Scottish & Irish*] ceilidh, disco, party.

danger *noun*
1 *Who knows what dangers lie ahead?* crisis, hazard, menace, peril, pitfall, threat, trap.
AN OPPOSITE IS safety.
2 *The forecast says there's a danger of frost.* chance, possibility, risk.

dangerous *adjective*
1 *We were in a dangerous situation.* alarming, hazardous, menacing, perilous, precarious, risky, unsafe.
2 *The police arrested him for dangerous driving.* careless, reckless.
3 *A dangerous criminal had escaped from prison.* desperate, ruthless, treacherous, violent.
4 *Lions are dangerous animals.* unpredictable, wild.
5 *It's wicked to empty dangerous chemicals into the river.* deadly, harmful, poisonous, toxic.
AN OPPOSITE IS harmless or safe.

dangle *verb*
There was a bunch of keys dangling from the chain. droop, flap, hang, sway, swing, trail, wave about.

dappled *adjective*
The ground under the trees is dappled with patches of sunlight. dotted, flecked, mottled, speckled, spotted, streaked.

dare *verb*
1 *I wouldn't dare to make a parachute jump.* have the courage, take the risk.
2 *He dared me to jump.* challenge, defy.

daring *adjective*
It was a very daring plan. bold, brave, courageous, fearless, intrepid, plucky, valiant.
AN OPPOSITE IS timid.
A daring person is a ***daredevil***.

dark *adjective*
1 *It was a very dark night.* black, gloomy, murky, pitch black, pitch dark.
AN OPPOSITE IS bright.
2 *She wore a dark green coat.*
AN OPPOSITE IS pale.

darken *verb*
The sky darkened. become overcast, blacken, cloud over.
AN OPPOSITE IS brighten.

darling *noun*
I love you, darling. dear, dearest, honey, love, sweetheart.

dash *noun*
1 *When the storm broke, we made a dash for shelter.* race, run, rush, sprint.
2 *I like just a dash of milk in my tea.* drop, small amount, splash, spot.

dash *verb*
1 *We dashed home because it was raining.* hasten, hurry, race, run, rush, speed, sprint, tear, zoom.
2 *She dashed her cup against the wall.* hurl, knock, smash, throw.

data *plural noun*
I entered all the data into the computer. details, facts, information.
Data can be in the form of ***figures***, ***numbers***, or ***statistics***.

date *noun*
I've made a date with a friend this evening. appointment, engagement, meeting

dawdle *verb*
Don't dawdle—we haven't got all day! be slow, delay, hang about, lag behind, linger, loiter, straggle.
AN OPPOSITE IS hurry.

dawn *noun* SEE **day**

day *noun*
1 *There are seven days in a week.*

VARIOUS TIMES OF THE DAY: dawn or daybreak or sunrise, morning, noon or midday, afternoon, evening, nightfall or sunset, dusk or twilight, night, midnight.

2 *Most people are awake during the day.* daytime.
AN OPPOSITE IS night.
3 *Things were different in his day.* age, epoch, era, period, time.

dazed *adjective*
He had a dazed expression on his face. bewildered, confused, muddled, perplexed.

dead *adjective*
1 *A dead fish floated by the side of the river.* deceased, lifeless.
Instead of 'the king who has just died', we can say 'the ***late*** king'.
Words for a dead body are ***carcass*** or ***corpse***.
AN OPPOSITE IS alive.
2 *Latin is a dead language.* extinct, obsolete.
AN OPPOSITE IS living.
3 *The battery was dead.* flat, not working, useless, worn out.
4 *The party was dead until the conjuror arrived.* boring, dull, slow, uninteresting.
AN OPPOSITE IS lively.

deaden *verb*
1 *The dentist gave me an injection to deaden the pain.* anaesthetize, lessen, reduce, suppress.
AN OPPOSITE IS increase.
2 *Double glazing deadens the noise of the traffic.* dampen, muffle, quieten.
AN OPPOSITE IS amplify.

deadly *adjective*
He gave her a deadly dose of poison. dangerous, destructive, fatal, harmful, lethal.
AN OPPOSITE IS harmless.

deafening *adjective*
We complained about the deafening noise. blaring, booming, loud, penetrating, thunderous.

deal *verb*
1 *Who is going to deal the cards?* distribute, give out, share out.
2 *My uncle used to deal in second-hand cars.* do business, trade.
to deal with something 1 *I can deal with this problem.* attend to, control, cope with, grapple with, handle, look after, manage, see to, solve, sort out.
2 *The book deals with the history of Rome.* be concerned with, cover, explain about.

deal *noun*
She made a deal with the garage for her new car. agreement, arrangement, bargain, contract.
a good deal, a great deal *We went to a great deal of trouble to do things properly.* a large amount, a lot.

dealer *noun*
If the goods are faulty, return them to the dealer. merchant, shopkeeper, supplier, trader, tradesman.

dear *adjective*
1 *She is a very dear friend.* beloved, close, loved, valued.
AN OPPOSITE IS distant.
2 *I didn't buy it because it was too dear.* costly, expensive.
AN OPPOSITE IS cheap.

death *noun*
1 *We mourned the death of our friend.* dying, end, passing.
2 *The accident resulted in several deaths.* fatality.

debatable *adjective*
It's debatable who was responsible for the accident. controversial, doubtful, questionable, uncertain.
AN OPPOSITE IS certain.

debate *noun*
We had a debate about animal rights. argument, discussion, dispute.
Something which people argue about a lot is a **controversy**.

debate *verb*
1 *We debated whether it is right to kill animals for food.* argue, discuss.
2 *I debated what to do next.* consider, deliberate, reflect on, weigh up.

debris *noun*
Debris from the crashed aircraft was scattered over a large area. fragments, pieces, remains, wreckage.

decay *verb*
Dead leaves fall to the ground and decay. break down, decompose, disintegrate, rot.

deceit *noun*
I saw through his deceit. bluff, cheating, deceitfulness, deception, dishonesty, fraud, lying, pretence, trickery.
AN OPPOSITE IS honesty.

deceitful *adjective*
Don't trust him—he's a deceitful person. cheating, dishonest, hypocritical, insincere, lying, [*informal*] sneaky, treacherous, two-faced, underhand.
AN OPPOSITE IS honest.

deceive *verb*
He intended to deceive you from the very beginning. cheat, [*slang*] con, [*informal*] diddle, double-cross, fool, mislead, swindle, take in, trick.

decent *adjective*
1 *I did the decent thing and owned up.* honest, honourable.
2 *My friend's jokes were not decent.* acceptable, appropriate, fitting, polite, proper, respectable, suitable.
AN OPPOSITE IS indecent.
3 *I haven't had a decent meal for ages!* agreeable, good, nice, satisfactory.
AN OPPOSITE IS bad.

deception *noun* SEE **deceit**

deceptive *adjective*
Appearances can be deceptive. misleading, unreliable.

decide *verb*
1 *We decided to finish our work instead of going out to play.* choose, elect, make a decision, make up your mind, opt, resolve.
2 *The referee decided that the player was offside.* conclude, judge, rule.
3 *The last lap decided the result of the race.* determine, settle.

decision *noun*
1 *Can you tell me what your decision is?* choice, preference.
2 *The judge announced his decision.* conclusion, findings, judgement, verdict.

decisive *adjective*
1 *A decisive piece of evidence proved that he was innocent.* convincing, crucial, definite.
AN OPPOSITE IS uncertain.
2 *A referee needs to be decisive.* firm, forceful, quick-thinking, resolute, strong-minded.
AN OPPOSITE IS hesitant.

declaration *noun*
The Prime Minister issued a formal declaration. announcement, proclamation, pronouncement, statement.

declare *verb*
He declared that he was innocent. announce, assert, make known, proclaim, pronounce, state, swear.

decline *verb*
1 *Our enthusiasm declined as the day went on.* decrease, diminish, dwindle, flag, lessen, tail off, wane, weaken.
AN OPPOSITE IS increase.
2 *Why did you decline my invitation to the party?* refuse, reject, turn down.
AN OPPOSITE IS accept.

decode *verb*
The spy tried to decode the secret message. figure out, interpret, make out, solve, understand, work out.

decompose *verb*
Dead leaves fall to the ground and decompose. break down, decay, disintegrate, rot.

decorate *verb*
1 *We decorated the church with flowers.* adorn, array, beautify, festoon.
To decorate a dish of food is to **garnish** it.
To decorate clothes with lace, etc., is to **trim** them.

2 *Dad is going to decorate my bedroom next weekend.* [*informal*] do up, paint, paper or wallpaper.
3 *They decorated her for bravery.* award or give a medal to, honour, reward.

> THINGS USED TO DECORATE VARIOUS THINGS INCLUDE: bunting, decorations, embroidery, flags, flowers, frills, lights, ornaments, pictures, plants, streamers, tinsel, trimming.

decorative *adjective*
The book had decorative designs in the margins. attractive, beautiful, colourful, elaborate, fancy, ornamental, pretty.
AN OPPOSITE IS plain.

decrease *verb*
1 *We decreased speed.* cut, lower, reduce, slacken.
2 *Our enthusiasm decreased as the day went on.* become less, decline, diminish, dwindle, flag, lessen, shrink, subside, tail off, wane, weaken.
AN OPPOSITE IS increase.

decrease *noun*
There has been a decrease in the bird population. cut, decline, drop, fall, reduction.
AN OPPOSITE IS increase *noun*.

decree *noun*
The king issued a decree that the day should be a holiday. command, declaration, order, proclamation.

decree *verb*
The government decrees what we must pay in taxes. declare, dictate, order, prescribe, proclaim, pronounce.

decrepit *adjective*
1 *Granny says she's not a decrepit old woman yet!* feeble, frail, infirm, weak, worn out.
2 *His hobby is restoring decrepit old cars.* battered, broken down, derelict.

dedicate *verb*
He dedicates himself entirely to his work. commit, devote.

dedicated *adjective*
Some dedicated fans waited all day to see the pop star. committed, devoted, enthusiastic, faithful, keen, zealous.

dedication *noun*
I admire her dedication to her work. commitment, devotion, enthusiasm (for).

deduce *verb*
The police managed to deduce who had committed the crime. conclude, decide, draw the conclusion, guess, reason, work out.

deduct *verb*
Tax is deducted from your salary. knock off, subtract, take away.
AN OPPOSITE IS add (to).

deduction *noun*
1 *My deduction was correct.* conclusion.
In this sense, *deduction* is related to the verb *deduce*
2 *He allowed me a deduction off the full price.* discount, reduction.
In this sense, *deduction* is related to the verb *deduct*.

deed *noun*
She was given a medal for her heroic deed. achievement, act, action, effort, exploit, feat.

deep *adjective*
1 *The well was very deep.*
AN OPPOSITE IS shallow.
2 *Her letter expressed her deep sympathy.* earnest, genuine, intense, sincere.
AN OPPOSITE IS insincere.
3 *He fell into a deep sleep.* heavy, sound.
AN OPPOSITE IS light.
4 *He spoke with a deep voice.* bass, low.
AN OPPOSITE IS high.

deer *noun*

DEER AND SIMILAR ANIMALS:
antelope, caribou, chamois, elk, gazelle, gnu, impala, moose, red deer, reindeer, wildebeest.
A male deer is a ***buck***, ***hart***, ***roebuck***, or ***stag***.
A female deer is a ***doe*** or ***hind***.
Deer's flesh used as food is ***venison***.

deface *verb*
Vandals defaced the statue. damage, mutilate, spoil, vandalize.

defeat *verb*
1 *We defeated our opponents soundly.* beat, get the better of, overcome, thrash, vanquish.
To defeat someone in chess is to ***checkmate*** them.
To be defeated is to ***lose***.
2 *They defeated their enemy in a bloody battle.* conquer, crush, overwhelm, rout, triumph over, win a victory over.
3 *They defeated moves to build a new road.* foil, frustrate.

defeat *noun*
They suffered a humiliating defeat. failure, humiliation, rout, [*informal*] thrashing.
AN OPPOSITE IS victory.

defect *noun*
The cars are tested for defects before they leave the factory. failure, fault, flaw, imperfection, shortcoming, weakness.
A defect in a computer program is a ***bug***.

defect *verb*
He defected to the enemy. desert, go over.
A person who defects to the other side is a ***traitor*** or ***turncoat***.

defective *adjective*
If the goods are defective, take them back to the shop. damaged, faulty, imperfect.
AN OPPOSITE IS perfect.

defence *noun*
1 *What was the accused woman's defence?* case, excuse, explanation, justification.
2 *We have no defence against this illness.* guard, protection, safeguard.
3 *The enemy soon broke through their defences.* barricade, fortification, rampart, shield.

defend verb
1 *We defended ourselves against the rival gang.* guard, keep safe, protect.
AN OPPOSITE IS attack.
2 *His lawyer defended him in court.* plead for, speak up for, stand up for, support.
AN OPPOSITE IS accuse.

defer verb
She decided to defer her departure until Saturday. delay, postpone, put off.

defiant adjective
He didn't like her defiant attitude. aggressive, disobedient, insolent, mutinous, obstinate, quarrelsome, rebellious, stubborn, uncooperative.
AN OPPOSITE IS cooperative.

deficient adjective
Their diet is deficient in vitamins. inadequate, insufficient, lacking, unsatisfactory, wanting.
AN OPPOSITE IS adequate.

defile verb
He felt that the filth he lived in defiled him. contaminate, degrade, dirty, infect, make dirty, pollute, soil, tarnish.

define verb
A thesaurus simply lists words, while a dictionary defines them. clarify, explain, give the meaning of, interpret.

definite adjective
1 *Is it definite that we're going to move?* certain, fixed, settled, sure.
2 *He's very definite in his opinions.* confident, decided, determined, emphatic, exact, precise, specific, unambiguous.
3 *She said there were definite signs of improvement in my work.* clear, distinct, marked, noticeable, obvious, positive, pronounced, unmistakable.
AN OPPOSITE IS indefinite.

definitely adverb
I'll definitely come tomorrow. beyond doubt, certainly, doubtless, for certain, positively, surely, unquestionably, without doubt, without fail.
AN OPPOSITE IS perhaps.

definition noun
The dictionary gives definitions for most words. explanation, interpretation.

deflate verb
1 *Vandals deflated the tyres of her car.* let down.
AN OPPOSITE IS inflate.
2 *She was deflated when she came last.* depress, humble, humiliate.

deflect verb
I was able to deflect the blow. avert, fend off, intercept, turn aside, ward off.

deformed adjective
He has a deformed foot. bent, buckled, crooked, distorted, gnarled, twisted, warped.

deft adjective
She folded the paper with deft movements of her fingers. agile, clever, expert, nimble, proficient, quick, skilful.
AN OPPOSITE IS clumsy.

defy verb
1 *It's not a good idea to defy the teacher.* confront, disobey, refuse to obey, resist, stand up to.
AN OPPOSITE IS obey.
2 *I defy you to produce evidence.* challenge, dare.
3 *The jammed door defied my attempts to open it.* beat, defeat, frustrate, resist, withstand.

degenerate verb
The game degenerated into a series of fouls. become worse, decline, deteriorate, sink, worsen.
AN OPPOSITE IS improve.

degrading adjective
It was a degrading experience. humiliating, shameful, undignified.

degree noun
She showed a high degree of skill in shaping the clay. extent, grade, level, measure, standard.

dejected *adjective*
I felt dejected when I failed the test.
depressed, desolate, discouraged,
[*informal*] down, downcast, forlorn,
gloomy, glum, [*informal*] low,
melancholy, miserable, sad, unhappy,
woeful, wretched.
AN OPPOSITE IS happy.

delay *verb*
1 *Please don't let me delay you.* detain,
hinder, hold up, keep waiting, make
late, slow down.
2 *They delayed the start of the race
because of the weather.* defer, postpone,
put off.
3 *You'll miss the bus if you delay.*
dawdle, [*informal*] hang about or
around, hesitate, linger, loiter, pause,
wait.

delay *noun*
What caused the delay? hold-up, pause,
wait.

delete *verb*
I deleted his name from the list. cancel,
cross out, erase, remove.

deliberate *adjective*
1 *It was a deliberate insult.* calculated,
conscious, intentional, planned,
premeditated.
AN OPPOSITE IS accidental or
unintentional.
2 *I walked with deliberate steps across
the icy pavement.* careful, cautious,
slow, unhurried.
AN OPPOSITE IS hasty or careless.

deliberate *verb*
*We deliberated where to go for the
summer holiday.* confer about,
consider, debate, discuss, think
carefully about, weigh up.

delicacy *noun*
1 *We admired the delicacy of the
embroidery.* daintiness, exquisiteness,
fineness, precision.
2 *She described the unpleasant details
with great delicacy.* sensitivity, tact.
3 *The table was loaded with delicacies.*
speciality, treat.

delicate *adjective*
1 *Her blouse had delicate embroidery
on the collar.* dainty, exquisite,
intricate.
2 *Take care not to damage the delicate
material.* fine, flimsy, fragile, soft, thin.
3 *Protect delicate plants if there's a
chance of frost.* sensitive, tender.
4 *He's often away from school—he has a
delicate constitution.* feeble, sickly,
unhealthy, weak.
5 *The nurse's fingers had a delicate
touch.* gentle, light, soft.
6 *He discussed the matter in a delicate
way.* careful, considerate, diplomatic,
discreet, prudent, sensitive, tactful.
7 *Can you help me with a delicate
problem?* awkward, embarrassing,
ticklish.

delicious *adjective*
The food was delicious. appetizing,
enjoyable, [*informal*] mouth-watering,
tasty.
SEE ALSO **taste** *verb*.
AN OPPOSITE IS horrible.

delight *noun*
*Imagine my delight when I saw my
friend again!* bliss, ecstasy, enjoyment,
happiness, joy, pleasure.

delight *verb*
The film's special effects delighted us.
amuse, charm, divert, enchant,
entertain, entrance, fascinate, please,
thrill.
AN OPPOSITE IS dismay.

delighted *adjective*
*The delighted spectators cheered the
victorious team.* ecstatic, elated,
exultant, joyful, happy, pleased,
thrilled.

delightful *adjective*
*The flower arrangements were
delightful.* attractive, beautiful,
charming, lovely, pleasant, pleasing.

delinquent *noun*
*The police know most of the delinquents
in our area.* criminal, hooligan, vandal,
young offender.

delirious *adjective*
The supporters were delirious with joy
when we scored the winning goal.
beside yourself, crazy, ecstatic, excited,
frantic, frenzied, hysterical, mad, wild.
AN OPPOSITE IS calm.

delirium *noun*
In his delirium he didn't know what he
was saying. excitement, fever, frenzy,
hysteria, madness.

deliver *verb*
1 How many letters does our postman
deliver each day? bring, convey,
distribute, hand over, present, supply,
take round.
2 The head delivered a lecture on good
behaviour. give, make, read out.

delude *verb*
He deluded us into thinking he could do
real magic. bluff, [slang] con, deceive,
fool, hoax, mislead, trick.

deluge *noun*
The crops were ruined in the deluge.
downpour, flood, inundation,
rainstorm.

deluge *verb*
They deluged me with questions.
overwhelm, swamp.

delusion *noun*
His belief that he ruled the world was a
delusion. dream, fantasy, self-
deception.

demand *verb*
1 I demand a refund! call for, claim,
insist on, require, want.
2 'What do you want?' she demanded.
ask, enquire, inquire.

demand *noun*
The manager agreed to the workers'
demands. claim, request, requirement.

demanding *adjective*
1 My baby sister is very demanding.
difficult, impatient, insistent, selfish.
AN OPPOSITE IS patient.
2 He has a very demanding job.
challenging, difficult, exhausting.
AN OPPOSITE IS easy.

democratic *adjective*
Britain has a democratic government.
elected.

demolish *verb*
They will have to demolish several
buildings to make way for the new
road. bulldoze, destroy, dismantle,
flatten, knock down, level, pull down,
tear down.
AN OPPOSITE IS build.

demonstrate *verb*
1 The teacher demonstrated how warm
air rises. explain, illustrate, show.
2 People were so angry about the heavy
lorries that they decided to demonstrate
in the street. march, parade, protest.

demonstration *noun*
1 She gave a demonstration of what the
new computer could do. display,
presentation, show.
2 Everyone joined the demonstration
against the heavy lorries. [informal]
demo, march, parade, protest, rally.

demote *verb*
At the end of the season, the team was
demoted to a lower division. put down,
relegate.
AN OPPOSITE IS promote.

den *noun*
We built a den in the garden. hideout,
hiding place, secret place, shelter.
The den of a wild animal is its **lair**.

denote *verb*
What does this symbol denote? be a sign
for, express, indicate, mean, signify,
stand for.

denounce *verb*
1 She denounced cruelty to animals.
complain about, condemn, deplore,
speak against.
2 Even his friends denounced him as a
traitor. accuse, blame, complain about,
condemn, inform against, report,
reveal.
AN OPPOSITE IS praise.

dense *adjective*
1 The accident happened in dense fog.
heavy, thick.
2 A dense crowd waited in the square.
compact, packed, solid.
3 [insulting] You are dense today! SEE
stupid.

dent *noun*
There was a large dent in the car door.
depression, hollow, indentation.

dent *verb*
He dented the car door. knock in, push in.

dentist *noun*

A dentist who specializes in straightening teeth is an **orthodontist**.

OTHER PEOPLE WHO WORK AT THE DENTIST'S: dental nurse, hygienist, receptionist.

THINGS THAT CAN BE DONE AT THE DENTIST'S: extractions, fillings, fitting a brace or a bridge, fitting a crown, fitting dentures, injections, scaling teeth, X-rays.
FOR OTHER PEOPLE WHO LOOK AFTER OUR HEALTH, SEE **medicine**.

deny *verb*
1 In spite of the evidence, he continued to deny the accusation. dispute, oppose, reject.
AN OPPOSITE IS accept.
2 Her parents don't deny her anything. deprive of, refuse.
AN OPPOSITE IS give.

depart *verb*
1 What time is the train due to depart? begin a journey, get going, leave, set off, set out, start.
2 It looks as if the criminals departed in a hurry. [informal] clear off, exit, go away, make off, retreat, withdraw.
AN OPPOSITE IS arrive.

department *noun*
I spent ages looking for the right department to pay my bill. branch, division, office, section.

depend *verb*
to depend on someone I depend on you to help me. bank on, count on, rely on, trust.
to depend on something My success will depend on good luck. be decided by, hinge on, rest on.

dependable *adjective*
We need dependable people who will finish the work on time. conscientious, honest, loyal, reliable, responsible, sound, steady, trustworthy.
AN OPPOSITE IS unreliable.

dependent *adjective*
dependent on 1 Everything is dependent on the weather. controlled by, determined by, subject to.
2 Don't ever become dependent on drugs. addicted to, [informal] hooked on, reliant on.

depict *verb*
1 The artist depicted the scene brilliantly. draw, paint, sketch.
2 The film depicted what life was like in medieval times. describe, illustrate, outline, portray, represent, show.

deplorable *adjective*
Their rudeness was deplorable. disgraceful, lamentable, scandalous, shameful, shocking, unforgivable.
AN OPPOSITE IS praiseworthy.

deplore *verb*
We all deplore cruelty to animals. condemn, disapprove of, hate.

deport *verb*
He was deported from Australia. banish, exile, expel, send abroad.

deposit *noun*
1 Dad paid the deposit on a new car. down-payment, first instalment, initial payment.
2 There was a deposit of mud at the bottom of the river. layer, sediment.

depot *noun*
The explorers set up a depot at the base of the mountain. base, store.
A depot where you store weapons is an **arsenal**.

depress *verb*
The weather depressed us. discourage, sadden.
AN OPPOSITE IS cheer.

depressed *adjective*
He was depressed by the news. dejected, desolate, discouraged, [*informal*] down, downcast, gloomy, glum, in despair, [*informal*] low, melancholy, miserable, sad, unhappy, wretched.
AN OPPOSITE IS cheerful.

depressing *adjective*
It was a depressing situation to be in. discouraging, distressing, gloomy, sad, unhappy, unwelcome.
AN OPPOSITE IS cheerful.

depression *noun*
1 She sank into a state of depression. dejection, desolation, despair, gloom, glumness, hopelessness, low spirits, melancholy, misery, pessimism, sadness, unhappiness.
AN OPPOSITE IS cheerfulness.
2 Most businesses do badly during a depression. recession, slump.
AN OPPOSITE IS boom.
3 The rain had collected in several depressions in the ground. dip, hole, hollow, indentation, pit, rut, sunken area.
AN OPPOSITE IS bump.

deprived *adjective*
The charity tries to help deprived families. needy, poor, underprivileged.
AN OPPOSITE IS privileged or wealthy.

deputize *verb*
to deputize for Will you deputize for the captain while she is ill? do the job of, replace, represent, stand in for, substitute for, take over from.

deputy *noun*
The deputy has been running the company for the last six months. assistant, second-in-command, stand-in, substitute.
There are several words with the prefix *vice-*, which mean 'the deputy for a particular person': e.g. *vice-captain*, *vice-president*, etc

derelict *adjective*
It's about time they pulled down those derelict buildings. abandoned, broken down, crumbling, decrepit, deserted, neglected, ruined.

derision *noun*
Her idea was greeted with shouts of derision. mockery, ridicule, satire, scorn.

derivation *noun*
It's interesting to learn about the derivation of words. origin, source.

derive *verb*
1 She derived a lot of pleasure from her garden. gain, get, obtain, receive.
2 He derived a lot of his ideas from a text book. borrow, collect, crib, draw, [*informal*] lift, pick up, take.

descend *verb*
1 After admiring the view, we began to descend the mountain. climb down, come down, go down, move down.
To descend through the air is to **drop** or **fall**.
To descend through water is to **sink**.
2 The road descends gradually into the valley. dip, drop, fall, incline, slope.
AN OPPOSITE IS ascend.
to be descended from someone She's descended from a French family. come from, originate from.
to descend from something I helped my little sister to descend from the pony. dismount from, get down from, get off.

descendant *noun*
A person's descendants are their **heirs** or **successors**.
AN OPPOSITE IS ancestor.

descent *noun*
The path makes a steep descent into the valley. dip, drop, fall, incline.
AN OPPOSITE IS ascent.

describe *verb*
1 An eyewitness described how the accident happened. depict, explain, outline, report, tell about.
2 She described him as a quiet, shy man. characterize, portray, present, represent.

description *noun*
1 I wrote a description of our day at the seaside. account, report, story.
2 We had to write a description of our favourite character in the novel. portrait, representation, sketch.

descriptive adjective
She said my writing was very descriptive. colourful, detailed, expressive, graphic, vivid.

desert noun

FEATURES OF A DESERT MIGHT BE: cactus, mirage, oasis, palm tree, sandhill, sandstorm.

ADJECTIVES WHICH MIGHT DESCRIBE A DESERT: arid, barren, dry, dusty, infertile, inhospitable, sandy, sterile, uncultivated, waterless.
A group of people travelling together across a desert is a *caravan*.
A desert island is an *uninhabited* island.
People who live in the desert are often *nomads*.

desert verb
He deserted his friends when they needed him most. abandon, betray, forsake, leave, [informal] walk out on.
To desert someone in a place they can't get away from is to *maroon* or *strand* them.

deserter noun
Deserters from the army are severely punished. absentee, runaway.

deserve verb
Her brave action deserves a reward. be worthy of, justify, merit, warrant.

design noun
1 We produced a design for a car of the future. blueprint, drawing.
A first example of something, used as a model for making others, is a *prototype*.
2 The head showed us some school uniforms and asked which design we liked best. style, type, version.
3 The wallpaper had a flowery design. arrangement, composition, pattern.

design verb
She designs all her own clothes. conceive, create, devise, sketch, think of.

desirable adjective
1 The house has many desirable features. appealing, attractive, interesting, irresistible, tempting.
AN OPPOSITE IS worthless.
2 It is desirable for you to come with us. advisable, prudent, sensible, wise.
AN OPPOSITE IS unwise.

desire verb
What do you most desire? crave, fancy, hanker after, long for, need, set your heart on, want, wish for, yearn for, yen.

desire noun
What is your greatest desire? ambition, craving, fancy, hankering, longing, urge, want, wish, yearning.
A desire for food is *appetite* or *hunger*.
A desire for drink is *thirst*
Excessive desire for money or other things is *greed*.

desolate adjective
1 He felt desolate when she died. dejected, depressed, forlorn, hopeless, lonely, melancholy, miserable, sad, wretched.
AN OPPOSITE IS cheerful.
2 No one wants to live in that desolate place. abandoned, bare, barren, bleak, cheerless, depressing, deserted, dismal, dreary, forsaken, gloomy, inhospitable, isolated, lonely, remote, uninhabited, wild.
AN OPPOSITE IS pleasant.

despair noun
She was overcome by feelings of despair. anguish, dejection, depression, desperation, gloom, hopelessness, melancholy, misery, pessimism, wretchedness.
AN OPPOSITE IS hope.

despatch noun, verb SEE dispatch noun, verb

desperate adjective
1 The refugees were in a desperate situation. critical, drastic, grave, hopeless, serious, severe.
2 The police warned people not to approach the desperate criminals. dangerous, reckless, violent.

despicable *adjective*
We were horrified by the despicable way
he treated his dog. contemptible,
disgraceful, hateful, shameful.

despise *verb*
He despises people who aren't good at
sport. be contemptuous of, deride, feel
contempt for, have a low opinion of,
look down on, scorn, sneer at.
AN OPPOSITE IS admire.

dessert *noun*
For dessert there's ice cream or fruit
salad. [informal] afters, pudding,
sweet.

destination *noun*
The train arrived at its destination five
minutes early. terminus.

destined *adjective*
1 My plans were destined to fail. bound,
certain, doomed, fated.
2 We felt that the disaster was destined.
inevitable, intended, unavoidable.

destiny *noun*
Was it destiny that brought us together?
fate, fortune.

destroy *verb*
1 An avalanche destroyed the village.
break down, crush, demolish,
devastate, flatten, knock down, level,
pull down, shatter, smash, sweep away.
2 He tried to destroy the good work we
had done. ruin, sabotage, undo, wreck.

destruction *noun*
The war caused terrible destruction of
life and property. annihilation,
demolition, devastation, elimination,
extermination, extinction, killing, ruin,
wrecking.
AN OPPOSITE IS conservation or
creation.

destructive *adjective*
The storm had a destructive effect on
the crops. catastrophic, damaging,
devastating, disastrous, harmful,
injurious, ruinous, violent.

detach *verb*
He detached the wires to make sure he
didn't get an electric shock. disconnect,
part, release, remove, separate, take
off, undo, unfasten.
To detach a caravan from a car, etc., is
to **unhitch** it.
To detach railway wagons from a
locomotive is to **uncouple** them.
To detach something by cutting it off is
to **sever** it.
AN OPPOSITE IS attach.

detached *adjective*
I don't support either team, so I can
watch from a detached point of view.
disinterested, impartial, independent,
neutral, objective, unbiased,
uncommitted, uninvolved,
unprejudiced.
AN OPPOSITE IS biased.

detail *noun*
Her account was accurate in every
detail. aspect, fact, feature, item,
particular, point, respect.

detain *verb*
1 The police detained the suspect.
arrest, capture, imprison, restrain.
AN OPPOSITE IS release.
2 I'll try not to detain you for long.
delay, hinder, hold up, keep waiting.

detect *verb*
The mechanic detected a fault in the
car. diagnose, discover, find, identify,
recognize, reveal, spot, track down.

deter *verb*
How can we deter the blackbirds from
eating the strawberries? discourage,
dissuade, prevent, put off, stop.
AN OPPOSITE IS encourage.

deteriorate *verb*
1 His health began to deteriorate.
decline, degenerate, get worse, go
downhill, worsen.
2 The buildings will deteriorate if we
don't maintain them. crumble, decay,
disintegrate.
AN OPPOSITE IS improve.

determination *noun*
Marathon runners show great
determination. commitment, courage,
dedication, drive, grit, [informal] guts,
perseverance, persistence, resolve,
spirit, will-power.

determine *verb*
Our task was to determine the height of
the tower. calculate, compute, decide,
figure out, reckon, work out.

determined *adjective*
1 She's a determined woman! assertive,
decisive, persistent, resolute, strong-
minded, tough.
AN OPPOSITE IS weak-minded.
2 I'm determined to win! committed,
resolved.

detest *verb*
I detest the smell of cigarette smoke.
dislike, hate, loathe.
Informal expressions are **can't bear**
and **can't stand**.
AN OPPOSITE IS love.

detestable *adjective*
I found the film's violence detestable.
[informal] awful, contemptible,
disgusting, hateful, horrible, horrid,
repulsive, revolting.
AN OPPOSITE IS adorable.

detonate *verb*
1 They set a timer to detonate the bomb.
explode, set off.
2 Fortunately the bomb didn't detonate.
blow up, go off.

detour *noun*
I wasted time by taking a detour.
diversion, indirect route, roundabout
route.

devastate *verb*
A hurricane devastated the town.
demolish, destroy, flatten, level, ruin,
wreck.

develop *verb*
1 The manager wants to develop the
business. build up, diversify, enlarge,
expand, extend.
2 The teacher said I should develop my
ideas. amplify, elaborate.
3 This group's music has developed in
their recent albums. advance, evolve,
get better, improve, progress.
4 The plants develop quickly in the
spring. grow, flourish.
5 How did he develop that posh accent?
acquire, cultivate, get, pick up.

development *noun*
1 Were there any developments while I
was away? change, happening,
incident, occurrence.
2 He is pleased with the development of
his business. expansion, growth,
improvement, progress, spread.
3 The land is set aside for industrial
development. building, exploitation,
use.

device *noun*
It's a device for opening tins more
easily. apparatus, appliance,
contraption, contrivance, gadget,
implement, instrument, tool.

devilish *adjective*
He showed devilish cunning. cruel,
diabolical, evil, fiendish, hellish,
infernal, savage, wicked.
AN OPPOSITE IS angelic.

devilment *noun*
[usually joking] What devilment have
you children been up to? mischief,
naughtiness, pranks, trouble.

devious *adjective*
1 I don't trust his devious explanations.
cunning, deceitful, dishonest, evasive,
furtive, insincere, misleading, sly,
[informal] sneaky, treacherous, wily.
2 Because of the roadworks, we took a
devious route home. indirect,
meandering, roundabout, winding.
AN OPPOSITE IS direct or
straightforward.

devise verb
We need to devise a strategy for Saturday's game. conceive, contrive, form, formulate, invent, make up, map out, organize, plan, prepare, think out, think up.

devote verb
They devote all their free time to sport. assign, commit, set aside.

devoted adjective
She's a devoted supporter of our team. committed, enthusiastic, faithful, loyal.
AN OPPOSITE IS apathetic.

devotion noun
She has always shown a great devotion to her children. adoration (of), commitment, love (of), loyalty.

devour verb
They devoured a whole plateful of sandwiches. consume, eat, gobble up, gulp down, swallow.

diabolical adjective
It was a diabolical plan. devilish, evil, fiendish, hellish, infernal, wicked.

diagnose verb
The doctor diagnosed the cause of my illness. detect, determine, identify, name, recognize.

diagnosis noun
What is the doctor's diagnosis? conclusion, explanation, interpretation, opinion, verdict.

diagram noun

VARIOUS KINDS OF DIAGRAM: block diagram, chart, cutaway diagram, figure, flow chart, graph, outline, pie chart, plan, sketch.

dial verb
I picked up the phone and dialled his number. call, phone, ring, telephone.

dialogue noun
The book consisted of a series of dialogues. chat, conversation, debate, discussion, exchange, talk.

dictate verb
to dictate to someone You've got no right to dictate to me! [informal] boss about, command, give orders to, impose on, [informal] lay down the law to, order about.

dictatorial adjective
I didn't like her dictatorial manner. [informal] bossy, tyrannical.

die verb
1 Her dog died last week. expire, pass away, perish.
To die of hunger is to **starve**.
2 The flowers will die if they don't have water. droop, fade, wilt, wither.
to die down The flames died down. become less, decline, decrease, dwindle, fizzle out, go out, subside, wane, weaken.
to die out When did the dinosaurs die out? become extinct, cease to exist, come to an end, disappear, vanish.

diet noun
The doctor asked me about my normal diet. food, nourishment, nutrition.
If you choose what to eat in order to lose weight, you are on a **slimming** diet.
If you don't eat meat, you are on a **vegetarian** diet.
If you don't eat any animal products at all, you are on a **vegan** diet.
SEE ALSO **food**.

differ verb
We differed about what to do. argue, clash, conflict, contradict each other, disagree, fall out, oppose each other, quarrel.
AN OPPOSITE IS agree.
to differ from My opinions differ from yours. be different from, contrast with.

difference noun
1 The salesman explained the difference between the computers we were looking at. contrast, distinction.
AN OPPOSITE IS similarity.
2 This will make a difference to our plans. alteration, change, modification, variation.

different *adjective*
1 *We have different opinions on this issue.* clashing, conflicting, contradictory, opposite.
2 *It's important that the teams wear different colours.* contrasting, dissimilar, distinguishable.
3 *The packet contains sweets of different flavours.* assorted, diverse, miscellaneous, mixed, numerous, several, various.
4 *We always go to the park—haven't you got any different ideas?* fresh, new, original.
5 *Everyone's handwriting is different.* distinct, distinctive, individual, special, unique.
AN OPPOSITE IS identical or similar.

difficult *adjective*
1 *The questions were very difficult.* baffling, complex, complicated, hard, involved, perplexing, tricky.
AN OPPOSITE IS simple.
2 *We were worn out by the difficult climb to the top of the hill.* challenging, demanding, exhausting, formidable, gruelling, laborious, strenuous, tough.
AN OPPOSITE IS easy.
3 *Mum says I was a difficult child when I was small.* annoying, awkward, disruptive, obstinate, stubborn, tiresome, troublesome, trying, uncooperative, unhelpful.
AN OPPOSITE IS cooperative.

difficulty *noun*
1 *The explorers were used to facing difficulty.* adversity, challenges, hardship, trouble.
2 *There were many difficulties to be overcome.* complication, dilemma, hitch, obstacle, problem, snag.

dig *verb*
1 *He spent the afternoon digging the garden.* cultivate, fork over, turn over.
2 *Rabbits dig holes in the ground.* burrow, excavate, gouge out, hollow out, scoop out, tunnel.
3 *Did you dig me in the back?* jab, poke, prod, punch, shove.

dignified *adjective*
She was a very dignified old lady. calm, formal, grave, proper, refined, sedate, serious.
AN OPPOSITE IS undignified.

dignity *noun*
1 *Please don't do anything to spoil the dignity of the occasion.* formality, importance, seriousness, solemnity.
2 *She handled the problem with dignity.* calmness, poise, self-control.

dilemma *noun*
I can wait for my friend and miss the bus, or catch the bus and leave her behind—it's a real dilemma! difficulty, problem.

dilute *verb*
You should dilute orange squash with water. thin, water down, weaken.
AN OPPOSITE IS concentrate.

dim *adjective*
1 *I could just see a dim outline in the mist.* blurred, cloudy, faint, fuzzy, hazy, indistinct, misty, pale, shadowy, vague.
AN OPPOSITE IS clear.
2 *The light is rather dim.* dark, dingy, dull, gloomy, murky.
AN OPPOSITE IS bright.

dimensions *plural noun*
We measured the dimensions of the room. capacity, extent, measurements, size.
FOR WORDS USED IN MEASURING, SEE **measurement**.

diminish *verb*
1 *Don't diminish his confidence by making fun of him.* lessen, make smaller, minimize, reduce.
2 *Our enthusiasm diminished as time went on.* become less, decline, decrease, dwindle, subside, wane.
AN OPPOSITE IS increase.

din *noun*
I can't hear you because of that awful din! clatter, hullabaloo, noise, racket, row.

dingy *adjective*
How can we brighten up this dingy room? colourless, dark, depressing, dim, dirty, dismal, drab, dreary, dull, faded, gloomy, grimy, murky, shabby.
AN OPPOSITE IS bright.

dip *verb*
1 *I dipped my hand in the water.* immerse, lower, plunge, submerge.
2 *The road dips down into the valley.* descend, go down, slope down.

dip *noun*
1 *There was a dip in the ground.* depression, hole, hollow, slope.
2 *It was so hot we decided to have a dip in the sea.* bathe, swim.

diplomacy *noun*
She showed great diplomacy in ending the dispute. delicacy, tact, tactfulness.

diplomatic *adjective*
Her questions were very diplomatic. careful, considerate, delicate, discreet, polite, sensitive, tactful.
AN OPPOSITE IS tactless.

dire *adjective*
It was a dire emergency when the bridge collapsed. acute, dangerous, dreadful, frightful, horrible, nasty, serious, terrible.

direct *adjective*
1 *Let's take the most direct route.* shortest, straight.
AN OPPOSITE IS indirect.
2 *Please give me a direct answer.* blunt, frank, honest, outspoken, plain, sincere, straightforward, unambiguous.
AN OPPOSITE IS evasive.

direct *verb*
1 *Can you direct me to the station?* guide, indicate the way, point, show the way, tell the way.
2 *They appointed someone to direct the company's affairs while the boss was ill.* administer, be in charge of, command, control, handle, lead, manage, run, superintend, supervise, take charge of. To direct an orchestra is to **conduct** it.
3 *He directed us to begin.* command, instruct, order, tell.

direction *noun*
Which direction did they go in? course, path, route, way.
directions *The kit comes with directions for assembling it.* guidance, guidelines, instructions, plans.

director *noun*
FOR PEOPLE IN CHARGE OF THINGS, SEE **chief** *noun*.

dirt *noun*
1 *The floor was covered in dirt.* dust, filth, grime, mess, muck, mud.
2 *Chickens scratched about in the dirt.* clay, earth, loam, mud, soil.

dirty *adjective*
1 *Those dirty clothes need washing.* dusty, filthy, foul, grimy, grubby, messy, mucky, muddy, soiled, sooty, stained.
AN OPPOSITE IS clean.
2 *We refused to drink the dirty water.* cloudy, impure, polluted.
AN OPPOSITE IS pure.
3 *The other team used dirty tactics.* dishonest, illegal, mean, unfair, unsporting.
AN OPPOSITE IS honest.
4 *He used a lot of dirty words.* coarse, crude, improper, indecent, obscene, offensive, rude, smutty, vulgar.
AN OPPOSITE IS decent.

disability *noun*
She leads a normal life in spite of her disabilities. affliction, complaint, handicap, impairment, infirmity.

disabled *adjective*
He has been disabled since the accident. handicapped.
A person who has difficulty in walking is *lame*.
A person who has to spend all the time in bed is *bedridden*.
A person who cannot move on their own is *immobile*.
A person who cannot move part of their body is *paralysed*.
A person who is paralysed in the legs is *paraplegic*.

disadvantage *noun*
It's a disadvantage to be small if you play basketball. drawback, handicap, hindrance, inconvenience, snag.

disagree *verb*
> *Unfortunately, my brother and I often disagree.* argue, clash, differ, fall out, quarrel, squabble.
> AN OPPOSITE IS agree.
> **to disagree with 1** *He disagrees with everything I say.* argue with, contradict, object to, oppose.
> **2** *Onions disagree with me.* have a bad effect on, upset.

disagreement *noun*
> *We had a disagreement about who should use the computer first.* argument, clash, conflict, debate, difference of opinion, dispute, quarrel, row, squabble.
> AN OPPOSITE IS agreement.

disagreeable *adjective*
> *There's no need to be so disagreeable.* annoying, horrible, nasty, offensive, spiteful, tiresome, uncooperative, unfriendly, unkind, unpleasant.
> AN OPPOSITE IS pleasant.

disappear *verb*
> **1** *The fog disappeared.* clear, disperse, dissolve, evaporate, fade away, melt away.
> **2** *The rabbits disappeared in the long grass.* become invisible, vanish.
> **3** *He disappeared round the corner.* depart, escape, flee, go away, run away, withdraw.
> AN OPPOSITE IS appear.

disappoint *verb*
> *I was disappointed by her behaviour.* dismay, displease, upset.
> AN OPPOSITE IS delight or satisfy.

disapproval *noun*
> *Her frown showed her disapproval.* condemnation, criticism, dislike, dissatisfaction.
> AN OPPOSITE IS approval.

disapprove *verb*
> **to disapprove of** *They all disapprove of smoking.* condemn, criticize, denounce, deplore, dislike, frown on, object to, take exception to, [*informal*] take a dim view of.
> AN OPPOSITE IS approve of.

disapproving *adjective*
> *She made some disapproving comments about my work.* critical, reproachful, uncomplimentary, unfavourable.
> AN OPPOSITE IS favourable.

disaster *noun*
> *The pilot managed to land the damaged plane and avoided a disaster.* calamity, catastrophe, tragedy.

> SOME DIFFERENT KINDS OF DISASTER: air crash, avalanche, collision, crash, derailment, earthquake, epidemic, fire, flood, hurricane, landslide, plague, road accident, shipwreck, tidal wave, tornado, volcanic eruption.

disastrous *adjective*
> *The disastrous fire cost millions of pounds.* calamitous, catastrophic, destructive, devastating, dire, dreadful, fatal, ruinous, terrible.

disc *noun*

> THINGS SHAPED LIKE A DISC: circle, counter, plate, record, wheel.

> VARIOUS KINDS OF RECORDED DISC: album, CD or compact disc, LP, recording, single.

> VARIOUS KINDS OF COMPUTER DISK: CD ROM, diskette, floppy disk, hard disk.
> Note that in computing, the word is usually spelt *disk*

discard *verb*
> *I discarded some old clothes and sent them to the jumble sale.* cast off, dispose of, dump, get rid of, reject, scrap, throw away.

discharge *verb*
> **1** *The accused man was found not guilty and discharged.* acquit, allow to leave, clear, free, let off, liberate, release.
> **2** *The chimney discharged thick smoke.* belch, eject, emit, expel, give off, give out, pour out, produce.

disciple *noun*
   The religious leader had many
   disciples. admirer, devotee, follower,
   supporter.
   The disciples of Jesus were the
   apostles.

discipline *noun*
   Discipline is important in the army.
   control, order.

disclose *verb*
   He never disclosed the truth. confess,
   make known, make public, reveal, tell.
   AN OPPOSITE IS conceal.

discolour *verb*
   The smoke discoloured the paint. mark,
   spoil the colour of, stain.

discomfort *noun*
   He still experiences a lot of discomfort
   from his injury. pain, soreness.

disconnect *verb*
   Disconnect the electricity supply before
   you start to mend the fuse. cut off,
   detach.

discontented *adjective*
   She felt very discontented with her job.
   dejected, dissatisfied, miserable,
   unhappy, upset.
   AN OPPOSITE IS happy.

discount *noun*
   I got a discount on the full price.
   allowance, concession, cut, deduction,
   reduction.

discourage *verb*
   1 Did her criticism discourage you?
   demoralize, depress, [informal] put you
   off.
   2 How can we discourage the
   blackbirds from eating the
   strawberries? deter, dissuade, prevent,
   restrain, stop.
   AN OPPOSITE IS encourage.

discover *verb*
   I discovered some old toys in the attic.
   come across, find, spot, stumble across,
   uncover.
   To discover something that has been
   buried is to **unearth** it.

To discover something that has been
under water is to **dredge it up**.
To discover something you have been
pursuing is to **track it down**.
AN OPPOSITE IS hide.

discovery *noun*
   Scientists have made an exciting new
   discovery. breakthrough, find.

discreet *adjective*
   I asked a few discreet questions about
   her illness. careful, cautious, delicate,
   diplomatic, polite, prudent, sensitive,
   tactful.
   AN OPPOSITE IS tactless.

discriminate *verb*
   It's sometimes hard to discriminate
   between poisonous mushrooms and
   edible ones. distinguish, judge the
   difference, tell the difference.
   to discriminate against It's wrong to
   discriminate against people because of
   their race, religion, or sex. be biased
   against, be intolerant of, be prejudiced
   against, persecute.

discrimination *noun*
   1 She shows discrimination in her
   choice of music. good judgement, good
   taste.
   2 Discrimination against people
   because of their race, religion, or sex is
   wrong. bias, intolerance, prejudice,
   unfairness.
   Discrimination against people because
   of their sex is **sexism**.
   Discrimination against people because
   of their race is **racism**.
   Discrimination against people of a
   different nation is **chauvinism**.

discuss *verb*
   He discussed the situation with his
   wife. confer about, debate, talk about.

discussion *noun*
   We had a lively discussion. argument,
   conversation, exchange of views.
   A formal discussion is a **conference** or
   debate.

disease *noun*
   He was suffering from a serious
   disease. affliction, ailment, [informal]
   bug, complaint, illness, sickness.
   SEE ALSO **illness**.

diseased *adjective*
Gardeners throw away diseased plants.
infected, sickly, unhealthy.
AN OPPOSITE IS healthy.
SEE ALSO **ill**.

disembark *verb*
The passengers disembarked from the
ferry. go ashore.
AN OPPOSITE IS embark.

disgrace *noun*
1 He never got over the disgrace of being
caught cheating. dishonour,
embarrassment, humiliation, shame.
2 The way he treats them is a disgrace!
outrage, scandal.

disgraceful *adjective*
We were horrified by their disgraceful
behaviour. appalling, outrageous,
scandalous, shameful, shocking.
AN OPPOSITE IS honourable.

disguise *verb*
I tried to disguise my feelings.
camouflage, conceal, cover up, hide,
mask.
to disguise yourself as The spy
disguised himself as a member of the
ship's crew. dress up as, pretend to be.

disguise *noun*
I didn't recognize him in that disguise.
camouflage, costume, make-up, mask.

disgust *noun*
I couldn't hide my disgust at his
behaviour. detestation, dislike, hatred,
horror, loathing, repulsion.
AN OPPOSITE IS liking.

disgust *verb*
Didn't those horrible pictures disgust
you? appal, distress, horrify, offend,
[informal] put you off, repel, revolt,
shock, sicken, [informal] turn your
stomach.
AN OPPOSITE IS please.

disgusting *adjective*
Cruelty to animals is disgusting.
appalling, horrible, loathsome, nasty,
offensive, repulsive, revolting,
sickening.
AN OPPOSITE IS delightful.

dish *noun*
1 She cooked the casserole in an
earthenware dish. basin, bowl.
A dish to serve soup from is a **tureen**.
SEE ALSO **container**.
2 What's your favourite dish? food, item
on the menu.

dishevelled *adjective*
He looked tired and dishevelled. messy,
ruffled, scruffy, untidy.
AN OPPOSITE IS neat.

dishonest *adjective*
1 There are too many dishonest traders
about. [informal] bent, cheating,
corrupt, criminal, [informal] crooked,
deceitful, disreputable, [informal]
dodgy, immoral, lying, [informal]
shady, swindling, thieving,
untrustworthy.
2 The judge reprimanded him for
making dishonest statements. devious,
false, fraudulent, misleading,
untruthful.
AN OPPOSITE IS honest.

dishonesty *noun*
He was accused of dishonesty. cheating,
corruption, [informal] crookedness,
deceit, deviousness, insincerity, lying.
AN OPPOSITE IS honesty.

disinfect *verb*
The nurse disinfected my wound.
cleanse, sterilize.
To disinfect an infected area is to
decontaminate it.
To disinfect a room with fumes is to
fumigate it.
AN OPPOSITE IS infect.

disinfectant *noun*
Mum poured disinfectant into the
drain. antiseptic.

disintegrate *verb*
1 Pounded by the waves, the wreck
disintegrated. break into pieces, break
up, crack up, fall apart.
2 Dead leaves fall to the ground and
gradually disintegrate. crumble, decay,
decompose, rot.

disinterested *adjective*
A referee must be disinterested.
detached, fair, impartial, neutral,
unbiased, unprejudiced.
AN OPPOSITE IS biased.

disk *noun* SEE **disc**

dislike *noun*
His colleagues regarded him with intense dislike. detestation, disapproval, disgust, hatred, loathing, revulsion.
AN OPPOSITE IS liking.

dislike *verb*
I dislike people who hunt wild animals. detest, disapprove of, hate, loathe.
·AN OPPOSITE IS like.

dislocate *verb*
1 He dislocated his shoulder playing rugby. [informal] put out, put out of joint.
2 Floods dislocated the train service. disrupt, interfere with, interrupt, throw into confusion or disorder, upset.

dislodge *verb*
The wind dislodged some tiles on the roof. displace, disturb, move, shift.

disloyal *adjective*
He was disloyal to his friends. faithless, false, treacherous, unfaithful, unreliable, untrustworthy.
AN OPPOSITE IS loyal.

dismal *adjective*
How can we brighten up this dismal room? cheerless, dark, depressing, dingy, drab, dreary, dull, gloomy, murky.
AN OPPOSITE IS bright or cheerful.

dismantle *verb*
After the school fair, we had to dismantle all the stalls. take apart, take down.
To dismantle a tent is to *strike* it.
AN OPPOSITE IS assemble.

dismay *noun*
We listened with dismay to the bad news. alarm, anxiety, disappointment, distress, gloom, shock.

dismayed *adjective*
I was dismayed by the failure of our plan. appalled, depressed, devastated, disappointed, discouraged, distressed, shocked, surprised.
AN OPPOSITE IS encouraged.

dismiss *verb*
1 The teacher dismissed the class. free, let go, release, send away.
2 The firm dismissed ten workers. [informal] fire, give notice to, make redundant, sack.
3 The weather was so bad that we dismissed the idea of having a picnic. discard, drop, reject.

dismount *verb*
I dismounted from my bike to open the gate. descend, get off.

disobedient *adjective*
She said she had never known such a disobedient child. badly behaved, contrary, defiant, disorderly, disruptive, mutinous, naughty, rebellious, uncontrollable, undisciplined, ungovernable, unmanageable, unruly.
AN OPPOSITE IS obedient.

disobey *verb*
1 You will be penalized if you disobey the rules. break, defy, disregard, ignore, violate.
2 Soldiers are trained never to disobey. be disobedient, mutiny, rebel, revolt.
AN OPPOSITE IS obey.

disorder *noun*
1 Police were called in to deal with the disorder. anarchy, brawling, commotion, disturbance, fighting, lawlessness, quarrelling, rioting, uproar.
2 It's time I tidied up the disorder in my room. chaos, confusion, mess, muddle, untidiness.
AN OPPOSITE IS order.

disorderly *adjective*
The head came in to reprimand the disorderly class. badly behaved, disobedient, uncontrollable, undisciplined, ungovernable, unmanageable, unruly.
AN OPPOSITE IS orderly.

dispatch *noun*
The messenger brought a dispatch from headquarters. bulletin, communication, letter, message, report.

dispatch *verb*
1 *They dispatched a letter to him.* post, send.
2 *They decided it was kindest to dispatch the wounded animal.* dispose of, [*informal*] finish off, kill.

dispense *verb*
1 *Villagers dispensed tea to the people who had been involved in the accident.* deal out, distribute, give out, provide, share out.
2 *The pharmacist dispenses medicine prescribed by the doctor.* make up, prepare, supply.
to dispense with *His leg had healed and he was able to dispense with his crutches.* dispose of, do without, get rid of, remove.

disperse *verb*
1 *The police dispersed the crowd.* break up, drive away, send away, send in different directions, separate.
2 *The crowd dispersed quickly after the match.* disappear, dissolve, melt away, scatter, spread out, vanish.
AN OPPOSITE IS gather.

displace *verb*
1 *The vibration displaced part of the mechanism.* dislodge, disturb, put out of place, shift.
2 *A brilliant new player displaced me in the team.* replace, succeed, take the place of.

display *verb*
We planned the best way to display our work. demonstrate, exhibit, present, put on show, set out, show, show off. To display something boastfully is to *flaunt* it.

display *noun*
We set out a display of our work. demonstration, exhibition, presentation, show.

displease *verb*
I didn't do anything to displease her. annoy, anger, exasperate, irritate, upset, vex.

dispose *verb*
to dispose of something *Let's dispose of this old carpet.* discard, [*informal*] dump, get rid of, give away, scrap, throw away.

to be disposed to do something *He didn't seem disposed to do anything about the problem.* be inclined to, be likely to, be ready to, be willing to.

disposition *noun*
He has a friendly disposition. character, nature, personality.

dispute *noun*
They settled the dispute about who should use the computer first. argument, controversy, debate, difference of opinion, disagreement, quarrel.

disqualify *verb*
She was disqualified from the competition. bar, prohibit.

disregard *verb*
I disregarded her advice. ignore, pay no attention to, reject, take no notice of.
AN OPPOSITE IS heed.

disrespect *noun*
She didn't intend any disrespect by the remark. insolence, rudeness.

disrespectful *adjective*
Don't be disrespectful towards her. bad-mannered, impolite, insolent, insulting, rude.
AN OPPOSITE IS respectful.

disrupt *verb*
Floods disrupted the train service. dislocate, interfere with, interrupt, throw into confusion or disorder, upset.

dissatisfied *adjective*
Dissatisfied customers may return the goods and get a refund. annoyed, disappointed, discontented, displeased, frustrated.
AN OPPOSITE IS satisfied.

dissolve *verb*
Stir your tea until the sugar dissolves. disintegrate, disperse, melt.

dissuade *verb*
to dissuade someone from doing something *We tried to dissuade him from going out in the storm.* argue someone out of, deter someone from, discourage someone from, persuade someone not to, warn someone against.
AN OPPOSITE IS persuade.

distance *noun*
What is the distance from here to London? measurement, mileage.
The distance across something is the **breadth** or **width**.
The distance along something is the **length**.
The distance between two points is a **gap** or **interval**.
FOR UNITS FOR MEASURING DISTANCE, SEE **measurement**.

distant *adjective*
1 *I'd love to travel to distant countries.* faraway, inaccessible, out-of-the-way, remote.
AN OPPOSITE IS close.
2 *His distant manner puts me off.* cool, formal, haughty, reserved, unapproachable, unfriendly, withdrawn.
AN OPPOSITE IS friendly.

distinct *adjective*
1 *You have made a distinct improvement.* definite, evident, noticeable, obvious, perceptible.
AN OPPOSITE IS imperceptible.
2 *It was a small photo, but the details were quite distinct.* clear, distinguishable, plain, recognizable, sharp, unmistakable, visible, well defined.
AN OPPOSITE IS indistinct.
3 *Organize your essay into distinct sections.* individual, separate.

distinction *noun*
1 *I can't see the distinction between the expensive coat and the cheap one.* contrast, difference, distinctiveness.
2 *My cousin had the distinction of getting the highest mark.* credit, glory, honour, merit, prestige.

distinctive *adjective*
We have a distinctive blue football strip. characteristic, different, recognizable, special, unique, unmistakable.

distinguish *verb*
1 *Can you distinguish between butter and margarine?* choose, decide, discriminate, make a distinction, tell apart.
2 *In the dark we couldn't distinguish who she was.* determine, identify, make out, perceive, recognize, single out, tell.

distinguished *adjective*
1 *The school has a distinguished academic reputation.* excellent, exceptional, first-rate, outstanding.
AN OPPOSITE IS ordinary.
2 *She's a very distinguished writer.* celebrated, eminent, famous, notable, prominent, renowned, well known.
AN OPPOSITE IS unknown.

distort *verb*
1 *When my bike hit the kerb, it distorted the wheel.* bend, buckle, contort, twist, warp.
2 *The newspaper distorted the facts.* slant, twist.

distract *verb*
Don't distract the driver. divert the attention of.

distress *noun*
1 *We tried to comfort her in her distress.* anguish, anxiety, dismay, grief, misery, pain, sadness, sorrow, suffering, torment, worry, wretchedness.
2 *We saw that the man in the boat was in distress.* danger, difficulty, trouble.

distress *verb*
We could see that the bad news distressed her. alarm, dismay, disturb, torment, trouble, upset, worry.
AN OPPOSITE IS comfort.

distribute *verb*
1 *They distributed free samples.* circulate, [*informal*] dish out, dispense, give out, hand round, issue, share out, take round.
2 *Distribute the seeds evenly.* disperse, scatter, spread.

district *noun*
Granny lives in a quiet district. area, locality, neighbourhood, region, vicinity.

distrust *verb*
I distrust her motives for being so nice to me. be sceptical about, be suspicious or wary of, doubt, feel uncertain or uneasy or unsure about, mistrust, question, suspect.
AN OPPOSITE IS trust.

disturb *verb*
1 *Don't disturb her if she's asleep.* annoy, bother, interrupt, pester.
2 *The bad new disturbed us.* alarm, distress, frighten, trouble, upset, worry.
3 *Don't disturb the papers on my desk.* mess about with, move, muddle.

disused *adjective*
They made the disused railway line into a cycle track. abandoned, closed down, unused.

ditch *noun*
They dug a ditch to help drain the marshy land. dike, drain, gully, trench.

dither *verb*
Don't dither—get on with it! delay, falter, hang about, hesitate, waver

dive *verb*
1 *She dived into the water.* jump, leap, plunge.
2 *The eagle dived towards its prey.* pounce, swoop.

diver *noun*
A diver who wears a rubber suit and flippers and breathes air from tanks carried on their back is a **scuba diver** or **frogman**.

diverse *adjective*
People from many diverse cultures live in the area. contrasting, different, differing, varied, various.

diversify *verb*
His business has diversified into a wider range of goods. branch out.

diversion *noun*
1 *Because of an accident, we had to follow a diversion.* detour, indirect route, roundabout route.
2 *His chief diversion is reading.* amusement, entertainment, recreation.

divert *verb*
1 *They diverted the plane to another airport.* direct, switch.
2 *She diverted herself by playing the piano.* amuse, cheer up, delight, entertain, keep happy.

divide *verb*
1 *We divided into two groups.* break up, move apart, part, separate, split.
AN OPPOSITE IS combine.
2 *He divided the food between us.* allot, deal out, dispense, distribute, give out, share out.
3 *Which way do we go? The path divides here.* branch, fork.
AN OPPOSITE IS converge.

divine *adjective*
1 *The holy book deals with divine things.* heavenly, holy, religious, sacred, spiritual.
2 *Ancient Greeks believed divine beings lived on Mount Olympus.* godlike, immortal.

division *noun*
1 *The government discussed the division of the country into smaller areas.* dividing, partition, splitting.
2 *There was a division in the government.* disagreement, split.
3 *There is a movable division between the two classrooms.* divider, dividing wall, partition, screen.
4 *Dad now works in a different division of his company.* branch, department, section, unit.

dizzy *adjective*
I feel dizzy when I look down from a height. dazed, faint, giddy, reeling, unsteady.

do *verb*
The verb *do* can mean many things. We give here only a few of the ways we use the word, and some of the many synonyms
1 *Can you do a job for me?* attend to, cope with, deal with, handle, look after, perform, undertake.
2 *I managed to do the job in two hours.* accomplish, achieve, carry out, complete, execute, finish.
3 *Can you do these sums?* answer, puzzle out, solve, work out.
4 *I tried to help, but it didn't do any good.* bring about, cause, produce, result in.
5 *You can do as you like.* act, behave, conduct yourself.

6 *He asked for £10, but he said £8 would do.* be acceptable, be enough, be satisfactory, be sufficient, serve.
to do away with *I would like to do away with homework.* abolish, eliminate, end, get rid of, put an end to.
to do up *Do up your coat before you go out.* button up, fasten.
SEE ALSO **fasten**.

docile *adjective*
Don't be afraid of the dog—he's quite docile. gentle, manageable, meek, obedient, safe, submissive, tame.
AN OPPOSITE IS fierce.

dock *noun*

> PLACES WHERE SHIPS TIE UP, UNLOAD, ETC.: berth, boatyard, dockyard, dry dock, harbour, jetty, landing stage, marina, pier, port, quay, wharf.

dock *verb*
We can't disembark until the ship docks. moor, tie up.

doctor *noun*
FOR PEOPLE WHO LOOK AFTER OUR HEALTH, SEE **medicine**.

doctrine *noun*
He explained the main doctrine of his religion. principle, teaching.
A set of doctrines of a particular religion is a **creed**.

document *noun*

> VARIOUS KINDS OF DOCUMENTS: birth certificate, death certificate, diploma, driver's licence, insurance certificate, insurance policy, marriage certificate, marriage licence, passport, television licence, visa.
> Legal documents concerning a house you own are the **deeds**.
> A legal document concerning a business agreement is a **contract**.
> A document stating what is to happen to your property when you die is a **will**.
> An official document giving people certain rights is a **charter**. ➡

> A document giving police a right to search a property is a **warrant**.
> Historical documents are **records**.
> A collection of documents relating to a particular thing or issue is the **documentation**.

dodge *verb*
I dodged the snowball she threw at me. avoid, evade.

dodge *noun*
He used various dodges to avoid paying tax. knack, manoeuvre, technique, trick.

dodgy *adjective*
Don't buy anything from him—he's a dodgy character. cunning, deceitful, dishonest, disreputable, shady, unreliable, wily.

dog *noun*

> A female dog is a **bitch**.
> A young dog is a **puppy** or **whelp**.
> An uncomplimentary word for a dog is **cur**.
> A dog of pure breed with known ancestors has a **pedigree**.
> A dog of mixed breeds is a **mongrel**.
> A dog used for hunting is a **hound**.
>
> SOME BREEDS OF DOG: Alsatian, basset-hound, beagle, bloodhound, boxer, bulldog, bull-terrier, cairn terrier, chihuahua, chow, cocker spaniel, collie, corgi, dachshund, Dalmatian, foxhound, fox terrier, Great Dane, greyhound, husky, Labrador, mastiff, Pekingese or Pekinese, Pomeranian, poodle, pug, retriever, Rottweiler, setter, spaniel, terrier, whippet.

dogged *adjective*
I admire the dogged way she kept going. determined, persistent, resolute, stubborn.
If you are dogged in an annoying or unhelpful way you are **obstinate** or **stubborn**.

domestic *adjective*
1 *At weekends I do various domestic chores.* family, household.
2 *Cats and dogs are popular domestic animals.* domesticated, tame.

domesticated *adjective*
Is your puppy domesticated yet? house-trained, trained.

dominant *adjective*
1 *Russia and the USA are two dominant world powers.* chief, dominating, leading, main, major, powerful, principal, supreme.
AN OPPOSITE IS unimportant.
2 *The castle is a dominant feature in the landscape.* big, conspicuous, eye-catching, imposing, large, obvious, outstanding.
AN OPPOSITE IS insignificant.

dominate *verb*
The visiting team dominated the game. control, govern, monopolize, take control of, take over.

donate *verb*
Will you donate something to our collection? contribute, give.

donor *noun*
A generous donor gave us money for new sports equipment. benefactor, contributor, sponsor.

doom *noun*
She went to her doom bravely. end, fate, ruin.

door *noun*

VARIOUS KINDS OF DOOR OR BARRIER: doorway, emergency exit, entrance, exit, French window, gate, gateway, patio door, portal, postern, revolving door, swing door, turnstile, way out.
A door in a floor or ceiling is a *trapdoor* or *hatch*.
The plank or stone underneath a door is the *threshold*.
The beam or stone above a door is the *lintel*.
The device on which most doors swing is the *hinge*.

---

dose *noun*
The nurse gave me a dose of the medicine. correct amount or quantity, measure.

dossier *noun*
The spy stole a dossier containing secret plans. file, folder, set of documents.

dot *noun*
She was furious when she saw dots of paint on the carpet. fleck, point, speck, spot.
*The dot you always put at the end of a sentence is a **full stop**.*

double *adjective*
There are several words which we use differently to mean *consisting of two* or *having two parts*: binary, dual, duplicate, paired, twin.

double *noun*
She's so like you—she's almost your double. [informal] lookalike, [informal] spitting image, twin.
A living organism created as an exact copy of another living organism is a *clone*.

double-cross *verb*
The gangsters hunted down the man who double-crossed them. betray, cheat.

doubt *noun*
1 *Have you any doubt about his honesty?* distrust, hesitation, mistrust, reservation, scepticism, suspicion.
AN OPPOSITE IS confidence.
2 *There's some doubt about what we're going to do.* ambiguity, confusion, question, uncertainty.
AN OPPOSITE IS certainty.

doubt *verb*
There is no reason to doubt her story. be sceptical about, be suspicious or wary of, distrust, feel uncertain or uneasy or unsure about, mistrust, question, suspect.
AN OPPOSITE IS trust.

doubtful *adjective*
1 *He looked doubtful, but agreed to let us go.* distrustful, hesitant, sceptical, suspicious, uncertain, unconvinced, unsure.

AN OPPOSITE IS certain.
2 *The referee made a doubtful decision there.* arguable, debatable, questionable.

downcast *adjective*
What's the matter? You seem downcast today. dejected, depressed, gloomy, glum, [*informal*] low, melancholy, miserable, sad, unhappy.
AN OPPOSITE IS cheerful.

downfall *noun*
After the government's downfall, we had a general election. collapse, fall, ruin.

downward *adjective*
We took the downward path into the valley. descending, downhill.
AN OPPOSITE IS upward.

doze *verb*
Dad often dozes in the evening. [*informal*] drop off, nod off, rest, sleep.

drab *adjective*
We brightened up the drab room with some new wallpaper. cheerless, colourless, dingy, dismal, dreary, dull, gloomy, grey.
AN OPPOSITE IS bright.

draft *noun*
I jotted down a draft of my story. outline, plan, rough version, sketch.

draft *verb*
I began to draft my story. plan, prepare, sketch, work out.

drag *verb*
The tractor dragged the car out of the ditch. draw, haul, lug, pull, tow, tug.
AN OPPOSITE IS push.
to drag something up *They dragged up a lot of rubbish from the bottom of the canal.* dredge, lift, raise.

drain *noun*
Surplus water runs away along a drain. channel, ditch, drainpipe, gutter, pipe, sewer.

drain *verb*
1 *If they drain the marsh, lots of waterbirds will die.* dry out, remove water from.

2 *She drained the oil from the engine.* draw off, empty.
3 *The water slowly drained away.* ooze, seep, trickle.
4 *The tough climb drained my energy.* consume, exhaust, use up.

drama *noun*
1 *Drama is one of my favourite subjects.* acting.
SEE ALSO **theatre**.
2 *I witnessed the drama of a real robbery.* action, excitement, suspense, turmoil.

dramatic *adjective*
We watched the dramatic rescue on TV. eventful, exciting, gripping, sensational, tense, thrilling.

dramatize *verb*
1 *They dramatized the story for TV.* adapt, make into a play.
2 *The policeman thought I was dramatizing what had happened.* exaggerate, make too much of.

drastic *adjective*
After being without food for three days, the explorers needed to take drastic action. desperate, extreme, harsh, severe.

draught *noun*
I felt a draught of air from the open window. breeze, current, movement, puff.

draw *verb*
1 *I drew pictures while she was talking.* doodle, sketch, trace.
2 *She told us to draw the castle.* depict, portray, represent.
3 *The horse was drawing a cart.* drag, haul, lug, pull, tow, tug.
4 *We expect tomorrow's match to draw a big crowd.* attract, bring in, pull in.
5 *The two teams drew 1–1.* finish equal, tie.
to draw near *As the ship drew near, I got more excited.* advance, approach, come near.

draw *noun*
Kinds of prize draw are a *lottery* and a *raffle*.

drawback *noun*
It's a drawback to be small if you play
basketball. disadvantage, handicap,
hindrance, inconvenience.

drawing *noun*

> VARIOUS KINDS OF DRAWING:
> caricature, cartoon, design, doodle,
> illustration, outline, sketch.
> Drawing done on a computer is
> *computer graphics*.
> SEE ALSO **picture** *noun*.

dread *noun*
He has a dread of spiders. anxiety
(about), fear, horror, phobia (about),
terror.

dreadful *adjective*
1 We saw a dreadful accident on the
motorway. alarming, appalling,
distressing, fearful, frightful, ghastly,
grisly, gruesome, horrible, horrifying,
shocking, terrible, tragic, upsetting.
2 We had dreadful weather on holiday.
abominable, awful, bad, dire,
[*informal*] filthy, foul, horrid, nasty.
AN OPPOSITE IS pleasant.

dream *noun*

> A bad dream is a *nightmare*.
> A dreamlike experience you have
> while awake is a *daydream*,
> *fantasy*, or *reverie*.
> Something you see in dreams or
> daydreams is a *vision*.
> The dreamlike state when you are
> hypnotized is a *trance*.
> Something you think you see that is
> not real is a *hallucination* or
> *illusion*.
> Something you dream of achieving in
> the future is an *ambition*.
> An ambition you dream of which is
> not likely to happen is a *pipedream*.

dream *verb*
I dreamed that I could fly. daydream,
fancy, have a vision, imagine.
To have a fantasy is to *fantasize*.

dreary *adjective*
1 Unfortunately, the lecturer had a
dreary voice. boring, dull, flat, tedious,
unexciting, uninteresting.
AN OPPOSITE IS lively.

2 When will this dreary weather end?
cheerless, depressing, dismal, dull,
gloomy, murky, overcast.
AN OPPOSITE IS bright or sunny.

drench *verb*
The rain drenched me to the skin. soak,
wet thoroughly.

dress *noun*
1 She bought a dress to wear to the
party. frock, gown.
2 She told us to wear appropriate dress
for a picnic. clothes, clothing, costume,
garments, outfit.
SEE ALSO **clothes**.

dress *verb*
1 I helped to dress my little brother.
clothe, put clothes on.
AN OPPOSITE IS undress.
2 A nurse dressed my wound. bandage,
bind up, put a dressing on.

dressing *noun*
1 Do you want dressing on your salad?
French dressing, mayonnaise.
2 The nurse put a dressing on the
wound. bandage, compress, plaster,
poultice.

dribble *verb*
1 Careful, the baby's dribbling on your
jumper. drool.
2 Water dribbled out of the hole in the
tank. drip, leak, ooze, seep, trickle.

drift *verb*
1 The boat drifted downstream. be
carried, float, move slowly.
2 The crowd lost interest and drifted
away. meander, ramble, stray, walk
aimlessly, wander.
3 The snow will drift in this wind.
accumulate, make drifts, pile up.

drift *noun*
1 The car was stuck in a snow drift.
accumulation, bank, heap, mound, pile,
ridge.
2 Did you understand the drift of the
speech? gist, main idea, point.

drill *noun*
1 Drill is an important part of a
soldier's life. practice, training.
2 You know the drill, so make a start on
erecting the tent. procedure, routine,
system.

drill verb
> It took a long time to drill through the concrete. bore, penetrate, pierce.

drink noun

SOME HOT DRINKS: chocolate, cocoa, coffee, tea.

SOME NON-ALCOHOLIC COLD DRINKS: barley water, cola, cordial, fruit juice, ginger beer, lemonade, lime juice, milk, milkshake, mineral water, orangeade, pop, sodawater, squash, tonic water, water.

SOME ALCOHOLIC DRINKS: ale, beer, champagne, cider, lager, mead, port, punch, red wine, shandy, sherry, white wine.
Very strong alcoholic drinks are **spirits**.
Specially flavoured spirits are **liqueurs**.

SOME SPIRITS: brandy, gin, rum, vodka, whisky.

THINGS YOU DRINK FROM: beaker, cup, glass, goblet, mug, tankard, tumbler, wineglass.

---

drink verb
> To drink greedily is to **gulp**, **guzzle**, or **swig**.
> To drink a small amount at a time is to **sip**.
> To drink with the tongue as a cat does is to **lap**.

drip noun
> Dad was worried by the drips of oil underneath the car. dribble, splash, spot, trickle.

drip verb
> The oil dripped onto the garage floor. dribble, drop, leak, splash, trickle.

drive verb
> 1 The dog drove the sheep through the gate. direct, guide, herd.
> 2 I couldn't drive the spade into the hard ground. hammer, plunge, push, ram, thrust.
> 3 When can I learn to drive a car? control, handle, manage.

> 4 Lack of money drove him to steal. compel, force, oblige.
> **to drive someone out** The invading soldiers drove the people out. eject, expel, throw out.
> To drive people out of their homes is to **evict** them.
> To drive people out of their country is to **banish** or **exile** them.

drive noun
> 1 We went for a drive in the country. excursion, jaunt, journey, outing, ride, trip.
> 2 Have you got the drive to succeed? ambition, determination, energy, enterprise, enthusiasm, initiative, keenness, motivation, persistence, zeal.

driver noun
> Many drivers go too fast. motorist.
> A person who drives someone's car as a job is a **chauffeur**.

droop verb
> Plants tend to droop in dry weather. be limp, bend, flop, sag, wilt.

drop noun
> 1 Large drops of rain began to fall. bead, blob, drip, droplet, spot.
> 2 Could I have another drop of milk in my tea? dash, small quantity.
> 3 We expect a drop in the price of fruit in the summer. cut, decrease, reduction.
> 4 There's a drop of two metres on the other side of the wall. descent, fall, plunge.

drop verb
> 1 The hawk dropped onto its prey. descend, dive, plunge, swoop.
> 2 I dropped to the ground exhausted. collapse, fall, sink, slump, subside, tumble.
> 3 Why did you drop me from the team? eliminate, exclude, leave out, omit.
> 4 They dropped the plan for a new bypass. abandon, discard, give up, reject, scrap.
> **to drop in** Drop in on your way home. call, pay a call, visit.
> **to drop out** Why did you drop out at the last minute? back out, pull out, [informal] quit, withdraw.

drown *verb*
The music drowned our conversation.
overwhelm.

drowsy *adjective*
If you feel drowsy, why not go to bed?
sleepy, tired, weary.

drug *noun*
The doctor knows which drugs will
make you better. medicine, remedy,
treatment.
A drug which relieves pain is an
analgesic or *painkiller*.
A drug which calms you down is a
sedative or *tranquillizer*.
Drugs which make you sleepy are
narcotics.
Drugs which make you more active are
stimulants
An informal word for addictive or
narcotic drugs is *dope*.

drum *noun*
We heard the warlike sound of drums
and trumpets.

VARIOUS DRUMS: bass drum, bongo
drum, kettledrum or timpani, side
drum, snare drum, tabor, tambour,
timpani, tom-tom.
FOR OTHER PERCUSSION
INSTRUMENTS, SEE **music**.

drunk *adjective*
He got drunk and had to be taken
home. intoxicated, [*informal*] tight.
AN OPPOSITE IS sober.

drunkard *noun*
He lost his job because he was a
drunkard. alcoholic, drunk.
AN OPPOSITE IS teetotaller.

dry *adjective*
1 Nothing will grow in this dry soil.
arid, barren, dehydrated, moistureless,
parched, waterless.
AN OPPOSITE IS wet.
2 He gave rather a dry speech. boring,
dreary, dull, tedious, uninteresting.
AN OPPOSITE IS interesting.
3 He has a dry sense of humour—you
can't tell whether he is joking or not.
ironic, quiet, subtle.

dry *verb*
1 She took the clothes out of the
washing machine and hung them up to
dry. dry out, get dry.
2 Will you please dry the dishes? wipe
dry.
to dry out, to dry up The young plants
all dried up in the drought. become dry,
shrivel, wilt, wither.
When you dry food to preserve it, you
dehydrate it.
When your throat feels very dry, you
are *parched*.
3 [*informal*] Why don't you just dry up!
become silent, stop talking.

dual *adjective*
There are several words which we use
differently to mean consisting of two or
having two parts: binary, double,
duplicate, paired, twin.

duck *noun*
A male duck is a *drake*.
A young duck is a *duckling*.

duck *verb*
1 I ducked when he threw a stone at me.
bend down, bob down, crouch, stoop.
2 They ducked me in the pool. immerse,
plunge, push under, submerge.

due *adjective*
1 The train is due in five minutes.
anticipated, expected.
2 Subscriptions are now due. owed,
owing, payable.
3 I give her due credit for what she did.
appropriate, deserved, fitting, proper,
suitable, well-earned.

dull *adjective*
1 I don't like the dull colours in this
room. dim, dingy, dismal, drab, dreary,
faded, gloomy, sombre, subdued.
AN OPPOSITE IS bright.
2 The sky was dull that day. cloudy,
grey, heavy, murky, overcast, sunless.
AN OPPOSITE IS clear.
3 I heard a dull thud from upstairs.
indistinct, muffled, muted.
AN OPPOSITE IS distinct.

4 *He's rather a dull student.* [*informal*]
dense, dim, obtuse, slow, stupid,
[*informal*] thick, unimaginative,
unintelligent.
AN OPPOSITE IS clever.
5 *The lecture was so dull that I fell
asleep.* boring, dry, monotonous,
tedious, unexciting, uninteresting.
AN OPPOSITE IS interesting.

dumb *adjective*
1 *I was struck dumb with amazement.*
If you do not speak, you are **mute** or
silent.
If you cannot speak because you are
surprised, confused, or embarrassed,
you are **speechless** or **tongue-tied**.
If you find it hard to express yourself,
you are **inarticulate**.
2 [*informal*] *He's too dumb to
understand.* [*informal*] dense, dim,
obtuse, slow, stupid, [*informal*] thick,
unintelligent.

dumbfounded *adjective*
*I was dumbfounded when I heard the
news.* amazed, astonished, astounded,
[*informal*] flabbergasted, speechless,
struck dumb, stunned.

dummy *noun*
*The revolver used in the robbery was a
dummy.* copy, imitation, toy.

dump *verb*
1 *I decided to dump the old toys I never
use.* discard, dispose of, get rid of,
scrap, throw away.
2 *Dump your things on the table.* drop,
place, put down, throw down, tip.

duplicate *noun*
*We made a duplicate of the original
document.* carbon copy, copy,
photocopy, reproduction.
An exact copy of a historic document or
manuscript is a **facsimile**.
An exact copy of a thing is a **replica**.
A person who looks like you is your
double or **twin**.
A living organism which is a duplicate
of another living organism is a **clone**.

duplicate *verb*
*She used the photocopier to duplicate
some papers.* copy, photocopy.

durable *adjective*
*These expensive trainers ought to be
more durable than the cheap ones.*
hard-wearing, lasting, robust, strong,
tough.
AN OPPOSITE IS flimsy.

duration *noun*
*They stayed there for the duration of the
holiday.* length, period.

dusk *noun*
I'll meet you at dusk. nightfall,
sundown, sunset, twilight.
AN OPPOSITE IS dawn.

dust *noun*
There was a lot of dust on the furniture.
dirt, particles, powder.

dust *verb*
1 *I dusted the bookshelves.* clean,
polish, wipe over.
2 *Mum dusted the top of the cake with
icing sugar.* powder, sprinkle.

dusty *adjective*
*The things we found in the attic were
very dusty.* dirty, grimy.
AN OPPOSITE IS clean.

dutiful *adjective*
She is a kind and dutiful daughter.
conscientious, devoted, faithful, loyal,
obedient, reliable, responsible,
thorough, trustworthy.
AN OPPOSITE IS irresponsible or lazy.

duty *noun*
1 *I have a duty to help my parents.*
obligation, responsibility.
2 *I carried out my duties
conscientiously.* assignment, job, task.
3 *You may have to pay a duty if you
bring things into the country from
abroad.* charge, tax.

dwarf *noun*
Other words for unusually small
people are **midget** and **pygmy**.
Note that these words may be insulting
AN OPPOSITE IS giant.

dwarf *verb*
*He was so tall that he dwarfed the
others.* look much bigger than, tower
over.

dwell *verb*
to dwell in *In ancient times people used to dwell in caves.* inhabit, live in, occupy, reside in.
to dwell on *Try not to dwell on things that happened in the past.* brood over, keep thinking about, worry about.

dwelling *noun* SEE **house** *noun*

dwindle *verb*
Our enthusiasm dwindled as the day went on. become less, decline, decrease, diminish, lessen, subside, wane, weaken.
AN OPPOSITE IS increase.

dying *adjective*
1 *The vet put the dying animal out of its misery.* expiring.
2 *I pulled up the dying plants.* drooping, fading, wilting, withering.
AN OPPOSITE IS lively or thriving.

dynamic *adjective*
The new captain gave the team the dynamic leadership it needed. active, energetic, enterprising, enthusiastic, forceful, lively, powerful, vigorous.
AN OPPOSITE IS apathetic.

Ee

eager *adjective*
We were eager to help. anxious, enthusiastic, keen.
AN OPPOSITE IS apathetic.

eagerness *noun*
The teacher was impressed by our eagerness to begin work. desire, enthusiasm, keenness.

early *adjective*
1 *The bus was early today.* ahead of schedule, ahead of time.
AN OPPOSITE IS late.
2 *The early computers were huge machines.* first, old.
AN OPPOSITE IS advanced or recent.

earmark *verb*
I decided to earmark £10 of my birthday money to buy a CD. reserve, set aside.

earn *verb*
1 *My cousin earns extra pocket money washing cars.* bring in, get, make, obtain, receive, work for.
2 *You trained hard and earned your success.* deserve, merit.

earnest *adjective*
He's a terribly earnest young man. grave, serious, sincere, solemn, thoughtful.
AN OPPOSITE IS casual or flippant.

earnings *plural noun*
My brother's earnings are not enough for him to live on. income, pay.
Earnings that you are paid week by week are your **wages**.
Regular yearly earnings, usually paid in monthly instalments, are your **salary**.
A payment someone receives for doing a single job is a **fee**.

earth *noun*
The earth was so dry that many plants died. ground, land, soil.
Rich, fertile earth is **loam**.
The top layer of fertile earth is **topsoil**.
Rich earth consisting of decayed plants is **humus**.
A heavy, sticky kind of earth is **clay**.

earthquake *noun*
When there is an earthquake, you feel a **shock** or **tremor**.
An instrument which detects and measures earthquakes is a **seismograph**.

ease *noun*
1 *He did the job with ease.* facility, skill, speed.
AN OPPOSITE IS difficulty.
2 *She leads a life of ease.* comfort, contentment, leisure, peace, quiet, relaxation, rest, tranquillity.
AN OPPOSITE IS stress.

ease *verb*
1 *The doctor gave her some pills to ease her pain.* lessen, moderate, relieve, soothe.
AN OPPOSITE IS aggravate.

2 *After taking the pills, the pain began to ease.* decrease, reduce, slacken.
AN OPPOSITE IS increase.
3 *We eased the piano into position.* edge, guide, manoeuvre, move gradually, slide, slip.

east *noun, adjective, adverb*
The parts of a country or continent in the east are the **eastern** parts.
The countries of east Asia, east of the Mediterranean, are called **oriental** countries.
To travel towards the east is to travel **eastward** or **eastwards** or **in an easterly direction**.
A wind from the east is an **easterly** wind.

easy *adjective*
1 *The work was easy.* effortless, light, undemanding.
2 *The instructions were easy to understand.* clear, elementary, plain, simple, straightforward.
3 *She is an easy person to get on with.* amiable, friendly, good-natured, informal, pleasant, tolerant.
4 *Our cat has an easy life.* carefree, comfortable, leisurely, peaceful, relaxed, relaxing, restful, tranquil, untroubled.
AN OPPOSITE IS difficult.

eat *verb*
He was eating a hot dog. consume, devour.
When cattle eat grass they are **grazing**.

VARIOUS WAYS TO EAT: bite, chew, crunch, gnaw, munch.
To eat very quickly is to **bolt** or **gobble** your food.
To eat a lot of food is to **gorge yourself** or **overeat**.
To eat in large mouthfuls is to **gulp** your food.
To eat in small mouthfuls is to **nibble** or **peck** at your food.
If you eat a little food to see what it is like, you **taste** it.
To eat a large, formal meal is to **banquet** or **dine** or **feast**.
FOR THINGS TO EAT, SEE **food**.

to eat something away *The flood began to eat away the river bank.* erode, wear away.

eatable *adjective*
Is the food eatable? edible, fit to eat, good, safe to eat.
AN OPPOSITE IS inedible or uneatable.

ebb *verb*
1 *The fishermen waited for the tide to ebb.* fall, flow back, go down, recede, retreat.
2 *She fell ill and her strength began to ebb.* decline, fade, lessen, wane, weaken.

eccentric *adjective*
What is the reason for his eccentric behaviour? abnormal, curious, odd, peculiar, strange, unconventional, unusual, weird, zany.
AN OPPOSITE IS conventional.

echo *verb*
1 *The sound echoed across the valley.* resound.
2 *'He's gone home.' 'Gone home?' she echoed.* repeat.

economic *adjective*
1 *The Chancellor of the Exchequer looks after the country's economic affairs.* business, financial.
2 *It's not economic to open the shop on Sundays.* profitable, worthwhile.

economical *adjective*
1 *My uncle is very economical with his money.* careful, frugal, prudent, thrifty.
If you are economical with money in a selfish way, you are **mean** or **miserly**.
AN OPPOSITE IS wasteful.
2 *It's an economical car to run.* cheap, inexpensive, reasonable.
AN OPPOSITE IS expensive.

economize *verb*
If you're poor you have to economize. be economical, cut back, spend less.

economy *noun*
1 *The Chancellor of the Exchequer looks after the national economy.* budget, economic affairs, wealth.
2 *They turned off the light for reasons of economy.* frugality, prudence, saving, thrift.

ecstasy *noun*
You should see my dog's ecstasy when I come home! bliss, delight, elation.

ecstatic *adjective*
> They gave me an ecstatic welcome.
> blissful, delighted, delirious, elated,
> enthusiastic, exultant, fervent,
> frenzied, gleeful, joyful, passionate.

edge *noun*

> The edge of a cliff or other steep
> place is the **brink**.
> The edge of a cup or other container
> is the **brim** or **rim**.
> The line round the edge of a circle is
> the **circumference**.
> The line round the edge of any other
> shape is its **outline**.
> The distance round the edge of an
> area is the **perimeter**.
> The stones along the edge of a road
> are the **kerb**.
> Grass along the edge of a road is the
> **verge**.
> The space down the edge of a page is
> the **margin**.
> The space round the edge of a
> picture is a **border**.
> Something that fits round the edge
> of a picture is a **frame**.
> The edge of a skirt, etc., is the **hem**.
> An edge with threads or hair
> hanging loosely down is a **fringe**.
> The edge of a crowd also is the
> **fringe** of the crowd.
> The area round the edge of a city is
> the **outskirts** or **suburbs**.
> The edge of a cricket field is the
> **boundary**.
> The edge of a football pitch is the
> **touchline**.

edge *verb*
> **1** I edged away from the lion. creep,
> move stealthily, slink, steal.
> **2** Mum edged the curtains with a
> fringe. trim.

edgy *adjective*
> The horses became edgy during the
> thunderstorm. agitated, anxious,
> excitable, fidgety, fraught, irritable,
> jumpy, nervous, restless, tense,
> [*informal*] uptight.
> AN OPPOSITE IS calm.

edible *adjective*
> Are these toadstools edible? eatable, fit
> to eat, good to eat, safe to eat.
> AN OPPOSITE IS poisonous or
> uneatable.

edit *verb*
> Her job was to edit the magazine.
> compile, get ready, organize, prepare,
> put together.

> WAYS YOU MIGHT EDIT
> CONTRIBUTIONS TO A MAGAZINE,
> ETC.: abridge or shorten, adapt or
> alter, censor, condense or cut or
> shorten, correct, format, proof-read,
> revise or rewrite.

edition *noun*
> **1** We prepared a Christmas edition of
> our magazine. copy, issue, number.
> **2** Our teacher bought the latest edition
> of the Junior Dictionary. version.

educate *verb*
> The job of a school is to educate young
> people. inform, instruct, teach, train.

educated *adjective*
> She is an educated woman. cultivated,
> cultured, knowledgeable, learned,
> literate, well informed, well read.

education *noun*
> Education is important if you want to
> get on in life. instruction, schooling,
> teaching, training.

> A programme of education is the
> **curriculum** or **syllabus**.
>
> PEOPLE WHO MAY HELP TO
> EDUCATE US: coach, counsellor,
> governess, headteacher, instructor,
> lecturer, professor, teacher, trainer,
> tutor.
>
> PLACES WHERE WE RECEIVE
> EDUCATION: academy, college,
> kindergarten, playgroup, primary
> school, secondary school, sixth-form
> college, university.

eerie *adjective*
> I heard some eerie sounds in the night.
> creepy, frightening, ghostly,
> mysterious, [*informal*] scary, sinister,
> [*informal*] spooky, strange, uncanny,
> unearthly, unnatural, weird.

effect *noun*
  1 *The effect of eating too much was that I became fat!* consequence, outcome, result, sequel, upshot.
  2 *Does this music have any effect on you?* impact, influence.
  3 *The lighting gives an effect of warmth.* feeling, illusion, impression, sense.

effective *adjective*
  1 *I wish they could find an effective cure for colds.* successful.
  2 *Our team needs an effective goalkeeper.* able, capable, competent, proficient, skilled.
  3 *He presented an effective argument against hunting.* compelling, convincing, impressive, persuasive, telling.
  AN OPPOSITE IS useless.

effervescent *adjective*
  He preferred effervescent drinks to the still kind. bubbly, fizzy, sparkling.
  AN OPPOSITE IS still.

efficient *adjective*
  1 *An efficient worker can do the job in an hour.* able, capable, competent, effective, proficient.
  2 *Dad tried to work out an efficient way of heating our house.* economic, productive.
  AN OPPOSITE IS inefficient.

effort *noun*
  1 *A lot of effort went into making that piece of work.* exertion, hard work, industry, labour, toil, work.
  2 *She congratulated us on a good effort.* attempt, endeavour, go, performance, try.

effortless *adjective*
  She's so good at it that she makes it look effortless. easy, painless, undemanding.
  AN OPPOSITE IS hard.

egg *verb*
  to egg someone on *We egged him on, even though we knew it was dangerous to climb the tree.* encourage, spur on.

eject *verb*
  1 *Lava was ejected from the volcano when it erupted.* discharge, emit.
  2 *The caretaker ejected an intruder from the building.* banish, evict, expel, kick out, remove, throw out, turn out.

elaborate *adjective*
  The plan was so elaborate that it was hard to remember all the details. complex, complicated, detailed, intricate, involved.
  AN OPPOSITE IS simple.

elaborate *verb*
  He refused to elaborate his plan. add to, amplify, develop, expand, fill out, improve on.
  AN OPPOSITE IS simplify.

elated *adjective*
  We were elated when we beat our rivals. delighted, delirious, ecstatic, exultant, gleeful, joyful, [*slang*] over the moon, pleased, thrilled.

elder *adjective*
  My elder brother is in the football team. older.

elderly *adjective*
  I helped the elderly couple to get on the bus. aged, rather old.
  AN OPPOSITE IS young.

eldest *adjective*
  Jane is my eldest sister. oldest.

elect *verb*
  We elected a new captain. appoint, vote for.

election *noun*
  We had an election to choose a new captain. ballot, poll, vote.

electricity *noun*
  Is the electricity on? current, power, power supply.

Someone whose job is to fit and repair electrical equipment is an ***electrician***.

SOME THINGS AN ELECTRICIAN MIGHT FIT OR REPAIR: adaptor, battery, cable, charger, ➡

circuit, dynamo, flex, fuse, generator, heating, insulation, lead, lighting, meter, plug, power point, socket, switch, terminal, transformer, wiring.

elegant *adjective*
She always wears elegant clothes. chic, fashionable, graceful, smart, sophisticated, stylish, tasteful.
AN OPPOSITE IS inelegant.

element *noun*
They discussed various elements of the book. component, constituent, feature, part.
to be in your element *A duck would be in its element in this wet weather.* be at home, be comfortable, be happy, enjoy yourself.
the elements 1 *The mountaineers battled against the elements.* the forces of nature, the weather.
SEE ALSO **weather.**
2 *We were taught the elements of algebra.* the basic facts, the fundamental facts, the principles.

elementary *adjective*
Anyone can solve such an elementary problem. basic, easy, fundamental, simple, straightforward, uncomplicated.
AN OPPOSITE IS advanced or complex.

eligible *adjective*
Children over twelve are not eligible to enter this race. allowed, authorized, qualified, suitable.
AN OPPOSITE IS ineligible.

eliminate *verb*
The government wants to eliminate crime. get rid of, put an end to.
To be eliminated from a competition is to be **knocked out**.

eloquent *adjective*
The lawyer's eloquent speech convinced the jury. articulate, expressive, fluent, persuasive.

elude *verb*
The police chased him, but he managed to elude them. avoid, escape from, evade, get away from.

elusive *adjective*
Deer are elusive animals. evasive, hard to find.

emancipate *verb*
Wilberforce worked for years to emancipate the slaves. free, liberate, release, set free.

embark *verb*
The passengers embarked in time for the ship to sail at high tide. board, go aboard.
AN OPPOSITE IS disembark.
to embark on something *Today we embarked on a big project.* begin, commence, start, undertake.

embarrass *verb*
Will it embarrass you if I tell people our secret? distress, humiliate, make you blush.

embarrassed *adjective*
Don't feel embarrassed—it happens to everyone! ashamed, awkward, bashful, distressed, flustered, humiliated, self-conscious, uncomfortable.

embers *plural noun*
The embers of the fire were still glowing next morning. ashes, cinders.

emblem *noun*
The dove is an emblem of peace. sign, symbol.

embrace *verb*
1 *She embraced him lovingly.* clasp, cuddle, hold, hug.
2 *She's always ready to embrace new ideas.* accept, adopt, take on, welcome.
3 *The syllabus embraces all aspects of the subject.* include, incorporate, take in.

embryo *noun*
A human embryo is in the mother's womb for nine months. foetus.

emerge *verb*
He didn't emerge from his bedroom until ten o'clock. appear, come out.

emergency *noun*
Try to keep calm in an emergency. crisis, danger, difficulty, serious situation.

emigrant *noun*
AN OPPOSITE IS immigrant.

emigrate *verb*
During the famine, many Irish people were forced to emigrate to America. leave the country, move abroad.
AN OPPOSITE IS immigrate.

eminent *adjective*
An eminent author came to give us a talk. celebrated, distinguished, famous, great, notable, prominent, renowned, respected, well known.
AN OPPOSITE IS unknown.

emit *verb*
1 *The exhaust pipe emitted clouds of smoke.* belch, blow out, discharge, expel, give off.
2 *The satellite was emitting radio signals.* give out, send out, transmit.
AN OPPOSITE IS receive.

emotion *noun*
His voice was full of emotion. feeling, fervour, passion, sentiment.

emotional *adjective*
1 *He made an emotional farewell speech.* moving, touching.
2 *The music for the love scenes was very emotional.* romantic, sentimental.
3 *She's a very emotional woman.* intense, passionate.
AN OPPOSITE IS unemotional.

emphasis *noun*
In the word 'dictionary' the emphasis is on the first syllable. accent, stress, weight.

emphasize *verb*
She emphasized the important points. dwell on, focus on, give emphasis to, highlight, stress, underline.

employ *verb*
1 *The new factory plans to employ 100 workers.* engage, give work to, hire, take on.
2 *The factory will employ the latest methods.* use, utilize.

employee *noun*
100 employees will work at the new factory. worker.
A word for all the employees of an organization is **staff** or **workforce**.

employer *noun*
He asked his employer for a pay rise. [*informal*] boss, chief, head, manager, owner.

employment *noun*
There are a lot of people in our area looking for employment. a job, an occupation, a profession, a trade, work.
FOR PARTICULAR KINDS OF EMPLOYMENT, SEE **job**.

empty *adjective*
1 *Please put the empty milk bottles outside the door.*
AN OPPOSITE IS full.
2 *The house next to ours has been empty for weeks.* deserted, uninhabited, unoccupied, vacant.
AN OPPOSITE IS occupied.
3 *After we put up our display, there was still some empty space on the wall.* bare, blank, clear, unused.

empty *verb*
1 *Empty the dirty water into the sink.* drain, pour out.
AN OPPOSITE IS fill.
2 *The building emptied when the fire alarm went off.* clear, evacuate.
3 *Did you empty all the shopping out of the trolley?* remove, unload.

enable *verb*
1 *The fine weather enabled us to do the job quickly.* aid, assist, help, make it possible for.
2 *A passport enables you to travel abroad.* allow, authorize, entitle, permit.
AN OPPOSITE IS prevent.

enchant *verb*
The ballet enchanted us. bewitch, charm, delight, entrance, fascinate.

enchantment *noun*
The forest had an air of enchantment. delight, magic, pleasure, wonder.

encircle *verb*
The pond was encircled by trees. ring, surround.

enclose verb
1 *The documents were enclosed in a brown paper envelope.* contain, insert, sheathe, wrap.
2 *The animals were enclosed within a wire fence.* confine, fence in, imprison, restrict, shut in.

enclosure noun
An animal's enclosure with bars is a *cage*.
An enclosure for chickens is a *coop* or *run*.
An enclosure for cattle and other animals is a *pen* or *corral*.
An enclosure for horses is a *paddock*.
An enclosure for sheep is a *fold*.
An enclosure for lost animals or towed-away vehicles is a *pound*.
An enclosure with buildings in it is a *compound*.
An enclosure for sporting events is an *arena* or *stadium*.

encounter verb
1 *He encountered her outside the station.* come face to face with, meet, run into.
2 *We encountered some problems.* come upon, confront, experience, be faced with.

encourage verb
1 *We went to the match to encourage our team.* applaud, cheer, egg on, inspire, motivate, spur on, support.
2 *Our doctor encourages people to stop smoking.* persuade, urge.
3 *Is advertising likely to encourage sales?* aid, boost, further, help, increase, promote, stimulate.
AN OPPOSITE IS discourage.

encouragement noun
Our team needs some encouragement. applause, incentive, inspiration, reassurance, stimulation, stimulus, support.

encouraging adjective
The results of the tests were encouraging. cheering, favourable, hopeful, optimistic, positive, promising, reassuring.

end noun
1 *The fence marks the end of the garden.* boundary, limit.
2 *The end of the film was the most exciting part.* close, conclusion, culmination, ending, finish.
The last part of a show or piece of music is the *finale*.
A section added at the end of a letter is a *postscript*.
A section added at the end of a story is an *epilogue*.
3 *I was tired by the time we got to the end of the journey.* destination, termination.
4 *We arrived late and found ourselves at the end of the queue.* back, rear, tail.
5 *What end did you have in view when you started?* aim, intention, objective, outcome, plan, purpose, result.

end verb
1 *We ended our work just in time for dinner.* break off, complete, conclude, finish, halt, [*informal*] round off.
2 *When did they end public executions?* abolish, do away with, eliminate, get rid of, put an end to.
3 *The concert ended with the National Anthem.* cease, close, come to an end, culminate, stop, terminate, wind up.

endanger verb
Bad driving endangers other people. put at risk, threaten.
AN OPPOSITE IS protect.

endeavour verb
Please endeavour to behave well. aim, attempt, make an effort, strive, try.

ending noun
The ending of the film was the most exciting part. close, conclusion, culmination, end, finish, last part.
The ending of a show or piece of music is the *finale*.

endless adjective
1 *Teachers need endless patience.* inexhaustible, infinite, limitless, unending, unlimited.
2 *There's an endless procession of cars along the main road.* ceaseless, constant, continual, continuous, everlasting, incessant, interminable, perpetual, unbroken, uninterrupted.

endurance *noun*
The climb was a test of their endurance.
determination, perseverance,
persistence, resolution, stamina.

endure *verb*
1 She had to endure a lot of pain. bear,
cope with, experience, go through, put
up with, stand, suffer, tolerate,
undergo.
2 These traditions have endured for
centuries. carry on, continue, keep
going, last, persist, survive.

enemy *noun*
They used to be friends but now they
are bitter enemies. adversary, foe,
opponent, rival.
AN OPPOSITE IS ally or friend.

energetic *adjective*
1 She's a very energetic person. active,
dynamic, enthusiastic, hard-working,
tireless.
2 It was a very energetic exercise
routine. brisk, fast, lively, quick
moving, strenuous, vigorous.
AN OPPOSITE IS lethargic.

energy *noun*
1 The dancers had tremendous energy.
drive, enthusiasm, liveliness, spirit,
stamina, strength, vigour, vitality, zest.
2 Industry needs a reliable supply of
energy. fuel, power.

enforce *verb*
The umpire's job is to enforce the rules.
administer, apply, carry out,
implement, impose, insist on, put into
effect.

engage *verb*
1 The builder engaged extra workers in
order to complete the job on time.
employ, hire, take on.
2 The general decided to engage the
enemy at dawn. attack, start fighting.
to engage someone in conversation
She engaged me in conversation and
I couldn't get away. converse with,
talk to.

engaged *adjective*
1 He was engaged in his work.
absorbed, busy, engrossed, immersed,
occupied, tied up.
AN OPPOSITE IS idle.
2 I tried to phone but the line was
engaged. being used, busy, unavailable.
AN OPPOSITE IS available.

engagement *noun*
1 Dad has a business engagement this
afternoon. appointment, commitment,
date, meeting.
2 The engagement between the two
armies was brief and bloody. action,
battle, clash, conflict, [plural]
hostilities.

engine *noun*

VARIOUS KINDS OF ENGINE: diesel
engine, electric motor, internal-
combustion engine, jet engine,
outboard motor, petrol engine, steam
engine, turbine, turbojet, turboprop.
A railway engine is a *locomotive*.

PARTS OF A PETROL ENGINE:
alternator, carburettor, cooling
system, crankshaft, cylinder block,
cylinders, distributor, fuel injection,
oil filter, pistons, starter motor,
throttle, valves.

engrave *verb*
An inscription was engraved on the
stone. carve, cut, etch.

engrossed *adjective*
She was engrossed in her work.
absorbed, busy, engaged, immersed,
occupied.

engulf *verb*
The tidal wave engulfed several villages
near the coast. drown, flood, immerse,
inundate, overwhelm, submerge,
swallow up, swamp.

enhance *verb*
The team's victory enhanced their
reputation. improve, strengthen.

enjoy *verb*
I really enjoyed the film. admire,
appreciate, be pleased by, get pleasure
from, like, love.

enjoyable *adjective*
It was an enjoyable party. agreeable, amusing, delightful, entertaining, pleasant.
AN OPPOSITE IS unpleasant.

enlarge *verb*
Business is so good that they plan to enlarge the shop. build on to, develop, expand, extend, increase the size of, make bigger.
To make something wider is to **broaden** or **widen** it.
To make something longer is to **extend**, **lengthen**, or **stretch** it.
To make something seem larger is to **magnify** it.
AN OPPOSITE IS reduce.

enlist *verb*
Many men decided to enlist in the army. enrol, join up, sign on, volunteer.

enormity *noun*
The enormity of the crime shocked the whole country. dreadfulness, evil, villainy, wickedness.

enormous *adjective*
Enormous waves battered the ship. colossal, gigantic, huge, immense, massive, monstrous, monumental, mountainous, towering, tremendous, vast.
AN OPPOSITE IS small.

enough *adjective*
Is there enough food for ten people? adequate, ample, sufficient.

enquire *verb*
He enquired if I was well. ask, inquire.
to enquire about *I enquired about train times to London.* ask for, get information about, investigate, request.

enquiry *noun*
The librarian help me with my enquiry. investigation, question, request, research.

enrage *verb*
I was enraged by their stupidity. anger, exasperate, incense, infuriate, madden, provoke.
AN OPPOSITE IS pacify.

enrol *verb*
I enrolled as a member of the drama club. join, put your name down, sign up, volunteer.

ensure *verb*
Please ensure that you lock the door before you go out. confirm, make certain, make sure, see.

enter *verb*
1 *Silence fell as I entered the room.* come in, walk in.
To enter a place without permission is to **invade** it.
AN OPPOSITE IS leave.
2 *The bullet entered his leg.* go into, penetrate, pierce.
3 *Can I enter my name on the list?* inscribe, insert, put down, record, register, set down, sign, write.
AN OPPOSITE IS cancel.
4 *We all decided to enter the competition.* enrol in, go in for, join in, participate in, sign up for, take part in, volunteer for.
AN OPPOSITE IS withdraw from.

enterprise *noun*
1 *She showed enterprise in starting her own business.* drive, initiative.
2 *The expedition was a very rash enterprise.* adventure, effort, mission, operation, project, undertaking, venture.

enterprising *adjective*
Some enterprising girls organized a sponsored walk. adventurous, ambitious, bold, courageous, daring, eager, energetic, enthusiastic, hard-working, imaginative, industrious, intrepid, keen.
AN OPPOSITE IS unadventurous.

entertain *verb*
1 *He entertained us for hours with his stories and jokes.* amuse, cheer up, divert, keep amused, make you laugh, please.
AN OPPOSITE IS bore.
2 *Members can entertain friends in the club's private dining room.* cater for, give hospitality to, receive, welcome.

entertainer noun

VARIOUS ENTERTAINERS: acrobat, actor, actress, ballerina, broadcaster, busker, clown, comedian or comic, conjuror, dancer, disc jockey or DJ, juggler, lion-tamer, magician, musician, singer, street entertainer, stunt man, trapeze artist, ventriloquist.
A famous entertainer is a *star* or *superstar*.
In past times, an entertainer in an important household was a *fool*, *jester*, or *minstrel*.

entertainment noun
We like to have our holiday in a place with plenty of entertainment.
amusements, diversions, enjoyment, fun, nightlife, pastimes, pleasure, recreation, sport.

VARIOUS KINDS OF ENTERTAINMENT: air show, ballet, cabaret, ceilidh, cinema, circus, comedy, concert, dance, disco, fair, firework display, flower show, gymkhana, motor show, musical, nightclub, opera, pageant, pantomime, play, radio, recitation, revue, rodeo, show, son et lumière, tattoo, television, theatre, variety show, waxworks, zoo.
SEE **music, sport**.

enthusiasm noun
1 *To be successful you need enthusiasm.*
ambition, commitment, drive, eagerness, keenness, zeal, zest.
AN OPPOSITE IS apathy.
2 *Gardening is one of her many enthusiasms.* craze, diversion, fad, hobby, interest, passion, pastime.

enthusiast noun
Her brother is a football enthusiast.
addict, devotee, fan, fanatic, [*informal*] freak, lover, supporter.

enthusiastic adjective
1 *He's an enthusiastic supporter of our local team.* avid, devoted, energetic, fervent, keen, passionate, zealous.

2 *The audience burst into enthusiastic applause.* eager, excited, exuberant, hearty, lively, vigorous.
AN OPPOSITE IS apathetic.

entire adjective
She spent the entire evening watching television. complete, full, total, whole.

entitle verb
The voucher entitles you to claim a discount. allow, authorize, enable, permit.

entrance noun
1 *Please pay at the entrance.* access, door, entry, gate, turnstile, way in.
When you go through the entrance to a building, you cross the *threshold*.
2 *I'll meet you in the entrance.* entrance hall, foyer, lobby, porch.
3 *Her sudden entrance took everyone by surprise.* appearance, arrival, entry.
AN OPPOSITE IS exit.

entrance verb
The music entranced us. charm, delight, enchant, please.

entrant noun
A prize of £50 will be awarded to the winning entrant. candidate, competitor, contender, contestant, participant.

entreat verb
We entreated him to drive slowly. ask earnestly, beg, implore, plead with, request.

entrust verb
to entrust someone with something
Can I entrust you with the money? let you look after, put you in charge of, trust you with.

entry noun
1 *Please don't block the entry.* access, door, entrance, gate, way in.
2 *Every evening I write an entry in my diary.* item, note.

envelop verb
Mist enveloped the top of the mountain. conceal, cover, hide, mask.

envious adjective
He was envious of his brother's success. jealous, resentful.

environment *noun*
Animals should live in their natural environment, not in cages. conditions, habitat, setting, situation, surroundings.
the environment We must do all we can to protect the environment. nature, the earth, the natural world, the world.

envy *noun*
I didn't feel any envy, even when I saw how rich she was. bitterness, jealousy, resentment.

envy *verb*
He envies her success. begrudge, grudge, resent.

episode *noun*
1 I paid for the broken window, and I want to forget the whole episode. event, experience, incident.
2 I missed last night's episode of my favourite programme. instalment, part.

equal *adjective*
1 Give everyone an equal amount. corresponding, equivalent, fair, identical, matching, similar.
2 The scores were equal at half-time. even, level, the same, square.

equalize *verb*
Our opponents equalized just before half-time. level the scores, make the scores equal or even.

equip *verb*
All the bedrooms are equipped with a colour television. provide, supply.
To equip soldiers with weapons is to *arm* them.
To equip a room with furniture is to *furnish* it.

equipment *noun*
Dad has got all the equipment you need to repair the car. apparatus, gear, implements, instruments, kit, machinery, materials, paraphernalia, tackle, things, tools.
Computing equipment is *hardware*.

equivalent *adjective*
You need 250 grams or an equivalent amount in ounces. corresponding, identical, matching, similar.

era *noun*
Shakespeare lived in the Elizabethan era. age, epoch, period, time.

erase
I erased the writing on the board. delete, get rid of, remove, rub out, wipe out.

erect *adjective*
The dog stood with its ears erect. perpendicular, upright, vertical.

erect *verb*
The town hall was erected in 1892. build, construct, put up, raise, set up.
To erect a tent is to *pitch* it.

erode *verb*
The flood water eroded the river bank. destroy, eat away, wear away.

errand *noun*
I went on an errand to the shop. assignment, job, journey, task, trip.

erratic *adjective*
Our goalkeeper's performance has been erratic this season. changeable, fluctuating, inconsistent, irregular, uneven, unpredictable, variable.
AN OPPOSITE IS consistent.

error *noun*
1 The accident was the result of an error by the driver. blunder, fault, lapse, mistake.
2 I think there is an error in your argument. fallacy, flaw, inaccuracy, inconsistency, misunderstanding.
The error of leaving something out is an *omission* or *oversight*.

erupt *verb*
Smoke began to erupt from the volcano. be discharged, be emitted, belch, burst out, gush, issue, pour out, shoot out, spout, spurt.

escalate *verb*
The police were afraid that the rioting would escalate. become worse, build up, develop, grow, increase, intensify.

escape *verb*
1 Why did you let him escape? break free, break out, get away, get out, [*informal*] give you the slip, run away.
2 She always escapes the nasty jobs. avoid, dodge, evade, get out of, shirk.

escape *noun*
1 *The prisoner's escape was filmed by security cameras.* breakout, flight, getaway.
2 *The explosion was caused by an escape of gas.* leak, leakage, seepage.

escort *noun*
1 *The president always has an escort to protect him.* bodyguard, guard.
2 *The actress arrived with her escort.* companion, partner.

escort *verb*
The queen was escorted by a number of attendants. accompany, guard, look after, protect.

especially *adverb*
I like biscuits, especially chocolate biscuits. above all, chiefly, most of all.

espionage *noun*
In a time of war, many people are involved in espionage. intelligence, spying.

essence *noun*
Don't give me all the details, but what is the essence of your problem? centre, core, gist, heart, substance.

essential *adjective*
Fresh fruit and vegetables are an essential part of our diet. basic, chief, crucial, fundamental, important, indispensable, necessary, principal, vital.

establish *verb*
1 *He plans to establish a new business.* begin, create, found, initiate, institute, introduce, launch, originate, set up, start.
2 *The police have not managed to establish his guilt.* confirm, prove, show to be true, verify.

establishment *noun*
1 *Since its establishment last year, many people have joined the drama club.* creation, formation, foundation, introduction.
2 *The restaurant is a very well run establishment.* business, concern, organization.

estate *noun*
1 *There's a new housing estate near our school.* area, development.
2 *The Duke does not allow hunting on his estate.* grounds, land.
3 *When he died, the millionaire left his estate to his partner.* fortune, possessions, property, wealth.

esteem *verb*
He was highly esteemed by all his colleagues. admire, appreciate, honour, look up to, respect, think highly of, value.

estimate *noun*
What is your estimate of how much it will cost? assessment, calculation, evaluation, guess, judgement, opinion.
An official estimate of the value of something is a **valuation**.
An official estimate of what a job is going to cost is a **quotation** or **tender**.

estimate *verb*
Dad asked the builder to estimate how much the job will cost. assess, calculate, compute, count up, evaluate, judge, reckon, think out, work out.

eternal *adjective*
1 *He seemed to have the secret of eternal youth.* everlasting, infinite, lasting, timeless, unending.
Beings with eternal life are said to be **immortal**.
2 *I'm sick of your eternal quarrelling!* ceaseless, constant, continual, incessant, never-ending, non-stop, perpetual, persistent, recurrent, repeated, unceasing.

evacuate *verb*
1 *The firemen had to evacuate us from the smoke-filled building.* clear, move out, remove, send away.
2 *You must evacuate the building when the fire alarm goes.* abandon, empty, leave, quit, withdraw from.

evade *verb*
Don't try to evade your responsibilities. avoid, dodge, escape from, fend off, shirk, steer clear of.
AN OPPOSITE IS confront.

evaluate *verb*
The government is evaluating the success of the training scheme. assess, calculate, estimate, judge, reckon, work out.

evaporate *verb*
Dew evaporates in the morning. disappear, disperse, dry up, melt away, vanish.
AN OPPOSITE IS condense.

evasive *adjective*
I still don't know the truth because his answers were so evasive. ambiguous, devious, indirect, oblique, roundabout, unhelpful.
AN OPPOSITE IS straightforward.

even *adjective*
1 *You need an even surface for cricket.* flat, level, smooth, straight.
AN OPPOSITE IS uneven.
2 *They travelled at an even pace.* monotonous, regular, rhythmical, steady, unvarying.
AN OPPOSITE IS irregular.
3 *He has an even temper.* calm, cool, placid, predictable, unexcitable.
AN OPPOSITE IS excitable.
4 *The scores were even at half-time.* equal, identical, level, matching, the same, square.
AN OPPOSITE IS different.
5 *2, 4, and 6 are even numbers.*
AN OPPOSITE IS odd.

even *verb*
to even something up *If I go over to their team, that will even up the numbers.* balance, equalize, level, match, square.

evening *noun*
Towards evening it clouded over and began to rain. dusk, nightfall, sundown, sunset, twilight.

event *noun*
1 *There were no unexpected events while you were away.* happening, incident, occurrence.
2 *They held a special event to celebrate the opening of the sports club.* ceremony, entertainment, function, occasion, party, reception.
3 *For some people, the Cup Final is the most important sporting event of the year.* competition, contest, engagement, fixture, game, match, meeting, tournament.

eventful *adjective*
We had an eventful journey. active, busy, exciting, interesting, lively.
AN OPPOSITE IS boring or restful.

eventual *adjective*
We worked hard, but we were delighted with the eventual outcome. ensuing, final, overall, resulting, ultimate.

eventually *adverb*
The journey took ages, but eventually we arrived safely. at last, finally, in the end, ultimately.

evergreen *adjective*
Most pine trees are evergreen.
AN OPPOSITE IS deciduous.

everlasting *adjective*
I'm sick of your everlasting chatter! ceaseless, constant, continual, eternal, incessant, never-ending, non-stop, perpetual, persistent, recurrent, repeated, unceasing, unending.
AN OPPOSITE IS occasional.
Everlasting life is ***immortality***.

everyday *adjective*
Don't bother to dress up—come in your everyday clothes. customary, normal, ordinary, regular, usual.

evict *verb*
The landlord threatened to evict the tenants. eject, expel, put out, remove, throw out, turn out.

evidence *noun*
I have evidence that what I say is true. confirmation, proof.
Evidence that someone accused of a crime was not there when the crime was committed is an ***alibi***.
Evidence given in a lawcourt is a ***testimony***.
To give evidence in court is to ***testify***.

evident *adjective*
It's evident that someone has made a mistake. apparent, certain, clear, noticeable, obvious, perceptible, plain, undeniable, unmistakable, visible.

evil *adjective*
1 *Whoever committed this murder is an evil person.* corrupt, immoral, perverted, sinful, treacherous, vicious, villainous, wicked.
2 *Who would do such an evil deed?* atrocious, cruel, diabolical, dreadful, fiendish, foul, hateful, malevolent, malicious, vile, wrong.
AN OPPOSITE IS good.

evil *noun*
1 *You cannot pretend there is no evil in the world.* corruption, crime, cruelty, dishonesty, immorality, malevolence, malice, mischief, sin, treachery, vice, villainy, wickedness, wrongdoing.
2 *Throughout history, people have endured many evils.* affliction, calamity, catastrophe, curse, disaster, misfortune, pain, suffering, wrong.

evolution *noun*
The evolution of life on earth has taken millions of years. development, emergence, growth, progress.

evolve *verb*
Over millions of years, simple forms of life evolved into complex organisms. develop, emerge, grow, mature, modify, progress.

exact *adjective*
1 *I gave the police an exact account of what happened.* accurate, correct, detailed, faithful, meticulous, precise, strict, true.
2 *Is this an exact copy of the original document?* identical, indistinguishable, perfect.
AN OPPOSITE IS inaccurate.

exaggerate *verb*
He tends to exaggerate his problems. inflate, magnify, make too much of, overdo.
AN OPPOSITE IS minimize.

examination *noun*
1 *The results of the examinations will be announced next month.* assessment, [*informal*] exam, test.
A sheet of questions to which you must write answers is an **exam paper**.
An examination in which you speak the answers is an **oral exam**.

2 *The judge made a thorough examination of the facts.* analysis, appraisal, inspection, investigation, review, study, survey.
3 *He was subjected to a long examination by the police.* cross-examination, interrogation, questioning.
4 *He was sent to hospital for an examination.* check-up.
A medical examination of a dead person is a **post-mortem**.

examine *verb*
1 *The judge examined the evidence.* analyse, appraise, explore, inquire into, inspect, investigate, look closely at, pore over, probe, scrutinize, sift, sort out, study, test, weigh up.
2 *The prosecution examined the witness.* cross-examine, grill, interrogate, question.

example *noun*
1 *Give me an example of what you mean.* case, illustration, instance, sample, specimen.
2 *She's an example to us all.* ideal, model.

exasperate *verb*
Dad was exasperated because the phone was continually engaged. [*informal*] aggravate, anger, annoy, irritate, provoke, upset, vex.

excavate *verb*
The builder excavated a trench for the foundations. dig, hollow out, scoop out.

exceed *verb*
She exceeded the previous long jump record by six centimetres. beat, better, excel, go over, outdo, pass, surpass.

exceedingly *adverb*
The team played exceedingly well. amazingly, especially, exceptionally, extraordinarily, extremely, outstandingly, specially, unusually, very.

excel *verb*
She's a good all-round player, but she excels at tennis. do best, shine, stand out.

excellent *adjective*
She's fairly good at most games, but she's excellent at tennis. [*informal*] brilliant, exceptional, extraordinary, [*informal*] fabulous, [*informal*] fantastic, first-class, first-rate, [*informal*] great, impressive, [*informal*] incredible, magnificent, marvellous, outstanding, [*informal*] phenomenal, remarkable, [*informal*] sensational, [*informal*] superb, superlative, [*informal*] supreme, [*informal*] terrific, tremendous, unequalled, wonderful.
AN OPPOSITE IS bad.

except *preposition*
Everyone got a prize except me. apart from, but, excluding, with the exception of.

exception *noun*
to take exception to something *She took exception to what he said about her clothes.* be upset by, complain about, disapprove of, dislike, object to.

exceptional *adjective*
It is exceptional to have such cold weather in June. abnormal, amazing, extraordinary, odd, peculiar, phenomenal, rare, special, strange, surprising, uncommon, unexpected, unheard-of, unusual.
AN OPPOSITE IS normal.

excerpt *noun*
She recited an excerpt from the poem. extract, part, passage, section.
A short excerpt is a *quotation*.
The most interesting excerpts from something are the *highlights*.
Excerpts from a film are *clips*.

excess *noun*
If there is an excess of something so that it is hard to sell it, there is a *glut*.
When a business has an excess of income over its expenses, it has a *profit* or a *surplus*.

excessive *adjective*
1 *I think his enthusiasm for football is excessive.* exaggerated, extreme, fanatical.
2 *Mum prepared excessive amounts of food for the party.* extravagant, needless, superfluous, unnecessary, unreasonable, wasteful.

exchange *verb*
The shop will exchange faulty goods. change, replace.
To exchange goods for other goods without using money is to *barter*.
To exchange an old thing for part of the cost of a new one is to *trade it in*.
To exchange things with your friends is to *swap* or *swop* them.
To exchange players for other players in football, etc., is to *substitute* them.

excitable *adjective*
Horses can be very excitable before a race. agitated, edgy, jumpy, nervous, restless.
AN OPPOSITE IS calm.

excite *verb*
The prospect of going to America really excited her. arouse, electrify, rouse, stimulate, stir up, thrill.
AN OPPOSITE IS calm.

excited *adjective*
On Christmas Eve he was too excited to sleep. animated, eager, elated, enthusiastic, exuberant, lively, thrilled.
AN OPPOSITE IS calm.

excitement *noun*
1 *The crowd's excitement increased as the final whistle drew near.* agitation, delirium, eagerness, elation, enthusiasm, exuberance, passion.
2 *I could hardly bear the excitement!* drama, stimulation, suspense, tension, thrill.

exciting *adjective*
The last minutes of the match were the most exciting of all! dramatic, electrifying, eventful, gripping, rousing, sensational, stimulating, stirring, thrilling.
AN OPPOSITE IS boring.

exclaim *verb*
'Get out of my house!' she exclaimed. call, cry out, shout, yell.

exclamation *noun*
He gave an exclamation of surprise. cry, shout, yell.
When we discuss language, the formal word for an exclamation is *interjection*.
An impolite exclamation is an *oath* or *swear word*.

exclude *verb*
1 *Anyone who doesn't pay the subscription is excluded from the club.* ban, banish, bar, keep out, prohibit, reject, remove, shut out.
2 *She's excluded dairy products from her diet.* leave out, omit.
AN OPPOSITE IS include.

exclusive *adjective*
It's a very exclusive hotel. [*informal*] posh, private, select, snobbish.

excursion *noun*
We went on an excursion to the seaside. expedition, jaunt, journey, outing, trip.

excuse *noun*
He had no excuse for his behaviour. defence, explanation, justification, reason.

excuse *verb*
I am prepared to excuse your bad behaviour on this occasion. forgive, overlook, pardon.
AN OPPOSITE IS punish.
to be excused something *May I be excused swimming?* be exempt from, be let off, be released from.

execute *verb*
1 *In some countries, criminals may still be executed.* put to death.

SOME METHODS USED TO EXECUTE PEOPLE: behead or decapitate or guillotine, burn, crucify, electrocute, gas, hang, inject, poison, shoot, stone.
To execute someone unofficially without a proper trial is to *lynch* them.

2 *She executed a perfect somersault.* accomplish, carry out, complete, perform, produce.

exempt *adjective*
Old age pensioners are exempt from paying for their prescriptions. excused, let off, spared.

exercise *noun*
Exercise helps to keep you fit. activity, effort, exertion.

SOME FORMS OF EXERCISE: aerobics, circuit training, dancing, games, gymnastics, jogging, keep fit, PE or physical education, running, sport, step aerobics, swimming, walking, workout.
SEE ALSO **sport.**

exercise book *I wrote a few notes in my exercise book.* jotter, notebook, writing pad.
exercises *Piano exercises are important if you want to improve your playing.* practice, training.

exercise *verb*
1 *If you exercise regularly, it helps you to keep fit.* exert yourself, keep fit, train.
2 *I sometimes exercise our neighbour's dog.* take for a walk, take out, walk.
3 *You must exercise patience.* apply, display, employ, show, use.

exert *verb*
He exerted all his strength to lift the box. apply, employ, use.

exertion *noun*
The exertion made him red in the face. effort, hard work, labour, toil.

exhaust *noun*
The exhaust from cars damages the environment. emissions, fumes, gases, smoke.

exhaust *verb*
1 *The steep climb up the hill exhausted me.* tire, wear out.
2 *We exhausted our supply of food before we'd gone half way!* consume, finish, go through, [*informal*] polish off, use up.

exhausted *adjective*
After a hard race, we lay exhausted on the grass. [*informal*] all in, breathless, fatigued, gasping, panting, [*informal*] puffed out, tired, weary, worn out.

exhausting *adjective*
Digging the garden is exhausting work. demanding, difficult, gruelling, hard, laborious, strenuous, tiring.
AN OPPOSITE IS easy.

exhaustion *noun*
He was overcome by sheer exhaustion.
fatigue, tiredness, weakness,
weariness.

exhibit *verb*
1 *Her paintings were exhibited in galleries all over Europe and America.*
arrange, display, present, put up, set
up, show.
2 *He was exhibiting signs of anxiety.*
demonstrate, reveal, show off.
AN OPPOSITE IS hide.

exhibition *noun*
We went to see an exhibition of paintings by Picasso. display, show.

exile *verb*
As a result of the war, many people were exiled from their own country. banish,
deport, drive out, eject, expel, send
away.

exile *noun*
He returned to his country after 24 years of exile. banishment, deportation,
expulsion.
A person who has been exiled is a
refugee.

exist *verb*
1 *Some people claim that ghosts actually exist.* be real, occur.
2 *We can't exist without food.* continue,
endure, keep going, last, live, remain
alive, survive.

existence *noun*
1 *I don't believe in the existence of ghosts.* reality.
2 *Our existence depends on preserving our environment.* life, survival.

existing *adjective*
1 *Many animals have become extinct, so we must protect existing species.* living,
remaining, surviving.
2 *Next season, the existing rules will be replaced by new ones.* current, present.

exit *noun*
1 *I'll wait for you by the exit.* barrier,
door, doorway, gate, way out.
2 *We made a hurried exit.* departure.

exit *verb*
The actors exited from the left of the stage. depart, go out, leave, withdraw.

exotic *adjective*
She's travelled to many exotic places.
alien, different, exciting, foreign,
remote, romantic, strange, unfamiliar,
wonderful.
AN OPPOSITE IS familiar.

expand *verb*
Business is good, and they hope to expand it. build up, develop, enlarge,
extend, increase, make bigger.
To become larger is to ***grow*** or ***swell***.
To become wider is to ***broaden***,
thicken, or ***widen***.
To become longer is to ***extend***,
lengthen, or ***stretch***.
AN OPPOSITE IS contract or reduce.

expanse *noun*
The explorers crossed a large expanse of desert. area, stretch, tract.
An expanse of water or ice is a ***sheet***.

expect *verb*
1 *I expect that it will rain.* anticipate,
forecast, foresee, imagine, predict,
prophesy.
2 *He expects complete obedience from his troops.* ask for, count on, demand,
insist on, require, want.
3 *I expect he missed the bus.* assume,
believe, guess, imagine, presume,
suppose, think.

expedition *noun*
An expedition into unknown territory
is an ***exploration***.
An expedition to see or hunt wild
animals is a ***safari***.
An expedition to find something is a
quest.
An expedition to carry out a special
task is a ***mission***.
An expedition to worship at a holy
place is a ***pilgrimage***.
SEE ALSO **travel**.

expel *verb*
1 *A fan expels the stale air and fumes.*
force out, send out.
2 *He was expelled from school.* ban,
dismiss, remove, send away, throw out.
To expel someone from their home is to
eject or ***evict*** them.
To expel someone from their country is
to ***banish*** or ***exile*** them.
To expel evil spirits is to ***exorcise***
them.

expense noun
He was worried about the expense involved in running a car. charges, cost, expenditure, overheads.

expensive adjective
Houses are very expensive in this area. costly, dear.
AN OPPOSITE IS cheap.

experience noun
1 She's had a lot of experience in the catering business. involvement, participation, practice.
2 I had an unusual experience today. event, happening, incident, occurrence.
An exciting experience is an **adventure**.
A frightening or difficult experience is an **ordeal**.

experienced adjective
She's an experienced nurse and is used to dealing with emergencies. expert, knowledgeable, professional, qualified, skilled, specialized, trained.
AN OPPOSITE IS inexperienced.

experiment noun
We carried out a scientific experiment. test, trial.
A series of experiments is **research** or an **investigation**.

experiment verb
We experimented to see if our invention would work. do tests.
To experiment on or with something is to **test** it or **try it out**.

expert noun
He's an expert at chess. authority, genius, specialist, wizard.

expert adjective
You need an expert craftsman to mend these antiques. brilliant, capable, clever, competent, experienced, knowledgeable, professional, proficient, qualified, skilful, skilled, specialized, trained.
AN OPPOSITE IS amateur or unskilful.

expertise noun
I haven't got the expertise you need to mend a computer. ability, competence, know-how, knowledge, skill, training.

expire verb
1 The television licence expires next month. become invalid, come to an end, finish, run out.
2 The animal expired before the vet arrived. die, pass away.

explain verb
1 The solicitor explained the procedure carefully. clarify, describe, give an explanation of, make clear.
2 I can explain my behaviour. account for, excuse, give reasons for, justify, make excuses for.

explanation noun
1 He'd better have a good explanation for his behaviour. excuse, justification, reason.
2 He gave us a brief explanation of how the device worked. account, demonstration, description.

explode verb
1 The firework exploded with a bang. blow up, burst, go off, make an explosion, shatter.
2 The slightest movement might explode the bomb. detonate, set off.

exploit noun
The book describes his exploits as a fighter pilot in the war. adventure, deed, escapade, feat, venture.

exploit verb
1 My music teacher says I should exploit my talent. build on, [informal] cash in on, develop, make use of, profit by, take advantage of, use, utilize.
2 Some workers are exploited by their employers. impose on, misuse, oppress, [slang] rip off, take unfair advantage of, treat unfairly.

explore verb
1 The spacecraft will explore the solar system. probe, search, survey, travel through.
2 We must explore all the possibilities. analyse, examine, inspect, investigate, look into, research, scrutinize.

explosion noun
The explosion rattled the windows. bang, blast, detonation.
An explosion from a volcano is an **eruption**.

An explosion of laughter is an
outburst.
The sound of a gun going off is a
report.
The sudden loud noise of thunder is a
clap of thunder.

explosive *noun*

SOME EXPLOSIVES: cordite,
dynamite, gelignite, gunpowder,
[*trademark*] Semtex, TNT.

export *verb*
*The factory exports a lot of the cars it
makes.* sell abroad, send abroad, ship
overseas.
AN OPPOSITE IS import.

expose *verb*
1 *He yawned, exposing a set of white
teeth.* uncover.
2 *He kept his secret for years, until a
newspaper exposed the truth.* betray,
disclose, make known, publish, reveal.

express *verb*
*He's always quick to express his
opinions.* communicate, convey,
phrase, put into words, voice.
To express yourself by word of mouth is
to **speak**.
To express yourself on paper is to
write.
To express your feelings is to **give vent**
to them.
SEE ALSO **talk** *verb*.

expression *noun*
1 *The English language contains many
colloquial expressions.* phrase, saying,
term, wording.
An expression that people use too
much is a **cliché**.
2 *Did you see her expression when I told
her the news?* appearance,
countenance, face, look.

SOME EXPRESSIONS YOU SEE ON
PEOPLE'S FACES: beam, frown, glare,
glower, grimace, grin, laugh, leer,
long face, poker-face, pout, scowl,
smile, smirk, sneer, wince, yawn.

3 *My sister plays the piano with great
expression.* emotion, feeling, sympathy,
understanding.

expressive *adjective*
1 *She gave me an expressive look.*
meaningful, revealing, significant,
telling.
2 *An actor needs to have an expressive
voice.* eloquent, lively, varied.
AN OPPOSITE IS expressionless.

exquisite *adjective*
*There was some exquisite embroidery
on the wedding dress.* beautiful, dainty,
delicate, intricate.

extend *verb*
1 *Delays on the motorway extended our
journey by an hour.* delay, draw out,
lengthen, make longer, prolong.
AN OPPOSITE IS shorten.
2 *He plans to extend his business.* add
to, build up, develop, enlarge, expand,
increase, widen the scope of.
AN OPPOSITE IS reduce.
3 *He sat back and extended his legs.*
hold out, put out, reach out, stick out,
stretch out.
4 *We extended a warm welcome to the
visitors.* give, offer.

extension *noun*
*They are building an extension to the
runway.* addition, continuation.

extensive *adjective*
*The palace gardens cover an extensive
area.* big, broad, large, spread out,
wide.
AN OPPOSITE IS small.

extent *noun*
1 *The map shows the extent of the
estate.* area, breadth, dimensions,
expanse, length, limits, measurement,
spread.
2 *After the storm we went out to see the
extent of the damage.* amount, degree,
level, magnitude, range, scope, size.

exterior *noun*
He painted the exterior of his house.
outside.
AN OPPOSITE IS interior.

exterminate *verb*
*They used poison to exterminate the
rats.* annihilate, destroy, get rid of, kill,
wipe out.

external *adjective*
> We liked the external appearance of the house, but inside it was rather gloomy. exterior, outer, outside.
> AN OPPOSITE IS internal.

extinct *adjective*
> An extinct species is one that has **died out** or **vanished**.
> An extinct volcano is an **inactive** volcano.

extinguish *verb*
> We managed to extinguish the fire before the fire engine arrived. put out, quench, smother.
> AN OPPOSITE IS ignite.

extra *adjective*
> 1 There is an extra charge for taking your bike on the train. added, additional, excess, further, increased, supplementary.
> 2 There is extra food in the kitchen if we need it. more, reserve, spare, surplus.

extract *noun*
> I read an extract from the book in a magazine. excerpt, part, passage, section.
> A short extract is a **quotation**.
> Specially interesting extracts from something are the **highlights**.
> An extract from a newspaper is a **cutting**.
> An extract from a film is a **clip**.

extract *verb*
> 1 The dentist decided to extract my tooth. draw out, pull out, remove, take out, [informal] whip out, withdraw.
> 2 She extracted passages from the book for the students to translate. derive, gather, get, obtain, quote, select.

extraordinary *adjective*
> I can't explain the extraordinary things that happened. abnormal, amazing, astonishing, curious, exceptional, [informal] fantastic, incredible, marvellous, miraculous, mysterious, odd, outstanding, peculiar, phenomenal, queer, rare, remarkable, special, strange, surprising, unbelievable, unheard of, unique, unusual, weird, wonderful.
> AN OPPOSITE IS ordinary.

extravagant *adjective*
> He held a large, extravagant party for all his friends. expensive, lavish, uneconomical, wasteful.
> AN OPPOSITE IS economical.

extreme *adjective*
> 1 They suffered dreadfully in the extreme cold. acute, excessive, great, intense, severe.
> 2 She lives on the extreme edge of the town. farthest, furthest.

exuberant *adjective*
> After our team's victory, we were in an exuberant mood. animated, boisterous, bubbly, cheerful, eager, elated, energetic, enthusiastic, excited, exultant, high-spirited, lively, sprightly, vivacious.
> AN OPPOSITE IS apathetic.

exultant *adjective*
> The fans were exultant after their team's victory. delighted, [slang] over the moon, pleased, thrilled.
> SEE ALSO **exuberant**.

eye *noun*

> PARTS OF YOUR EYE: cornea, eyeball, eyebrow, eyelash, eyelid, iris, lens, pupil, retina.
>
> SOME PROBLEMS WITH EYESIGHT: astigmatism, long-sightedness, myopia or short-sightedness.
>
> SOME DISEASES OF THE EYE: cataract, glaucoma.
> A person who tests your eyesight is an **optician**.
> A specialist in eye diseases is an **oculist**.
> An adjective describing things connected with the eyes is **optical**.
> Instruments you look through are **optical instruments**.

eye *verb*
> The dog eyed the sausages hungrily. contemplate, gaze at, look at, regard, stare at, watch.

eyewitness *noun*
> An eyewitness described the accident. bystander, observer, onlooker, spectator, witness.

Ff

fabric *noun*
*Mum bought some fabric to make
curtains.* cloth, material, stuff.
A plural word is *textiles*.
FOR VARIOUS KINDS OF FABRIC, SEE
cloth.

fabulous *adjective*
1 [*informal*] *We had a fabulous time at
the party.* [*informal*] brilliant,
excellent, [*informal*] fantastic, first-
class, marvellous, outstanding,
[*informal*] smashing, superb,
tremendous, wonderful.
2 *Dragons are fabulous creatures.*
fictitious, imaginary, legendary,
mythical.

face *noun*
1 *You could tell by her face that she had
bad news.* countenance, expression,
features, look.
SEE ALSO **expression**.
2 *Put the cards face down.* front.
3 *A cube has six faces.* side, surface.

face *verb*
1 *Stand and face your partner.* be
opposite to, look towards.
2 *I had to face all my problems on my
own.* confront, cope with, encounter,
face up to, meet, stand up to, tackle.
AN OPPOSITE IS avoid.

facetious *adjective*
Don't make facetious remarks. cheeky,
flippant.

facility *noun*
1 *The crèche is a useful facility for busy
parents.* amenity, convenience,
resource, service.
2 *The facility with which he did the job
surprised me.* ease, skill.

fact *noun*
*It's a fact that cuckoos lay their eggs in
other birds' nests.* certainty, reality,
truth.
AN OPPOSITE IS fiction.

the facts *The police want to know all
the facts.* circumstances, details,
information, particulars.
Facts which are useful in trying to
prove something are *evidence*.
Facts expressed as numbers are
statistics.
Facts which you put into a computer
are *data*.

factor *noun*
*Hard work was an important factor in
her success.* aspect, component,
element, influence, ingredient.

factory *noun*

> PLACES WHERE THINGS ARE
> MANUFACTURED: assembly line,
> forge, foundry, manufacturing plant,
> mill, production line, refinery,
> workshop.

factual *adjective*
1 *The documentary provides a factual
account of what actually happened.*
accurate, authentic, correct, exact,
genuine, objective, precise, reliable,
true.
AN OPPOSITE IS false.
2 *The film is based on factual
occurrences.* real, real life, true.
A film or story based on a person's life
is *biographical*.
A film or story based on history is
historical.
A film telling you about real events is a
documentary.
AN OPPOSITE IS fictional.

fade *verb*
1 *Sunlight has faded the curtains.*
bleach, make paler, whiten.
AN OPPOSITE IS brighten.
2 *After a couple of days, the flowers
faded.* droop, flag, shrivel, wilt, wither.
AN OPPOSITE IS flourish.
3 *Gradually, the light began to fade.*
decline, diminish, disappear, dwindle,
fail, melt away, vanish, wane, weaken.
AN OPPOSITE IS increase.

fail *verb*
1 *Peace talks between the two sides
have failed.* be unsuccessful, come to
an end, fall through, [*informal*] flop,
founder, meet with disaster.

AN OPPOSITE IS succeed.
2 *The plane's engines failed just after it had taken off.* break down, cut out, give up, stop working.
3 *The light began to fail.* decline, diminish, disappear, dwindle, fade, get worse, vanish, wane, weaken.
AN OPPOSITE IS improve.
4 *She failed to keep her appointment.* forget, neglect, omit.
AN OPPOSITE IS remember.

failing *noun*
She loved him, despite his failings. bad habit, defect, fault, imperfection, shortcoming, weakness.

failure *noun*
1 *There was a failure in the computer system.* breakdown, collapse, crash, stoppage.
2 *Our attempt to beat the record ended in failure.* defeat, disappointment, disaster, [*informal*] a flop, [*slang*] a wash-out.
AN OPPOSITE IS success.

faint *adjective*
1 *The picture was faint and I couldn't make out the details.* blurred, dim, faded, hazy, indistinct, misty, pale, shadowy, unclear, vague.
AN OPPOSITE IS clear.
2 *I noticed a faint smell of roses.* delicate, slight.
AN OPPOSITE IS strong.
3 *I heard a faint cry for help.* distant, hushed, low, muffled, muted, soft, thin, weak.
AN OPPOSITE IS loud.
4 *He was so hungry that he felt faint.* dizzy, exhausted, feeble, giddy, light-headed, unsteady, weak.

faint *verb*
He thought he was going to faint. become unconscious, collapse, [*informal*] flake out, pass out, [*old use*] swoon.

faint-hearted *adjective*
This is not time to be faint-hearted. apprehensive, fearful, nervous, timid, unadventurous.
AN OPPOSITE IS bold.

fair *adjective*
1 *I think the referee made a fair decision.* disinterested, fair-minded, honest, honourable, impartial, just, proper, right, unbiased, unprejudiced.
AN OPPOSITE IS unfair.
2 *The twins both have fair hair.* blond or blonde, golden, light, yellow.
AN OPPOSITE IS dark.
3 *Her work is fair, but not outstanding.* acceptable, adequate, average, moderate, passable, reasonable, respectable, satisfactory, tolerable.
4 *The forecast says the weather will be fair today.* bright, clear, cloudless, dry, favourable, fine, pleasant, sunny.

fair *noun*

PLACES AND EVENTS WITH OUTDOOR AMUSEMENTS: amusement park, carnival, fairground or funfair, gala, theme park.

SOME AMUSEMENTS YOU FIND IN FAIRS: big dipper, big wheel, bouncy castle, bumper cars or dodgems, coconut shy, fortune-teller, ghost train, helter-skelter, merry-go-round, roller coaster, roundabout, shooting gallery, sideshow, slot-machine, stalls, swingboat, switchback.

OTHER KINDS OF FAIR WHERE THINGS ARE ON EXHIBITION OR FOR SALE: antiques fair, bazaar, Christmas fair, craft fair, market.

fairly *adverb*
1 *We were not treated fairly.* honestly, impartially, justly, properly.
2 *I saw a fairly good film on TV last night.* moderately, [*informal*] pretty, quite, rather, reasonably, somewhat, tolerably, up to a point.

fairy *noun*
FOR OTHER LEGENDARY CREATURES, SEE **legendary**.

faith noun
1 *I have the utmost faith in you.* belief, confidence, trust.
AN OPPOSITE IS doubt.
2 *The school is attended by pupils of many different faiths.* creed, doctrine, religion.

faithful adjective
1 *His dog is his faithful friend.* close, constant, dependable, devoted, firm, loyal, reliable, trustworthy.
AN OPPOSITE IS unfaithful.
2 *It's a faithful reproduction of the original painting.* accurate, exact, precise, true.

fake noun
I thought the painting might be valuable, but it was a fake. copy, forgery, imitation, replica, reproduction.
An event which fakes a real event is a **hoax**, or **sham**, or **simulation**.
A person who pretends to be another person is an ***impostor***.

fake verb
He tried to fake a posh accent. copy, imitate, pretend, put on, reproduce, simulate.
To fake someone's signature is to ***forge*** it.

fall verb
The verb *to fall* can be used in many ways. These are some of the ways we use it, and some of the synonyms we could use
1 *He fell off the wall.* crash down, pitch, topple, tumble.
2 *I fell into the water.* drop, plunge, sink.
3 *The tide began to fall.* ebb, go down, subside.
4 *The water-level in the reservoir fell during the summer.* become lower, decline, decrease, diminish, dwindle, lessen.
5 *Prices are likely to fall after Christmas.* be reduced, come down, slump.
6 *After a long siege, the town fell to the enemy.* give in, surrender.
7 *Millions of soldiers fell in the war.* die.

8 *We arrived at the hotel as night was falling.* come, happen, occur.
9 *His eyes fell on an advertisement in the paper.* be directed at, come to rest on.
to fall in *We were afraid the roof would fall in.* cave in, collapse.
to fall out *Those two fall out over the slightest little thing!* argue, differ, disagree, quarrel, squabble.
to fall through *Our plans for a picnic fell through because of the rain.* be unsuccessful, come to nothing, fail, founder.

fall noun
1 *He had a fall and cut his knee.* tumble.
2 *I noticed a fall in the water-level.* drop, lowering.
3 *There has been a fall in the price of vegetables.* decline, decrease, reduction.
4 *The fall of the town led to the signing of a peace treaty.* defeat, surrender.

fallacy noun
It is a fallacy to think that money always makes people happy. error, falsehood, mistake.

false adjective
1 *The police charged him with giving false information.* deceptive, fallacious, fictitious, inaccurate, incorrect, invented, misleading, mistaken, untrue, wrong.
AN OPPOSITE IS correct.
2 *He was arrested for travelling with a false passport.* bogus, counterfeit, fake.
AN OPPOSITE IS authentic.
3 *She's wearing false eyelashes.* artificial, imitation.
AN OPPOSITE IS real.
4 *He turned out to be a false friend.* deceitful, dishonest, disloyal, treacherous, unfaithful, unreliable, untrustworthy.
AN OPPOSITE IS trustworthy.

falsehood noun
1 *She accused me of falsehood.* deceit, dishonesty.
2 *He accused them of spreading falsehoods about him.* fib, lie.

falter *verb*
1 *She didn't falter as she walked up to the lion's cage.* flinch, hesitate, hold back, lose confidence, pause, stumble, waver.
To falter in your speech is to **stammer** or **stutter**.
2 *My courage began to falter.* become weaker, flag, wane, weaken.

fame *noun*
The film brought him international fame. distinction, eminence, glory, honour, importance, prestige, prominence, renown.

familiar *adjective*
1 *Starlings are a familiar sight in our garden.* accustomed, common, customary, everyday, frequent, mundane, normal, ordinary, regular, routine, usual, well known.
AN OPPOSITE IS rare.
2 *I thought he was a bit too familiar with me.* chatty, close, confidential, friendly, informal, intimate, relaxed.
AN OPPOSITE IS formal or unfriendly.
to be familiar with something *Are you familiar with this music?* be acquainted with, be aware of, be an expert in, know.

family *noun*
My family lives in Scotland. relations, relatives.

Your family is your **relations** or **relatives**.
An old-fashioned term for your family is your **kin**.

MEMBERS OF A FAMILY MAY INCLUDE: adopted child, aunt, brother, child, cousin, daughter, father, foster-child, foster-parent, grandchild, grandparent, guardian, husband, mother, nephew, niece, parent, sister, son, step-child, step-parent, uncle, ward, wife.
The official term for your closest relative is **next of kin**.
A single stage in a family is a **generation**.
The line of ancestors from which a family is descended is its **ancestry** or **pedigree**. ➡

A diagram showing how people in your family are related is a **family tree** or **genealogy**.
A powerful family which goes on from generation to generation is a **dynasty**.
A number of families with the same ancestor, especially in Scotland, is a **clan**.
In certain societies, a group of families living together is a **tribe**.
The children in a family are the **offspring**.
A family of young birds is a **brood**.
A family of puppies, etc., is a **litter**.

famine *noun*
The drought caused widespread famine. hunger, malnutrition, scarcity, shortage, starvation, want.
AN OPPOSITE IS plenty.

famished *adjective*
What's for dinner? I'm famished! hungry, ravenous, [*informal*] starving.
If you are rather hungry, you are **peckish**.

famous *adjective*
He's one of the world's most famous actors. celebrated, distinguished, eminent, notable, outstanding, prominent, renowned, well known.
AN OPPOSITE IS unknown.

fan *noun*
1 *I switched on the fan in the kitchen.* blower, extractor fan, ventilator.
2 *I used to be a Manchester United fan.* admirer, devotee, enthusiast, follower, supporter.

fanatic *noun*
My brother is a football fanatic. addict, devotee, enthusiast, [*informal*] freak.

fanatical *adjective*
He is a fanatical supporter of our local team. enthusiastic, extreme, fervent, over-enthusiastic, passionate, rabid, zealous.
AN OPPOSITE IS moderate.

fanciful *adjective*
His story included some fanciful ideas about fairies and goblins. fantastic, fictitious, imaginary, unrealistic.
AN OPPOSITE IS realistic.

fancy *adjective*
The furniture was very fancy.
decorative, elaborate, ornamental,
pretty.
AN OPPOSITE IS plain.

fancy *verb*
1 *What do you fancy to eat?* feel like,
long for, prefer, want, wish for.
2 *I fancied I heard a noise downstairs.*
imagine, think.

fantastic *adjective*
1 *He told some fantastic story about
little green men.* amazing,
extraordinary, fanciful, far-fetched,
incredible, strange, unbelievable,
unlikely, unrealistic, weird.
AN OPPOSITE IS realistic.
2 [*informal*] *We had a fantastic time.*
[*informal*] brilliant, excellent,
[*informal*] fabulous, first-class,
marvellous, outstanding, [*informal*]
smashing, superb, tremendous,
wonderful.

fantasy *noun*
*Those ideas about becoming rich and
famous are all his fantasy.* daydream,
delusion, dream, fancy, hallucination,
vision.

far *adjective*
1 *She lives in the far north.* distant,
faraway, remote.
2 *The ferry took us to the far side of the
river.* opposite, other.
AN OPPOSITE IS near.

farcical *adjective*
The whole idea is farcical. absurd,
laughable, ludicrous, ridiculous.

fare *noun*
*How much is the fare on the train to
London?* charge, cost, payment, price.

far-fetched *adjective*
*His explanations sounded a bit far-
fetched to me.* amazing, extraordinary,
fanciful, fantastic, incredible, strange,
unbelievable, unlikely, unrealistic.
AN OPPOSITE IS likely.

farm *noun*

KINDS OF FARM: arable farm, cattle
farm, dairy farm, fish farm, fruit
farm, hill farm, mixed farm, pig
farm, poultry farm, stud farm. ➡

The formal word for farming is
agriculture.
A farm which uses no artificial
fertilizers or chemicals is an
organic farm.
A very small farm is a
smallholding.
A small farm growing fruit and
vegetables is a **market garden**.
A small farm in Scotland is a **croft**.
A large cattle farm in America is a
ranch.

FARM BUILDINGS: barn, battery
unit, byre or cowshed, dairy, Dutch
barn, farmhouse, granary, milking
parlour, outhouse, pigsty, stable.

OTHER PARTS OF A FARM: barnyard
or farmyard, cattle pen, fallow or set-
aside land, fields, haystack, meadow,
paddock, pasture, rick, sheep fold,
silo.

ITEMS OF FARM EQUIPMENT: baler,
combine harvester, cultivator, drill,
harrow, harvester, irrigation system,
manure spreader, mower, planter,
plough, tedder, tractor, trailer.

PEOPLE WHO WORK ON A FARM:
agriculturalist, agricultural worker,
[*old use*] dairymaid, farm labourer,
farm manager, ploughman,
shepherd, stockbreeder, tractor
driver.

ACTIVITIES THAT TAKE PLACE ON A
FARM: breeding animals, cultivating
or tilling the land, fertilizing the
land, growing crops, harvesting,
irrigation, ploughing, reaping,
rearing livestock, sowing.

CROPS GROWN ON FARMS: barley,
cereals or corn, fodder, fruit, maize,
oats, potatoes, rape, rye, sugar beet,
sweet corn, vegetables, wheat.

SOME FARM ANIMALS: bull, bullock,
chicken or hen, cow, duck, goat,
goose, horse, pig, sheep, turkey.
Birds kept on a farm are **poultry**.
Animals kept for milk or beef are
cattle.
Farm animals in general are
livestock.

fascinate *verb*
I was fascinated by his stories. attract,
bewitch, captivate, charm, delight,
enchant, entrance, interest, please.
AN OPPOSITE IS bore.

fashion *noun*
1 *He behaved in a strange fashion.*
manner, way.
2 *She always dresses according to the
latest fashion.* craze, fad, look, style,
taste, trend.

fashion *verb*
*We fashioned the clay into animal
figures.* form, make, mould, shape.

fashionable *adjective*
She always wears fashionable clothes.
chic, contemporary, current, elegant,
the latest, modern, smart,
sophisticated, stylish, tasteful,
[*informal*] trendy, up-to-date.
AN OPPOSITE IS unfashionable.

fast *adjective*
1 *He made a fast exit when he saw me
coming.* brisk, hasty, headlong, high-
speed, hurried, lively, quick, rapid,
smart, speedy, swift, unhesitating.
Something which goes faster than
sound is **supersonic**.
AN OPPOSITE IS slow.
2 *Make the rope fast.* firm, secure,
tight.
AN OPPOSITE IS loose.
3 *Before you put clothes in the washing
machine, make sure the colours are
fast.* indelible, permanent.

fast *adverb*
1 *He was driving too fast.* briskly,
quickly, rapidly, swiftly.
2 *The boat was stuck fast on the rocks.*
firmly, tightly.

fast *verb*
The monks used to fast on holy days. go
hungry, go without food.

fasten *verb*
He fastened the strap to the camera.
attach, connect, fix, join, link, secure.

To fasten something with rope, etc.,
is to **bind**, **hitch**, **knot**, **lash**, or **tie**
it.
To fasten something with adhesive is
to **glue**, **paste**, or **stick** it. ➡

To fasten a door, you **bolt**, **lock**, or
padlock it.
To fasten a caravan or railway
wagon to something, you **couple**
them, or **hitch** them up.
To fasten the front of your coat, etc.,
you **button** it, **zip** it, or **do it up**.
To fasten an envelope, you **seal** it or
stick it down.
To fasten pieces of paper together,
you **clip**, **pin**, or **staple** them.
To fasten pieces of wood together,
you **nail** or **screw** them.
To fasten pieces of metal together,
you **rivet**, **solder**, or **weld** them.
To secure a boat is to **anchor** or
moor it.
To secure an animal is to **tether** it.

THINGS YOU CAN USE FOR
FASTENING VARIOUS THINGS:
adhesive, anchor, bolt, buckle,
button, catch, chain, clamp, clasp,
clip, drawing pin, glue, gum, hook,
knot, lace, latch, lock, nail, padlock,
painter, paste, peg, pin, rivet, rope,
safety pin, screw, seal, [*trademark*]
Sellotape, solder, staple, strap,
string, tack, tape, tether, tie,
[*trademark*] Velcro, wedge, zip.

fastener, fastening *nouns*
FOR THINGS YOU CAN USE AS
FASTENINGS, SEE **fasten**.

fat *adjective*
1 *You'll get fat if you eat so much
chocolate!* chubby, dumpy, flabby, gross,
heavy, overweight, plump, podgy,
portly, round, stout.
Note that synonyms for *fat* are often
insulting
2 *She was reading a fat book.* bulky,
thick, weighty.
AN OPPOSITE IS thin.

fat *noun*

KINDS OF FAT USED IN COOKING:
butter, dripping, ghee, lard,
margarine, olive oil, suet, various
vegetable oils.
Different kinds of fat are **saturated
fats** and **polyunsaturated fats**.

fatal *adjective*
  1 *If it had been an inch lower, the wound would have been fatal.* deadly, lethal, mortal.
  A fatal illness is an *incurable* or *terminal* illness.
  2 *He made a fatal mistake half way through the match.* calamitous, disastrous, dreadful.

fatality *noun*
  Did the accident result in fatalities? casualty, death, loss.

fate *noun*
  1 *Fate was kind to her.* chance, destiny, fortune, luck.
  2 *He met a terrible fate.* death, end.

fatigue *noun*
  By the end of the journey, I was overcome with fatigue. exhaustion, tiredness, weakness, weariness.

fatigued *adjective*
  We were all fatigued by the time we got home. [*informal*] all in, exhausted, tired, weary, worn out.

fatty *adjective*
  I don't like fatty food. fat, greasy, oily.

fault *noun*
  1 *There's a fault in the loudspeakers.* defect, flaw, weakness.
  2 *I'm really sorry about the confusion—it's all my fault.* responsibility.

faultless *adjective*
  It was a faultless piece of work. flawless, ideal, perfect.
  AN OPPOSITE IS imperfect.

faulty *adjective*
  1 *The stereo was faulty, so Dad took it back to the shop.* broken, damaged, defective, out of order, unusable.
  2 *She said that my argument was faulty.* flawed, illogical, inaccurate, incorrect, invalid.
  AN OPPOSITE IS perfect.

favour *noun*
  1 *He did me a favour.* courtesy, good deed, good turn, kindness, service.
  2 *They looked on him with favour.* approval, friendliness, goodwill.

3 *We complained that the referee showed favour towards the other side.* bias, favouritism, preference, prejudice.
  to be in favour of something *I didn't expect you to be in favour of fox hunting.* approve of, like, support.

favour *verb*
  1 *I favour our original plan.* advocate, approve of, back, be in sympathy with, choose, [*informal*] fancy, [*informal*] go for, like, opt for, prefer.
  AN OPPOSITE IS oppose.
  2 *In the second half, the strong wind favoured our team.* aid, be advantageous to, help.
  AN OPPOSITE IS hinder.

favourable *adjective*
  1 *The weather conditions were very favourable.* advantageous, helpful.
  AN OPPOSITE IS unfavourable.
  2 *The film received favourable reviews.* agreeable, approving, complimentary, encouraging, friendly, generous, kind, positive, reassuring.
  AN OPPOSITE IS critical or hostile.

favourite *adjective*
  What is your favourite book? best-loved, dearest, preferred, top.

favouritism *noun*
  A referee must not show favouritism. bias, one-sidedness, prejudice.

fear *noun*
  She huddled in the corner, trembling with fear. alarm, anxiety, apprehension, dread, fright, horror, panic, terror, timidity, uneasiness, worry.

A formal word for a special type of fear is *phobia*.
A fear of open spaces is *agoraphobia*.
A fear of spiders is *arachnophobia*.
A fear of enclosed spaces is *claustrophobia*.
A fear or dislike of foreigners is *xenophobia*.

AN OPPOSITE IS courage.

fear *verb*
  What do you fear most? be afraid or frightened of, dread, worry about.

fearful *adjective*
   1 *There was a fearful look in his face.*
   afraid, anxious, apprehensive,
   frightened, nervous, scared, terrified,
   timid.
   AN OPPOSITE IS brave.
   2 *The erupting volcano was a fearful
   sight.* dreadful, fearsome, frightening,
   horrifying, intimidating, [*informal*]
   scary, terrifying.
   3 [*informal*] *Your friends made a
   fearful mess in the kitchen.* awful,
   frightful, horrid, nasty, unpleasant,
   upsetting.

fearless *adjective*
   *The fearless explorers pressed on into
   the unknown.* brave, courageous,
   daring, heroic, intrepid, plucky,
   valiant.
   AN OPPOSITE IS cowardly.

fearsome *adjective*
   *The tiger yawned, revealing a fearsome
   set of teeth.* dreadful, fearful,
   frightening, horrifying, intimidating,
   [*informal*] scary, terrifying.

feasible *adjective*
   1 *Is it feasible to get to London and
   back before teatime?* possible,
   practicable, practical, realistic,
   workable.
   AN OPPOSITE IS impractical.
   2 *He gave a feasible excuse, but I don't
   know whether to believe it.* credible,
   likely, reasonable.
   AN OPPOSITE IS incredible.

feast *noun*
   *The king held a great feast to celebrate
   his coronation.* banquet, dinner.
   SEE ALSO **meal**.

feat *noun*
   *The trapeze artists performed many
   daring feats.* achievement, act, action,
   deed, exploit, performance.

feather *noun*
   A large feather is a ***plume***.
   All the feathers on a bird are its
   plumage.
   Soft, fluffy feathers are ***down***.
   A feather used as a pen is a ***quill***.

feathery *adjective*
   The duvet is full of feathery stuff. fluffy,
   light, soft.

feature *noun*
   1 *The crime had several unusual
   features.* aspect, characteristic, detail,
   peculiarity, point.
   A person's features are their ***face***.
   2 *There was a feature about our school
   in the local paper last week.* article,
   item, piece, report, story.

feature *verb*
   1 *The film features a brilliant new
   actor.* give prominence to, highlight,
   star.
   2 *A brilliant new actor features in this
   film.* appear, figure, star, take part.

fee *noun*
   *If you want to join, there's an annual
   membership fee of £10.* charge, cost,
   payment, price.
   A fee to use a private road or bridge is
   a ***toll***.

feeble *adjective*
   1 *I still feel feeble after my illness.*
   delicate, exhausted, faint, frail,
   listless, poorly, puny, sickly, useless,
   weak, weary, weedy.
   AN OPPOSITE IS strong.
   2 *I made a feeble attempt to stop the
   ball.* hesitant, indecisive, ineffectual.
   AN OPPOSITE IS decisive.
   3 *Do you expect me to believe that feeble
   excuse?* flimsy, lame, poor, tame,
   unconvincing, weak.
   AN OPPOSITE IS convincing.

feed *verb*
   It costs a lot to feed a family. cater for,
   give food to, nourish, provide for.
   to feed on *Sheep feed on grass.*
   consume, eat.

feel *verb*
   1 *I let the baby feel the cat's warm fur.*
   caress, stroke, touch.
   2 *When the light went out, I had to feel
   my way to the door.* fumble, grope.
   3 *It feels cold today.* appear, seem.
   4 *Old people tend to feel the cold.* be
   aware of, be conscious of, experience,
   notice, suffer from.
   5 *I feel that it's time to go home.* believe,
   consider, think.

feeling *noun*
1 *She lost the feeling in her right hand.* sensation, sense of touch, sensitivity.
2 *Cruelty to animals arouses strong feelings.* emotion, passion, sentiment.
3 *My sister has a feeling for this kind of music.* fondness, sympathy, understanding (of).
4 *I have a feeling that something is wrong.* belief, hunch, idea, impression, instinct, intuition, notion, thought.
5 *There was a good feeling at the party.* atmosphere, mood.

female *adjective*
FOR FEMALE HUMAN BEINGS, SEE **woman**.
FOR FEMALE ANIMALS, SEE **animal**.
AN OPPOSITE IS male.

feminine *adjective*
Her style of dress is very feminine. AN OPPOSITE IS masculine.

fence *noun*

THINGS USED TO SURROUND A PIECE OF LAND: electric fence, fencing, hedge, paling, palisade, railing, stockade, wall, wire fence.

THINGS SET UP TO BLOCK THE WAY: barricade, barrier, hurdle, obstacle.

fence *verb*
The farmyard was fenced with a thorn hedge. encircle, enclose, surround.
to fence something in *The animals are fenced in at night.* confine, coop up, wall in.

fend *verb*
to fend for yourself *It's time you learned to fend for yourself!* care for, look after, take care of.
to fend someone or **something off** *He raised his arm to fend off the blow.* drive away, fight off, hold off, push away, repel, ward off.

ferment *verb*
Dad left his home-made wine to ferment in a glass jar. bubble, fizz, foam, seethe.

ferment *noun*
The country was in a state of ferment. agitation, commotion, confusion, excitement, tumult, turbulence, turmoil, unrest, upheaval.

ferocious *adjective*
The ferocious dog made me very nervous. dangerous, fearsome, fierce, savage, vicious, violent, wild.
AN OPPOSITE IS tame.

ferry *verb*
The lifeboat ferried passengers to safety. carry, convey, ship, take, transfer, transport.

fertile *adjective*
The surrounding countryside was green and fertile. flourishing, fruitful, productive.
AN OPPOSITE IS barren or sterile.

fertilize *verb*
If you want good crops, you must fertilize the soil. cultivate, enrich, feed, manure.

THINGS USED TO FERTILIZE THE SOIL: chemical fertilizer, compost, dung or manure, mulch, organic fertilizer.

fervent *adjective*
She's a fervent supporter of the local team. avid, committed, enthusiastic, fanatical, keen, passionate, vigorous, zealous.
AN OPPOSITE IS apathetic.

festival *noun*
The town holds a festival every summer. carnival, celebration, fair, feast, fête, gala, jamboree.
A celebration of a special anniversary is a *jubilee*.

festive *adjective*
The opening of the new community centre was a festive occasion. cheerful, happy, jolly, jovial, joyful, joyous, light-hearted, merry.
AN OPPOSITE IS gloomy.

fetch *verb*
1 *I fetched the shopping from the car.*
bring, carry, collect, convey, get, obtain,
pick up, retrieve, transfer, transport.
2 *If we sell our car, how much will it
fetch?* be sold for, bring in, earn, go for,
make, raise, sell for.

feud *noun*
*The feud between the gangs resulted in
violence.* antagonism, conflict, dispute,
enmity, fighting, hostility, quarrel,
rivalry, strife.

feverish *adjective*
1 *I had a feverish cold.*
When you are feverish you are **hot** and
shivery.
With a bad fever you may become
delirious.
2 *There was feverish activity to get the
hall ready before everyone arrived.*
agitated, busy, excited, frantic,
frenzied, hectic, hurried, impatient,
restless.

few *adjective*
*Yesterday was one of the few times I
have been absent from school.*
infrequent, rare, uncommon.
AN OPPOSITE IS many.

fibre *noun*
*Cloth consists of many fibres woven
together.* filament, hair, strand, thread.

fickle *adjective*
*His supporters turned out to be very
fickle.* changeable, disloyal, erratic,
inconsistent, unfaithful, unpredictable,
unreliable.
AN OPPOSITE IS loyal.

fiction *noun*
1 *I enjoy reading fiction.*
FOR VARIOUS KINDS OF LITERATURE,
SEE **writing**.
2 *Her account of what happened was a
fiction from start to finish.* fantasy,
invention, lie.
AN OPPOSITE IS fact.

fictional *adjective*
I enjoy fictional writing best. creative,
imaginative.
AN OPPOSITE IS factual.

fictitious *adjective*
1 *Peter Pan is a fictitious character.*
imaginary, invented, made-up, non-
existent, unreal.
AN OPPOSITE IS real.
2 *He gave the police a fictitious name.*
assumed, bogus, fake, false,
fraudulent.
AN OPPOSITE IS genuine.

fiddle *verb*
1 *Don't fiddle with the knobs on the TV.*
fidget, meddle, mess about, play about,
tamper, twiddle.
2 *[informal] He tried to fiddle his
expenses.*
To fiddle something is to **be dishonest**
about it, or to **cheat** or **swindle**
someone.

fiddling *adjective*
*I don't want to go into a lot of fiddling
details.* insignificant, minor, petty,
small, tedious, trivial, unimportant.
AN OPPOSITE IS important.

fiddly *adjective*
Mending this torch is a fiddly job.
awkward, complicated, intricate,
involved.
AN OPPOSITE IS straightforward.

fidelity *noun*
*The dog displayed amazing fidelity to
its owner.* devotion, faithfulness,
loyalty.

fidget *verb*
I begin to fidget when I'm bored. be
restless, fiddle about, mess about,
move restlessly, play about.

fidgety *adjective*
*After waiting an hour, we began to get
fidgety.* agitated, impatient, restless.
AN OPPOSITE IS calm.

field *noun*
1 *Cattle were grazing in the field.*
meadow, pasture.
A small field for horses is a **paddock**.
An area of grass in a village is a **green**.
2 *The field is too wet for games today.*
ground, pitch, playing field, recreation
ground.
3 *Electronics is not my field.* area of
study, special interest, speciality,
special subject.

fiendish *adjective*
The tyrant used fiendish methods to gain power. cruel, devilish, diabolical, evil, hellish, infernal, savage, wicked.
AN OPPOSITE IS angelic.

fierce *adjective*
1 *The travellers were killed in a fierce attack by armed bandits.* brutal, cruel, ferocious, fiendish, merciless, murderous, pitiless, ruthless, sadistic, savage, vicious, violent, wild.
2 *We played against fierce opposition last Saturday.* aggressive, competitive, eager, keen, passionate, relentless, strong.
3 *We walked out into the fierce heat of the sun.* blazing, intense, raging.

fiery *adjective*
1 *We could feel the fiery heat of the furnace.* blazing, burning, fierce, flaming, glowing, hot, intense, raging, red, red-hot.
2 *Take care—he has a fiery temper.* angry, excitable, furious, irritable, passionate, violent.

fight *noun*
1 *He's always getting into fights with other boys.*

Fighting is *combat* or *hostilities*.
A fight between armies is an *action* or a *battle*.
A minor unplanned battle is a *skirmish*.
A series of actions or battles is a *campaign* or a *war*.
A confused fight in a public place is a *brawl*, *punch-up*, or *scuffle*.
A minor fight over something unimportant is a *scrap*, *squabble*, or *tussle*.
A long-lasting series of fights or squabbles is a *feud*.
A fight arranged between two people is a *duel*.
A fight in a boxing or wrestling ring is a *bout* or *match*. ➡

Fighting sports such as karate and judo are *martial arts*.
A fight between knights on horseback in the Middle Ages was a *joust* or *tilting match*.

2 *We must continue the fight against poverty.* crusade, struggle.

fight *verb*
1 *Two men were fighting in the street.* exchange blows, have a fight, scrap, scuffle.
2 *The two countries fought each other in the war.* attack, do battle with, wage war with.
Fighting with foils or swords is *fencing*.
Fighting with fists is *boxing*.
A fight in which you try to throw your opponent to the ground is *wrestling*.
3 *Local people decided to fight the decision to build a bypass.* campaign against, make a stand against, oppose, protest against, resist.

fighter *noun*

PEOPLE WHO FIGHT IN A WAR OR CONFLICT: freedom fighter, gladiator, guerrilla, gunman, knight, sniper, soldier, swordsman, terrorist, warrior.

PEOPLE WHO FIGHT AS A SPORT: boxer, contender, contestant, wrestler.
FOR PEOPLE WHO FIGHT IN THE ARMY, ETC., SEE **armed services**.

figure *noun*
1 *Write the figure '8' on the blackboard.* digit, integer, number, numeral.
2 *Bargaining over the price of the new car, the salesman asked Dad what figure he had in mind.* amount, price, sum, value.
3 *She's always had a very good figure.* body, build, form, shape.
4 *She was looking at a small bronze figure of a horse.* carving, sculpture, statue.

figure   162   **filthy**

5 *The figure on page 22 shows the average rainfall for the area.* diagram, drawing, graph, illustration.
figures *You must be good with figures to work in the bank.* accounts, mathematics, statistics, sums.

figure *verb*
The same character figures in many of her novels. appear, feature, take part.
to figure out 1 *Have you figured out how much this holiday will cost?* add up, calculate, compute, count, reckon, work out.
2 *I can't figure out what this means.* comprehend, follow, make out, puzzle out, see, understand.

figure of speech *noun*

SOME COMMON FIGURES OF SPEECH: alliteration, assonance, hyperbole, irony, metaphor, onomatopoeia, personification, simile.

file *noun*
1 *I keep my papers in a file.* binder, cover, folder.
A file containing information, especially secret information, is a **dossier**.
2 *Please walk in a single file.* column, line, procession, queue, rank, row.

file *verb*
1 *I file all my letters in a pink folder.* organize, put away, store.
2 *We filed into the hall for assembly.* march, parade, troop, walk in a line.

fill *verb*
1 *We filled the trolley with shopping.* cram, load, pack, stuff, top up.
To fill a tyre with air is to **inflate** it.
AN OPPOSITE IS empty.
2 *What can I use to fill this hole?* block up, close up, plug, seal, stop up.
3 *Sightseers filled the streets.* block, [*informal*] bung up, crowd, jam, obstruct.

filling *noun*
The chair has a padded seat with a foam filling. padding, stuffing.

film *noun*
1 *I watched a good film last night.* [*American*] motion picture, movie, video.

To go to a cinema to see a film is to **go to the pictures**.
A long film is a **feature film**.
A short excerpt from a film is a **clip**.
A script for a film is a **screenplay**.

KINDS OF FILM: biopic, cartoon, comedy, documentary, horror film, love story or romance, space or science fiction film, war film, western.

2 *There was a film of oil on the water.* coat, coating, covering, layer, sheet, skin.
A large patch of oil floating on water is a **slick**.

filter *noun*
A filter used to separate tea leaves from tea, etc., is a **strainer**.
A device used in the kitchen to separate lumps from liquid or from flour, etc., is a **sieve**.
A coarse sieve used in the garden is a **riddle**.

filter *verb*
Dad filters his home-made wine to get rid of the cloudiness. clarify, purify, strain.

filth *noun*
The floor was covered with a layer of filth. dirt, grime, mess, muck, mud, scum, slime, sludge.

filthy *adjective*
1 *Your shoes are filthy!* dirty, grimy, grubby, messy, mucky, muddy, soiled, stained.
AN OPPOSITE IS clean.
2 *You mustn't drink that filthy water!* cloudy, contaminated, foul, impure, polluted, slimy, smelly, stinking.
AN OPPOSITE IS pure.
3 *We were offended by their filthy language.* coarse, crude, dirty, improper, indecent, obscene, offensive, rude, vulgar.
AN OPPOSITE IS decent.

final *adjective*
1 *The final moments of the game were very tense.* closing, concluding, last.
AN OPPOSITE IS opening.
2 *What was the final result?* eventual, ultimate.

finale *noun*
The fireworks were the finale to the whole festival. conclusion, culmination, end.

finance *noun*
I'm not very interested in finance. commerce, economics, investments, money.
finances *What's the state of your finances?* bank account, funds, money, resources, wealth.

finance *verb*
The bank helped them finance the business. back, invest in, pay for, provide money for, subsidize, support.

find *verb*
1 *Did you find the money you lost?* get back, recover, retrieve, trace, track down.
AN OPPOSITE IS lose.
2 *Did you find what you wanted?* come across, discover, encounter, locate, see, spot, stumble across, unearth.
3 *Did the doctor find what was wrong?* detect, diagnose, identify.
4 *I think you will find that digging is hard work.* become aware, learn, notice, realize, recognize.

findings *plural noun*
The judge announced his findings. conclusion, decision, judgement, verdict.

fine *adjective*
1 *We applauded his fine performance.* admirable, commendable, excellent, first-class, good.
AN OPPOSITE IS bad.
2 *As the weather was fine, we took a picnic.* bright, clear, cloudless, fair, pleasant, sunny.
AN OPPOSITE IS dull.

3 *The spider spins a very fine thread.* delicate, flimsy, fragile, slender, slim, thin.
AN OPPOSITE IS thick.
4 *The dunes were made of fine sand.* dusty, powdery.
AN OPPOSITE IS coarse.

fine *noun*
She had to pay a fine for speeding. penalty.

finger *noun*

Your short fat finger is your **thumb**. The finger next to your thumb is your **index finger**, because it is the finger you point with or indicate things with.
The next finger is your **middle finger**.
The next finger is your **ring finger**, because you can wear a wedding or engagement ring on that finger of your left hand.
Your small thin finger is your **little finger**.
The joints in your fingers are your **knuckles**.

finger *verb*
Please don't finger the food on the table. feel, touch.

finicky *adjective*
Our cat is finicky about her food. [*informal*] choosy, fussy, hard to please, particular.

finish *verb*
1 *When are you likely to finish your work?* cease, complete, reach the end of, round off, stop.
2 *The concert is likely to finish at about nine o'clock.* conclude, end, reach the end, terminate, [*informal*] wind up.
3 *I've finished my chocolates.* consume, exhaust, get through, [*informal*] polish off, use up.
AN OPPOSITE IS start.

finish *noun*
The finish of the race was very exciting. close, completion, conclusion, end, result, termination.
AN OPPOSITE IS start.

fire *noun*
1 *A crowd gathered to watch the fire.* blaze, flames.
2 *The heat of the fire melted the steel frame.* burning, combustion.

A very big hot fire is an *inferno*.
An open fire out of doors is a *bonfire*.
A metal container for an outdoor fire is a *brazier*.
A metal container for burning rubbish is an *incinerator*.
An enclosed fire which produces great heat is a *furnace*.
An enclosed fire for cooking food is an *oven*.
An enclosed fire for making pottery, etc., is a *kiln*.

VARIOUS KINDS OF HEATING APPARATUS AT HOME, IN SCHOOL, ETC.: boiler, central heating, convector, electric fire, fan heater, fireplace, gas fire, immersion heater, radiator, stove, underfloor heating.

---

fire *verb*
1 *Vandals fired the barn.* burn, ignite, kindle, light, put a light to, set alight, set fire to.
2 *You fire pottery in a kiln.* bake, harden, heat.
3 *He claimed that he fired the gun by mistake.* discharge, let off, set off, shoot.
To fire a missile is to *launch* it.
4 [*informal*] *The boss fired him because he was continually late for work.* dismiss, sack.
to fire at something *I fired at the target.* aim at, shoot at.

firework *noun*

VARIOUS FIREWORKS: banger, cascade, Catherine wheel, cracker or firecracker, fountain, rocket, Roman candle, sparkler, squib.

---

firm *noun*
Mum works for a firm that sells computers. business, company, concern, organization.

firm *adjective*
1 *Make sure the ladder rests on firm ground.* hard, solid.
AN OPPOSITE IS soft.
2 *Is the ladder firm?* fixed, secure, stable, steady.
AN OPPOSITE IS unsteady.
3 *She has a firm belief in fate.* decided, definite, determined, obstinate, persistent, resolute, sure.
AN OPPOSITE IS unsure.
4 *I trust him—he's a firm friend.* close, constant, dependable, devoted, faithful, loyal, reliable, trustworthy.
AN OPPOSITE IS unreliable.

first *adjective*
1 *The first cars were slow and unreliable.* earliest, original.
2 *The first thing to do in an emergency is to keep calm.* basic, chief, fundamental, key, main, principal.
at first *At first, I thought the lesson was going to be boring, but then I got interested.* at the beginning, initially, originally, to start with.

first-class, first-rate *adjectives*
The team's performance was first-class. excellent, outstanding, supreme, unequalled.

INFORMAL SYNONYMS: brilliant, fabulous, fantastic, great, tremendous.

first-hand *adjective*
Do you have first-hand knowledge of this firm? direct, personal.

fish *noun*

VARIOUS FISH: brill, carp, catfish, chub, cod, conger, cuttlefish, dace, eel, flounder, goldfish, grayling, gudgeon, haddock, hake, halibut, herring, jellyfish, lamprey, ling, mackerel, minnow, mullet, perch, pike, pilchard, piranha, plaice, roach, salmon, sardine, sawfish, shark, skate, sole, sprat, squid, starfish, stickleback, sturgeon, swordfish, trout, tuna, turbot, whitebait, whiting.
Bloater and ***kipper*** are kinds of smoked herring.
Young fish are *fry*.
An informal word for a very small fish is a *tiddler*. ➡

A large number of fish swimming together is a *shoal*.
A fisherman who uses a rod and line is an *angler*.
A man whose job is to catch fish at sea is a *trawlerman*.
The sport or job of catching fish is *fishing*.
Fishing with a rod and line is *angling*.
Fishing with nets from a boat is *trawling*.
Fishing equipment is *tackle*.

SOME EQUIPMENT USED IN FISHING: bait, creel, float, fly, gaff, hook, keepnet, line, lure, net, reel, rod, trawl line, trawl net.

fishy *adjective*
[*informal*] *Tell the police if you see anything fishy going on.* shady, suspicious.

fit *adjective*
1 *They gave us a dinner fit for a king!* appropriate, fitting, good enough, proper, right, suitable.
AN OPPOSITE IS unsuitable.
2 *You should try to keep fit.* healthy, in good form, robust, strong, well.
AN OPPOSITE IS unhealthy.
3 *We worked till we were fit to collapse.* liable, likely, ready.

fit *verb*
1 *My new jeans don't seem to fit.* be the right size.
2 *We need to fit a new lock on the door.* install, put in place.
3 *The pieces of this jigsaw don't fit.* go together, join up, match.
4 *Wear clothes to fit the occasion.* be suitable for, go with, suit.

fit *noun*
I had a fit of coughing. attack, bout, outburst.

fitting *adjective*
Scoring the winning goal was a fitting end to his great career. appropriate, apt, proper, suitable.
AN OPPOSITE IS inappropriate.

fix *verb*
1 *He fixed a bayonet to the end of his rifle.* attach, connect, fasten, join, link.
SEE ALSO **fasten**.
2 *We set the post in concrete to fix it in its proper position.* make firm, secure, stabilize.
3 *Let's fix a time for the party.* agree on, arrange, decide, establish, settle, specify.
4 [*informal*] *Dad says he can fix my bike.* mend, put right, repair.

fix *noun*
[*informal*] *Can you help me? I'm in a fix.* difficulty, dilemma, [*informal*] jam, mess, plight.

fixture *noun*
Our team has three fixtures next week. date, engagement, game, match.

fizz *verb*
The lemonade fizzed when I opened the bottle. bubble, foam, froth, hiss.

fizzy *adjective*
The baby hates fizzy drinks. bubbly, effervescent, foaming, sparkling.
AN OPPOSITE IS still.

flabbergasted *adjective* [*informal*]
I was flabbergasted when they said I had won first prize. amazed, astonished, astounded, dumbfounded, speechless, stunned, surprised, taken aback.

flabby *adjective*
This exercise is good for flabby thighs. fat, fleshy, out of condition, slack.
AN OPPOSITE IS firm.

flag *noun*
The street was decorated with flags for the carnival. banner, pennant, streamer.
The flag of a regiment is its *colours* or *standard*.
A flag flown on a ship is an *ensign*.

flag *verb*
Our enthusiasm flagged as the day went on. decline, decrease, diminish, dwindle, lessen, tail off, wane, weaken.

flames *plural noun*
Don't put your hand near the flames. blaze, fire.

flap *verb*
The sail flapped in the wind. flutter, sway, thrash about, wave about.

flare *verb*
to flare up 1 *The bonfire flared up when he threw dry grass on it.* blaze, burn brightly, flame.
2 *She flares up at the slightest provocation.* become angry, lose your temper.

flash *noun, verb*
FOR VARIOUS EFFECTS OF LIGHT, SEE **light** *noun*.

flat *adjective*
1 *You need a flat surface to write on.* even, level, smooth.
AN OPPOSITE IS uneven.
2 *I lay flat on the ground.* horizontal, outstretched, spread out.
AN OPPOSITE IS upright.
To be lying face downwards is to be **prone**.
To be lying face upwards is to be **supine**.
3 *He spoke in a flat, quiet voice.* boring, dull, lifeless, monotonous, tedious, uninteresting.
AN OPPOSITE IS lively.
4 *The front tyre of my bike was flat.* deflated, punctured.
AN OPPOSITE IS inflated.

flat *noun*
FOR PLACES WHERE PEOPLE LIVE, SEE **house**.

flatten *verb*
1 *She flattened the crumpled paper.* smooth.
To flatten clothes that have been washed is to **iron** or **press** them.
2 *They flattened the old buildings and built a new road.* demolish, destroy, knock down, level, pull down.
3 *The wheat had been flattened by the rain.* crush, squash.

flaunt *verb*
He likes to flaunt his expensive clothes. display, exhibit, show off.

flavour *noun*
1 *I don't like the flavour of raw onions.* taste.
FOR WORDS TO DESCRIBE HOW THINGS TASTE, SEE **taste** *verb*.
2 *Which flavour of ice cream do you like best?* kind, sort, variety.

flavour *verb*
To flavour food with salt, pepper, etc., is to **season** it.

flaw *noun*
1 *Pride was the greatest flaw in his character.* imperfection, weakness.
2 *There's a flaw in your argument.* error, fallacy, inaccuracy, mistake, slip.
3 *There's a small flaw in the glass.* blemish, break, chip, crack.

fleck *noun*
He brushed a few flecks of dust from his jacket. dot, mark, speck, spot.

flee *verb*
When they saw the police arrive, the attackers fled. escape, get away, retreat, run away.

fleet *noun*
A group of ships or vehicles travelling together is a **convoy**.
A fleet of warships is an **armada**.
A number of ships belonging to a particular country is its **navy**.

fleeting *adjective*
I only caught a fleeting glimpse of him. brief, momentary, quick, short.
AN OPPOSITE IS lengthy or permanent.

flesh *noun*
Your flesh is **muscle** and **fat**.
An animal's flesh used for food is **meat**.

flex *noun*
Don't trip over the flex of the iron! cable, lead, wire.

flexible *adjective*
1 *The wire was flexible enough to wind round the post.* pliable, soft, springy, supple.
AN OPPOSITE IS rigid.

2 *My plans are flexible, so I can come at any time.* adjustable, alterable, variable.
AN OPPOSITE IS fixed.
3 *He's quite flexible—he'll play in any position.* adaptable, versatile.
AN OPPOSITE IS inflexible.

flicker *verb*
The candlelight flickered in the draught. glimmer, quiver, tremble, twinkle, waver.

flight *noun*
1 *The Wright brothers played an important part in the history of flight.* aviation, flying.
2 *The refugees began their flight from danger under cover of darkness.* escape.

flimsy *adjective*
1 *A butterfly's wings are so flimsy that the slightest touch damages them.* brittle, delicate, fine, fragile, frail, light, thin.
2 *The gale blew down our flimsy shelter.* rickety, shaky, weak, wobbly.
AN OPPOSITE IS strong.

flinch *verb*
She didn't even flinch when he threatened her. back off, draw back, falter, recoil, shrink back, start, wince.

fling *verb*
I flung a stone into the pond. cast, [*informal*] chuck, hurl, pitch, sling, throw, toss.

flippant *adjective*
Don't make flippant remarks about people's misfortunes. facetious, frivolous, silly, stupid.
AN OPPOSITE IS serious.

float *verb*
1 *The raft floated gently down the river.* drift, sail.
2 *There wasn't enough water to float the ship.* launch.
AN OPPOSITE IS sink.

flock *noun*
FOR VARIOUS GROUPS, SEE **group** *noun*.

flock *verb*
People flocked round to see what was happening. crowd, gather, herd, jostle.

flog *verb*
He flogged the poor donkey mercilessly. beat, cane, lash, thrash, [*slang*] wallop, whack, whip.

flood *noun*
The flood of water swept away the bridge. deluge, inundation, rush, torrent.

flood *verb*
The river burst its banks and flooded the valley. cover, drown, engulf, immerse, inundate, overwhelm, submerge, swamp.
to flood in *Donations to the charity flooded in.* flow in, keep coming, pour in.

floor *noun*
1 *There weren't enough chairs, so I had to sit on the floor.*

SOME THINGS USED TO MAKE OR COVER A FLOOR: carpet, flagstones, floorboards, lino or linoleum, mat, matting, parquet, rug, tiles, vinyl.

2 *Her flat is on the top floor.* level, storey.
A floor on a ship is a ***deck***.

flop *verb*
1 *I was so tired that I just flopped onto my bed.* collapse, drop, fall, slump.
2 *The plants in the hanging basket will flop if you don't water them.* dangle, droop, hang down, sag, wilt.
3 [*informal*] *Their first single flopped, but their second was a big hit.* be unsuccessful, fail, founder, meet with disaster.

floppy *adjective*
The dog had long, floppy ears. droopy, limp, soft.

flounder *verb*
1 *We floundered through the mud.* stagger, struggle, stumble, wallow.
2 *The question took him by surprise and he began to flounder.* falter, get confused, make mistakes, talk aimlessly.

flourish *verb*
1 *The plants may flourish if we get some rain.* be fruitful, bloom, blossom, flower, grow, thrive.
AN OPPOSITE IS die.
2 *The company has continued to flourish.* be successful, boom, develop, do well, increase, prosper, succeed.
AN OPPOSITE IS fail.
3 *He flourished his umbrella to attract the taxi driver's attention.* brandish, shake, twirl, wave.

flow *verb*
Water flowed along the gutter. glide, run, stream.
To flow slowly is to *dribble*, *drip*, *ooze*, *seep*, or *trickle*.
To flow fast is to *cascade* or *pour*.
To flow with sudden force is to *spurt*, *squirt*, or *well up*.
To flow over the edge of something is to *overflow* or *spill*.
When blood flows from a wound, we say that it *bleeds*.
When the tide flows out, it *ebbs*.

flow *noun*
1 *It's hard work rowing against the flow.* current, stream, tide.
2 *There was a steady flow of water into the pond.* cascade, flood, gush, rush.

flower *noun*

A single flower is a *bloom*.
A mass of small flowers growing together is *blossom*.
Flowers in a vase are an *arrangement*.
A bunch of flowers arranged for a special occasion is a *bouquet*, *posy*, or *spray*.
Flowers arranged to make a circle are a *garland* or *wreath*.

SOME WILD FLOWERS: bluebell, buttercup, catkin, celandine, coltsfoot, cornflower, cowslip, daisy, dandelion, foxglove, harebell, kingcup, orchid, poppy, primrose.

SOME POPULAR CULTIVATED FLOWERS: begonia, candytuft, carnation, chrysanthemum, columbine, crocus, cyclamen, daffodil, dahlia, forget-me-not, freesia, geranium, gladiolus, ➡

hollyhock, hyacinth, iris, lilac, lily, lupin, marigold, nasturtium, pansy, pelargonium, peony, petunia, phlox, pink, polyanthus, rose, snowdrop, sunflower, tulip, wallflower, water lily.

PARTS OF A FLOWER: axil, bract, calyx, carpel, corolla, perianth, pistil, pollen, sepal, stamen, whorl.

flower *verb*
Most plants flower in the summer. bloom, blossom, have flowers.

fluent *adjective*
I wish I was fluent in French. articulate, eloquent.
AN OPPOSITE IS hesitant.

fluffy *adjective*
Seven fluffy ducklings were swimming in the pond. downy, feathery, furry, fuzzy, hairy, soft.

fluid *noun*
Fluids are either *liquids* or *gases*.
AN OPPOSITE IS solid.

fluke *noun*
It was just a fluke that the ball went into the net. accident, chance, stroke of good luck.

flush *verb*
He flushed with embarrassment. blush, colour, go red, redden.

flustered *adjective*
I get flustered when I have to read in assembly. confused, mixed up, nervous.
AN OPPOSITE IS confident.

flutter *verb*
The moth's wings fluttered. flap, quiver, tremble, vibrate.

fly *noun*
FOR VARIOUS INSECTS, SEE **insect**.

fly *verb*
1 *The swallows were flying high in the sky.* flit, glide, hover, rise, soar, swoop.
2 *The ship was flying the British flag.* display, hang up, hoist, raise, show, wave.
3 *Doesn't time fly!* go quickly, pass quickly, rush by.

foam *noun*
1 *This detergent makes a lot of foam.*
bubbles, froth, lather, suds.
2 *These cushions are filled with foam.*
sponge, spongy rubber.

foam *verb*
The lemonade foamed as I poured it into the glass. boil, bubble, fizz, froth up.

focus *noun*
1 *Can you adjust the focus on the projector?* clarity, sharpness.
2 *The club's new player is the focus of attention in the papers.* centre, focal point.
in focus *These photos are not in focus.* clear, focused, sharp, well defined.
out of focus *The photos are out of focus.* blurred, foggy, fuzzy, hazy, indistinct, unclear, unfocused.

focus *verb*
Can you focus the projector? adjust the focus of, get into focus.
to focus on *We ought to focus on the main problem.* concentrate on, examine, look at, think about.

fog *noun*
There was fog on the motorway. bad visibility.
Thin fog is *haze* or *mist*.
A thick mixture of fog and smoke is *smog*.

foggy *adjective*
1 *Dad doesn't like driving in this foggy weather.* hazy, misty, murky.
2 *The photo was foggy.* blurred, fuzzy, indistinct.
AN OPPOSITE IS clear.

foil *verb*
1 *The security officer foiled the attempted robbery.* block, check, halt, prevent, stop.
2 *The security officer foiled the thieves.* frustrate, outwit.

fold *verb*
Fold the paper along the dotted line. bend, crease, double over.

fold *noun*
1 *She smoothed the soft folds of her dress.*
A fold which is part of the way a garment is made is a *pleat*.
2 *The dog drove the sheep into the fold.* enclosure, pen.

folder *noun*
I keep my project work in a folder. cover, file.

follow *verb*
1 *James I followed Elizabeth I.* come after, replace, succeed, take the place of.
AN OPPOSITE IS precede.
2 *Follow that car!* chase, go after, keep up with, pursue.
3 *The lion followed its prey.* hunt, stalk, tail, track, trail.
4 *Try to follow his example.* be guided by, imitate, model yourself on.
5 *Follow the rules.* heed, keep to, obey, observe, pay attention to, take notice of.
6 *Do you follow snooker?* be a fan of, know about, support, take an interest in.
7 *Try to follow what I say.* comprehend, grasp, understand.
8 *It's sunny now, but it doesn't follow that it'll be fine tonight.* be inevitable, come about, ensue, happen, mean, result.

follower *noun*
Someone who follows you in a job, etc., is your *successor*.
Someone who follows a person or animal to try to catch them is a *hunter* or *pursuer*.
Someone who continually follows a person about is a *stalker*.
Someone who follows a person's teaching is a *disciple*.
Someone who follows a football team, etc., is a *fan* or *supporter*.

fond *adjective*
1 *He gave me a fond kiss.* affectionate, loving, tender.
2 *Winning the lottery is just a fond dream.* fanciful, silly, unrealistic.
to be fond of *I'm very fond of her.* admire, adore, like, love.

food *noun*
All living things need food.
nourishment.

The food that we normally eat or that we choose to eat is our *diet*.
Something specially tasty to eat is a *delicacy*.
Food for farm animals is *fodder*.
A word used for the food which plants need is *nutrients*.

PRINCIPAL CONSTITUENTS OF OUR FOOD: carbohydrate, fat, fibre, protein, roughage, starch, vitamins.

Cereal foods

VARIOUS CEREALS: barley, maize or sweetcorn, oats, rice, rye, wheat.

SOME FOODS MADE FROM CEREALS: bran, cornflakes, cornflour, flour, muesli, oatmeal, porridge.

FOODS MADE LARGELY FROM FLOUR: batter, biscuits, bread, cake, dumplings, noodles, pancakes, pasta, pastry, pizza, tortilla, Yorkshire pudding.

VARIOUS KINDS OF BREAD: bagel, baguette, brown bread, chapatti, French bread or French stick, fruit loaf, granary bread, matzo, nan, rye bread, white bread, wholemeal bread.
You can use bread to make *sandwiches* or *toast*.

SOME KINDS OF CAKE: bun, doughnut or donut, fruitcake, gingerbread, meringue, muffin, scone, shortbread, sponge cake.

KINDS OF PASTA: lasagne, macaroni, ravioli, spaghetti, tagliatelle.

THINGS MADE WITH PASTRY: flan, pasty, pie, quiche, samosa, sausage roll, tart.

Food from animals

Different kinds of meat: bacon, beef, chicken, duck, game, gammon, goose, ham, lamb, mutton, pork, turkey, veal, venison. ➡

DIFFERENT WAYS A BUTCHER CUTS AND SELLS MEAT: burgers, chops, cutlets, mince, roasting joint, sausages, steak.

SOME FOODS OFTEN MADE WITH MEAT: casserole, chop suey, chow mein, curry, fritters, goulash, hash, hotpot, kebab, meat pie, paté, rissoles, stew.

Other foods which come from animals are *eggs* and *milk*.

FOODS MADE WITH EGGS: omelette, soufflé.

FOODS MADE WITH MILK: blancmange, butter, cheese, cream, custard, ice cream, milk pudding, yoghurt.
A diet which includes no meat is a *vegetarian* diet.
A diet which includes no animal products is a *vegan* diet.

Fish used as food

SOME FISH THAT PEOPLE EAT: bream, cod, eel, haddock, halibut, herring, mackerel, pilchard, plaice, salmon, sardine, sole, sprat, trout, tuna.
Bloaters and *kippers* are kinds of smoked herring.
An expensive food from a fish called *sturgeon* is *caviare*.
Very small young herrings or sprats are called *whitebait*.

SOME SHELLFISH THAT PEOPLE EAT: crab, lobster, mussels, oysters, prawn, scampi, shrimp, whelks.
A mixture of fish, shellfish, etc., is *seafood*.

Fruits and vegetables
FOR FRUITS AND VEGETABLES, SEE *fruit, vegetable*.

Sweet foods

THINGS WE USE TO MAKE FOOD TASTE SWEET INCLUDE: artificial sweeteners, honey, saccharin, sugar, syrup, treacle.

SWEET FOODS USUALLY CONTAINING A LOT OF SUGAR INCLUDE: biscuit, cake, chocolate, gateau, ice cream, icing, jam, jelly, marmalade, pudding, sweet. ➡

SOME PUDDINGS OR DESSERTS:
charlotte, cheesecake, crumble, fool,
fruit pies, fruit salad, fruit tarts,
gateau, milk pudding, mousse,
sundae, trifle.

Other ingredients and flavourings

KINDS OF FAT USED IN FOOD: butter,
dripping, ghee, lard, margarine,
olive oil, suet, vegetable oil.

THINGS YOU ADD TO FOOD TO MAKE
THE TASTE MORE INTERESTING:
chilli, chutney, curry powder,
dressing, garlic, gravy, herbs,
ketchup, mayonnaise, mustard,
pepper, pickle, salt, sauce, spice,
sugar, vinegar.
Things like salt and pepper which
you add to food are *condiments* or
seasoning.
Artificial chemicals added to food
before you buy it are called
additives.
Additives may be *colourings*,
flavourings, or *preservatives*.

fool *noun*
1 *Only a fool would have believed him.*
ass, clown, dope, idiot, moron.
Fool and its synonyms are used
informally, and they are insulting if
you use them to describe other people
2 [*old use*] *The king's fool entertained
the court.* jester.

fool *verb*
He fooled you completely! bluff, [*slang*]
con, deceive, [*informal*] have you on,
hoax, [*informal*] kid, mislead, take you
in, trick.
to fool about *The teacher told us not to
fool about.* be naughty, misbehave, play
about.

foolish *adjective*
What a foolish thing to do! absurd,
crazy, idiotic, irresponsible, pointless,
ridiculous, senseless, silly, stupid,
thoughtless, unintelligent, unwise.
AN OPPOSITE IS sensible.

foolproof *adjective*
The plan was completely foolproof.
certain, guaranteed, infallible, safe,
sure, unfailing.

foot *noun*
1 *These shoes hurt my feet.*
An animal's foot is a *paw*.
A horse's foot is a *hoof*.
A pig's foot is a *trotter*.
A bird's feet are its *claws*.
The feet of a bird of prey are its *talons*.
2 *We set up camp at the foot of the
mountain.* base, bottom.

footprint *noun*
We followed the footprints in the snow.
footmark, track.

forbid *verb*
*I think they ought to forbid smoking in
public places.* ban, bar, make illegal,
prohibit, rule out, stop.
AN OPPOSITE IS allow.

forbidding *adjective*
*Despite her forbidding appearance,
she's actually quite a kind woman.*
gloomy, grim, menacing, ominous,
stern, threatening, unfriendly,
unwelcoming.
AN OPPOSITE IS friendly.

force *noun*
1 *I had to use all my force to open the
door.* effort, energy, might, power,
strength.
2 *The force of the explosion broke all the
windows.* effect, impact, shock,
violence.
3 *They sent a military force to stop the
riots.* army, troops.
in force *Is that rule still in force?*
effective, legal, valid.

force *verb*
1 *You can't force me to do it.* compel,
make, order, require.
2 *They forced the change on us.* impose,
inflict.
3 *We had to force the door.* break open,
burst open, prise open, smash, wrench,
[*informal*] yank.

forceful *adjective*
*I'm a bit afraid of her forceful
personality.* dominant, energetic,
overpowering, powerful, strong.
AN OPPOSITE IS weak.

ford *verb*
*There's no bridge, but you can ford the
stream here.* drive through, ride
through, wade across.

forecast *noun*
The forecast is for more rain. outlook, prediction.

forecast *verb*
Did they forecast rain for today? foresee, foretell, predict.

foreground *noun*
I painted my dog in the foreground of my picture. front, nearest part.
AN OPPOSITE IS background.

foreign *adjective*
1 You see a lot of foreign people in London. overseas, visiting.
AN OPPOSITE IS native.
2 I would love to travel to foreign places. distant, exotic, far-away, remote, strange, unfamiliar.
AN OPPOSITE IS familiar.
3 Lying is foreign to her nature. uncharacteristic (of), untypical (of).
AN OPPOSITE IS natural.

foreigner *noun*
Many foreigners visit the centre every year. alien, immigrant, outsider, overseas visitor, stranger.
A formal word is **alien**.
A word describing people who come from abroad to live in a country is **immigrant**.

foremost *adjective*
He is one of the foremost actors of our time. best known, chief, distinguished, eminent, leading, major, most important, outstanding, principal, prominent.
AN OPPOSITE IS unimportant.

foresee *verb*
I foresaw what would happen. anticipate, forecast, foretell, predict, prophesy.

forest *noun*

VARIOUS KINDS OF AREA WHERE TREES GROW: coppice, copse, jungle, plantation, wood, woodland.

foretell *verb*
1 He foretold that an accident would happen. forecast, foresee, predict, prophesy.
2 The cold wind foretold a change in the weather. herald, signify.

forfeit *noun*
He had to pay a forfeit. fine, penalty.

forfeit *verb*
If you broke the rules, you'll have to forfeit your prize. give up, lose, surrender.

forge *verb*
1 He forged the iron into a sword. beat into shape, cast, hammer out, shape.
2 It is a serious offence to forge someone's signature. copy, counterfeit, fake.
to forge ahead After a slow start, the company is now forging ahead. advance quickly, make good progress, make headway, progress quickly.

forgery *noun*
The painting was a forgery. copy, counterfeit, fake, fraud, imitation, replica, reproduction.

forget *verb*
1 I forgot my toothbrush when I packed my suitcase. leave out, miss out, omit.
2 I forgot my umbrella when I got off the bus. leave behind, overlook.
AN OPPOSITE IS remember.

forgetful *adjective*
You'd better remind him—he's so forgetful! absent-minded, careless, inattentive, negligent, unreliable, vague.

forgive *verb*
Please forgive me—I won't do it again! excuse, let off, pardon.

fork *verb*
The path forks here, and I don't know which way to go. branch, divide, split.

forlorn *adjective*
I felt quite forlorn after she had left. abandoned, alone, deserted, forsaken, friendless, lonely, sad, solitary, unhappy.
AN OPPOSITE IS cheerful.

form *noun*
1 *I made out the form of a man through the mist.* figure, outline, shape, silhouette.
2 *Ice is a form of water.* kind, sort, type, variety.
3 *My brother moves up into a higher form next term.* class, group, level, set, stream, tutor-group.
4 *If you want to join the club, sign this form.* document, paper.

form *verb*
1 *The potter formed the clay into a tall vase.* cast, mould, shape.
2 *We formed a chess club.* bring into existence, create, establish, found, make, organize, set up.
3 *Two friends and I form the committee.* act as, compose, constitute, make up.
4 *Icicles formed under the bridge.* appear, come into existence, develop, grow, take shape.

formal *adjective*
1 *I went to the formal opening of the sports centre.* ceremonial, official.
2 *We shook hands in a formal way.* conventional, correct, dignified, proper, solemn.

format *noun*
1 *They've changed the format of the newspaper.* appearance, design, presentation, style.
The format of a document includes its *layout*, *shape*, and *size*.
2 *I'd like to change the format of our weekly meetings.* arrangements, organization, plan.

former *adjective*
In former times, the house was an inn. earlier, previous.

formula *noun*
What is your formula for success? blueprint, method, prescription, procedure, recipe, set of rules.

formulate *verb*
We formulated a plan so that everyone knew exactly what to do. define, express clearly, set out in detail, work out.

forsake *verb*
She knew he would never forsake her. abandon, desert, leave.

fort, fortification *nouns*

> VARIOUS FORTIFIED PLACES: castle, citadel, fortress, garrison, military camp, stronghold, tower.

fortify *verb*
1 *The soldiers tried to fortify the town.* defend, protect, reinforce, secure.
2 *A good breakfast will fortify you for the day ahead.* bolster, boost, cheer, encourage, strengthen, sustain.
AN OPPOSITE IS weaken.

fortunate *adjective*
We were fortunate to have good weather. in luck, lucky.

fortune *noun*
1 *Mum had the good fortune to win a prize in a raffle.* accident, chance, luck.
2 *The millionaire left his fortune to a charity.* assets, estate, [*informal*] millions, possessions, property, riches, wealth.

forward *adjective*
1 *It's a good idea to do some forward planning.* advance, early.
2 *Wasn't he rather forward, telling the teacher what to do?* bold, cheeky, eager, familiar, impudent.

forwards *adverb*
1 *The queue moved forwards very slowly.* along, on, onwards.
2 *Will you all face forwards, please.* ahead, to or toward the front.
AN OPPOSITE IS backwards.

foster *verb*
My aunt decided to foster a child. bring up, care for, look after, take care of.
To *adopt* a child is to make the child legally a full member of your family.

foul *adjective*
1 *The refugees were living in foul conditions.* dirty, disgusting, filthy, loathsome, messy, mucky, offensive, repulsive, revolting, rotten, smelly, stinking, vile.
AN OPPOSITE IS clean.
2 *Foul drinking water was blamed for the epidemic.* contaminated, impure, infected, polluted, slimy, unclean.
AN OPPOSITE IS pure.

3 *He was sent off for using foul language.* abusive, blasphemous, coarse, crude, dirty, improper, indecent, insulting, obscene, offensive, rude, vulgar.
AN OPPOSITE IS decent.
4 *The referee blew her whistle for a foul tackle.* illegal, prohibited, unfair.
AN OPPOSITE IS fair.

found *verb*
The school was founded a hundred years ago. begin, create, establish, initiate, institute, set up, start.

foundation *noun*
1 *Dad and I laid the foundation for a garden shed.* base.
2 *There's no foundation for the rumour they are spreading.* basis, grounds.
3 *It's a hundred years since the foundation of the hospital.* beginning, establishment, setting up, starting.

founder *verb*
1 *The ship struck a rock and foundered.* go under, sink.
2 *The project foundered because of a lack of money.* be unsuccessful, come to an end, fail, fall through, [*informal*] flop, meet with disaster.

fountain *noun*
A fountain of water shot into the air. jet, spout, spray, spurt.

fox *noun*
*A female fox is a **vixen**.*
*A young fox is a **cub**.*

fox *verb*
The riddle completely foxed me. baffle, bewilder, deceive, mystify, perplex, puzzle.

foyer *noun*
We'll meet you in the cinema foyer. entrance, entrance hall, lobby, reception.

fraction *noun*
I can afford only a fraction of what they asked for. bit, part, portion.

fractionally *adverb*
Their house is fractionally bigger than ours. a little, marginally, slightly.

fracture *verb*
He fell off his bike and fractured a bone in his arm. break, chip, crack.

fracture *noun*
The X-ray showed a fracture in the bone. break, breakage, chip, crack.

fragile *adjective*
Old people's bones are more fragile than ours. breakable, brittle, delicate, easily damaged, frail, weak.
AN OPPOSITE IS strong.

fragment *noun*
1 *I dug up a fragment of broken pottery.* bit, chip, piece, sliver.
2 *She overheard fragments of their conversation.* part, portion, scrap.

fragrant *adjective*
The room was fragrant with the smell of roses. perfumed, scented, sweet smelling.

frail *adjective*
1 *She still feels rather frail after her illness.* feeble, unsteady, weak.
2 *The balcony looks a bit frail.* delicate, easily damaged, flimsy, fragile, rickety, unsound.
AN OPPOSITE IS strong.

frame *noun*
1 *The frame of the building is made of steel girders.* framework, shell, skeleton.
2 *I put the photo of my friend in a frame.* border, case, edging, mount.
frame of mind *Let's wait till he's in a better frame of mind.* humour, mood, temper.

frank *adjective*
Please give me a frank reply, even if it is bad news. blunt, direct, genuine, honest, outspoken, plain, sincere, straightforward, truthful.
AN OPPOSITE IS insincere or tactful.

frantic *adjective*
1 *She was frantic with worry.* berserk, beside yourself, delirious, fraught, hysterical, uncontrollable, worked up.
2 *There was frantic activity to get everything ready before the visitors arrived.* desperate, excited, frenzied, furious, hectic, wild.
AN OPPOSITE IS calm.

fraud *noun*
1 *He was guilty of fraud.* [slang] con-trick, deceit, deception, dishonesty, forgery, swindling, trickery.
2 *The 'special offer' was a fraud.* hoax, pretence, sham, swindle, trick.
3 *The salesman was a fraud.* cheat, hoaxer, impostor, swindler.

fraudulent *adjective*
He was accused of fraudulent business activities. bogus, cheating, corrupt, criminal, [informal] crooked, deceitful, devious, dishonest, illegal, lying, swindling, underhand.
AN OPPOSITE IS honest.

frayed *adjective*
I can't wear this shirt—the collar is frayed. tattered, worn.

freak *noun*
[informal] *My sister is a keep-fit freak.* addict, devotee, enthusiast, fanatic.

freakish *adjective*
We've had freakish weather conditions this summer. abnormal, exceptional, extraordinary, odd, peculiar, queer, unpredictable, unusual.
AN OPPOSITE IS normal.

free *adjective*
1 *We are free to do what we want.* able, allowed, at liberty, permitted.
AN OPPOSITE IS restricted.
2 *After ten years in prison, he was free at last.* emancipated, freed, independent, liberated, released.
AN OPPOSITE IS enslaved or imprisoned.
3 *I got a free drink with my burger.* complimentary, free of charge.
4 *Look out—the end of that rope has worked free.* loose, untied.
AN OPPOSITE IS secure.
5 *Is the bathroom free?* available, unoccupied, vacant.
AN OPPOSITE IS engaged.
6 *He is free with his money.* generous, lavish, liberal.
AN OPPOSITE IS mean.

free *verb*
1 *The soldiers freed the prisoners of war.* liberate, release, rescue, save, set free.

To free slaves is to **emancipate** them. To free prisoners by paying money to the captors is to **ransom** them.
AN OPPOSITE IS imprison.
2 *We freed the dogs and let them run about.* loose, turn loose, untie.
AN OPPOSITE IS confine.
3 *The judge freed the accused man.* acquit, clear, discharge, let go, let off, pardon.
AN OPPOSITE IS condemn.
4 *Can you free those tangled ropes?* undo, untangle.
AN OPPOSITE IS tangle.

freedom *noun*
We all like to have the freedom to do what we want. independence, liberty.

freeze *verb*
1 *Water begins to freeze at 0°C.* become ice, harden, solidify.
2 *If you freeze food, you can store it for a long time.* refrigerate.
To make food cold to store it for a short time is to **chill** it.
3 *They decided to freeze prices until next year.* fix, hold, keep as they are.

freight *noun*
They unloaded the freight from the wagons. cargo, goods, load.

frequent *adjective*
1 *I've given you frequent warnings about your behaviour.* constant, continual, countless, many, numerous, recurrent, recurring, repeated.
AN OPPOSITE IS infrequent.
2 *Cuckoos used to be frequent visitors to this part of the country.* common, familiar, habitual, ordinary, persistent, regular.
AN OPPOSITE IS rare.

frequent *verb*
The restaurant is frequented by actors from the nearby theatre. visit.

fresh *adjective*
1 *The youth club needs some fresh ideas.* additional, different, extra, up-to-date.
AN OPPOSITE IS old.
2 *We need some fresh bread.* freshly baked, new.
AN OPPOSITE IS stale.

3 *I prefer fresh fruit to tinned.* natural, raw, unprocessed.
AN OPPOSITE IS preserved or tinned.
4 *After being indoors all day, I felt like some fresh air.* clean, cool, invigorating.
AN OPPOSITE IS stuffy.
5 *Can I get a fresh duvet cover out of the cupboard?* clean, laundered, washed.
AN OPPOSITE IS dirty.
6 *Having a shower makes me feel nice and fresh.* energetic, healthy, invigorated, lively, revived, vigorous.
AN OPPOSITE IS weary.
7 *When you are camping, you need a supply of fresh water.* drinkable, pure.
AN OPPOSITE IS salty.

freshen *verb*
to freshen someone up *The swim had freshened her up.* invigorate, revive.

fret *verb*
The dog frets if we leave her tied up. be anxious, be upset, become stressed, worry.

friction *noun*
1 *Bike brakes work by friction against the wheel.* resistance, rubbing, scraping.
2 *There was some friction between the two sides.* antagonism, conflict, disagreement, hostility, opposition, quarrelling.

friend *noun*
I was playing with my friends.
companion, comrade, [*informal*] mate, [*informal*] pal.
A friend you play games with is a ***playmate***.
A friend you work with or live with is your ***partner***.
A friend you write to but don't normally meet is a ***penfriend***.
A friend you know only slightly is an ***acquaintance***.
AN OPPOSITE IS enemy.

friendless *adjective*
I felt quite friendless when everyone went away on holiday. abandoned, alone, deserted, forlorn, forsaken, lonely, solitary, unloved.

friendly *adjective*
1 *You will like her—she's a friendly person.* affectionate, amiable, amicable, approachable, genial, good-natured, gracious, helpful, kind, kind-hearted, likeable, sympathetic.
2 *Those two have a very friendly relationship.* close, familiar, intimate, loving.
3 *They gave me a friendly welcome.* civil, courteous, hospitable, neighbourly, polite, warm, welcoming.
AN OPPOSITE IS unfriendly.

friendship *noun*
Their friendship has lasted for many years. affection, association, attachment, closeness, comradeship, familiarity, fellowship, fondness.
A formal friendship between countries or parties is an ***alliance***.
AN OPPOSITE IS hostility.

frieze *noun*
We painted a decorative frieze around the wall. border, edging.

fright *noun*
1 *She jumped up in fright and began to scream.* alarm, dismay, dread, fear, horror, panic, terror.
2 *The explosion gave us a dreadful fright!* scare, shock, surprise.

frighten *verb*
Sorry—I didn't mean to frighten you. alarm, horrify, make afraid, petrify, scare, shock, startle, terrify.
AN OPPOSITE IS reassure.

frightened *adjective*
If we stick together, there's no need to be frightened. afraid, alarmed, apprehensive, dismayed, fearful, nervous, panicky, scared, terrified.

frightening *adjective*
The film was very frightening. creepy, eerie, ghostly, horrifying, nightmarish, [*informal*] scary, sinister, spine-chilling, [*informal*] spooky.

frightful *adjective*
1 *There was a frightful accident on the motorway.* alarming, appalling, awful, dreadful, fearful, ghastly, grisly, gruesome, hideous, horrible, horrid, horrific, horrifying, shocking.
2 [*informal*] *It was a frightful shame you couldn't come to my party.* dreadful, great, terrible.

fringe *noun*
1 *She fiddled with the fringe of the tablecloth.* border, edging, frill.
2 *We live on the fringe of the town.* border, edge, margin, outskirts.

frisk *verb*
to frisk about *Lambs were frisking about in the field.* bound, caper, dance, frolic, hop about, jump about, leap about, play about, prance, romp, skip.

fritter *verb*
If you fritter your money on sweets, you'll have nothing to spend on holiday. spend unwisely, squander, use up, waste.

frivolous *adjective*
1 *We were in a frivolous mood before we went on holiday.* flippant, frisky, high-spirited, jaunty, joking, jolly, light-hearted, lively, playful, sprightly.
2 *Don't waste my time asking frivolous questions.* facetious, foolish, petty, pointless, ridiculous, silly, stupid, superficial, trivial, unimportant, worthless.
AN OPPOSITE IS serious.

frock *noun*
FOR THINGS YOU WEAR, SEE **clothes**.

frolic *verb*
Lambs were frolicking in the field. bound, caper, dance, frisk about, have fun, hop about, jump about, leap about, play about, prance, romp, skip.

front *noun*
1 *We stood at the front of the queue.* head.
The front of a ship is the ***bow*** or ***prow***.
The front of a picture is the ***foreground***.
AN OPPOSITE IS back.
2 *Troops were sent to the front.* battle area, danger zone, front line.

front *adjective*
The front runners came into sight round the corner. first, leading, most advanced.
AN OPPOSITE IS back.

frontier *noun*
We crossed the frontier between France and Belgium. border, boundary.

frosty *adjective*
It was a clear, frosty night. cold, crisp, freezing, icy, wintry.

froth *noun*
I love the froth you get on hot chocolate. bubbles, foam.
The froth on top of soapy water is ***lather*** or ***suds***.
Dirty froth is ***scum***.

frown *noun*
FOR EXPRESSIONS ON PEOPLE'S FACES, SEE **expression**.

frugal *adjective*
1 *We try to be frugal with our pocket money.* careful, economical, prudent, sparing, thrifty.
AN OPPOSITE IS wasteful.
2 *I had very little money left, so I had a frugal meal.* cheap, inexpensive.
AN OPPOSITE IS lavish.

fruit *noun*

VARIOUS FRUITS WHICH PEOPLE USE AS FOOD: apple, apricot, avocado, banana, bilberry, blackberry, blackcurrant, cherry, coconut, crab apple, cranberry, damson, date, fig, gooseberry, grape, greengage, guava, kiwi fruit, loganberry, lychee, mango, melon, nuts, olive, pawpaw or papaya, peach, pear, pineapple, plum, pomegranate, quince, raspberry, redcurrant, rosehip, sloe, strawberry, tomato.

CITRUS FRUITS: grapefruit, lemon, lime, nectarine, orange, satsuma, tangerine.

DRIED FRUITS: currant, prune, raisin, sultana.

Rhubarb is not a fruit, but we eat it as if it was a fruit.

fruitful *adjective*
1 *Did you have a fruitful shopping trip?* profitable, rewarding, successful, useful, worthwhile.
AN OPPOSITE IS fruitless.
2 *We drove through miles of fruitful farmland.* fertile, flourishing, productive.
AN OPPOSITE IS unproductive.

fruitless *adjective*
I looked everywhere for my purse, but it was a fruitless search. futile, pointless, unproductive, unprofitable, unsuccessful, useless, vain.
AN OPPOSITE IS successful.

frustrate *verb*
The police frustrated an attempted robbery. baffle, block, check, defeat, foil, halt, hinder, prevent, stop.

fry *verb*
FOR WAYS TO COOK THINGS, SEE **cook** *verb*.

fuel *noun*

Fuels found in the earth which are formed from decomposed living matter are *fossil fuels*.

KINDS OF FOSSIL FUEL: coal, crude oil or petroleum, natural gas.

FUELS REFINED FROM CRUDE OIL: diesel, gasoline, paraffin, petrol.

KINDS OF COAL INCLUDE: anthracite, coke, smokeless coal.

OTHER KINDS OF SOLID FUEL: charcoal, logs, peat.

OTHER FUELS INCLUDE: butane, [*trademark*] Calor gas, electricity, methylated spirit, nuclear fuel, propane.

fugitive *noun*
Police searched for the fugitives. deserter, outlaw, runaway.
Someone who is a fugitive from war or persecution is a *refugee*.

fulfil *verb*
1 *She fulfilled her ambition to play at Wimbledon.* accomplish, achieve, attain, bring about, carry out, complete, succeed in.
2 *To be a member of the team, you must fulfil certain conditions.* meet, satisfy.

full *adjective*
1 *The basin was full, so I turned the tap off.* brimming, filled, overflowing, topped-up.
AN OPPOSITE IS empty.
2 *The shopping centre was full on Saturday.* busy, congested, crammed, crowded, jammed, packed.
AN OPPOSITE IS uncrowded.
3 *The head wanted a full explanation of what had happened.* complete, comprehensive, detailed, entire, whole.
AN OPPOSITE IS incomplete.
4 *We drove at full speed.* greatest, highest, maximum, top.
AN OPPOSITE IS minimum.
5 *She was wearing a full skirt.* broad, loose, wide.
AN OPPOSITE IS tight.

fumes *plural noun*
People could hardly breathe because of the fumes. exhaust, gases, pollution, smoke.

fun *noun*
Let's have some fun! amusement, diversion, enjoyment, entertainment, games, jokes, laughter, merriment, play, pleasure, recreation, sport.
to make fun of someone *It was cruel to make fun of her when she fell over.* jeer at, laugh at, mock, ridicule, taunt, tease.
To make fun of someone in a story, poem, or play, etc., is to *satirize* them.

function *noun*
1 *The function of a doctor is to cure sick people.* duty, job, responsibility, task, work.
2 *They held an official function to open the new sports centre.* ceremony, event, reception.

function *verb*
The computer doesn't function properly. go, operate, work.

functional *adjective*
1 *The drinks machine is functional again.* going, operating, usable, working.
2 *The kitchen was small but functional.* practical, useful.

fundamental *adjective*
He taught me the fundamental rules of chess. basic, elementary, essential, important, main, necessary, principal, underlying.
AN OPPOSITE IS advanced.

funds *plural noun*
He invested all his funds. capital, money, riches, savings, wealth.

funeral *noun*

> A funeral at which a dead person is buried is an ***interment***.
> An interment takes place in a ***cemetery*** or ***graveyard***.
> A funeral at which a dead person's body is burned is a ***cremation***.
> A cremation takes place in a ***crematorium***.
> A vehicle which carries a dead person to a funeral is a ***hearse***.
> A formal funeral procession is a ***cortège***.
> People who attend a funeral are ***mourners***.
> A person who organizes funerals is an ***undertaker***.

funfair *noun* SEE **fair** *noun*

funny *adjective*
1 *He told us a funny joke.* amusing, comic, diverting, entertaining, hilarious, humorous, [*informal*] priceless, witty.
AN OPPOSITE IS serious.
2 *There's a funny smell in here.* abnormal, curious, mysterious, odd, peculiar, puzzling, queer, strange, unusual, weird.

fur *noun*

> VARIOUS COVERINGS ON ANIMALS' SKINS: bristles, coat, down, fleece, hair, hide, pelt, wool.

furious *adjective*
1 *He was furious because he didn't win.* angry, enraged, fuming, incensed, infuriated, livid, mad, raging, seething.
2 *We worked at a furious rate to try to get things finished.* desperate, excited, frantic, frenzied, hectic, intense, tempestuous, tumultuous, turbulent, violent, wild.
AN OPPOSITE IS calm.

furniture *noun*

> VARIOUS ITEMS OF FURNITURE FOR SITTING OR SLEEPING ON: armchair, bed, bunk, chair, cot, couch, cradle, dining chair, divan, pew, pouffe, rocking chair, seat, settee, sofa, stool.
>
> VARIOUS ITEMS OF FURNITURE TO KEEP THINGS IN OR PUT THINGS ON: bench, bookcase, bureau, cabinet, chest of drawers, coffee table, cupboard, desk, dresser, dressing table, filing cabinet, sideboard, table, trestle table, wardrobe, workbench.
> A set of pieces of furniture that go together is a ***suite***.
> The soft covering on armchairs, sofas, etc., is ***upholstery***.
> Old and valuable pieces of furniture are ***antiques***.

furrow *noun*
A furrow to sow seeds in is a ***drill***.
A furrow made by the wheels of vehicles is a ***rut***.
A furrow in someone's skin is a ***wrinkle***.

furry *adjective*
A small, furry creature was curled up inside the box. downy, feathery, fleecy, fuzzy, hairy, woolly.

further *adjective*
We need further information. additional, extra, fresh, more, new, supplementary.

further *verb*
We want to further the cause of peace. advance, aid, assist, back, encourage, help along, promote, support, urge on.

furthermore *adverb*
> *We started late and, furthermore, we ran out of petrol on the motorway.* additionally, also, besides, moreover, too.

furtive *adjective*
> *She cast a furtive glance over her shoulder and then unlocked the door.* cautious, concealed, crafty, disguised, secretive, sly, [*informal*] sneaky, stealthy, underhand.

fury *noun*
> **1** *He didn't disguise his fury at what had happened.* anger, indignation, rage, wrath.
> **2** *There was no shelter from the fury of the storm.* ferocity, fierceness, force, intensity, power, savagery, tempestuousness, turbulence, violence.

fuse *verb*
> *The metals had fused together into a solid mass.* blend, combine, join, melt, merge, unite.
> To fuse metals together when you are making or mending something is to **solder** or **weld** them.

fuss *noun*
> *There was a lot of fuss when someone was accused of cheating.* bother, commotion, excitement, hullabaloo, trouble.

fuss *verb*
> *Please don't fuss!* get excited, make a commotion, worry.

fussy *adjective*
> **1** *Our cat is fussy about her food.* [*informal*] choosy, finicky, hard to please, particular.
> **2** *I don't like clothes with fussy designs.* complicated, detailed, elaborate.

futile *adjective*
> *I made a futile attempt to stop him going.* fruitless, pointless, unproductive, unprofitable, unsuccessful, useless, vain, wasted.
> AN OPPOSITE IS successful.

future *noun*
> *Now that we have sponsorship, the team's future looks bright.* outlook, prospects.
> AN OPPOSITE IS past.

fuzzy *adjective*
> **1** *The TV picture has gone fuzzy.* blurred, cloudy, hazy, indistinct, out of focus, unclear, unfocused.
> AN OPPOSITE IS clear.
> **2** *She was wearing a fuzzy sweater.* fleecy, fluffy, woolly.

Gg

gadget *noun*
> *It's a handy little gadget.* contraption, device, implement, instrument, tool.

gain *verb*
> **1** *They had nothing to gain by lying.* acquire, earn, get, obtain, win.
> AN OPPOSITE IS lose.
> **2** *They finally gained the shore.* achieve, get to, reach.

gains *plural noun*
> *The stock market saw large gains yesterday.* increases, profits.

gala *noun*
> *The village annual gala is in July.* carnival, fair, festival, fête.

gallant *adjective*
> **1** *In the old days, a gallant knight defended the weak and the poor.* brave, courageous, fearless, heroic, valiant.
> AN OPPOSITE IS cowardly.
> **2** *The gallant young man did everything he could to make the ladies comfortable.* gentlemanly, polite.
> AN OPPOSITE IS rude.

gamble *verb*
> *He gambled £10 on the horse.* bet, risk, wager.

> DIFFERENT WAYS OF GAMBLING: betting, bingo, cards, dice, lottery, the pools, raffle.

game *noun*
> **1** *Their favourite game was hide-and-seek.* amusement, fun, pastime, sport.
> **2** *I've been selected to play in the game on Saturday.* competition, contest, match, tournament.

GAMES YOU USUALLY PLAY INDOORS: bagatelle, billiards, bingo, cards, charades, chess, darts, dice, dominoes, draughts, lotto, ludo, marbles, ping-pong, pool, skittles, snooker, solitaire, table tennis, tiddlywinks, tombola.

CHILDREN'S GAMES OFTEN PLAYED OUT OF DOORS: conkers, hide-and-seek, hopscotch, leapfrog, roller skating, skateboarding, skating, sledging, tag.
OTHER OUTDOOR GAMES, SEE **sport**.

gang *noun*
A gang of workmen dug a hole in the road. crowd, group, team.

gangster *noun*
The film was about a group of ruthless gangsters. criminal, [*informal*] crook, gunman.

gaol *verb*
The thief was gaoled for six months. detain, imprison, lock up, [*informal*] shut away.

gap *noun*
1 *The animals escaped through a gap in the fence.* breach, break, hole, opening.
2 *She returned to work after a gap of two years.* interval, pause, rest.

gaping *adjective*
He nearly fell into a gaping hole. broad, wide, wide open, yawning.

garbage *noun*
Put the garbage in the bin. junk, litter, refuse, rubbish, trash, waste.

garden *noun*

VARIOUS FEATURES OF A GARDEN: border, compost heap, flower bed, greenhouse, hedge, lawn, orchard, path, patio, pond, rockery or rock garden, shed, shrubbery, terrace, trellis.
SEE ALSO **flower, fruit, tree, vegetable**.

TOOLS GARDENERS USE: cultivator, fork, hoe, lawnmower, rake, ➡

riddle, secateurs, shears, shovel, sieve, spade, trowel, watering can.

SUBSTANCES USED IN THE GARDEN: compost, fertilizer, insecticide, manure, peat, pesticide, weedkiller.

garment *noun* SEE **clothes**

gas *noun*
A cloud of poisonous gas escaped from the factory. fumes, vapour.

SOME KINDS OF GAS: carbon dioxide, carbon monoxide, coal gas, helium, hydrogen, methane, nitrogen, oxygen, ozone, sulphur dioxide, tear gas.

gash *noun*
The broken glass made a nasty gash in my foot. cut, slash, slit, wound.

gasp *verb*
At the end of the race we lay down gasping for breath. gulp, pant.

gate *noun*
We waited at the gate to be let in. barrier, entrance, gateway.

gather *verb*
1 *A crowd gathered to watch the performers.* assemble, collect, come together, swarm round.
AN OPPOSITE IS disperse.
2 *The captain gathered her team to give them a talk.* bring together, get together, muster, round up.
3 *They were gathering mushrooms in the forest.* collect, harvest, pick.
4 *I gather that you've just been on holiday.* hear, learn, understand.

gathering *noun*
There was a big family gathering for her birthday. assembly, crowd, meeting, party.

gaudy *adjective*
He wore a rather gaudy shirt. brightly coloured, flashy, showy.

gauge *verb*
I tried to gauge how much further she had to go. assess, estimate, judge, measure.

gaze
The dog gazed hungrily at the food.
look, stare.

gear *noun*
We put the fishing gear in the back of the car. equipment, paraphernalia, tackle, things.

gem *noun*
The gems glittered under the bright lights. jewel, precious stone.
SEE ALSO **jewel**.

gender *noun*
The gender of a man is ***male*** or ***masculine***.
The gender of a woman is ***female*** or ***feminine***.
The gender of a thing is ***neuter***.

general *adjective*
1 *There's a general feeling that our team will win.* common, popular, prevailing, prevalent, widespread.
2 *I've only got a general idea of where we are.* approximate, broad, indefinite, vague.

generally *adverb*
We generally buy our food at the shop down the road. as a rule, chiefly, commonly, mainly, mostly, normally, on the whole, principally, usually.

generate *verb*
The shop generated a lot of business when it started giving away free gifts. bring about, create, give rise to, produce.

generous *adjective*
1 *It was generous of you to give him your last sweet.* charitable, unselfish.
AN OPPOSITE IS selfish.
2 *We all had generous second helpings.* ample, large, liberal.
AN OPPOSITE IS meagre.

genial *adjective*
His genial smile made us feel welcome. cheerful, friendly, good-natured, kind, pleasant, warm-hearted.
AN OPPOSITE IS unfriendly.

genius *noun*
She's a genius at maths. expert, mastermind, wizard.

gentle *adjective*
1 *The vet is very gentle with the sick animals.* good-tempered, humane, kind, tender.
2 *She had a gentle voice.* low, mild, peaceful, pleasant, quiet, reassuring, soft.
3 *The yacht hardly moved in the gentle wind.* faint, imperceptible, light, slight.
AN OPPOSITE IS rough or severe.

genuine *adjective*
1 *Is that a genuine diamond?* actual, authentic, real.
AN OPPOSITE IS fake.
2 *He seemed like a very genuine person.* honest, sincere, true.
AN OPPOSITE IS false.

germs *plural noun*
Many germs cause diseases. bacteria, [*informal*] bugs, microbes, viruses.

germinate *verb*
The seeds will germinate when the weather gets warmer. sprout, start growing.

gesture *noun*
She made an angry gesture. action, movement, sign.

get *verb*
1 *It's getting cold.* become, grow, turn.
2 *I got a new bike yesterday.* acquire, buy, obtain, purchase, receive.
3 *What time did you get home?* arrive, reach.
4 *The dog got the ball.* bring, fetch, find, pick up, retrieve.
5 *Shall I get the tea?* make ready, prepare.
6 *Get him to do the washing up.* order, persuade.
7 *I don't get what you mean.* comprehend, follow, grasp, understand.
to get on with something *She told us to get on with our work.* continue, concentrate on, keep on with, persevere with.
to get out of something *He always gets out of the hard jobs.* avoid, shirk.
to get over something *Have you got over your cold?* get better from, recover from.

ghastly *adjective*
We saw a ghastly accident on the motorway. appalling, awful, dreadful, frightful, grim, grisly, horrible, horrifying, shocking, terrible.

ghost *noun*
Do you believe in ghosts? spectre, spirit.

giant *adjective*
The giant tree towered above us. colossal, enormous, gigantic, huge, immense, mammoth, massive, monstrous.
SEE ALSO **big**.
AN OPPOSITE IS tiny.

giddy *adjective*
I felt giddy when I stood at the edge of the cliff. dizzy, faint, unsteady.

gift *noun*
1 *I received some nice gifts on my birthday.* present.
2 *She has a gift for music.* genius, talent.

gifted *adjective*
There are some gifted players in the team. able, accomplished, clever, skilful, talented.

gigantic *adjective*
There was a gigantic statue in the square. colossal, enormous, giant, huge, immense, mammoth, massive, monstrous.
AN OPPOSITE IS tiny.

girder *noun*
The roof was supported by a framework of iron girders. bar, beam.

girl *noun*
A synonym used in some parts of Britain is *lass*.
Old-fashioned words are *damsel*, *maid*, and *maiden*.

give *verb*
1 *He gave each person a present.* deal out, distribute, hand over, issue, pass, supply.
2 *The sponsors gave a prize to the winner.* award, offer, present.
3 *Will you give something to our collection for charity?* contribute, donate.
4 *He gave a laugh.* let out, utter.
5 *We gave a concert at the end of term.* arrange, organize, perform, present, put on.
6 *Will this branch give if I sit on it?* bend, break, buckle, collapse, give way.
to give in *They gave in after a long fight.* submit, surrender, yield.
to give up *We gave up trying to beat the record.* abandon, end, finish, [*informal*] scrap.

glad *adjective*
I was glad to hear that she was feeling better. delighted, happy, pleased.
AN OPPOSITE IS sad.

glamorous *adjective*
She looks very glamorous in that dress. attractive, beautiful, gorgeous, [*informal*] sexy.
AN OPPOSITE IS unattractive.

glamour *noun*
She was excited by the glamour of a career in television. appeal, attraction, excitement, fascination.

glance *verb*
1 *I glanced at my watch.* look quickly, peep.
2 *The ball glanced off the edge of the bat.* bounce, ricochet.

glare *verb*
He glared angrily at me. frown, glower, scowl.

glare *noun*
1 *The glare of the lights dazzled me.* brightness, brilliance.
SEE ALSO **light** *noun*.
2 *She gave me an angry glare.* frown, nasty look, scowl.

glaring *adjective*
1 *The car's glaring headlights nearly caused an accident.* blinding, bright, brilliant, dazzling.
2 *The book was full of glaring mistakes.* conspicuous, gross, noticeable, obvious.

glass, glasses *nouns*

WORDS FOR GLASS USED IN WINDOWS: double glazing, glazing, pane, plate glass.

KINDS OF GLASS FOR DRINKS OR LIQUIDS: beaker, goblet, tumbler, wineglass. ➡

GLASSES YOU WEAR TO HELP YOU
SEE OR TO PROTECT YOUR EYES:
bifocals, contact lenses, goggles,
reading glasses, spectacles,
sunglasses.

INSTRUMENTS WITH LENSES TO
MAKE THINGS LOOK BIGGER:
binoculars, field glasses, magnifying
glass, microscope, opera glasses,
telescope.

glassy *adjective*
1 *The road was glassy after the frost.*
icy, shiny, slippery, smooth.
2 *He stared at us with glassy eyes.*
blank, dull, empty, expressionless,
glazed, staring, vacant.

gleam *noun*
*I saw a gleam of moonlight between the
clouds.* glimmer, glint, ray, shaft.

gleam *verb*
The lights gleamed on the water.
glimmer, glint, glisten, shimmer, shine.

gleeful *adjective*
She gave a gleeful laugh. delighted,
exultant, happy, joyful, pleased.
AN OPPOSITE IS gloomy.

glide *verb*
The boat glided gently across the lake.
move smoothly, slide, slip.

glimpse *verb*
*He glimpsed a deer running through
the forest.* catch sight of, make out, see,
spot.

glint *verb*
*The sunlight glinted on the polished
brass.* flash, glitter, sparkle.

glisten *verb*
*The reflection of the lights glistened on
the wet road.* gleam, shine.

glitter *verb*
*The jewels glittered under the bright
lights.* flash, shine, sparkle, twinkle.

gloat *verb*
*There's no need to gloat, even if you did
win by five goals!* boast, crow, exult,
show off.

global *adjective*
*The global effects of pollution are
alarming.* international, universal,
worldwide.

globe *noun*
1 *I'd like to travel all round the globe.*
earth, planet, world.
2 *The light was enclosed in a glass
globe.* ball, sphere.

gloom *noun*
1 *We could hardly see in the gloom.*
darkness, dimness, shade, shadow.
The gloomy light late in the evening is
dusk or *twilight*.
2 *We were filled with gloom when we
heard the news.* dejection, depression,
misery, sadness, unhappiness.

gloomy *adjective*
1 *It was a gloomy day.* cloudy, dark,
dim, murky, overcast, shadowy.
2 *What are you looking so gloomy
about?* dejected, depressed, glum,
melancholy, miserable, sad, unhappy.
3 *This gloomy room needs some bright
curtains to cheer it up.* depressing,
dingy, dismal, dreary, sombre.
AN OPPOSITE IS bright or cheerful.

glorify *verb*
*They didn't like the film because it
glorified war.* celebrate, honour, praise.

glorious *adjective*
1 *It was a glorious victory.* celebrated,
famous, heroic, illustrious, noble,
renowned, triumphant.
AN OPPOSITE IS shameful.
2 *Look at that glorious sunset!*
beautiful, gorgeous, lovely,
magnificent, spectacular, splendid,
superb, wonderful.
AN OPPOSITE IS ugly.

glossy *adjective*
The book was printed on glossy paper.
gleaming, lustrous, shining, shiny.
AN OPPOSITE IS dull.

glow *noun*
1 *The fire gave out a warm glow.*
brightness, heat, redness, warmth.
2 *She felt a glow of pleasure when she
passed the exam.* feeling, sensation.

glow *verb*
The embers of the bonfire glowed in the dark. gleam, shine.
FOR VARIOUS EFFECTS OF LIGHT, SEE **light** *noun*.

glower *verb*
He glowered at them when they interrupted him. frown, glare, scowl, stare angrily.

glue *noun*

VARIOUS THINGS YOU USE FOR GLUING: adhesive, cement, gum, paste, sealant, [*trademark*] Sellotape, sticky tape, wallpaper paste.

glum *adjective*
What are you looking so glum about? dejected, depressed, gloomy, melancholy, miserable, sad, unhappy.
AN OPPOSITE IS cheerful.

gluttonous *adjective*
She has a gluttonous appetite for ice cream! greedy, insatiable.

gnarled *adjective*
The branches of the tree were gnarled with age. bent, crooked, distorted, knobbly, knotty, lumpy, twisted.

gnaw *verb*
The dog gnawed at his bone. bite, chew.

go *verb*
The verb *to go* can be used in many ways. We give just some of the common ways here
1 *I'd like to go round the world one day.* journey, travel.
SEE ALSO **travel**.
2 *We'll go in a minute.* be off, depart, get away, leave, proceed, set out, start.
3 *This road goes to Bristol.* extend, lead, reach, stretch.
4 *The milk went sour.* become, turn.
5 *My watch isn't going.* function, operate, work.
6 *Plates go on that shelf.* belong, have a place.

7 *The show went well.* happen, pass, proceed, take place.
to go off *The bomb went off.* detonate, explode.
to go on 1 *What went on while I was away?* happen, occur, take place.
2 *Please go on with what you're saying.* carry on, continue, keep going, persevere, proceed.

go *noun*
Whose go is it next? chance, opportunity, try, turn.

goal *noun*
What is your goal in life? aim, ambition, intention, object, objective, purpose, target.

gobble *verb*
They gobbled up all the food. bolt, eat quickly, gulp, guzzle.

good *adjective*
We use the adjective *good* to describe anything we like or approve of. Therefore the number of possible synonyms is almost endless. We give here just some of the many words you could use
1 *We had a good time at the party.* agreeable, [*informal*] brilliant, delightful, enjoyable, excellent, [*informal*] fabulous, [*informal*] fantastic, fine, [*informal*] incredible, lovely, marvellous, nice, outstanding, perfect, pleasant, pleasing, remarkable, satisfactory, [*informal*] sensational, splendid, superb, [*informal*] terrific, wonderful.
2 *She's a good friend.* caring, charitable, considerate, decent, friendly, helpful, humane, loving, loyal, merciful, noble.
3 *They promised they would be good in future.* honest, just, law-abiding, moral, obedient, truthful, virtuous.
4 *He's a good tennis player.* able, accomplished, capable, clever, competent, efficient, gifted, proficient, skilful, skilled, talented.
5 *She did a good job.* commendable, competent, correct, creditable, conscientious, neat, praiseworthy, thorough, well done.

6 *After our long walk we were looking forward to a good meal.* delicious, eatable, healthy, nourishing, nutritious, tasty, well-cooked, wholesome.
AN OPPOSITE IS bad.

good-looking *adjective*
He's a very good-looking man.
attractive, handsome.
AN OPPOSITE IS ugly.

good-natured *adjective*
He told us what we did wrong in a good-natured way, so no one got upset.
considerate, friendly, helpful, kind, pleasant, sympathetic.
AN OPPOSITE IS unkind.

goods *plural noun*
Lorries take the goods from the ship to the warehouse. cargo, freight, merchandise, produce, wares.

goodwill *noun*
The meeting was a success because of the goodwill shown by both sides.
friendliness, good intentions.

gorgeous *adjective*
She always wore gorgeous clothes.
beautiful, colourful, lovely, magnificent, splendid, superb.
AN OPPOSITE IS ugly.

gossip *verb*
Those two are always gossiping!
chatter, spread rumours, tell tales.

gossip *noun*
1 *Don't believe all the gossip you hear.*
chat, chatter, rumour, scandal.
2 *He's an awful gossip.* busybody, chatterbox, nosy parker, telltale.

gouge *verb*
He gouged a hole in the wall. cut, dig, hollow out, scoop out.

govern *verb*
They governed the country fairly.
administer, be in charge of, control, direct, look after, manage, regulate, rule, run, supervise.

government *noun*

DIFFERENT TYPES OF GOVERNMENT: democracy, dictatorship, monarchy, republic.

GROUPS OF PEOPLE INVOLVED IN GOVERNMENT: the Cabinet, the civil service, government departments or ministries, local authorities, parliament.

INDIVIDUAL PEOPLE INVOLVED IN GOVERNMENT: Chancellor of the Exchequer, civil servants, Members of Parliament, ministers, politicians, the premier, the President, the Prime Minister, Secretaries of State, senators.

PEOPLE INVOLVED IN LOCAL GOVERNMENT: councillors, the mayor.

PEOPLE WHO WORK FOR THEIR GOVERNMENT IN FOREIGN COUNTRIES: ambassadors, consuls, diplomats.

grab *verb*
I grabbed the reins of the runaway horse. catch, clutch, get hold of, grasp, seize, snatch.

graceful *adjective*
I admired the dancer's graceful movements. flowing, nimble, pliant, supple.
AN OPPOSITE IS clumsy.

gracious *adjective*
She gave a gracious smile. agreeable, courteous, good-natured, kind, pleasant, polite.
AN OPPOSITE IS rude or unkind.

grade *noun*
The butcher sells only top grade meat.
class, quality, standard.

grade *verb*
Eggs are graded according to size.
classify, group, sort.

gradient *noun*
They struggled up the steep gradient.
ascent, bank, hill, incline, rise, slope.

gradual *adjective*
There has been a gradual increase in prices. even, gentle, moderate, regular, slow, steady.
AN OPPOSITE IS sudden.

grain *noun*
1 They grow a lot of grain in this part of the country. cereals, corn.
2 He had some grains of sand in his shoes. bit, particle, speck.

grand *adjective*
The wedding was a grand occasion. big, great, important, imposing, impressive, magnificent, [*informal*] posh, splendid, stately.
AN OPPOSITE IS insignificant.

grant *verb*
They granted his request for leave. allow, give, let you have, permit.

grant *noun*
She got a grant to help her pay for a music course. allowance, award, scholarship, sponsorship, subsidy.

graphic *adjective*
The newspaper printed a graphic account of the battle. clear, descriptive, detailed, lifelike, lively, vivid.

graphics *plural noun*
The graphics were produced by computer. diagrams, drawings, pictures.

grapple *verb*
They grappled with the intruder, but he got away. struggle, wrestle.

grasp *verb*
1 He grasped the end of the rope. catch, clutch, grab, grip, hang on to, hold, seize, take hold of.
2 The ideas were quite difficult to grasp. appreciate, comprehend, follow, understand.

grasp *noun*
She has a good grasp of mathematics. comprehension, understanding.

grasping *adjective*
He's a grasping old miser. greedy, miserly, money-grabbing, selfish, tight.
AN OPPOSITE IS generous.

grass *noun*

VARIOUS GRASS-COVERED AREAS: field, green, lawn, meadow, pasture, playing field, prairie, recreation ground, savannah, steppe, village green.

grate *verb*
1 I grated the cheese. shred.
2 The chalk grated on the board. rub, scrape, scratch.
to grate on The parrot's screeching grates on me. annoy, irritate, upset, vex.

grateful *adjective*
I'm grateful for your help. appreciative, thankful.
AN OPPOSITE IS ungrateful.

grating *noun*
There was an iron grating over the top of the well. framework, grid, grill.

gratitude *noun*
How can we show our gratitude for her help? appreciation, thanks.

grave *noun*

THINGS PUT UP TO MARK A GRAVE: gravestone, headstone, memorial, monument, plaque, tombstone.

PLACES WHERE DEAD PEOPLE ARE BURIED: catacomb, cemetery, crypt, graveyard, mausoleum, tomb, vault.

grave *adjective*
1 They looked grave when they heard the news. grim, sad, serious, thoughtful.
AN OPPOSITE IS cheerful.
2 She made a grave mistake. crucial, important, serious, vital.
AN OPPOSITE IS trivial.

graveyard *noun*
He was buried in the local graveyard. burial ground, cemetery, churchyard.

graze *verb*
I grazed my knee when I fell off my bike. scrape, scratch.

greasy *adjective*
I don't like greasy foods. fatty, oily.

great *adjective*
1 *Our voices echoed round the great cavern.* big, enormous, extensive, huge, immense, large, tremendous, vast.
AN OPPOSITE IS small.
2 *Crime is a great problem in this area.* considerable, crucial, major, serious, severe.
AN OPPOSITE IS trivial.
3 *The opening of the Olympic Games is a great event.* grand, important, large scale, magnificent, spectacular.
AN OPPOSITE IS unimportant.
4 *Shakespeare was a great writer.* brilliant, celebrated, classic, exceptional, famous, notable, outstanding, well-known.
AN OPPOSITE IS ordinary.

greed *noun*
Because of his greed, there was nothing left for me! gluttony, overeating, selfishness.

greedy *adjective*
1 *She was so greedy that she ate all the cakes.* gluttonous, [*informal*] piggish.
2 *The greedy shopkeeper cheated his customers.* grasping, miserly, money-grabbing, selfish, tight-fisted.
AN OPPOSITE IS generous or unselfish.

green *adjective, noun*

VARIOUS SHADES OF GREEN: emerald, grass-green, jade, khaki, lime, olive, pea-green, turquoise.

greens *plural noun* SEE **vegetable**

greet *verb*
She greeted me with a friendly wave. hail, receive, salute, welcome.

greeting *noun*

GREETINGS USED WHEN WE MEET SOMEONE: good day (good morning, etc.), hallo or hello or hullo, how do you do, welcome.

GREETINGS USED ON CARDS FOR SPECIAL OCCASIONS: congratulations, happy anniversary, happy birthday, many happy returns, merry Christmas, well done.

grey *adjective, noun*

VARIOUS SHADES OF GREY: ashen, blackish, leaden, off-white, silvery, slate grey, smoky, sooty, whitish.

grid *noun*
There was an iron grid covering the hole. framework, grating, grill.

grief *noun*
He could not hide his grief when his grandfather died. anguish, misery, regret, sadness, sorrow, unhappiness.
AN OPPOSITE IS joy.

grievance *noun*
If you have a grievance, speak to the manager. complaint, grumble.

grieve *verb*
1 *They are still grieving over her death.* lament, mourn, weep.
AN OPPOSITE IS rejoice.
2 *Her bad behaviour grieved her parents.* distress, hurt, sadden, upset.
AN OPPOSITE IS please.

grievous *adjective*
1 *Her death was a grievous loss.* distressing, sad, tragic.
2 *The school suffered grievous damage in the storm.* grave, heavy, serious, severe.

grim *adjective*
1 *I could tell she was angry by the grim expression on her face.* bad-tempered, severe, stern, unfriendly.
AN OPPOSITE IS friendly.
2 *The monster's grim appearance made us shudder.* frightening, frightful, grisly, gruesome, hideous, horrible, menacing, terrible, threatening.
AN OPPOSITE IS attractive.

grime *noun*
The windows were covered in grime. dirt, dust, filth.

grin *verb*
FOR VARIOUS WAYS TO SHOW AMUSEMENT, SEE **laugh**.

grind *verb*
1 *He ground the coffee beans.* crush, mill, powder, pulverize.
2 *He ground the blades of the lawn mower.* polish, sharpen.

grip *verb*
1 *Grip the handle tightly.* clutch, grasp, hold, seize.
2 *The audience was gripped by the film.* absorb, engross, fascinate.

grisly *adjective*
We found the grisly remains of a dead sheep. dreadful, gory, gruesome, hideous, horrible, nasty, revolting, sickening.

grit *noun*
1 *I've got some grit in my shoe.* gravel, stones.
2 *The runners in the marathon showed real grit.* bravery, courage, determination, endurance, [*informal*] guts, pluck, toughness.

groan *verb*
He groaned with pain. cry out, moan, sigh, wail.

groom *verb*
The stable girl was grooming the horse. brush, clean, smarten, tidy.

groove *noun*
He cut a groove in the table. channel, cut, furrow, rut, scratch, slot.

grope *verb*
I groped in the dark for the light switch. feel about, fumble.

gross *adjective*
1 *He was so gross he could hardly fit into the chair.* fat, heavy, overweight.
2 *I was disgusted by their gross behaviour.* coarse, indecent, offensive, rude, shocking, vulgar.
3 *It was a gross injustice.* conspicuous, extreme, glaring, noticeable, obvious.

grotesque *adjective*
1 *He can twist himself into grotesque shapes.* deformed, distorted, fantastic, strange, unnatural, weird.
2 *It was a grotesque idea.* absurd, ludicrous, ridiculous.

ground *noun*
1 *I planted some seeds in the ground.* earth, land, soil.
2 *The ground was too wet to play on.* arena, field, pitch, stadium.
grounds *What were her grounds for accusing you?* argument, basis, justification, reason.

group *noun*
1 *I like to feel I'm a member of a group.* community, family, society.
2 *People with similar interests often form a group.* alliance, association, club, guild, league, society, union.
3 *We formed a group to discuss sports day.* assembly, committee, gathering, meeting.
4 *She sorted her clothes into different groups.* category, collection, pack, set.
5 *A group of soldiers marched down the road.* army, company, force, platoon, squad, squadron, troop.

SPECIAL WORDS FOR GROUPS OF PEOPLE:
a **band** of musicians.
a **class** of children in school.
a **company** of actors.
a **congregation** of worshippers in church.
a **coven** of witches.
a **crew** of sailors.
a **gang** of workers.
a **horde** of invaders.
a **mob** of rioters.
a **rabble** of troublemakers.
a **team** of players.

SPECIAL WORDS FOR GROUPS OF ANIMALS:
a **brood** of chicks.
a **covey** of partridges.
a **flock** of sheep or birds.
a **gaggle** of geese.
a **herd** of cattle or elephants.
a **litter** of pigs or puppies.
a **pack** of wolves.
a **pride** of lions.
a **school** of whales.
a **shoal** of fish.
a **swarm** of insects.

SPECIAL WORDS FOR GROUPS OF THINGS:
a **battery** of guns.
a **bunch** of flowers.
a **clump** of trees.
a **clutch** of eggs in a nest.
a **constellation** or **galaxy** of stars.
a **convoy** or **fleet** of ships.

group *verb*
I want you to group in fours for the next game. assemble, collect, come together, gather, get together, swarm round, team up.

grouse *verb*
He's always grousing about work. complain, grumble, moan, object, protest, whine.

grow *verb*
1 *The flowers I planted are growing fast.* become bigger, develop, get bigger, spring up, sprout, swell.
2 *His business has grown this year.* build up, enlarge, expand, flourish, increase, prosper.
3 *She likes growing roses.* cultivate, produce, raise.
4 *You'll grow more confident with practice.* become, get.
to grow up *She's growing up fast.* become adult, mature.

growth *noun*
1 *He is pleased with the growth of his business.* development, enlargement, expansion, increase, spread.
2 *The doctor examined the growth on my foot.* lump, swelling, tumour.

grub *noun*
I found a grub in my apple. caterpillar, larva, maggot.

grubby *adjective*
Wash your hands if they are grubby. dirty, grimy, messy, mucky, soiled.
AN OPPOSITE IS clean.

grudge *verb*
to grudge someone something *I don't grudge him his success.* be jealous or resentful about, envy, resent.

gruelling *adjective*
The marathon is a gruelling race. challenging, exhausting, hard, laborious, strenuous, tough.
AN OPPOSITE IS easy.

gruesome *adjective*
The battlefield was a gruesome sight. appalling, bloody, dreadful, frightful, gory, grisly, hideous, horrible, nasty, revolting, sickening, terrible.

gruff *adjective*
He spoke in a gruff voice. harsh, hoarse, husky, rough.

grumble *verb*
She grumbles if I'm late. complain, grouse, moan, object, protest, whine.

grumpy *adjective*
He's grumpy because he's got a headache. bad-tempered, cross, ill-tempered, irritable, short-tempered, sour.
AN OPPOSITE IS good-tempered.

guarantee *verb*
They guaranteed that they'd deliver it today. pledge, promise, undertake, vow.

guard *verb*
1 *We had injections to guard us against various diseases.* defend, protect, safeguard, shield.
2 *Two policemen guarded the prisoner.* escort, keep watch on, look after, mind, stand guard over, tend, watch over.

guard *noun*
A guard was on duty at the gate. lookout, security officer, sentinel, sentry, warder, watchman.

guardian *noun*
The guardian of the treasure was a fierce dragon. defender, keeper, minder, protector.

guess *noun*
My answer was just a guess. estimate, feeling, hunch.

guess *verb*
1 *I didn't know the answer, so I guessed.* estimate, have a shot, make a guess.
2 *I guess you are tired after your journey.* assume, imagine, suppose, think.

guest *noun*
We had guests on Sunday. caller, visitor.

guide *noun*
1 *The guide showed us around.* courier, escort, leader, tour leader.
2 *We bought a useful guide to the city.* guidebook, handbook.

guide *verb*
She guided me out of the maze. direct, escort, lead, show the way, steer.

guidelines *plural noun*
She gave us some guidelines to help us with our project. advice, a brief, guidance, instructions, tips.

guilt *noun*
1 He admitted his guilt. guiltiness, wickedness, wrongdoing.
2 You could see the look of guilt on her face. bad conscience, penitence, regret, remorse, shame.
AN OPPOSITE IS innocence.

guilty *adjective*
1 The jury found him guilty. at fault, in the wrong, liable, responsible, to blame.
AN OPPOSITE IS innocent.
2 She had a guilty look on her face. ashamed, conscience-stricken, penitent, remorseful, repentant.
AN OPPOSITE IS unrepentant.

gulf *noun*
There's a great gulf between their points of view. difference, gap, opening, separation, split.

gullible *adjective*
He's so gullible he'll believe anything. innocent, naive, trusting, unsuspecting.

gulp *verb*
1 Don't gulp your food. bolt, gobble, guzzle.
2 She gulped in amazement. gasp, swallow.

gun *noun*
FOR VARIOUS TYPES OF GUN, SEE **weapon**.

gush *noun*
There was a gush of water from the pipe. cascade, flood, jet, spout, spurt, stream, torrent.

gush *verb*
Oil gushed from the well. burst, erupt, flood, flow, pour, rush, spout, spurt, squirt, stream.

guts *plural noun*
[informal] The players showed real guts. bravery, courage, determination, endurance, grit, pluck, toughness.

guzzle *verb*
They guzzled down all the cakes. bolt, gobble, gulp.

Hh

habit *noun*
1 It was his habit to go for a walk each morning. convention, custom, practice, routine.
2 He has a habit of scratching his head. mannerism, way.

habitual *adjective*
1 She soon recovered her habitual good humour. accustomed, customary, normal, ordinary, predictable, regular, routine, standard, traditional, usual.
AN OPPOSITE IS abnormal.
2 He is a a habitual smoker. addicted, confirmed, dependent, persistent.

hack *verb*
They hacked through the undergrowth. chop, cut, slash, slice.
SEE ALSO **cut** *verb*.

haggard *adjective*
He looked haggard after his ordeal. exhausted, gaunt, ill, thin, tired out, withered, worn out.
AN OPPOSITE IS healthy.

haggle *verb*
They haggled over the price. argue, bargain, negotiate.

hair *noun*

> WORDS FOR THE HAIR ON YOUR HEAD: hank, lock, [informal] mop, tress.
>
> VARIOUS HAIRSTYLES: bob, braids, crew-cut, curls, dreadlocks, fringe, Mohican, perm or permanent wave, pigtail, plaits, ponytail, quiff, ringlets, short back and sides, sideboards, sideburns, topknot. ➡

PEOPLE WHO CUT AND CARE FOR YOUR HAIR: barber, coiffeur or coiffeuse, hairdresser, hairstylist.

WORDS TO DESCRIBE THE COLOUR OF HAIR: auburn, [*male*] blond, [*female*] blonde, brunette, [*informal*] carroty, dark, fair, flaxen, ginger, grey, grizzled, mousy, platinum blonde, red, silver.

FALSE HAIR: hairpiece, toupee, wig.

HAIR ON AN ANIMAL: bristles, down, fleece, fur, mane.

hair-raising *adjective*
The drive along the mountain road was hair-raising. alarming, dangerous, frightening, scary, terrifying.

hairy *adjective*
The dog had a thick hairy coat. bristly, furry, fuzzy, hirsute, long-haired, shaggy, woolly.

half-hearted *adjective*
There's no point playing if you're going to be half-hearted about it. apathetic, indifferent, lukewarm, uncommitted, unenthusiastic.
AN OPPOSITE IS enthusiastic.

hall *noun*
1 *The hall was full for the concert.* assembly hall, auditorium, concert hall, theatre.
2 *When you go through the front door, you find yourself in the hall.* entrance hall, foyer, hallway, lobby.

hallucination *noun*
She's been having hallucinations. delusion, dream, fantasy, illusion, mirage, vision.

halt *verb*
1 *A traffic jam halted the traffic.* check, obstruct, stop.
2 *The car halted at the red light.* come to a halt, draw up, pull up, stop, wait.
3 *Work halted when the whistle went.* break off, cease, end, terminate.
AN OPPOSITE IS go or start.

halve *verb*
1 *Halve the tomatoes and scoop out the seeds.* cut in half, divide into halves, split in two.
2 *The workforce has been halved in the last five years.* cut by half, reduce by half.

hammer *verb*
I hammered on the door, but no one answered. [*informal*] bash, batter, beat, knock, strike.
SEE ALSO **hit** *verb*.

hamper *verb*
Bad weather hampered the rescuers. curb, foil, frustrate, get in the way of, handicap, hinder, hold up, interfere with, obstruct, restrict, slow down.
AN OPPOSITE IS help.

hand *noun*
When you clench your hand you make a *fist*.
The flat part of the inside of your hand is the *palm*.

hand *verb*
Hand your essay in at the end of the week. deliver, give, offer, pass, present, submit.
to hand something down *The family home was handed down from generation to generation.* bequeath, leave as a legacy, pass down, pass on.

handicap *noun*
1 *In this job, lack of experience can be a handicap.* difficulty, disadvantage, drawback, hindrance, inconvenience, nuisance, obstacle, problem.
AN OPPOSITE IS advantage.
2 *He was born with a visual handicap.* disability, impairment.

handicap *verb*
Lack of money handicapped the research project. create problems for, hamper, hinder, hold back, restrict.
AN OPPOSITE IS help.

handicraft *noun*
FOR VARIOUS ARTS AND CRAFTS, SEE **art**.

handiwork *noun*
Is this your handiwork? creation, doing, invention, work.

handle *noun*
The handle on my bag has broken. grip, handgrip.
The handle of a sword is the *hilt*.

handle *verb*
1 It's important to handle the puppies very carefully. feel, finger, grasp, hold, stroke, touch.
2 The referee handled the game well. conduct, control, cope with, deal with, look after, manage, supervise.

handsome *adjective*
1 He's a very handsome man. attractive, good-looking.
AN OPPOSITE IS unattractive.
2 The stately home was full of handsome furniture. admirable, beautiful, elegant, tasteful, well-made.
AN OPPOSITE IS ugly.
3 They made a handsome profit when they sold the house. big, large, sizeable, valuable.
AN OPPOSITE IS mean.

handy *adjective*
1 It's a handy gadget for peeling potatoes. convenient, easy to use, helpful, practical, useful, well-designed.
AN OPPOSITE IS awkward.
2 Keep your tools handy. accessible, available, close at hand, easy to reach, nearby, ready.
AN OPPOSITE IS inaccessible.

hang *verb*
1 A blue flag hung from the flagpole. dangle, droop, swing, trail down.
2 I hung the picture on the wall. attach, fasten, fix, peg, pin, stick, suspend.
3 Smoke hung in the air. drift, float, hover.
to hang about or **around** Don't hang about, we'll miss the bus. dawdle, linger, loiter.
to hang on [informal] Try to hang on a bit longer. carry on, continue, hold on, keep going, persevere, persist, stick it out, wait.
to hang on to something 1 Hang on to the rope. catch, grasp, hold, seize.
2 Hang on to your ticket in case they ask to see it. keep, retain, save.

haphazard *adjective*
The arrangement of the exhibition was haphazard. arbitrary, chaotic, confusing, disorderly, disorganized, higgledy-piggledy, random, unplanned.
AN OPPOSITE IS orderly.

happen *verb*
Did anything interesting happen? arise, come about, crop up, emerge, occur, result, take place.

happening *noun*
There have been some strange happenings here lately. event, incident, occurrence, phenomenon.

happiness *noun*
Her face glowed with happiness. bliss, cheerfulness, contentment, delight, ecstasy, elation, exuberance, gaiety, gladness, high spirits, joy, jubilation, light-heartedness, merriment, pleasure, well-being.
AN OPPOSITE IS sorrow.

happy *adjective*
1 She came in looking happy and excited. cheerful, contented, delighted, ecstatic, elated, exultant, glad, gleeful, good-humoured, joyful, light-hearted, merry, overjoyed, over the moon, pleased, proud, radiant, thrilled.
2 They spent many happy days on the beach. blissful, heavenly, idyllic, joyous.
AN OPPOSITE IS unhappy.

harass *verb*
The dog had been harassing the sheep on the farm. annoy, badger, bait, bother, disturb, hound, molest, persecute, pester, plague, torment, trouble.

harassed *adjective*
She felt tired and harassed. distressed, hassled, irritated, stressed, troubled, vexed, worried.
AN OPPOSITE IS carefree.

harbour *noun*

PLACES WHERE SHIPS CAN TIE UP OR SHELTER: anchorage, dock, haven, jetty, landing stage, marina, moorings, pier, port, quay, wharf.

harbour *verb*
He was suspected of harbouring an escaped criminal. conceal, give refuge to, give sanctuary to, hide, protect, shelter, shield.

hard *adjective*
1 *The ground was hard and covered with frost.* dense, firm, flinty, rigid, rocky, solid, stony.
AN OPPOSITE IS soft.
2 *Shovelling the snow from the drive was very hard work.* exhausting, gruelling, heavy, laborious, strenuous, tiring, tough, wearying.
AN OPPOSITE IS easy.
3 *That's a hard question to answer.* baffling, complex, complicated, confusing, difficult, intricate, involved, perplexing, puzzling.
AN OPPOSITE IS simple.
4 *It's been a long, hard winter.* disagreeable, harsh, painful, severe, unpleasant.
AN OPPOSITE IS pleasant.
5 *He was a hard man.* callous, cruel, hard-hearted, heartless, intolerant, merciless, pitiless, ruthless, severe, stern, strict, unfeeling, unkind.
AN OPPOSITE IS kind.
6 *She gave the rope a hard pull.* energetic, forceful, heavy, powerful, strong, violent.
AN OPPOSITE IS slight.
hard up *They are too hard up to buy new clothes.* badly off, needy, poor.

harden *verb*
We left the cement to harden. set, solidify, stiffen.
If you harden clay in a kiln, you *bake* or *fire* it.
AN OPPOSITE IS soften.

hardly *adverb*
I could hardly see in the fog. barely, only just, scarcely, with difficulty.

hardship *noun*
They suffered years of hardship during the war. adversity, affliction, difficulty, misery, misfortune, suffering, trouble, unhappiness, want.

hardware *noun*
The ship's cargo consisted entirely of military hardware. equipment, implements, instruments, machines, machinery, tools.
FOR VARIOUS TOOLS, SEE **tool**.

hard-wearing *adjective*
Denim is a hard-wearing material. durable, lasting, stout, strong, sturdy, tough, well-made.
AN OPPOSITE IS flimsy.

hardy *adjective*
You must be hardy to go camping in this weather. fit, healthy, hearty, robust, strong, sturdy, tough, vigorous.
AN OPPOSITE IS tender.

harm *verb*
1 *His captors didn't harm him.* hurt, ill-treat, injure, misuse, treat badly, wound.
2 *Too much direct sunlight may harm this plant.* damage, ruin, spoil.

harm *noun*
I didn't mean to cause him any harm. damage, hurt, injury, pain.
AN OPPOSITE IS benefit.

harmful *adjective*
The harmful effects of smoking are now well known. bad, damaging, dangerous, deadly, injurious, poisonous, unhealthy, unwholesome.
AN OPPOSITE IS beneficial or harmless.

harmless *adjective*
1 *It was just a bit of harmless fun.* acceptable, innocuous, safe.
2 *The dog looks fierce, but really he's quite harmless.* innocent, inoffensive, mild.
AN OPPOSITE IS dangerous or harmful.

harmonize *verb*
Choose colours which will harmonize in an attractive way. blend, coordinate, go together, match, suit each other.

harmony *noun*
They lived together in perfect harmony. agreement, compatibility, cooperation, friendliness, goodwill, peace, sympathy, understanding.
AN OPPOSITE IS disagreement.

harness noun

> PARTS OF A HORSE'S HARNESS: bit, blinker, bridle, collar, crupper, girth, halter, headstall, noseband, pommel, rein, saddle, spurs, stirrups, trace.

harness verb
Attempts have been made to harness the sun's energy. control, make use of, use, utilize.

harsh adjective
1 *She had a loud harsh voice.* croaking, disagreeable, grating, jarring, rasping, raucous, rough, shrill, strident, unpleasant.
AN OPPOSITE IS gentle.
2 *We blinked in the harsh light.* bright, brilliant, dazzling, gaudy, glaring, lurid.
AN OPPOSITE IS subdued.
3 *Conditions in the prison are harsh.* arduous, difficult, hard, severe, stressful, tough, uncomfortable.
AN OPPOSITE IS easy.
4 *The material had a harsh, unpleasant texture.* abrasive, coarse, rough.
AN OPPOSITE IS smooth.
5 *He has had to endure a lot of harsh criticisms.* brutal, cruel, hard-hearted, merciless, pitiless, severe, stern, strict, unforgiving, unkind, unsympathetic.
AN OPPOSITE IS lenient.

harvest noun
The farmers had a good harvest this year. crop, return, yield.
Things grown on a farm are **produce**.

harvest verb
The weather was too wet for the wheat to be harvested. bring in, collect, gather, mow, pick, reap, take in.

hassle noun
[*informal*] *They had a lot of hassle getting their money back.* argument, bother, fuss, inconvenience, trouble.

haste noun
More haste, less speed. hurry, rush, speed, urgency.

hasty adjective
1 *They made a hasty exit.* abrupt, fast, headlong, hurried, quick, rapid, speedy, sudden, swift.
2 *He soon regretted his hasty decision.* foolhardy, impulsive, rash, reckless, thoughtless.
AN OPPOSITE IS careful or leisurely.

hat noun

> THINGS PEOPLE WEAR ON THE HEAD: balaclava, baseball cap, bearskin, beret, boater, bonnet, bowler, cap, coronet, crash helmet, crown, fez, hard hat, headband, headdress, helmet, hood, mitre, mortarboard, skullcap, sou'wester, stetson, sunhat, tiara, top hat, trilby, turban, wig, yarmulke.

hatch verb
Those troublemakers are hatching a plot. conceive, contrive, [*informal*] cook up, devise, [*informal*] dream up, invent, plan, plot, scheme, think up.

hate verb
1 *He hates spiders.* can't bear, can't stand, detest, dislike, loathe.
2 *I hate her superior attitude.* deplore, despise, resent, scorn.
AN OPPOSITE IS like or love.

hateful adjective
That was a hateful thing to do. awful, contemptible, despicable, detestable, disgusting, foul, horrible, nasty, vile.
AN OPPOSITE IS lovable.

hatred noun
She looked at him with hatred. animosity, antagonism, contempt, detestation, dislike, enmity, hate, hostility, intolerance, loathing.
AN OPPOSITE IS love.

haughty adjective
She had a haughty expression. arrogant, boastful, conceited, lofty, lordly, pompous, presumptuous, proud, [*informal*] stuck-up, superior.
AN OPPOSITE IS modest.

haul verb
He hauled his bike out of the shed. drag, draw, pull, tow.

haunt *verb*
1 *He returned to one of the cafés he used to haunt when he was younger.* frequent, visit frequently.
2 *The sight haunted me for years.* linger in the memory, obsess, prey on.

have *verb*
The verb *have* has many meanings and can be used in many ways. Here are just some of the ways you might use it
1 *I have my own radio.* own, possess.
2 *Our house has six rooms.* consist of, include, incorporate.
3 *We had a good party.* enjoy.
4 *She had a bad time.* endure, experience, feel, go through, live through, put up with, suffer.
5 *I had some really nice presents.* be given, get, obtain, receive.
6 *She had the last toffee.* consume, eat, steal, take.
to have someone on [*informal*] *Don't believe him—he's having you on.* deceive, fool, hoax, mislead, trick.
to have to do something *They had to pay for the damage.* be compelled or forced to, have an obligation to, must, need to, ought to, should.

haven *noun*
The lake is a haven for a variety of wild birds. refuge, place of safety, sanctuary, shelter.
SEE **harbour** *noun*.

hazard *noun*
Beware of the hazards along the way. danger, pitfall, risk, snag, threat, trap.

hazardous *adjective*
He made the hazardous journey to the South Pole. dangerous, risky, unsafe.
AN OPPOSITE IS safe.

haze *noun*
I could hardly see through the haze. cloud, fog, mist, steam, vapour.

hazy *adjective*
1 *The things in the distance were rather hazy.* blurred, dim, faint, misty, unclear.
2 *He's only got a hazy knowledge of history.* uncertain, vague.
AN OPPOSITE IS clear.

head *noun*
1 *Use your head!* ability, brains, intellect, intelligence, mind, understanding.

> PARTS OF YOUR HEAD: brain, brow, cheek, chin, cranium, crown, dimple, ear, eye, forehead, gums, hair, jaw, jowl, lip, mouth, nose, nostril, scalp, skull, teeth, temple, tongue.
> FOR OTHER PARTS OF YOUR BODY, SEE **body**.

2 *She's head of a large business.* [*informal*] boss, controller, director, manager.
SEE ALSO **chief** *noun*.

head *verb*
1 *The department is headed by a government minister.* be in charge of, command, control, direct, govern, guide, lead, manage, rule, run, superintend, supervise.
2 *At the end of the day we headed for home.* aim, go, make, set out, start, steer, turn.
to head someone or **something off** *Police headed off the approaching cars.* deflect, divert, intercept, turn aside.

headache *noun*
Severe kinds of headache are *migraine* and *neuralgia*.

heading *noun*
Each chapter had a different heading. caption, headline, title.

headlong *adjective*
We made a headlong dash to get out of the rain. breakneck, hasty, hurried, impulsive, quick, reckless.

headquarters *plural noun*
They phoned headquarters for instructions. base, depot, head office, [*informal*] HQ.

headteacher *noun*
The headteacher runs the school. headmaster or headmistress, principal.

headway *noun*
They are making little headway with the negotiations. advance, breakthrough, progress.

heal *verb*
1 *It took two months for my leg to heal properly.* get better, knit, mend, recover.
2 *Part of a doctor's job is to heal the sick.* cure, make better, restore, treat.

health *noun*
1 *Unfortunately, his health is poor.* condition, constitution.
2 *He's bursting with health and vitality.* fitness, strength, vigour, well-being.
FOR VARIOUS MEDICAL TREATMENTS, SEE **medicine**.
FOR VARIOUS ILLNESSES, SEE **illness**.

healthy *adjective*
1 *He's always been a healthy child.* fit, flourishing, [*informal*] in good shape, robust, sound, strong, sturdy, vigorous, well.
AN OPPOSITE IS ill.
2 *The air in the mountains is said to be very healthy.* bracing, health-giving, invigorating, wholesome.
AN OPPOSITE IS unhealthy.

heap *noun*
There was an untidy heap of books on her desk. collection, mass, mound, mountain, pile, stack.
heaps of [*informal*] *We had heaps of food.* ample, lots of, plenty of.

heap *verb*
We heaped up all the rubbish. bank, collect, pile, stack.

hear *verb*
1 *Did you hear what she said?* catch, listen to, overhear, pay attention to, pick up.
2 *Have you heard the news?* be told, discover, find out, gather, learn, receive.

heart *noun*
1 *Have you no heart?* affection, compassion, feeling, humanity, kindness, love, sympathy, tenderness, understanding.
2 *It's a new hotel, located right in the heart of the city.* centre, middle.
3 *They tried to get to the heart of the problem.* core, essence.

heartbreaking *adjective*
The sick animal's condition was heartbreaking. distressing, moving, pitiful, tragic.
AN OPPOSITE IS cheering.

heartbroken *adjective*
He was heartbroken when his dog died. dejected, depressed, desolate, grieving, miserable, sad, sorrowful, tearful.
AN OPPOSITE IS cheerful.

heartless *adjective*
How could she be so heartless? callous, cruel, hard-hearted, inhuman, pitiless, ruthless, unfeeling, unkind.
AN OPPOSITE IS kind.

hearty *adjective*
1 *He gave me a hearty slap on the back.* forceful, strong, vigorous.
AN OPPOSITE IS feeble.
2 *He had a hearty appetite after his walk.* big, healthy.
AN OPPOSITE IS poor.
3 *They gave us a hearty welcome.* enthusiastic, sincere, warm.
AN OPPOSITE IS unenthusiastic.

heat *noun*
1 *The cat basked in the heat of the fire.* glow, hotness, warmth.
2 *Last summer, the heat made me feel ill.* closeness, high temperatures, hot weather.
A long period of hot weather is a *heatwave*.

heat *verb*

> VERBS WHICH MEAN TO BE HOT, TO BECOME HOT, OR TO MAKE SOMETHING HOT: bake, blister, boil, burn, cook, fry, grill, inflame, make hot, melt, reheat, roast, scald, scorch, simmer, sizzle, smoulder, steam, stew, swelter, toast, warm up.
> AN OPPOSITE IS cool.

heath *noun*
I took the dog for a walk across the heath. common land, moor, moorland, open country, wasteland.

heave *verb*
They heaved the sacks onto a lorry. drag, draw, haul, hoist, lift, lug, pull, raise, throw, tug.

heaven *noun*
1 *They believed that when they died they would go to heaven.* the afterlife, eternal rest, the next world, paradise.
AN OPPOSITE IS hell.
2 *Lying by the pool with a good book is her idea of heaven.* bliss, contentment, delight, ecstasy, happiness, joy, pleasure.
the heavens *The rocket soared into the heavens.* the sky, space.

heavenly *adjective*
[*informal*] *The weather was heavenly.* beautiful, blissful, delightful, [*informal*] divine, exquisite, lovely, [*informal*] out of this world, wonderful.
AN OPPOSITE IS horrible.

heavy *adjective*
1 *The box was too heavy for me to lift.* bulky, burdensome, large, massive, ponderous, weighty.
2 *Digging the garden is heavy work.* back-breaking, exhausting, gruelling, hard, laborious, strenuous, tiring, tough, wearying.
3 *The book made heavy reading.* deep, demanding, intellectual, serious.
4 *The heavy rain caused flooding.* severe, torrential.
5 *In the morning there was a heavy mist.* dense, thick.
6 *The apple tree had a heavy crop of fruit.* abundant, copious, profuse.
7 *She said goodbye with a heavy heart.* depressed, gloomy, miserable, sad, sorrowful, unhappy.
AN OPPOSITE IS light.

hectic *adjective*
The next few days were hectic. bustling, busy, chaotic, feverish, frantic, lively.
AN OPPOSITE IS leisurely.

hedge *verb*
1 *The garden was hedged with privet.* encircle, enclose, fence in, surround.
2 *When she asked for an answer, he hedged.* be evasive.

heed *verb*
She didn't heed his warning. attend to, consider, listen to, mark, mind, note, notice, obey, pay attention to, regard, take notice of.
AN OPPOSITE IS ignore.

heedless *adjective*
Heedless of other people, they raced through the streets. inconsiderate, neglectful, thoughtless, unconcerned (about), unsympathetic (towards).
AN OPPOSITE IS careful.

hefty *adjective*
The wrestler was a hefty man. [*informal*] beefy, big, brawny, burly, heavy, hulking, large, mighty, muscular, powerful, solid, strong, tough.
AN OPPOSITE IS slight.

height *noun*
The plane was flying at its normal height. altitude, elevation.

heighten *verb*
The crowd's excitement heightened as the kick-off approached. increase, intensify.
AN OPPOSITE IS lessen.

hell *noun*
Some people believe that sinners go to hell. eternal punishment, the lower regions, the underworld.
AN OPPOSITE IS heaven.

helmet *noun*
A helmet worn by builders, etc., is a **hard hat**.
A helmet worn by motor cyclists is a **crash helmet**.
Part of a helmet that protects the face is a **visor**.

help *noun*
Thank you for your help. advice, aid, assistance, backing, benefit, collaboration, cooperation, friendship, guidance, support.
AN OPPOSITE IS hindrance.

help *verb*
1 *She helped him when he was in trouble.* advise, aid, assist, back, befriend, be helpful to, collaborate with, cooperate with, [*informal*] give a hand to, serve, side with, stand by, support, take pity on.
AN OPPOSITE IS hinder.

2 *This medicine will help your cough.*
cure, ease, improve, make better,
relieve.
AN OPPOSITE IS aggravate.
3 *I can't help coughing.* avoid, prevent,
stop.

helpful *adjective*
1 *The staff were friendly and helpful.*
considerate, cooperative, kind,
neighbourly, obliging, sympathetic,
thoughtful.
AN OPPOSITE IS unhelpful.
2 *She gave us some helpful advice.*
beneficial, profitable, useful, valuable,
worthwhile.
AN OPPOSITE IS worthless.

helping *noun*
I got a huge helping of ice cream.
amount, plateful, portion, ration,
serving, share.

helpless *adjective*
Kittens are born blind and helpless.
defenceless, dependent, feeble,
powerless, weak.
AN OPPOSITE IS independent.

hem *verb*
to hem someone in *They were
hemmed in by the crowd.* encircle,
surround.

herald *noun*
*The cuckoo is said to be the herald of
spring.* announcer, messenger.

herald *verb*
*Thunder often heralds a change in the
weather.* advertise, announce, foretell,
indicate, make known, predict,
proclaim, promise.

herb *noun*

VARIOUS HERBS USED FOR
FLAVOURING: balm, balsam, basil,
borage, camomile, caraway, chervil,
chicory, chive, coriander, cumin, dill,
fennel, fenugreek, hyssop, liquorice,
lovage, marjoram, mint, oregano,
parsley, peppermint, rosemary, rue,
sage, savory, spearmint, tansy,
tarragon, thyme.

herd *noun*
FOR WORDS FOR GROUPS OF ANIMALS,
SEE **group** *noun*.

hereditary *adjective*
Cystic fibrosis is a hereditary disease.
handed down, inherited, passed on.

heritage *noun*
*These ancient buildings are part of our
heritage.* culture, history, inheritance,
legacy, tradition.

hero, heroine *nouns*
*Everyone turned out to welcome the
heroes.* champion, idol, victor, winner.

heroic *adjective*
He made a heroic effort to rescue her.
bold, brave, courageous, daring,
fearless, gallant, intrepid, noble,
selfless, valiant.
AN OPPOSITE IS cowardly.

hesitant *adjective*
*He was hesitant about accepting their
offer.* cautious, dithering, faltering,
hesitating, nervous, shy, timid,
uncertain, undecided, unsure, wary,
wavering.
AN OPPOSITE IS confident.

hesitate *verb*
She hesitated, unsure of what to say. be
cautious, delay, dither, falter, hang
back, pause, [*informal*] think twice,
wait, waver.

hidden *adjective*
1 *She kept the money hidden in a
drawer.* concealed, covered, invisible,
out of sight, private, shrouded, unseen.
AN OPPOSITE IS visible.
2 *There's a hidden meaning in the
message.* coded, mysterious, obscure,
secret.
AN OPPOSITE IS obvious.

hide *verb*
1 *Quick!—someone's coming—we'd
better hide.* go into hiding, go to
ground, lie low, lurk, take cover, take
refuge.
AN OPPOSITE IS reveal yourself.
2 *They hid the gold in a cave.* bury,
conceal, put out of sight, secrete.
AN OPPOSITE IS discover.
3 *The clouds hid the sun.* blot out,
cover, mask, screen, shroud, veil.
AN OPPOSITE IS uncover.

4 *I tried to hide my feelings.*
camouflage, cloak, disguise, keep
secret, suppress.
AN OPPOSITE IS show.

hideous *adjective*
*His smile made him look even more
hideous than before.* appalling,
dreadful, frightful, ghastly, gruesome,
repulsive, shocking, terrible, ugly.
AN OPPOSITE IS beautiful.

hideout *noun*
We made a hideout in the garden. den,
hiding place, lair, refuge.

hiding *noun*
His father gave him a hiding. beating,
caning, thrashing.

high *adjective*
1 *The house was surrounded by a high
wall.* high-rise, lofty, soaring, tall,
towering.
2 *The lounge was a spacious room with
a high ceiling.* elevated, raised.
3 *His father was a high official in the
Civil Service.* chief, distinguished,
eminent, important, leading, powerful,
prominent, top.
4 *House prices are very high at the
moment.* dear, excessive, expensive,
unreasonable.
5 *A high wind was blowing.*
exceptional, great, intense, strong.
6 *She had a high squeaky voice.* high-
pitched, piercing, sharp, shrill.
A high singing voice is **soprano** or
treble.

highlight *noun*
*The day in Paris was the highlight of
the trip.* best moment, high spot.

hike *verb*
They hiked across the moors. ramble,
tramp, trek, walk.

hilarious *adjective*
They thought the film was hilarious.
amusing, comic, funny, [*informal*]
hysterical.

hill *noun*
1 *From the top of this hill you can see
for miles around.* mound, mountain,
peak, ridge, summit.
2 *She pushed her bike up the steep hill.*
ascent, gradient, incline, rise, slope.

hinder *verb*
Snowdrifts hindered their progress.
bar, check, curb, delay, deter, frustrate,
get in the way of, hamper, handicap,
hold up, obstruct, prevent, restrict,
slow down, stand in the way of, stop.
AN OPPOSITE IS help.

hindrance *noun*
*Lack of money was a hindrance to the
progress of the research.* difficulty,
disadvantage, drawback, handicap,
inconvenience, obstacle.
AN OPPOSITE IS help.

hinge *verb*
to hinge on *Everything hinges on your
decision.* depend on, rely on, rest on.

hint *noun*
I've no idea what it is—give me a hint.
clue, indication, inkling, sign,
suggestion.

hint *verb*
She hinted that we'd get a surprise. give
a hint, imply, indicate, suggest.

hire *verb*
If you hire a bus or aircraft you
charter it.
If you hire someone to do a job you
engage or **employ** them.
If you hire a building for a time you
lease or **rent** it.

historic *adjective*
Notice that there is a difference
between *historic*, which means famous
or important in history, and *historical*,
which simply refers to anything that
happened in the past
*The Battle of Hastings was a historic
event.* celebrated, eminent, famous,
important, momentous, notable,
renowned, significant, well-known.
AN OPPOSITE IS unimportant.

historical *adjective*
See note under *historic*.
*No one is sure whether Robin Hood is a
historical character.* actual, authentic,
past, real, real-life, true.
AN OPPOSITE IS fictitious.

history *noun*
1 *I'm interested in our country's history.* heritage, past.
2 *He wrote a history of the First World War.* account, chronicle, record.

hit *noun*
1 *He got a nasty hit on the head.* bang, blow, bump, knock, whack.
A hit with your fist is a *punch*.
A hit with your open hand is a *clap* or *slap* or *smack*.
A hit with a bat or club is a *drive* or *stroke* or *swipe*.
2 *The new record was an instant hit.* success, triumph, [*informal*] winner.

hit *verb*
1 *She hit him on the head with her umbrella.*

THERE ARE VARIOUS WAYS TO HIT THINGS: To hit with your fist is to *punch*.
To hit with the palm of your hand is to *clap*, *slap*, *spank*, or *smack*.
To punish someone by hitting them is to *beat*, *birch*, *cane*, *flog*, *lash*, *scourge*, *thrash*, or *whip* them.
To hit someone with a stick or blunt instrument is to *club*, *cosh*, or *cudgel* them.
To hit your toe on something is to *stub* it.
To hit a ball with a bat or club is to *drive* it.
To kill an insect by hitting it is to *swat* it.
To hit something repeatedly is to *batter* or *pound* it.
To hit another vehicle in an accident is to *collide* with it or *ram* it.

OTHER WORDS MEANING TO HIT: These words can be used as nouns as well as verbs. Many of them are used informally. bang, bash, belt, biff, bump, butt, clonk, clout, crack, cuff, jab, jog, kick, knock, nudge, prod, rap, slam, slap, slog, sock, strike, swipe, tap, thump, thwack, wallop, whack, wham.

2 *The drought hit the farmers.* affect, bring disaster to, damage, do harm to, harm, hurt, ruin.
to hit on something *They hit on a new way of making money.* discover, think of.

hoard *noun*
He kept a hoard of sweets in his drawer. heap, pile, stockpile, store, supply.

hoard *verb*
Squirrels hoard nuts. collect, gather, keep, pile up, put by, save, store.

hoarse *adjective*
Her voice was hoarse after shouting so much. croaking, grating, growling, gruff, harsh, husky, rough.

hoax *noun*
The telephone call was a hoax. fake, fraud, joke, practical joke, trick.

hobby *noun*
What's your favourite hobby? activity, interest, pastime, pursuit, recreation, relaxation.

hoist *verb*
The crane hoisted the crates onto a ship. heave, lift, pull up, raise, winch up.

hold *noun*
She took a firm hold on the dog's lead. clasp, clutch, grasp, grip, purchase.

hold *verb*
1 *Please hold the dog's lead.* clasp, cling to, clutch, grasp, grip, hang on to, seize.
2 *Can I hold the baby?* embrace, hug.
3 *They held the suspect until the police arrived.* confine, detain, keep, stop.
4 *Will the shelf hold all these books?* bear, carry, support, take.
5 *If our luck holds, we could reach the final.* carry on, continue, last, persist, stay.
6 *She holds strong opinions.* believe in, maintain, stick to.
to hold out 1 *Hold out your hand.* extend, offer, reach out, stick out, stretch out.
2 *They can't hold out much longer.* carry on, continue, endure, hang on, keep going, last, persevere, persist, resist, stand fast.
to hold something up 1 *Hold up your hand.* lift, put up, raise.
2 *The accident held up the traffic.* delay, halt, hinder, obstruct, slow down.

hold-up noun

1 *As long as there aren't any hold-ups, we should arrive before lunch.* delay, interruption.
2 *There was a hold-up at the bank.* robbery.

hole noun

VARIOUS KINDS OF HOLE IN THE GROUND: abyss, burrow, cave, cavern, cavity, chasm, crater, depression, excavation, hollow, mine, pit, pothole, shaft, tunnel, underground passage.

VARIOUS HOLES RIGHT THROUGH THINGS: breach, break, chink, crack, cut, gap, gash, leak, opening, perforation, puncture, slit, split, tear, vent, window.

holiday noun

I spent my summer holiday in France. break, day off, leave, time off, vacation.

TIMES WHEN MANY PEOPLE DO NOT GO TO WORK OR SCHOOL: bank holiday, half-term, holy day, school holidays, weekend.

VARIOUS KINDS OF HOLIDAY: camping, caravanning, cruise, honeymoon, pony-trekking, safari, seaside holiday, touring, travelling, walking.

PLACES WHERE YOU MIGHT STAY ON HOLIDAY: apartment, bed and breakfast, boarding house, campsite, cruise ship, flat, guesthouse, hostel, hotel, motel, self-catering apartment or studio, villa.

hollow adjective

Tennis balls are hollow. empty, unfilled.
AN OPPOSITE IS solid.

hollow verb

Some birds make their nests by hollowing out holes in tree trunks. dig, excavate, gouge, scoop.

hollow noun

The cat tried to hide in a hollow in the ground. crater, dent, depression, dip, hole.
A hollow between two hills is a *valley*.

holy adjective

1 *The pilgrims knelt to pray in the holy shrine.* blessed, divine, revered, sacred.
2 *The pilgrims were holy people.* pious, religious, righteous, saintly.

home noun

The floods forced people to flee their homes. abode, dwelling, house, lodging, residence.
SEE ALSO **house**.
A home for the sick is a **convalescent home** or **nursing home**.
A place where a bird or animal lives is its **habitat**.

homely adjective

It's a traditional hotel with a homely atmosphere. comfortable, cosy, easygoing, friendly, informal, natural, ordinary, relaxed, simple.
AN OPPOSITE IS sophisticated.

homework noun

I have to do homework every night. assignments, [*informal*] prep, preparation, private study.

honest adjective

1 *He's an honest boy, so he gave the money back.* conscientious, good, honourable, law-abiding, moral, reliable, trustworthy, upright, virtuous.
AN OPPOSITE IS dishonest.
2 *She gave me an honest reply.* direct, frank, genuine, outspoken, plain, sincere, straight, straightforward, truthful, unbiased.
AN OPPOSITE IS insincere.

honesty noun

1 *I don't doubt your honesty.* goodness, honour, integrity, morality, reliability, trustworthiness, truthfulness, uprightness, virtue.
AN OPPOSITE IS dishonesty.
2 *I was surprised by the honesty of his comments.* directness, frankness, outspokenness, plainness, sincerity, straightforwardness.
AN OPPOSITE IS insincerity.

honour noun

1 *Her success brought honour to the school.* credit, fame, good reputation, renown, respect.
2 *It's an honour to meet you.* distinction, privilege.

honour *verb*
> The winners were honoured at a special ceremony. celebrate, give credit to, glorify, pay respect or tribute to, praise.

honourable *adjective*
> 1 He's an honourable man. decent, fair, good, honest, loyal, moral, respectable, respected, righteous, sincere, trustworthy, trusty, upright, virtuous, worthy.
> 2 It was an honourable thing to do. admirable, creditable, noble, praiseworthy.
> AN OPPOSITE IS unworthy.

hook *verb*
> 1 He hooked the trailer to the car. connect, couple, fasten, hitch, link.
> 2 He hooked an enormous fish. capture, catch, take.

hooligan *noun*
> Hooligans did a lot of damage in the park. delinquent, lout, ruffian, troublemaker, vandal.

hooter *noun*
> A hooter sounded to warn everyone of the danger. horn, siren, whistle.

hop *verb*
> They were hopping about in excitement. bound, caper, dance, jump, leap, prance, skip, spring.

hope *noun*
> 1 Her dearest hope was to see her family again. ambition, desire, dream, wish.
> 2 There's hope of better weather tomorrow. expectation, likelihood, prospect.

hope *verb*
> I hope that we win the championship. be hopeful or optimistic, expect, have faith, trust, wish.

hopeful *adjective*
> 1 She was in a hopeful mood. confident, expectant, optimistic, positive.
> AN OPPOSITE IS pessimistic.
> 2 The future is beginning to look more hopeful. encouraging, favourable, promising, reassuring.
> AN OPPOSITE IS discouraging.

hopeless *adjective*
> 1 The situation seems hopeless. beyond hope, desperate, wretched.
> AN OPPOSITE IS hopeful.
> 2 I'm hopeless at cricket. bad, incompetent, poor, useless, worthless.
> AN OPPOSITE IS competent.

horde *noun*
> Hordes of people were queuing for tickets. crowd, gang, group, mob, swarm, throng.

horizontal *adjective*
> He lay in a horizontal position. flat, level.
> AN OPPOSITE IS vertical.

horrible *adjective*
> What a horrible smell! appalling, awful, beastly, disagreeable, disgusting, dreadful, ghastly, hateful, horrid, loathsome, nasty, objectionable, offensive, repulsive, revolting, terrible, unpleasant.
> AN OPPOSITE IS pleasant.

horrid *adjective* SEE **horrible**

horrific *adjective*
> The accident was horrific. appalling, atrocious, disgusting, dreadful, frightening, ghastly, grisly, gruesome, hideous, horrifying, shocking, sickening.

horrify *verb*
> We were horrified by the news. appal, disgust, frighten, scare, shock, sicken, terrify.

horror *noun*
> 1 He has a horror of snakes. detestation, disgust, dislike, dread, fear, loathing, terror.
> 2 Photographs showed the full horror of the tragedy. awfulness, frightfulness, ghastliness, gruesomeness, hideousness.

horse *noun*

> VARIOUS KINDS OF HORSE: bronco, carthorse, [old use] charger, cob, colt, filly, foal, gelding, hunter, mare, [informal] nag, piebald, pony, race horse, Shetland pony, shire-horse, skewbald, stallion, steed, warhorse. ➡

PEOPLE WHO RIDE HORSES:
cavalryman, equestrian, horseman
or horsewoman, jockey, rider.
SEE ALSO **harness** *noun*.
A cross between a donkey and a
horse is a ***mule***.

hospitable *adjective*
She's a very hospitable woman.
friendly, generous, sociable, warm,
welcoming.
AN OPPOSITE IS unfriendly.

hospital *noun*

PLACES WHERE PEOPLE GO FOR
MEDICAL TREATMENT: clinic,
convalescent home, hospice,
infirmary, nursing home,
sanatorium.

PARTS OF A HOSPITAL: accident and
emergency, dispensary, intensive
care unit, operating theatre,
outpatients, pharmacy, X-ray
department, ward.
SEE ALSO **medicine**.

hospitality *noun*
They thanked us for our hospitality.
friendliness, sociability, welcome.

hostage *noun*
*The hijackers treated their hostages
well.* captive, prisoner.

hostile *adjective*
1 *The supporters of the other team
looked hostile.* aggressive,
antagonistic, inhospitable, malevolent,
unfriendly, unwelcoming, warlike.
AN OPPOSITE IS friendly.
2 *The weather conditions were too
hostile to make the journey.* adverse,
bad, unfavourable, unhelpful.
AN OPPOSITE IS favourable.

hostility *noun*
*The hostility between the opposing sides
was obvious.* aggression, antagonism,
bad feeling, detestation, dislike,
enmity, hate, hatred, ill will,
malevolence, opposition,
unfriendliness.
AN OPPOSITE IS friendship.

hot *adjective*
1 *The sun was extremely hot.* blistering,
burning, roasting, scorching.
2 *Do you like this hot weather?* humid,
oppressive, steamy, stifling,
sweltering, tropical, warm.
3 *Careful—the soup's really hot.* baking
hot, boiling, piping hot, scalding,
sizzling, steaming.
4 *I like curry, but only if it's not too hot.*
gingery, peppery, spicy.
5 *He's got a hot temper.* angry,
emotional, excited, fierce, impatient,
passionate, violent.
AN OPPOSITE IS cold or mild.

house *noun*

WORDS FOR THE PLACE YOU LIVE
IN: abode, dwelling, home, lodging,
quarters, residence.

BUILDINGS WHERE PEOPLE LIVE:
apartment, bungalow, chalet,
cottage, council house, croft,
detached house, farmhouse, flat,
hovel, hut, igloo, lodge, maisonette,
manor, manse, mansion, rectory,
semi-detached house, shack, shanty,
terraced house, thatched house,
vicarage, villa.
FOR ROOMS IN A HOUSE, SEE **room**.

house *verb*
*The refugees were housed in temporary
accommodation.* accommodate, board,
lodge, place, put up, shelter, take in.

hover *verb*
1 *Army helicopters hovered overhead.*
fly.
2 *He hovered in the doorway, afraid to
go inside.* dally, dither, hang about,
hesitate, linger, loiter, pause, wait
about.

howl *verb*
FOR VARIOUS WAYS TO MAKE SOUNDS,
SEE **sound** *verb*.

huddle *verb*
We huddled together to get warm.
cluster, crowd, cuddle, flock, gather,
nestle, snuggle, squeeze.
AN OPPOSITE IS scatter.

hue *noun*
FOR VARIOUS COLOURS, SEE **colour**
noun.

hug *verb*
*She flung her arms round him and
hugged him tight.* clasp, cling to,
cuddle, embrace, hold close, snuggle
against, squeeze.

huge *adjective*
Elephants are huge animals. colossal,
enormous, giant, gigantic, great,
[*informal*] hulking, immense,
imposing, impressive, massive, mighty,
monstrous, monumental, stupendous,
[*informal*] terrific, towering,
tremendous, vast, weighty.
AN OPPOSITE IS tiny.

hum *noun*
She could hear the hum of bees. buzz,
drone, murmur.

human *adjective*
She'll forgive you—she's quite human.
SEE **humane**.

human beings *plural noun*
*Human beings are supposed to be more
intelligent than animals.* folk,
humanity, humans, mankind, men and
women, mortals, people.

humane *adjective*
*A humane society should treat animals
well.* benevolent, charitable, civilized,
compassionate, human, humanitarian,
kind, kind-hearted, loving, merciful,
sympathetic, tender, warm-hearted.
AN OPPOSITE IS cruel.

humble *adjective*
1 *Her humble manner makes you forget
how famous she is.* docile, meek,
modest, polite, respectful, submissive,
unassertive.
AN OPPOSITE IS proud.
2 *She comes from a humble
background.* commonplace, lowly,
obscure, ordinary, simple,
undistinguished, unimportant.
AN OPPOSITE IS important.

humid *adjective*
I don't like this humid weather. muggy,
steamy, sticky, sweaty.
AN OPPOSITE IS fresh.

humiliate *verb*
*He humiliated her in front of all her
colleagues.* crush, deflate, disgrace,
embarrass, humble, make ashamed,
[*informal*] put you in your place,
shame, [*informal*] take you down a peg.

humiliating *adjective*
They suffered a humiliating defeat.
crushing, degrading, embarrassing,
humbling, undignified.
AN OPPOSITE IS glorious.

humility *noun*
*They were impressed by his gentleness
and humility.* humbleness, meekness,
modesty.
AN OPPOSITE IS pride.

humorous *adjective*
*She made a humorous and entertaining
speech.* amusing, comic, funny, witty.
AN OPPOSITE IS serious.

humour *noun*
1 *His stories were full of humour.* sense
of humour, wit.
2 *The arguments had not improved her
humour.* disposition, frame of mind,
mood, spirits, temper.

hump *noun*
Camels have humps on their backs.
bulge, bump, lump, swelling.

hump *verb*
He humped the suitcases upstairs.
carry, cart, fetch, haul, lift, lug, take,
transfer.

hunch *noun*
I have a hunch that she won't come.
feeling, guess, idea, impression,
inkling, intuition, suspicion.

hunch *verb*
He hunched his shoulders. arch, bend,
curl, curve, hump, shrug.

hunger *noun*
*Many people died from cold and
hunger.* famine, lack of food,
starvation.
Bad health caused by not having
enough food is ***malnutrition***.

hungry *adjective*
Our dog always seems to be hungry.
famished, greedy, [*informal*] peckish,
ravenous, starving.

hunt *noun*
> After searching for hours, the police abandoned the hunt. chase, pursuit, quest, search.

hunt *verb*
> **1** I think it's cruel to hunt animals. chase, hound, pursue, stalk, track, trail.
> **2** I hunted in the attic for our old photos. ferret, look, rummage, search, seek.

hunting *noun*

> KINDS OF HUNTING: badger-baiting, beagling, deer stalking, falconry, ferreting, fishing, fox-hunting, hare coursing, hawking, shooting, whaling.

hurdle *noun*
> **1** I jumped over the hurdle easily. barricade, barrier, fence, hedge, obstacle.
> **2** There are many hurdles to overcome in life. difficulty, handicap, hindrance, obstruction, problem, snag, stumbling block.

hurl *verb*
> I hurled the ball as far as I could. cast, [informal] chuck, fling, launch, pitch, sling, throw, toss.

hurry *verb*
> **1** If you want to catch the bus, you'd better hurry. [informal] buck up, dash, fly, hasten, hurtle, rush, speed.
> AN OPPOSITE IS dawdle.
> **2** It's no good trying to hurry him. quicken, speed up.
> AN OPPOSITE IS slow down.

hurry *noun*
> What's the hurry for? haste, rush, speed, urgency.

hurt *verb*
> **1** Put that knife down—you might hurt someone. damage, harm, injure, wound.
> To hurt someone deliberately is to **torment** or **torture** them.
> **2** My feet hurt. ache, be painful, smart, sting, throb, tingle.
> **3** The insult hurt her. distress, grieve, upset.

hurtle *verb*
> The train hurtled along at top speed. charge, dash, fly, race, rush, shoot, speed, tear, zoom.

hush *verb*
> He told us all to hush. be quiet, be silent, [informal] pipe down, shut up, stop talking.
> **to hush something up** They tried to hush up the scandal. conceal, cover up, hide, keep quiet, keep secret, suppress.

husky *adjective*
> **1** Her voice is still a bit husky. croaking, grating, gravelly, growling, gruff, harsh, hoarse, rough.
> **2** The wrestler was a big, husky fellow. [informal] beefy, brawny, burly, hefty, large, mighty, muscular, powerful, solid, strong, tough.

hustle *verb*
> The police hustled him into a car. bustle, force, hasten, hurry, push, rush, shove.

hut *noun*
> He keeps his fishing tackle in a hut by the river. cabin, chalet, den, shack, shanty, shed.

hybrid *noun*
> An animal that combines two different species is a **cross-breed**.
> A dog that combines two different breeds is a **mongrel**.

hygienic *adjective*
> Hygienic conditions are essential in hospital. clean, disinfected, germ free, healthy, sanitary, sterilized, unpolluted, wholesome.
> AN OPPOSITE IS unhygienic.

hypocrisy *noun*
> He accused the newspapers of hypocrisy. falsity, insincerity.

hypocritical *adjective*
> It's hypocritical to say one thing and do another. false, insincere, two-faced.

hypothesis *noun*
> His hypothesis was proved to be correct. suggestion, supposition, theory.

hypothetical *adjective*
This is a hypothetical situation, not a real one. academic, imaginary, supposed, theoretical.
AN OPPOSITE IS actual.

hysteria *noun*
Hysteria swept the town when a tiger escaped from the zoo. frenzy, hysterics, madness.

hysterical *adjective*
1 *The fans became hysterical when the band appeared.* crazy, delirious, frenzied, mad, raving, uncontrollable, wild.
2 [*informal*] *Listen to his joke—it's hysterical.* funny, hilarious, ridiculous.

ice *noun*

> KINDS OF ICE: black ice, floe, frost, glacier, iceberg, icicle.

icy *adjective*
1 *You need to dress warmly in icy weather.* arctic, bitter, cold, crisp, freezing, frosty, wintry.
2 *Icy roads are dangerous.* frozen, glassy, slippery.

idea *noun*
1 *I've got a great idea!* inspiration, plan, proposal, scheme, suggestion.
2 *She has some funny ideas about life.* belief, concept, conception, hypothesis, notion, opinion, theory, view.
3 *What's the main idea of this poem?* intention, meaning, point, thought.
4 *Give me an idea of what you are planning.* clue, hint, impression, inkling.

ideal *adjective*
It's ideal weather for a picnic. the best, excellent, faultless, perfect, suitable.

identical *adjective*
The twins were wearing identical clothes. alike, indistinguishable, interchangeable, matching, similar.
AN OPPOSITE IS different.

identify *verb*
1 *The police asked if I could identify the thief.* distinguish, name, pick out, recognize, single out.
2 *The doctor couldn't identify what was wrong.* diagnose, discover, [*informal*] put a name to, spot.
to identify with *Can you identify with the hero of the story?* feel for, [*informal*] put yourself in the shoes of, sympathize with, understand.

idiom *noun*
It's hard for foreigners to understand English idioms. choice of words, expression, manner of speaking, phrase, phrasing, usage.

idiotic *adjective*
It was an idiotic thing to do. daft, foolish, irrational, mad, ridiculous, silly, stupid, thoughtless, unintelligent, unwise.
AN OPPOSITE IS sensible.

idle *adjective*
1 *He lost his job for being so idle.* apathetic, lazy, slothful, uncommitted.
AN OPPOSITE IS enthusiastic.
2 *The machines lay idle during the strike.* doing nothing, inactive, inoperative, unemployed, unused.
AN OPPOSITE IS busy.

idol *noun*
1 *The people worshipped the idol.* deity, god, image, statue.
2 *He was a pop idol of the fifties.* favourite, hero, star.

idolize *verb*
She idolized her mother. adore, be devoted to, love, worship.

ignite *verb*
1 *We ignited the lantern with a match.* kindle, light, set alight, set on fire.
2 *The fire refused to ignite.* burn, catch fire.

ignorant *adjective*
1 *He was ignorant of the facts.* lacking knowledge, unacquainted (with), unaware, unconscious, unfamiliar (with).
AN OPPOSITE IS knowledgeable.
2 *He's an ignorant young man.* illiterate, uneducated.
AN OPPOSITE IS educated.
3 [*informal and insulting*] *You're just ignorant!* SEE **stupid**.

ignore *verb*
1 *He ignored the warning and got into difficulties.* disobey, disregard, take no notice of, [*informal*] turn a blind eye to.
2 *I ignored the difficult questions.* leave out, miss out, neglect, omit, overlook, skip.

ill *adjective*
1 *You can't work properly if you are ill.* ailing, bedridden, diseased, feeble, frail, infected, infirm, poorly, queasy, sick, sickly, suffering, under the weather, unfit, unhealthy, unwell, weak.
AN OPPOSITE IS healthy or well.
2 *Did the plants suffer ill effects in the frost?* adverse, bad, damaging, harmful, injurious, unfavourable.
AN OPPOSITE IS good.
FOR VARIOUS ILLNESSES, SEE **illness**.

illegal *adjective*
Stealing is illegal. against the law, banned, criminal, forbidden, outlawed, prohibited, unlawful, wrong.
AN OPPOSITE IS legal.

illegible *adjective*
His signature was illegible. unclear, unreadable.
AN OPPOSITE IS legible.

illiterate *adjective*
They're illiterate because they didn't go to school. unable to read, uneducated.
AN OPPOSITE IS literate.

illness *noun*
What kind of illness is he suffering from? abnormality, affliction, ailment, attack, [*informal*] bug, complaint, condition, disability, disease, disorder, health problem, infection, infirmity, sickness, [*informal*] upset.

A sudden illness is an **attack** or **fit**.
A period of illness is a **bout**.
A general outbreak of illness in a particular area is an **epidemic**.

VARIOUS ILLNESSES OR COMPLAINTS: acne, allergy, anaemia, appendicitis, arthritis, asthma, bronchitis, cancer, cataract, catarrh, chickenpox, chilblains, chill, cholera, cold, colic, constipation, convulsions, cough, diabetes, diarrhoea, diphtheria, dysentery, eczema, epilepsy, fever, flu, gangrene, gastric flu, glandular fever, haemorrhage, hay fever, headache, hernia, hypothermia, indigestion, influenza, jaundice, laryngitis, leprosy, leukaemia, lumbago, malaria, measles, meningitis, migraine, multiple sclerosis, mumps, neuralgia, piles, plague, pneumonia, polio or poliomyelitis, rabies, rheumatism, rickets, scarlet fever, sciatica, scurvy, shingles, smallpox, spina bifida, stomach-ache, stroke, tetanus, thrombosis, tonsillitis, tuberculosis, typhoid, typhus, ulcer, whooping cough.
SEE ALSO **medicine**.

illogical *adjective*
His argument was illogical. absurd, fallacious, inconsistent, irrational, senseless, silly, unreasonable.
AN OPPOSITE IS logical.

illuminate *verb*
1 *The floodlights illuminated the pitch.* light up.
2 *Her explanation illuminated the problem.* clarify, clear up, explain, make clear, throw light on.

illusion *noun*
The magician fooled us with his illusions. conjuring, deception, trick.

illustrate *verb*
1 *I used some photos to illustrate my story.* depict, picture, portray.
2 *The accident illustrates the importance of road safety.* demonstrate, make clear, show.

illustration 209 **immersed**

illustration *noun*
1 *She likes books with illustrations.*
decoration, diagram, drawing,
photograph, picture, sketch.
2 *I'll give you an illustration of what I
mean.* demonstration, example,
instance, specimen.

image *noun*
1 *The film contained frightening
images of war.* depiction, picture,
portrayal, representation.
2 *The temple contained images of the
gods.* carving, figure, idol, statue.
3 *You can see your image in the mirror.*
likeness, reflection.
4 *She's the image of her mother.* double,
twin.

imaginary *adjective*
Her fears were imaginary. fanciful,
fictional, fictitious, imagined, invented,
made up, non-existent, unreal.
AN OPPOSITE IS real.

imagination *noun*
Use your imagination. artistry,
creativity, fancy, ingenuity,
inventiveness, originality, sensitivity,
thought, vision.

imaginative *adjective*
His paintings were very imaginative.
artistic, attractive, beautiful, clever,
creative, fanciful, ingenious, inspired,
inventive, original, poetic, sensitive,
thoughtful, vivid.
AN OPPOSITE IS boring or
unimaginative.

imagine *verb*
1 *Imagine what it would be like to be
rich.* conjure up, dream up, fancy, make
up, picture, pretend, think up,
visualize.
2 *I imagine you'd like a drink.* assume,
believe, guess, presume, suppose.

imitate *verb*
1 *She was very good at imitating his
voice.* counterfeit, impersonate, make
fun of, mimic, parody, reproduce,
[*informal*] send up, simulate.
2 *Try to imitate my example.* copy,
follow, match.

imitation *adjective*
*The coat was made from imitation
leather.* artificial, counterfeit, dummy,
model, sham, simulated.
AN OPPOSITE IS real.

imitation *noun*
It's an imitation, not the real thing.
copy, counterfeit, dummy, duplicate,
fake, forgery, impersonation,
impression, likeness, mock-up, model,
replica, reproduction, sham,
simulation.
An imitation which you want people to
laugh at is a **caricature** or **parody**.

immature *adjective*
She's very immature for her age.
babyish, childish, infantile, juvenile.
AN OPPOSITE IS mature.

immediate *adjective*
1 *Please can I have an immediate reply.*
direct, instantaneous, prompt, quick,
[*informal*] snappy, speedy, swift, top
priority, urgent.
AN OPPOSITE IS slow.
2 *Fortunately we get on well with our
immediate neighbours.* adjacent,
closest, nearest.
AN OPPOSITE IS distant.

immediately *adverb*
I want you to do it immediately! at
once, directly, instantly, now, promptly,
right away, straight away.

immense *adjective*
It was an immense building. big,
colossal, enormous, giant, gigantic,
great, huge, imposing, impressive,
large, majestic, massive, mighty,
monstrous, monumental, stupendous,
towering, tremendous, vast.
AN OPPOSITE IS tiny.

immerse *verb*
*I immersed the potatoes in cold water to
cool them down.* dip, lower, plunge,
submerge.

immersed *adjective*
*I didn't hear because I was immersed in
my work.* absorbed, busy, engrossed,
interested, involved, occupied,
preoccupied.

immobile *adjective*
He sat immobile in his chair.
motionless, stationary, still, unmoving.
AN OPPOSITE IS mobile.

immobilize *verb*
The car was immobilized by water in
the engine. cripple, disable, paralyse,
put out of action, stop.

immoral *adjective*
We were shocked by their immoral
behaviour. bad, corrupt, deceitful,
dishonest, evil, impure, indecent,
naughty, scandalous, sinful, wicked,
wrong.
AN OPPOSITE IS moral.

immortal *adjective*
They believed their gods were immortal.
ageless, everlasting, undying.
AN OPPOSITE IS mortal.

immune *adjective*
immune from or **to** We are immune to
many diseases. free from, immunized
against, inoculated against, protected
from, resistant to, safe from,
unaffected by, vaccinated against.

immunize *verb*
You can be immunized by **inoculation**
or **vaccination**.

impact *noun*
1 Was the car damaged in the impact?
bang, blow, bump, collision, crash,
knock, smash.
2 Computers have a big impact on our
lives. effect, influence.

impair *verb*
Very loud noise can impair your
hearing. damage, harm, weaken.

impartial *adjective*
The referee must be impartial.
disinterested, fair, fair-minded,
independent, just, neutral, objective,
open-minded, unbiased, unprejudiced.
AN OPPOSITE IS biased.

impassable *adjective*
The road was impassable because of the
flood. blocked, closed, obstructed,
unusable.

impatient *adjective*
1 Don't be so impatient! eager, in a
hurry, keen.
2 We were impatient because of the
delay. agitated, anxious, edgy, fidgety,
irritable.
3 He was very impatient with her.
abrupt, hasty, quick-tempered.
AN OPPOSITE IS patient.

imperceptible *adjective*
He gave an almost imperceptible smile.
faint, gradual, insignificant, invisible,
negligible, slight, undetectable,
unnoticeable.
AN OPPOSITE IS noticeable.

imperfect *adjective*
The goods are rejected if they are
imperfect. broken, damaged, defective,
deficient, faulty, incomplete, marked,
spoilt, unfinished.
AN OPPOSITE IS perfect.

impersonal *adjective*
He was put off by her impersonal
manner. cool, detached, distant,
formal, official, remote,
unapproachable, unemotional,
unfriendly, uninvolved,
unsympathetic.
AN OPPOSITE IS friendly.

impersonate *verb*
He made us laugh by impersonating the
Prime Minister. counterfeit, disguise
yourself as, imitate, mimic, parody,
[informal] send up, simulate.

impertinent *adjective*
He made some rather impertinent
remarks. cheeky, disrespectful,
impolite, impudent, insolent,
irreverent, rude, saucy.
AN OPPOSITE IS respectful.

implement *noun*
We have a cupboard full of implements
for doing jobs round the house.
appliance, device, gadget, instrument,
tool, utensil.

implement *verb*
The bad weather made it impossible to
implement the plan. bring about, carry
out, execute, fulfil, perform, put into
practice, try out.

implore verb
We implored her to help us. beg,
entreat, plead with.

imply verb
He implied that they were wrong. hint,
indicate, suggest.

impolite adjective
There's no need to be impolite when
someone asks a civil question. abrupt,
abusive, bad-mannered, disrespectful,
impertinent, insulting, rude,
uncomplimentary, uncouth.
AN OPPOSITE IS polite.

import verb
The country has to import most of the
oil it uses. bring in, ship in.
AN OPPOSITE IS export.

important adjective
1 The World Cup is an important
sporting event. big, central, historic,
major, momentous, outstanding,
significant.
2 They have some important things to
do. pressing, serious, urgent, weighty.
3 The prime minister is an important
person. distinguished, eminent,
famous, great, influential, leading,
notable, powerful, prominent,
renowned, well-known.
AN OPPOSITE IS unimportant.

impose verb
1 The plans for a bypass were imposed
against the wishes of local people.
enforce, insist on, introduce.
2 The government imposed a tax on
fuel. fix, inflict, prescribe, set.
to impose on I don't want to impose on
you. put a burden on, take advantage
of.

imposing adjective
The castle is an imposing building. big,
dignified, grand, great, impressive,
magnificent, majestic, splendid,
stately, striking.
AN OPPOSITE IS insignificant.

impossible adjective
Years ago, people said that space travel
was impossible. absurd, hopeless,
impracticable, impractical, insoluble,
out of the question, ridiculous.
AN OPPOSITE IS possible.

impostor noun
The man who claimed to be a detective
was an impostor. cheat, [slang] con
man, impersonator, swindler, trickster.

impracticable adjective
The scheme turned out to be
impracticable. absurd, hopeless,
impossible, impractical, out of the
question, ridiculous.
AN OPPOSITE IS possible.

impractical adjective
1 He's impractical when it comes to
doing jobs round the house. clumsy,
incompetent, ineffective, ineffectual,
useless.
2 The inventor's designs were
impractical. impossible, impracticable,
inconvenient, unachievable,
unrealistic.
AN OPPOSITE IS practical.

impress verb
They were impressed by his hard work.
influence, leave its mark on, make an
impression on, stick in your mind.
to impress something on someone
She impressed on us the need to be
careful. emphasize, stress.

impression noun
1 She had the impression something
was wrong. feeling, hunch, idea,
notion, sense, suspicion.
2 The film made a big impression on
them. effect, impact, influence, mark.
3 She does a good impression of the
boss. imitation, impersonation,
[informal] send-up.

impressive adjective
The cathedral is an impressive
building. grand, great, important,
imposing, large, magnificent, majestic,
remarkable, spectacular, splendid,
stately, striking.
AN OPPOSITE IS insignificant.

imprison verb
The thief was imprisoned for two years.
commit to prison, confine, detain, gaol
or jail, [informal] keep under lock and
key, lock up, [informal] put away.
AN OPPOSITE IS liberate.

imprisonment *noun*
*He was sentenced to two years'
imprisonment.* confinement, detention,
gaol or jail.
A person who is held by the police is *in
custody*.
A person who is in prison awaiting
trial is *on remand*.

improbable *adjective*
It seemed a rather improbable story.
far-fetched, incredible, questionable,
unbelievable, unconvincing, unlikely.
AN OPPOSITE IS probable.

impromptu *adjective*
*The musicians gave us an impromptu
concert.* ad lib, improvised,
spontaneous, unplanned, unprepared,
unrehearsed.
AN OPPOSITE IS rehearsed.

improper *adjective*
1 *Improper use of the equipment may
cause damage.* careless, inappropriate,
incorrect, irresponsible, silly, wrong.
2 *They used language that was
considered improper.* coarse, crude,
dirty, indecent, obscene, offensive,
rude, smutty, unseemly, vulgar.
AN OPPOSITE IS proper.

improve *verb*
1 *Her work improved during the term.*
advance, develop, get better, move on,
progress.
AN OPPOSITE IS deteriorate.
2 *Has he improved since his illness?*
pick up, rally, recover, revive.
AN OPPOSITE IS get worse.
3 *How can I improve this story?* amend,
correct, enhance, make better, refine,
revise.
4 *She got a grant to improve the house.*
decorate, modernize, upgrade.
To improve something by making small
changes is to *touch it up*.

improvement *noun*
1 *There's been an improvement in her
health.* advance, gain, progress,
recovery.
2 *He made some improvements to the
article.* amendment, correction,
revision.

3 *They've made a lot of improvements to
the house since they moved in.*
decoration, modernization,
modification.

improvise *verb*
*We had nothing ready, so we had to
improvise.* ad lib, make it up, perform
impromptu.

impudent *adjective*
She made some impudent remarks.
bold, brazen, cheeky, disrespectful,
forward, impertinent, impolite,
insolent, insulting, irreverent, rude,
saucy, shameless.
AN OPPOSITE IS respectful.

impulse *noun*
1 *He did it on a sudden wild impulse.*
desire, instinct, urge.
2 *What was the impulse behind your
decision?* force, motive, pressure,
stimulus.

impulsive *adjective*
*I didn't think about it: it was just an
impulsive action.* hasty, impromptu,
instinctive, intuitive, involuntary,
natural, spontaneous, sudden,
thoughtless, unconscious, unplanned,
unrehearsed, unthinking, wild.
AN OPPOSITE IS deliberate.

impure *adjective*
*He became ill through drinking impure
water.* contaminated, defiled, dirty,
infected, polluted, unclean.
AN OPPOSITE IS pure.

inaccessible *adjective*
1 *The medicines were inaccessible on
the top shelf.* hard to find,
inconvenient, out of reach, out of the
way.
2 *The plane crashed in an inaccessible
area.* desolate, isolated, lonely,
outlying, out-of-the-way, remote,
unfrequented.
AN OPPOSITE IS accessible.

inaccurate *adjective*
*The police said that the witness's story
was inaccurate.* faulty, imperfect,
incorrect, inexact, misleading,
mistaken, unreliable, untrue, wrong.
AN OPPOSITE IS accurate.

inactive *adjective*
Hedgehogs are inactive in winter.
asleep, doing nothing, hibernating,
idle, immobile, passive, quiet, sleepy,
slow.
AN OPPOSITE IS active.

inadequate *adjective*
The inadequate rainfall means that
water must be rationed. insufficient,
limited, meagre, poor, scanty, scarce,
unsatisfactory.
AN OPPOSITE IS adequate.

inanimate *adjective*
Rocks and stones are inanimate. dead,
inactive, lifeless.
AN OPPOSITE IS animate.

inappropriate *adjective*
Her remarks were thought to be
inappropriate. improper, out of place,
tactless, unseemly, unsuitable,
untimely, wrong.
AN OPPOSITE IS appropriate.

inattentive *adjective*
She shouts at him if he's inattentive.
absent-minded, careless, daydreaming,
dreaming, heedless, lacking
concentration, negligent, unobservant.
AN OPPOSITE IS attentive.

inaudible *adjective*
Their cries for help were inaudible.
faint, indistinct, low, muffled, muted,
unclear, weak.
AN OPPOSITE IS audible.

incapable *adjective*
He's incapable of doing things for
himself. helpless, incompetent,
ineffective, ineffectual, stupid, useless.
All these synonyms are followed by *at*
rather than *of*
AN OPPOSITE IS capable.

incentive *noun*
They were offered incentives to work
harder. encouragement, inducement,
motivation, stimulus.

incessant *adjective*
They were tired of his incessant
complaints. ceaseless, chronic,
constant, continual, endless, eternal,
everlasting, never-ending, non-stop,
perpetual, persistent, relentless,
unceasing, unending.
AN OPPOSITE IS occasional.

incident *noun*
He told us about an amusing incident
that happened last week. event,
happening, occasion, occurrence.

incidental *adjective*
Let's discuss the main point, not
incidental details. inessential, minor,
odd, secondary, subordinate,
unimportant.
AN OPPOSITE IS essential.

inclination *noun*
He has an inclination to eat too much.
bias, disposition, instinct, leaning,
readiness, tendency, willingness.

incline *verb*
The yacht inclined to one side in the
strong wind. bend, lean, slant, slope,
tilt, tip.
to be inclined He's inclined to eat too
much. be disposed, have a habit (of), be
liable, like, prefer, tend.

incline *noun*
We had to push the car up the incline.
gradient, hill, rise, slope.

include *verb*
This CD includes some of my favourite
songs. combine, comprise, consist of,
contain, incorporate, take in.
AN OPPOSITE IS exclude.

income *noun*
She gets a monthly income from her
employer. pay, salary, wage.
Income that you get from savings is
interest.
Income that a retired person gets is a
pension.
AN OPPOSITE IS expenditure.

incompatible *adjective*
They split up because they were
incompatible. unsuited.
AN OPPOSITE IS incompatible.

incompetent *adjective*
He was so incompetent that he had to
do the work again. hopeless,
ineffective, inefficient, unsatisfactory,
unskilful, useless.
AN OPPOSITE IS competent.

incomplete *adjective*
She was punished because her work
was incomplete. imperfect, unfinished.
AN OPPOSITE IS complete.

incomprehensible *adjective*
Can you explain this incomprehensible
message? baffling, meaningless,
obscure, perplexing, puzzling, unclear,
unintelligible.
AN OPPOSITE IS intelligible.

incongruous *adjective*
His business suit seemed incongruous
at a pop concert. inappropriate, odd,
out of place, unsuitable, unsuited.
AN OPPOSITE IS appropriate.

inconsiderate *adjective*
It's inconsiderate to play the radio so
loudly. insensitive, rude, selfish,
tactless, thoughtless, uncaring,
unfriendly, unhelpful, unkind,
unthinking.
AN OPPOSITE IS considerate.

inconsistent *adjective*
1 His performance has been
inconsistent this season. changeable,
erratic, fickle, unpredictable,
unreliable, variable.
2 The stories of the two witnesses are
inconsistent. contradictory, different.
AN OPPOSITE IS consistent.

inconspicuous *adjective*
The policeman thought he would be
inconspicuous in plain clothes.
camouflaged, hidden, insignificant,
invisible, unnoticed.
AN OPPOSITE IS conspicuous.

inconvenience *noun*
She said she didn't want to cause any
inconvenience. annoyance, bother,
disadvantage, disruption, drawback,
encumbrance, hindrance, irritation,
nuisance, trouble.

inconvenient *adjective*
The visitors arrived at an inconvenient
moment. annoying, awkward, difficult,
embarrassing, irritating, tiresome,
troublesome, unsuitable.
AN OPPOSITE IS convenient.

incorporate *verb*
The CD incorporates some of his
favourite songs. combine, comprise,
consist of, contain, include, take in.
AN OPPOSITE IS exclude.

incorrect *adjective*
Nine out of ten of his answers were
incorrect. false, inaccurate, mistaken,
wrong.
AN OPPOSITE IS correct.

increase *verb*
1 They plan to increase the size of the
road to cope with more traffic. add to,
broaden, develop, enlarge, expand,
make bigger, widen.
2 They increased the time allowed for
the work. extend, lengthen, prolong.
3 The police increased their efforts to
find the murderer. intensify, step up.
4 They've increased the bus fares. put
up, raise.
5 Can you increase the volume of the
TV? amplify, boost, turn up.
6 The number of cars on the roads
continues to increase. become bigger,
build up, escalate, go up, grow, mount,
multiply, rise, soar.
AN OPPOSITE IS decrease.

incredible *adjective*
Do you expect us to believe that
incredible story? amazing,
extraordinary, fantastic, far-fetched,
improbable, surprising, unbelievable,
unconvincing, unlikely, untrustworthy.
AN OPPOSITE IS credible.

incredulous *adjective*
She seemed incredulous when told
she'd won. disbelieving, distrustful,
sceptical, suspicious, uncertain,
unconvinced.

incurable *adjective*
Sadly, he has an incurable illness.
fatal, hopeless, untreatable.

indecent *adjective*
We were embarrassed by their indecent behaviour. coarse, crude, dirty, improper, obscene, offensive, rude, smutty, vulgar.
AN OPPOSITE IS decent.

indefinite *adjective*
His answer was rather indefinite. ambiguous, general, uncertain, unclear, vague.
AN OPPOSITE IS definite.

independence *noun*
They value their independence. freedom, liberty.

independent *adjective*
1 She led an independent life. carefree, free.
AN OPPOSITE IS dependent.
2 He wanted an independent opinion about the matter. disinterested, impartial, neutral, objective, open-minded, unbiased, unprejudiced.
AN OPPOSITE IS biased.

indicate *verb*
1 She indicated where we could get a drink. describe, make known, point out, show, specify.
2 A red light indicates danger. communicate, convey, denote, express, mean, signal, signify, stand for, symbolize.

indication *noun*
He gave no indication that he felt ill. clue, evidence, hint, inkling, sign, signal, symptom, token, warning.

indicator *noun*
The indicators showed that the machine was working normally. clock, dial, display, gauge, instrument, meter, pointer, screen, sign, signal.

indifferent *adjective*
1 They were indifferent to the result of the game. apathetic, not bothered, unconcerned, unenthusiastic, uninterested.
AN OPPOSITE IS enthusiastic.
2 The food was indifferent. fair, mediocre, ordinary, unexciting.
AN OPPOSITE IS excellent.

indignant *adjective*
We were indignant about the way they mistreated the animals. angry, annoyed, cross, exasperated, furious, infuriated, irritated, resentful, [*informal*] sore.

indirect *adjective*
1 She was late because she came by an indirect route. devious, meandering, rambling, roundabout, winding, zigzag.
2 He gave an indirect answer to the question. disguised, euphemistic, implied, oblique.
AN OPPOSITE IS direct.

indispensable *adjective*
He is an indispensable member of the team. crucial, essential, necessary, vital.
AN OPPOSITE IS unnecessary.

indistinct *adjective*
1 The photo was rather indistinct. blurred, faint, fuzzy, hazy, indefinite, obscure, shadowy, unclear.
AN OPPOSITE IS clear.
2 They could hear indistinct sounds of people talking. deadened, incomprehensible, muffled, mumbled, unintelligible, vague.
AN OPPOSITE IS distinct.

indistinguishable *adjective*
The two sisters look almost indistinguishable. identical, interchangeable, the same.
AN OPPOSITE IS different.

individual *adjective*
Her singing has an individual style. characteristic, different, distinct, distinctive, personal, special, unique.

individual *noun*
Who was that odd individual? character, man, person, woman.

induce *verb*
1 She couldn't be induced to take part. coax, encourage, persuade, prevail on, tempt.
2 Her illness was induced by stress. bring on, cause, give rise to, lead to, produce, provoke.

indulge *verb*
They indulged their children too much.
humour, pamper, spoil, treat.
to indulge in *I indulged in a nice hot
bath.* enjoy, wallow in.

indulgent *adjective*
They are very indulgent parents.
easygoing, generous, lenient, liberal,
permissive, tolerant.
AN OPPOSITE IS strict.

industrious *adjective*
She's a very industrious worker. busy,
conscientious, enterprising, hard-
working, keen, persistent, productive,
tireless, zealous.
AN OPPOSITE IS lazy.

industry *noun*
1 *Many people in the town work in
industry.* business, commerce,
manufacturing, trade.
2 *He admired her for her industry.*
application, commitment,
determination, effort, energy, hard
work, industriousness, keenness,
perseverance, persistence, zeal.

ineffective *adjective*
1 *Sadly, the medicine was ineffective.*
fruitless, futile, unproductive,
unsuccessful, useless, vain, worthless.
AN OPPOSITE IS effective.
2 *He was an ineffective leader.* SEE
ineffectual.

ineffectual *adjective*
He was an ineffectual captain of the
team. feeble, inadequate, incompetent,
ineffective, inefficient, unconvincing,
unsuccessful, weak.
AN OPPOSITE IS competent.

inefficient *adjective*
1 *He lost his job for being inefficient.*
ineffective, slow, unproductive, useless.
2 *The car was inefficient in its use of
fuel.* extravagant, prodigal,
uneconomical, wasteful.
AN OPPOSITE IS efficient.

inert *adjective*
He lay inert on the pavement. immobile,
lifeless, motionless, still.

inertia *noun*
It was sheer inertia that stopped her
from doing anything. apathy, idleness,
inactivity, laziness.
AN OPPOSITE IS liveliness.

inevitable *adjective*
When two men were sent off, it was
inevitable that they would lose the
game. certain, sure, unavoidable.

inexhaustible *adjective*
The supply of fossil fuels is not
inexhaustible. endless, infinite,
limitless, never-ending, unlimited.

inexpensive *adjective*
He bought some inexpensive clothes in
the market. cheap, cut-price, low-
priced, reasonable.
AN OPPOSITE IS expensive.

inexplicable *adjective*
The origins of the universe are an
inexplicable mystery. baffling,
bewildering, incomprehensible,
insoluble, mysterious, mystifying,
puzzling, unsolvable.
AN OPPOSITE IS understandable.

infallible *adjective*
She has an infallible way of making me
laugh. certain, dependable, foolproof,
never-failing, perfect, reliable, sound,
sure, trustworthy, unbeatable.
AN OPPOSITE IS unreliable.

infamous *adjective*
Dick Turpin was an infamous
highwayman. notorious, villainous,
wicked.

infant *noun*
He was a very demanding infant. baby,
small child, toddler.

infantile *adjective*
[*uncomplimentary*] She said their
behaviour had been infantile. babyish,
childish, immature, silly.
AN OPPOSITE IS mature.

infect *verb*
They were afraid that chemicals had
infected the water supply. contaminate,
defile, poison, pollute, spoil.

infected *adjective*
The nurse treated the infected wound with antiseptic. inflamed, poisoned, septic.

infection *noun*
The infection spread rapidly. blight, contagion, contamination, epidemic, virus.
FOR VARIOUS ILLNESSES, SEE **illness**.

infectious *adjective*
The flu is very infectious. catching, contagious, transmittable.

infer *verb*
Note: *infer* and *imply* are not synonyms
He inferred from her silence that she agreed. assume, conclude, deduce, gather, guess, work out.

inferior *adjective*
1 The clothes were of inferior quality. bad, cheap, indifferent, mediocre, poor, shoddy, [*informal*] tacky, trashy.
2 The officer can give orders to everyone of inferior rank. junior, lesser, lower, subordinate.
AN OPPOSITE IS superior.

infested *adjective*
The garden shed was infested with mice. alive, crawling, overrun, plagued, swarming, teeming.

infiltrate *verb*
Spies infiltrated the enemy's camp. enter secretly, penetrate.

infinite *adjective*
There's an infinite number of stars in the sky. countless, endless, inexhaustible, innumerable, limitless, never-ending, uncountable, unending, unlimited, untold.
AN OPPOSITE IS finite.

infirm *adjective*
Infirm people need a lot of help. elderly, feeble, frail, ill, old, poorly, weak.
People who have to stay in bed are **bedridden**.
AN OPPOSITE IS healthy.

inflame *verb*
The sight of the badly treated animals inflamed our anger. arouse, kindle, provoke, rouse, stimulate.
AN OPPOSITE IS soothe.

inflamed *adjective*
The nurse put antiseptic on the inflamed wound. infected, poisoned, red, septic.

inflammation *noun*
This ointment will soothe the inflammation. infection, redness, soreness.

inflate *verb*
1 The tyres need to be inflated. blow up, pump up.
2 Don't inflate the importance of the experiment. exaggerate, make too much of.

inflexible *adjective*
1 The material becomes inflexible as it dries. firm, hard, rigid, solid, stiff, unbending, unyielding.
2 The rules of the game are inflexible. invariable, unalterable.
3 This referee is inflexible about applying the rules. obstinate, resolute, strict, stubborn, uncompromising.
AN OPPOSITE IS flexible.

inflict *verb*
I hate seeing someone inflict pain on an animal. administer, apply, deal out, impose.

influence *noun*
The influence of parents is important for children. authority, control, dominance, effect, guidance, impact, power.

influence *verb*
The money he was offered influenced his decision. affect, change, control, direct, guide, have an effect on, modify, motivate.

influential *adjective*
Members of the government are influential people. important, leading, powerful, significant.
AN OPPOSITE IS unimportant.

inform *verb*
I'll inform you if I can't come. advise, let you know, notify, tell.
to inform against The spy informed against his colleague. accuse, betray, denounce, give information about, report, [*informal*] sneak on, [*slang*] split on, [*informal*] tell tales about.

informal *adjective*
1 *They were surprised how informal she was.* approachable, easygoing, familiar, free and easy, friendly, homely, natural, ordinary, relaxed.
2 *I can wear informal clothes to the party.* casual, comfortable, everyday.
3 *He talked to us in a quite informal way.* chatty, colloquial, personal, slangy.
AN OPPOSITE IS formal.

information *noun*

VARIOUS KINDS OF INFORMATION: data, evidence, facts, intelligence, knowledge, propaganda, public records, statistics.

VARIOUS WAYS INFORMATION IS PASSED ON: advertisements, announcements, a brief, a bulletin, communications, gossip, instructions, the Internet, letters, the media, messages, the news, notices, reports, statements, teaching.

VARIOUS WAYS INFORMATION CAN BE STORED: database, documents, dossier, file.

informative *adjective*
The travel agent gave us an informative booklet about holidays abroad. helpful, illuminating, instructive, revealing, useful.
AN OPPOSITE IS unhelpful.

informer *noun*
The informer gave the police some vital information. informant, spy, telltale.

infrequent *adjective*
This bird is an infrequent visitor to this area. irregular, occasional, rare, uncommon, unusual.
AN OPPOSITE IS frequent.

infuriate *verb*
He was infuriated by their bad behaviour. anger, enrage, exasperate, incense, provoke.

ingenious *adjective*
It seemed like an ingenious plan. artful, brilliant, clever, crafty, cunning, imaginative, inspired, inventive, original, shrewd, skilful, subtle.

inhabit *verb*
People inhabited the caves thousands of years ago. dwell in, live in, make a home in, occupy, reside in, settle in, set up home in.

inhabitant *noun*
The inhabitants of the remote island had few visitors. citizen, occupant, occupier, resident.
The inhabitants of a town, etc., are the town's **population**.

inhabited *adjective*
Is the castle inhabited? lived-in, occupied.
AN OPPOSITE IS uninhabited.

inherent *adjective*
The instinct to survive is inherent in all animals. fundamental, hereditary, ingrained, inherited, natural.

inheritance *noun*
She was left a small inheritance in her uncle's will. bequest, legacy.

inherited *adjective*
Eye colour is an inherited characteristic. hereditary, passed down.

inhibited *adjective*
He was too inhibited to join the fun. bashful, prim and proper, reserved, self-conscious, shy, tense, [*informal*] uptight.
AN OPPOSITE IS uninhibited.

inhospitable *adjective*
1 *They were so inhospitable that he didn't even get a cup of tea.* cool, hostile, unfriendly, unsociable, unwelcoming.
AN OPPOSITE IS hospitable.
2 *The explorers were glad to leave those inhospitable mountains.* comfortless, desolate, forbidding.

inhuman *adjective*
She thought it was inhuman to hunt animals. barbaric, barbarous, bloodthirsty, cruel, diabolical, fiendish, heartless, merciless, pitiless, ruthless, savage.
AN OPPOSITE IS humane.

initial *adjective*
The initial work on the bypass starts next week. earliest, first, introductory, opening, preliminary.
AN OPPOSITE IS final.

initiate *verb*
We initiated negotiations to buy a new house. begin, commence, enter into, launch, open, start.
AN OPPOSITE IS finish.

initiative *noun*
She was given the job because she showed initiative. ambition, drive, enterprise, leadership, originality.

injection *noun*
The nurse gave me an injection. inoculation, [*informal*] jab, vaccination.

injure *verb*
Was anyone injured in the accident? harm, hurt, wound.
FOR VARIOUS KINDS OF INJURY, SEE **wound** *verb*.

injustice *noun*
The injustice of the decision made them angry. bias, dishonesty, favouritism, illegality, prejudice, unfairness, unlawfulness.
AN OPPOSITE IS justice.

inner *adjective*
1 The inner rooms of the palace are not open to visitors. central, inside, interior, internal, middle.
2 She tried to hide her inner feelings. concealed, hidden, innermost, intimate, inward, personal, private, secret.
AN OPPOSITE IS outer.

innocent *adjective*
1 The jury found him innocent. blameless, free from blame, guiltless.
AN OPPOSITE IS guilty.
2 Sleeping babies look so innocent. angelic, faultless, harmless, inexperienced, naïve, pure, simple, sinless, virtuous.
AN OPPOSITE IS wicked.

innovation *noun*
The club introduced some innovations this year. change, new feature, reform.

innovator *noun*
George Stephenson was an important innovator in the history of railways. discoverer, experimenter, inventor, pioneer, reformer.

innumerable *adjective*
There are innumerable stars in the sky. countless, numberless, uncountable, untold.

inquest *noun*
They held an inquest to determine how she died. hearing, inquiry, investigation.

inquire *verb*
If you have any problems, please inquire at the desk. ask, enquire, seek help.

inquiry *noun*
There will be an inquiry into how the accident happened. enquiry, inquest, investigation.

inquisitive *adjective*
Who's that inquisitive man asking all those questions? curious, inquiring, interfering, meddling, nosy, prying, snooping.
An inquisitive person is a **busybody**.

insane *adjective*
Although they are often used as a joke, synonyms of *insane* are usually insulting, and show that the person using the word does not understand mental illnesses
crazy, daft, mad, [*informal*] out of your mind, unbalanced, unhinged.

inscribe *verb*
He read the words inscribed on the tomb. engrave, set down, write.

inscription *noun*
He read the inscription on the tomb. engraving, wording, writing.

insect *noun*

VARIOUS INSECTS: ant, aphid, bee, beetle, blackbeetle, blackfly, bluebottle, bumble-bee, butterfly, cicada, cockroach, cricket, daddy-long-legs, damselfly, dragonfly, earwig, firefly, fly, glow-worm, gnat, grasshopper, hornet, ladybird, locust, mantis, mayfly, midge, ➡

mosquito, moth, termite, tsetse fly, wasp, weevil.

OTHER FORMS OF AN INSECT: caterpillar, chrysalis, grub, larva, maggot, pupa.

CRAWLING CREATURES WHICH PEOPLE OFTEN CALL INSECTS WHICH STRICTLY SPEAKING ARE NOT INSECTS: arachnid, centipede, earthworm, mite, slug, spider, woodlouse, worm.

insecure *adjective*
1 *Be careful—that scaffolding is insecure.* dangerous, loose, precarious, shaky, unsafe, unstable, unsteady, wobbly.
2 *She felt insecure in her new job.* anxious, apprehensive, nervous, uncertain, unconfident, uneasy.
AN OPPOSITE IS secure.

insensitive *adjective*
Her remarks were a bit insensitive. callous, cruel, tactless, thoughtless, uncaring, unfeeling, unsympathetic.
AN OPPOSITE IS sensitive.

insert *verb*
He inserted the key into the lock. drive in, introduce, push in, put in, tuck in.

inside *adjective*
We painted the inside walls of the hut with emulsion. indoor, inner, interior, internal.
AN OPPOSITE IS outside.

inside *noun*
The inside of the apple was rotten. centre, core, heart, interior, middle.
AN OPPOSITE IS outside.

insignificant *adjective*
There was an insignificant amount of rainfall last month. inconsiderable, negligible, small, trivial, unimportant, unimpressive, valueless, worthless.
AN OPPOSITE IS significant.

insincere *adjective*
He paid her some rather insincere compliments. deceitful, deceptive, dishonest, false, flattering, hypocritical, lying, pretended, [*informal*] two-faced.
AN OPPOSITE IS sincere.

insist *verb*
He insisted that he was innocent. assert, declare, emphasize, maintain, state, stress, swear, vow.
to insist on *She insists on obedience.* demand, expect, require.

insistent *adjective*
In the end he gave in to their insistent requests. assertive, emphatic, forceful, persistent, relentless, repeated, unrelenting, urgent.

insolence *noun*
He was punished for his insolence. arrogance, boldness, cheek, disrespect, forwardness, impertinence, impudence, rudeness, [*informal*] sauce.
AN OPPOSITE IS politeness.

insolent *adjective*
Her insolent stare annoyed him. arrogant, bold, brazen, [*informal*] cheeky, disrespectful, forward, impertinent, impolite, impudent, insulting, rude, saucy, shameless, sneering.
AN OPPOSITE IS polite.

insoluble *adjective*
The problem seemed insoluble. baffling, incomprehensible, inexplicable, mysterious, mystifying, puzzling, unanswerable, unsolvable.
AN OPPOSITE IS soluble.

inspect *verb*
The builders inspected the damage done by the storm. check, examine, investigate, scrutinize, study, survey.

inspection *noun*
They had a school inspection last term. check, check-up, examination, investigation, review, scrutiny, survey.

inspector *noun*
The inspector checked the standard of work. examiner, investigator, official, tester.

inspiration *noun*
  1 *What was the inspiration behind your story?* impulse, motivation, stimulus.
  2 *I had a sudden inspiration.* idea, thought.

inspire *verb*
  The crowd inspired them to play well. animate, arouse, egg on, encourage, motivate, prompt, stimulate.

install *verb*
  They installed the central heating boiler in the bathroom. establish, fix, place, position, put in, set up.
  AN OPPOSITE IS remove.

instalment *noun*
  Did you see the first instalment of the new serial? episode, part.

instance *noun*
  Give me an instance of what you mean. case, example, illustration, sample.

instant *adjective*
  Gardeners don't expect instant results. direct, fast, immediate, instantaneous, prompt, quick, rapid, snappy, speedy, swift.

instant *noun*
  The shooting star was gone in an instant. flash, moment, second, split second.

instantaneous *adjective* SEE **instant** *adjective*

instinct *noun*
  1 *Animals have an instinct to look after their young.* impulse, inclination, tendency, urge.
  2 *Some instinct told him that they would come today.* feeling, hunch, intuition.

instinctive *adjective*
  1 *It's instinctive for a mother to protect her baby.* inherent, intuitive, natural.
  2 *Blinking in bright light is an instinctive reaction.* automatic, impulsive, involuntary, reflex, spontaneous, unconscious, unthinking.
  AN OPPOSITE IS deliberate.

institute *verb*
  They've instituted a one-way system in town. create, establish, initiate, introduce, launch, set up, start.

institution *noun*
  1 *It was an institution for blind people.* academy, college, foundation, home, hospital, institute, organization, school, society.
  2 *Sunday dinner is a regular institution in their house.* convention, custom, habit, ritual, routine, tradition.

instruct *verb*
  1 *The teacher instructed them in how to use the new computer.* coach, teach, train.
  2 *He instructed us to wait.* command, order, tell.

instructive *adjective*
  It was instructive watching the professional players training. educational, helpful, illuminating, informative, revealing.
  AN OPPOSITE IS unhelpful.

instructor *noun*
  The swimming instructor taught them life-saving. coach, teacher, trainer.

instrument *noun*
  The surgeon uses instruments specially designed for doing operations. appliance, contraption, device, gadget, implement, tool, utensil.
  FOR MUSICAL INSTRUMENTS, SEE **music**.

instrumental *adjective*
  She was instrumental in getting him a job. active, helpful, influential, useful.

insufficient *adjective*
  Many plants died because there was insufficient rain. inadequate, meagre, poor, scanty, scarce, unsatisfactory.
  AN OPPOSITE IS enough or excessive.

insulate *verb*
  He insulated the water pipes to prevent loss of heat. cover, enclose, lag, protect, surround, wrap up.

insult *verb*
  It was wrong to insult him in public. abuse, call you names, mock, sneer at, snub, taunt.
  AN OPPOSITE IS compliment.

insult noun
She was offended by his insults. abuse, cheek, impudence, insulting behaviour, rudeness, slur, snub, taunt.
AN OPPOSITE IS compliment.

insulting adjective
She was infuriated by his insulting remarks. abusive, contemptuous, impolite, insolent, mocking, offensive, rude, scornful.
AN OPPOSITE IS complimentary.

insurance noun
Have you got insurance against loss or accident? cover, protection.
The insurance document is the **policy**.

intact adjective
The vase remained intact despite being dropped. complete, [informal] in one piece, perfect, unbroken, undamaged, unharmed.

integral adjective
1 The boiler is an integral part of the heating system. essential, indispensable, necessary.
2 The equipment is supplied as an integral unit. combined, complete, full, integrated, whole.

integrate verb
They decided to integrate the two groups. amalgamate, bring together, combine, harmonize, join, merge, put together, unify, unite.
AN OPPOSITE IS separate verb.

integrity noun
You can trust her integrity. fidelity, goodness, honesty, honour, loyalty, reliability, sincerity, trustworthiness, virtue.
AN OPPOSITE IS dishonesty.

intellect noun SEE **intelligence**

intellectual adjective
1 It was an intellectual book about philosophy. demanding, difficult, educational, improving.
2 The professor is very intellectual. academic, brainy, clever, cultured, intelligent, scholarly, studious, thoughtful.

intelligence noun
1 Use your intelligence! ability, brains, cleverness, genius, insight, intellect, judgement, mind, reason, sense, understanding, wisdom, wit.
2 They received intelligence about the enemy's plans. data, facts, information, knowledge, news, reports, warnings.

intelligent adjective
The professor must be a very intelligent person. able, brainy, bright, brilliant, clever, intellectual, perceptive, quick, sharp, shrewd, smart, wise.
AN OPPOSITE IS stupid.

intelligible adjective
The message was not very intelligible. clear, comprehensible, legible, lucid, meaningful, plain, straightforward, unambiguous, understandable.
AN OPPOSITE IS incomprehensible.

intend verb
1 What do you intend to do? aim, have in mind, mean, plan, plot, propose.
2 The surprise was intended to please you. design, set up.

intense adjective
1 She suffered the intense pain bravely. acute, agonizing, extreme, great, severe, sharp, strong, violent.
AN OPPOSITE IS slight.
2 The contest aroused intense feelings. burning, deep, emotional, fanatical, passionate, powerful, profound.
AN OPPOSITE IS mild.

intensify verb
1 They intensified their attack in the second half of the game. boost, make greater, reinforce, sharpen, step up, strengthen.
2 The excitement intensified. become greater, build up, escalate, heighten, increase.
AN OPPOSITE IS reduce.

intensive adjective
They made an intensive search. concentrated, detailed, thorough.
AN OPPOSITE IS superficial.

intent adjective
She had an intent look on her face. absorbed, concentrating, eager, engrossed, interested, preoccupied.

intention *noun*
It's his intention to work with
computers. aim, ambition, goal, intent,
objective, plan, target.

intentional *adjective*
He was penalized for an intentional
foul. calculated, conscious, deliberate,
intended, planned, wilful.
AN OPPOSITE IS accidental.

intercept *verb*
He managed to intercept the pass.
catch, check, cut off, deflect, head off,
stop.

interest *verb*
Astronomy interests a lot of people.
absorb, appeal to, attract, capture the
imagination of, excite, fascinate,
intrigue, stimulate.
AN OPPOSITE IS bore.

interest *noun*
1 Did he show any interest? attention,
concern, curiosity, involvement.
2 The information was of no interest to
anyone. consequence, importance,
significance, value.
3 He asked him about his interests.
activity, diversion, hobby, pastime,
pursuit.

interesting *adjective*
They listened intently to the interesting
story. absorbing, appealing, curious,
engrossing, entertaining, exciting,
fascinating, intriguing, riveting,
stimulating.
AN OPPOSITE IS boring.

interfere *verb*
Don't interfere in other people's affairs.
be a busybody, butt in, interrupt,
intervene, intrude, meddle, [*informal*]
poke your nose in, pry, snoop.
to interfere with The bad weather
interfered with the plans for sports day.
get in the way of, hamper, hinder,
obstruct.

interior *adjective, noun* SEE **inside**
adjective, noun

intermediate *adjective*
She's reached an intermediate stage in
her studies, but she's still got a long
way to go. half-way, middle, midway,
transitional.

intermittent *adjective*
The TV has an intermittent fault.
irregular, occasional, recurrent.
AN OPPOSITE IS continual.

internal *adjective*
She didn't know much about the
internal parts of computers. inner,
inside, interior.
AN OPPOSITE IS external.

international *adjective*
Interpol is an international police
organization. global, inter-continental,
worldwide.

interpret *verb*
Can you interpret this old writing?
clarify, decipher, decode, explain, make
clear, make sense of, paraphrase,
translate, understand.

Interrogate *verb*
The police interrogated the suspect for
several hours. cross-examine, examine,
grill, interview, question.

interrupt *verb*
1 Please don't interrupt while I am
speaking. barge in, break in, butt in,
cut in, intervene.
2 A fire alarm interrupted work. cut
short, disrupt, halt, hold up, stop,
suspend.
3 The new houses interrupt their view.
get in the way of, interfere with,
obstruct, spoil.

interruption *noun*
They worked for an hour without any
interruption. break, check, disruption,
gap, halt, pause, stop, suspension.

intersection *noun*
Drivers need to take special care at the
intersection. crossroads, interchange,
junction.

interval *noun*
1 There was an interval of two hours
before they came back. break, delay,
lapse, lull, pause, wait.
Another word for an interval in a play
or film is *interlude* or *intermission*.
An interval in a meeting is a *recess*.
An interval when you take a rest is a
breather or *breathing space*.
2 There were signs at regular intervals
along the road. distance, gap, space.

intervene *verb*
1 *Many events intervened before he saw her again.* come between, happen, occur.
2 *He intervened to stop the fight.* butt in, interfere, interrupt, [*informal*] step in.

interview *verb*
If you witnessed the accident, the police will want to interview you. examine, interrogate, question, sound you out.

intimate *adjective*
1 *They have been intimate friends for many years.* affectionate, close, familiar, friendly, loving.
AN OPPOSITE IS impersonal.
2 *He had no right to ask for intimate details of her life.* confidential, personal, private, secret.

intimidate *verb*
They attempted to intimidate witnesses in the trial. bully, frighten, menace, persecute, scare, terrify, terrorize, threaten.

intolerable *adjective*
The doctor will give you an injection if the pain becomes intolerable. impossible to bear, unacceptable, unbearable, unendurable.
AN OPPOSITE IS tolerable.

intolerant *adjective*
Don't be so intolerant—try to understand their point of view. biased, chauvinistic, narrow-minded, prejudiced, racialist, racist, sexist.
AN OPPOSITE IS tolerant.

intoxicated *adjective*
He couldn't drive because he was intoxicated. drunk, [*informal*] tight.
AN OPPOSITE IS sober.

intoxicating *adjective*
1 *Children are not allowed to buy intoxicating drinks.* alcoholic, strong.
2 *Reaching the top of the mountain was an intoxicating experience.* exciting, stimulating.

intricate *adjective*
The clock has an intricate mechanism. complex, complicated, elaborate, involved, sophisticated.
AN OPPOSITE IS simple.

intrigue *verb*
1 *Science intrigues me.* appeal to, attract, fascinate, interest.
2 *Guy Fawkes intrigued against Parliament.* conspire, plot, scheme.

introduce *verb*
1 *Let me introduce you to my friend.* make known, present.
2 *It was his job to introduce the various acts in the concert.* announce, give an introduction to, lead into.
3 *They introduced a new bus service.* begin, bring in, commence, create, establish, initiate, set up, start.

introduction *noun*
Something which happens as an introduction to a bigger event is a ***prelude***.
An introduction to a book is a ***preface***.
An introduction to a play is a ***prologue***.
A piece played as an introduction to a concert or opera is an ***overture***.

introductory *adjective*
The chairman made some introductory remarks. initial, opening, preliminary.
AN OPPOSITE IS final.

intrude *verb*
This is a private conversation—please don't intrude! break in, butt in, interfere, intervene, push in.

intruder *noun*
They called the police when they saw an intruder in the garden. burglar, prowler, trespasser.

intuition *noun*
I had an intuition that you'd come today. feeling, hunch, instinct.

invade *verb*
The country has been invaded many times in its history. attack, enter, march into, occupy, raid.

invalid *adjective*
1 *The passport is invalid because the photograph has come off.* out-of-date, unacceptable, unusable, worthless.
2 *The arguments that he used were invalid.* fallacious, false, illogical, irrational, unconvincing.
AN OPPOSITE IS valid.

invaluable *adjective*
Your help was invaluable. precious,
priceless, useful, valuable.
AN OPPOSITE IS worthless.

invariable *adjective*
It's an invariable rule that we must
wash our hands before meals. constant,
inflexible, unalterable, unchangeable.
AN OPPOSITE IS variable.

invasion *noun*
Fortunately, the expected invasion
never happened. attack, raid.

invent *verb*
Who invented computers? conceive,
create, design, devise, originate, think
up.

invention *noun*
1 This system is his own invention.
[*informal*] brainchild, creation, design,
discovery.
2 She made a lot of money from her new
invention. contraption, device.
3 Her story was pure invention. deceit,
fantasy, fiction, lies.

inventive *adjective*
She's full of inventive ideas. creative,
enterprising, imaginative, ingenious,
inspired, original.

inventor *noun*
The device was sold to a big company
by its inventor. creator, designer,
discoverer, originator.

investigate *verb*
They were investigating the possibility
of establishing a new business.
consider, examine, explore, follow up,
gather evidence about, [*informal*] go
into, inquire into, look into, research,
scrutinize, study.

investigation *noun*
An investigation showed how the
accident happened. enquiry,
examination, inquiry, inspection,
research, study, survey.

invigorating *adjective*
He took an invigorating shower.
healthy, refreshing, stimulating,
reviving.
AN OPPOSITE IS tiring.

invisible *adjective*
They planted trees so that the sewage
works will be invisible from the road.
camouflaged, concealed, covered,
disguised, hidden, inconspicuous,
obscured, out of sight, undetectable,
unnoticeable, unnoticed, unseen.
AN OPPOSITE IS visible.

invite *verb*
He invited them to join in. ask,
encourage, request, urge.

inviting *adjective*
An inviting smell came from the
kitchen. appealing, attractive,
encouraging, irresistible, tantalizing,
tempting.
AN OPPOSITE IS repulsive.

involuntary *adjective*
Blinking is an involuntary movement.
impulsive, instinctive, reflex,
spontaneous, unconscious, unthinking.
AN OPPOSITE IS deliberate.

involve *verb*
1 What does the job involve? comprise,
contain, incorporate, take in.
2 Protecting the environment involves
us all. affect, concern, interest.

involved *adjective*
1 The problem was too involved for
him. complex, complicated, confusing,
difficult, elaborate, intricate.
AN OPPOSITE IS simple.
2 Once she started the work, she got
really involved. absorbed, active, busy,
committed, engrossed, enthusiastic,
interested, keen, preoccupied.
AN OPPOSITE IS uninterested.

irrational *adjective*
They couldn't understand his irrational
behaviour. absurd, crazy, illogical,
mad, nonsensical, senseless, silly,
unreasonable.
AN OPPOSITE IS rational.

irregular *adjective*
1 The buses run at irregular times.
erratic, haphazard, intermittent,
occasional, odd, random,
unpredictable, unreliable, varying.
AN OPPOSITE IS regular.

2 *His behaviour is highly irregular.*
abnormal, exceptional, illegal,
improper, unconventional, unusual.
AN OPPOSITE IS normal.

irrelevant *adjective*
She left out the irrelevant details.
inappropriate, inessential,
meaningless, pointless, unnecessary.
AN OPPOSITE IS relevant.

irresistible *adjective*
*On such a hot day, ice cream was an
irresistible temptation!* overpowering,
overwhelming, persuasive, powerful,
unavoidable.

irresponsible *adjective*
It's irresponsible to drive too fast.
immoral, inconsiderate, negligent,
reckless, selfish, thoughtless,
uncaring, untrustworthy.
AN OPPOSITE IS responsible.

irreverent *adjective*
*They were reprimanded for their
irreverent behaviour in church.*
blasphemous, disrespectful, rude.
AN OPPOSITE IS reverent.

irritable *adjective*
She's in an irritable mood! angry, bad-
tempered, grumpy, ill-tempered,
impatient, short-tempered, touchy.

irritate *verb*
She was irritated by their attitude.
anger, annoy, bother, exasperate,
provoke, vex.

island *noun*
A small island is an **islet**.
A coral island is an **atoll**.
A group of islands is an **archipelago**.

isolate *verb*
1 *The police isolated the troublemakers.*
keep apart, segregate, separate, single
out.
2 *The hospital isolates infectious
patients.* place in quarantine, set apart.

isolated *adjective*
1 *The isolated farm had few visitors.*
desolate, inaccessible, lonely, outlying,
out-of-the-way, remote, unfrequented.
AN OPPOSITE IS accessible.

2 *There had been a few isolated cases of
cheating.* abnormal, exceptional,
single, uncommon, unique, unusual.
AN OPPOSITE IS common.

issue *verb*
1 *They issued blankets to the refugees.*
distribute, give out, supply.
2 *They have issued a new set of stamps.*
bring out, circulate, print, produce,
publish, put out, release.
3 *Smoke issued from the chimney.*
appear, come out, emerge, erupt, flow
out, gush.

issue *noun*
1 *Do they deal with the issue of
passports here?* distribution, issuing.
2 *The new issue of the magazine comes
out this week.* copy, edition, number,
publication.
3 *They print stories about local issues
in the magazine.* affair, controversy,
dispute, matter, problem, question,
subject, topic.
4 *They were eager to know the issue of
the election.* consequence, effect,
outcome, result, upshot.

itch *noun*
1 *She had an itch in her foot.* irritation,
tickle, tingling.
2 *He had an itch to travel.* ache, desire,
impulse, longing, restlessness, urge,
wish, yearning.

item *noun*
1 *There were some interesting items in
the sale.* article, bit, object, thing.
2 *Did you read this item in the paper?*
article, feature, piece, report.

jab *verb*
She jabbed me in the ribs. elbow, nudge, poke, prod, stab, thrust.

jacket *noun*
1 He took off his jacket and hung it in the wardrobe. SEE **coat** *noun*.
2 The hot water tank has an insulating jacket. cover, covering, sheath, wrapper, wrapping.

jaded *adjective*
I felt tired and jaded at the end of a long day. bored, [*informal*] fed up, listless, weary.
AN OPPOSITE IS lively.

jagged *adjective*
The knife had a jagged edge. rough, uneven, zigzag.
AN OPPOSITE IS smooth.

jail *noun* SEE **prison**

jam *noun*
1 She was delayed in a jam on the motorway. blockage, bottleneck, hold-up, tailback, traffic jam.
2 [*informal*] I'm in a bit of a jam. difficulty, dilemma, [*informal*] tight corner.

jam *verb*
1 The door was jammed open. prop, stick, wedge.
2 Cars jammed the street. block, [*informal*] bung up, fill, obstruct.
3 I jammed my kit into a holdall. cram, crowd, crush, pack, ram, squash, squeeze, stuff.

jangle *verb*
A bell jangled loudly. clang, clink, jingle, ring, tinkle.

jar *noun*
VARIOUS KINDS OF JAR: carafe, flagon, glass, jam jar, jug, mug, pitcher, pot, urn.
FOR OTHER CONTAINERS, SEE **container**.

jar *verb*
He jarred his back badly when he fell. jerk, jolt, shake, shock.

jarring *adjective*
Her voice was jarring. disagreeable, discordant, grating, grinding, harsh, unpleasant.

jaunt *noun*
They're planning a jaunt to Paris. excursion, expedition, outing, trip.

jaunty *adjective*
He whistled a jaunty tune. bright, carefree, cheerful, lively, sprightly.
AN OPPOSITE IS gloomy.

jazzy *adjective*
The band were playing some jazzy music. lively, rhythmic, spirited, syncopated.

jealous *adjective*
He's jealous because I won. bitter, envious, grudging, resentful.

jeer *verb*
to jeer at Some of the younger men jeered at him. barrack, boo, deride, hiss, laugh at, make fun of, mock, ridicule, scoff at, sneer at, taunt.
AN OPPOSITE IS cheer.

jerk *verb*
He jerked the fishing rod out of the water. pluck, pull, tug, twitch, wrench, yank.

jerky *adjective*
The coach drew to a jerky halt. bouncy, bumpy, jolting, jumpy, shaky, uneven.
AN OPPOSITE IS steady.

jest *noun, verb* SEE **joke** *noun, verb*

jester *noun*
The king's jester kept the court amused. clown, entertainer, fool, joker.

jet *noun*
A jet of water shot high in the air. fountain, gush, rush, spout, spurt, squirt, stream.

jetty *noun*
A boat tied up at the jetty. landing stage, pier, quay.

jewel, jewellery *nouns*

> VARIOUS ITEMS OF JEWELLERY:
> anklet, bangle, beads, bracelet,
> brooch, chain, charm, choker, clasp,
> cufflinks, earring, engagement ring,
> locket, necklace, pendant, pin, ring,
> signet ring, tiepin, wedding ring.
>
> VARIOUS STONES OR GEMS USED TO
> MAKE JEWELLERY: agate, amber,
> amethyst, aquamarine, beryl,
> carnelian or cornelian, coral,
> diamond, emerald, garnet, jade,
> jasper, jet, lapis lazuli, onyx, opal,
> pearl, ruby, sapphire, topaz,
> turquoise.
>
> METALS USED TO MAKE
> JEWELLERY: gold, platinum, silver.

jingle *verb*
Coins jingled as he emptied his pocket.
chink, clink, ring, tinkle.

job *noun*
1 *He's got a well-paid job.* appointment,
business, career, employment,
livelihood, living, occupation, position,
post, profession, trade, work.
The job you particularly want to do is
your **mission** or **vocation**.
2 *It's not my job to do the washing-up.*
assignment, chore, duty, errand, task.

> JOBS PEOPLE DO: accountant,
> architect, artist, banker, barber,
> barmaid or barman, barrister,
> blacksmith, bookseller, brewer,
> bricklayer, broadcaster, builder,
> cameraman, caretaker, carpenter,
> cashier, caterer, chauffeur, chef,
> cleaner, clergyman, clerk,
> coastguard, composer, conductor,
> cook, courier, curator, decorator,
> dentist, designer, detective, driver,
> docker, doctor, dustman, electrician,
> engineer, entertainer, estate agent,
> executive, farmer, fireman, forester,
> gamekeeper, gardener, groundsman,
> hairdresser, handyman, hotelier,
> industrialist, interpreter, joiner,
> journalist, labourer, lawyer, lecturer,
> librarian, machinist, mason,
> mechanic, midwife, milkman, miller,
> miner, model, musician,
> nightwatchman, nurse, ➡

> nurseryman, office worker, optician,
> pharmacist, photographer,
> physiotherapist, pilot, plumber,
> policeman or policewoman,
> politician, porter, postman, printer,
> probation officer, professor,
> programmer, projectionist,
> psychiatrist, publisher, receptionist,
> reporter, sailor, scientist, secretary,
> shepherd, shopkeeper, signalman,
> social worker, soldier, solicitor,
> steward or stewardess, stockbroker,
> surgeon, surveyor, tailor, teacher,
> technician, telephonist, test pilot,
> traffic warden, typist, undertaker,
> vet, waiter or waitress.

jog *verb*
1 *He jogs round the park every
morning.* go jogging, run, trot.
2 *She jogged my elbow.* jar, jerk, jolt,
knock, nudge, push.
3 *The photograph may jog her memory.*
prompt, refresh, set off, stimulate, stir.

join *noun*
*They mended it so well that you can't
see the join.* joint, link, mend, seam.

join *verb*
1 *The countries joined together to
abolish trade restrictions.* amalgamate,
combine, come together, merge, unite.
AN OPPOSITE IS separate.
2 *Join one section of pipe to the other.*
attach, connect, fasten, fix, link, put
together, tack on.
SEE ALSO **fasten.**
AN OPPOSITE IS detach.
3 *Two roads join here.* converge, meet,
merge.
AN OPPOSITE IS divide.
4 *I joined the crowd going into the
cinema.* follow, go with, tag along with.
AN OPPOSITE IS leave.
5 *He joined the navy.* become a member
of, enlist in, enrol in, volunteer for.
AN OPPOSITE IS resign from.

joint *adjective*
*The preparation of the meal was a joint
effort.* combined, communal,
cooperative, shared, united.
AN OPPOSITE IS individual.

joint *noun*

> IMPORTANT JOINTS IN YOUR BODY:
> ankle, elbow, hip, knee, knuckle,
> shoulder, vertebra, wrist.

joist *noun*
Long joists support the ceiling. beam,
girder, rafter.

joke *noun*
Do you know any good jokes? funny
story, [*informal*] gag, jest, pun.

joke *verb*
They're always laughing and joking. be
facetious, clown, jest, make jokes.

jolly *adjective*
We had a jolly time last night. cheerful,
happy, joyful, merry.
AN OPPOSITE IS gloomy.

jolt *verb*
The car jolted over the track. bounce,
bump, jar, jerk, jog, shake.

jostle *verb*
*He was jostled by the journalists and
photographers.* crowd in on, hustle,
press, push, shove.

jot *verb*
I quickly jotted down some ideas. note,
scrawl, scribble, write.

jotter *noun*
He made some notes in his jotter.
exercise book, notebook, writing pad

journal *noun*
1 *He subscribes to several medical
journals.* magazine, newspaper, paper,
periodical, publication.
2 *The captain kept a journal of the
voyage.* account, chronicle, diary, log,
record.

journalist *noun*
*She works as a journalist on the local
newspaper.* contributor, correspondent,
reporter, writer.

journey *noun*
*His journey took him through France,
Germany, and Italy.* itinerary, route,
travels.
SEE ALSO **travel**.

jovial *adjective*
He was in a very jovial mood. cheerful,
good-humoured, happy, jolly, joyful,
merry, warm-hearted.
AN OPPOSITE IS sad.

joy *noun*
Her eyes filled with tears of joy. bliss,
cheerfulness, delight, ecstasy, elation,
exultation, gaiety, gladness, glee,
happiness, joyfulness, jubilation,
mirth, rejoicing.
AN OPPOSITE IS sorrow.

joyful *adjective*
*They arrived home amid joyful scenes
in London.* cheerful, delighted,
ecstatic, elated, exultant, gleeful,
happy, jolly, jovial, joyous, jubilant,
merry, rejoicing, triumphant.
AN OPPOSITE IS sad.

judge *noun*
A judge in a local court is a
magistrate.
A judge in a dispute is an **arbitrator**
or a **mediator**.
A judge in a competition is an
adjudicator.
A judge in a sport is a **linesman**,
referee, **referee's assistant**, **touch
judge**, or **umpire**.

judge *verb*
1 *He was judged and found innocent.*
examine, try.
2 *The umpire judged that the ball was
out.* adjudicate, decide, decree, pass
judgement, rule.
3 *She has been asked to judge the
entries in the art competition.* appraise,
assess, evaluate, give your opinion of.
4 *They judged him to be about 25 years
old.* consider, estimate, gauge, guess,
reckon, suppose.

judgement *noun*
1 *The judgement was given by the
chairman of the committee.* arbitration,
award, conclusion, decision, decree,
finding, outcome, result, ruling,
verdict.
2 *His comments show a lack of political
judgement.* common sense,
discrimination, expertise, good sense,
intelligence, reason, wisdom.

3 *They have formed an unfair judgement of his character.* belief, estimation, evaluation, impression, opinion, point of view.

judicious *adjective*
It was a judicious change of tactics. clever, prudent, sensible, shrewd, thoughtful, well-judged, wise.
AN OPPOSITE IS unwise.

juice *noun*
The juice from the vegetables was kept in the fridge. fluid, liquid, sap.

jumble *noun*
There was a jumble of books on the floor. chaos, clutter, confusion, mess, muddle.

jumble *verb*
The drawer was full of letters jumbled together. mess up, mix up, muddle, shuffle.
AN OPPOSITE IS arrange.

jump *verb*
1 *Lambs were jumping about in the field.* bound, leap, spring.
2 *I bet you can't jump the fence.* clear, vault.
When a cat jumps it **pounces**.

jump *noun*
The horse easily cleared the last jump. ditch, fence, gate, hurdle, obstacle.

junction *noun*
Two cars collided at the junction. crossroads, interchange, intersection, T-junction.

junior *adjective*
1 *The junior members of the club go swimming on Thursdays.* younger.
2 *He's only a junior employee in the firm.* inferior, lesser, lower, minor, subordinate.
AN OPPOSITE IS senior.

junk *noun*
The garage is full of junk. clutter, garbage, jumble, lumber, oddments, odds and ends, rubbish, scrap, trash, waste.

just *adjective*
It was a just punishment, considering the crime. appropriate, deserved, fair, justified, legitimate, merited, proper, reasonable, rightful, unbiased, unprejudiced.
AN OPPOSITE IS unjust.

justice *noun*
1 *Justice demands that everyone should be treated the same.* fairness, honesty, impartiality, integrity, right.
AN OPPOSITE IS injustice.
2 *They were tried in a court of justice.* law.

justifiable *adjective*
He had a justifiable reason for being late. acceptable, defensible, excusable, forgivable, justified, permissible, reasonable, right.
AN OPPOSITE IS unjustifiable.

justify *verb*
1 *He attempted to justify his actions.* defend, excuse, explain.
2 *The dreadful crime justifies the severe punishment.* deserve, merit, warrant.

jut *verb*
The mantelpiece juts over the fireplace. extend, overhang, poke out, project, protrude, stick out.

juvenile *adjective*
The government introduced new measures to deal with juvenile offenders. adolescent, young, youthful.
AN OPPOSITE IS adult or mature.

Kk

keel *verb*
to keel over *The boat keeled over in the wind.* capsize, lean, overturn, tilt.

keen *adjective*
1 *All the players are very keen.* ambitious, committed, diligent, eager, enthusiastic, fervent, industrious, interested, motivated, zealous.
AN OPPOSITE IS apathetic.

2 *The carving knife has a keen edge.*
cutting, razor-sharp, sharp, sharpened.
AN OPPOSITE IS blunt.
3 *Owls must have keen eyesight.* acute,
perceptive, sensitive, sharp.
AN OPPOSITE IS poor.
4 *A keen wind was blowing and flakes
of snow began to fall.* bitter, cold, icy,
penetrating, severe.
AN OPPOSITE IS mild.

keep *verb*
1 *I'll keep these things for later.*
conserve, guard, hang on to, hold on to,
preserve, retain, safeguard, save, store
up.
AN OPPOSITE IS abandon or lose.
2 *Please keep still.* remain, stay.
3 *She kept laughing.* carry on,
continue, keep on, persevere in, persist
in.
4 *You're late. What kept you?* delay,
detain, hamper, hinder, hold up,
obstruct, restrain.
5 *Will the milk keep until tomorrow?* be
preserved, be usable, last, stay good.
6 *They kept chickens and a few pigs.*
look after, manage, mind, own.
7 *It costs a lot to keep a family.* feed,
maintain, pay for, provide for, support.
to keep something up *Keep up the
good work!* carry on, continue,
maintain.

keeper *noun*
The keeper of something precious is
the **custodian**.
The keeper of a museum is the
curator.
The keeper of a prison is a **jailer** or
warder.
The keeper of a hostel is the **warden**.

key *noun*
*The key to his behaviour may lie in his
unhappy past.* answer, clue,
explanation, solution.

keyboard *noun*

VARIOUS KEYBOARD INSTRUMENTS:
accordion, celesta, electronic
keyboard, harmonium, harpsichord,
organ, piano, spinet, synthesizer.

kidnap *verb*
She was kidnapped by terrorists.
abduct, carry off, run away with,
snatch.

kill *verb*
1 *He was killed by a gunman.* [*slang*]
bump off, dispatch, do away with,
[*informal*] finish off, [*old use*] slay.
2 *Careless driving can kill.* take life.

To kill people deliberately is to
murder them.
To kill people brutally is to **butcher**
them.
To kill large numbers of people is to
annihilate, **exterminate**, or
massacre them.
To kill people as a punishment is to
execute them or **put them to
death**.
To kill people for political reasons is
to **assassinate** them.
To kill people for their beliefs is to
martyr them.
To kill an animal humanely is to **put
it down** or **put it to sleep**.
To kill an animal for food is to
slaughter it.
To kill animals selectively is to **cull**
them.

VARIOUS WAYS TO KILL: behead,
choke, crucify, decapitate, drown,
electrocute, garrotte, gas, guillotine,
hang, knife, lynch, poison, shoot,
smother, stab, starve, stone,
strangle, suffocate, throttle.

PEOPLE WHO KILL FOR VARIOUS
REASONS: assassin, butcher, cut-
throat, executioner, gunman, hunter,
murderer, slayer, trapper.

VARIOUS KINDS OF KILLING:
assassination, euthanasia,
execution, homicide, manslaughter,
martyrdom, murder, suicide.

THE KILLING OF LARGE NUMBERS
OF PEOPLE OR ANIMALS:
annihilation, bloodshed, butchery,
carnage, elimination, extermination,
extinction, genocide, massacre,
slaughter.

kind noun
1 *I like all kinds of music.* category, class, sort, type.
2 *What kind of animal is that?* breed, family, race, species.
3 *What kind of baked beans do you prefer?* brand, make, variety.

kind adjective
It was very kind of you to help me. affectionate, amiable, benevolent, brotherly, caring, charitable, comforting, compassionate, considerate, courteous, fatherly, friendly, generous, genial, gentle, good-natured, good-tempered, gracious, helpful, hospitable, humane, indulgent, kind-hearted, kindly, lenient, loving, merciful, motherly, neighbourly, obliging, polite, sensitive, sisterly, soft-hearted, sweet, sympathetic, tactful, tender, thoughtful, understanding, unselfish, warm-hearted, well-meaning.
AN OPPOSITE IS unkind.

kindle verb
1 *The sparks kindled the dry grass.* ignite, light, set fire to, set light to.
2 *The damp wood refused to kindle.* burn, catch fire, start burning.

kindly adjective SEE **kind** adjective

king noun SEE **ruler**

kink noun
The rope had a kink in it. bend, coil, knot, loop, tangle, twist.

kiosk noun
He bought a newspaper at the kiosk. bookstall, booth, news-stand, stall.

kit noun
1 *I've forgotten my games kit.* gear, outfit, paraphernalia, tackle.
2 *I've bought a repair kit for my bike.* equipment, set of tools.

kitchen noun

EQUIPMENT YOU MIGHT FIND IN A KITCHEN: blender, cooker, crockery, cutlery, dish rack, dishwasher, draining board, extractor fan, food processor, freezer, fridge, grill, ➡

kettle, liquidizer, microwave oven, mincer, mixer, oven, percolator, refrigerator, scales, sink, stove, thermos, toaster, tray, vacuum flask.
FOR VARIOUS COOKING UTENSILS, SEE **cook, crockery, cutlery**.

knack noun
You need a special knack to do this. expertise, gift, skill, talent, trick.

knead verb
He kneaded the athlete's tired muscles. manipulate, massage, pound, press, squeeze.

knickers plural noun SEE **underclothes**

knife noun

VARIOUS KINDS OF KNIFE: butter knife, carving knife, clasp-knife, cleaver, dagger, flick knife, machete, penknife, pocket knife, scalpel, sheath knife.
FOR OTHER KINDS OF CUTLERY, SEE **cutlery**.

knob noun
The trunk of the gnarled old tree was covered with knobs. bulge, bump, lump, projection, swelling.
A knob on a door is a **handle**.
A knob in the middle of a shield is a **boss**.

knock verb
I knocked my head on a beam. [*informal*] bash, bump, smack, strike, thump. SEE **hit** verb.
to knock off 1 [*informal*] *They knocked off work early today.* cease, end, finish, stop.
2 [*informal*] *He's planning to knock off some videos.* [*informal*] make off with, [*slang*] pinch, steal, take, walk off with.

knot verb
We knotted the two ropes together. bind, do up, entwine, fasten, join, lash, link, tie.
AN OPPOSITE IS untie.

VARIOUS KNOTS: bow, bowline, clovehitch, fisherman's knot, granny knot, hitch, noose, reef knot, sheepshank, sheetbend, slipknot.

know *verb*
1 *I don't know how to mend a puncture.* comprehend, have experience of, remember, understand.
2 *The police know who committed the crime.* be certain, have confidence.
3 *As soon as he saw her, he knew who she was.* identify, perceive, recognize, realize.
4 *Do you know Martin well?* be acquainted with, be familiar with, be a friend of.

knowing *adjective*
She gave him a knowing look. expressive, meaningful.

knowledge *noun*
1 *She has the knowledge and ability to do well in the exam.* awareness, background, education, experience, grasp, know how, learning, skill, talent, training, understanding, wisdom.
AN OPPOSITE IS ignorance.
2 *An encyclopedia contains a lot of knowledge.* data, facts, information, learning, scholarship, science.

knowledgeable *adjective*
He's very knowledgeable about antiques. familiar (with), learned, well educated, well informed.
SEE ALSO **clever**.
AN OPPOSITE IS ignorant.

label *noun*
The washing instructions are on the label. sticker, tag, ticket.

label *verb*
They labelled all the boxes, so they know what's in them. identify, mark, name, put a label on, tag.

laborious *adjective*
It was a laborious climb to the top of the hill. difficult, exhausting, gruelling, hard, stiff, strenuous, tiring, tough.
AN OPPOSITE IS easy.

labour *noun*
1 *They were paid for their labour.* effort, exertion, industry, pains, toil, work.
2 *The firm took on extra labour.* employees, workers.
3 *She began labour in the night, and the baby was born by morning.* childbirth, labour pains.
Labour pains are also called ***contractions***.

labour *verb*
They laboured to get the job finished on time. exert yourself, [*informal*] slave away, toil, work hard.

labyrinth *noun*
He got lost in the labyrinth of corridors. maze, network, tangle.

lace *noun*
1 *They have lace curtains in their front room.* net, netting.
2 *He left the laces on his trainers undone.* cord, string.

lack *noun*
The judge dismissed the case because of a lack of evidence. absence, scarcity, shortage, want.
A general lack of food is a ***famine***.
A general lack of water is a ***drought***.
AN OPPOSITE IS abundance.

lack *verb*
The game lacked excitement. be short of, be without, miss, need, require, want.

laden *adjective*
We came home laden with shopping. burdened, loaded, weighed down.

lady *noun* SEE **woman**

ladylike *adjective*
She behaved in a ladylike manner. cultured, modest, polite, [*informal*] posh, prim and proper, refined, respectable, well-bred.
AN OPPOSITE IS vulgar.

lag *verb*
1 *He soon became tired and started lagging behind.* dawdle, drop behind, fall behind, linger, loiter, straggle, trail.
2 *We lagged our water pipes to conserve heat.* insulate, wrap up.

lair *noun*
> They tracked the animal back to its
> *lair.* den, hideout, hiding place, refuge,
> shelter.

lake *noun*
> We rowed across the lake. boating lake,
> lagoon, [*Scottish*] loch, pond, pool,
> reservoir.

lame *adjective*
> **1** The horse was lame and had to be
> withdrawn from the race. crippled,
> disabled, limping, maimed.
> **2** He didn't believe her lame excuse.
> feeble, flimsy, inadequate, poor, tame,
> unconvincing, weak.

lament *verb*
> They lamented the death of their friend.
> grieve for, mourn, shed tears for, weep
> for.

lamp *noun* SEE **light** *noun*

land *noun*
> **1** They returned to their native land
> after many years abroad. country,
> nation, region, state, territory.
> **2** This land produces good crops. earth,
> farmland, ground, soil.
> **3** The duke owns this land. estate,
> grounds, property.

land *verb*
> **1** The plane landed exactly on time.
> arrive, touch down.
> **2** They landed at Dover. berth, come
> ashore, disembark, dock.

landlady, landlord *nouns*
> The landlady or landlord of a pub is the
> *licensee*.
> The landlady or landlord of a rented
> property is the *owner* or *proprietor*.

landscape *noun*
> We sat on the hill and admired the
> landscape. countryside, panorama,
> scene, scenery, view.

lane *noun* SEE **road**

language *noun*

> The words we know and use are the
> *lexical items* or *vocabulary* of our
> language.
> The rules for using words are the
> *grammar* of the language.
> A computer language is a *code*. ➡

WAYS WE USE LANGUAGE: listening,
reading, speaking or speech, writing.

VARIETIES OF LANGUAGE: colloquial
language, dialect, formal language,
informal language, jargon, register,
slang.

PARTS OF A WORD: letter, consonant,
vowel; syllable, prefix, suffix.

UNITS OF LANGUAGE WE USE IN
WRITING: clause, paragraph, phrase,
sentence, word.

NAMES OF PARTS OF SPEECH:
adjective, adverb, conjunction,
exclamation or interjection, noun,
preposition, pronoun, verb.

PUNCTUATION MARKS USED IN
WRITING: apostrophe, brackets,
colon, comma, dash, exclamation
mark, full stop, hyphen, question
mark, quotation marks or speech
marks, semicolon.

WORDS USED TO DESCRIBE THE WAY
LANGUAGE SOUNDS: accent,
intonation, pronunciation.

---

lanky *adjective*
> The lanky figure ran clumsily.
> awkward, bony, gaunt, lean, long,
> skinny, tall, thin, ungraceful, weedy.
> AN OPPOSITE IS graceful or sturdy.

lap *noun*
> **1** The cat sat on my lap. knees, thighs.
> **2** The cars were on the last lap of the
> race. circuit.

lapse *noun*
> **1** She made a mistake because of a
> lapse in concentration. failure, fault,
> flaw, shortcoming, slip, weakness.
> **2** He's started playing tennis again
> after a lapse of six months. break, gap,
> interruption, interval, lull, pause.

larder *noun*
> There's some cheese in the larder. food
> cupboard, pantry.

large *adjective*
> **1** Elephants are large animals. big,
> bulky, colossal, enormous, giant,
> gigantic, great, heavy, hefty, huge,
> immense, mighty, monstrous, weighty.

2 *She gave them large helpings of food.* above average, abundant, ample, generous, substantial, tremendous.
3 *The cathedral is a large building.* grand, high, imposing, lofty, massive, tall, towering, vast.
4 *They need a large room if they're going to dance.* roomy, sizeable, spacious.
5 *The gales caused damage over a large area.* broad, extensive, vast, wide.
6 *The meeting was attended by a large number of people.* considerable, incalculable.
AN OPPOSITE IS small.

lash *verb*
1 *It was terrible to see him lash the poor donkey.* beat, flog, strike, thrash, whip.
2 *They lashed oil drums together with rope to make a raft.* bind, fasten, secure, tie.

last *adjective*
1 *Z is the last letter of the alphabet.* closing, concluding, final, terminating, ultimate.
AN OPPOSITE IS first.
2 *What was his last record called?* latest, most recent.
AN OPPOSITE IS next.

last *verb*
1 *I hope the fine weather lasts.* carry on, continue, endure, hold, keep on, persist, remain, stay.
2 *They don't expect the sick animal to last much longer.* hold out, keep going, linger, live, survive.

latch *noun*
Make sure the latch is holding the door shut. bolt, catch, fastener.

late *adjective*
1 *The bus is late.* delayed, overdue.
AN OPPOSITE IS early or punctual.
2 *They had a great deal of respect for the late king.* dead, deceased, former.

latent *adjective*
She was encouraged to develop her latent talent. hidden, potential, undeveloped, undiscovered.

laugh *verb*

> VARIOUS WAYS TO SHOW AMUSEMENT: beam, burst into laughter, chortle, chuckle, giggle, go into hysterics, grin, guffaw, roar with laughter, simper, smile, smirk, sneer, snigger, titter.
> **to laugh at** *Don't laugh at people less fortunate than you.* deride, make fun of, mock, ridicule, scoff at, tease.

laughable *adjective*
They found the idea laughable. absurd, comic, funny, hilarious, ludicrous, ridiculous, silly.

laughter *noun*
She heard peals of laughter coming from the room. hilarity, merriment, mirth.

launch *verb*
1 *They watched the rocket being launched.* blast off, fire, send off, set off.
2 *She has launched a new business.* begin, embark on, establish, found, initiate, open, set up, start.

lavatory *noun*
They put up a notice showing where the lavatory is. cloakroom, convenience, [*informal*] loo, public convenience, toilet, WC.

lavish *adjective*
1 *She was lavish with her gifts for the children.* extravagant, free, generous.
AN OPPOSITE IS mean.
2 *There was a lavish supply of food.* abundant, bountiful, copious, liberal, plentiful.
AN OPPOSITE IS meagre.

law *noun*

> A law passed by parliament is an ***act***.
> A proposed law to be discussed by parliament is a ***bill***.
> The process of making laws is ***legislation***.
> The laws of a game are ***regulations*** or ***rules***.
> A regulation which must be obeyed is a ***commandment***, ***decree***, ***edict***, or ***order***. ➡

A set of laws or rules is a **code**.

EVENTS THAT TAKE PLACE IN A LAWCOURT: court martial, hearing, inquest, lawsuit, legal proceedings, trial.

PEOPLE WHO MAY BE INVOLVED IN A LAWCOURT: the accused, advocate, barrister, clerk, coroner, counsel for the defence, counsel for the prosecution, defendant, judge, juror, lawyer, magistrate, plaintiff, police, prosecutor, solicitor, usher, witness.

TERMS OFTEN USED IN LAWCOURTS: accusation, appeal, arrest, bail, case, charge, dock, evidence, judgement, plea, probation, punishment, remand, sentence, suing, summons, testimony, verdict.

lawful *adjective*
Stealing is not a lawful act. allowed, just, legal, legitimate, permissible, permitted, right.
AN OPPOSITE IS illegal.

lawless *adjective*
A lawless mob attacked the building. anarchic, badly behaved, disobedient, disorderly, mutinous, rebellious, riotous, rowdy, turbulent, uncontrolled, undisciplined, unruly, wild.
AN OPPOSITE IS well behaved.

lay *verb*
1 *She laid her books on the table.* deposit, leave, place, position, put down, set down, spread.
2 *Please lay the table for dinner.* arrange, set out.

layer *noun*
1 *The walls needed two layers of paint.* coat, coating, covering, film, sheet, skin, thickness.
2 *You can see layers of white and pink rock in the cliff.* seam, stratum.

laze *verb*
I spent most of the holiday lazing in the sun. be lazy, do nothing, lie about, loaf, lounge, relax, [*informal*] unwind.

laziness *noun*
He was annoyed by the laziness of his workers. idleness, inactivity, sloth, slowness.

lazy *adjective*
She accused him of being lazy. idle, slack, slothful, slow, unenterprising.
AN OPPOSITE IS hard-working.

lead *verb*
1 *The rescuers led them to safety.* conduct, escort, guide, pilot, steer.
AN OPPOSITE IS follow.
2 *Scott led an expedition to the South Pole.* be in charge of, direct, head, manage, preside over, supervise.
3 *She led from the start of the race.* be in front, be in the lead, head the field.

lead *noun*
1 *We followed the captain's lead.* example, guidance, leadership.
2 *He was in the lead from the start.* first place, front position.
3 *He was given the lead in the play.* chief part, starring role, title role.
4 *Keep the dog on a lead.* chain, leash, strap.
5 *Don't trip over the electrical lead.* cable, flex, wire.

leader *noun*
The leader of a team is the **captain**.
The leader of a business is the **boss**, **director**, or **head**.
The leader of a group of wrongdoers is the **ringleader**.
The leader of a military expedition is the **commander**.
The leader of a party of tourists is a **courier** or **guide**.
The leader of a tribe is the **chief** or **chieftain**.
The leader of a government is the **premier** or **prime minister**.
The leader of a country is the **president** or **ruler**.
SEE ALSO **ruler**.

leaf *noun*
1 *Deciduous trees lose their leaves in autumn.*
A mass of leaves is **foliage** or **greenery**.
2 *She tore a leaf out of her book.* page, sheet.

leaflet *noun*
People keep on putting advertising leaflets through our door. brochure, circular, pamphlet.

league *noun*
to be in league with someone *The two criminals are in league with each other.* collaborate with, conspire with, join forces with, plot with, scheme with.

leak *noun*
The plumber mended a leak in the water tank. crack, drip, hole.
A leak in a tyre is a ***puncture***.

leak *verb*
1 *The oil made a mess when it leaked onto the floor.* drip, escape, ooze, seep, trickle.
2 *The plan was leaked to the newspaper.* disclose, give away, let out, make known, pass on, reveal.

lean *verb*
1 *I leaned against the wall.* prop yourself, recline, rest, support yourself.
2 *The yacht leaned to one side in the wind.* bank, incline, list, slant, slope, tilt, tip.

lean *adjective*
The athlete has a strong, lean figure. slender, slim, thin, wiry.
SEE ALSO **thin**.
AN OPPOSITE IS fat.

leap *verb*
The dog leaped in the air to catch the ball. bound, jump, spring, vault.

learn *verb*
1 *They learned a lot on the school trip.* discover, find out, gain understanding of, gather, grasp, pick up.
2 *I've got to learn my words for the play.* learn by heart, memorize.

learned *adjective*
The author of this book is very learned. academic, clever, cultured, educated, intellectual, knowledgeable, scholarly.
AN OPPOSITE IS ignorant or uneducated.

learner *noun*
He's a very slow learner. beginner, novice, starter.
Someone learning things at school or college is a ***pupil*** or ***student***.

Someone learning a trade is an ***apprentice*** or ***trainee***.
Someone being trained for the armed services or the police is a ***cadet***.

learning *noun*
She's a woman of great learning. culture, education, knowledge, scholarship, wisdom.

least *adjective*
1 *Whoever has the least points has to drop out of the game.* fewest, lowest.
2 *The least amount of this poison is deadly.* slightest, smallest, tiniest.

leave *verb*
1 *Do you have to leave now?* depart, go away, go out, make off, say goodbye, set off, take your leave, withdraw.
AN OPPOSITE IS arrive or enter.
2 *Don't leave me here on my own!* abandon, desert, forsake.
3 *All the passengers left the damaged ship.* evacuate, get out of.
4 *He has left his job.* give up, quit, resign from, [*informal*] walk out of.
5 *Leave the milk bottles by the front door.* deposit, place, position, put down, set down.
6 *He left all the arrangements to her.* entrust, refer.
7 *She left him some money in her will.* bequeath, hand down.
to leave someone or **something out**
They left him out of the team. exclude, miss out, omit, reject.

leave *noun*
1 *Will you give me leave to speak?* freedom, liberty, permission.
2 *She gets 30 days' leave a year.* holiday, time off, vacation.

lecture *noun*
1 *They heard an interesting lecture on astronomy.* address, speech, talk.
2 *She gave them a lecture on how to behave.* reprimand, [*informal*] telling off, warning.

lecture *verb*
He lectured on English literature. give a lecture, speak, talk.

lecturer *noun* SEE **teacher**

ledge *noun*
The climbers rested on a ledge of rock.
projection, shelf.
A ledge under a door is a **sill**.
A ledge under a window is a
windowsill.

left *adjective*
The left side of a ship when you face
the bow is the **port** side.
AN OPPOSITE IS right.

leg *noun*

PARTS OF YOUR LEG: ankle, calf,
foot, knee, shin, thigh.

WORDS WHICH DESCRIBE PEOPLE'S
LEGS: bandy, bow-legged, knock-
kneed.

legacy *noun*
He left her a legacy in his will. bequest,
inheritance.

legal *adjective*
It's not legal for children to buy
cigarettes. allowed, lawful, legalized,
legitimate, permissible, permitted.
AN OPPOSITE IS illegal.

legalize *verb*
They won't ever legalize the sale of
cigarettes to children. allow, make
legal, permit.
AN OPPOSITE IS ban.

legendary *adjective*
Unicorns are legendary beasts.
fabulous, fictional, fictitious, invented,
made-up, mythical, non-existent.
AN OPPOSITE IS real.

CREATURES YOU READ ABOUT IN
LEGENDS: brownie, centaur, dragon,
dwarf, elf, fairy, giant, gnome, goblin,
griffin, imp, leprechaun, leviathan,
mermaid, monster, nymph, ogre,
phoenix, pixie, troll, unicorn,
vampire, werewolf, witch, wizard.

legible *adjective*
She has good, legible handwriting.
clear, neat, readable.
AN OPPOSITE IS illegible.

legitimate *adjective*
Are you the legitimate owner of this
car? authorized, legal, licensed,
permitted, proper, rightful.

leisure *noun*
He has plenty of leisure since he retired.
holiday time, recreation, relaxation,
rest, spare time, time off.

leisurely *adjective*
She went for a leisurely walk by the
river. gentle, lingering, peaceful,
relaxed, relaxing, restful, slow,
unhurried.
AN OPPOSITE IS fast.

lend *verb*
She lent him £5. loan.
AN OPPOSITE IS borrow.

length *noun*
The passengers complained about the
length of the delay. duration, time.

lengthen *verb*
1 She had to lengthen the skirt after she
bought it. extend, make longer.
2 The days lengthen in spring. draw
out, get longer.
AN OPPOSITE IS shorten.

lengthy *adjective*
She had a lengthy wait for the bus.
drawn out, extended, long, longish,
prolonged, time-consuming.
AN OPPOSITE IS short.

lenient *adjective*
The teacher was lenient and let her off.
easygoing, forgiving, indulgent, kind,
merciful, soft-hearted, tolerant.
AN OPPOSITE IS strict.

lessen *verb*
1 The nurse gave him some ointment to
lessen the pain. minimize, reduce,
relieve.
2 The force of the storm lessened during
the night. become less, decrease, die
away, diminish, dwindle, ease off,
moderate, slacken, subside, tail off,
weaken.
AN OPPOSITE IS increase.

let *verb*
1 *His parents wouldn't let him go out.*
allow, give permission to, permit.
AN OPPOSITE IS forbid.
2 *They are letting the house next door.*
hire, lease, rent.

lethal *adjective*
A tiny amount of this drug is lethal.
deadly, fatal, mortal, poisonous.

letter *noun*

LETTERS WE USE TO MAKE WORDS
IN WRITING: The letters a, e, i, o, u,
and sometimes y, are vowels. The
other letters are consonants.

LETTERS WE SEND TO EACH OTHER:
correspondence, mail, post.

VARIOUS LETTERS AND WRITTEN
MESSAGES: business letter, card,
circular, communication, dispatch,
greetings card, love letter,
memorandum, note, postcard.
The letters which form part of the
New Testament are *epistles*.

level *adjective*
1 *You need a level field for playing
rounders.* even, flat, horizontal,
smooth.
AN OPPOSITE IS uneven.
2 *At half-time the scores were level.*
equal, even, matching, [*informal*] neck-
and-neck, the same.

level *verb*
1 *He levelled the garden to make a
lawn.* even out, flatten, smooth.
2 *A serious earthquake levelled the
town.* demolish, destroy, devastate,
knock down.

level *noun*
1 *The water had reached a high level.*
height.
2 *The lift takes you up to the sixth level.*
floor, storey.
3 *What level have you reached in your
piano exams?* grade, stage, standard.
4 *She was promoted to a higher level in
the firm.* degree, position, rank,
standing, status.

lever *verb*
I levered the lid off the box. force, prise,
wrench.

liable *adjective*
1 *He is liable to make mistakes when
he's tired.* disposed, inclined, likely,
prone, ready.
AN OPPOSITE IS unlikely.
2 *The drunken driver was liable for the
accident.* responsible, to blame.

liar *noun*
*She didn't trust him—she knew he was
a liar.* deceiver, fibber.

liberal *adjective*
1 *He poured a liberal amount of milk
into his tea.* abundant, bountiful,
copious, lavish, plentiful.
AN OPPOSITE IS miserly.
2 *She has a liberal attitude towards
most things.* broad-minded, easygoing,
indulgent, lenient, permissive,
tolerant, unprejudiced.
AN OPPOSITE IS strict.

liberate *verb*
*There was great rejoicing when they
liberated the prisoners.* discharge,
emancipate, free, let out, release,
rescue, save, set free, untie.
AN OPPOSITE IS imprison.

liberty *noun*
1 *They had the liberty to do what they
wanted.* freedom, independence.
2 *Eventually the slaves were given their
liberty.* emancipation, liberation,
release.

licence *noun*
He has a licence to practise as a doctor.
certificate, document, permit, warrant.

license *verb*
*Certain shops are licensed to sell
alcohol.* allow, authorize, entitle,
permit.

lid *noun*
She couldn't get the lid off the jar. cap,
cover, covering, top.

lie *noun*
They weren't taken in by his lies. deceit,
dishonesty, falsehood, fib.
AN OPPOSITE IS truth.

lie *verb*
1 *It's twelve o'clock and he's still lying
in bed!* lounge, recline, rest, sprawl,
stretch out.
To lie face down is to be *prone*.

To lie face upwards is to be **supine**.
2 *The house lies in a valley.* be located, be situated.
3 *I don't trust her—I think she's lying.* bluff, deceive someone, fib.
to lie low *We'll lie low until the danger passes.* go into hiding, hide, take cover, take refuge.

life *noun*
1 *He has a very easy life.* existence, way of life.
2 *His life depended on finding water.* survival.
3 *You seem to be full of life today!* animation, energy, liveliness, spirit, sprightliness, vigour, vitality.
4 *She was reading a life of Elvis Presley.* autobiography, biography.

lifeless *adjective*
1 *The lifeless body lay on the bed.* dead, deceased, killed.
AN OPPOSITE IS living.
2 *Nothing grows in that lifeless desert.* arid, barren, sterile.
AN OPPOSITE IS fertile.
3 *He lay lifeless on the ground.* inanimate, inert, motionless, unconscious.
AN OPPOSITE IS conscious or moving.

lifelike *adjective*
The waxworks are very lifelike. convincing, natural, realistic, true to life.
AN OPPOSITE IS unrealistic.

lift *verb*
1 *The crane lifted the girder.* elevate, hoist, pick up, pull up, raise.
2 *The plane lifted off the ground.* ascend, rise, soar.

light *noun*

VARIOUS KINDS OF NATURAL LIGHT: daylight, half-light, moonlight, starlight, sunlight, twilight.

SOURCES OF ARTIFICIAL LIGHT: arc light, bulb, candle, chandelier, electric light, floodlight, fluorescent lamp, headlamp or headlight, illuminations, lamp, lantern, laser, neon light, pendant light, searchlight, spotlight, standard lamp, street light, strobe, taper, torch. ➡

LIGHTS USED AS SIGNALS: beacon, flare, traffic lights, warning light.

LIGHTS USED TO IGNITE THINGS: cigarette lighter, lighter, match, pilot light.

DIFFERENT EFFECTS OF LIGHT WHICH YOUR EYE CAN DETECT: beam, blaze, brightness, diffused light, flame, flash, flicker, fluorescence, glare, gleam, glint, glitter, glow, halo, illumination, lustre, phosphorescence, radiance, ray, reflection, shaft.

ADJECTIVES WHICH DESCRIBE DIFFERENT KINDS OF LIGHT: bright, blazing, dazzling, flashing, flickering, fluorescent, glaring, gleaming, glimmering, glinting, glistening, glittering, glowing, luminous, lustrous, phosphorescent, reflected, shimmering, shining, sparking, sparkling, twinkling.

light *adjective*
1 *They had a light and airy room to work in.* bright, illuminated, well-lit.
AN OPPOSITE IS dim or gloomy.
2 *She was wearing light blue jeans.* pale.
AN OPPOSITE IS dark.
3 *Modern laptop computers are very light.* lightweight, portable.
AN OPPOSITE IS heavy.
4 *A light wind rippled the surface of the water.* faint, gentle, imperceptible, slight.
AN OPPOSITE IS strong.
5 *Since his illness he can only do light work.* easy, undemanding.
AN OPPOSITE IS strenuous.
6 *She prefers light music.* cheerful, entertaining, pleasant.
AN OPPOSITE IS serious.

light *verb*
1 *It was so cold that she lit the fire.* fire, ignite, kindle, set alight, set fire to, put a match to, switch on.
AN OPPOSITE IS extinguish.
2 *The bonfire lit the sky.* brighten, illuminate, light up, shed light on, shine on.
AN OPPOSITE IS darken.

like *preposition*
She bought some jeans like her sister's.
indistinguishable from, resembling,
similar to, the same as.

like *verb*
What sort of films do you like? admire,
appreciate, approve of, be fond of, be
interested in, be partial to, be pleased
by, delight in, enjoy, prefer.
AN OPPOSITE IS dislike.

likeable *adjective*
She's a very likeable person. attractive,
charming, friendly, lovable, nice,
pleasant.
AN OPPOSITE IS hateful.

likely *adjective*
It's likely that we'll win on Saturday.
anticipated, expected, foreseeable,
predictable, probable.
AN OPPOSITE IS unlikely.

likeness *noun*
1 There's a strong likeness between the
two sisters. resemblance, similarity.
AN OPPOSITE IS difference.
2 This photo is a good likeness of him.
copy, image, picture, portrait,
representation.

liking *noun*
She has a liking for classical music.
affection, fondness, love, preference,
taste.
AN OPPOSITE IS dislike.

limb *noun*
Your limbs are your *arms* and *legs*.
Birds have *wings*.
Seals, etc., have *flippers*.
An octopus has *tentacles*.
The limbs of a tree are its *boughs* or
branches.

limit *noun*
1 She put a limit of ten on the number
he could invite to the party. ceiling,
maximum, restriction.
A limit on time is a *deadline* or *time
limit*.
2 The fence marks the limit of the school
grounds. border, boundary, bounds,
edge, extent, perimeter.

limit *verb*
They had to limit the number of tickets
they sold for the concert. control, put a
limit on, ration, restrict.

limited *adjective*
1 The supply of food was limited. finite,
fixed, inadequate, insufficient,
rationed, restricted, short,
unsatisfactory.
2 It was hard to move about in the
limited space. cramped, narrow, small.
AN OPPOSITE IS limitless.

limitless *adjective*
What would you do if you had a
limitless amount of money? endless,
inexhaustible, infinite, never-ending,
unending, unlimited, vast.
AN OPPOSITE IS limited.

limp *verb*
She managed to limp home after she
cut her foot. falter, hobble, hop.

limp *adjective*
The leaves of the plant looked limp.
drooping, flabby, flexible, floppy,
sagging, soft, wilting.
AN OPPOSITE IS rigid.

line *noun*

LINES MARKED ON PAPER OR OTHER
SURFACES: dash, streak, stripe,
stroke, underlining.

LINES CUT OR FOLDED INTO THE
SURFACE OF SOMETHING: crease,
furrow, groove, score, scratch, slash,
wrinkle.

LINES OF PEOPLE: column, cordon,
crocodile, file, procession, queue,
rank.

LINES OF THINGS: rank, row, series,
stream.

LINES WHICH MARK THE EDGE OF
SOMETHING: border, boundary,
edging, frontier.

LINES USED TO FASTEN THINGS:
cord, hawser, rope, string, thread,
wire. ➡

LINES WHICH CARRY ELECTRICITY:
cable, flex, lead, wire.

VARIOUS KINDS OF RAILWAY LINE:
branch line, commuter line, main
line, route, track.

line *verb*
to line up *They lined up to get into the cinema.* form a line, queue.

linger *verb*
1 *The smell of burning lingered after the fire was put out.* continue, last, persist, remain, stay.
AN OPPOSITE IS disappear.
2 *Don't linger outside in this cold weather.* dawdle, delay, hang about, lag behind, loiter, stay behind, wait about.
AN OPPOSITE IS hurry.

link *noun*
The two countries have close links with each other. association, connection, relationship.
FOR THINGS YOU CAN USE TO LINK THINGS TOGETHER, SEE **fasten**.

link *verb*
They linked the trailer to the tractor. attach, connect, couple, fasten, join.
to link up *The two teams linked up for training sessions.* amalgamate, merge, unite.
AN OPPOSITE IS separate.

liquid *adjective*
He poured the liquid jelly into a mould. flowing, fluid, molten, runny, sloppy, thin, watery, wet.
AN OPPOSITE IS solid.

liquid *noun*
Substances which flow like liquids and gases are **fluids**.

list *noun*
A list of people's names is a **roll**.
A list of people with their addresses and phone numbers is a **directory**.
A list of the pupils attending school is a **register**.
A list of people who have tasks to do is a **rota**.
A list of books in the library or of goods for sale is a **catalogue**.

A list of topics mentioned in a book is an **index**.
A list of numbers or facts is a **table**.
A list of things to choose from is a **menu**.
A list of things to be done is a **schedule**.

list *verb*
1 *I helped to list the books in the library.* catalogue, index, make a list of, record, register, write down.
2 *The damaged ship listed to one side.* incline, lean, slope, tilt, tip.

listen *verb*
to listen to something *They listened carefully to what he said.* attend to, concentrate on, hear, heed, overhear, pay attention to, take notice of.

listless *adjective*
The audience was listless because it was so hot. apathetic, feeble, lifeless, tired, unenthusiastic, uninterested, weary.
AN OPPOSITE IS lively.

literal *adjective*
She gave a literal translation of the Latin motto. exact, precise, strict, word for word.

literary *adjective*
She's a literary person—she has read a lot of books. cultured, educated, refined, well-read.

literature *noun*
1 *He has read a lot of English literature.* books, writings.
FOR KINDS OF LITERATURE, SEE **writing**.
2 *The travel agent gave them some literature about their holiday destination.* brochures, handouts, leaflets, pamphlets.

litter *noun*
The street was covered with litter. clutter, garbage, junk, mess, odds and ends, refuse, rubbish, waste.

litter *verb*
Why are these bits of paper littered round the room? scatter, strew.

little *adjective*
1 *He's got a little dictionary that fits in his pocket.* compact, miniature, small, tiny.
2 *Did you see those little lambs?* newborn, young.
AN OPPOSITE IS big.

live *adjective*
You can see live animals in the zoo. SEE **living** *adjective*.

live *verb*
Will these plants live through the winter? continue, exist, flourish, last, remain, stay alive, survive.
AN OPPOSITE IS die.
to live in a place *We live in a flat.* dwell in, inhabit, occupy, reside in.
to live on *What do polar bears live on?* eat, feed on.

livelihood *noun* SEE **living** *noun*

lively *adjective*
A lively crowd enjoyed an entertaining match. animated, boisterous, bubbly, bustling, cheerful, energetic, enthusiastic, excited, exuberant, frisky, high-spirited, merry, spirited, sprightly.
AN OPPOSITE IS apathetic.

living *adjective*
1 *She has no living relatives.* alive.
AN OPPOSITE IS dead.
2 *There are no dinosaurs still living.* existing, surviving.
AN OPPOSITE IS extinct.

living *noun*
1 *He makes a living from painting.* income, livelihood.
2 *What does she do for a living?* career, job, occupation, profession, trade.

load *noun*
1 *I could hardly carry such a big load.* burden, weight.
2 *A lorry was delivering its load to the supermarket.* cargo, consignment, freight, goods.

load *verb*
1 *We loaded the luggage into the car.* heap, pack, pile, stow.
2 *They loaded him with their shopping.* weigh down.

loaf *verb*
He loafed about all day without offering to help us. dawdle, loiter, mess about, [*informal*] stand around, waste time.

loan *noun*
She needs a loan to pay for her holiday. advance.
A system which allows you to pay for something later is **credit**.
A loan to buy a house is a **mortgage**.

loan *verb*
Can you loan me 50p? advance, lend.
AN OPPOSITE IS borrow.

loathe *verb*
He loathes football. despise, detest, dislike, hate.

loathsome *adjective*
Rats are loathsome creatures. abominable, despicable, detestable, disgusting, foul, hated, horrible, nasty, repellent, repulsive, revolting, unpleasant, vile.
AN OPPOSITE IS lovable.

lobby *noun*
They waited for him in the lobby. entrance hall, foyer, hall.

local *adjective*
He always uses the local shops. nearby, neighbourhood, neighbouring.

locality *noun*
There are some good schools in the locality. area, community, district, neighbourhood, parish, region, residential area, town, vicinity.

locate *verb*
1 *She located the book she wanted in the library.* detect, discover, find, search out, unearth.
AN OPPOSITE IS lose.
2 *They located the new offices in the middle of town.* build, establish, place, position, put, set up, situate, station.

location *noun*
The coastguard asked the yachtsman to give his location. place, position, situation, spot, whereabouts.

lock *noun*
He fixed a lock on the shed door. bolt, catch, padlock.

lock *verb*
Make sure you lock the door when you go out. bolt, close, fasten, seal, secure, shut.

lodge *verb*
1 Where are you lodging at present? rest, stay.
2 The authorities lodged the homeless family in a hostel. accommodate, board, house, put up.
3 The ball lodged in a tree. became fixed, get caught or jammed or stuck.

lodger *noun*
She earns some money taking in lodgers. boarder, paying guest.

lodgings *noun*
Where can we find lodgings for a few nights? accommodation, a boarding house, [informal] digs, a lodging house, quarters, rooms, temporary home.

lofty *adjective*
You can see the church's lofty spire from miles away. high, soaring, tall, towering.
AN OPPOSITE IS low.

log *noun*
1 They collected logs to burn on the fire. FOR VARIOUS FORMS OF TIMBER, SEE **wood**.
2 The ship's captain kept a log of the voyage. account, diary, journal, record.

logic *noun*
He admired the logic of her argument. clarity, good sense, orderly thinking, reasoning, validity.

logical *adjective*
She presents ideas in a logical way. clear, intelligent, lucid, methodical, rational, reasonable, sensible, systematic, valid.
AN OPPOSITE IS illogical.

loiter *verb*
They were late because they loitered on the way. be slow, dawdle, hang back, linger, loaf about, mess about, straggle.

lone *adjective*
A lone rider galloped past. isolated, single, solitary, unaccompanied.

lonely *adjective*
1 He felt lonely while his friends were away. alone, desolate, forlorn, forsaken, friendless, neglected, solitary.
2 The climbers sheltered in a lonely hut. abandoned, distant, faraway, isolated, out-of-the-way, remote, secluded.

long *adjective*
It seemed a long time before the bus came. endless, interminable, lengthy, longish, prolonged, unending.
AN OPPOSITE IS short.

long *verb*
to long for something I'm longing for a drink. [informal] be dying for, crave, desire, fancy, have an appetite for, itch for, pine for, want, wish for, yearn for.
If you long for food or drink you are **hungry** or **thirsty**.

look *verb*
1 Look carefully so that you recognize it when you see it again. keep your eyes open, take note, watch.
2 You look pleased today. appear, seem.
to look after someone or **something** He looked after their things while they went swimming. care for, guard, keep an eye on, mind, protect, tend, watch over.
To look after sick people is to **nurse** them.
to look at something 1 We stopped to look at the view. contemplate, eye, gape at, gaze at, observe, peep at, peer at, regard, scan, see, stare at, survey, view.
2 She looked at their work. cast an eye over, consider, examine, glance at, inspect, scrutinize, skim through, study, take a look at.
to look down on someone Don't look down on them just because they are younger than you. despise, scorn, sneer at.
to look for something He spent ages looking for his keys. hunt for, search for, seek.
to look out If you don't look out, you'll get wet. beware, keep an eye open, pay attention, take care, watch out.
to look up to someone He looks up to his older sister. admire, have a high opinion of, respect, think highly of.

look *noun*

1 *Did you have a look at what she was wearing?* glance, glimpse, peep, sight, view.
2 *She has a friendly look.* air, appearance, aspect, bearing, countenance, expression, face, manner.

lookout *noun*

The lookout reported that a stranger was approaching. guard, sentinel, sentry, watchman.

loom *verb*

1 *A figure loomed out of the mist.* appear, arise, emerge.
2 *The grim castle loomed above us.* rise, stand out, stick up, tower.

loop *noun*

His foot was caught in a loop in the rope. bend, circle, coil, curl, hoop, kink, noose, ring, twist.

loop *verb*

The sailor looped the rope round a bollard. bend, coil, curl, turn, twist, wind.

loose *adjective*

1 *The fire was started by a loose wire.* detached, disconnected, unattached.
AN OPPOSITE IS secure.
2 *These guy ropes are too loose.* slack.
AN OPPOSITE IS tight.
3 *Don't stumble on these loose stones.* insecure, movable, shaky, unsteady, wobbly.
AN OPPOSITE IS firm.
4 *The animals wander loose in the safari park.* at large, free, roaming, uncaged, unconfined, unrestricted.
AN OPPOSITE IS confined.

loosen *verb*

Can you loosen these knots? ease, free, loose, release, slacken, undo, unfasten, unloose, untie.
AN OPPOSITE IS tighten.

loot *noun*

The loot was buried near the church. haul, plunder, takings.

loot *verb*

Rioters looted the shops. pillage, plunder, raid, ransack, rob, steal from.

lopsided *adjective*

The lopsided load on the lorry looked dangerous. crooked, tilting, unbalanced, uneven.

lorry *noun*

FOR VARIOUS VEHICLES, SEE **vehicle**.

lose *verb*

1 *She's lost her purse.* be unable to find, mislay.
2 *He lost his way in the forest.* miss, stray from.
AN OPPOSITE IS find.
3 *Unfortunately, we lost on Saturday.* be defeated or unsuccessful, get beaten, suffer a defeat.
AN OPPOSITE IS win.

loss *noun*

1 *The loss of their water supply caused a lot of problems.* deprivation, disappearance, failure.
2 *He was devastated by the loss of his friend.* death.

lot *noun*

a lot of, lots of *She gave him a lot of help. He's got lots of money.* a large amount of, ample, heaps of, much, plenty of.
the lot *I don't want any, so you can give her the lot.* all, everything.

lotion *noun*

He needed some lotion for his sunburn. cream, ointment.

loud *adjective*

1 *She couldn't sleep because of the loud noise.* audible, blaring, booming, deafening, echoing, noisy, penetrating, piercing, resounding, rowdy, shrieking, shrill, [*informal*] terrific, thunderous.
A noise which is loud enough to hear is **audible**.
AN OPPOSITE IS quiet.
2 *They were wearing rather loud shirts.* bright, flashy, gaudy, showy.
AN OPPOSITE IS soft.

lounge *verb*

They lounged in the garden all day. be lazy, hang about, idle, laze, loaf, lie around, loiter, mess about, relax, sprawl, stand about, take it easy, waste time.

lovable *adjective*
She's got a lovable little puppy.
adorable, appealing, attractive,
charming, cuddly, enchanting, likeable,
lovely.
AN OPPOSITE IS hateful.

love *noun*
He talked about her love for him.
admiration, adoration, affection,
devotion, fondness, friendship, liking,
passion.
to be in love with *My sister is in love
with a boy at her college.* be devoted to,
be fond of.
love affair *Do you think their love affair
will lead to marriage?* affair, courtship,
relationship, romance.

love *verb*
1 *They love each other and want to get
married.* admire, adore, be in love
with, care for, cherish, have a passion
for, idolize, treasure, value, worship.
2 *I love fish and chips.* appreciate,
approve of, be fond of, be partial to,
enjoy.
AN OPPOSITE IS hate.

lovely *adjective*
The flowers look lovely. appealing,
attractive, beautiful, charming,
delightful, enjoyable, fine, nice,
pleasant, pretty, sweet.
AN OPPOSITE IS nasty.

lover *noun*
*People send cards to their lovers on
Valentine's Day.* boyfriend, fiancé,
fiancée, girlfriend, sweetheart,
valentine.

loving *adjective*
She gave him a loving kiss.
affectionate, devoted, fond, friendly,
kind, passionate, tender, warm.
AN OPPOSITE IS unfriendly.

low *adjective*
1 *The low land is often flooded in
winter.* low-lying, sunken.
2 *He resented his low status in the firm.*
humble, inferior, junior, lowly, modest.
3 *We spoke in low whispers.* muffled,
muted, quiet, soft, subdued.
4 *The tuba plays low notes.* bass, deep.
AN OPPOSITE IS high.

lower *verb*
1 *The supermarket has lowered its
prices.* bring down, cut, decrease,
lessen, reduce, [*informal*] slash.
2 *Will you please lower the volume of
your radio?* quieten, turn down.
3 *At sunset they lower the flag.* dip,
haul down, let down, take down.
AN OPPOSITE IS raise.

lowly *adjective*
*He has a lowly position at present, but
he hopes he'll be promoted soon.*
humble, inferior, insignificant, junior,
low, modest.

loyal *adjective*
She has always been a loyal friend.
constant, dependable, devoted,
faithful, reliable, sincere, true,
trustworthy.
AN OPPOSITE IS disloyal.

lubricate *verb*
*He spent the morning lubricating his
bike.* grease, oil.

lucid *adjective*
*She gave a lucid explanation of the
process.* clear, logical, rational,
sensible, unambiguous,
understandable.
AN OPPOSITE IS confused.

luck *noun*
1 *He found his watch by luck.* accident,
chance, coincidence, destiny, fate,
fluke.
2 *She had a bit of luck today.* good
fortune, happiness, success.

lucky *adjective*
1 *He made a lucky discovery.*
accidental, chance, unintentional,
unplanned.
2 *Some lucky person won a million
pounds.* favoured, fortunate, happy,
successful.
AN OPPOSITE IS unlucky.

ludicrous *adjective*
They laughed at such a ludicrous idea.
absurd, daft, foolish, laughable,
ridiculous, senseless, silly.

luggage noun
> They packed their luggage in the boot of the car. baggage, belongings, paraphernalia, things.

> VARIOUS ITEMS OF LUGGAGE: bag, basket, box, briefcase, case, chest, hamper, handbag, hand luggage, haversack, holdall, knapsack, pannier, purse, rucksack, satchel, suitcase, trunk, wallet.

lull verb
> She lulled the baby by singing quietly. calm, hush, pacify, quieten, soothe, subdue.

lull noun
> He took advantage of a lull in the storm and ran home. break, calm, gap, interval, pause.

lumber noun
> They cleared the lumber out of the garage. bits and pieces, clutter, jumble, junk, odds and ends, rubbish, trash.

lumber verb
> **1** A rhinoceros lumbered towards them. blunder, move clumsily, shamble.
> **2** [informal] They lumbered him with the clearing up. burden, [informal] saddle.

luminous adjective
> The alarm clock has a luminous dial. glowing, phosphorescent, shining.

lump noun
> **1** Lumps of sticky clay stuck to his boots. cake, chunk, mass, slab.
> A round lump of something is a **ball**.
> An oblong lump of something is a **brick**.
> A lump of metal is an **ingot**.
> A lump of gold is a **nugget**.
> A lump of wood is a **block**.
> A lump of earth is a **clod**.
> A lump of blood is a **clot**.
> **2** After the stone hit him he got a lump on his head. bulge, bump, protrusion, swelling.

lump verb
> **to lump things together** Just lump the ingredients together and give them a stir. blend, combine, mingle, mix.

lunge verb
> **1** Robin lunged at the sheriff with his sword. jab, stab, strike, thrust.
> **2** The policeman lunged after the escaping robber. charge, dash, dive, pounce, rush, throw yourself.

lurch verb
> **1** The passengers lurched forward as the bus stopped suddenly. reel, stagger, stumble, sway, totter.
> **2** The ship lurched as the waves pounded it. heave, lean, list, pitch, roll, wallow.

lure verb
> They lured him into their trap. attract, coax, draw, invite, persuade, tempt.

lurk verb
> The lion lurked in wait for its prey. crouch, hide, lie in wait, lie low.

luscious adjective
> She ate a bowl of luscious strawberries. appetizing, delicious, juicy, sweet.

lust noun
> He had a lust for power. appetite, craving, desire, greed, hunger, itch, longing, passion.

luxurious adjective
> They were amazed by the luxurious surroundings in the hotel. comfortable, costly, expensive, grand, lavish, lush, magnificent, rich, splendid, wealthy.
> AN OPPOSITE IS austere or poor.

luxury noun
> It must be nice to live a life of luxury. affluence, comfort, ease, extravagance, pleasure, self-indulgence, wealth.
> AN OPPOSITE IS poverty.

lying noun
> The judge accused him of lying. deceit, dishonesty, falsehood.

lyrical adjective
> His writing had a very lyrical quality. emotional, expressive, songlike.

Mm

machine *noun*
Do you know how this machine works?
apparatus, appliance, contraption,
contrivance, device, engine, gadget,
instrument, robot, tool.
A collection of machines is *machinery*.
The moving parts of a machine is the
mechanism or *works*.

machinery *noun*
1 *A lot of machinery has been installed.*
equipment, machines, plant.
2 *They set out to reform the machinery
of government.* method, organization,
procedure, system.

mad *adjective*
1 *You must be mad to go swimming on
a day like this.* crazy, daft, insane,
irrational, manic, mental, out of your
mind, out of your senses, unbalanced,
unstable.
Note that these words are used
informally, and they are often insulting
AN OPPOSITE IS sane.
2 [*informal*] *He's mad about football.*
enthusiastic, fanatical, keen (on),
passionate.
3 *He was mad with rage.* angry,
berserk, beside yourself, frenzied,
hysterical.

madden *verb*
*She was maddened beyond endurance
by his behaviour.* anger, enrage,
exasperate, incense, inflame, infuriate,
make mad, provoke, vex.

madman *noun*
*He must be a madman to drive like
that.* lunatic, maniac.
It is important to avoid giving offence
when using words connected with
mental illness.

madness *noun*
He was driven to the brink of madness.
frenzy, hysteria, insanity, lunacy,
mania, mental illness.
Make sure that if you use a synonym
listed here it will not be insulting.

magazine *noun*
1 *She bought a magazine to read on the
train.* comic, journal, paper, periodical,
publication.
2 *The ammunition was stored in a
secret magazine.* ammunition dump,
arsenal, storehouse.

magic *adjective*
He disappeared as if by a magic trick.
conjuring, magical, miraculous,
supernatural.

magic *noun*
Do you believe in magic? charms,
enchantments, sorcery, spells,
witchcraft, wizardry.

magician *noun*
1 *They hired a magician for the
children's party.* conjuror.
2 *According to legend, King Arthur was
helped by the medieval magician
Merlin.* sorcerer, witch, wizard.

magnetize *verb*
*His dark brown eyes magnetized those
around him.* attract, captivate, charm,
fascinate, hypnotize.
AN OPPOSITE IS repel.

magnificent *adjective*
1 *The mountain scenery was
magnificent.* beautiful, glorious,
gorgeous, impressive, majestic, noble,
spectacular, splendid, superb.
2 *The President lived in a magnificent
palace.* dignified, grand, imposing,
[*informal*] posh, stately.
3 *It was a magnificent meal.* excellent,
[*informal*] fabulous, [*informal*]
fantastic, first-class, marvellous,
wonderful.
AN OPPOSITE IS ordinary.

magnify *verb*
1 *The image was magnified to 100
times its actual size.* [*informal*] blow
up, enlarge, make larger.
AN OPPOSITE IS reduce.

2 *She tended to magnify the faults of the people she disliked.* exaggerate, make too much of, maximize, overdo.
AN OPPOSITE IS minimize.
magnifying glass SEE **glass**.

magnitude *noun*
He exaggerates the magnitude of his problems. dimensions, extent, importance, size.

mail *noun*
The postman brings the mail. correspondence, letters and parcels, post.

mail *verb*
He mailed the birthday card too late to get there in time. dispatch, post, send.

maim *verb*
He was maimed for life after the car accident. cripple, disable, injure, mutilate, wound.

main *adjective*
1 *What was the main point of the story?* basic, central, chief, crucial, dominant, essential, fundamental, greatest, important, outstanding, predominant, primary, prime, supreme.
2 *They are the main suppliers of coal in the district.* biggest, foremost, largest, leading, major, principal.
AN OPPOSITE IS minor or unimportant.

mainly *adverb*
The chimpanzees eat mainly fruit and vegetables. chiefly, especially, generally, in the main, largely, mostly, normally, on the whole, predominantly, primarily, principally, usually.

maintain *verb*
1 *It pays to maintain your bike in good order.* keep, look after, preserve, take care of.
2 *He has always maintained that he was innocent.* argue, assert, claim, contend, declare, insist, proclaim, state.
3 *It costs a lot to maintain a family.* feed, keep, pay for, provide for, support.

maintenance *noun*
The maintenance of an old car can be expensive. care, repairs, servicing, upkeep.

majestic *adjective*
The town was dominated by the majestic castle. awe-inspiring, awesome, dignified, grand, imposing, impressive, magnificent, noble, splendid, stately.
AN OPPOSITE IS commonplace.

major *adjective*
1 *They decided to keep to the major roads.* bigger, chief, greater, larger, primary, principal.
2 *She had a major part in the play.* big, considerable, great, important, leading, outstanding, significant.
AN OPPOSITE IS minor.

majority *noun*
The majority of the people prefer television to radio. bulk, greater number, most.
AN OPPOSITE IS minority.
to be in the majority *Those who agreed with the decision were in the majority.* be greater, dominate, outnumber the others, predominate.

make *verb*
The verb *make* is used in many ways. We give just a selection of the main ways you can use the word here
1 *They made a shelter out of leaves and branches.* assemble, build, construct, produce, put together.
To make a cake is to ***bake*** or ***cook*** it.
To make clothes, etc., is to ***knit***, ***sew***, or ***weave*** them.
To make a model, statue, etc., is to ***carve***, ***cast***, or ***mould*** it.
To make something in a factory is to ***manufacture*** or ***mass-produce*** it.
2 *They're always making trouble.* bring about, cause, give rise to, provoke.
3 *They made me captain.* appoint, elect, nominate.
4 *They've made the attic into a games room.* alter, change, convert, modify, transform, turn.
5 *She'll make a good actress when she's older.* become, change into, grow into, turn into.
6 *The regulations were made to protect children.* agree, decide on, establish, fix.
7 *You made me jump!* cause you to.
8 *If I don't want to come, you can't make me.* compel, force, order.

9 *He made a lot of money last year.*
earn, gain, get, obtain, receive, win.
10 *The swimmer just made the shore.*
arrive at, get as far as, get to, reach.
11 *What do you make the total?*
calculate, compute, count, estimate,
reckon.
12 *2 and 2 make 4.* add up to, come to,
total.
13 *The garage made an offer for her
car.* propose, suggest.
14 *Have you made your bed this
morning?* arrange, tidy.
to make fun of *Don't make fun of her.*
deride, jeer at, laugh at, mock, ridicule,
scoff at, [*informal*] send up, tease.
to make off *The thieves made off in a
stolen car.* depart, disappear, go away,
leave, set off.
to make someone or **something out** *I
can't make out why everything went
wrong.* appreciate, comprehend,
fathom, make sense of, recognize,
understand, work out.
to make up *She made up a lot of lies.*
compose, create, invent, originate,
think up.
to make up your mind *Make up your
mind about what you want to do.*
choose, decide, make a decision,
resolve.

make *noun*
*There were many different makes of
computer.* brand, kind, model, sort,
type, variety.

make-believe *noun*
His story was all make-believe. fantasy,
imagination, pretence, pretending,
sham.

maker *noun*
*The company is the country's largest
car maker.* manufacturer, producer.

make-up *noun*
She hardly ever wears make-up.
cosmetics.
FOR VARIOUS ITEMS OF MAKE-UP, SEE
cosmetics.

male *adjective*
FOR MALE HUMAN BEINGS, SEE **man**.
FOR MALE CREATURES, SEE **animal**.
AN OPPOSITE IS female.

malevolent *adjective* SEE **malicious**

malice *noun*
He gave her a look of pure malice.
enmity, hatred, hostility, ill will,
malevolence, nastiness, spite,
spitefulness, viciousness.
AN OPPOSITE IS kindness.

malicious *adjective*
*They've been spreading malicious
rumours.* bitchy, evil-minded, hateful,
ill-natured, malevolent, mischievous,
nasty, revengeful, spiteful, vicious,
wicked.
AN OPPOSITE IS kind.

mammal *noun*
FOR VARIOUS KINDS OF ANIMAL, SEE
animal.

man *noun*

A polite word for a man is
gentleman.
Informal words are ***bloke***, ***chap***,
fellow, ***guy***.
A married man is a ***husband***.
A man who has children is a ***father***.
An unmarried man is a ***bachelor***.
A man whose wife has died is a
widower.
A man on his wedding day is a
bridegroom.
A man who is engaged to be married
is a ***fiancé***.
A man who is going out with a
woman is her ***boyfriend***.
Words for a young man are ***boy***, ***lad***,
youth.

manage *verb*
1 *How much work can you manage
before dinner?* achieve, bring about,
carry out, cope with, deal with, do,
finish, perform.
2 *You'll have to manage with what
you've got.* be satisfied, cope, make do.
3 *If you can't pay it all, pay what you
can manage.* afford, spare.
4 *His eldest son manages the business
now.* administer, administrate, be in
charge of, be the manager of, direct,
govern, lead, look after, preside over,
regulate, rule, run, superintend,
supervise, take control of.
5 *She has a knack for managing
difficult horses.* control, dominate,
handle.

manager *noun*
If you have a problem, talk to the manager. [*informal*] boss, chief, director, proprietor.
FOR PEOPLE IN CHARGE OF VARIOUS THINGS, SEE **chief** *noun*.

mangle *verb*
His hand was mangled in the machine. crush, damage, injure, maim, mutilate, squash, tear, wound.

manhandle *verb*
1 The journalists were manhandled by the security guards. [*informal*] beat up, knock about, mistreat, misuse, treat roughly.
2 They had to manhandle the piano up the stairs. carry, haul, heave, hump, lift, pull, push.

mania *noun*
A mania for the pop group swept the country. craze, enthusiasm, fad, hysteria, obsession, passion.
SEE ALSO **madness**.

maniac *noun* SEE **madman**

manic *adjective* SEE **mad**

manifesto *noun*
Each political party issues a manifesto before an election. declaration, policy, statement.

manipulate *verb*
1 He carefully manipulated the dials of the radio set. control, guide, handle, manage, steer.
2 She uses her charm to manipulate people. exploit, impose on, take advantage of, use.

mankind *noun*
Conservation of this planet is important for all mankind. human beings, humanity, the human race, men and women, people.

manner *noun*
1 She does things in a professional manner. fashion, style, way.
2 He had a very cheeky manner. air, attitude, bearing, behaviour, character, conduct, disposition, look.
good manners, or simply **manners** He has no manners at all. courtesy, good behaviour, politeness.

manoeuvre *noun*
1 Their victory was the result of a very skilful manoeuvre. dodge, plan, plot, scheme, strategy, tactic, trick.
2 Getting the car into the garage is a tricky manoeuvre. move, operation.

manoeuvre *verb*
The captain manoeuvred the ship into the dock. guide, move, pilot, steer.

mansion *noun*
We had to pay £3 each to look round the mansion. manor, manor house, palace, stately home.
SEE ALSO **house** *noun*.

manufacture *verb*
The factory manufactures pine furniture. assemble, build, fabricate, make.
Manufacturing something in large quantities is **mass-production**.

many *adjective*
I have been to London many times. countless, frequent, innumerable, numerous, untold, various.
AN OPPOSITE IS few.

map *noun*
He drew us a map to show us how to get to the party. chart, diagram, plan.
A book of maps is an **atlas** or a **roadbook**.

map *verb*
They had to map the area around the school. chart, survey.
to map something out They sat down and mapped out a strategy for the next game. arrange, devise, organize, plan, prepare, work out.

mar *verb*
The match was marred by bad weather. make a mess of, mess up, ruin, spoil.

marauder *noun*
Marauders came down from the hills to attack the village. bandit, invader, plunderer, raider.

march *verb*
Soldiers marched into the town. file, parade, stride, troop.

margin *noun*
Don't write in the margin of the paper. border, edge.

marginal *adjective*
The difference between the two estimates is marginal. borderline, minimal, negligible, small, unimportant.
AN OPPOSITE IS great.

mark *noun*
1 There were dirty marks all over the kitchen floor. blemish, blot, blotch, dot, fingermark, line, scar, scratch, scribble, smear, smudge, smut, spot, stain, streak.
A mark on a person's skin is a **birthmark**, **freckle**, **mole**, or **tattoo**.
2 The flag was at half-mast as a mark of respect for the dead man. emblem, indication, sign, symbol, token.
3 The manufacturer's mark is on the label. badge, brand, seal, stamp.

mark *verb*
1 He picked up the photograph gently, careful not to mark it. damage, deface, smudge, stain.
To mark your skin is to **bruise**, **cut**, **graze**, **scar**, or **scratch** it.
2 She had a pile of English essays to mark. assess, correct, grade.
3 There will be trouble, you mark my words! attend to, heed, listen to, mind, note, notice, observe, take note of.

market *noun*

PLACES WHERE THINGS ARE BOUGHT AND SOLD: auction, bazaar, car boot sale, fair, sale, street market.
SEE ALSO **shop**.

market *verb*
The company needs to market its goods in Europe. advertise, promote, sell, trade in.

maroon *verb*
They were marooned on a desert island. abandon, cast away, desert, forsake, leave, put ashore, strand.

marriage *noun*
1 My grandparents celebrated 40 years of marriage. matrimony.
2 Today is the anniversary of their marriage. wedding.

marsh *noun*
The birds breed on coastal marshes. bog, fen, mud, swamp.

marshy *adjective*
His feet squelched in the marshy ground. boggy, muddy, soft, soggy, swampy, waterlogged, wet.
AN OPPOSITE IS firm or dry.

marvel *noun*
The exhibition featured all the marvels of modern science. miracle, wonder.

marvel *verb*
to marvel at She marvelled at his courage. admire, applaud, be amazed by, be astonished by, be surprised by, wonder at.

marvellous *adjective*
1 Medical science can do marvellous things these days. amazing, astonishing, extraordinary, incredible, miraculous, phenomenal, remarkable, surprising, unbelievable, wonderful.
2 She looked marvellous. excellent, [informal] fabulous, [informal] fantastic, glorious, magnificent, sensational, [informal] smashing, spectacular, splendid, superb.
AN OPPOSITE IS ordinary.

masculine *adjective*
He was rugged, handsome, and very masculine. male, manly.
AN OPPOSITE IS feminine.

mash *verb*
Mash the fruit into a pulp. beat, crush, pound, smash, squash.
To make something into powder is to **grind** or **pulverize** it.

mask *verb*
The factory was masked by a row of poplar trees. camouflage, cloak, conceal, cover, disguise, hide, obscure, screen, shield, shroud, veil.

mass *noun*
She began sifting through the mass of papers on her desk. accumulation, heap, [informal] load, lot, lump, mound, pile, quantity, stack.

massacre *verb* SEE **kill**

massage *verb*
> She massaged his aching back. knead,
> manipulate, rub.

massive *adjective* SEE **huge**

mast *noun*
> A radio mast is an ***aerial*** or
> ***transmitter***.
> A mast to fly a flag on is a ***flagpole***.
> A mast to carry power lines is a ***pylon***.

master *noun*
> A master in a school is a
> ***schoolmaster*** or ***teacher***.
> The master of a dog is its ***keeper*** or
> ***owner***.
> The master of a ship is the ***captain***.
> A master in a particular sport or skill
> is an ***ace***, ***expert***, or ***genius***.

master *verb*
> Some people think it is sexist to use
> the verb *master*
> **1** *I've mastered the basic moves of chess.*
> [*informal*] get the hang of, grasp, learn,
> understand.
> **2** *She succeeded in mastering her fear
> of heights.* conquer, control, curb,
> defeat, dominate, get the better of,
> govern, manage, overcome, regulate,
> restrain, subdue, tame, triumph over.

mastermind *noun*
> **1** *She's a scientific mastermind.* expert,
> genius, intellectual.
> **2** *Who was the mastermind behind the
> plan?* brains, creator, inventor,
> originator, planner.

masterpiece *noun*
> This piece of music is a masterpiece.
> classic.

mastery *noun*
> **1** *He struggled to gain mastery over his
> emotions.* authority, control,
> dominance, power, [*informal*] the
> upper hand.
> **2** *His tactical mastery helped him to
> win the match.* cleverness, knowledge,
> skill.

match *noun*
> **1** *The semi-final was a really exciting
> match.* competition, contest, game, tie,
> tournament.
> **2** *The jacket and tie are a good match.*
> combination, double, pair.

match *verb*
> Does this tie match my shirt? be
> compatible with, be the same colour as,
> be similar to, blend with, combine
> with, correspond with, fit with, go with,
> harmonize with, tone in with.
> AN OPPOSITE IS contrast.

matching *adjective*
> He wore a blue shirt with a matching
> tie. comparable, compatible,
> complimentary, coordinating,
> corresponding, equivalent,
> harmonizing, similar, twin.
> AN OPPOSITE IS contrasting.

mate *noun*
> **1** [*informal*] *He's one of my best mates.*
> [*informal*] chum, friend, [*informal*] pal.
> **2** *He's got a job as a plumber's mate.*
> assistant, colleague, companion,
> helper, partner.

mate *verb*
> Many birds mate in spring. become
> partners, copulate, have intercourse,
> have sex.

material *noun*
> **1** *She's collecting material for a
> newspaper article.* data, facts, ideas,
> information, notes, subject matter.
> **2** *He needed to buy some cleaning
> materials.* building materials, raw
> materials, stuff, substances, things.
> FOR VARIOUS BUILDING MATERIALS,
> SEE **building**.
> **3** *Her skirt was made of soft, woollen
> material.* cloth, fabric.
> FOR VARIOUS KINDS OF FABRIC, SEE
> **cloth**.

mathematics *noun*
> He had to finish his mathematics
> homework before going out. [*informal*]
> maths, number work.

VARIOUS BRANCHES OF
MATHEMATICS: algebra, arithmetic,
geometry, statistics.

WORDS FOR THINGS YOU DO IN
MATHS: addition or adding,
calculation or calculating, counting,
division or dividing, investigating,
measuring, multiplication or
multiplying, subtraction or
subtracting, sums. ➡

VARIOUS MATHEMATICAL
INSTRUMENTS: calculator,
compasses, computer, dividers,
protractor, ruler, set square.

SOME WORDS YOU MIGHT USE IN
MATHS: angle, answer, area, binary
system, capacity, concentric,
congruence, decimal fraction,
decimal point, diagonal, diameter,
difference, digit, equation,
equilateral, factor, figure, fraction,
function, graph, index, locus,
logarithm, matrix, measurement,
mensuration, minus, negative,
number, parallel, pattern,
percentage, perpendicular, plus,
positive, problem, radius, ratio, right
angle, shape, sine, sum, symmetry,
tangent, tessellation, theorem,
times, total, unit, volume.
FOR OTHER WORDS YOU MIGHT USE
IN MATHS, SEE **measurement,
shape**.

matted *adjective*
Her hair was dirty and matted.
knotted, tangled, uncombed.

matter *noun*
1 The manager will deal with this
matter. affair, business, concern,
incident, issue, situation, subject,
thing, topic.
2 Peat consists mainly of vegetable
matter. material, stuff, substance.
3 What's the matter with the car?
difficulty, problem, trouble, worry.

matter *verb*
Will it matter if I'm late? be important,
count, make a difference.

mature *adjective*
1 She's mature for her age. adult,
advanced, grown-up, well developed.
2 There is a large garden, with mature
chestnut and oak trees. established,
fully grown.
AN OPPOSITE IS immature.

maximum *adjective*
The maximum number of people
allowed in the minibus is 16. biggest,
fullest, greatest, highest, largest, top.
AN OPPOSITE IS minimum.

maximum *noun*
Temperatures usually reach their
maximum after noon. ceiling, highest
point, peak, top, upper limit.

maybe *adverb*
Maybe I'll come, maybe I won't!
perhaps, possibly.
AN OPPOSITE IS definitely.

maze *noun*
They were lost in a confusing maze of
corridors. labyrinth, network, tangle,
web.

meadow *noun*
Cows were grazing in the meadow.
field, pasture.

meagre *adjective*
She was forced to supplement her
meagre wages by taking another job.
inadequate, insufficient, [*informal*]
measly, scanty, small, stingy.

meal *noun*

MEALS YOU HAVE AT VARIOUS
TIMES OF DAY: breakfast, dinner,
[*informal*] elevenses, high tea, lunch
or luncheon, supper, tea.
A big formal meal is a **banquet** or
feast.
A quick informal meal is a **snack**.
A meal you eat out of doors is a
barbecue or **picnic**.
A meal where you help yourself to
food is a **buffet**.
A meal you buy ready cooked is a
takeaway.

VARIOUS COURSES OF A MEAL:
[*informal*] afters, dessert, main
course, pudding, starter, sweet.
SEE ALSO **food**.

mean *adjective*
1 He's too mean to give to charity.
[*informal*] mingy, miserly, selfish,
stingy, tight, uncharitable.
AN OPPOSITE IS generous.
2 That was a mean trick to play.
callous, contemptible, cruel,
despicable, malicious, nasty, shabby,
shameful, [*informal*] sneaky, spiteful,
unkind, vicious.
AN OPPOSITE IS kind.

mean *verb*
1 *What does that sign mean?*
communicate, convey, denote, express,
hint at, imply, indicate, say, signify,
stand for, suggest, symbolize.
2 *I mean to work harder.* aim, desire,
intend, plan, propose, want, wish.

meander *verb*
*We meandered round the town looking
at the shops.* ramble, roam, stray,
wander.

meaning *noun*
*The expression has several different
meanings in English.* definition,
explanation, interpretation, sense,
significance.

meaningless *adjective*
1 *She felt that her life was meaningless.*
empty, futile, pointless, worthless.
2 *I can't speak Japanese, so it was
meaningless to me.* incomprehensible,
nonsensical, pointless, senseless.

means *plural noun*
1 *Scientists now have the means to
travel to other planets.* ability, capacity,
method, process, way.
2 *He hasn't got the means to buy a
house.* capital, finances, funds, income,
money, resources, riches, wealth.

measly *adjective*
[*informal*] *They offered him a measly
£2 for all the work he did.* inadequate,
insufficient, meagre, poor, scanty,
small, [*informal*] stingy.

measure *verb*
*Measure the length and width of the
window.* assess, calculate, compute,
gauge, survey, take measurements of.

measure *noun*
1 *They now know the measure of the
problem.* extent, magnitude,
measurement, size.

2 *The government introduced new
measures to curb crime.* act, action, law,
procedure, step.

measurement *noun*
*What are the measurements of this
room?* dimensions, extent, measure,
size.

METRIC UNITS USED TO MEASURE
DISTANCE (BREADTH OR WIDTH,
GAUGE, HEIGHT, AND LENGTH):
millimetre, centimetre, metre,
kilometre.

OLD UNITS USED TO MEASURE
DISTANCE (BREADTH OR WIDTH,
GAUGE, HEIGHT, AND LENGTH):
inch, foot, yard, furlong, mile.

UNIT USED TO MEASURE DISTANCE
IN SPACE: light year.

UNIT USED TO MEASURE DEPTH AT
SEA: fathom.

METRIC UNITS USED TO MEASURE
AREA: square centimetre (metre,
etc.), hectare.

OLD UNITS USED TO MEASURE
AREA: square inch (foot, etc.), acre.

METRIC UNITS USED TO MEASURE
CAPACITY OR VOLUME: millilitre,
cubic centimetre, litre.

OLD UNITS USED TO MEASURE
CAPACITY OR VOLUME: cubic inch,
pint, quart, gallon.

METRIC UNITS USED TO MEASURE
WEIGHT: milligram, gram, kilo or
kilogram, tonne.

OLD UNITS USED TO MEASURE
WEIGHT: ounce, pound, stone,
hundredweight, ton.

UNITS USED TO MEASURE TIME:
second, minute, hour, day, week,
month, year, decade, century,
millennium.

UNITS USED TO MEASURE SPEED OR
VELOCITY: kilometres per hour,
miles per hour, [*informal*] ton.

UNIT USED TO MEASURE SPEED AT
SEA: knot. ➡

UNITS USED TO MEASURE TEMPERATURE: degrees Celsius, degrees centigrade, degrees Fahrenheit.

INFORMAL MEASUREMENTS OF AMOUNT OR QUANTITY: cupful, handful, pinch, plateful, spoonful.

meat *noun*

KINDS OF MEAT: bacon, beef, chicken, game, gammon, ham, lamb, mutton, pork, poultry, turkey, veal, venison.

VARIOUS CUTS OR JOINTS OF MEAT: breast, brisket, chops, cutlet, fillet, leg, loin, rib, rump, scrag, shoulder, silverside, sirloin, spare-rib, steak, topside.

INNER ORGANS OF ANIMALS WHICH CAN BE EATEN: liver, kidney, offal, tripe.

KINDS OF PROCESSED MEAT: brawn, burger, corned beef, hamburger, mince, pasty, pâté, pie, potted meat, rissole, sausage.

mechanic *noun*
The mechanic said it would take an hour to mend the engine. engineer, technician.

medal *noun*

OTHER THINGS GIVEN TO PEOPLE FOR SOMETHING GOOD OR BRAVE THEY HAVE DONE: award, certificate, decoration, honour, medallion, prize, reward, ribbon, rosette, star, trophy.

medallist *noun*
Everyone cheered when the medallists received their awards. champion, victor, winner.

meddle *verb*
1 *She's always meddling in other people's affairs.* interfere, intervene, intrude, [*informal*] poke your nose in, pry.
2 *Don't meddle with my things.* fiddle about, tinker.

media *plural noun* SEE **medium** *noun*

medicine *noun*
1 *Has he taken his medicine?* drug, medication, prescription, remedy, treatment.
An amount of medicine taken at one time is a **dose**.
2 *My cousin is at university studying medicine.* healing, therapy, treatment of diseases.

COMMON MEDICINES AND TREATMENTS: anaesthetic, antibiotic, antidote, antiseptic, aspirin, gargle, herbs, iodine, linctus, morphia, narcotic, painkiller, penicillin, sedative, tonic, tranquillizer.

FORMS IN WHICH YOU TAKE MEDICINE: capsule, inhaler, injection, lotion, lozenge, ointment, pastille, pill, tablet.

THINGS USED TO DRESS WOUNDS: bandage, dressing, lint, plaster, poultice.

EQUIPMENT USED IN MEDICAL TREATMENT: forceps, hypodermic syringe, scalpel, sling, splint, stethoscope, syringe, thermometer, tweezers.

PLACES WHERE YOU CAN GET MEDICAL TREATMENT: clinic, doctor's surgery, health centre, hospital, infirmary, nursing home, sickbay.

VARIOUS DEPARTMENTS AND AREAS IN A HOSPITAL: accident and emergency, dispensary, intensive-care unit, operating theatre, outpatients' department, ward, X-ray department.

PEOPLE WHO LOOK AFTER OUR HEALTH:
A person trained to heal sick people is a **doctor** or **physician**.
A doctor who works in a local health centre is a **general practitioner**.
A person trained to look after sick people is a **nurse**.
Someone who performs medical operations is a **surgeon**. ➡

A specialist in repairing people's faces or bodies after accidents is a *plastic surgeon*.
A person who puts you to sleep during operations is an *anaesthetist*.
A person who takes X-rays is a *radiologist*.
A person who tests your hearing is an *audiometrician*.
A person who tests your eyes is a *optician*.
A person who looks after your feet is a *chiropodist*.
People who look after your teeth: *dentist* and *hygienist*.
A specialist in skin problems is a *dermatologist*.
A specialist in what you eat is a *dietician*.
A specialist in women's health is a *gynaecologist*.
A specialist in childbirth is an *obstetrician*.
Someone who helps to deliver babies is a *midwife*.
A specialist in children's health is a *paediatrician*.
A specialist in mental illnesses is a *psychiatrist*.
People who treat you by rubbing or twisting your body in various ways: *chiropractor*, *masseur*, *osteopath*, and *physiotherapist*.
SEE ALSO **ill, illness**.

mediocre *adjective*
I thought the film was rather mediocre. indifferent, inferior, ordinary, second-rate, undistinguished, unexciting.

meditation *noun*
Monks spend a lot of their time in meditation. contemplation, prayer, reflection.

meditate *verb*
She sat in silence, meditating on the day's events. brood (over), contemplate, deliberate (on), ponder, reflect (on), think (about).

medium *adjective*
The man was of medium height. average, middle, moderate, normal, ordinary, usual.

medium *noun*
This artist's favourite medium is watercolour. means of expression, method, way.
the media or **the mass media**
Media is plural, so we should not say a media, but the media

THE MEDIA, OR THE MASS MEDIA, INCLUDE: advertising, broadcasting, cable television, magazines, newspapers, the press, radio, satellite television, terrestrial television.

meek *adjective*
She looks meek, but she has a fierce temper. docile, gentle, humble, mild, modest, obedient, patient, quiet, resigned, tame.
AN OPPOSITE IS aggressive.

meet *verb*
1 *A week later, I met him in the street.* [*informal*] bump into, come across, encounter, run into, see.
2 *My parents met me at the station.* greet, pick up, welcome.
3 *We were told to meet in the playground.* assemble, collect, gather, muster, rally.
4 *Two roads meet here.* come together, connect, converge, cross, intersect, join, link up, merge, unite.
5 *Improvements were carried out to meet the new safety requirements.* agree to, comply with, fulfil, satisfy.

meeting *noun*
A meeting of children in school is an *assembly*.
A formal meeting to discuss business is a *committee* or *council*.
A meeting to discuss and learn about a particular topic is a *conference* or *congress*.
A meeting to receive information from someone is a *briefing*.
A meeting to give information to reporters is a *press conference*.
A large meeting to show support for something, often out of doors, is a *rally*.
A meeting for worship is a *service*.

A meeting with a friend is a
rendezvous or *date*.
A formal meeting with a king or queen
is an *audience*.

melancholy *adjective*
*She sat on her own with a melancholy
look on her face.* cheerless, dejected,
depressed, gloomy, miserable,
mournful, sad, sombre, sorrowful,
unhappy, woeful.
AN OPPOSITE IS cheerful.

mellow *adjective*
1 *The fruit had a ripe, mellow flavour.*
pleasant, rich, smooth, sweet.
AN OPPOSITE IS sharp.
2 *The subdued lighting gave the room a
mellow atmosphere.* agreeable,
comforting, friendly, peaceful,
reassuring, soft, warm.
AN OPPOSITE IS harsh.

melody *noun*
*He picked up the guitar and began to
play a familiar melody.* air, theme,
tune.

melt *verb*
The ice melted in the sun. soften, thaw,
unfreeze.
To melt frozen food is to *defrost* it.
To treat ore to get metal from it is to
smelt it.
to melt away *The crowd melted away.*
disappear, disperse, dissolve, dwindle,
fade, go away, vanish.

member *noun*
to be a member of something *She's a
member of the local tennis club.* belong
to, join, subscribe to.

memorable *adjective*
*The atmosphere, music, and beautiful
surroundings created a truly
memorable occasion.* impressive,
notable, outstanding, remarkable,
striking, unforgettable.
AN OPPOSITE IS ordinary.

memorial *noun* SEE **monument**

memorize *verb*
*I tried to memorize my words for the
play.* commit to memory, learn, learn
by heart, remember.
AN OPPOSITE IS forget.

memory *noun*
*He has lots of happy memories of his
holiday in America.* impression,
recollection, remembrance, reminder,
reminiscence.

menace *verb*
*They were menaced by a man wielding
a knife.* bully, intimidate, terrorize,
threaten.

menace *noun*
1 *People who drink and drive are a
menace to society.* danger, threat.
2 *That cat is an absolute menace!*
annoyance, inconvenience, irritation,
nuisance.

mend *verb*
1 *Workmen were mending holes in the
roof.* fix, put right, renovate, repair,
restore.
2 *Those socks need mending.* darn,
patch, sew up, stitch up.

mental *adjective*
1 *She is getting old, but her mental
powers are as sharp as ever.*
intellectual, rational.
2 *After his accident, he was in a
dreadful mental state.* emotional,
psychological.

mention *verb*
1 *She mentioned the idea to her boss.*
comment on, hint at, refer to, speak
about, touch on.
2 *He mentioned that his father was
meeting him later.* [*informal*] let out,
remark, say.
3 *The speaker mentioned all the
prizewinners.* acknowledge, draw
attention to, name.

merciful *adjective*
Perhaps the judge will be merciful.
compassionate, forgiving, generous,
gracious, humane, humanitarian, kind,
lenient, mild, pitying, sympathetic,
tender-hearted, tolerant.
AN OPPOSITE IS merciless.

merciless *adjective*
It was a merciless attack on the two people. barbaric, callous, cruel, hard, hard-hearted, harsh, heartless, intolerant, pitiless, relentless, remorseless, ruthless, savage, severe, stern, strict, unfeeling, unforgiving, unkind, unrelenting, vicious.
AN OPPOSITE IS merciful.

mercy *noun*
Their attackers showed no mercy. charity, compassion, feeling, forgiveness, goodwill, grace, humanity, kindness, lenience, love, pity, sympathy, understanding.
AN OPPOSITE IS cruelty.

merge *verb*
1 *The authorities merged two schools.* amalgamate, combine, integrate, join together, link up, put together, unite.
2 *Motorways merge in one mile.* come together, converge, join, meet.
AN OPPOSITE IS separate.

merit *noun*
It's a painting of considerable merit. distinction, excellence, quality, talent, value, virtue, worth.

merit *verb*
Her suggestion merits careful consideration. be entitled to, deserve, earn, justify, rate, warrant.

merriment *noun*
Her eyes sparkled with merriment. amusement, gaiety, hilarity, joking, jollity, joviality, laughter, mirth.

merry *adjective*
He walked off, whistling a merry tune. bright, carefree, cheerful, happy, jolly, jovial, joyful, light-hearted, lively, spirited.
AN OPPOSITE IS gloomy.

mess *noun*
1 *Clear up this mess!* chaos, clutter, confusion, dirt, disorder, jumble, litter, muddle, [*informal*] shambles, untidiness.
2 *I made a real mess of it.* [*informal*] hash, mix-up.
3 *I got into a mess.* difficulty, dilemma, [*informal*] fix, [*informal*] jam, plight, problem.

mess *verb*
to mess about *We were just messing about.* loaf, lounge about, [*informal*] muck about, play about.
to mess things up *I hope you haven't messed up my tapes.* confuse, jumble, make a mess of, mix up, muddle, tangle.
to mess something up *He said he knew how to do it, but he messed it up.* bungle, [*informal*] make a hash of.

message *noun*
Did you get my message? communication.

VARIOUS KINDS OF MESSAGE: announcement, bulletin, cable, dispatch, letter, memo or memorandum, note, notice, phone call, report, statement.

PEOPLE WHO DELIVER MESSAGES: bearer, carrier, courier, dispatch rider, go-between, herald, messenger, postman, runner.

messy *adjective*
Her bedroom is really messy. chaotic, dirty, disorderly, filthy, grubby, mucky, muddled, untidy.
AN OPPOSITE IS neat.

metal *noun*

SOME COMMON METALS: aluminium, chromium, copper, gold, iron, lead, magnesium, mercury, nickel, platinum, silver, tin, zinc.

SOME METAL ALLOYS: brass, bronze, gunmetal, pewter, solder, steel.

metallic *adjective*
1 *The copper vase had a metallic sheen.* gleaming, lustrous, shiny.
2 *A funny metallic sound came from inside the engine.* clanking, clinking, ringing.

method *noun*
1 *She had a secret method for baking cakes.* procedure, process, technique, way.

A specially skilful method for doing something is a **knack**.
2 *There's method in everything he does.* a design, order, organization, a pattern, a plan, a routine, a system.

methodical *adjective*
She's very methodical and keeps a record of everything. businesslike, careful, deliberate, efficient, logical, meticulous, neat, orderly, organized, systematic, tidy.
AN OPPOSITE IS careless.

microbe *noun*
Microbes are **bacteria**, **germs**, **micro-organisms**, or **viruses**.

middle *adjective*
The ball knocked the middle stump out of the ground. central, inner, inside, midway.

middle *noun*
There's a maggot in the middle of this apple. centre, core, heart.
The middle of a wheel is the **hub**.
The middle part of an atom or cell is the **nucleus**.

might *noun*
I banged at the door with all my might. energy, force, power, strength, vigour.

mighty *adjective*
He split the log with one mighty blow. big, enormous, forceful, great, hefty, muscular, powerful, strong, vigorous.
AN OPPOSITE IS weak.

mild *adjective*
1 *He's a mild person who never complains.* amiable, docile, easygoing, gentle, good-tempered, harmless, kind, lenient, merciful, placid, soft-hearted.
2 *The weather has been mild for this time of year.* pleasant, temperate, warm.
AN OPPOSITE IS severe.

militant *adjective*
The protesters became more militant. aggressive, assertive, attacking, fighting, hostile, warlike.

milk *noun*

> KINDS OF MILK: condensed, dried, evaporated, long-life, pasteurized, skimmed, UHT.
> Foods made from milk are **dairy products**.
>
> SOME DAIRY PRODUCTS: butter, cheese, cream, custard, fromage frais, junket, milk pudding, yoghurt.

milky *adjective*
The sun was hazy in the milky grey sky. cloudy, misty, opaque, whitish.
AN OPPOSITE IS clear.

mill *verb*
Wheat is milled to make flour. grind.
to mill about *Everyone was milling about wondering what to do.* move aimlessly, swarm, throng.

mimic *verb*
Children often mimic their teachers. copy, do impressions of, imitate, impersonate, pretend to be, [*informal*] take off.
If you mimic people specially to make fun of them, you **caricature** or **parody** them.

mind *noun*
1 *Her mind was as sharp as ever.* brain, head, intellect, intelligence, judgement, mental powers, reasoning, sense, understanding, wits.
2 *He changed his mind.* beliefs, intentions, opinion, outlook, point of view, view, way of thinking, wishes.

mind *verb*
1 *Will you mind my bag for a minute?* care for, guard, [*informal*] keep an eye on, look after, watch.
2 *Mind the step.* be careful about, beware of, heed, look out for, note, pay attention to, remember, take notice of, watch out for.
3 *I won't mind if you're late.* be upset, bother, care, complain, disapprove, grumble, object, take offence, worry.

mine *noun*
A coal mine is a **colliery** or **pit**.
A place where coal is removed from the surface of the ground is an **opencast mine**.
A place where stone or slate is removed is a **quarry**.

mine *verb*
People used to mine lead in these caves. dig for, excavate, extract, remove.

mingle *verb*
The detectives mingled with the crowd. blend, combine, get together, mix.

miniature *adjective*
A piccolo looks like a miniature flute. minute, tiny, toy.
SEE ALSO **small**.

minimum *adjective*
This task can be done with the minimum amount of effort. least, littlest, lowest, smallest.
AN OPPOSITE IS maximum.

minor *adjective*
1 *They decided to travel on the minor roads.* lesser, less important, secondary, smaller.
2 *I only had a minor part in the play.* inferior, insignificant, little, small, subordinate, trivial, unimportant.
3 *He was guilty of a minor crime.* petty.
AN OPPOSITE IS major.

minority *noun*
Only a minority are opposed to the scheme. lesser number, smaller number.
AN OPPOSITE IS majority.
to be in a minority *Some of them opposed the scheme, but they were in a minority.* be outnumbered, lose.

mint *adjective*
His bike was in mint condition. brand new, fresh, new, perfect, unmarked, unused.

minute *adjective*
You can hardly see it, it's so minute. insignificant, little, microscopic, negligible, tiny.
AN OPPOSITE IS large.

miracle *noun*
It was a miracle that she recovered from her illness. marvel, mystery, wonder.

miraculous *adjective*
She made a miraculous recovery. amazing, astonishing, extraordinary, incredible, inexplicable, marvellous, mysterious, unbelievable, wonderful.

mirage *noun*
He thought he saw a lake in the distance, but it was a mirage. illusion, vision.

misbehave *verb*
She has been misbehaving in class again. behave badly, be naughty, disobey, do wrong, fool about, make mischief, mess about, [*informal*] muck about.
AN OPPOSITE IS behave.

misbehaviour *noun*
We were punished for our misbehaviour. disobedience, mischief, naughtiness, rudeness, wrongdoing.

miscellaneous *adjective*
The box was full of miscellaneous odds and ends. assorted, different, mixed, various.

mischief *noun*
She'll make sure he doesn't get into any mischief. misbehaviour, naughtiness, pranks, scrapes, trouble.

mischievous *adjective*
The mischievous puppy chewed up my slippers. badly behaved, boisterous, disobedient, impish, naughty, playful, roguish, wicked.
AN OPPOSITE IS well behaved.

miserable *adjective*
1 *You look miserable—what's the matter?* anguished, broken-hearted, dejected, depressed, distressed, gloomy, glum, melancholy, mournful, sad, sorrowful, tearful, unhappy, woeful.
AN OPPOSITE IS cheerful or happy.

2 *The poor animals lived in miserable conditions.* distressing, heartbreaking, pathetic, pitiful, squalid, uncomfortable, wretched.
AN OPPOSITE IS comfortable.
3 *The weather was cold and miserable.* depressing, dismal, dreary, grey, unpleasant.
AN OPPOSITE IS pleasant.

miserly *adjective*
He was too miserly to contribute to the collection. [*informal*] grasping, mean, mercenary, [*informal*] mingy, stingy.
AN OPPOSITE IS generous.

misery *noun*
He saw the misery in her eyes. anguish, dejection, depression, despair, distress, gloom, grief, heartache, melancholy, sadness, sorrow, suffering, unhappiness, wretchedness.
AN OPPOSITE IS happiness.

misfortune *noun*
She seems to revel in the misfortunes of other people. adversity, affliction, bad luck, calamity, catastrophe, disaster, hardship, mishap, tragedy, trouble.
AN OPPOSITE IS good luck.

mishap *noun*
She had a slight mishap with the car. accident, calamity, catastrophe, disaster, misfortune.

mislay *verb*
I mislaid my purse. lose.
AN OPPOSITE IS find.

mislead *verb*
Don't try to mislead us! bluff, confuse, deceive, fool, [*informal*] kid, trick.

misleading *adjective*
The article in the paper contained a number of misleading statements. ambiguous, confusing, deceptive, muddling, puzzling, unclear, unreliable, wrong.

miss *verb*
1 *I missed the bus.* be too late for.
2 *The arrow missed the target.* fall short of, go wide of.
3 *If we leave now, we should miss the traffic.* avoid.

4 *I missed dad when he was in hospital.* grieve for, long for, need, pine for, want, yearn for.
to miss something out *I missed out the boring parts of the story.* ignore, leave out, omit, overlook, skip.

missile *noun*
FOR VARIOUS MISSILES, SEE **weapon**.

missing *adjective*
We found the missing cat two days later. absent, lost, straying.

mission *noun*
1 *His mission was to improve staff morale.* aim, campaign, job, objective, purpose, task.
2 *The devices were tested on a recent space mission.* expedition, exploration, journey, voyage.

mist *noun*
1 *We drove slowly through the mist.* cloud, drizzle, fog, haze.
2 *I can't see out because of the mist on the windows.* condensation, steam.

mistake *noun*
Her work is always full of mistakes. blunder, error, inaccuracy, lapse, slip, slip-up.
A spelling mistake is a ***misspelling***.
A mistake where something is left out is an ***omission***.
A mistake in a printed book is a ***misprint***.

mistake *verb*
She mistook my meaning entirely. get wrong, misunderstand, mix up.

mistreat *verb*
A dog which has been mistreated will remain wary of strangers. abuse, hurt, misuse, treat badly.

mistrust *verb*
He had no reason to mistrust her. be sceptical about, distrust, have doubts about, suspect.
AN OPPOSITE IS trust.

misty *adjective*
1 *The weather forecast said that it will be misty.* foggy, hazy.
2 *I can't see out because the windows are misty.* cloudy, opaque, smoky, steamy.

3 *I could just make out a misty shape in the distance.* blurred, dim, faint, fuzzy, indistinct, shadowy, vague.
AN OPPOSITE IS clear.

misunderstand *verb*
He misunderstood her remarks. get wrong, miss the point of, mistake.
AN OPPOSITE IS understand.

misunderstanding *noun*
The problem was due to a misunderstanding on my part. error, mistake, [*informal*] mix-up.

misuse *verb*
They felt that they had been deceived and misused. abuse, hurt, mistreat, treat badly.

mix *verb*
Mix the ingredients in a bowl. blend, combine, mingle.
to mix something up *Don't mix up those papers—I've only just sorted them out.* confuse, jumble, muddle.
To mix up playing cards is to **shuffle** them.

mixed *adjective*
Add a teaspoon of mixed herbs. assorted, different, miscellaneous, various.
AN OPPOSITE IS separate.

mixture *noun*
1 *Whisk the ingredients and put the mixture in a saucepan.* blend, combination, mix.
2 *There's an odd mixture of things in this drawer.* assortment, collection, jumble, variety.
A mixture of metals is an **alloy**.
A mixture of two different species of plant or animal is a **hybrid**.
A mixture of a solid in a liquid is an **emulsion**.

moan *verb*
1 *He moaned in pain.* cry, groan, sigh, wail.
2 *We moaned about the food.* complain, grouse, grumble.

mob *noun*
Troops were called in to control the mob. bunch, crowd, gang, horde, riot, throng.

mob *verb*
Autograph hunters mobbed the pop star. crowd round, hem in, jostle, surround, swarm round, throng round.

mobile *adjective*
1 *A mobile library visits once a fortnight.* movable, travelling.
Something that you can carry about is **portable**.
2 *It wasn't long after the accident before he was mobile again.* active, moving about, [*informal*] up and about.
AN OPPOSITE IS immobile.

mobilize *verb*
The organizers of the demonstration mobilized a lot of supporters. enlist, gather, get together, muster, organize, rally, summon.

mock *verb*
The winner mocked the other competitors. deride, jeer at, laugh at, make fun of, ridicule, scoff at, scorn, [*informal*] send up, sneer at.

mockery *noun*
His smile was full of mockery. derision, jeering, laughter, ridicule, scorn, sneering.
Mocking someone by saying the opposite of what you mean is **sarcasm**.
A piece of writing which mocks someone or something is **parody** or **satire**.

model *adjective*
1 *They've decided to build a model railway.* miniature, toy.
2 *She's a model pupil.* ideal, perfect.

model *noun*
1 *They bought a little model of the aeroplane.* copy, replica, toy.
2 *This year's models will be on display at the motor show.* design, type, version.
3 *She's a model of good behaviour.* example, ideal.

model *verb*
He models figures in clay. construct, fashion, make, mould, shape.

moderate *adjective*
The company offers good quality work at moderate prices. average, fair, medium, modest, normal, ordinary, reasonable, sensible.
AN OPPOSITE IS excessive.

moderate *verb*
1 *The storm moderated.* become less severe, decrease, die down, ease off, subside, wear off.
2 *They moderated their demands.* lessen, reduce.

moderately *adverb*
He answered the questions moderately well. fairly, [*informal*] pretty, quite, rather, reasonably, to some extent.

modern *adjective*
1 *All the equipment in their kitchen was modern.* advanced, the latest, up to date.
AN OPPOSITE IS out of date.
2 *She always dresses in modern clothes.* contemporary, fashionable, present-day, progressive, [*informal*] trendy.
AN OPPOSITE IS old-fashioned.

modernize *verb*
The farmhouse had been fully modernized. improve, rebuild, update.

modest *adjective*
1 *He's modest about his success.* bashful, coy, humble, quiet, shy.
AN OPPOSITE IS conceited.
2 *There has been a modest increase in sales.* average, medium, moderate, reasonable.

modify *verb*
The present law needs to be modified. adapt, adjust, alter, change, refine, revise, vary.

moist *adjective*
1 *The walls of the cellar were moist.* clammy, damp, watery, wet.
2 *Tropical plants grow well in this moist atmosphere.* humid, muggy, rainy, steamy.
AN OPPOSITE IS dry.

moisture *noun*
Moisture caused the model to disintegrate. condensation, damp, dampness, dew, mist, steam, vapour, water, wetness.

molest *verb*
The crowd were shouting abuse and molesting the two police officers. abuse, annoy, assault, attack, bother, harass, interfere with, irritate, pester, torment, vex, worry.

molten *adjective*
The molten metal is poured into a mould. liquid, melted.

moment *noun*
1 *I'll be ready in a moment.* [*informal*] flash, instant, minute, second.
2 *It was one of the great moments of aviation history.* occasion, time.

momentary *adjective*
His momentary lack of concentration almost caused an accident. brief, fleeting, short, temporary.
AN OPPOSITE IS permanent.

momentous *adjective*
It was a momentous decision to declare war. critical, crucial, decisive, historic, important, serious, significant.
AN OPPOSITE IS unimportant.

monarch *noun* SEE **ruler**

money *noun*
I haven't got any money. [*slang synonyms*] bread, dough, lolly.

DIFFERENT FORMS IN WHICH YOU CAN SPEND MONEY: banknotes, cash, change, cheques, coins, credit card, currency, notes, traveller's cheques.

WORDS FOR THE MONEY PEOPLE MAY OWN: finances, fortune, funds, resources, riches, wealth.

DIFFERENT FORMS IN WHICH YOU CAN OWN MONEY: assets, capital, estate, investments, property, savings.

MONEY YOU RECEIVE FOR DOING A JOB: earnings, income, pay, salary, wages.

MONEY YOU RECEIVE FOR OTHER REASONS: dividends, grant, interest, pension, pocket money, profits, winnings. ➡

MONEY YOU OWE OR PAY TO OTHER PEOPLE: debts, duty, tax.

MONEY WHICH SOMEONE LENDS YOU: advance, loan, mortgage.

monkey *noun*

VARIOUS KINDS OF MONKEY: ape, baboon, chimpanzee, gibbon, gorilla, marmoset, orang-utan.

monopolize *verb*
He monopolized the conversation all evening. hog, keep others out of, take over.
AN OPPOSITE IS share.

monotonous *adjective*
Her monotonous voice almost sent me to sleep. boring, dreary, dull, flat, tedious, unchanging, unexciting, uninteresting.
AN OPPOSITE IS interesting.

monster *noun*
The film featured several frightening monsters. beast, brute, giant, ogre.

monstrous *adjective*
1 The monstrous tidal wave swamped the surrounding countryside. big, colossal, enormous, gigantic, great, huge, hulking, immense, mighty, towering, vast.
2 The whole nation was shocked by the monstrous crime. abhorrent, atrocious, cruel, dreadful, evil, gross, gruesome, hideous, horrible, horrifying, inhuman, obscene, outrageous, repulsive, shocking, terrible, villainous, wicked.

monument *noun*

VARIOUS THINGS SET UP AS MONUMENTS: column, cross, gravestone or headstone or tombstone, mausoleum, memorial, obelisk, pillar, shrine, statue, tombstone.

mood *noun*
What sort of mood is he in today? disposition, humour, state of mind, temper.

moody *adjective*
1 She had been moody and withdrawn for several weeks. bad-tempered, cross, depressed, gloomy, grumpy, melancholy, miserable, sulky, sullen.
AN OPPOSITE IS cheerful.
2 He's such a moody person that I don't know whether to joke with him or not. changeable, touchy, unpredictable, unreliable.

moor *verb*
We moored the boat in the harbour. fasten, make fast, secure, tie up.

mope *verb*
It's no use moping—things could be worse. be sad, brood, grieve, pine, sulk.

moral *adjective*
1 We have a moral responsibility to help people in need. ethical.
2 She's a very moral person. honest, innocent, law-abiding, pure, righteous, trustworthy, truthful, upright, virtuous.
AN OPPOSITE IS immoral.

moral *noun*
The moral of this story is that crime does not pay. lesson, meaning, message.
morals Hasn't he got any morals? decency, goodness, honesty, ideals, integrity, morality, principles, standards.

morale *noun*
The team's morale is high, so we have a good chance of winning. attitude, confidence, courage, mood, spirit, state of mind.

more *adjective*
The soup needs more pepper. added, additional, extra, further.
AN OPPOSITE IS less.

moreover *adverb*
They know the painting is a forgery. Moreover, they know who painted it. also, besides, further, furthermore, in addition.

morsel *noun*
She hadn't eaten a morsel of food all day. bite, crumb, fragment, mouthful, nibble, piece, scrap, taste.

mortal *adjective*
1 *All human beings are mortal.* bodily, earthly, human, physical.
AN OPPOSITE IS immortal.
2 *He received a mortal wound.* deadly, fatal, lethal.

mortality *noun*
Sadly, there is high mortality among young birds. death rate, fatalities, loss of life.
AN OPPOSITE IS survival.

mostly *adverb*
Nowadays, houses are mostly lit by electricity. chiefly, commonly, generally, largely, mainly, normally, predominantly, primarily, principally, typically, usually.

motherly *adjective*
All her motherly instincts were aroused by the sight of the babies. caring, kind, loving, maternal, protective, tender.

motion *noun*
He summoned the waiter with a motion of his hand. gesture, movement.

motionless *adjective*
The cat sat motionless, watching the bird. immobile, stationary, still, unmoving.
AN OPPOSITE IS moving.

motivate *verb*
He was motivated solely by the desire for power. encourage, induce, persuade, prompt, provoke, spur, stimulate, urge.

motive *noun*
The police believe jealousy was the motive for the crime. cause, motivation, purpose, reasoning, thinking.

motor *noun*
The toy train had an electric motor. engine.
motor car SEE **car**.

motorist *noun*
Some motorists drive too fast in bad weather. driver.

mottled *adjective*
The sunlight made a mottled pattern under the trees. dappled, patchy, speckled, spotty.

motto *noun*
Her motto has always been, 'keep smiling'. catchphrase, proverb, saying, slogan.

mould *verb*
We moulded the figures from clay. fashion, form, model, shape.

mouldy *adjective*
There was nothing in the fridge but some mouldy cheese. damp, decaying, decomposing, musty, rotten, rotting.

mound *noun*
1 *She sat at her desk, surrounded by mounds of paper.* heap, mass, pile, stack.
2 *There used to be a castle on top of that mound.* hill, hump, rise.
An ancient mound of earth over a grave is a ***barrow***.

mount *verb*
1 *She mounted the pony and rode off.* get on, jump onto.
2 *He mounted the steps.* ascend, climb, go up.
3 *The gallery is mounting an exhibition of 16th century drawings.* display, put up, set up.
to mount up *Her debts were beginning to mount up.* accumulate, get bigger, grow, increase, pile up.

mountain *noun*
The top of a mountain is the ***peak*** or ***summit***.
A line of mountains is a ***range***.
A long, narrow mountain is a ***ridge***.
A mountain with a hole at the top caused by an eruption is a ***volcano***.

mountainous *adjective*
1 *Travelling is difficult in mountainous country.* alpine, hilly, rugged.
2 *The ship was battered by mountainous waves.* colossal, enormous, gigantic, high, huge, steep, towering.

mourn *verb*
He mourned for his dead dog. go into mourning, grieve, lament, pine, weep.
AN OPPOSITE IS rejoice.

mournful adjective
1 *The farewell party was a mournful occasion.* dismal, distressing, gloomy, sad, sorrowful, tearful, unhappy.
2 *They could hear the mournful cries of the abandoned animals.* desolate, distressed, forlorn, melancholy, woeful.
AN OPPOSITE IS cheerful.

mouth noun
1 *Don't talk with your mouth full.* jaws, lips.
A dog's nose and mouth is its **muzzle**.
2 *They travelled the whole length of the river, from its source to its mouth.* outlet.
A wide river mouth is an **estuary**.
A river mouth where the river divides into branches is a **delta**.
3 *She saw the mouth of a cave in the cliff above her.* entrance, opening.

move noun
1 *Don't make a move!* movement.
2 *What will his next move be?* action, deed, manoeuvre, step.
3 *It's your move next.* chance, go, opportunity, turn.

move verb
People and things can move in many different ways. We give some of the commoner senses of the word, followed by synonyms you could use
1 *To move things from one place to another.* carry, remove, shift, transfer, transport.
2 *To move from a certain position.* budge, depart, go, leave, quit.
3 *To move restlessly.* fidget, flap, shake, stir, toss, turn, twist, twitch.
4 *To move from side to side.* swing, wag, wave, wiggle.
5 *To move along.* make progress, proceed, travel, walk.
6 *To move along quickly.* career, dash, fly, hasten, hurry, hurtle, race, run, rush, shoot, speed, sweep, zoom.
7 *To move along slowly.* amble, crawl, dawdle, stroll.
8 *To move towards something.* advance, approach, come, proceed, progress.
9 *To move away from something.* back, retreat, reverse, withdraw.
10 *To move downwards.* descend, drop, fall, sink, swoop.

11 *To move upwards.* arise, ascend, climb, mount, rise, soar.
12 *To move round and round.* revolve, roll, rotate, spin, turn, twirl, twist, wheel, whirl.
13 *To move gracefully.* dance, flow, glide.
14 *To move clumsily.* flounder, lumber, lurch, shuffle, stagger, stumble, totter, trip, trundle.
15 *To move stealthily.* crawl, creep, edge, slink.

movement noun
1 *He felt incapable of movement.* action, gesture, motion, moving.
2 *Has there been any movement in their attitude?* change, development, progress, shift.
3 *She's keen to join the anti-hunting movement.* campaign, crusade, group, organization, party.

moving adjective
His moving story nearly made her cry. emotional, inspiring, stirring, [informal] tear-jerking, touching.

muck noun
They were clearing the muck out of the stable. dirt, dung, filth, grime, manure, mud, rubbish, sewage, slime, sludge.

mucky adjective
His hands are all mucky. dirty, filthy, foul, grimy, grubby, messy, muddy, soiled, squalid.
AN OPPOSITE IS clean.

mud noun
The tractor left a trail of mud on the road. clay, dirt, muck, slime, sludge, soil.

muddle noun
1 *There was a muddle over the arrangements.* confusion, misunderstanding, [informal] mix-up.
2 *There was a muddle of clothes on the floor.* jumble, mess, tangle.

muddle verb
1 *He muddled all the books on her desk.* jumble up, make a mess of, [informal] mess up, mix up, shuffle, tangle.
AN OPPOSITE IS tidy.
2 *Don't talk so fast—you'll muddle him.* bewilder, confuse, mislead, perplex, puzzle.

muddy *adjective*
1 *Take off your muddy shoes before you come in.* caked, dirty, filthy, messy, mucky, soiled.
AN OPPOSITE IS clean.
2 *I got filthy walking across the muddy ground.* boggy, marshy, soft, spongy, waterlogged, wet.
AN OPPOSITE IS dry or firm.

muffle *verb*
1 *They muffled themselves up to play in the snow.* cover, wrap.
2 *She tried to muffle her sneeze.* deaden, disguise, mask, silence, stifle, suppress.

muffled *adjective*
She could hear muffled voices coming from next door. indistinct, muted, unclear, woolly.
AN OPPOSITE IS clear.

muggy *adjective*
The weather's been very muggy recently. close, damp, humid, moist, oppressive, steamy.
AN OPPOSITE IS fresh.

multiply *verb*
Mice multiply quickly. breed, increase, reproduce, spread.

multitude *noun*
She's got a multitude of things to do. crowd, host, large number, mass.

mumble *verb*
He was mumbling and they could hardly understand what he was saying. mutter, talk indistinctly.

munch *verb*
He sat munching crisps through the whole film. chew, crunch.

murder *noun*
A synonym commonly used in America is **homicide**.
The murder of an important person is an **assassination**.
The murder of a king is **regicide**.
Killing someone without meaning to do so is **manslaughter**.
SEE ALSO **kill**.

murderous *adjective*
They launched a murderous attack on their enemy. bloodthirsty, brutal, cruel, deadly, ferocious, fierce, pitiless, ruthless, savage, vicious, violent.

murky *adjective*
It was so murky that they had to put the headlights on. cloudy, dark, dim, dull, foggy, gloomy, grey, misty, sombre.
AN OPPOSITE IS clear.

murmur *noun*
There was a murmur of voices from the next room. buzz, drone, hum, whispering.

muscular *adjective*
The wrestler was a muscular man. [*informal*] beefy, brawny, burly, hefty, husky, powerful, robust, strong, sturdy, tough, well built, well developed.
AN OPPOSITE IS puny or weak.

music *noun*

DIFFERENT KINDS OF MUSIC: blues, classical music, country and western, dance music, disco music, folk music, gospel, jazz, orchestral music, pop music, punk, ragtime, rap, reggae, rock, soul, swing.

MUSICAL COMPOSITIONS FOR SINGING: anthem, ballad, carol, hymn, lullaby, sea shanty, song, spiritual.

LONG MUSICAL COMPOSITIONS FOR SINGING OR DANCING: ballet, musical, opera, operetta, oratorio.

SOME OTHER KINDS OF MUSICAL COMPOSITION: concerto, fanfare, fugue, march, nocturne, overture, prelude, rhapsody, sonata, symphony.

Musical instruments

FAMILIES OF MUSICAL INSTRUMENTS: brass, keyboard, percussion, strings, woodwind.

STRINGED INSTRUMENTS THAT CAN BE PLAYED WITH A BOW: cello, double bass, viola, violin or fiddle. ➡

INSTRUMENTS WITH STRINGS PLAYED BY PLUCKING OR STRUMMING: banjo, guitar, harp, lute, lyre, sitar, ukulele, zither.

BRASS INSTRUMENTS: bugle, cornet, euphonium, flugelhorn, French horn, trombone, trumpet, tuba.

OTHER INSTRUMENTS YOU PLAY BY BLOWING: bagpipes, bassoon, clarinet, cor anglais, flute, harmonica or mouth organ, oboe, piccolo, recorder, saxophone.

KEYBOARD INSTRUMENTS: accordion, harmonium, harpsichord, keyboard, organ, piano, synthesizer.

PERCUSSION INSTRUMENTS: bass drum, bongo drum, castanets, celesta, chime bars, cymbals, drum, glockenspiel, gong, kettledrum, maracas, marimba, rattle, side drum, snare drum, tabor, tambour, tambourine, timpani, tom-tom, triangle, tubular bells, vibraphone, wood block, xylophone.

Musicians

DIFFERENT SINGING VOICES: alto, bass, contralto, soprano, tenor, treble.

PEOPLE WHO PLAY VARIOUS INSTRUMENTS: bugler, cellist, clarinettist, drummer, fiddler, flautist, guitarist, harpist, oboist, organist, percussionist, pianist, piper, timpanist, trombonist, trumpeter, violinist.

VARIOUS OTHER MUSICIANS: accompanist, composer, conductor, instrumentalist, singer, vocalist.

GROUPS OF MUSICIANS: band, choir or chorus, duet or duo, ensemble, group, orchestra, quartet, quintet, trio.

Musical terms

TERMS USED IN MUSIC: chord, chromatic scale, counterpoint, diatonic scale, discord, harmony, melody, note, octave, pitch, ➡

rhythm, scale, semitone, tempo, theme, tone, tune.

NAMES OF NOTES IN WRITTEN MUSIC: crotchet, minim, quaver, semibreve, semiquaver.

OTHER SIGNS USED IN WRITTEN MUSIC: clef sign, flat, key signature, natural, sharp, stave, time signature.

musical *adjective*
She has a very musical voice. harmonious, melodious, pleasant, sweet sounding, tuneful.

muster *verb*
Can they muster a full team for Saturday? assemble, call together, collect, gather, get together, mobilize, rally, round up.

musty *adjective*
There's a musty smell in the spare room. airless, damp, mouldy, stale, stuffy.
AN OPPOSITE IS fresh.

mute *adjective*
He stared in mute amazement. dumb, silent, speechless, tongue-tied.

mutilate *verb*
The soldier was horribly mutilated in the explosion. cripple, injure, lame, maim, mangle, wound.

mutinous *adjective*
The captain was unable to control his mutinous crew. defiant, disobedient, rebellious, uncontrollable.

mutiny *verb*
The sailors mutinied because of the bad conditions on their ship. disobey, rebel, revolt, rise up.

mutter *verb*
I can't understand what you're saying when you mutter. mumble, murmur, talk indistinctly.

mutual *adjective*
They had a mutual interest in doing the deal. common, joint, reciprocal, shared.

mysterious *adjective*
1 *The doctors were puzzled by her mysterious illness.* baffling, incomprehensible, inexplicable, miraculous, mystifying, perplexing, puzzling, unexplained.
2 *Someone had drawn a mysterious sign on the wall.* eerie, obscure, secret, strange, uncanny, weird.

mystery *noun*
What really happened was a mystery. miracle, mysterious happening, puzzle, riddle, secret.

mystify *verb*
He was mystified by her disappearance. baffle, bewilder, perplex, puzzle.

mythical *adjective*
The unicorn is a mythical beast. fabulous, fanciful, fictional, imaginary, invented, legendary, mythological, non-existent, unreal.
AN OPPOSITE IS real.

Nn

nag *verb*
He was always nagging her to work harder. badger, pester, scold.

naïve *adjective*
He's so naïve that he believes her promises. gullible, inexperienced, innocent, simple-minded.

naked *adjective*
He walked naked into the bathroom. bare, nude, stripped, unclothed, undressed.
AN OPPOSITE IS clothed.

name *noun*
The official names you have are your *first names* or *forenames*, and *surname*.
Names a Christian is given at baptism are *Christian names*.
A false name is an *alias*.
A name people use instead of your real name is a *nickname*.

A false name an author uses is a *pen name* or *pseudonym*.
The name of a book is its *title*.

name *verb*
His parents named him Antony. call.
To name someone at the ceremony of baptism is to *baptize* or *christen* them.

nap *noun*
to take a nap *He always takes a nap on Sunday afternoons.* doze, nod off, rest, sleep.

narrate *verb*
He narrated the story of his life. recount, relate, tell.

narration *noun*
Who did the narration in that film? commentary, description, storytelling.

narrative *noun*
The sailor wrote an exciting narrative of his lonely voyage. account, chronicle, history, story, tale, [*informal*] yarn.

narrow *adjective*
He squeezed through a narrow opening. slender, slim, thin.
AN OPPOSITE IS wide.

narrow-minded *adjective*
She has a very narrow-minded view of life. biased, conservative, intolerant, prejudiced, prim.
AN OPPOSITE IS broad-minded.

nasty *adjective*
The adjective *nasty* can refer to almost anything you don't like. We give some of the common uses of the word, followed by synonyms you could use instead
1 *A nasty person.* cruel, unfriendly, unkind, unpleasant.
2 *A nasty experience.* awful, dreadful, fearful, frightening, grim, horrifying, [*informal*] scary, terrifying.
3 *A nasty problem.* baffling, complicated, difficult, hard, insoluble, puzzling, ticklish, tricky.
4 *A nasty mess.* dirty, disgusting, filthy, horrible, loathsome, [*informal*] mucky, revolting, squalid.
5 *A nasty smell.* bad, disagreeable, foul, objectionable, repulsive, rotten, sickening, stinking.

6 *A nasty crime.* barbaric, beastly, brutal, cruel, ruthless, savage, vicious.
7 *A nasty film.* immoral, indecent, obscene, offensive, shocking, [*informal*] sick, violent.
8 *A nasty illness.* acute, critical, dangerous, life threatening, painful, serious, severe.
AN OPPOSITE IS nice.

nation *noun*
1 *The president addressed the nation on television.* community, population, society.
2 *People from many nations compete in the Olympic Games.* country, land, state.

national *adjective*
1 *She bought the national and local newspapers.* general, nationwide.
AN OPPOSITE IS local.
2 *It's interesting to learn about other people's national customs.* ethnic.

nationalist *noun*
People who love their country are ***patriots***.
People who think their country is better than any other are ***chauvinists***.

natural *adjective*
1 *It's natural for birds to defend their territory.* inherited, instinctive, intuitive.
2 *It's natural for most people to write with the right hand.* normal, ordinary, spontaneous, usual.
AN OPPOSITE IS unnatural.

nature *noun*
1 *I like TV programmes about nature.* the countryside, natural history, wildlife.
2 *He has a kind nature.* character, disposition, manner, personality.
3 *I collect coins, medals, and things of that nature.* description, kind, sort, type, variety.

naughty *adjective*
The naughty children felt ashamed of themselves. bad, badly behaved, bad-mannered, disobedient, impolite, mischievous, rebellious, rude, stubborn, troublesome, uncontrollable, unmanageable, unruly, wicked.
AN OPPOSITE IS well behaved.
to be naughty behave badly, disobey, [*informal*] mess about, misbehave.

navigate *verb*
The captain navigated his ship between the dangerous rocks. direct, guide, manoeuvre, pilot, sail, steer.

navy *noun*
WORDS FOR GROUPS OF SHIPS: armada, convoy, fleet.

near *adjective*
1 *We get on well with our near neighbours.* adjacent, close, next door.
2 *My birthday is near.* approaching, coming.
3 *I invited all my near relatives to the party.* close, dear, familiar, intimate.
AN OPPOSITE IS distant.

nearly *adverb*
It's nearly dinner time. almost, approaching, not quite, practically, virtually.

neat *adjective*
1 *My friend keeps her bedroom neat.* clean, orderly, tidy, uncluttered.
2 *Mum always looks neat when she goes out.* elegant, smart, spruce, trim.
3 *He congratulated me on doing a neat job.* accurate, deft, expert, meticulous, precise, skilful.
AN OPPOSITE IS untidy.

necessary *adjective*
The policeman said that the repairs to the car were absolutely necessary. compulsory, essential, indispensable, inevitable, needed, unavoidable.
AN OPPOSITE IS unnecessary.

necessity *noun*
Is it a necessity, or can we do without it? essential, requirement.

need *noun*
There's a need for more shops in our area. call, demand, requirement.

need *verb*
1 *I need £10.* be short of, lack, require, want.
2 *The charity needs our support.* depend on, rely on.

needless *adjective*
Why are they making that needless noise? excessive, superfluous, unnecessary, unwanted.

needlework *noun*
Gran says you need good eyesight for needlework. embroidery, sewing.

needy *adjective*
Don't you think we should help needy people? badly off, hard up, poor.
AN OPPOSITE IS rich.

negative *adjective*
He has a very negative attitude to his job. contrary, grudging, obstinate, pessimistic, uncooperative, unenthusiastic, unhelpful, unwilling.
AN OPPOSITE IS positive.

neglect *verb*
She's been neglecting her work. abandon, disregard, forget, ignore, leave alone, overlook, pay no attention to, shirk.

negligent *adjective*
The doctor was accused of being negligent. careless, forgetful, inattentive, inconsiderate, irresponsible, slack, sloppy, slovenly, thoughtless, uncaring, unprofessional, unthinking.
AN OPPOSITE IS careful.

negligible *adjective*
There has been a negligible amount of rain this summer. imperceptible, insignificant, slight, small, tiny, trivial, unimportant.
AN OPPOSITE IS considerable.

negotiate *verb*
1 *She negotiated with the car salesman.* bargain, confer, discuss terms, haggle.
2 *The driver failed to negotiate the bend and crashed the car.* get past, manoeuvre round.

negotiation *noun*
Instead of fighting, the two sides settled the dispute by negotiation. arbitration, bargaining, diplomacy, discussion.

neighbourhood *noun*
They live in a very nice neighbourhood. area, community, district, locality, vicinity.

neighbouring *adjective*
She invited people from the neighbouring houses to her party. adjacent, bordering, close, near, nearby, nearest, next door.

neighbourly *adjective*
It was neighbourly to water their plants while they were away. friendly, helpful, kind.
AN OPPOSITE IS unfriendly.

nerve *noun*
1 *That steeplejack has some nerve!* bravery, courage, daring, pluck.
2 *She's got a nerve, taking my pen without asking!* cheek, impertinence, impudence, rudeness.

nerve-racking *adjective*
His driving test was a nerve-racking experience. agonizing, distressing, tense, worrying.
AN OPPOSITE IS relaxing.

nervous *adjective*
She always feels nervous before an exam. agitated, anxious, apprehensive, edgy, fearful, fidgety, flustered, insecure, jumpy, on edge, tense, uneasy, [*informal*] uptight, worried.
AN OPPOSITE IS calm.

nestle *verb*
The puppies nestled against their mother. cuddle, curl up, lie comfortably, snuggle.

net, network *nouns*

THINGS WITH A CRISS-CROSS ARRANGEMENT OF LINES, ETC.: grid, lace, lattice, mesh, net, netting, network, trellis, web.
A network of paths is a *labyrinth* or *maze*.
An organization with many connected parts, like a railway network, is a *system*.

neutral *adjective*
1 *A referee has to be neutral.*
disinterested, impartial, unbiased,
unprejudiced.
AN OPPOSITE IS prejudiced.
2 *The room was decorated in neutral
colours.* drab, indefinite, pale.
AN OPPOSITE IS distinctive.

new *adjective*
1 *Start on a new sheet of paper.* brand
new, clean, fresh, unused.
A new stamp or coin is in ***mint***
condition.
2 *They went to the motor show to see the
new models.* current, latest, modern,
recent, up to date.
3 *She thought she'd sorted everything
out, but then a new problem arose.*
additional, different, extra,
unexpected, unfamiliar.
4 *Haven't you got any new ideas?*
innovative, radical, revolutionary.
AN OPPOSITE IS old.

newcomer *noun*
*The teacher introduced the newcomer to
the class.* arrival, beginner, new boy,
new girl.
A person who has just come to a new
country is an ***immigrant*** or ***settler***.

news *noun*
What's the latest news? information,
[*old use*] tidings, word.

VARIOUS FORMS IN WHICH YOU GET
NEWS: announcement, bulletin,
dispatch, message, newsflash,
newsletter, newspaper, notice,
poster, press release, proclamation,
report, statement.
SEE ALSO **communication**.

next *adjective*
1 *He lives in the house next to the chip
shop.* adjacent, closest, nearest.
AN OPPOSITE IS distant.
2 *If she's not on this bus, she's bound to
be on the next one.* following,
subsequent.
AN OPPOSITE IS previous.

nice *adjective*
People often use the adjective *nice*
because it can refer to almost anything
we like; but its meaning is vague, and
there are a lot of more precise words
we can use. We give here some of the
uses of the word, followed by synonyms
you could use instead
1 *A nice person.* friendly, generous,
helpful, kind, likeable.
2 *A nice experience.* delightful,
enjoyable, good.
3 *Nice food.* delicious, satisfying, tasty,
well cooked.
4 *A nice smell.* agreeable, fragrant.
5 *Nice weather.* fine, sunny, warm.
6 *Nice manners.* courteous, elegant,
polished, polite, refined.
7 *A nice picture.* attractive, beautiful,
pleasing.
AN OPPOSITE IS nasty.
Other senses in which you can use the
word *nice*:
1 *There is a nice distinction between
borrowing and stealing.* delicate, fine.
2 *A watchmaker must have a nice eye
for small details.* accurate,
discriminating, exact, meticulous,
precise.

nimble *adjective*
*She soon sewed the button on with her
nimble fingers.* agile, deft, quick, quick-
moving, skilful.
AN OPPOSITE IS clumsy.

nip *verb*
1 *She nipped her finger in the door.*
pinch, snip, squeeze.
2 *The dog nipped my leg.* bite.
3 [*informal*] *She nipped along to the
shops.* dash, go, [*informal*] pop, run,
rush.

noble *adjective*
1 *She comes from an ancient noble
family.* aristocratic, high-born, upper-
class.
AN OPPOSITE IS ordinary.
2 *The rescue team were congratulated
for their noble efforts.* brave,
chivalrous, courageous, gallant, heroic,
honourable, virtuous, worthy.
AN OPPOSITE IS cowardly or unworthy.

3 *The noble building could be seen from miles around.* dignified, distinguished, elegant, grand, great, imposing, impressive, magnificent, majestic, splendid, stately.
AN OPPOSITE IS insignificant.

nobleman, noblewoman *nouns*
aristocrat, noble.
FOR VARIOUS NOBLE TITLES, SEE **title**.

nod *verb*
He nodded his head in agreement.
bend, bob, bow.
to nod off *He sometimes nods off in front of the television.* be drowsy, doze, fall asleep, have a nap, rest, sleep.

noise *noun*
There's a dreadful noise coming from the house. din, hullabaloo, pandemonium, racket, row, screaming, screeching, shrieking, shouting, tumult, uproar, yelling.
FOR VARIOUS WAYS TO MAKE SOUNDS, SEE **sound** *verb*.

noisy *adjective*
1 *They complained about the noisy children.* chattering, rowdy, screaming, screeching, shrieking, shrill, talkative.
2 *The people next door were playing noisy music.* blaring, booming, deafening, ear-splitting, loud, thunderous.
AN OPPOSITE IS quiet.

nominate *verb*
They nominated her as captain.
appoint, choose, elect, name, select.

non-existent *adjective*
The danger was non-existent. fictitious, imaginary, imagined, made-up.
AN OPPOSITE IS real.

nonsense *noun*
She's talking nonsense! (These synonyms are normally used *informally*) bilge, rot, rubbish, stuff and nonsense, tripe.

nonsensical *adjective*
His nonsensical idea just wasn't worth talking about. absurd, crazy, foolish, illogical, incomprehensible, irrational, laughable, ludicrous, meaningless, ridiculous, senseless, silly, stupid, unreasonable.
AN OPPOSITE IS sensible.

non-stop *adjective*
1 *Their non-stop chattering annoyed her.* ceaseless, constant, continual, continuous, endless, incessant, never-ending, unbroken, unceasing.
2 *They took a non-stop train from Leicester to London.* direct, express, fast.

normal *adjective*
1 *He had a normal kind of day at work.* average, common, customary, familiar, habitual, ordinary, predictable, regular, routine, standard, typical, unsurprising, usual.
2 *No normal person would sleep on a bed of nails.* healthy, rational, reasonable, sane.
AN OPPOSITE IS abnormal.

north *noun, adjective, adverb*
The parts of a continent or country in the north are the **northern** parts.
To travel towards the north is to travel **northward** or **northwards** or **in a northerly direction**.
A wind from the north is a **northerly** wind.
A person who lives in the north of Britain is a **northerner**.

nose *noun*
1 *Someone punched him on the nose.*
The openings in your nose are **nostrils**.
Words for an animal's nose are **muzzle** or **snout**.
2 *She sat in the nose of a boat looking out for dangerous rocks.* bow, front, prow.

nostalgia *noun*
He felt a nostalgia for the old days.
longing, pining, yearning.

nostalgic *adjective*
He has nostalgic memories of his childhood. emotional, romantic, sentimental, wistful.

nosy *adjective* [*informal*]
  She resented his nosy questions about her private life. inquisitive, interfering, meddlesome, prying.

notable *adjective*
  1 *Many notable writers and artists were present at the ceremony.* celebrated, distinguished, eminent, famous, important, outstanding, prominent, renowned, well known.
  2 *The Prince's visit was a notable event.* memorable, rare, remarkable, uncommon, unusual.
  AN OPPOSITE IS insignificant or ordinary.

note *noun*
  1 *He sent a note thanking her for the present.* communication, letter, message.
  2 *There was a note of anger in her voice.* feeling, quality, sound, tone.

note *verb*
  1 *He noted the car number on a piece of paper.* jot down, make a note of, record, scribble, write down.
  2 *Did you note what he was wearing?* heed, mark, notice, observe, pay attention to, see, take note of.

notebook *noun*
  She jotted down a few ideas in a notebook. diary, exercise book, jotter, writing book.

nothing *noun*
  Four minus four equals nothing. nought, zero.
  In cricket a score of nothing is a ***duck***, in tennis it is ***love***, and in football it is ***nil***.

notice *noun*
  Someone put up a notice about the meeting. advertisement, placard, poster, sign, warning.
  to take notice of something *She took notice of the warning.* heed, pay attention to.

notice *verb*
  1 *Did you notice what he was wearing?* heed, mark, note, observe, pay attention to, see, take note of.
  2 *I noticed a funny smell.* become aware of, detect.

noticeable *adjective*
  1 *There has been a noticeable improvement in the weather.* definite, distinct, measurable, notable, perceptible, significant.
  2 *The power station is noticeable from many miles away.* conspicuous, visible.
  3 *He spoke with a noticeable foreign accent.* audible, obvious, pronounced, unmistakable.
  AN OPPOSITE IS imperceptible.

notion *noun*
  He has some strange notions about life. belief, concept, idea, opinion, theory, thought, view.

notorious *adjective*
  The police finally arrested the notorious criminal. infamous, outrageous, scandalous, shocking, well known, wicked.

nourish *verb*
  Plants are nourished by water drawn up through their roots. feed, strengthen, sustain.

nourishing *adjective*
  The refugees were in need of nourishing food. health-giving, nutritious, sustaining, wholesome.

novel *adjective*
  The designer had a novel approach to fashion. different, fresh, imaginative, innovative, new, original, uncommon, unconventional, unfamiliar, unusual.
  AN OPPOSITE IS familiar.

novel *noun*
  FOR VARIOUS KINDS OF WRITING, SEE **writing**.

now *adverb*
  1 *She is now living in Glasgow.* at present, at the moment, currently.
  2 *The job must be done now.* immediately, straight away, without delay.

nude *adjective*
  Several children swam nude. bare, naked, stripped, undressed.
  AN OPPOSITE IS clothed.

nudge *verb*
  She nudged me with her elbow. bump, jog, jolt, poke, prod, shove, touch.

nuisance *noun*
The dog's constant barking is a real nuisance. annoyance, bother, inconvenience, irritation, menace, pest, worry.

numb *adjective*
My toes are numb with cold. dead, frozen, insensitive, paralysed.
AN OPPOSITE IS sensitive.

number *noun*
1 He added the numbers together to get the answer. figure, numeral.
Any of the numbers from 0 to 9 is a **digit**.
A negative or positive whole number is an **integer**.
An amount used in measuring or counting is a **unit**.
2 A large number of people welcomed the team home. collection, crowd, multitude.
3 He'd lost the current number of the magazine. edition, issue.
4 The band played some well-known numbers. piece, song.

numerous *adjective*
The car had numerous faults. abundant, countless, innumerable, many, plenty of, untold.
AN OPPOSITE IS few.

nurse *verb*
1 He nursed her while she was ill. care for, look after, tend.
2 She nursed the baby in her arms. cradle, cuddle, hold, hug.

nursery *noun*
1 Her little brother starts at a nursery next month. crèche, kindergarten, nursery school.
2 They went to the nursery to buy plants for the garden. garden centre.

nut *noun*

KINDS OF NUT: almond, brazil, cashew, chestnut, cobnut, coconut, filbert or hazelnut, peanut, pecan, pistachio, walnut.

oath *noun*
1 He swore a solemn oath that he was telling the truth. pledge, promise, vow, word of honour.
2 He let out a terrible oath when the door slammed on his finger. blasphemy, curse, exclamation, swear word.

obedient *adjective*
The dog seemed very obedient. disciplined, docile, manageable, submissive, well behaved.
AN OPPOSITE IS disobedient.

obey *verb*
1 The soldiers refused to obey orders. abide by, adhere to, carry out, follow, heed, implement, keep to, observe, submit to.
2 He obeyed without question. be obedient, conform, do what you are told, take orders.
AN OPPOSITE IS disobey.

object *noun*
1 She saw some strange objects in the museum. article, item, thing.
2 What is the object of this exercise? aim, goal, intention, objective, point, purpose.

object *verb*
to object to something He objected to the plan. argue against, be opposed to, complain about, disapprove of, grumble about, mind, protest against, raise questions about, take exception to.
AN OPPOSITE IS accept or agree to.

objection *noun*
Her objections were ignored. complaint, disapproval, opposition, outcry, protest, query, question.

objectionable *adjective*
  The drains were giving off an objectionable smell. disagreeable, disgusting, foul, hateful, intolerable, loathsome, nasty, offensive, repellent, revolting, sickening, undesirable, unpleasant.
  AN OPPOSITE IS acceptable.

objective *adjective*
  1 *There was no objective evidence of his guilt.* actual, real, scientific.
  2 *He gave an objective account of what happened.* disinterested, factual, impartial, rational, unbiased, unemotional, unprejudiced.
  AN OPPOSITE IS subjective.

objective *noun*
  Their objective was to reach the top of the hill. aim, ambition, goal, intention, object, purpose, target.

obligation *noun*
  Everyone has an obligation to pay taxes. commitment, duty, liability, requirement, responsibility.
  AN OPPOSITE IS option.

obligatory *adjective*
  The wearing of seat belts is obligatory. compulsory, necessary, required.
  AN OPPOSITE IS optional.

oblige *verb*
  Would you oblige me by passing the salt? help, please.

obliged *adjective*
  1 *He felt obliged to help them.* bound, compelled, forced, required.
  2 *I'm much obliged to you for your kindness.* appreciative, grateful, indebted, thankful.

oblique *adjective*
  1 *After the earthquake, the floor ended up at an oblique angle.* inclined, slanting, sloping, tilted.
  2 *She made some oblique remarks about his appearance.* indirect, roundabout.

oblong *noun* rectangle.
  FOR OTHER SHAPES, SEE **shape** *noun*.

obscene *adjective*
  We were shocked by her obscene language. coarse, crude, disgusting, filthy, foul, improper, indecent, objectionable, offensive, pornographic, rude, shocking, smutty, vulgar.
  AN OPPOSITE IS decent.

obscure *adjective*
  1 *An obscure figure could be seen in the distance.* blurred, dim, hidden, indistinct, misty, murky, shadowy, unclear, vague.
  AN OPPOSITE IS clear.
  2 *His joke seemed rather obscure.* confusing, incomprehensible, puzzling.
  AN OPPOSITE IS obvious.
  3 *Henry Kirke White is an obscure poet.* forgotten, minor, undistinguished, unheard of, unimportant, unknown.
  AN OPPOSITE IS famous.

obscure *verb*
  Mist obscured the view. block out, conceal, cover, disguise, envelop, hide, mask, screen, shroud.
  AN OPPOSITE IS reveal.

observant *adjective*
  If you're observant, you might see a kingfisher by the river. alert, attentive, perceptive, sharp-eyed, vigilant, watchful.
  AN OPPOSITE IS inattentive.

observation *noun*
  1 *They took him to hospital for observation.* scrutiny, study, watching.
  2 *She made observations about their behaviour.* comment, opinion, remark, statement.

observe *verb*
  1 *Astronomers observed the eclipse last night.* look at, study, view, watch.
  2 *They observed a change in his behaviour.* detect, discern, note, notice, perceive, see, spot, witness.
  3 *It's important to observe the rules.* abide by, adhere to, follow, heed, keep to, obey, respect, submit to.
  4 *She observed that it was a nice day.* comment, declare, mention, remark, say.

obsession *noun*
  Football is his obsession. addiction, mania, passion.

obsolete *adjective*
Computers quickly become obsolete.
antiquated, dated, discarded, disused,
old-fashioned, out of date.
AN OPPOSITE IS current *adjective*.

obstacle *noun*
1 *They drove around the obstacles in
the road.* barricade, barrier,
obstruction.
2 *His age was an obstacle to his career.*
catch, difficulty, hindrance, hurdle,
problem, snag.

obstinate *adjective*
The obstinate donkey would not move.
contrary, defiant, perverse, stubborn,
uncooperative, unreasonable, wilful.
AN OPPOSITE IS cooperative.

obstruct *verb*
1 *The path was obstructed.* block, make
impassable.
2 *The demonstrators obstructed the
traffic for over an hour.* check, curb,
halt, hamper, hinder, hold up, restrict,
slow down, stop.

obtain *verb*
*The police wanted to know where he
had obtained the money.* acquire, come
by, find, get, get hold of, [*informal*] pick
up.
To obtain something by paying for it is
to **buy** or **purchase** it.

obtuse *adjective*
*He was too obtuse to understand her
point.* [*informal*] dense, dull, slow,
stupid, [*informal*] thick, unintelligent.

obvious *adjective*
1 *It was silly to make so many obvious
mistakes.* glaring, noticeable,
pronounced.
2 *The castle is an obvious landmark.*
conspicuous, distinct, notable,
prominent, visible.
AN OPPOSITE IS inconspicuous.
3 *She didn't say much, but what she
was thinking was obvious.* clear,
evident, plain, unconcealed,
undisguised, unmistakable.
AN OPPOSITE IS hidden.

occasion *noun*
1 *They needed to wait for the right
occasion to tell him.* chance, moment,
opportunity, time.
2 *The wedding was a happy occasion.*
affair, celebration, ceremony, event,
happening, incident, occurrence.

occasional *adjective*
*The weather forecaster predicted
occasional showers.* infrequent,
intermittent, irregular, odd, scattered,
unpredictable.
AN OPPOSITE IS frequent or regular.

occupant *noun*
*The present occupants of the house are
moving out shortly.* inhabitant,
occupier, resident, tenant.

occupation *noun*
1 *He's not happy with his present
occupation.* business, employment, job,
post, profession, trade, work.
FOR VARIOUS OCCUPATIONS, SEE **job**.
2 *His favourite occupation is reading.*
activity, hobby, pastime, pursuit.

occupied *adjective*
She's very occupied in her work.
absorbed, busy, engaged, engrossed,
involved.
AN OPPOSITE IS idle.

occupy *verb*
1 *They occupy the house next door.*
dwell in, inhabit, live in, reside in.
2 *She got rid of the piano because it
occupied too much space.* fill, take up,
use up.
3 *Troops occupied the town.* capture,
conquer, invade, take over, take
possession of.

occur *verb*
1 *She told us what had occurred.* arise,
come about, develop, happen, take
place.
2 *The disease only occurs in certain
parts of the world.* crop up, exist, turn
up.

occurrence *noun*
*An eclipse of the sun is an unusual
occurrence.* event, happening, incident,
occasion, phenomenon.

ocean *noun*

> THE GREAT OCEANS OF THE WORLD:
> Antarctic, Arctic, Atlantic, Indian,
> Pacific.

odd *adjective*
1 *Her behaviour seemed very odd.*
abnormal, curious, eccentric, funny,
peculiar, puzzling, queer, strange,
unconventional, unusual, weird.
AN OPPOSITE IS normal.
2 *He could only find a couple of odd
socks.* left over, single, spare.
3 *He does odd jobs to earn money.*
casual, irregular, occasional, various.

oddments *plural noun*
She put the oddments in a box. bits,
bits and pieces, fragments, leftovers,
odds and ends, offcuts, remnants,
scraps.

odour *noun*
*There's a nasty odour coming from the
fridge.*
A nice smell is a **fragrance** or
perfume.
A nasty smell is a **reek**, **stench**, or
stink.

offence *noun*
He was punished for his offence. crime,
fault, outrage, sin, wrongdoing.
In games, an offence is a **foul** or an
infringement.
to give offence SEE **offend**.

offend *verb*
1 *His remarks offended her.* anger,
annoy, disgust, give offence to, hurt
your feelings, insult, upset, vex.
2 *You'll be punished if you offend again.*
break the law, do wrong.

offensive *adjective*
1 *She was shocked by their offensive
language.* abusive, disgusting,
impolite, insulting, nasty, obscene,
revolting, rude, sickening, unpleasant,
vulgar.
AN OPPOSITE IS pleasant.
2 *The police arrested him for carrying
an offensive weapon.* aggressive,
dangerous, threatening, warlike.

offer *verb*
1 *A reward was offered for his capture.*
make available, propose, put forward,
suggest.
2 *He offered to help with the work.*
volunteer.

offer *noun*
*Their offer of help was gratefully
received.* proposal, suggestion.

office *noun*

> PEOPLE WHO WORK IN AN OFFICE:
> cashier, clerk, filing clerk, office boy
> or office girl, receptionist, secretary,
> shorthand typist, telephonist, typist,
> word processor operator.
>
> EQUIPMENT USED IN AN OFFICE:
> answering machine, calculator,
> computer, copier, desk, diary,
> dictating machine, duplicator, fax,
> files, filing cabinet, intercom,
> photocopier, stapler, stationery,
> telephone, typewriter, word
> processor.

officer *noun*
FOR POLICE OFFICERS, SEE **police**.
FOR OFFICERS IN THE ARMED
SERVICES, SEE **rank**.

official *adjective*
It was an official announcement.
approved, authentic, authorized,
formal, genuine, legitimate, proper.
AN OPPOSITE IS unofficial.

official *noun*
*We spoke to an official of the
organization.* officer, organizer, person
in charge, representative.

> OFFICIALS IN A CLUB OR
> ORGANIZATION: chairman or
> chairperson or chairwoman,
> secretary, treasurer.
>
> OFFICIALS AT A SPORTING EVENT:
> assistant referee, linesman,
> marshal, referee, steward, touch
> judge, umpire.

officious *adjective*
*He got annoyed with the officious car
park attendant.* [*informal*] bossy,
interfering, zealous.

often *adverb*
It often rains in April. again and again, constantly, frequently, many times, regularly, repeatedly, time after time.

oil *verb*
He oiled the hinge to stop it squeaking. grease, lubricate.

oily *adjective*
Fried food is too oily for me. fatty, greasy.

ointment *noun*
The nurse gave her some ointment for the rash. cream, lotion.

old *adjective*
1 *She doesn't like growing old.* aged, decrepit, doddery, elderly, [*slang*] past it.
AN OPPOSITE IS young.
2 *The old church was being restored.* ancient, crumbling, decayed, decaying, ruined.
Something that you respect because it is old is **venerable**.
3 *I put on old clothes to do some gardening.* scruffy, shabby, worn, worn out.
AN OPPOSITE IS new.
4 *The car he used to drive was an old model.* antiquated, early, obsolete, old-fashioned, out of date, primitive.
Valuable old cars are **veteran** or **vintage** cars.
Other things which are valuable because they are old are **antique**.
AN OPPOSITE IS up to date.
5 *She wondered what life was like in the old days.* earlier, former, past, previous, remote.
Times before written records were kept are **prehistoric** times.
The ancient Greeks and Romans lived in **classical** times.
The Middle Ages are **medieval** times.
AN OPPOSITE IS modern.

old-fashioned *adjective*
He has some rather old-fashioned ideas. obsolete, out of date, traditional, unfashionable.
AN OPPOSITE IS modern or stylish.

omen *noun*
They hoped that the storm was not an omen of disaster. indication, sign, warning.

ominous *adjective*
The rumble of thunder was an ominous sign of a coming storm. forbidding, grim, menacing, sinister, threatening, unlucky.

omission *noun*
There are some surprising omissions from the list. exclusion, gap, oversight.

omit *verb*
1 *His article was omitted from the magazine.* cut, eliminate, exclude, leave out, miss out, overlook, pass over, skip.
2 *Don't omit to turn off the lights.* fail, forget, neglect.

one-sided *adjective*
The driver gave a very one-sided account of the accident. biased, prejudiced, unfair.

onlooker *noun*
The onlookers did nothing to stop the fight. bystander, eyewitness, observer, spectator, witness.

ooze *verb*
Oil was oozing out of the damaged tank. dribble, leak, seep.

opaque *adjective*
The dirt had turned the window opaque. cloudy, dull, hazy, muddy, murky, obscure, unclear.
AN OPPOSITE IS transparent.

open *adjective*
1 *The puppy escaped through the open door.* ajar, gaping, unfastened, unlocked, wide open.
AN OPPOSITE IS closed.
2 *There aren't many open spaces where children can play.* accessible, clear, empty, extensive, public, uncrowded, unrestricted.
AN OPPOSITE IS enclosed.
3 *He was open about what he had done wrong.* communicative, frank, honest, outspoken, sincere, straightforward.
AN OPPOSITE IS deceitful.

4 *The captain faced open rebellion from the crew.* obvious, plain, unconcealed, undisguised.
AN OPPOSITE IS concealed.
5 *It's an open question as to whether they'll win the next election.* arguable, debatable, unanswered, undecided, unfinished, unresolved.

open *verb*
1 *Please open the door.* unbolt, unfasten, unlock.
To open a locked door is to **unbolt**, **unfasten**, or **unlock** it.
To open an umbrella is to **unfurl** it.
To open a wine bottle is to **uncork** it.
To open a map is to **unfold** or **unroll** it.
To open a parcel is to **undo** or **unwrap** it.
2 *The jumble sale opens at 2 p.m.* begin, commence, [*informal*] get going, start.
3 *A new rail service has just been opened.* initiate, launch, set up.
AN OPPOSITE IS close.

opening *noun*
1 *The animals got out through an opening in the fence.* breach, break, gap, hole, split.
2 *We enjoyed the opening of the concert.* beginning, commencement, start.
3 *I attended the opening of the new sports centre.* initiation, launch.
4 *The job offers a good opening for a keen young person.* chance, opportunity.

open-minded *adjective*
She has an open-minded attitude to new ideas. fair, impartial, neutral, objective, unbiased, unprejudiced.
AN OPPOSITE IS biased.

operate *verb*
1 *This watch operates even under water.* function, go, perform, work.
2 *Do you know how to operate this machine?* deal with, drive, handle, manage, use, work.
3 *The surgeon operated to remove her appendix.* carry out an operation, perform surgery.

operation *noun*
1 *Her main concern was the safe operation of the machines.* functioning, performance, working.

2 *He had an operation to remove his appendix.* surgery.
3 *Tracking down those ruthless criminals was a dangerous operation.* action, activity, enterprise, exercise, manoeuvre, process, project, task.

opinion *noun*
He was asked for his honest opinion. attitude, belief, comment, conclusion, feeling, idea, impression, judgement, notion, point of view, theory, thought, view.

opponent *noun*
He fought fiercely against his opponent. adversary, challenger, enemy, foe, rival.
Your opponents in a game are the **opposition**.
AN OPPOSITE IS ally.

opportunity *noun*
1 *There were few opportunities to relax.* chance, moment, occasion, time.
2 *The job offers a good opportunity for a keen young person.* [*informal*] break, opening.

oppose *verb*
Many people opposed the building of the new road. argue against, attack, be against, be hostile towards, disapprove of, fight against, [*informal*] make a stand against, resist.

opposite *adjective*
1 *They have opposite views about politics.* conflicting, contradictory, contrary, contrasting, different, incompatible, opposed, opposing.
AN OPPOSITE IS similar.
2 *She lives on the opposite side of the road.* facing.

opposite *noun*
She says one thing and does the opposite. contrary, converse, reverse.

opposition *noun*
1 *She hadn't expected so much opposition to her idea.* disapproval, hostility, resistance, scepticism, unfriendliness.
AN OPPOSITE IS support.
2 *The opposition were stronger than they expected.* opponents, rivals.

oppress *verb*
1 *The people were oppressed by the military government.* abuse, crush, exploit, misuse, persecute.
2 *The atmosphere in the room oppressed them.* concern, grieve, sadden, trouble, upset, weigh down, worry.

oppressive *adjective*
1 *The oppressive ruler made the people's lives miserable.* brutal, cruel, harsh, repressive, severe, tyrannical, unjust.
2 *This weather feels very oppressive.* airless, close, heavy, hot, humid, muggy, stifling, stuffy.

optical *adjective*

VARIOUS OPTICAL INSTRUMENTS: bifocals, binoculars, field glasses, glasses, lens, magnifier, magnifying glass, microscope, opera glasses, periscope, spectacles, sunglasses, telescope.

optimistic *adjective*
She's optimistic about her chances of success. buoyant, cheerful, confident, expectant, hopeful, positive.
AN OPPOSITE IS pessimistic.

option *noun*
He had the option of staying or leaving. alternative, choice, possibility.

optional *adjective*
Everyone has to pay for the basic holiday, but the excursions are optional extras. possible, voluntary.
AN OPPOSITE IS compulsory.

oral *adjective*
He gave an oral report of what happened. spoken, verbal.
AN OPPOSITE IS written.

orbit *verb*
The earth orbits the sun in about 365 days. circle, travel round.

ordeal *noun*
He went through a horrific ordeal. difficulty, experience, [*informal*] nightmare, suffering, test, torture.

order *noun*
1 *The captain gave the order to abandon ship.* command, instruction.
2 *She gave the newsagent an order for the new magazine.* application, demand, request, reservation.
3 *The army restored order after the riot.* calm, control, discipline, good behaviour, law and order, obedience, organization, peace.
4 *They put the library books in alphabetical order.* arrangement, sequence, series, succession.
5 *She keeps her bike in good order.* condition, state.

order *verb*
1 *She ordered them to be quiet.* command, instruct, require, tell.
2 *He ordered the new magazine.* apply for, book, request, reserve.

orderly *adjective*
1 *Her work was always very orderly.* careful, methodical, neat, organized, systematic, tidy, well arranged, well organized.
AN OPPOSITE IS untidy.
2 *The police expect orderly behaviour at the demonstration.* law-abiding, obedient, peaceful, restrained, well behaved, well disciplined.
AN OPPOSITE IS disorderly.

ordinary *adjective*
1 *It was just an ordinary sort of day.* customary, everyday, familiar, habitual, normal, regular, routine, standard, typical, usual.
2 *She's just an ordinary sort of person.* average, common, conventional, humble, modest, plain, simple, undistinguished, unexceptional, unexciting.
3 *It was a very ordinary game.* indifferent, mediocre, unimpressive, uninteresting.
AN OPPOSITE IS special or unusual.

organic *adjective*
Some farmers are going back to using organic fertilizers instead of chemical ones. biological, living, natural.

organism *noun*
Evolution has produced millions of different organisms. creature, living thing.

organization noun
1 *She works for a charitable organization.* institution, [*informal*] set-up.

BUSINESS ORGANIZATIONS: business, company, corporation, firm.

ORGANIZATIONS FOR LEISURE, SPORT, ETC.: association, club, league, society.

POLITICAL ORGANIZATIONS: confederation, federation, party, union.

2 *Who was responsible for the organization of the conference?* arrangement, coordination, organizing, planning, running.

organize verb
1 *It took her ages to organize the car-boot sale.* coordinate, make arrangements for, plan, run, see to, set up.
2 *The librarian has to organize the books in the library.* arrange, classify, put in order, sort out, tidy up.

organized adjective
It was an organized fire drill. methodical, orderly, planned, systematic, well run.
AN OPPOSITE IS chaotic.

origin noun
1 *We know very little about the origin of life on earth.* beginning, birth, cause, creation, source, start.
AN OPPOSITE IS end *noun*.
2 *He became very rich, despite his humble origins.* ancestry, background, descent, family, parentage, pedigree, stock.

original adjective
1 *The settlers drove out the original inhabitants.* aboriginal, earliest, first, initial, native.
2 *The story was very original.* creative, fresh, imaginative, inspired, inventive, new, novel, unconventional, unfamiliar, unusual.
3 *Is that an original work of art or a copy?* authentic, genuine, real, unique.

originate verb
1 *Where did the idea originate?* begin, commence, crop up, emerge, start.
2 *They originated a new style of dancing.* be the inventor of, conceive, create, design, give birth to, introduce, invent, launch.

ornament noun
A few ornaments will make the place more attractive. adornment, decoration.

ornamental adjective
He bought an ornamental glass vase. attractive, decorative, pretty.

orthodox adjective
He disagreed with her orthodox views about religion. accepted, approved, conventional, customary, established, normal, official, ordinary, regular, standard, traditional, usual, well established.
AN OPPOSITE IS unconventional.

outbreak noun
1 *Everyone feared an outbreak of disease.* epidemic, plague.
2 *The armies prepared for the outbreak of war.* beginning, commencement, start.

outburst noun
There was an outburst of laughter from the next room. eruption, explosion, storm.

outcome noun
What was the outcome of the meeting? consequence, effect, result, upshot.

outcry noun
There was an outcry over the closure of the hospital. fuss, protest, uproar.

outdoor adjective
The hotel had an outdoor swimming pool. open-air, out of doors, outside.

outer adjective
He was wearing a thick jumper and waterproof outer garments. exterior, external, outside.
AN OPPOSITE IS inner.

outfit *noun*
1 *She bought a new outfit for the wedding.* costume, suit.
2 *The puncture repair outfit is in the boot.* equipment, gear, paraphernalia.

outing *noun*
They've gone on their annual outing to London. excursion, expedition, jaunt, picnic, trip.

outlaw *noun*
A band of outlaws held up the train. bandit, brigand, criminal, fugitive, outcast, robber.

outlet *noun*
If you instal a fire, you must provide an outlet for the fumes. channel, mouth, opening, way out.

outline *noun*
1 *She could see the outline of the house in the dim light.* form, profile, shadow, shape, silhouette.
2 *He gave us a brief outline of his plan.* framework, précis, rough idea, summary.

outline *verb*
He outlined his plan. describe, summarize.

outlook *noun*
1 *The house has a pleasant outlook over the valley.* prospect, scene, sight, view.
2 *He has a rather gloomy outlook on life.* attitude, frame of mind, point of view, view.
3 *The outlook for the weekend is bright and sunny.* expectations, forecast, prediction.

outlying *adjective*
Children from the outlying areas came to school by bus. distant, far, outer, remote.

outrage *noun*
1 *There was public outrage at the government's decision.* anger, disgust, fury, horror, indignation, resentment, revulsion, sense of shock.
2 *The area has been the scene of some of the worst terrorist outrages.* atrocity, crime, disgrace, scandal.

outrageous *adjective*
1 *His behaviour was outrageous.* atrocious, disgraceful, disgusting, offensive, scandalous, shocking.
2 *They charge outrageous prices at that shop.* excessive, unreasonable.
AN OPPOSITE IS acceptable or reasonable.

outside *adjective*
Emulsion paint is not for outside use. exterior, external, outer.

outside *noun*
We looked at the outside of a house, but we couldn't get in. exterior, shell, surface.
AN OPPOSITE IS inside.

outsider *noun*
She's lived there for years, but local people still treat her as an outsider. alien, foreigner, immigrant, newcomer, stranger, visitor.

outskirts *plural noun*
We live on the outskirts of town. edge, fringe, outer areas.
The outskirts of a big town are the **suburbs**.
AN OPPOSITE IS centre.

outspoken *adjective*
He's always been an outspoken critic of the government. blunt, frank, honest, plain, straightforward.
AN OPPOSITE IS tactful.

outstanding *adjective*
1 *She will be an outstanding tennis player in a few years.* celebrated, conspicuous, distinguished, eminent, excellent, exceptional, extraordinary, great, impressive, notable, prominent, remarkable, superlative, well known.
AN OPPOSITE IS ordinary.
2 *There are still some outstanding bills to pay.* overdue, owing, unpaid.

outward *adjective*
Outward appearances can be deceptive. exterior, external, outer, outside, superficial, surface, visible.

outwit *verb*
The fox succeeded in outwitting the hounds. baffle, cheat, deceive, fool, trick.

oval *adjective*
The cake was on an oval plate. egg-shaped, elliptical.

oven *noun*
The meat was roasting in the oven. cooker, stove.
A special oven for firing pottery, etc., is a *kiln*.

overcast *adjective*
It's a bit overcast—it might rain. black, cloudy, dark, dismal, dull, gloomy, grey, leaden, stormy, threatening.

overcome *verb*
1 He's finally managed to overcome his fear of flying. conquer, cope with, deal with, defeat, sort out.
2 She was overcome by the fumes. get the better of, make helpless, overpower, overwhelm.

overflow *verb*
The river had overflowed its banks. flood, pour over, spill over.

overgrown *adjective*
The back garden was completely overgrown. tangled, untidy, unweeded, weedy, wild.

overhang *verb*
Part of the cliff overhangs the beach. jut over, project over, protrude over, stick out over.

overhaul *verb*
1 The boiler was recently overhauled. check over, examine, inspect, put right, repair, restore, service.
2 The express overhauled a goods train. leave behind, overtake, pass.

overhead *adverb*
A seagull flew overhead. above, high up, in the sky.

overlook *verb*
1 He seems to have overlooked one important fact. fail to see, miss.
2 She's always willing to overlook his faults. disregard, excuse, forget about, ignore, pardon, pay no attention to, [informal] turn a blind eye to.
3 The chateau overlooked fields of corn and olive trees. face, have a view of, look on to.

overpower *verb*
It took three police officers to overpower him. beat, conquer, defeat, get the better of, overcome, subdue.

overpowering *adjective*
I felt an overpowering need to sneeze. compelling, irresistible, overwhelming, powerful, strong, uncontrollable.

overrun *verb*
The barn was overrun with rats and mice. invade, take over.

oversight *noun*
The mix-up was due to an oversight on the part of the travel agent. carelessness, an error, a mistake, an omission.

overtake *verb*
We overtook the car in front. leave behind, overhaul, pass.

overthrow *verb*
The rebels overthrew the President. beat, conquer, defeat, [informal] throw out, topple.

overturn *verb*
1 The boat overturned. capsize, tip over, turn over, turn turtle.
2 She leapt to her feet, overturning her chair. knock over, spill, tip over, topple, upset.

overwhelm *verb*
1 The troops were overwhelmed by superior enemy forces. beat decisively, crush, defeat, overcome, overpower.
2 A tidal wave overwhelmed the village. bury, devastate, engulf, flood, inundate, submerge, swallow up.

overwhelming *adjective*
He was elected by an overwhelming majority. crushing, decisive, devastating, great.
An overwhelming victory at an election is a *landslide*.

owe *verb*
If you owe money to someone, you are *in debt*.

owing *adjective*
> There is still £50 owing. due,
> outstanding, overdue, owed, unpaid.
> **owing to** *Owing to the rain, the match
> is cancelled.* as a result of, because of,
> on account of, thanks to.

own *verb*
> It was the first car she'd owned. be the
> owner of, possess.
> **to own up** *No one owned up to
> breaking the window.* admit your guilt,
> confess.

Pp

pace *noun*
> 1 *Move forward two paces.* step, stride.
> 2 *The front runner set a fast pace.* rate,
> speed.
> A formal word is **velocity**.

pacify *verb*
> She was furious at first, but he
> managed to pacify her eventually.
> appease, calm, humour, quieten,
> soothe.
> AN OPPOSITE IS anger or annoy.

pack *noun*
> 1 *There were four candles in each pack.*
> bale, bundle, package, packet.
> 2 *The hikers picked up their packs and
> trudged off.* haversack, knapsack,
> rucksack.

pack *verb*
> 1 *She packed her suitcase and called a
> taxi.* fill, load up.
> 2 *I forgot to pack my hairdryer.* stow
> away, wrap up.
> 3 *They packed as many passengers as
> possible onto the train.* cram, crowd,
> jam, squeeze, stuff, wedge.

package *noun*
> The postman delivered a package.
> bundle, packet, parcel.

pad *noun*
> 1 *She put a pad of cotton wool over the
> wound.* wad.
> A pad to make a chair or bed
> comfortable is a **cushion** or **pillow**.
> A pad to kneel on in church is a
> **hassock** or **kneeler**.
> 2 *There's a pad for messages next to the
> phone.* jotter, notebook, writing pad.

pad *verb*
> The seats are padded with foam rubber.
> fill, pack, stuff.
> To put covers and padding on furniture
> is to **upholster** it.

padding *noun*
> The padding is coming out of this
> armchair. filling, stuffing.
> The covers and padding on furniture is
> **upholstery**.

paddle *verb*
> 1 *The children paddled at the water's
> edge.* dabble, splash about.
> To walk through deep water is to
> **wade**.
> 2 *He paddled his canoe along the canal.*
> To move a boat along with two oars is
> to **row** it.

paddock *noun*
> The horses were kept in a paddock
> behind the farm. enclosure.
> Other grassy areas are **field**, **meadow**,
> or **pasture**.

page *noun*
> 1 *Several pages have been torn out of
> this book.* leaf, sheet.
> 2 *He wrote two pages of notes.* side.
> 3 *[old use] The king summoned his
> page.* attendant, boy, servant.

pageant *noun*
> A pageant was put on to mark the
> centenary of the event. display,
> entertainment, parade, procession,
> spectacle.

pageantry *noun*
> He was greeted with all the pageantry
> of an official state visit. ceremony,
> display, grandeur, magnificence, pomp,
> show, spectacle, splendour.

pail noun
He used a pail of water to put out the fire. bucket.
FOR OTHER CONTAINERS, SEE **container**.

pain noun
Her back has been causing her a lot of pain. anguish, suffering.

A dull pain is an **ache** or **soreness**.
Severe pain is **agony**, **torment**, or **torture**.
A slight pain is **discomfort**.
A slight pain which doesn't last long is a **twinge**.
A sudden pain is a **pang** or **stab**.
Pain in your head is a **headache**.
Pain in your tooth is **toothache**.
The pains a woman feels when giving birth are **contractions** or **labour pains**.
To cause pain or to feel pain is to **hurt**.

painful adjective
1 My shoulder's still really painful. aching, agonizing, hurting, inflamed, raw, smarting, stinging, sore, tender, throbbing.
2 The conversation brought back many painful memories. distressing, nasty, unpleasant, upsetting.
AN OPPOSITE IS painless.

painless adjective
1 The treatment is quite painless. comfortable, pain free.
2 This is a quick and painless way to learn a foreign language. easy, effortless, simple, trouble free.
AN OPPOSITE IS painful.

painstaking adjective
The discovery is the result of ten years' painstaking research. careful, conscientious, methodical, meticulous, systematic, thorough.
AN OPPOSITE IS careless.

paint noun

KINDS OF PAINT: distemper, emulsion, enamel, lacquer, oil colour, oil paint, pastel, primer, stain, tempera, undercoat, varnish, ➡

water colour, whitewash.
A layer of paint is a **coat** of paint.
Paint which stays shiny when it dries is **gloss** paint.
Paint which goes dull when it dries is **matt** paint.

paint verb
1 The walls were painted yellow. colour, decorate.
2 He painted the view from his bedroom window. depict, portray, represent.

painter noun
A person who paints houses, etc., is a **decorator**.
A person who paints pictures is an **artist**.

painting noun SEE **picture** noun

pair noun
A pair of people who go out together are a **couple**.
Two people who sing or play music together are a **duet**.
Two people who work together are **partners** or a **partnership**.
Two babies born together are **twins**.

palace noun
The palace was open to the public at weekends. castle, mansion, stately home.

pale adjective
1 His illness made him look pale. pallid, pasty, unhealthy, white.
If you suffer from a poor condition of the blood which makes you pale, you are **anaemic**.
AN OPPOSITE IS ruddy.
2 I don't like pale colours. bleached, dim, faded, faint, light.
Pale colours which you use deliberately to get a soft effect are **pastel** colours.
AN OPPOSITE IS bright.

pamper verb
He's been pampered by his parents ever since he was a baby. humour, indulge, spoil.

pamphlet noun
We were given a pamphlet about road safety. booklet, brochure, leaflet.

pan *noun*
>FOR UTENSILS USED IN COOKING, SEE
>**cook** *verb*.

pandemonium *noun*
>*Pandemonium broke out when the*
>*results were announced.* bedlam, chaos,
>confusion, din, disorder, excitement,
>fuss, hullabaloo, racket, row, tumult,
>turbulence, turmoil, upheaval, uproar.

pane *noun*
>*There was a small crack in the pane of*
>*glass.* sheet of glass, window.

panel *noun*
>*A panel of experts was consulted.* group,
>team.

panic *noun*
>*People fled the streets in panic.* alarm,
>hysteria.

panic *verb*
>*If a fire starts, don't panic!* become
>hysterical, [*informal*] lose your head,
>stampede.

panicky *adjective*
>*The animals became panicky during*
>*the thunderstorm.* alarmed, frantic,
>frightened, hysterical, overexcited.
>AN OPPOSITE IS calm.

panorama *noun*
>*A beautiful panorama of lakes and*
>*mountains spread out in front of them.*
>landscape, perspective, prospect,
>scene, view.

pant *verb*
>*He was panting by the time he reached*
>*the top.* breathe quickly, gasp, puff.

pants *plural noun*
>FOR UNDERCLOTHES, SEE
>**underclothes**.

paper *noun*
>**1** *She sat at the desk with pen and*
>*paper ready.*

>VARIOUS KINDS OF MATERIAL FOR
>WRITING OR DRAWING ON: card,
>cardboard, cartridge paper, manila,
>notepaper, postcard, stationery,
>tracing paper, writing paper.
>A piece of paper is a *leaf* or a
>*sheet*. ➡

>EARLY MATERIALS FOR WRITING ON
>WERE: papyrus, parchment, vellum.

>OTHER KINDS OF PAPER: tissue
>paper, toilet paper, wallpaper,
>wrapping paper.

>**2** *There were some important papers in*
>*his briefcase.*

>PAPERS WHICH MAY BE IMPORTANT:
>accounts, certificates, deeds,
>documents, forms, licences, receipts,
>records.

>**3** *The story made the front page of the*
>*local paper.* newspaper.

parade *noun*
>*The crowd cheered as the parade*
>*passed along the street.* display,
>procession, show.
>A parade of people on horseback is a
>***cavalcade***.
>A parade of soldiers is a ***march past***.

parade *verb*
>*The demonstrators paraded through*
>*the city.* assemble, file past, line up,
>make a procession, march past.

paradoxical *adjective*
>*It seems paradoxical to make weapons*
>*in order to keep peace.* absurd,
>contradictory, illogical.

parallel *noun*
>*There is a parallel between their*
>*situations.* analogy, comparison,
>likeness, match, resemblance,
>similarity.

paralyse *verb*
>*The shock paralysed him.* cripple,
>deaden, immobilize.

paraphernalia *noun*
>*The hall was full of the builder's*
>*paraphernalia.* baggage, belongings,
>equipment, gear, odds and ends, stuff,
>tackle, things.

paraphrase *verb*
>*He paraphrased the story to make it*
>*easier to understand.* interpret,
>translate.

parcel *noun*
>*The postman delivered a parcel.*
>package, packet.

parched *adjective*
1 *Nothing was growing in the parched earth.* arid, baked, barren, dry, scorched, sterile, waterless.
2 *I'm parched!* thirsty.

pardon *verb*
Hundreds of political prisoners were pardoned and released. excuse, forgive, free, let off, release, set free, spare.
To pardon someone who is condemned to death is to **reprieve** them.

pardon *noun*
She knew she had done wrong, but she hoped for pardon. forgiveness, mercy.
A pardon for someone who is condemned to death is a **reprieve**.
A general pardon for a whole group of people is an **amnesty**.

pardonable *adjective*
It was a pardonable mistake. excusable, forgivable, minor, negligible, understandable.
AN OPPOSITE IS unforgivable.

parent *noun*
FOR FAMILY RELATIONSHIPS, SEE **family**.

park *noun*

DIFFERENT KINDS OF PARK:
amusement park, arboretum, botanical gardens, forest park, nature reserve, public gardens, recreation ground, safari park, theme park.
A park with fields and trees around a big house is an **estate** or **parkland**.

park *verb*
He parked her car outside her house. leave, place, position, station.

parliament *noun*
The British parliament consists of the **House of Commons** and the **House of Lords**.
FOR RELATED WORDS, SEE **government**.

parody *noun*
The film was a parody of a horror story. An informal synonym is **send-up**.
A piece of writing which uses humour to make us think about how silly someone or something is, is a **satire**.
A description which exaggerates amusing things about a person is a **caricature**.

parson *noun* SEE **clergyman**

part *noun*
1 *All the parts of the engine are now working properly.* bit, component, constituent.
2 *I only saw the first part of the programme.* element, piece, portion, section.
3 *Which part of this organization deals with complaints?* branch, department, division.
4 *Granny lives in another part of the town.* area, district, neighbourhood, region, sector.
5 *He's just right to act the part of Romeo.* character, role.

part *verb*
1 *It was the first time she'd been parted from her parents.* divide, remove, separate.
AN OPPOSITE IS join.
2 *They exchanged a final kiss before they parted.* depart, go away, leave, say goodbye, split up.
AN OPPOSITE IS meet.

partial *adjective*
The play was only a partial success. imperfect, incomplete, limited.
AN OPPOSITE IS complete.
to be partial to *He's partial to a hot drink at bedtime.* appreciate, be fond of, be keen on, enjoy, like.

participate *verb*
She participates actively in local politics. be involved, cooperate, help, join in, share, take part.

particle *noun*
The camera lens was covered with particles of dust. bit, fragment, grain, piece, scrap, shred, sliver, speck.
In science, particles of matter include **atoms**, **neutrons**, and **protons**.

particular *adjective*
  1 *He usually agreed with her, but in this particular case he thought she was wrong.* distinct, individual, unique.
  2 *She took particular care not to damage the parcel.* exceptional, notable, outstanding, special, unusual.
  3 *The cat's very particular about his food.* choosy, finicky, fussy, hard to please.

particulars *plural noun*
  The police officer took down all the particulars. circumstances, details, facts, information.

parting *noun*
  Parting from him was very difficult. departure, going away, leaving, saying goodbye, separation, splitting up.
  AN OPPOSITE IS meeting.

partition *noun*
  A partition separates the two classrooms. room divider, screen.

partly *adverb*
  It was partly my fault. in part, to some extent, up to a point.
  AN OPPOSITE IS entirely.

partner *noun*
  He's a good friend, as well as my business partner. ally, associate, colleague.
  In marriage, your partner is your **spouse** or your **husband** or **wife**.
  An animal's partner is its **mate**.

party *noun*
  1 *They had a party at the end of term.* celebration, festivity, function, [*informal*] get-together.

VARIOUS KINDS OF PARTY: ball, banquet, barbecue, birthday party, ceilidh, Christmas party, dance, disco, feast, house-warming, picnic, reception, reunion, tea party, wedding.

  2 *A party of tourists was going round the museum.* band, crowd, group.
  3 *They support different political parties.* alliance, association, league.

pass *verb*
  1 *We watched the procession pass.* go by, move past.
  2 *She tried to pass the car in front.* overhaul, overtake.
  3 *We passed over the bridge.* advance, go, proceed, progress.
  4 *Could you pass me the vegetables, please?* deliver, give, hand over, offer, present.
  5 *Do you think you will pass your music exam?* be successful in, get through, succeed in.
  6 *How did you pass the time on holiday?* occupy, spend, use.
  7 *The pain will soon pass.* disappear, fade, go away, vanish.
  8 *Parliament has passed a new law against computer hacking.* approve, confirm, decree, establish.

pass *noun*
  1 *He has a pass which allows him to fish in the lake.* licence, permit, ticket.
  2 *The horses filed through a pass between the hills.* canyon, gap, gorge, ravine, valley.

passable *adjective*
  1 *She has a passable knowledge of German.* acceptable, adequate, fair, satisfactory, tolerable.
  AN OPPOSITE IS unacceptable.
  2 *The flooded road is passable again.* clear, open, unblocked, usable.
  AN OPPOSITE IS impassable.

passage *noun*
  1 *They discovered a secret passage.* corridor, passageway, tunnel.
  2 *The police forced a passage through the crowd.* path, route, way.
  3 *A sea passage takes longer than going by air.* crossing, journey, voyage.
  4 *She asked them to choose a favourite passage from a book.* episode, excerpt, extract, piece, quotation, section.
  5 *He hadn't changed, despite the passage of time.* advance, passing, progress.

passenger *noun*
  The bus has seats for 55 passengers. traveller.
  Passengers who travel regularly to work are **commuters**.

passer-by *noun*
The policeman asked if any passer-by had witnessed the accident. bystander, onlooker, witness.

passion *noun*
1 *'Romeo and Juliet' is a story of youthful passion.* emotion, love.
2 *She has a passion for adventure.* appetite, craving, desire, eagerness, enthusiasm, obsession, thirst, urge, zest.

passionate *adjective*
1 *It was a passionate speech.* emotional, intense, strong.
AN OPPOSITE IS unemotional.
2 *He is a passionate follower of football.* avid, enthusiastic, fervent, zealous.
AN OPPOSITE IS apathetic.

passive *adjective*
Instead of fighting back, the demonstrators remained passive. docile, inactive, patient, resigned, submissive, unresisting.
AN OPPOSITE IS active.

past *noun*
In the past, things were different. days gone by, old days, olden days, past times.
The study of what happened in the past is *history*.
The things and ideas that have come down to us from the past are our *heritage*.
AN OPPOSITE IS future.

past *adjective*
Things were very different in past centuries. earlier, former, old, previous.
AN OPPOSITE IS future.

pasta *noun*

SOME KINDS OF PASTA: cannelloni, lasagne, macaroni, noodles, ravioli, spaghetti, tagliatelle, vermicelli.

paste *noun*
She used some paste to stick pictures into the album. adhesive, glue, gum.

pastime *noun*
What's your favourite pastime? activity, amusement, diversion, entertainment, game, hobby, occupation, recreation, relaxation, sport.
SEE ALSO **game, sport.**

pasture *noun*
Cattle were grazing on the pasture. field, grassland, meadow.

pasty *adjective*
He has a pasty complexion. pallid, pale, unhealthy, white.

pat *verb*
He patted her on the head. tap, touch.
To hit someone hard with an open hand is to *slap* them.
To stroke someone with an open hand is to *caress* them.
To touch something gently with something soft is to *dab* it.

patch *verb*
I need to patch my jeans. mend, repair.
Another way to mend holes in clothes is to *darn* them or *stitch* them up.

patchy *adjective*
The weather forecast warned of patchy outbreaks of rain. inconsistent, irregular, uneven, unpredictable, varying.
AN OPPOSITE IS uniform.

path *noun*

VARIOUS KINDS OF PATH: bridle path or bridleway, cart track, footpath, footway, pathway, pavement or [*American*] sidewalk, track, trail, walk, walkway.
A path above a beach is an *esplanade* or *promenade*.
A path along a canal is a *towpath*.
A path between buildings is an *alley*.
SEE ALSO **road.**

pathetic *adjective*
1 *The refugees were a pathetic sight.* distressing, heartbreaking, moving, pitiful, sad, touching, tragic.
2 *The goalkeeper made a pathetic attempt to stop the ball.* inadequate, incompetent, laughable, useless, weak.

patience *noun*
> *She waited with great patience for an hour.* calmness, endurance, perseverance, persistence, resignation, restraint, self-control, tolerance.
> AN OPPOSITE IS impatience.

patient *adjective*
> **1** *She was very patient with the children.* calm, docile, easygoing, even-tempered, mild, philosophical, quiet, resigned, serene, tolerant, uncomplaining.
> **2** *After hours of patient effort, the job was finished.* determined, persevering, persistent, steady, unhurried, untiring.
> AN OPPOSITE IS impatient.

patrol *verb*
> *Police patrolled the area all night.* guard, keep watch over, tour.

> VARIOUS PEOPLE WHO PATROL:
> guard, lookout, nightwatchman, policeman, policewoman, scout, security officer, sentinel, sentry, watchman.

patron *noun*
> *The theatre asked local business people to be patrons.* backer, benefactor, sponsor, subscriber, supporter.

patter *verb*
> FOR VARIOUS SOUNDS, SEE **sound**.

pattern *noun*
> **1** *Do you like the pattern on this wallpaper?* decoration, design.
> **2** *She used a pattern when she was making the skirt.* example, guide, model, specimen, standard.

pause *noun*
> *There was a pause while they got their breath back.* break, gap, halt, lull, rest, stop, wait.
> A pause in the middle of a performance is an **interlude** or **interval**.
> A pause in the middle of a cinema film is an **intermission**.
> A pause caused by something unexpected is an **interruption** or **stoppage**.

pause *verb*
> **1** *She paused uncertainly, not sure what she should do.* hang back, hesitate, wait.
> **2** *They paused to let the others catch up.* break off, halt, rest, stop, take a break.

pave *verb*

> MATERIALS USED TO PAVE PATHS, ETC.: asphalt, cobbles, concrete, crazy paving, flagstones, paving stones, setts, tiles.

paw *noun*
> *The cat left prints of her paws in the wet concrete.* foot.
> A horse's foot is a **hoof**.
> A pig's feet are its **trotters**.
> A bird's feet are its **claws**.

pay *verb*
> **1** *She paid a lot for her new car.* [*informal*] fork out, give, hand over, spend.
> **2** *He always pays his debts.* clear, pay off, refund, repay, settle.
> **3** *They paid for all the damage they caused.* compensate, pay back.
> **4** *Do you think the new business is likely to pay?* be profitable.
> **5** *I'll make you pay for this!* suffer.

payment *noun*

> PAYMENTS WHICH YOU MAKE TO OTHER PEOPLE:
> The total of all the payments you make is your **expenditure**.
> Payment made by a man or woman to a divorced wife or husband is **alimony**.
> A payment to make up for some wrong that you have done is **compensation**.
> A voluntary payment to a charity is a **contribution** or **donation**.
> A first payment of part of the price of something is a **deposit**.
> The payment you make to travel on public transport is the **fare**.
> A payment you have to make as a punishment is a **fine**.
> A payment for an insurance policy is a **premium**.
> A payment made to free a hostage or prisoner is a **ransom**. ➡

A payment you make which shows that you appreciate something someone has done is a **reward**.
A payment to join a club is a **subscription**.
If you have to make an extra payment on top of the normal price, it is a **supplement** or **surcharge**.
A payment to use a private road or bridge is a **toll**.
A voluntary payment to a waiter, etc., is a **tip**.

PAYMENTS WHICH OTHER PEOPLE MAKE TO YOU:
Payments you get for work you have done are your **pay**, **salary**, or **wages**.
A payment you get for doing a single job is a **fee**.
Regular payments you get when you have retired from work are your **pension**.
Payment that you receive regularly from parents is **pocket money**.
A payment you get if you paid too much for something is a **refund**.

peace noun
1 *After the war there was a period of peace.* agreement, friendliness, harmony.
2 *She enjoys the peace of the countryside.* calmness, peacefulness, quiet, serenity, silence, stillness, tranquillity.

peaceful adjective
They enjoyed a peaceful day fishing. calm, gentle, placid, pleasant, quiet, relaxing, restful, serene, soothing, still, tranquil, undisturbed, untroubled.
AN OPPOSITE IS noisy or troubled.

peak noun
1 *The peak of the mountain was covered in snow.* cap, summit, tip, top.
2 *At the peak of the storm I thought the house would be blown away!* climax, crisis, culmination, height, highest point.

peal verb
The bells pealed to celebrate the wedding. chime, ring.
If a bell rings slowly at a funeral, etc., it **tolls**.

pebble noun
A quantity of pebbles on a beach is **shingle**.
Round stones like large pebbles are **cobbles**.

peculiar adjective
1 *What's that peculiar smell?* abnormal, curious, extraordinary, funny, out of the ordinary, queer, strange, unusual.
AN OPPOSITE IS ordinary.
2 *He seemed a bit peculiar.* eccentric, odd, suspicious, weird.
3 *He recognized her peculiar way of writing.* characteristic, different, distinctive, identifiable, individual, particular, personal, special, unique.

peculiarity noun
Did you notice any peculiarity which would help us identify the man? abnormality, characteristic, eccentricity, oddity.

pedigree noun
They have a complete record of the dog's pedigree. ancestry, descent, family history.

peel noun
Orange peel is used in marmalade. rind, skin.

peep, peer verbs SEE **look** verb

peer, peeress nouns
aristocrat, noble, nobleman or noblewoman.
FOR TITLES OF NOBLES, SEE **title**.

pelt verb
They pelted each other with snowballs. attack, bombard, shower.
SEE ALSO **throw**.

pen noun
1 *My pen has run out of ink.* ballpoint, felt-tipped pen, fountain pen.
2 *The dog drove the sheep into the pen.* enclosure, fold.

penalize verb
In football, you will be penalized if you handle the ball. punish.

penalty noun
The maximum penalty for this crime is ten years in prison. punishment.

penetrate *verb*
1 *He stepped on a nail that penetrated his foot.* bore through, get through, make a hole in, pierce.
When something penetrates a tyre, it *punctures* it.
2 *The soldiers penetrated the enemy's defences.* enter, get past, infiltrate.

penitent *adjective*
He was penitent about his mistake. apologetic, ashamed, regretful, remorseful, repentant, sorry.
AN OPPOSITE IS unrepentant.

people *plural noun*
1 *There's always a lot of people in town on Saturdays.* folk, men and women and children.
People as opposed to animals are *humans* or *human beings* or *mankind*.
2 *The people will decide who governs the country.* citizens, common people, population, the public, society.
3 *It would be wonderful if the peoples of the world could live in peace.* nation, race.

peppery *adjective*
He's not keen on food with a peppery taste. hot, spicy.

perceive *verb*
1 *They perceived a shape on the horizon.* become aware of, catch sight of, make out, notice, observe, recognize, see, spot.
2 *He began to perceive what she meant.* comprehend, grasp, realize, understand.

perceptible *adjective*
There was a perceptible note of anger in his voice. clear, definite, distinct, evident, noticeable, obvious, recognizable, unmistakable, visible.
AN OPPOSITE IS imperceptible.

perceptive *adjective*
She's very perceptive about people. acute, alert, clever, observant, quick, sensitive, sharp, shrewd.
AN OPPOSITE IS unobservant.

perch *verb*
He perched on top of the wall. balance, rest, settle, sit.

percussion *noun*
FOR VARIOUS PERCUSSION INSTRUMENTS, SEE **music**.

perfect *adjective*
1 *She has a perfect set of teeth.* complete, faultless, flawless, ideal, intact, undamaged, whole.
A perfect stamp or coin is *in mint condition*.
2 *This photocopier makes perfect copies every time.* accurate, correct, exact, faithful, precise.
AN OPPOSITE IS imperfect.
3 *He was a perfect stranger.* absolute, total, utter.

perfect *verb*
He spent years perfecting his technique. improve, polish up, refine.

perforate *verb*
She perforated the paper with a pin. bore through, pierce, prick, puncture.

perform *verb*
1 *He's too shy to perform on a stage.* act, appear, dance, play, sing.
2 *They performed a play about Cinderella.* present, produce, put on, take part in.
3 *Soldiers are expected to perform their duty.* carry out, do, execute, fulfil.
To perform a crime is to *commit* a crime.

performance *noun*
1 *He really enjoyed the performance he saw at the theatre.* presentation, production, show.
FOR DIFFERENT KINDS OF PERFORMANCE, SEE **entertainment**.
2 *She congratulated them on their good performance.* achievement, attempt, behaviour, conduct, effort, endeavour, exertion, work.

performer *noun* SEE **entertainer**

perfume *noun*
The perfume of roses filled the room. fragrance, scent, smell.

perhaps *adverb*
Perhaps the weather will be better tomorrow. maybe, possibly.
AN OPPOSITE IS definitely.

peril *noun*
They bravely faced the peril which lay ahead. danger, risks, threat.
AN OPPOSITE IS safety.

perilous *adjective*
They made a perilous trek through the mountains. dangerous, hazardous, risky.
AN OPPOSITE IS safe.

perimeter *noun*
They put up a fence round the perimeter of the field. border, boundary, edge.
The distance round the edge of something is the **circumference**.

period *noun*
1 After a long period of hard work they had a rest. span, spell, stretch, time.
2 The book is about the Victorian period. age, epoch, era.

periodical *noun*
She bought a computing periodical to read on the train. journal, magazine.

perish *verb*
1 Many birds perish in cold weather. be killed, die, expire, pass away.
2 There was a leak where the rubber hose had perished. crumble away, decay, decompose, disintegrate, go bad, rot.

permanent *adjective*
1 She told him to do a permanent repair, not just to patch it up. durable, lasting.
2 If you live in a city, traffic noise is a permanent problem. chronic, constant, continual, endless, everlasting, incessant, never-ending, perennial, perpetual, persistent, unending.
3 Marriage is a permanent relationship. lifelong, long-lasting, stable, steady.
AN OPPOSITE IS temporary.

permissible *adjective*
It is not permissible to smoke in here. acceptable, allowed, lawful, legal, permitted, right.
AN OPPOSITE IS forbidden.

permission *noun*
They had the teacher's permission to leave. agreement, approval, consent, [informal] go-ahead.

permissive
His parents have a permissive attitude—they let him do what he wants. easy-going, indulgent, lenient, tolerant.
AN OPPOSITE IS intolerant.

permit *verb*
The council doesn't permit fishing in the lake. agree to, allow, approve of, authorize, consent to, give permission for, license, tolerate.
Another way to say 'Permit me to speak' is to say '**Let** me speak'.

permit *noun*
You need a permit to fish in the river. licence, pass, ticket.

perpendicular *adjective*
The Leaning Tower of Pisa is not perpendicular. upright, vertical.

perpetual *adjective*
The perpetual roar of traffic is very annoying. ceaseless, chronic, constant, continual, continuous, endless, eternal, everlasting, incessant, never-ending, non-stop, perennial, permanent, persistent, unceasing, unending.
AN OPPOSITE IS temporary.

perplex *verb*
The question perplexed him. baffle, bewilder, confuse, muddle, mystify, puzzle, worry.

persecute *verb*
People were persecuted for their religious beliefs. bully, discriminate against, harass, intimidate, oppress, terrorize, torment, torture.

persevere *verb*
She persevered despite all the difficulties. continue, go on, [informal] keep at it, keep going, persist, [informal] stick at it.
AN OPPOSITE IS give up.

persist *verb*
1 He persists in his beliefs, despite the evidence. be obstinate, keep on, persevere.
AN OPPOSITE IS stop.
2 How long will this snow persist? last, linger, remain.
AN OPPOSITE IS disappear.

persistent *adjective*
1 *There are persistent rumours that she is getting married.* constant, continual, endless, eternal, everlasting, incessant, never-ending, repeated, unceasing.
2 *He had a persistent cold all winter.* ceaseless, chronic, permanent, recurrent, recurring.
3 *That dog is very persistent—he won't go away.* determined, obstinate, patient, persevering, resolute, steadfast, stubborn, tireless.

person *noun*
Who was that person I saw you with last night? character, human being, individual.
An adult person is a **man** or **woman**.
A young person is a **baby**, **infant**, **child**, or **adolescent**.

personal *adjective*
1 *They have personal business to discuss.* confidential, intimate, private, secret.
2 *Don't make personal remarks!* critical, insulting, offensive, rude.

personality *noun*
1 *She has an attractive personality.* character, disposition, make-up, nature.
2 *A crowd gathered to watch the show business personalities arrive.* celebrity, famous person, idol, public figure, star.

personnel *noun*
The company promised that all personnel would get a pay rise. employees, staff, workers.

perspire *verb*
He perspires a lot in hot weather. sweat.

persuade *verb*
I persuaded him to come with us. coax, convert, convince.
To persuade someone to do something is also to **talk them into** doing it.
AN OPPOSITE IS dissuade.

persuasion *noun*
It took a lot of persuasion to make him change his mind. argument, coaxing, convincing, persuading, reasoning.

persuasive *adjective*
She used some very persuasive arguments. convincing, credible, effective, logical, reasonable, sound, strong, valid.
AN OPPOSITE IS unconvincing.

perverse *adjective*
He was acting in a rather perverse way. contrary, illogical, obstinate, stubborn, tiresome, uncooperative, unhelpful, unreasonable.
AN OPPOSITE IS reasonable.

pervert *verb*
The police claimed that he had tried to pervert the course of justice. interfere with, lead astray, undermine.

perverted *adjective*
His perverted behaviour got him into trouble with the police. abnormal, corrupt, evil, immoral, improper, obscene, twisted, unnatural, warped, wicked, wrong.
AN OPPOSITE IS normal.

pessimistic *adjective*
They were pessimistic about their chances of winning. cynical, despairing, gloomy, hopeless, negative, without hope.
AN OPPOSITE IS optimistic.

pest *noun*
1 *He won't use chemicals to get rid of garden pests.*
Pests in general are **vermin**.
An informal word for insect pests is **bugs**.
A pest which lives on or in another creature is a **parasite**.
2 *Don't be a pest!* annoyance, bother, nuisance.

pester *verb*
Please don't pester me while I'm busy! annoy, [*informal*] badger, bother, harass, nag, plague, provoke, trouble, try, worry.

pet *noun*

CREATURES COMMONLY KEPT AS PETS INCLUDE: budgerigar, canary, cat, dog, ferret, fish, gerbil, goldfish, guinea pig, hamster, mouse, parrot, pigeon, rabbit, rat, tortoise.

petrify verb
He was so petrified that he couldn't move. frighten, horrify, scare, shock, terrify.

petrol noun
In America, petrol is **gas** or **gasoline**.

petty adjective
There were a lot of annoying petty rules. insignificant, minor, small, trivial, unimportant.
AN OPPOSITE IS important.

pharmacy noun
He went to the pharmacy for his medicine. chemist's, dispensary.

phase noun
Going to a new school is the start of a new phase in your life. period, stage, step, time.

phenomenal adjective
The winner of the quiz had a phenomenal memory. amazing, exceptional, extraordinary, [informal] fantastic, incredible, outstanding, remarkable, unbelievable, unusual, wonderful.
AN OPPOSITE IS ordinary.

phenomenon noun
1 Snow is a common phenomenon in winter. event, fact, happening, occurrence.
2 The six-year old pianist was quite a phenomenon. curiosity, marvel, wonder.

philosophical adjective
1 They had a philosophical debate about the meaning of life. abstract, academic, analytical, intellectual, learned, logical, rational, reasoned, theoretical.
AN OPPOSITE IS practical.
2 He was quite philosophical about losing the race. calm, patient, reasonable, resigned, sensible, stoical, unemotional.
AN OPPOSITE IS emotional.

philosophy noun
Her philosophy can be summed up in the phrase, 'Respect all living things'. beliefs, convictions, values, way of thinking.

phobia noun
He has a phobia about spiders. anxiety, dislike, dread, fear, [informal] hang-up, hatred, horror.

> A fear of open spaces is
> **agoraphobia**.
> A fear of spiders is **arachnophobia**.
> A fear of enclosed spaces is
> **claustrophobia**.
> A fear of strangers or foreigners is
> **xenophobia**.

phone verb
He phoned her to tell her the news. call, dial, ring, telephone.

photocopy verb
She photocopied the article. copy, duplicate, print off, reproduce

photograph noun
Have the holiday photographs been developed yet? photo, shot, snap or snapshot.

> The photographs you get when a film is processed are **prints**.
> A photograph on the original film from which you have to make a print is a **negative**.
> A photograph which is larger than a normal print is an **enlargement**.
> A photograph for projecting onto a screen is a **slide** or **transparency**.

photograph verb
She photographed him in fancy dress. shoot, snap, take a picture of.

> PHOTOGRAPHIC EQUIPMENT
> INCLUDES: [old use] box camera, cine-camera, darkroom, enlarger, exposure meter or light meter, [trademark] Polaroid camera, SLR or single lens reflex camera, telephoto lens, tripod, zoom lens.

phrase noun
'I don't believe it!' is a common phrase. expression, saying.

phrase verb
She tried to phrase it politely. express, put into words.

physical *adjective*
1 *There's a lot of physical contact in rugby.* bodily.
Physical punishment is **corporal** punishment.
2 *Ghosts have no physical presence.* actual, earthly, real, solid, substantial.

pick *verb*
1 *They picked partners for the game.* choose, decide on, opt for, select, settle on, single out.
2 *They decided to pick a new captain.* elect, nominate, vote for.
3 *She picked some flowers from the garden.* collect, cut, gather.
4 *I picked an apple off the tree.* pluck, pull off, take.

picture *noun*
There were some good pictures in the book. illustration, image, likeness, portrayal, representation.

> PICTURES PRODUCED BY VARIOUS METHODS: cartoon, collage, doodle, drawing, engraving, etching, identikit picture, mosaic, oil painting, photograph, print, sketch, slide, snap or snapshot, transfer, transparency, water colour.
> A picture which represents a particular person is a **portrait**.
> A picture which gives a side view of someone is a **profile**.
> A picture which exaggerates some aspect of a person is a **caricature**.
> A picture which gives just the general shape of someone or something is an **outline** or **silhouette**.
> A picture drawn quickly without much thought is a **doodle**.
> A picture which represents a group of objects is a **still life**.
> A picture which represents a country scene is a **landscape**.
> A picture which does not represent any person, thing, or scene is an **abstract**.
> A picture painted on a wall is a **fresco** or a **mural**. ➡

> A picture painted by a famous painter of the past is an **old master**.
> A copy of a painting is a **reproduction**.
> Pictures on a computer are **graphics**.
> Moving pictures are **films**.

picture *verb*
1 *They were pictured against a background of flowers.* depict, illustrate, portray, represent, show.
2 *Can you picture what the world will be like in 100 years?* imagine, visualize.

picturesque *adjective*
1 *They stayed in a picturesque thatched cottage.* attractive, charming, pretty, quaint.
AN OPPOSITE IS ugly.
2 *It was a picturesque account of life in the Middle Ages.* colourful, descriptive, expressive, graphic, imaginative, lively, poetic, vivid.

piece *noun*

> A SUBSTANTIAL PIECE OF SOMETHING: bar, block, chunk, hunk, length, lump, part, sample, section, segment, slab, stick.
>
> A PIECE BROKEN OR CUT OFF SOMETHING: bit, chip, crumb, fragment, morsel, particle, scrap, shred, slice.
>
> A PIECE OF SOMETHING TO EAT: bite, crumb, helping, morsel, portion, share.
>
> ONE OF THE PIECES THAT SOMETHING IS MADE OF: component, constituent, element, part, unit.
> A piece of clothing is an **article** or **item** of clothing.
> FOR WORDS FOR A PIECE OF MUSIC OR WRITING, SEE **music, writing**.

pier *noun*
1 *The passengers disembarked at the pier.* jetty, landing stage, quay, wharf. A structure built out into the sea as a protection against the waves is a **breakwater**.
2 *The flood nearly swept away the piers supporting the bridge.* column, pile, pillar, support.

pierce *verb*
This new drill will pierce almost anything. bore through, drill through, enter, go through, make a hole in, penetrate.
To pierce a hole through paper is to **punch** a hole or **perforate** it.
To pierce a hole in a tyre is to **puncture** it.
To pierce someone with a spike is to **impale** or **spear** them.

piercing *adjective*
He heard a piercing scream. deafening, high-pitched, loud, penetrating, sharp, shrill.

pig *noun*

An old word for pigs is **swine**.
A wild pig is a **wild boar**.
A male pig is a **boar** or **hog**.
A female pig is a **sow**.
A baby pig is a **piglet**.
A family of piglets is a **litter**.
The smallest piglet in a litter is the **runt**.

pile *noun*
1 *Where did this pile of rubbish come from?* accumulation, heap, mass, mound, quantity, stack.
2 *The pier is built on piles driven into the mud.* column, pier, post, support.

pile *verb*
Pile everything in the corner and we'll sort it out later. accumulate, assemble, bring together, build up, collect, concentrate, gather, heap up, stack.

pill *noun*
The doctor told her to swallow the pills with some water. capsule, pellet, tablet.

pillar *noun*
The roof was supported by tall pillars. column, pier, pile, post, prop, support.

pillow *noun*
A long kind of pillow is a **bolster**.
A kind of pillow for a chair or sofa is a **cushion**.

pilot *verb*
She piloted the aircraft back to safety. fly, guide, lead, navigate, steer.

pimple *noun*
He had a pimple on his nose. boil, spot, swelling.
A lot of pimples or spots on your skin is a **rash**.

pin *noun*
A pretty pin you might wear on a dress is a **brooch**.
A pin to fix something on a noticeboard is a **drawing pin**.
A pin to fix a baby's nappy in place is a **safety pin**.

pinch *verb*
1 *He pinched his fingers in the door.* crush, nip, squeeze.
2 [*informal*] *Who pinched my pen?* [*informal*] lift, [*informal*] make off with, pilfer, steal, take, [*informal*] walk off with.

pine *verb*
The dog pined when its master died. mope, mourn, sicken, waste away.
to pine for *She was pining for her mother.* crave, long for, want, yearn for.

pioneer *noun*
1 *They learned about the pioneers who first settled in America.* colonist, discoverer, explorer, settler.
2 *Alexander Bell was a pioneer in the history of telecommunications.* innovator, inventor, originator.

pious *adjective*
The pious pilgrims knelt down when they reached the sacred place. holy, religious, reverent, saintly.

pip *noun*
A pip in an apple, orange, etc., is a **seed**.
The pips on dice are **spots**.
The pips of a time signal are **bleeps**.

pipe *noun*
The water flows away along this pipe.
tube.
A length of pipe is **piping** or **tubing**.
The system of water pipes in a house is
the **plumbing**.
A pipe used for watering the garden is
a **hose**.
A pipe in the street which supplies
water for fighting fires, etc., is a
hydrant.
A pipe which carries oil, etc., over long
distances is a **pipeline**.

pipe *verb*
1 *They pipe water from the Welsh hills
to Birmingham.* convey, transmit.
2 *She began to pipe a tune on her
recorder.* blow, play, sound, whistle.

pirate *noun*
In the old days ruthless pirates sailed
the high seas. buccaneer, marauder.

pistol *noun*
FOR VARIOUS GUNS, SEE **weapon**.

pit *noun*
1 *They dug a deep pit.* abyss, chasm,
crater, depression, excavation, hole,
hollow, mine, pothole, quarry.
2 *At one time, a lot of coal was mined
from the pits in this area.* coal mine,
colliery.

pitch *noun*
The groundsman worked hard to
prepare the pitch for the game. ground,
playing field.

pitch *verb*
1 *They pitched the rubbish into the
skip.* [*slang*] bung, cast, [*informal*]
chuck, fling, heave, hurl, lob, sling,
throw, toss.
2 *It was hard trying to pitch the tent in
the rain!* erect, put up, set up.
3 *He lost his balance and pitched into
the water.* drop, fall heavily, plunge,
topple.
4 *The ship pitched about in the storm.*
dip, lurch, rock, roll, toss.

pitfall *noun*
They tried to avoid the obvious pitfalls.
catch, danger, difficulty, hazard, snag,
trap.

pitiful *adjective*
1 *We could hear pitiful cries for help.*
distressing, miserable, moving,
pathetic, sad, touching, wretched.
2 *The goalkeeper made a pitiful attempt
to stop the ball.* contemptible, hopeless,
inadequate, incompetent, laughable,
pathetic, ridiculous, useless.

pitiless *adjective*
They kept up a pitiless bombardment
until the town was flattened. barbaric,
bloodthirsty, brutal, callous, cruel,
heartless, inhuman, merciless,
relentless, remorseless, ruthless,
sadistic, savage, vicious.
AN OPPOSITE IS merciful.

pity *noun*
The thugs showed no pity. compassion,
feeling, humanity, kindness, mercy,
regret, sympathy, tenderness,
understanding.
AN OPPOSITE IS cruelty.

pity *verb*
She pitied anyone who was out in the
storm. feel for, feel pity for, sympathize
with, weep for.

pivot *noun*
The point on which a lever turns is the
fulcrum.
The point on which a spinning object
turns is its **axis**.
The point on which a wheel turns is the
axle or **hub**.

placard *noun*
They put up a placard announcing the
sale. advertisement, bill, notice, poster,
sign.

place *noun*
1 *They couldn't find the place on the
map.* location, point, position,
situation, spot.
A place where there is a particular
building or something interesting is a
site.
2 *This would be a nice place for a
holiday.* area, country, district, locality,
neighbourhood, region, vicinity.
3 *Save me a place on the bus.* seat.

place *verb*
1 *The council placed a recycling centre next to the car park.* locate, situate.
2 *They placed guards at regular intervals along the route.* position, stand, station.
3 *Place your things on the table.* arrange, deposit, dump, lay, leave, put down, rest, set down.

placid *adjective*
1 *He won't get upset—he's a very placid character.* cool, even-tempered, level-headed, mild, sensible, unexcitable.
AN OPPOSITE IS excitable or quarrelsome.
2 *They had a placid voyage.* calm, peaceful, quiet, restful, tranquil, unruffled, untroubled.
AN OPPOSITE IS stormy.

plague *noun*
1 *Doctors worked hard to prevent the plague from spreading.* epidemic, infection, outbreak.
2 *There was a plague of wasps this summer.* invasion, swarm.

plague *verb*
1 *Ants have plagued us all summer.* afflict, be a nuisance to, torment.
To be plagued by insects or vermin is to be *infested* by them.
2 *She had been plagued by bad luck.* annoy, irritate, nag, pester, trouble, vex, worry.

plain *adjective*
1 *The room was very plain.* austere, homely, modest, simple, undecorated.
AN OPPOSITE IS elaborate.
2 *Some people say she looks plain compared with her sister.* ordinary, unattractive.
AN OPPOSITE IS attractive.
3 *It was quite plain what he meant.* clear, comprehensible, definite, distinct, evident, obvious, unambiguous, unmistakable.
AN OPPOSITE IS unclear.
4 *He told her in plain words what he thought.* blunt, direct, frank, honest, outspoken, sincere, straightforward.

plain *noun*
A grassy plain in a hot country is called *savannah*.
The large plains of North America are the *prairies*.
The large plains of Russia are the *steppes*.

plaintive *adjective*
He played a plaintive tune on his saxophone. melancholy, mournful, sad, sorrowful, wistful.
AN OPPOSITE IS cheerful.

plan *noun*
1 *The captain explained her plan to the rest of the team.* aim, idea, intention, policy, project, proposal, scheme, strategy.
A plan to do something bad is a *plot*.
2 *They looked at the plans for the new sports centre.* blueprint, design, diagram, drawing.
3 *He drew a plan of the village.* chart, map, sketch map.

plan *verb*
1 *They planned a money-raising campaign.* arrange, contrive, design, devise, formulate, map out, organize, outline, prepare, think out, work out.
To plan to do something bad is to *plot*.
2 *What do you plan to do next?* aim, intend, mean, propose.

plane *noun* SEE **aircraft**

planet *noun*
Is there life on other planets? world.

PLANETS OF THE SOLAR SYSTEM:
Earth, Jupiter, Mars, Mercury, Neptune, Pluto, Saturn, Uranus, Venus.
The path followed by a planet is its *orbit*.
Minor planets orbiting the sun are *asteroids*.
Something which orbits a planet is a *satellite*.
The earth's large satellite is the *moon*.

plank *noun* SEE **timber**

plant *noun*

> SOME KINDS OF PLANT: algae, bulb,
> cactus, cereal, fern, flower, fungus,
> grass, herb, lichen, moss, shrub,
> tree, vegetable, waterplant.
> SEE ALSO **flower, fruit, tree,**
> **vegetable.**
>
> PARTS OF VARIOUS PLANTS: bloom,
> blossom, branch, bud, flower, fruit,
> leaf, petal, pod, root, shoot, stalk,
> stem, trunk, twig.
>
> THINGS THAT PLANTS GROW FROM:
> bulb, corm, cutting, seed, tuber.
> *Annual* plants live for just one year.
> *Biennial* plants live for two years.
> *Perennial* plants continue to live
> year after year.
> A plant which is growing where you
> don't want it is a *weed*.
> A young plant is a *seedling*.
> A word for plants in general is
> *vegetation*.
> A formal scientific word for plants in
> general is *flora*.
> The scientific study of plants is
> *botany*.

plant *verb*
>They will plant the seeds in April. set
>out, sow.
>To move a plant from where it was
>growing and plant it somewhere else is
>to *transplant* it.

plaster *noun*
>The nurse put a plaster on the cut.
>dressing, sticking plaster.

plate *noun*
>1 She piled their plates with food.
>FOR ITEMS OF CROCKERY, SEE
>crockery.
>2 The sides of the warship were
>protected by steel plates. panel, sheet.
>3 There were some attractive plates in
>the book. illustration, photo, picture.

platform *noun*
>She stood on the platform to make the
>speech. stage.

play *noun*
>1 There was a good play on TV last
>night. comedy, drama, performance,
>production, tragedy.
>2 It is important to balance work and
>play. amusement, fun, games, playing,
>recreation, sport.
>FOR VARIOUS GAMES AND SPORTS,
>SEE **game, sport.**

play *verb*
>1 The children went out to play. amuse
>yourself, have fun, romp about.
>2 Would you like to play with us? join
>in, participate, take part.
>3 I'll play you at snooker. challenge,
>compete against, oppose.
>4 She played the piano at the school
>concert. perform on.
>5 He often plays tapes in the car. have
>on, listen to, put on.
>6 She played Mary in the nativity play.
>act, portray, represent, take the part of.
>**to play about, to play up** She gets
>angry if anyone starts to play up while
>she's reading a story. behave badly, fool
>around, make mischief, mess about,
>misbehave.

player *noun*
>1 You need four players for this game.
>competitor, contestant, participant.
>2 How many players were there in the
>band? instrumentalist, musician,
>performer.
>Someone who plays music on their own
>is a *soloist*.
>FOR VARIOUS PERFORMERS, SEE
>**entertainer, music.**

playful *adjective*
>They were in a playful mood. cheerful,
>frisky, frivolous, impish, jaunty, joking,
>lively, mischievous, skittish, sprightly.
>AN OPPOSITE IS serious.

playing field *noun*
>They couldn't play because the playing
>field was too wet. ground, pitch,
>recreation ground, sports ground.

plea *noun*
>The judge ignored the accused man's
>plea for mercy. appeal, entreaty,
>request.

plead *verb*
He pleaded to be let off. appeal, ask, beg, entreat, implore, request.

pleasant *adjective*
The adjective *pleasant* can refer to anything which pleases you, and there are many possible synonyms. We just give some common ones here
1 He seems to be a pleasant person. amiable, amicable, approachable, cheerful, decent, friendly, genial, good-natured, hospitable, kind, likeable, sympathetic.
2 We had a pleasant time. agreeable, delightful, enjoyable, entertaining, excellent, pleasing, relaxing.
3 You get pleasant views from the upstairs windows. attractive, beautiful, charming, lovely, pretty.
4 The weather is quite pleasant today. bright, clear, fine, mild, sunny, warm.
5 They played pleasant music while they had their dinner. gentle, peaceful, soothing.
AN OPPOSITE IS unpleasant.

please *verb*
1 He did it to please her. amuse, entertain, give pleasure to, make happy, satisfy.
2 Do as you please. want, wish.

pleased *adjective*
Why do you look so pleased today? contented, delighted, elated, glad, grateful, happy, satisfied, thankful, thrilled.
AN OPPOSITE IS annoyed.

pleasure *noun*
1 She gets a lot of pleasure from her garden. comfort, contentment, delight, enjoyment, gladness, happiness, joy, satisfaction.
Very great pleasure is **bliss** or **ecstasy**.
2 He talked about the pleasures of living in the country. amusement, diversion, entertainment, luxury, recreation.

pleat *noun*
It takes ages to iron the pleats in the skirt. crease, fold, tuck.

pledge *noun*
She gave a pledge that the work will be done on time. assurance, guarantee, oath, promise, vow, word.

plentiful *adjective*
They had a plentiful supply of food. abundant, ample, generous, inexhaustible, lavish, liberal, profuse.
AN OPPOSITE IS scarce.

plenty *noun*
Don't buy any milk—there's plenty in the fridge. an abundance, a lot, a profusion.
More than you know what to do with is a **glut** or **surplus**.
AN OPPOSITE IS scarcity.
plenty of They've got plenty of food. abundant, ample, heaps of, [*informal*] loads of, a lot of, lots of, [*informal*] masses of, piles of.

pliable *adjective*
She showed him how to weave a basket out of pliable twigs. flexible, springy, supple.
AN OPPOSITE IS rigid.

plight *noun*
He was concerned about the plight of the homeless. difficulty, dilemma, problem.

plod *verb*
1 We plodded through the mud. tramp, trudge.
2 She plodded away at her work without much enthusiasm labour at, persevere with.

plot *noun*
1 Guy Fawkes was involved in a plot against the government. conspiracy, scheme, secret plan.
2 It was hard to follow the plot of the film. narrative, story, thread.
3 He bought a plot of ground to build a retirement home. area, lot, patch, piece.
A plot of ground for growing flowers or vegetables is an **allotment** or **smallholding**.
A large plot of land is a **tract** of land.

plot *verb*
1 They plotted to rob a bank. conspire, intrigue, scheme.
2 They were plotting mischief. [*informal*] cook up, hatch.

plough *verb*
> After one crop is harvested, they plough the ground for the next one. cultivate, till, turn over.

pluck *verb*
> **1** He had to pluck the chicken before cooking it. remove the feathers from, strip.
> **2** They plucked the apples off the tree. collect, gather, harvest, pick, pull off.
> **3** A seagull plucked her sandwich out of her hand. grab, jerk, pull, seize, snatch, tug, yank.
> **4** He began to pluck the strings of his guitar.
> To run your finger or plectrum across the strings of a guitar is to **strum**.
> To pluck the strings of a violin or cello is to play **pizzicato**.

plucky *adjective* SEE **brave**

plug *noun*
> They put a plug in the hole. bung, cork, stopper.

plug *verb*
> **1** She tried to plug a leak in the water tank. block up, bung up, close, fill, seal, stop up.
> **2** [informal] They asked the local radio station to plug our concert. advertise, mention frequently, promote, publicize, recommend.

plump *adjective*
> He's getting a bit plump. chubby, dumpy, podgy, portly, round, squat, stout.
> AN OPPOSITE IS skinny.

plunder *verb*
> Rioters plundered the shops. loot, pillage, raid, ransack, rob, steal from.

plunge *verb*
> **1** She plunged into the water. dive, drop, fall, jump, leap, pitch, swoop down, tumble.
> **2** I plunged my hand in the water. dip, immerse, lower, sink, submerge.
> **3** He plunged his spear into the animal's side. force, push, stab, thrust.

plural *adjective*
> AN OPPOSITE IS singular.

pneumatic *adjective*
> The tricycle has pneumatic tyres. air-filled, pumped up.

poach *verb*
> Robin Hood used to poach deer in Sherwood Forest. hunt illegally, steal.

podgy *adjective*
> She needs more exercise—she's getting podgy. chubby, dumpy, plump, portly, round, stout.
> AN OPPOSITE IS skinny.

poem *noun*

> Poems are **poetry**, **rhymes**, or **verse**.
>
> SOME KINDS OF POEM: ballad, free verse, haiku, limerick, narrative poem, nonsense verse, nursery rhyme, ode, sonnet.
> A poem divided into groups of lines with a regular pattern of rhymes is in **stanzas**.
> A poem with pairs of lines that rhyme is in **couplets**.
> Poor verse with silly-sounding rhymes is **doggerel**.
> A short poem which is meant to be set to music is a **lyric**.

poetic *adjective*
> They used poetic language in their descriptions. emotional, [uncomplimentary] flowery, imaginative, lyrical, poetical.

point *noun*
> **1** She hurt herself on that sharp point. prong, spike, tip.
> **2** Remember to put in the decimal point. dot, full stop, mark, spot.
> **3** He marked on the map the exact point where the accident happened. location, place, position, site, situation.
> **4** At that point the rain started to come down. instant, moment, time.
> **5** She said that his last point was a good one. detail, idea, thought.
> **6** Honesty is one of his good points. characteristic, feature, peculiarity.
> **7** What is the point of that story? aim, intention, meaning, purpose, use, usefulness.

point verb

1 *She pointed the way.* draw attention to, indicate, point out, show, signal.
2 *Can you point me in the right direction for the station?* aim, direct, guide, lead, steer.

pointless adjective

It's pointless to argue with him—he's so stubborn. futile, useless, vain.
AN OPPOSITE IS worthwhile.

poise noun

She showed great poise on her first public appearance. calmness, coolness, dignity, self-confidence.

poise verb

He poised himself on a narrow ledge. balance, support, suspend.

poison noun

A poison to kill plants is **herbicide** or **weedkiller**.
A poison to kill insects is **insecticide** or **pesticide**.
The poison in a snake bite is **venom**.
Food poisoning can be caused by bacteria such as **salmonella**.

SOME POISONOUS SUBSTANCES: arsenic, belladonna, cyanide, DDT, hemlock, paraquat, strychnine, warfarin.
A substance which can save you from the effects of a poison is an **antidote**.

poisonous adjective

He became very ill after receiving a poisonous snake bite. deadly, lethal, toxic, venomous.

poke verb

He poked me in the back with a stick. dig, jab, prod, stab, thrust.
to poke out *She saw the kitten's head poking out of the basket.* project, protrude, stick out.

polar adjective

The polar night lasts for months. antarctic or arctic.

pole noun

Four poles marked the corners of the field. bar, post, rod, shaft, stick.
A pole that you use when walking or as a weapon is a **staff**.
A pole for a flag to fly from is a **flagpole**.
A pole to support sails on a boat, etc., is a **mast** or **spar**.
A pole with a pointed end to stick in the ground is a **stake**.
Poles which a circus entertainer walks on are **stilts**.

police officer noun

ORDINARY POLICE OFFICERS: [*informal*] bobby, constable, [*slang*] cop or copper, policeman or policewoman.

POLICE OFFICERS HIGHER IN RANK THAN A CONSTABLE: chief constable, inspector, sergeant, superintendent.
Someone training for the police force is a **cadet**.
Someone who investigates crimes is a **detective**.

policy noun

She explained the government's policy on education. approach, plan of action, strategy.
A document which officially explains someone's policy is a **manifesto**.

polish verb

She was polishing the car. rub down, shine, wax.
to polish something off *They polished off the rest of the work quickly.* complete, conclude, end, finish, round off.

polish noun

He rubbed hard to get a good polish on the car. brightness, brilliance, glaze, gloss, lustre, sheen, shine, sparkle.

polished adjective

1 *She could see her face in the polished surface.* bright, glassy, gleaming, glossy, lustrous, shining, shiny.
AN OPPOSITE IS dull.
2 *They gave a polished performance.* elegant, faultless, perfect, stylish, well prepared.
AN OPPOSITE IS rough.

polite *adjective*
He's always very polite to me.
chivalrous, civil, civilized, considerate,
correct, courteous, gallant, obliging,
respectful, tactful, well mannered, well
spoken.
AN OPPOSITE IS rude.

politics *noun*

THE MAIN POLITICAL PARTIES IN
BRITAIN: Conservative or Tory,
Labour, Liberal Democrat.

WORDS TO DESCRIBE VARIOUS
POLITICAL BELIEFS: anarchist,
capitalist, communist, conservative,
democratic, fascist, liberal, Marxist,
moderate, monarchist, nationalist,
radical, republican, socialist.

WORDS TO DESCRIBE PEOPLE WITH
EXTREME POLITICAL VIEWS:
extremist, revolutionary.
A politician who wants to make
important changes can be described
as **radical**.

DIFFERENT POLITICAL SYSTEMS:
anarchy, capitalism, communism,
democracy, dictatorship, monarchy,
republic.

poll *noun*
The result of the poll has been declared.
ballot, election, vote.
A vote on a particular question by all
the people in a country is a
referendum.
An official survey to find out about the
population is a **census**.

pollute *verb*
The river has been polluted by
chemicals. contaminate, infect, poison.

pomp *noun*
The coronation was conducted with
great pomp. ceremony, display,
formality, grandeur, magnificence,
pageantry, spectacle, splendour.

pompous *adjective*
He spoke in a rather pompous manner.
arrogant, haughty, self-important,
snobbish, [*informal*] stuck-up.
AN OPPOSITE IS modest.

pond *noun* SEE **pool**

pool *noun*
There are fish in that pool. pond.
A larger area of water is a **lake**.
A small shallow area of water is a
puddle.
A pool of water in the desert is an
oasis.
A pool specially made to swim in is a
swimming pool or **swimming bath**.

poor *adjective*
1 You can't afford luxuries if you are
poor. badly off, deprived, hard up,
needy, penniless, underprivileged.
AN OPPOSITE IS rich.
2 Her work was very poor. bad,
[*informal*] hopeless, inadequate,
incompetent, inefficient, inferior,
mediocre, shoddy, unsatisfactory,
useless, weak, worthless.
AN OPPOSITE IS good or superior.
3 They pitied the poor animals
standing in the rain. forlorn,
miserable, pathetic, sad, unfortunate,
unhappy, unlucky, wretched.
AN OPPOSITE IS lucky.

poorly *adjective*
He stayed at home because he felt
poorly. ill, sick, unfit, unwell.
AN OPPOSITE IS well.

popular *adjective*
Disney has made a lot of popular
children's films. celebrated, favourite,
loved, well-known, well-liked, well-
loved.
Clothes which are popular are
fashionable or **trendy**.
AN OPPOSITE IS unpopular.

populated *adjective*
They stayed in a village populated
mainly by holidaymakers. inhabited,
lived in, occupied.

population *noun*
The whole population turned out to
welcome the victorious football team.
citizens, community, inhabitants,
residents.

porch *noun*
She waited in the porch until the rain
eased off. doorway, entrance.

pore *verb*
to pore over *The engineers pored over the printout of the computer programme to find out what was wrong.* examine, inspect, look closely at, scrutinize, study.

porous *adjective*
Porous substances soak up liquid. absorbent, spongy.

port *noun*
The ship entered the port. anchorage, dock, harbour, haven, seaport.
A harbour for yachts and pleasure boats is a ***marina***.

portable *adjective*
They took a portable TV on holiday. easy to carry, handy, light, lightweight.
A portable phone is a ***mobile phone***.
A portable computer is a ***laptop***.

portion *noun*
He asked for a small portion of pie. bit, helping, part, piece, quantity, ration, serving, share, slice.

portrait *noun*
There's a portrait of the queen on every stamp. image, likeness, picture, profile, representation.

portray *verb*
The film portrays what life was like 1000 years ago. depict, describe, illustrate, represent, show.

pose *noun*
1 *He adopted a suitable pose so that she could take a photo.* attitude, position, posture.
2 *Don't take his behaviour seriously—it's only a pose.* act, pretence.

pose *verb*
She posed in front of the camera. model, sit.
to pose as someone *The burglar posed as a gas man.* impersonate, pretend to be.

posh *adjective*
1 [*informal*] *They stayed in a posh hotel.* elegant, fashionable, high-class, [*uncomplimentary*] snobbish.
2 [*informal*] *He put on posh clothes for the visit.* decent, formal, smart.

position *noun*
1 *Mark the position on the map.* location, place, point, site, spot, whereabouts.
2 *He shifted his position to avoid getting cramp.* pose, posture.
3 *Losing all her money put her in a difficult position.* circumstances, condition, situation, state.
4 *A referee should adopt a neutral position.* attitude, opinion, outlook, view.
5 *She has a responsible position in her firm.* appointment, function, job.

positive *adjective*
1 *He was positive that he was right.* certain, confident, convinced, definite, emphatic, sure.
AN OPPOSITE IS uncertain.
2 *The teacher gave her some positive advice.* beneficial, constructive, helpful, optimistic, useful, worthwhile.
AN OPPOSITE IS negative.

possess *verb*
He doesn't possess a car. have, own.

possessions *plural noun*
Many of their possessions were taken in the burglary. belongings, goods, property.

possibility *noun*
There's a possibility that it may rain later. chance, danger, likelihood, risk.

possible *adjective*
1 *Is it possible that life exists on other planets?* credible, likely, probable.
2 *It wasn't possible to move the piano.* feasible, practicable, practical.
AN OPPOSITE IS impossible.

possibly *adverb*
Possibly they'll arrive next week. maybe, perhaps.

post *noun*
1 *He put up some posts for a new fence.* A long round post is a ***pole***.
A post or pole which you use to support something is a ***prop***.
A post driven into the ground to make a foundation for a building, etc., is a ***pile***.
A post supporting a roof, etc., is a ***column*** or ***pillar***.
A post supporting a bridge is a ***pier***.

A post with a sharpened end to be driven into the ground is a **stake**.
A short post in the road or on a traffic island is a **bollard**.
The post which marks the finish of a race is the **winning post**.
2 *The post was delivered late.* cards, letters, mail, packets, parcels, postcards.
3 *She has been appointed to a new post.* appointment, job, position, situation.
If you are looking for a post, you are looking for **employment** or **work**.

post *verb*
1 *Did you post those letters?* despatch or dispatch, mail, send.
2 *The captain posted the team for Saturday's game on the noticeboard.* advertise, display, pin up, put up, stick up.

poster *noun*
They put up a poster to advertise sports day. advertisement, announcement, bill, notice, placard, sign.

postpone *verb*
As the weather was bad, they decided to postpone the game. defer, delay, put off.
To stop what you are doing for a time, intending to start again later, is to **adjourn** or **suspend** it.

posture *noun*
You can tell he's a soldier because of his upright posture. bearing.

pot *noun*

VARIOUS POTS YOU MIGHT FIND IN A KITCHEN: basin, bowl, casserole, cauldron, crock, dish, jar, pan, saucepan, teapot, urn.
SEE ALSO **container**.

potent *adjective*
1 *The chemicals had a potent smell.* overpowering, overwhelming, powerful, strong.
A potent drink is an **alcoholic** or **intoxicating** drink.
2 *It was a very potent argument.* effective, forceful, influential.
AN OPPOSITE IS weak.

potential *adjective*
1 *He's a potential champion.* budding, future, likely, possible, probable, promising.
2 *These floods are a potential disaster for the farmers.* looming, threatening.

potion *noun*
She drank a magic potion. drug, medicine, mixture.

pottery *noun*

A formal word for the art of making pottery is **ceramics**.

KINDS OF POTTERY: bone china, china, earthenware, porcelain, stoneware, terracotta.
The kind of pottery we eat and drink from is **crockery**.

THINGS OFTEN MADE OF POTTERY INCLUDE: basin, bowl, cup, dish, flowerpot, jug, mug, plate, pot, saucer, teapot, tureen, vase.

pouch *noun*
He kept his money in a leather pouch. bag, purse, sack.

poultry *noun*

KINDS OF POULTRY: bantam, chicken, duck, fowl, goose, guinea fowl, hen, pullet, turkey.
A male chicken specially fattened for eating is a **capon**.

pounce *verb*
to pounce on *The cat pounced on the mouse.* ambush, attack, jump on, leap on, seize, snatch, spring at, swoop down on.

pound *verb*
Huge waves pounded the stranded ship. batter, beat, hit, smash.
To pound something hard until it is powder is to **crush**, **grind**, or **pulverize** it.
To pound something soft is to **knead**, **mash**, or **pulp** it.

pour *verb*
1 *Water poured through the hole.* flow, gush, run, spill, spout, stream.
2 *I poured the milk out of the bottle.* serve, tip.

poverty *noun*
His poverty led him into crime.
hardship, need, shortage, want.
If you owe people money, you are *in debt*.
If you can't pay your debts, you are *bankrupt*.
AN OPPOSITE IS wealth.

powder *noun*
The powder got up her nose and made her sneeze. dust, particles.

powder *verb*
After bathing the baby, she powdered his bottom. cover with powder, dust, sprinkle.

powdered *adjective*
She used powdered coffee to make her drink. crushed, granulated, ground, pulverized.
Powdered milk, etc., is *dehydrated* or *dried* milk.

powdery *adjective*
The wind blew the powdery soil away.
dry, dusty, fine, loose.

power *noun*
1 They were impressed by the power of the machine. energy, force, might, strength.
2 He has the power to keep an audience interested. ability, competence, skill, talent.
3 A policeman has the power to arrest someone. authority, privilege, right.
4 The king had power over everyone.
command, control, dominance, domination, influence.

powerful *adjective*
1 He is the most powerful person in the land. dominant, forceful, important, influential.
2 The wrestler was a powerful man.
muscular, strong, tough, vigorous.
3 The enemy had a powerful army.
formidable, invincible, irresistible, mighty, potent.
4 He used some powerful arguments.
convincing, effective, impressive, persuasive.
AN OPPOSITE IS powerless or weak.

powerless *adjective*
The town was powerless against the enemy's might. defenceless, feeble, helpless, ineffective, weak.
AN OPPOSITE IS powerful.

practicable *adjective*
Is the plan practicable? achievable, attainable, feasible, possible, practical, realistic, workable.
AN OPPOSITE IS impracticable.

practical *adjective*
1 She is very practical—she does her own car repairs. capable, competent, expert, proficient, skilled.
2 He has a set of practical tools to make the heavy jobs easier. convenient, handy, usable, useful.
3 He's very practical in a crisis.
businesslike, efficient, helpful, realistic, sensible.
AN OPPOSITE IS impractical.
practical joke The plastic spider in his lunch box was meant to be a practical joke. hoax, prank, trick.

practically *adverb*
Keep going—we're practically there!
almost, as good as, just about, nearly, virtually.

practice *noun*
1 They need more practice if they want to win. exercises, preparation, rehearsal, training.
2 What will the plan involve in practice? action, operation, reality, use.
3 Smoking used to be a common practice. custom, habit, routine, tradition.

practise *verb*
1 The gymnastics coach keeps telling them to practise. do exercises, rehearse, train.
To practise just before you take part in an event is to *warm up*.
2 Practise what you preach. apply, carry out, do, follow, perform, put into practice.

praise *verb*
1 The critics praised their performance in the concert. commend, compliment, congratulate, exalt, pay tribute to, rave about.

To show that you think something is very good you can **applaud**, **cheer**, or **clap**.
AN OPPOSITE IS criticize.
2 *People go to church to praise God.* adore, glorify, honour, worship.

praise *noun*
She received a lot of praise for her work. admiration, applause, approval, compliments, congratulations, thanks, tribute.

prance *verb*
They started prancing about in a silly way. caper, cavort, dance, frisk, frolic, gambol, jump, leap, play, romp, skip.

prayer *noun*

Your private prayers are your **devotions** or **meditation**.
An **intercession** is a prayer to God on behalf of someone else.
A **petition** or **supplication** is a prayer to God on your own behalf.
An **invocation** is a prayer asking for God's help.
A **doxology** is a prayer of praise to God.
Prayer in which the congregation alternates with the priest or minister is a **litany**.
A **collect** is a short prayer in the Church of England and the Roman Catholic Church.
The prayer which Jesus taught his followers is the **Lord's Prayer**.
The **Fatiha** is a section of the Koran used as a prayer by Muslims.
The **Kaddish** is a daily prayer in praise of God in Jewish services.

preach *verb*
1 *The vicar preached about the Good Samaritan.* give a sermon.
2 *She's a fine one to preach about punctuality—she's always late!* give advice, lecture people, tell people what to do.

preacher *noun*
Someone who preaches about the Christian gospel is an **evangelist**.
Someone who goes to another country to preach is a **missionary**.
SEE ALSO **clergyman**.

precarious *adjective*
1 *The climbers were in a precarious situation on a narrow ledge.* dangerous, insecure, perilous, risky.
2 *Take care—that ladder looks precarious!* rickety, shaky, unsafe, unstable, unsteady, wobbly.
AN OPPOSITE IS secure.

precaution *noun*
She took the precaution of locking everything in the safe. defence, insurance, protection, safeguard, safety measure.

precede *verb*
1 *A police motorcyclist preceded the procession.* come before, go before, lead.
2 *The minister preceded his talk with an announcement.* introduce, lead into, start.
AN OPPOSITE IS follow.

precious *adjective*
1 *Your health is the most precious thing you have.* beneficial, important, invaluable, useful, valuable, worthwhile.
AN OPPOSITE IS unimportant.
2 *The crown glittered with precious gems.* costly, expensive, valuable.
AN OPPOSITE IS worthless.

precipice *noun*
The climber fell down a precipice. cliff, crag, drop.

précis *noun*
He gave a précis of the talk they heard yesterday. outline, summary.

precise *adjective*
1 *They must have precise measurements before they lay the new carpet.* accurate, correct, exact, meticulous, right.
AN OPPOSITE IS inaccurate.
2 *He gave us precise instructions about how to get to his house.* careful, clear, definite, detailed, specific.
AN OPPOSITE IS vague.

predator *noun*
The heron is one of the frog's predators. hunter.

predatory *adjective*
Predatory magpies stole eggs from a blackbird's nest. greedy, hunting, marauding, pillaging, plundering, preying.

predict *verb*
You can't predict what may happen in the future. forecast, foresee, foretell, prophesy.

predictable *adjective*
It was predictable that it would rain. expected, foreseeable, likely, probable.
AN OPPOSITE IS unpredictable.

predominate *verb*
Girls predominate in the rounders team. be in the majority, dominate.

preface *noun*
If you read the preface you'll find out what the book is about. introduction, prologue.

prefer *verb*
Do you prefer tea or coffee? choose, fancy, favour, incline towards, like, plump for, want.

preferable *adjective*
preferable to *She finds country life preferable to living in the city.* better than, more attractive than, more desirable than, nicer than, preferred to.

preference *noun*
1 *He has a preference for sweet things.* desire, fancy, liking, wish.
2 *There's milk or cream—what's your preference?* choice, inclination, option, pick.

prefix *noun*
AN OPPOSITE IS suffix.

pregnant *adjective*
She went regularly to the clinic for a check-up when she was pregnant. carrying a child, [*informal*] expecting.
A pregnant woman is an **expectant mother**.

prehistoric *adjective*

SOME PREHISTORIC REMAINS YOU MIGHT VISIT: barrow or tumulus, cromlech or stone circle, dolmen, hill fort, menhir or standing stone. ➡

The prehistoric period when the best tools and weapons were made of stone was the **Stone Age**.
Formal names for the Old, Middle, and New Stone Ages are **Palaeolithic**, **Mesolithic**, and **Neolithic** periods.
The period when the best tools and weapons were made of bronze was the **Bronze Age**.
The period when the best tools and weapons were made of iron was the **Iron Age**.
A person who studies prehistory by excavating and analysing remains is an **archaeologist**.
A person who studies fossils and ancient forms of life is a **palaeontologist**.

prejudice *noun*
1 *The referee was accused of showing prejudice.* bias, favouritism, unfairness.
AN OPPOSITE IS impartiality.
2 *They campaigned against racial prejudice.* discrimination, intolerance, narrow-mindedness.
Prejudice against other races is **racism**.
Prejudice against other nations is **xenophobia**.
Prejudice against the other sex is **sexism**.
Male prejudice against women is sometimes called **male chauvinism**.
Prejudice against other people because of your religion, etc., is **bigotry**.
AN OPPOSITE IS tolerance.

prejudiced *adjective*
The players thought the referee was prejudiced. biased, intolerant, narrow-minded, one-sided, unfair.
To be prejudiced against other races is to be **racist**.
To be prejudiced against other nations is to be **xenophobic**.
To be prejudiced against the other sex is to be **sexist**.
To be prejudiced against other people because of your religion, etc., is to be **bigoted**.
AN OPPOSITE IS impartial or tolerant.

preliminary *adjective*
   1 *Preliminary results with the new medicine are encouraging.* early, experimental, first, initial, provisional, trial.
   2 *She made some preliminary remarks before starting the main part of her talk.* introductory, opening, preparatory.
   The preliminary rounds of a competition are the *qualifying* rounds.

prelude *noun*
   The first match was an exciting prelude to the season. beginning, introduction, opening, preparation, start.
   The introduction to an opera, etc., is also called an *overture*.
   The introduction to a book is a *preface* or *prologue*.
   AN OPPOSITE IS conclusion or epilogue.

premises *plural noun*
   Keep out—these are private premises. buildings, property.

preoccupied *adjective*
   preoccupied in something *She didn't see me because she was preoccupied in her work.* absorbed in, concentrating on, engrossed in, intent on, interested in, involved in, obsessed with.

preparation *noun*
   The concert involved a lot of preparation. getting ready, making arrangements, organization, rehearsal.

prepare *verb*
   1 *There are things to prepare if you're going to have visitors.* arrange, get ready, make arrangements for, organize, plan, set up.
   2 *A teacher prepares pupils for exams.* educate, instruct, teach.
   To prepare for a play is to *rehearse*.
   To prepare people to take part in a sport is to *coach* them.
   To prepare yourself to take part in a sport is to *train*.
   To prepare yourself for an exam is to *revise*.
   to be prepared *He wanted a volunteer who was prepared to stay behind and wash up.* be able, be ready, be willing.

prescribe *noun*
   1 *The doctor prescribed some medicine.* advise, recommend, suggest.
   2 *The law prescribes heavy penalties for this offence.* assign, fix, lay down, specify.

presence *noun*
   Your presence is required. attendance.

present *adjective*
   1 *Is everyone present?* at hand, here, in attendance.
   2 *Who are the present champions?* current, existing.

present *noun*
   Did you get any presents on your birthday? gift.
   Money that you give to a waiter, etc., is a *gratuity* or *tip*.
   Money that you give to a charity, etc., is a *contribution* or *donation*.

present *verb*
   1 *The mayor presents the prizes on sports day.* award, hand over.
   2 *They presented a play about the history of the town.* act, perform, put on.
   3 *He presented the new designs for approval.* display, exhibit, show.
   4 *They were presented to the Prime Minister.* introduce, make known.

preserve *verb*
   1 *It's more difficult to preserve food in hot weather.* keep, save, store.

WORDS TO DESCRIBE PRESERVED FOODS: bottled, canned, chilled, cured, dehydrated, desiccated, dried, freeze-dried, frozen, pickled, refrigerated, salted, smoked, tinned.

   2 *It's important to preserve the countryside.* conserve, defend, guard, look after, maintain, protect, safeguard.
   AN OPPOSITE IS destroy.

preside *verb*
   The chairman was unable to preside at the meeting. be in charge, take charge.

president *noun*
   FOR PEOPLE IN CHARGE OF VARIOUS THINGS, SEE **chief** *noun*.

press verb
1 *Those things will fit in the case if you press them down.* compress, cram, crush, force, push, shove, squash, squeeze.
2 *She pressed her jeans.* flatten, iron, smooth.
3 *They pressed him to stay a bit longer.* beg, entreat, implore, persuade, put pressure on, urge.

press noun
1 *She read about the accident in the press.* magazines, newspapers.
2 *The press came to the opening of the new sports centre.* journalists, photographers, reporters.

pressure noun
1 *The pressure of the huge crowd broke down the barrier.* force, heaviness, pushing, shoving, squeezing, weight.
2 *They kept up the pressure but couldn't score a winning goal.* attack.
3 *If you were prime minister, could you stand the pressure?* [informal] hassle, strain, stress, tension.

pressurize verb
They pressurized him to join the gang. force, persuade, put pressure on, urge.

prestige noun
Their prestige suffered when they lost. credit, fame, glory, good name, honour, renown, reputation.

presume verb
1 *I presume you'd like something to eat.* assume, believe, guess, imagine, suppose, take it for granted, think.
2 *He wouldn't presume to tell her what to do!* be bold enough, be presumptuous enough, dare, take the liberty (of), venture.

presumptuous adjective
It was presumptuous of him to take charge. arrogant, bold, cheeky, forward, impertinent, impudent, self-important.

pretence noun
She didn't fool them—they saw through her pretence. act, acting, deceit, deception, disguise, insincerity, lying, make-believe, pose, posing, pretending, sham, show, trickery.

pretend verb
1 *Don't believe her—she's pretending.* act, bluff, deceive someone, fool, hoax, [informal] kid, lie, mislead someone, play a part, pose, put on an act.
To pretend that something happens is to **fake**, **imagine**, or **simulate** it.
2 *He pretended that he could play the piano.* allege, claim, declare, make out.
to pretend to be someone or **something** *She was pretending to be a policewoman.* disguise yourself as, imitate, impersonate, play the part of, pose as, profess to be, put on an act as.

pretty adjective
1 *They saw some pretty scenery in the hills.* attractive, beautiful, lovely, nice, picturesque, pleasing.
2 *The girl was wearing a pretty little dress.* charming, [informal] cute, dainty.
AN OPPOSITE IS ugly.

pretty adverb
[informal] *That's pretty good!* fairly, moderately, quite, rather, somewhat.
AN OPPOSITE IS very.

prevail verb
1 *In Britain, south-westerly winds prevail.* dominate, predominate.
2 *I think the more experienced team will prevail.* be victorious, come out on top, succeed, triumph, win.

prevailing, prevalent adjectives
What's the prevailing colour in this year's fashions? accepted, common, current, dominant, fashionable, general, influential, normal, ordinary, orthodox, popular, predominant, principal, usual, widespread.
AN OPPOSITE IS unusual.

prevent verb
1 *The driver could do nothing to prevent the accident.* avert, avoid.
2 *The police prevented an attempted bank raid.* block, foil, frustrate, intercept.
3 *There's not much you can do to prevent colds.* stave off, take precautions against, ward off.
4 *The scarecrow prevents the birds from eating the seed.* deter, discourage, frighten off, stop.

previous *adjective*
1 *She had enjoyed her previous visits to the museum.* earlier, former.
2 *He had phoned the previous day.* preceding.
AN OPPOSITE IS subsequent.

prey *noun*
The lion killed its prey. quarry, victim.

prey *verb*
to prey on *Owls prey on small animals.* eat, feed on, hunt, kill.

price *noun*
£30 is a reasonable price for a second-hand bike. amount, cost, expense, figure, payment, sum.
The price you pay for a journey on public transport is a *fare*.
The price you pay to send a letter is the *postage*.
The price you pay to use a private road, bridge, or tunnel is a *toll*.
The prices you have to pay at a hotel, etc., are their *charges*, *rates*, or *terms*.

priceless *adjective*
1 *The museum contained many priceless antiques.* costly, dear, expensive, precious, rare, valuable.
2 [*informal*] *The joke she told was priceless.* amusing, comic, funny, hilarious, witty.

prick *verb*
He pricked the balloon with a pin. jab, perforate, pierce, puncture, stab.

prickle *noun*
She fell into a bush full of prickles. barb, needle, spike, spine, thorn.

prickly *adjective*
The bush was a bit prickly. bristly, scratchy, sharp, spiky, spiny, thorny.

pride *noun*
1 *She looked with pride at what she had achieved.* dignity, satisfaction, self-respect.
2 [*uncomplimentary*] *Pride goes before a fall.* arrogance, conceit, pomposity, self-importance, self-righteousness, snobbery, vanity.
AN OPPOSITE IS humility.

priest *noun*
A priest of an ancient Celtic religion in Britain and France was a *Druid*.
A Buddhist priest is a *lama*.
SEE ALSO **clergyman**.

priggish *adjective*
They hated the priggish way he looked down on the rest of them. pious, pompous, prim, self-righteous, snobbish, [*informal*] stuck-up, superior.
AN OPPOSITE IS humble.

prim *adjective*
She's too prim to enjoy rude jokes! narrow-minded, priggish, proper, puritanical.
AN OPPOSITE IS broad-minded.

primarily *adverb*
He likes all kinds of music but primarily he's interested in jazz. above all, basically, chiefly, especially, first of all, fundamentally, mainly, mostly, predominantly, principally.

primary *adjective*
Their primary aim was to win the game. basic, chief, dominant, first, foremost, fundamental, greatest, leading, main, major, most important, outstanding, prime, principal, supreme, top.

prime *adjective*
1 *Her prime concern was to protect her children.* SEE **primary**.
2 *The local shop only sells prime beef.* best, excellent, first-class, select, top.

primitive *adjective*
1 *Primitive humans were hunters rather than farmers.* ancient, early, prehistoric, primeval.
AN OPPOSITE IS civilized.
2 *These days steam engines seem very primitive.* backward, basic, crude, elementary, obsolete, simple, undeveloped.
AN OPPOSITE IS advanced.

principal *adjective*
Their principal aim is to bring peace. basic, chief, dominant, first, foremost, fundamental, greatest, leading, main, major, most important, outstanding, primary, prime, supreme, top.

principle *noun*
> She taught him the principles of geometry. belief, rule, theory.
> **principles** He seemed to have no principles when it came to making money. morals, standards.

print *verb*
> 1,000 copies of the book were printed. issue, publish.

print *noun*
> 1 She found the tiny print difficult to read. characters, lettering, letters, printing, type.
> 2 I followed the prints of his feet in the snow. impression, mark.
> 3 It's a print, not an original painting. copy, duplicate, photocopy, reproduction.
> Something printed from information stored in a computer is a **printout** or **hard copy**.

priority *noun*
> Traffic on the main road has priority. precedence, right of way.

prise *verb*
> She tried to prise the lid off the box. force, lever, wrench.

prison *noun*
> He was sentenced to six months in prison. confinement, imprisonment.

> PLACES WHERE VARIOUS PEOPLE MAY BE DETAINED: [old use] Borstal, compound, concentration camp, detention centre, [old use] dungeon, gaol or jail, guardhouse, [informal] lock-up, open prison, [American] penitentiary, police cell, [American] reformatory.
> People detained in their own home are **under house arrest**.
> People detained before their trial are **in custody** or **on remand**.
> Before the trial they may be detained in a **remand centre**.

prisoner *noun*
> The prisoner tried to escape from jail. captive, convict.
> A person who is held prisoner until some demand is met is a **hostage**.

private *adjective*
> 1 Keep out—this is private property. privately owned.
> 2 What I write in my diary is private. confidential, intimate, personal, secret. Secret official documents are **classified** or **restricted** documents.
> 3 Can we go somewhere a little more private? concealed, hidden, isolated, little known, quiet, secluded.
> AN OPPOSITE IS public.

privilege *noun*
> Club members enjoy special privileges. advantage, benefit, concession, right.

privileged *adjective*
> Rich people are in a privileged position compared with poor people. advantageous, favoured, powerful, special, superior.

prize *noun*
> He held on to his lead and won the first prize. award, reward, trophy.
> Money that you win as a prize or in gambling is your **winnings**.
> Prize money that keeps increasing until someone wins it is a **jackpot**.

prize *verb*
> The necklace was one that her mother had prized for years. appreciate, cherish, esteem, hold dear, like, rate, regard, revere, treasure, value.
> AN OPPOSITE IS dislike.

probable *adjective*
> If you've got toothache, it's probable that you need a filling. expected, feasible, likely, predictable, presumed.
> AN OPPOSITE IS improbable.

probe *noun*
> They were conducting a probe into corruption within the company. examination, inquiry, investigation, study.

probe *verb*
> 1 The doctor probed the wound. poke, prod.
> 2 New equipment can probe the depths of the sea. explore, penetrate, see into.
> 3 The programme probed corruption within the police force. examine, inquire into, investigate, look into, scrutinize, study.

problem *noun*
1 *Can you help me solve this problem?*
dilemma, mystery, poser, puzzle,
question.
A puzzling question which people ask
as a joke is a **conundrum** or **riddle**.
2 *Not having any money is a big
problem.* difficulty, [*informal*]
headache, snag, trouble, worry.

procedure *noun*
*She explained the procedure for making
pastry.* course of action, method, plan
of action, process, system, technique,
way.
A procedure which you follow regularly
is a **routine**.
A procedure which you are planning is
a **scheme** or **strategy**.

proceed *verb*
Settle down, then we can proceed. carry
on, continue, go ahead, go on, make
progress, move forward, progress.

proceedings *plural noun*
1 *The proceedings were interrupted by a
fire alarm.* events, [*informal*] goings-
on, happenings, matters, things.
2 *He threatened to start proceedings if
she didn't pay her debts.* a lawsuit,
legal action.

proceeds *plural noun*
*They added up the proceeds from the
sale.* earnings, income, profit, revenue,
takings.

process *noun*
*They have developed a new process for
making steel rustproof.* method,
operation, procedure, system,
technique.

process *verb*
*They process crude oil before we use it
as fuel.* alter, change, convert, deal
with, prepare, refine, transform, treat.

procession *noun*
*The procession made its way slowly
down the hill.* column, line, parade.
A procession of people on horses is a
cavalcade.
A procession of motor vehicles is a
motorcade.
A procession of people in costume is a
pageant.
A funeral procession is a **cortège**.

proclaim *verb*
*The judges proclaimed that the winner
was disqualified.* announce, declare,
make known, pronounce.

prod *verb*
He prodded me in the back with a ruler.
dig, jab, nudge, poke, push.

produce *verb*
1 *Some lorries produce a lot of fumes.*
cause, create, generate, give rise to.
2 *The tree produced a good crop of
apples this year.* grow, yield.
3 *The factory produces cars and vans.*
construct, make, manufacture.
4 *The referee's decision produced angry
shouts from the crowd.* arouse, provoke,
result in, stimulate.
5 *As a journalist, she has to produce
interesting articles every day.* compose,
invent, think up.
6 *She can produce evidence to prove she
was right.* bring out, present, put
forward, reveal, supply.

produce *noun*
The shop sells home-grown produce.
fruit and vegetables, greengrocery.
The produce of a farm is its **crops** or
harvest.

product *noun*
1 *The company launched a new range
of beauty products.* article, item,
substance.
2 *The problems with the car are the
product of years of neglect.*
consequence, outcome, result, upshot.

production *noun*
1 *Production at the factory has
increased this year.* output.
2 *They went to see a new production at
the Arts Theatre.* performance, play,
show.

productive *adjective*
1 *The soil is rich and productive.*
fertile, fruitful.
2 *It wasn't a very productive meeting.*
beneficial, constructive, effective,
profitable, rewarding, useful, valuable,
worthwhile.
AN OPPOSITE IS unproductive.

profession *noun*
Nursing is a worthwhile profession.
business, career, employment, job,
occupation, work.

professional *adjective*
1 *She sought the advice of professional
builders.* competent, efficient, expert,
qualified, responsible, skilled, trained.
2 *It's a very professional piece of work.*
competent, efficient, proficient, skilful.
AN OPPOSITE IS incompetent.
3 *His ambition is to be a professional
footballer.* paid.
AN OPPOSITE IS amateur.

proficient *adjective*
She's a very proficient typist.
accomplished, capable, efficient,
experienced, expert, skilful, skilled.
AN OPPOSITE IS incompetent

profile *noun*
1 *I didn't see his face properly—I just
saw his profile.* outline, side view,
silhouette.
2 *The local paper published a profile of
each of the candidates.* account,
biography, sketch.

profit *noun*
1 *They sold the business and bought a
yacht with the profit.* gain, surplus.
The extra money you get on your
savings is *interest*.
2 *There's no profit in shouting at the
referee from the bench.* advantage,
benefit.

profit *verb*
1 *Did you profit from the sale?* gain,
make money.
2 *It won't profit anyone to get angry.*
benefit, help.

profitable *adjective*
1 *Selling things at a car-boot sale can
be profitable.* advantageous, beneficial,
productive, rewarding, worthwhile.
2 *The business has been very profitable
in recent years.* commercial,
moneymaking, paying, profit-making.
AN OPPOSITE IS unprofitable.

profound *adjective*
1 *They expressed their profound
sympathy.* deep, sincere.
AN OPPOSITE IS insincere.

2 *The book is full of original and
profound insights.* intellectual,
knowledgeable, learned, philosophical,
serious, thoughtful.
AN OPPOSITE IS superficial.

profuse *adjective*
*He offered his profuse apologies for the
mistake.* abundant, ample,
extravagant, lavish, plentiful.
AN OPPOSITE IS meagre.

programme *noun*
1 *We worked out a programme for
sports day.* plan, schedule, timetable.
A list of things to be done at a meeting
is an ***agenda***.
2 *There was a really good programme
on TV last night.* broadcast,
performance, production,
transmission.

progress *noun*
1 *I traced their progress on the map.*
advance, journey, movements, route,
travels, way.
2 *Progress in computer technology has
been amazingly rapid.* development,
evolution, growth, improvement.
An important piece of progress is a
breakthrough.

progress *verb*
1 *Work on the new building was
progressing rapidly.* advance, continue,
forge ahead, go on, make headway,
make progress, move forward, proceed.
2 *Technology is bound to progress even
further.* develop, evolve, improve.
AN OPPOSITE IS retreat.

progression *noun*
*He followed the progression of events
with interest.* advance, development,
evolution, sequence, series, succession.

progressive *adjective*
1 *There's been a progressive
improvement in their performance this
season.* accelerating, continuous,
escalating, growing, increasing,
ongoing, steady.
AN OPPOSITE IS erratic.
2 *The new manager has progressive
ideas.* advanced, forward-looking, go-
ahead, up-to-date.
AN OPPOSITE IS conservative.

prohibit *verb*
> They decided to prohibit smoking on the buses. ban, forbid, make illegal, outlaw, rule out, stop, veto.
> AN OPPOSITE IS allow.

project *noun*
> 1 We did a history project on the Victorians. activity, assignment, piece of research, task.
> 2 The council announced a project to build a bypass. plan, proposal, scheme.

project *verb*
> 1 A narrow ledge projects from the cliff. bulge, extend, jut out, overhang, protrude, stand out, stick out.
> 2 The lighthouse projects a beam of light. cast, shine, throw out.

prolong *verb*
> They prolonged their visit by a few days. draw out, extend, increase, lengthen, make longer, stretch out.
> AN OPPOSITE IS shorten.

prominent *adjective*
> 1 He has very prominent cheekbones. bulging, jutting out, projecting, protruding, sticking out.
> 2 The windmill on the hill is a prominent landmark. conspicuous, noticeable, obvious, recognizable.
> AN OPPOSITE IS inconspicuous.
> 3 She's a prominent member of the society. celebrated, distinguished, eminent, famous, important, leading, major, notable, outstanding, renowned, well-known.
> AN OPPOSITE IS unknown.

promise *noun*
> 1 We had promises of help from many people. assurance, guarantee, pledge, vow, word, word of honour.
> 2 That young actor shows promise. potential, talent.

promise *verb*
> 1 She promised to come. agree, consent, undertake.
> 2 He promised that he would pay me back. assure someone, give your word, guarantee, swear, take an oath, vow.

promising *adjective*
> 1 The new goalkeeper made a promising first appearance on Saturday. encouraging, hopeful.
> 2 He's a promising young actor. budding, likely, talented, [informal] up-and-coming.

promontory *noun*
> They stood on the promontory, looking out to the sea. cape, headland, peninsula.

promote *verb*
> 1 He was promoted to captain. elevate, exalt, move up, raise, upgrade.
> 2 They gave away free samples to promote the new shampoo. advertise, make known, market, [informal] plug, publicize, sell.
> 3 The conference aimed to promote trade between the two countries. back, encourage, help, support.

promoter *noun*
> One of the festival's promoters withdrew their support. backer, sponsor.

prompt *adjective*
> She received a prompt reply to her letter. immediate, instant, punctual, quick, rapid, swift, unhesitating.
> AN OPPOSITE IS delayed.

prompt *verb*
> 1 The demonstration prompted the police to increase security in the town. encourage, motivate, persuade, provoke, stimulate.
> 2 The speaker was hesitant and the chairman had to prompt her. jog your memory, remind.

prone *adjective*
> 1 The victim was lying prone on the floor. face down, on the front.
> To lie face upwards is to be **supine**.
> 2 She's prone to exaggerate. inclined, liable, likely.

prong *noun*
> Pierce the sausage with the prongs of a fork. point, spike.

pronounce *verb*
1 *Try to pronounce the words clearly.*
articulate, say, sound, speak, utter.
2 *The doctor pronounced her fully recovered.* announce, declare, judge, proclaim.

pronounced *adjective*
She walked with a pronounced limp.
clear, conspicuous, definite, distinct, evident, marked, noticeable, obvious, perceptible, prominent, striking, unmistakable.
AN OPPOSITE IS imperceptible.

pronunciation *noun*
The announcer's pronunciation was not very clear. accent, articulation, intonation.

proof *noun*
The police say they have proof of her guilt. confirmation, evidence.

prop *noun*
The construction was supported by 300 steel props. strut, support.
A stick to prop yourself on when you hurt a leg is a **crutch**.
Part of a building which props up a wall is a **buttress**.

prop *verb*
He propped his bike against the kerb.
lean, rest, stand.
to prop something up *The roof will have to be propped up while the repairs are carried out.* hold up, reinforce, support.

propaganda *noun*
The play is nothing but political propaganda. advertising, indoctrination, publicity.

propel *verb*
The boat is propelled by using a long paddle. drive forward, move forward, push forward.

propeller *noun*
The large horizontal propeller of a helicopter is a **rotor**.
The underwater propeller of a ship is a **screw**.

proper *adjective*
1 *They had not followed the proper procedures.* acceptable, correct, normal, right, suitable, usual.
AN OPPOSITE IS wrong or incorrect.
2 *He should get the proper punishment for the crime.* appropriate, deserved, fair, fitting, just, lawful, legal, suitable, valid.
AN OPPOSITE IS inappropriate.
3 *In those days, it wasn't thought proper for a woman to go on the stage.* decent, respectable, tasteful.
AN OPPOSITE IS rude.
4 [*informal*] *He's in a proper mess!* absolute, complete, great, perfect, thorough, total, utter.

property *noun*
1 *He owns a great deal of property.* assets, belongings, goods, possessions. Property in the form of money is a **fortune** or **riches** or **wealth**.
2 *Keep off! Private property!* buildings, estate, land, premises.
3 *An unusual property of this gas is its smell.* characteristic, feature, peculiarity, quality.

prophecy *noun*
Her prophecy came true. forecast, prediction.

prophesy *verb*
She prophesied that it would rain. forecast, foresee, foretell, predict.

prophet, prophetess *nouns*

> PEOPLE WHO ARE SUPPOSED TO BE ABLE TO FORETELL THE FUTURE: clairvoyant, forecaster, fortune-teller, mystic, oracle, seer, soothsayer.

proportion *noun*
1 *A large proportion of the audience were delighted.* fraction, part, section, share.
2 *What is the proportion of girls to boys in your class?* balance, ratio.
proportions *The sports centre is a building of large proportions.* dimensions, measurements, size.

proposal *noun*
>The council discussed a proposal to build a supermarket. plan, project, recommendation, scheme, suggestion.

propose *verb*
>1 He proposed a change in the rules. ask for, recommend, suggest.
>2 He proposes to attend next month's meeting. aim, intend, mean, plan.
>3 She was proposed as a candidate in the local election. nominate, put forward.

proprietor *noun*
>He is the proprietor of a local restaurant. [informal] boss, manager, owner.

prosecute *verb*
>They prosecuted him for dangerous driving. accuse (of), bring to trial, charge (with), start legal proceedings against.
>To take someone to court to try to get money from them is to **sue** them.

prospect *noun*
>1 There's a prospect of a change in the weather. chance, expectation, hope, likelihood, possibility, probability, promise.
>2 The hotel has a lovely prospect across the valley. outlook, panorama, view.

prospect *verb*
>The petrol company is prospecting for oil. explore, search, survey.

prosper *verb*
>He expects his business to prosper this year. become prosperous, be successful, boom, do well, expand, flourish, grow, progress, succeed, thrive.
>AN OPPOSITE IS fail.

prosperity *noun*
>Tourism has brought prosperity to the region. affluence, [informal] boom, growth, plenty, success, wealth.

prosperous *adjective*
>The north of the country is more prosperous than the south. affluent, rich, successful, wealthy, well off.
>AN OPPOSITE IS poor.

protect *verb*
>1 A sentry was posted outside to protect the palace. defend, guard, keep safe, safeguard, secure.
>2 I put up an umbrella to protect myself from the sun. insulate, preserve, screen, shade, shield.

protection *noun*
>Use a sun cream that will give you adequate protection against harmful ultra-violet rays. cover, defence, insulation, shelter.

>PEOPLE WHO PROTECT YOU: defender, guard, protector.
>A guard who protects a person's life is their **bodyguard**.
>An informal word for a bodyguard is **minder**.
>Someone who protects someone's interests is their **benefactor** or **patron**.

protest *noun*
>1 The scheme was dropped following protests from local residents. complaint, objection.
>A general protest is an **outcry**.
>2 There was a big protest in the square. [informal] demo, demonstration, march, rally.

protest *verb*
>1 Local residents protested about the introduction of the scheme. argue, complain, express disapproval, grouse, grumble, make a protest, object (to).
>2 A big crowd protested in the square. demonstrate, [informal] hold a demo, march.

protrude *verb*
>His stomach protrudes above his waistband. bulge, jut out, poke out, project, stand out, stick out, swell.

proud *adjective*
>1 Her father's really proud of her. delighted (with), pleased (with).
>AN OPPOSITE IS disgusted (with).
>2 [uncomplimentary] He's too proud to mix with the likes of us! arrogant, [informal] cocky, conceited, grand, haughty, self-important, self-righteous, snobbish, [informal] stuck-up, superior, vain.
>AN OPPOSITE IS humble.

prove *verb*
>The evidence will prove that he is innocent. confirm, demonstrate, establish, verify.
>AN OPPOSITE IS disprove.

proverb *noun* SEE **saying**

proverbial *adjective*
>'Many hands make light work' is a proverbial saying. conventional, famous, traditional, well-known.

provide *verb*
>**1** We'll provide the food if you bring something to drink. arrange for, contribute, donate, lay on.
>To provide food and drink for people is to **cater** for them.
>**2** The council provided money for new equipment. allot, allow, [informal] fork out, give, grant.
>To provide money which you promise to give back later is to **lend** or **loan** it.
>**3** They provided us with the essential equipment. equip, supply.
>**to provide for 1** He had provided for an emergency of this sort. get ready for, prepare for, take precautions against.
>**2** Parents have to provide for their children. care for, look after, support, take care of.

provision *noun*
>Many parents would welcome the provision of childcare facilities at work. providing, setting up, supply, supplying.
>**provisions** We had enough provisions for two weeks. food, groceries, rations, stores, supplies.

provisional *adjective*
>The list of players is only provisional. preliminary, temporary.
>AN OPPOSITE IS permanent.

provocation *noun*
>The dog won't attack without some provocation. [informal] aggravation, challenge, inducement, taunting, teasing.

provoke *verb*
>**1** I didn't do anything to provoke him. [informal] aggravate, anger, annoy, exasperate, incense, infuriate, irritate, offend, taunt, tease, torment, vex, worry.
>AN OPPOSITE IS pacify.

>**2** His jokes provoked a lot of laughter. arouse, bring about, cause, generate, give rise to, induce, produce, prompt, spark off, stimulate, stir up, whip up.

prowl *verb*
>Guard dogs prowled about the grounds of the palace. creep, roam, slink, sneak, steal.

prudent *adjective*
>It would be prudent to start saving some money. careful, cautious, sensible, shrewd, thoughtful, wise.
>AN OPPOSITE IS reckless or unwise.

prune *verb*
>Mum prunes her roses every spring. cut back, trim.

pry *verb*
>Don't pry—it's none of your business! be curious, be inquisitive, [informal] be nosy, interfere, [informal] nose about or around, snoop.
>**to pry into something** Don't pry into my affairs! inquire into, interfere in, investigate, meddle in, [informal] poke your nose into, spy on.

pseudonym *noun*
>George Orwell isn't his real name—it's a pseudonym. alias, assumed name, false name.

psychic *adjective*
>She was said to have psychic powers. supernatural, telepathic.

psychological *adjective*
>The doctor said the patient's problem was psychological. emotional, mental.

pub *noun*
>They went to the pub for a drink. [old use] inn, [informal] local, public house, [old use] tavern.
>Other places where alcoholic drinks are served are a **bar** or **wine bar**.

puberty *noun*
>You reach puberty in your teens. adolescence, sexual maturity.

public *adjective*
>**1** There have been proposals to ban smoking in all public places. accessible, communal, open, shared.
>AN OPPOSITE IS private.

2 *It's public knowledge that he went to prison.* common, familiar, general, popular, unconcealed, universal, well-known.
AN OPPOSITE IS secret.

public *noun*
the public *The public has a right to know how government works.* citizens, the community, everyone, the nation, people in general, the population, society, the voters.
in public *Should people be allowed to smoke in public?* anywhere, in the open, openly, publicly.

publication *noun*
She's celebrating the publication of her first novel. issuing, printing, production.
Various publications are *books* and *magazines*.

publicity *noun*
1 *Did you see the publicity for the play?* advertisements, advertising, promotion.
2 *Famous people don't always enjoy publicity.* being in the limelight, fame, notoriety.

publicize *verb*
They asked the local radio station to publicize the concert. advertise, announce, make known, market, [*informal*] plug, promote.

publish *verb*
1 *The magazine is published every week.* bring out, circulate, issue, print, produce, release.
2 *When will they publish the results?* announce, communicate, declare, disclose, make known, make public, publicize, report, reveal.
To publish information which is supposed to be secret is to *leak* it.
To publish information on radio or TV is to *broadcast* it.

pudding *noun*
Do you want any pudding? dessert, sweet.
FOR VARIOUS FOODS, SEE **food**.

puff *noun*
1 *A puff of wind caught his hat.* breath, flurry, gust.
2 *A puff of smoke rose from the chimney.* cloud, whiff.

puff *verb*
1 *The engine puffed black smoke into the blue sky.* belch, blow out, emit, send out.
2 *By the end of the race I was puffing.* breathe heavily, gasp, pant, wheeze.
3 *The sails puffed out as the wind rose.* become inflated, billow, swell.

pull *verb*
1 *He pulled the chair nearer the desk.* drag, draw, haul, lug, tow, trail.
AN OPPOSITE IS push.
2 *Be careful—you nearly pulled my arm off!* jerk, pluck, rip, tug, wrench.
to pull out 1 *She pulled the cork out of the bottle.* extract, remove, take out.
2 *He had to pull out of the race.* back out, retire, withdraw.
to pull someone's leg *I hope you aren't pulling my leg!* make fun of you, play a trick on you, tease you.
to pull through *It was a bad accident, but the doctors expect her to pull through.* get better, recover, revive, survive.
to pull up *She pulled up at the traffic lights.* draw up, halt, put the brakes on, stop.

pulp *verb*
The strawberries were pulped and mixed with the ice cream. crush, liquidize, mash, squash.

pulse *noun*
You can feel the pulse of blood in your veins. beat, drumming, throb.

pump *verb*
The fire brigade pumped water out of the cellar. drain, draw off, empty, raise.
To move liquid from a higher container to a lower one through a tube is to *siphon* it.

punch *verb*
1 *He punched me on the nose!* jab, poke, prod, thump.
SEE ALSO **hit** *verb*.
2 *I need to punch another hole in my belt.* bore, pierce.

punctual *adjective*
The bus was punctual today. in good time, on time, prompt.
AN OPPOSITE IS late.

punctuation *noun*

PUNCTUATION MARKS: apostrophe, brackets, colon, comma, dash, exclamation mark, full stop, hyphen, question mark, quotation marks or speech marks, semicolon, square brackets.

OTHER MARKS YOU USE IN WRITING: accent, asterisk or star, bullet point, slash.

puncture *noun*
1 *I had a puncture on the way home.* burst tyre, flat tyre.
2 *I found the puncture in my tyre.* hole, leak, pinprick.

puncture *verb*
A nail punctured my tyre. deflate, let down, perforate, pierce.

punish *verb*
Those responsible for this crime will be severely punished. make an example of, penalize.

punishment *noun*
Many people believe that the punishment should fit the crime. correction, penalty.
Making someone suffer because they have harmed you is *revenge*.

Punishing someone by taking their life is *capital punishment* or *execution*.

FORMS OF CAPITAL PUNISHMENT: beheading or decapitation or the guillotine, burning, crucifixion, electrocution, firing squad or shooting, gassing, hanging, injection, poisoning, stoning.

Punishing someone by hurting them physically is *corporal punishment*.

FORMS OF CORPORAL PUNISHMENT: a beating, the birch, the cane, flogging, [*informal*] a hiding, a spanking, torture, whipping. ➡

OTHER FORMS OF PUNISHMENT: banishment or exile, [*old use*] Borstal, community service, confiscation of property, deportation, detention, a fine, a forfeit, gaol or jail, an imposition, imprisonment, probation.

FORMS OF PUNISHMENT YOU MAY READ ABOUT IN HISTORY BOOKS: ducking-stool, keelhauling, the pillory, the stocks, the treadmill.

puny *adjective*
He's rather a puny child. delicate, feeble, frail, pathetic, weak, weedy.
AN OPPOSITE IS strong.

pupil *noun*
There are 33 pupils in our class. learner, scholar, schoolchild, student.
Someone who follows a great teacher is a *disciple*.

purchase *verb*
He used the money to purchase a new bike. acquire, buy, get, obtain, pay for.

purchase *noun*
1 *She opened her bag and examined her purchases.* acquisition.
2 *The climbers had difficulty getting any purchase on the rock face.* grasp, hold, leverage.

pure *adjective*
1 *The bracelet is made of pure gold.* authentic, genuine, real.
2 *He was talking pure nonsense.* absolute, complete, perfect, sheer, total, utter.
3 *Their products are made from pure ingredients.* natural, wholesome.
4 *They swam in the pure, clear water of the lake.* clean, fresh, unpolluted.
Water which is purified by boiling it and condensing the vapour is *distilled* water.
AN OPPOSITE IS impure.

purge *verb*
The boss took action to purge all dishonest employees. expel, get rid of, remove, root out.

purify *verb*
You can't drink this water unless you purify it. clean, make pure.
You destroy germs by **disinfecting** or **sterilizing** things.
You take solid particles out of liquids by **filtering** them.
To purify water by boiling it and condensing the vapour is to **distil** it.
To purify crude oil is to **refine** it.

puritanical *adjective*
He's rather puritanical about moral matters. austere, narrow-minded, prim, severe, strict.
AN OPPOSITE IS broad-minded.

purpose *noun*
1 Have you got a particular purpose in mind? aim, ambition, end, goal, hope, intention, objective, outcome, plan, result, target, wish.
2 What's the purpose of this gadget? point, use, usefulness, value.

purposeful *adjective*
Her purposeful look showed she meant business. decisive, determined, positive.
AN OPPOSITE IS aimless or hesitant.

purposeless *adjective*
He felt he was leading a purposeless existence. aimless, pointless, senseless, unnecessary, useless.
AN OPPOSITE IS useful.

purposely *adverb*
Was it an accident, or did he do it purposely? consciously, deliberately, intentionally, knowingly, on purpose.
AN OPPOSITE IS accidentally.

purse *noun*
She lost all her money when her purse was stolen. bag, handbag, pouch.
A container for paper money, credit cards, etc., is a **wallet**.

pursue *verb*
1 He ran off, pursued by two police officers. chase, follow, go in pursuit of, hound, hunt, run after, tail, track down.
2 She pursued her acting career with great determination. carry on, continue, keep up with, proceed with, work at.

pursuit *noun*
1 The pursuit of the fox lasted for hours. chase, hunt, tracking down, trail.
2 They both enjoyed outdoor pursuits. activity, hobby, interest, occupation, pastime, pleasure.

push *verb*
1 They pushed us out of the way. barge, drive, elbow, force, hustle, jostle, propel, shove, thrust.
AN OPPOSITE IS pull.
2 He pushed his things into a bag. compress, cram, crush, insert, pack, press, put, ram, squash, squeeze.
3 They pushed him to work even harder. bully, [informal] lean on, persuade, pressurize, put pressure on, urge.
4 The firm is pushing its new product hard. advertise, market, [informal] plug, promote, publicize.

put *verb*
1 The council plans to put a recycling centre next to the car park. locate, situate.
2 Put the books on the shelf. arrange, dump, leave, place, set down, stand.
3 Put your head on the cushion. lay, lean, rest.
4 I'll put some pictures on the wall. attach, fasten, fix, hang.
5 They put guards outside the bank. position, stand, station.
6 She wanted to put her point of view. express, say, state.
to put something off They had to put off their visit because of the fog. defer, delay, postpone.
to put something out The firemen quickly put out the blaze. extinguish, quench, smother.
to put something up 1 It doesn't take long to put up the tent. construct, erect, set up.
2 I'm going to buy a new bike before they put up the price. increase, raise.
to put up with something I don't know how you put up with that noise. bear, endure, stand, tolerate.

puzzle *noun*
Can you solve this puzzle for me? difficulty, dilemma, mystery, [informal] poser, problem, question.

puzzle *verb*
1 *I was very puzzled by her reply.* baffle, bewilder, confuse, fox, mystify, perplex.
2 *We puzzled over the problem for hours.* brood, meditate, ponder, think, worry.

puzzling *adjective*
There were many puzzling aspects of the affair. baffling, bewildering, confusing, inexplicable, insoluble, mysterious, mystifying, perplexing.
AN OPPOSITE IS straightforward.

quadrangle *noun*
The covered path round the inside of a courtyard next to a cathedral or monastery is the ***cloisters***.

quail *verb*
She quailed at the furious expression on his face. back away, falter, flinch, hesitate, quake, recoil, show fear, shrink back, tremble.

quaint *adjective*
They stayed in a quaint thatched cottage. antiquated, charming, curious, old-fashioned, picturesque.

quake *verb*
The whole building quaked when the bomb went off. quiver, rock, shake, sway, tremble, vibrate, wobble.

qualification *noun*
He gave his approval to the scheme, but with several qualifications. condition, exception, reservation.
qualifications *Have you got the qualifications to do the job properly?* ability, competence, experience, know-how, knowledge, skill, suitability, training.

qualified *adjective*
1 *This job needs a qualified electrician.* competent, experienced, professional, skilled, trained.
AN OPPOSITE IS amateur.

2 *He's not qualified for a lorry driver's job.* appropriate, eligible, suitable.
3 *He received qualified praise for his efforts.* cautious, half-hearted, limited, modified.

qualify *verb*
1 *She doesn't qualify for unemployment benefit.* be eligible, be qualified, have the qualifications.
2 *The first three runners will qualify to take part in the final.* get through, pass.
3 *She felt the need to qualify her last statement.* limit, modify, restrict, soften, weaken.

quality *noun*
1 *The butcher sells top quality meat.* class, grade, standard, value.
2 *The most obvious quality of rubber is that it stretches.* characteristic, feature, peculiarity, property.

quantity *noun*
1 *The council deals with a large quantity of rubbish every week.* amount, bulk, [*informal*] load, mass, volume, weight.
2 *We had a large quantity of empty bottles to get rid of.* number.
When we add up numbers, we get a ***sum*** or ***total***.
FOR WORDS WE USE WHEN MEASURING VARIOUS QUANTITIES, SEE **measurement**.

quarrel *noun*
We have quarrels, but really we are good friends. argument, clash, conflict, difference of opinion, disagreement, dispute, misunderstanding, row, squabble.
Continuous quarrelling is ***strife***.
A long-lasting quarrel is a ***feud*** or ***vendetta***.
A quarrel in which people become violent is a ***brawl*** or ***fight***.

quarrel *verb*
They quarrelled about money. argue, clash, differ, disagree, fall out, fight, row, squabble.
to quarrel with something *I can't quarrel with your decision.* complain about, disagree with, object to, oppose, question, take exception to.

quarrelsome *adjective*
He's a very quarrelsome man.
aggressive, bad-tempered, defiant, excitable, hostile, impatient, irritable, mutinous, quick-tempered, rebellious.
AN OPPOSITE IS placid.

quarry *noun*
1 *This quarry produces limestone for road building.* excavation.
A place with shafts and tunnels where minerals are dug out is a *mine* or *pit*.
2 *The lion stalked its quarry.* prey, victim.

quarters *plural noun*
The soldiers stayed in quarters in the town. accommodation, billets, housing, living quarters, lodgings.

quaver *verb*
His voice quavered. falter, quake, quiver, shake, tremble, waver.

quay *noun*
The ship unloaded its cargo onto the quay. berth, dock, harbour, jetty, landing stage, pier, wharf.

queasy *adjective*
The sea was rough and I began to feel a bit queasy. ill, poorly, queer, sick, unwell.

queer *adjective*
1 *I heard a queer noise.* curious, eerie, funny, inexplicable, mysterious, puzzling, strange, uncanny, unusual, weird.
2 *There's something queer going on.* abnormal, [*informal*] fishy, odd, peculiar, shady, suspicious.
3 *He was feeling rather queer after eating so much chocolate.* poorly, queasy, sick, unwell.
SEE ALSO **ill**.
AN OPPOSITE IS normal.

quench *verb*
1 *The iced lemonade soon quenched her thirst.* cool, satisfy.
2 *They dumped sand on the embers to quench the fire.* extinguish, put out, smother.

query *noun, verb* SEE **question** *noun, verb*

quest *noun*
The quest for a vaccine for the disease continues. hunt, search.

question *noun*
1 *I'll try to answer your question.* demand, enquiry or inquiry, query.
A question which someone asks as a joke is a *brain-teaser* or *conundrum* or *riddle*.
A series of questions asked as a game is a *quiz*.
A set of questions which someone asks in order to get information is a *questionnaire* or *survey*.
2 *There's some question about his honesty.* argument, controversy, debate, dispute, doubt, problem, uncertainty.

question *verb*
1 *Four men were being questioned about the burglary.* ask, cross-examine, examine, grill, interrogate, interview, quiz.
2 *He questioned the referee's decision.* argue over, challenge, dispute, object to, quarrel with, query.

questionable *adjective*
1 *It's questionable how necessary these changes are.* debatable, doubtful, uncertain, unclear.
2 *The police said her evidence was questionable.* unconvincing, unreliable.

questionnaire *noun*
They were asked to fill in a questionnaire. opinion poll, survey.

queue *noun*
There was a queue of cars at the level crossing. column, file, line, row, string, tailback.

queue *verb*
Please queue at the door. form a queue, line up, wait in a queue.

quick *adjective*
1 *You'd better be quick—the bus leaves in 10 minutes.* fast, rapid, swift.
2 *He made a quick exit.* hasty, headlong, hurried, [*informal*] nippy, speedy, sudden.
3 *Do you mind if we have a quick rest?* brief, momentary, short.

4 *I hope to get a quick reply.* early, immediate, instant, instantaneous, prompt, punctual, snappy, unhesitating.
5 *She's very quick at mental arithmetic.* acute, alert, bright, clever, perceptive, sharp, smart.
AN OPPOSITE IS leisurely or slow.

quicken *verb*
Their pace quickened. accelerate, become faster, hasten, hurry up, speed up.

quiet *adjective*
1 *The deserted house was quiet.* noiseless, silent, soundless.
AN OPPOSITE IS noisy.
2 *They spoke in quiet whispers.* hushed, low, soft.
Something that is so quiet that you can't hear it is **inaudible**.
AN OPPOSITE IS loud.
3 *She's a very quiet, modest person.* reserved, retiring, shy, thoughtful, uncommunicative.
AN OPPOSITE IS talkative.
4 *We were in a quiet mood.* calm, peaceful, placid, restful, serene, tranquil, untroubled.
AN OPPOSITE IS excited.
5 *We found a quiet place for a picnic.* isolated, lonely, private, secluded.
AN OPPOSITE IS busy.

quieten *verb*
1 *Her mother was trying to quieten her.* calm, hush, pacify, soothe.
2 *A silencer quietens the noise of the engine.* deaden, muffle, soften, suppress.
To use a special device to make a musical instrument quieter is to **mute** it.

quit *verb*
1 *Police were called in when he refused to quit the building.* abandon, depart from, desert, forsake, go away from, leave.
2 *When he became ill, he had to quit his job.* give up, resign from.
3 [*informal*] *Quit pushing!* cease, leave off, stop.

quite *adverb*
Take care how you use *quite*, as the two senses are almost opposites
1 *Yes, I have quite finished.* absolutely, altogether, completely, entirely, perfectly, totally, utterly, wholly.
2 *They played quite well, but far from their best.* fairly, moderately, [*informal*] pretty, rather.

quiver *verb*
The jelly quivered when the table was banged. quake, quaver, shake, shiver, shudder, tremble, vibrate, wobble.

quiz *verb*
Four men have been quizzed about the crime. ask, cross-examine, examine, grill, interrogate, interview, question.

quota *noun*
Make sure everyone gets their proper quota of food. allowance, helping, portion, ration, share.

quotation *noun*
I copied a short quotation from the book. excerpt, extract, passage, piece.
A piece taken from a newspaper is a **cutting**.
A piece taken from a film or TV programme is a **clip**.
quotation marks *In writing, you put quotation marks round the words someone has said.* inverted commas, speech marks.

quote *verb*
He quoted a passage from the Bible. repeat, speak.

Rr

race *noun*
1 *They had a race to see who could get there first.* chase, competition, contest.

VARIOUS KINDS OF COMPETITIVE RACING: cross-country, cycle racing, horse racing, hurdles, marathon, motor racing, regatta, relay race, road race, rowing, speedway racing, running races, sprinting, ➡

steeplechase, stock-car racing, swimming races.
A race to decide who will take part in the final is a *heat*.

VARIOUS PLACES WHERE RACES TAKE PLACE: circuit, dog track, racecourse, racetrack, stadium.
Once round a circuit or racetrack is a *lap*.

2 *We belong to different races but we are all humans.* ethnic group, nation, people.
A group of related families is a *clan*.
A group of families living together ruled by a chief is a *tribe*.

race *verb*
1 *They raced each other to the end of the road.* compete with, have a race with, try to beat.
2 *She had to race home because she was late.* dash, fly, gallop, hurry, move fast, run, rush, sprint, tear, zoom.

racism *noun*
Sadly, racism still exists in society. bias, chauvinism, discrimination, intolerance, prejudice, racial hatred, xenophobia.

rack *noun*
He made a rack for his tools in the garage. frame, framework, shelf, stand.

racket *noun*
1 *A racket is used to hit the ball in tennis.*
In cricket and other games you hit the ball with a *bat*.
In golf you hit the ball with a *club*.
2 *She complained about the racket from next door.* commotion, disturbance, hullabaloo, noise, pandemonium, row, tumult, uproar.
3 [slang] *The police were investigating an insurance racket.* fraud, [slang] rip-off, swindle.

radiant *adjective*
Her radiant smile made everyone feel better. beautiful, bright, cheerful, happy, sunny, warm.

radiate *verb*
1 *This fire radiates a lot of heat.* emit, give off, send out.
2 *The bus routes radiate from the centre of town.* spread out.

radical *adjective*
1 *We need a radical examination of what went wrong.* basic, drastic, fundamental, thorough.
AN OPPOSITE IS superficial.
2 *Some people were suspicious of the politician's radical views.* extreme, revolutionary.
AN OPPOSITE IS moderate.

radio *noun*
He turned on the radio. radio set, receiver, transistor, [old use] wireless.
Equipment which has a radio and also plays CDs and cassettes is a *stereo* or *hi-fi*.
The radio receiver in hi-fi equipment is a *tuner*.
A portable stereo is a *personal stereo* or [trademark] *Walkman*.
Radio equipment which sends out programmes is a *transmitter*.
Sending out radio programmes is *broadcasting*.

rag *noun*
She wiped the floor with a rag. cloth, scrap of cloth.

rage *noun*
He was trembling with rage. anger, fury, indignation, [old use] wrath.
A child's rage is a *tantrum* or *temper*.

rage *verb*
She raged about the delays. be angry, be fuming, flare up, lose your temper, seethe, storm.

ragged *adjective*
1 *Who was the man wearing ragged clothes?* frayed, old, patched, ripped, shabby, tattered, tatty, threadbare, torn, worn out.
2 *A ragged line of refugees struggled along the road.* irregular, uneven.

raid *noun*
The enemy raid caught them by surprise. assault, attack, blitz, invasion.

raid *verb*
1 *Police raided the house.* attack, descend on, invade, pounce on, rush, storm, swoop on.
2 *They raided the larder when they were hungry.* loot, pillage, plunder, rob, steal from.

raider *noun*
Raiders swooped down from the mountains. attacker, brigand, invader, looter, marauder, robber, thief.
Someone who raids ships at sea is a **pirate**.
Someone who raids and steals cattle is a **rustler**.

rail *noun*
The fence was made of iron rails. bar, rod.
A fence made of rails is also called **railings**.

railway *noun*

The rails which trains run on are the **line** or **permanent way** or **track**. The American term is **railroad**.

DIFFERENT KINDS OF RAILWAY: branch line, cable railway, funicular, light railway, main line, metro, mineral line, monorail, mountain railway, narrow gauge railway, rack-and-pinion railway, rapid transit system, sidings, standard gauge railway, tramway, the tube, underground railway.

VARIOUS KINDS OF TRAIN: diesel, electric train, express, freight train or goods train, intercity, sleeper, steam train, stopping train, tram, underground train.
Vehicles which run on the railway are **locomotives** and **rolling stock**.

VARIOUS KINDS OF LOCOMOTIVE AND ROLLING STOCK: buffet car, cable car, carriage, coach, container wagon, dining car, engine, goods van, goods wagon, guard's van, locomotive, Pullman carriage, shunter, sleeping car, steam engine, tender, truck, wagon. ➡

THINGS YOU MIGHT SEE ALONG THE LINE: cutting, halt, level crossing, marshalling yard, points, signal-box, signals, sleepers, station, track, tunnel, viaduct.
The end of the line is the **terminus**.

THINGS YOU MIGHT SEE AT A STATION: booking office, buffers, buffet, information centre, left-luggage office, luggage trolley, platform, ticket office, timetable, waiting room.

PEOPLE WHO WORK FOR THE RAILWAY INCLUDE: announcer, booking clerk, conductor, crossing keeper, driver, engineer, fireman, guard, platelayer, porter, signalman, station manager, stationmaster, steward.

rain *noun, verb*

VARIOUS KINDS OF RAIN: cloudburst, deluge, downpour, drizzle, rainstorm, shower, squall.

VARIOUS WAYS IT CAN RAIN: drizzle, pelt, pour, [*informal*] rain cats and dogs, spit.
A formal word for rain, snow, etc., is **precipitation**.
The rainy season in south and southeast Asia is the **monsoon**.
When there is no rain for a long time you have a **drought**.
FOR OTHER WORDS TO DO WITH WEATHER, SEE **weather**.

raise *verb*
The verb *to raise* can be used in many ways. We give some of the common ways you can use it here
1 *Raise your hand if you need help.* hold up, lift, put up.
2 *They raised a monument to the victims of the earthquake.* build, construct, erect, set up.
3 *The box was too heavy for him to raise.* lift, pick up.
To raise a flag or sail is to **hoist** it.
To raise a vehicle off the ground is to **jack it up**.
To raise the barrel of a big gun is to **elevate** it.

To raise prices is to *increase* them.
To raise someone to a higher rank is to
promote them.
4 *They aimed to raise £1000 for charity.*
collect, get, make.
5 *He raised some questions about the
new policy.* bring up, introduce,
mention, put forward, refer to, suggest.
6 *The doctor didn't want to raise their
hopes.* build up, encourage, stimulate.
7 *The farmer raises prize cattle.* breed,
rear.
8 *She sold some of the tomato plants I
had raised.* cultivate, grow, produce.
9 *It's hard work trying to raise a family.*
bring up, care for, educate, look after,
nurture.

rally *noun*
*Some demonstrators held a rally in the
town square.* [*informal*] demo,
demonstration, march, meeting,
protest.

ram *verb*
The car rammed the one in front. bump,
collide with, crash into, hit, smash into,
strike.

ramble *verb*
1 *They rambled round the country
park.* hike, meander, range, roam,
rove, stroll, walk, wander.
2 *He tends to ramble when he talks.*
stray from the point, talk aimlessly.

rambling *adjective*
1 *They followed a rambling path.*
indirect, meandering, roundabout,
twisting, winding, zigzag.
AN OPPOSITE IS direct.
2 *She was bored by his rambling
speech.* aimless, confused, wordy.
AN OPPOSITE IS eloquent.
3 *They stayed in a rambling old
farmhouse.* sprawling, straggling.
AN OPPOSITE IS compact.

rampage *verb*
Hooligans rampaged through the town.
go berserk, go wild, race about, rush
about.

random *adjective*
*The inspectors looked at a random
sample of their work.* arbitrary, casual,
chance, haphazard, unplanned.
AN OPPOSITE IS deliberate.

range *noun*
1 *There was a range of mountains to
the south.* chain, line, row, series,
string.
2 *Supermarkets sell a wide range of
goods.* selection, spectrum, variety.
3 *The pianist said that playing jazz
was outside his range.* limit, scope.
4 *He can hit a target at a range of a
hundred yards.* distance.

range *verb*
1 *Prices range from £10 to £15.* differ,
extend, fluctuate, vary.
2 *The flower pots were ranged in rows
on the windowsill.* arrange, display, lay
out, line up, set out.
3 *Sheep range over the hills.* ramble,
roam, rove, stray, wander.

rank *noun*
1 *They lined up in a single rank.*
column, file, line, row, series.
2 *After he'd gained experience, he was
promoted to a higher rank.* grade, level,
position, status.

RANKS IN THE AIR FORCE, IN
DESCENDING ORDER OF SENIORITY:
Marshal of the RAF, Air Chief
Marshal, Air Marshal, Air Vice-
Marshal, air commodore, group
captain, wing commander, squadron
leader, flight lieutenant, flying
officer, pilot officer, warrant officer,
flight sergeant, chief technician,
sergeant, corporal, junior technician,
senior aircraftman, leading
aircraftman, aircraftman.

RANKS IN THE ARMY, IN
DESCENDING ORDER OF SENIORITY:
Field Marshal, general, lieutenant
general, major general, brigadier,
colonel, lieutenant colonel, major,
captain, lieutenant, second
lieutenant or subaltern, warrant
officer, staff sergeant, sergeant,
corporal, lance corporal, private. ➡

RANKS IN THE NAVY, IN
DESCENDING ORDER OF SENIORITY:
Admiral of the Fleet, admiral, vice-
admiral, rear admiral, commodore,
captain, commander, lieutenant
commander, lieutenant, sub-
lieutenant, chief petty officer, petty
officer, leading rating, able rating,
ordinary rating.

ransack *verb*
  1 *She ransacked the house looking for
her purse.* comb, rummage through,
scour, search, [*informal*] turn upside
down.
  2 *Rioters ransacked the shops.* loot,
pillage, plunder, wreck.

rap *verb*
  He rapped on the door. knock, tap.

rapid *adjective*
  They made rapid progress. brisk, fast,
quick, speedy, swift.
  AN OPPOSITE IS slow.

rare *adjective*
  1 *She died of a rare disease.* abnormal,
curious, odd, peculiar, strange,
uncommon, unusual.
  2 *A cuckoo is a rare sight in this area.*
exceptional, infrequent, occasional,
surprising.
  AN OPPOSITE IS common.

rarely *adverb*
  She rarely went out. infrequently,
occasionally, seldom.
  AN OPPOSITE IS often.

rash *adjective*
  He regretted his rash decision. careless,
hasty, hurried, impulsive, incautious,
reckless, risky, thoughtless.
  AN OPPOSITE IS careful.

rash *noun*
  1 *She had a rash on her skin.* spots.
  2 *There's been a rash of burglaries in
the area.* outbreak.

rate *noun*
  1 *They set out at a fast rate.* pace,
speed.
  A formal word is ***velocity***.
  2 *What's the usual rate for washing a
car?* amount, charge, cost, fee, figure,
payment, price, wage.

rate *verb*
  *How do you rate their chance of
winning?* consider, estimate, evaluate,
judge, regard.

rather *adverb*
  1 *She was rather ill.* fairly, moderately,
[*informal*] pretty, quite, slightly,
somewhat.
  2 *He said he'd rather not come.*
preferably, sooner.

ratio *noun*
  The ratio of boys to girls is about 50–50.
balance, fraction, proportion.
  You can express a ratio as a
percentage.

ration *noun*
  They had their ration of sweets.
allowance, helping, measure, portion,
quota, share.
  rations *The expedition carried enough
rations to last a month.* food,
necessities, provisions, stores,
supplies.

ration *verb*
  *In time of war the government may
ration food supplies.* allot, control,
distribute fairly, limit, restrict, share
equally.

rational *adjective*
  1 *No rational person would do such a
silly thing.* intelligent, normal,
reasonable, sane, sensible, thoughtful,
wise.
  2 *Don't get angry—let's have a rational
discussion.* balanced, logical, lucid,
reasoned, sound.
  AN OPPOSITE IS irrational.

rationalize *verb*
  1 *The new manager tried to rationalize
the company.* reorganize, sort out.
  2 *He couldn't rationalize his absurd
fear of spiders.* be rational about,
explain, justify, think through.

rattle *noun, verb*
  FOR VARIOUS WAYS TO MAKE SOUNDS,
SEE **sound** *verb*.

rave *verb*
1 *He raved about the film he saw last week.* be enthusiastic, talk wildly.
2 *The head raved angrily about our bad behaviour.* rage, roar, shout, storm, yell.

ravenous *adjective*
He felt ravenous and ate a huge dinner. famished, greedy, hungry, starved, starving.

raw *adjective*
1 *Raw vegetables are supposed to be good for you.* uncooked.
AN OPPOSITE IS cooked.
2 *The factory imports a lot of raw materials from abroad.* crude, natural, unprocessed, untreated.
AN OPPOSITE IS manufactured or processed.
3 *The raw beginners didn't know what to do.* ignorant, new, untrained.
AN OPPOSITE IS experienced.
4 *Her knee felt raw after she fell off her bike.* bloody, inflamed, painful, red, rough, sore, tender.
5 *The raw wind made him shiver.* bitter, chilly, cold, unpleasant.

ray *noun*
A ray of light shone between the curtains. beam, shaft, stream.
A strong narrow ray of light used in various technological devices is a **laser**.

razor *noun*
A razor you throw away after using it is a **disposable razor**.
An electric razor is also called a **shaver**.

reach *verb*
1 *They hoped to reach Oxford by lunch time.* arrive at, get to, go as far as, make.
2 *The appeal fund has reached its target.* achieve, attain.
3 *He could just reach the handle.* get hold of, grasp, touch.
to reach out *Reach out your hand.* extend, hold out, put out, raise, stick out, stretch out.

reach *noun*
1 *The shelf was just within his reach.* grasp.
2 *The shops are within easy reach.* distance, range.

react *verb*
How did she react when you asked for money? answer, behave, reply, respond.

reaction *noun*
What was his reaction when you said it was too expensive? answer, reply, response.
Information about how people have reacted to something is **feedback**.

read *verb*
He couldn't read her handwriting. decipher, make out, understand.
To read through something very quickly is to **skim through** it.
To read here and there in a book is to **dip into** it.
A device which enables a computer to read things is a **scanner** which **scans** pages.

readable *adjective*
1 *It was a very readable book.* enjoyable, entertaining, interesting, well written.
AN OPPOSITE IS boring.
2 *Is his handwriting readable?* clear, decipherable, legible, plain, understandable.
AN OPPOSITE IS illegible.

readily *adverb*
1 *She readily agreed to help.* eagerly, gladly, happily, voluntarily, willingly.
2 *The recipe uses ingredients which are readily available.* conveniently, easily, quickly.

ready *adjective*
1 *Dinner is ready.* available, done, obtainable, prepared, set out, waiting.
AN OPPOSITE IS not ready.
2 *He's always ready to help.* eager, glad, keen, pleased, willing.
AN OPPOSITE IS reluctant.
3 *She's always got a ready reply.* immediate, prompt, quick, sharp, smart.
AN OPPOSITE IS slow.
4 *This balloon is ready to burst at any moment!* liable, likely.

real *adjective*
1 *History is about real events.* actual, factual, true, verifiable.
AN OPPOSITE IS fictitious or imaginary.

2 *She likes stories about real life.*
everyday, ordinary.
AN OPPOSITE IS unreal.
3 *There was real cream in the coffee.*
authentic, genuine, natural, pure.
AN OPPOSITE IS artificial.
4 *You're a real friend!* dependable,
reliable, sound, trustworthy.
AN OPPOSITE IS untrustworthy.
5 *She doesn't often show her real
feelings.* honest, sincere, true.
AN OPPOSITE IS insincere.

realistic *adjective*
1 *The film gives a realistic idea of what
happened.* authentic, convincing, fair,
faithful, genuine, lifelike, reasonable,
recognizable, true to life, truthful.
2 *Some people say it's not realistic to
ban traffic from the city centre.* feasible,
possible, practicable, practical,
sensible, workable.
AN OPPOSITE IS unrealistic.

reality *noun*
Stop daydreaming and face reality. the
facts, the real world, the truth.

realize *verb*
*It took him a long time to realize what
she meant.* appreciate, become aware
of, [*informal*] catch on to, comprehend,
grasp, recognize, see, [*informal*]
tumble to, [*informal*] twig, understand.

really *adverb*
1 *Are you really going to Australia?*
actually, certainly, definitely,
genuinely, honestly, in fact, truly.
2 *I saw a really good film last night.*
exceptionally, extremely, unusually,
very.

realm *noun*
The king ruled the realm for fifty years.
country, domain, empire, kingdom.

reap *verb*
1 *They used to reap corn with scythes.*
cut, gather in, harvest, mow.
2 *They hoped they would reap some
benefit from all their efforts.* gain, get,
obtain, receive, win.

reappear *verb*
*The swallows reappeared after the
winter.* appear again, come back,
return.

rear *adjective*
*They found seats in the rear coach of
the train.* back, end, last.
The rear legs of an animal are its **hind**
legs.
AN OPPOSITE IS front.

rear *noun*
*They walked through to the rear of the
train.* back, end, tail-end.
The rear of a ship is the **stern**.

rear *verb*
1 *They have reared three children.*
bring up, care for, feed, look after,
nurture.
2 *Farmers rear cattle.* breed, produce,
raise.
3 *The horse reared.* rise up.
4 *The deer reared their heads when they
caught his scent.* hold up, lift, raise.

reason *noun*
1 *What was the reason for his
behaviour?* cause, excuse, explanation,
incentive, justification, motive.
2 *Reason is what distinguishes us from
other animals.* brains, intelligence,
judgement, reasoning, understanding,
wisdom.
3 *She tried to make him see reason.*
common sense, logic, sense.

reason *verb*
1 *He reasoned that if they started early
they would reach their destination by
noon.* calculate, conclude, deduce, draw
the conclusion, infer, judge, work out.
2 *She tried to reason with him, but he
wouldn't change his mind.* argue,
debate, use reason.

reasonable *adjective*
1 *He'll understand—he's a very
reasonable person.* calm, intelligent,
rational, realistic, sane, sensible,
thoughtful, wise.
AN OPPOSITE IS irrational.
2 *Her argument seemed very
reasonable.* believable, credible,
justifiable, logical, sound.
AN OPPOSITE IS illogical.
3 *£10 is a reasonable price.* acceptable,
average, fair, moderate, normal,
proper, respectable.
AN OPPOSITE IS excessive.

reasonably *adverb*
1 *They all behaved reasonably.*
intelligently, rationally, sanely,
sensibly.
2 *It is reasonably warm for the time of
year.* fairly, moderately, [*informal*]
pretty, quite, rather, tolerably.

reasoning *noun*
She couldn't follow his reasoning.
analysis, argument, case, deduction,
line of thought, logic, reasons,
thinking.

reassure *verb*
*He reassured them and said everything
would be all right.* calm, comfort,
encourage, give confidence to, support.
AN OPPOSITE IS threaten.

rebel *verb*
*The dictator feared that the people
would rebel.* revolt, rise up.
To rebel against the captain of a ship is
to ***mutiny***.
AN OPPOSITE IS obey.

rebel *noun*
A person who rebels violently against
the government is a ***revolutionary***.
A person who thinks that all
governments and laws are bad is an
anarchist.
A person who rebels against the
captain of a ship is a ***mutineer***.

rebellion *noun*
1 *As conditions got worse there were
signs of rebellion among the men.*
disobedience, rebelliousness,
resistance.
2 *The dictator sent soldiers to put down
the rebellion.* revolt, revolution,
uprising.
A rebellion on a ship is a ***mutiny***.

rebellious *adjective*
1 *Troops were sent to deal with the
rebellious citizens.* disloyal, mutinous,
revolutionary.
2 *He was a very rebellious boy.* defiant,
difficult, disobedient, quarrelsome,
uncontrollable, unmanageable, unruly,
wild.
AN OPPOSITE IS obedient.

rebound *verb*
The ball rebounded off the wall. bounce
back, spring back.
If a bullet rebounds off a wall, etc., it is
said to ***ricochet***.

rebuild *noun*
*After the earthquake they started to
rebuild the town.* build again, renew,
repair, restore.

recall *verb*
1 *The manufacturer recalled the faulty
cars.* bring back, call back.
2 *Try to recall what happened.*
recollect, remember, think back to.

recapture *verb*
*They spent ages trying to recapture my
rabbit.* get back, retrieve.

recede *verb*
*When the rain stopped the flood
receded.* decline, ebb, go back, retreat,
subside.

receipt *noun*
*Keep the receipt in case you need to take
the goods back.* account, bill, proof of
purchase, ticket.
receipts *He was pleased with the shop's
receipts last month.* gains, income,
profits, takings.

receive *verb*
1 *The captain went up to receive the
winners' cup.* accept, be given, collect,
take.
AN OPPOSITE IS give or present.
2 *He received some serious injuries.*
experience, suffer, sustain, undergo.
AN OPPOSITE IS inflict.
3 *We went to the front door to receive
our visitors.* greet, meet, welcome.

recent *adjective*
1 *He told her about the recent changes
to the rules.* fresh, new.
2 *She watches the news to keep up with
recent events.* contemporary, current,
up to date.

reception *noun*
1 *They gave him a friendly reception.*
greeting, welcome.
2 *They enjoyed themselves at the
wedding reception.* celebration, party.
More formal synonyms are ***function*** or
gathering.

recess *noun*
1 *There was a statue in a recess in the wall.* alcove, bay, corner.
2 *They had a recess for refreshments halfway through the meeting.* adjournment, break, interlude, intermission, interval, rest.

recession *noun*
Many people lost their jobs in the recession. depression, slump.

recipe *noun*
He was able to make a cake by following the recipe. directions, instructions, list of ingredients.

recital *noun*
1 *He had to listen to a long recital of all her problems.* account, narration, repetition.
2 *He gave a short recital of piano music.* concert, performance.

recitation *noun*
She enjoyed his recitation of the poem. narration, performance, speaking, telling.

recite *verb*
She recited a poem she had written. deliver, narrate, perform.

reckless *adjective*
The police arrested him for reckless driving. careless, dangerous, hasty, impulsive, inattentive, incautious, irresponsible, negligent, rash, thoughtless, wild.
AN OPPOSITE IS careful.

reckon *verb*
1 *I tried to reckon how much she owed me.* add up, assess, calculate, compute, count, estimate, figure out, total, work out.
2 *I reckon it's going to rain.* believe, feel, guess, think.

reclaim *verb*
1 *They ought to reclaim all this derelict land.* make usable, restore, save.
2 *They were able to reclaim their bus fares after the journey.* get back, put in a claim for, recover.

recline *verb*
He reclined lazily on the sofa. lean back, lie, loll, lounge, rest, sprawl, stretch out.

recognizable *adjective*
He is recognizable because he's much taller than the rest of us. distinctive, distinguishable, identifiable, unmistakable.

recognize *verb*
1 *If you saw him again, would you recognize him?* distinguish, identify, know, make out, notice, pick out, recall, recollect, remember, see, spot.
2 *He should recognize that what he did was wrong.* accept, acknowledge, admit, be aware, confess, grant, realize, [*informal*] twig, understand.

recoil *verb*
She recoiled when she saw the blood. back away, draw back, falter, flinch, quail, shrink back, wince.

recollect *verb*
1 *She didn't recollect what happened.* have a memory of, recall, remember.
2 *They sat for hours recollecting old times.* be nostalgic about, reminisce about, tell stories about, think back to.
AN OPPOSITE IS forget.

recollection *noun*
They exchanged recollections of last summer's holiday. memory, reminiscence.

recommend *verb*
1 *The doctor recommended a complete rest.* advise, advocate, counsel, prescribe, propose, suggest, urge.
2 *The critics recommended the film.* approve of, commend, praise, speak well of.

recommendation *noun*
1 *He acted on the doctor's recommendation.* advice, encouragement, suggestion.
2 *It was her recommendation that got him the job.* approval, backing, praise, support.

reconcile *verb*
She managed to reconcile them after their quarrel. bring together, reunite.
reconcile yourself to something *He could never reconcile himself to being dropped from the team.* accept, put up with, tolerate.

record *noun*
  1 *They spent the evening chatting and playing records.*

> KINDS OF RECORD: album, compilation, EP or extended play, single.
>
> KINDS OF RECORDING: audiotape, cassette, CD-ROM, compact disc or CD, digital recording, long-playing record or LP, tape recording, video, video cassette, video disc, videotape.

  2 *He broke the world record for the high jump.* [*informal*] best, best performance.
  3 *She kept a record of what she did on holiday.* account, diary, file, journal, report.
  The record of what happened at a meeting is the **minutes**.
  The record of a ship's voyage is the **log**.
  A record of people's names and information about them is a **register**.
  Records consisting of historical documents are **archives**.

record *verb*
  1 *She recorded the concert.* tape, video.
  2 *He recorded what he saw in a notebook.* enter, note, put down, set down, write down.

record player *noun*
  FOR EQUIPMENT FOR MAKING AND PLAYING RECORDINGS, SEE **audio-visual**.

recover *verb*
  1 *It took him a long time to recover after his illness.* come round, get better, heal, improve, mend, pull through, rally, revive.
  2 *They managed to recover the football they kicked over the fence.* find, get back, reclaim, retrieve, trace, track down.

recovery *noun*
  1 *His recovery from his illness took a long time.* convalescence, cure, healing, revival.
  2 *The police didn't offer much hope for the recovery of the stolen goods.* restoration, retrieval, salvaging.

recreation *noun*
  The people deserved some recreation after their hard work. amusement, diversion, enjoyment, entertainment, fun, leisure, play, pleasure, relaxation.
  A particular activity you do as recreation is a **hobby** or **pastime**.

recruit *noun*
  The new recruits were very inexperienced. beginner, learner, new member, novice.
  A recruit learning a trade is an **apprentice** or **trainee**.

recruit *verb*
  The youth club needs to recruit new members. advertise for, bring in, enrol, take on.
  To be recruited into the armed services is to **enlist** or **sign on**.

rectangle *noun* oblong.

recur *verb*
  Go to the doctor if the symptoms recur. come again, happen again, persist, reappear, repeat itself, return.

recycle *verb*
  We should recycle as much waste as we can. reclaim, recover, retrieve, reuse, salvage, use again.

red *adjective, noun*

> WORDS TO DESCRIBE VARIOUS SHADES OF RED: blood-red, brick-red, cherry, crimson, flame-coloured, maroon, pink, rose, ruby, scarlet, vermilion, wine-coloured.
> Something which is rather red is **reddish**.
>
> WORDS TO DESCRIBE SOMEONE'S RED CHEEKS: blushing, flushed, glowing, rosy, ruddy.
>
> WORDS TO DESCRIBE REDDISH HAIR: auburn, carroty, ginger.
>
> WORDS TO DESCRIBE RED EYES: bloodshot, inflamed.

redden *verb*
  His face reddened with embarrassment. become red, blush, colour, flush, glow.

redeem verb
He redeemed his watch from the pawnbroker's. buy back, reclaim, recover.

reduce verb
He reduced the time he spent reading so he had more time for football. cut, cut back, lessen, make less.
To reduce something by half is to **halve** it.
To reduce the width of something is to **narrow** it.
To reduce the length of something is to **shorten** or **trim** it.
To reduce the height or level of something is to **bring it down** or **lower** it.
To reduce speed is to **decelerate** or **slow down**.
To reduce someone to a lower rank is to **demote** them.
To reduce the strength of a liquid is to **dilute** it.
AN OPPOSITE IS increase.

reduction noun
1 The company announced a reduction in prices. cut, decrease, drop.
AN OPPOSITE IS increase.
2 With this voucher, you get a reduction of £5. concession, discount, refund.

redundant adjective
The work was finished, so his offer of help was redundant. superfluous, unnecessary, unwanted.
AN OPPOSITE IS essential.

reel noun
She wound the tape onto the reel. spool.

reel verb
1 The blow made his head reel. spin, whirl.
2 He reeled along the road as if he was drunk. lurch, roll, stagger, stumble, sway, totter, wobble.

refer verb
1 She had to refer the decision to her boss. hand over, pass on.
2 If they don't have what he wants, they'll refer him to another shop. direct, recommend, send.

to refer to 1 Don't refer to this matter again. allude to, bring up, comment on, draw attention to, make reference to, mention, speak of.
2 If he can't spell a word, he refers to his dictionary. consult, go to, look up, turn to.

referee noun
A person who helps the referee in football is a **linesman** or **touch judge** or **assistant referee**.
A person who makes sure players keep to the rules in some other games is an **umpire**.
A person who acts as a judge in a competition is an **adjudicator**.

reference noun
1 Don't make any reference to her dirty clothes. comment (about), mention (of), remark (about).
2 Which book does this reference come from? example, illustration, quotation.
3 When you apply for a job you need a reference. recommendation.

refill verb
She refilled her glass. top up.
To refill a fuel tank is to **refuel**.

refine verb
1 They have to refine crude oil before it can be used. distil, process, purify.
2 She wrote a rough outline and then refined it. amend, correct, improve, modify.

refined adjective
It was nice to meet someone who was so refined. civil, civilized, cultivated, cultured, polite, [informal] posh, sophisticated, well brought-up, well educated, well mannered, well spoken.
AN OPPOSITE IS vulgar.

reflect verb
1 Cat's-eyes reflect the light from a car's headlights. send back, shine back, throw back.
2 Their success reflects their hard work. demonstrate, exhibit, indicate, reveal, show.

to reflect on She had time to reflect on what had happened. brood over, consider, contemplate, meditate on, ponder, think about.

reflection *noun*
  1 *He could see his reflection in the glass.* image, likeness.
  2 *Their success is a reflection of their hard work.* indication, outcome, result.
  3 *She needed some time for reflection.* contemplation, meditation, thinking.

reflective *adjective*
  1 *You should wear reflective patches if you ride your bike at night.* reflecting, shiny.
  2 *You seem to be in a reflective mood.* serious, thoughtful.

reflex *adjective*
  Blinking is usually a reflex action. automatic, instinctive, involuntary, spontaneous, unthinking.
  AN OPPOSITE IS conscious.

reform *verb*
  She told him to reform his behaviour or be thrown out. amend, change, correct, improve, make better, modify.

reform *noun*
  The club introduced several reforms. amendment, change, improvement, modification.

refrain *verb*
  to refrain from *Please refrain from smoking.* avoid, [*informal*] quit, stop.

refresh *verb*
  1 *They refreshed themselves with a cup of tea.* cool, freshen, invigorate, restore, revive, stimulate.
  2 *Let me refresh your memory.* jog, prod, prompt.

refreshments *plural noun*
  Refreshments were served during the interval. drinks, food, a snack.

refrigerate *verb*
  Food keeps longer if it is refrigerated. chill, cool, freeze, keep cold.

refuge *noun*
  The climbers looked for refuge from the blizzard. cover, a haven, a hiding place, protection, safety, sanctuary, security, shelter.

refugee *noun*
  The refugees had no food or shelter. exile, outcast.

refund *verb*
  She asked them to refund her money. give back, pay back, repay, return.

refuse *verb*
  1 *He refused the invitation.* decline, reject, say no to, turn down.
  AN OPPOSITE IS accept.
  2 *They were refused help.* deny, deprive of, withhold.
  AN OPPOSITE IS allow.

refuse *noun*
  The refuse was taken to the tip. garbage, junk, litter, rubbish, scrap, trash, waste.

regain *verb*
  1 *The troops regained possession of the town.* get back, recapture, win back.
  2 *They were glad to regain the safety of the harbour.* get back to, return to.

regard *verb*
  1 *He regarded her as his best friend.* consider, judge, think of, value.
  2 *The cat regarded him curiously.* contemplate, eye, gaze at, look at, scrutinize, stare at, view, watch.

regard *noun*
  1 *She quailed under his stern regard.* gaze, look, scrutiny, stare.
  2 *Little regard was shown for their feelings.* attention, consideration, heed, notice, thought.
  3 *They have a great regard for her ability.* admiration, affection, esteem, respect.

regarding *preposition*
  He had received no answer regarding his request. about, concerning, connected with, involving, on the subject of, with reference to, with regard to.

regardless *adjective*
  regardless of *He leapt into the water regardless of the danger.* careless about, heedless of, indifferent to, not caring about, unconcerned about.

region *noun*
  1 *The Antarctic is a cold region.* area, expanse, part of the world, place, territory, tract.
  2 *There are two local radio stations serving this region.* area, district, locality, neighbourhood, vicinity, zone.

register *verb*
  1 *They registered as members of the club.* enlist, enrol, join, sign on.
  2 *The parents registered the birth of their child.* record, set down, write down.
  3 *The thermometer registered a very high temperature.* indicate, reveal, show.

regret *noun*
  1 *He felt no regret for his actions.* guilt, penitence, remorse, repentance, shame.
  2 *With great regret, I have to tell you that your friend is very ill.* grief, sadness, sorrow, sympathy.

regret *verb*
  1 *She regrets losing her temper.* be sorry, feel regret, repent, reproach yourself.
  2 *Everyone regretted his death.* feel sad about, grieve, lament, mourn.

regretful *adjective*
  1 *She gave him a regretful smile and said sorry.* apologetic, ashamed, conscience-stricken, penitent, remorseful, repentant, sad.
  AN OPPOSITE IS unrepentant.
  2 *He said a regretful goodbye to his friends.* melancholy, reluctant, sad, sorrowful, wistful.
  AN OPPOSITE IS happy.

regrettable *adjective*
  It was a regrettable accident. deplorable, disgraceful, distressing, lamentable, shameful, shocking, undesirable, unfortunate, unlucky.
  AN OPPOSITE IS fortunate.

regular *adjective*
  1 *You ought to have meals at regular times.* evenly spaced, fixed, predictable.
  Words to describe various regular intervals are **daily**, **hourly**, **monthly**, **weekly**, **yearly**.

  2 *She has beautiful regular teeth.* even, symmetrical.
  AN OPPOSITE IS uneven.
  3 *The drummer kept up a regular rhythm.* consistent, constant, measured, repeated, steady, uniform, unvarying.
  AN OPPOSITE IS erratic.
  4 *They went home by their regular route.* accustomed, customary, familiar, habitual, normal, ordinary, routine, usual.
  AN OPPOSITE IS unusual.
  5 *She applied through the regular channels.* common, conventional, correct, official, proper, standard, traditional.
  AN OPPOSITE IS unusual.
  6 *I'm a regular customer at the sweet shop.* dependable, faithful, frequent, reliable.
  AN OPPOSITE IS irregular or abnormal.

regulate *verb*
  1 *Just turn the knob to regulate the temperature.* adjust, alter, change, get right, vary.
  2 *The council has a new scheme to regulate the traffic.* control, direct, govern, limit, manage, organize, restrict, supervise.

regulation *noun*
  The traffic regulations should be obeyed. law, requirement, restriction, rule.
  A regulation which applies in a particular area is a **by-law**.
  A regulation imposed on you by someone of higher rank is a **decree** or **order**.

rehearsal *noun*
  They had a rehearsal for the play. practice, preparation, [*informal*] try-out.

rehearse *verb*
  They had to rehearse the scene all over again. go over, practise, try out.

reign *verb*
  Which British monarch reigned the longest? be king or queen, be on the throne, govern, have power, rule.

reinforce *verb*
1 *He put up a concrete post to reinforce the fence.* prop up, strengthen, support.
2 *They sent another hundred soldiers to reinforce the army.* add to, assist, back up, help.

reinforcements *plural noun*
The officer asked headquarters to send reinforcements. [*informal*] back-up, help, reserves, support.

reject *verb*
1 *She rejected his invitation.* decline, refuse, say no to, turn down, veto.
2 *Shops reject poor quality goods.* discard, eliminate, get rid of, scrap, send back, throw away, throw out.
AN OPPOSITE IS accept.

rejoice *verb*
They rejoiced when their team won the cup. be happy, celebrate, delight, exult.
AN OPPOSITE IS grieve.

relate *verb*
1 *Doctors relate all these illnesses to poor diet.* associate, compare, connect, link.
2 *The TV programme related to the music industry.* be relevant, concern, refer.
3 *She related her story.* describe, narrate, report on, tell.

relation *noun*
FOR YOUR VARIOUS RELATIONS, SEE **family**.

relationship *noun*
1 *Is there a relationship between wealth and happiness?* association, bond, connection, link.
The relationship between two numbers is a ***ratio***.
2 *The twins have a close relationship.* attachment, friendship, understanding.
3 *Are those two having a relationship?* love affair, romance.

relative *noun*
FOR YOUR VARIOUS RELATIVES, SEE **family**.

relative *adjective*
1 *The police gathered evidence relative to the crime.* allied, associated (with), connected (with), related, relevant.
AN OPPOSITE IS irrelevant.
2 *They live in relative comfort.* comparative.

relax *verb*
1 *They did some exercises to relax their cramped muscles.* ease, loosen.
AN OPPOSITE IS tighten.
2 *Don't relax your efforts!* lessen, reduce.
AN OPPOSITE IS increase.
3 *She likes to relax in front of the TV.* be relaxed, get comfortable, let up, rest, [*informal*] unwind.

relaxation *noun*
People need some relaxation after work. informality, leisure, peace and quiet, recreation, relaxing, rest, tranquillity.
AN OPPOSITE IS tension.

relaxed *adjective*
They enjoyed the relaxed atmosphere of the party. calm, carefree, casual, comfortable, contented, cosy, easygoing, friendly, good-humoured, happy, informal, leisurely, light-hearted, peaceful, restful, serene, tranquil, unhurried, untroubled.
AN OPPOSITE IS tense.

relay *verb*
He relayed the information to the police. communicate, pass on, send out, spread, transmit.

relay *noun*
1 *The rescuers worked in relays.* shift, turn.
2 *There will be a live relay from the pop concert on TV.* broadcast, programme, transmission.

release *verb*
1 *The prisoners were released early.* allow out, discharge, free, let go, liberate, rescue, save, set free.
To release slaves is to ***emancipate*** them.
AN OPPOSITE IS imprison.

2 *The dog was tied up—who released him?* let loose, set loose, unfasten, unleash, untie.
3 *The group were about to release their new CD.* issue, make available, publish, send out.

relegate *verb*
At the end of the season the team was relegated to a lower division. demote, put down.

relent *verb*
She relented and let them off their punishment. be lenient, give in, show pity, soften, weaken, yield.

relentless *adjective*
1 *The guns continued a relentless bombardment.* cruel, fierce, merciless, pitiless, remorseless, ruthless, unfeeling.
2 *They were sick of the relentless rain.* ceaseless, constant, continual, continuous, everlasting, incessant, never-ending, perpetual, persistent, unceasing.

relevant *adjective*
1 *The arguments she used weren't relevant to the case.* applicable, appropriate, connected, linked, related, significant, suitable.
2 *Don't interrupt unless your comments are relevant.* to the point.
AN OPPOSITE IS irrelevant.

reliable *adjective*
1 *She's a reliable friend.* constant, dependable, devoted, faithful, loyal, responsible, trustworthy.
2 *I wish the weather was more reliable.* certain, consistent, predictable.
3 *They have a reliable water supply.* regular, safe, sound, steady, sure.
AN OPPOSITE IS unreliable.

relic *noun*
The museum contains interesting relics from the past. reminder, souvenir, survival.

relief *noun*
The pills gave some relief from the pain. comfort, ease, help, relaxation, release, rest.

relieve *verb*
The doctor said the pills would relieve the pain. calm, comfort, diminish, ease, help, lessen, lighten, make less, moderate, reduce, relax, soothe.
AN OPPOSITE IS intensify.

religion *noun*
People from all religions went to the service. belief, creed, cult, doctrine, faith, sect.

SOME OF THE PRINCIPAL RELIGIONS OF THE WORLD: Buddhism, Christianity, Hinduism, Islam, Judaism, Shintoism, Sikhism, Taoism, Zen.
The study of religion is *divinity* or *scripture* or *theology*.

religious *adjective*
1 *They went to a religious service.* divine, holy, sacred.
2 *He's very religious.* pious, reverent, spiritual.

reluctant *adjective*
He was reluctant to help. grudging, half-hearted, hesitant, uncooperative, unenthusiastic, unhelpful, unwilling.
AN OPPOSITE IS eager.

rely *verb*
You can rely on him. bank on, count on, depend on, have confidence in, trust.

remain *verb*
1 *Fog remained on the motorway all day.* continue, [*informal*] hang about, linger, stay.
2 *Please remain as you are.* carry on, continue, keep on, stay, wait.
3 *Little remained of the house after the fire.* be left, survive.

remainder *noun*
Keep the remainder of the food for later. remains, remnants, rest, surplus.

remains *plural noun*
He cleared away the remains of the party. debris, fragments, odds and ends, remnants, scraps, traces.
The remains at the bottom of a cup are *dregs*.
Remains of food after a meal are *leftovers*.
The remains of a building or wall, etc., which has collapsed are *rubble*.

Remains still standing after a building has collapsed are **ruins**.
The remains of a crashed aircraft, ship, or vehicle are **wreckage**.
The remains of a dead person are **ashes** or **bones** or the **corpse**.
The remains of a dead animal are the **carcass**.
Historic remains are **relics** or our **heritage**.

remark *verb*
He remarked that it was a nice day. comment, declare, mention, note, observe, say, state.

remark *noun*
They exchanged a few remarks about the weather. comment, mention, observation, statement, thought, word.

remarkable *adjective*
To win the competition three years running is a remarkable achievement. amazing, exceptional, extraordinary, important, impressive, interesting, notable, out of the ordinary, outstanding, phenomenal, special, strange, striking, surprising, tremendous, uncommon, unusual, wonderful.
AN OPPOSITE IS ordinary.

remedy *noun*
1 *There is no known remedy for his illness.* cure, medicine, relief, therapy, treatment.
A remedy to act against a poison is an **antidote**.
2 *It's a big problem, and I don't know the remedy.* answer, solution.

remember *verb*
1 *She couldn't remember his name.* have a memory of, recall, recognize, recollect.
2 *He was trying to remember his lines for the play.* get off by heart, keep in mind, learn, memorize.
AN OPPOSITE IS forget.
3 *She likes to remember the old days.* be nostalgic about, reminisce about, tell stories about, think back to.

remind *verb*
Remind me to buy some potatoes. jog your memory, prompt.

reminder *noun*
1 *They sent him a reminder to pay the bill.* cue, hint, prompt.
2 *He bought the picture as a reminder of his holidays.* relic, souvenir.

reminisce *verb*
to reminisce about *He likes to reminisce about his school days.* be nostalgic about, recall, remember, tell stories about, think back to.

reminiscence *noun*
He told us his reminiscences of his childhood. memory, recollection.

remnants *plural noun*
They spent ages clearing up the remnants of the party. debris, fragments, odds and ends, remains, scraps, traces.

remorse *noun*
He showed no remorse for what he'd done. grief, guilt, penitence, pricking of conscience, regret, repentance, sadness, shame, sorrow.

remorseful *adjective*
She seemed remorseful about her actions. apologetic, ashamed, conscience-stricken, penitent, regretful, repentant, sorry.
AN OPPOSITE IS unrepentant.

remorseless *adjective*
They continued their remorseless bombardment of the town. constant, continual, continuous, cruel, fierce, incessant, merciless, never-ending, perpetual, persistent, pitiless, relentless, ruthless, unceasing, unfeeling.

remote *adjective*
1 *He liked to travel to remote parts of the world.* distant, faraway, inaccessible, isolated, lonely, out of reach, out of the way, unfrequented.
AN OPPOSITE IS accessible.
2 *The chances of him winning are remote.* improbable, negligible, poor, slender, slight, small, unlikely.
AN OPPOSITE IS likely.

removal noun
1 *The dentist said the removal of the tooth would be painless.* extraction, taking out.
2 *The police were called to deal with the removal of the intruders.* dismissal, ejection, expulsion.

remove verb
1 *Please remove your rubbish.* clear away, take away.
2 *The police removed the people who were causing trouble.* eject, expel, [*informal*] kick out, send away, throw out, turn out.
To remove people from a house where they are living is to **evict** them.
To remove a monarch from the throne is to **depose** him or her.
3 *They removed the rude words from the film.* censor, cut out, delete, eliminate, erase, get rid of.
4 *The men removed the furniture to her new house.* move, transfer, transport.
5 *The dentist removed my bad tooth.* draw out, extract, pull out, take out, [*informal*] whip out.
6 *She removed her coat.* dispense with, peel off, strip off, take off.

render verb
1 *The shock rendered her speechless.* leave, make.
2 *She rendered him a great service.* give, provide.

rendezvous noun
1 *They arranged a rendezvous for six o'clock.* appointment, engagement, meeting.
A rendezvous with your boyfriend or girlfriend is a **date**.
2 *Their usual rendezvous is by the swings in the park.* meeting place.

renew verb

> VARIOUS WAYS TO RENEW THINGS:
> bring up to date, [*informal*] do up, mend, modernize, overhaul, recondition, redecorate, redesign, redo, refit, remake, renovate, repaint, repair, replace, replenish, restore, resume, resurrect, revitalize, revive, touch up, update.

renown noun
He achieved great renown for his daring exploits. distinction, eminence, fame, glory, honour, prestige, prominence.

renowned adjective
The shop is renowned for its pork pies. celebrated, distinguished, famous, notable, outstanding, prominent, well known.
AN OPPOSITE IS unknown.

rent verb
They rented a van to move their things. charter, hire.
to rent something out *The garage down the road rents out various vehicles.* lease, let.

repair verb
1 *It took them a week to repair the damaged car.* fix, mend, overhaul, patch up, put right, service.
2 *He tried to repair the hole in his jeans.* darn, patch, sew up.

repay verb
They repaid her expenses. pay back, refund.
To pay someone money for damage you have done is to **compensate** them.

repeat verb
1 *She had to repeat her story all over again.* retell, say again.
2 *He repeated everything she said.* echo, quote, tell.
3 *They had to repeat the exercise.* do again, redo.
4 *That shot was a fluke—he couldn't repeat it.* copy, duplicate, reproduce.

repeat noun
Their new song is really just a repeat of their last one. copy, duplicate, replica, repetition.

repeatedly adverb
He was warned repeatedly about his behaviour. again and again, constantly, continually, frequently, often, persistently, regularly, time after time.

repel *verb*

1 *The soldiers managed to repel the attack.* drive off, fend off, fight off, force away, hold off, push away, resist, ward off.
2 *They were repelled by his bad language.* disgust, horrify, offend, revolt, sicken, [*slang*] turn you off.

repellent *adjective*

She found him quite repellent. disgusting, foul, hateful, hideous, horrible, loathsome, objectionable, offensive, repulsive, revolting, sickening, vile.
AN OPPOSITE IS attractive.

repent *verb*

Do you truly repent your sins? be repentant about, regret, reproach yourself for.

repentance *noun*

She showed genuine repentance for her sins. guilt, penitence, regret, remorse, sorrow.

repentant *adjective*

She was repentant when she saw what she'd done. apologetic, ashamed, conscience-stricken, penitent, regretful, remorseful, sorry.
AN OPPOSITE IS unrepentant.

repetitive *adjective*

The work was very repetitive. boring, monotonous, tedious.

replace *verb*

1 *He replaced the books on the shelf.* put back, restore (to), return (to).
2 *Who will replace the captain when he leaves?* be a substitute for, come after, follow, succeed, take over from, take the place of.
3 *They had to replace the tyres on the car.* change, renew.

replacement *noun*

They had to find a replacement for the injured player. [*informal*] stand-in, substitute.
Someone who replaces an actor who is ill, etc., is an **understudy**.

replica *noun*

1 *The picture is a replica of a famous painting.* copy, duplicate, reproduction.
An exact copy of a document is a **facsimile**.
2 *They saw a replica of a space module.* model, reconstruction.

reply *noun*

She didn't get a reply to her letter. acknowledgement, answer, reaction, response.
An angry reply is a **retort**.

reply *verb*

to reply to *It took him a long time to reply to her letter.* acknowledge, answer, give a reply to, react to, respond to.

report *verb*

1 *The newspapers reported what happened.* announce, declare, describe, give an account of, proclaim, publish, record, state, tell.
2 *He was told to report to reception when he arrived.* announce yourself, introduce yourself, make yourself known, present yourself.
3 *She reported him to the police.* complain about, denounce, inform against, tell of.

report *noun*

1 *There was a report in the paper about the crash.* account, article, description, news, record, story.
2 *He was startled by the report of the gun.* bang, blast, crack, detonation, noise.

reporter *noun*

A TV reporter interviewed them about the accident they witnessed. correspondent, journalist.

represent *verb*

1 *The picture represents a hunting scene.* act out, depict, describe, illustrate, picture, portray, show.
You can represent things by **drawing** or **painting** them.
2 *Santa Claus represents the spirit of Christmas.* stand for, symbolize.
3 *He appointed a lawyer to represent him.* speak for.

representation *noun*
There was a representation of Santa Claus at the side of the stage. image, likeness, model, picture, portrait, portrayal.

repress *verb*
1 *She always repressed her feelings.* bottle up, control, curb, restrain, stifle, suppress.
AN OPPOSITE IS express.
2 *The people were repressed by the government.* control, keep down, oppress.

repressive *adjective*
The people eventually rebelled against the repressive government. cruel, dictatorial, harsh, oppressive, severe, totalitarian, tyrannical, undemocratic.
AN OPPOSITE IS liberal.

reprieve *verb*
The condemned man was reprieved only minutes before the execution. let off, pardon, set free, spare.

reprimand *verb*
He reprimanded them for their bad behaviour. condemn, criticize, reproach, scold, tell off, [*informal*] tick off.
AN OPPOSITE IS praise.

reprisal *noun*
She refused to name the criminals because she feared reprisals. revenge, vengeance.

reproach *verb*
She reproached him for letting her down. criticize, find fault with, reprimand, scold, show disapproval of, [*informal*] tell off, [*informal*] tick off.
AN OPPOSITE IS praise.

reproduce *verb*
1 *The parrot can reproduce human voices.* imitate, mimic, simulate.
2 *The photocopier will reproduce as many copies as you want.* copy, duplicate, photocopy, print, reprint.
3 *Mice reproduce amazingly quickly.* breed, increase, multiply, produce offspring.

Fish reproduce by *spawning*.
To reproduce plants is to *propagate* them.
To reproduce exact copies of living things is to *clone* them.

reproduction *noun*
1 *Nature has devised many ways of reproduction.*
The reproduction of animals is *breeding*.
The reproduction of plants is *propagation*.
The reproduction of exact copies of living things is *cloning*.
2 *Is that an original painting or a reproduction?* copy, duplicate, imitation, likeness, print, replica.
A reproduction of something which is intended to deceive people is a *fake* or *forgery*.
An exact reproduction of a document is a *facsimile*.

reptile *noun*

> SOME REPTILES: alligator, basilisk, chameleon, crocodile, lizard, salamander, snake, tortoise, turtle.
> FOR OTHER ANIMALS, SEE **animal**.

repulsive *adjective*
They were put off by the animal's repulsive appearance. disgusting, foul, hateful, hideous, horrible, loathsome, objectionable, offensive, repellent, revolting, sickening, vile.
AN OPPOSITE IS attractive.

reputation *noun*
His reputation spread throughout the world. distinction, eminence, fame, name, prestige, renown.

request *verb*
They requested his help. appeal for, apply for, ask for, beg for, call for, entreat, implore, invite, pray for, seek.

request *noun*
He wouldn't listen to their request for help. appeal, call, cry, demand, entreaty, plea.
A request for a job, etc., is an *application*.
A request signed by a lot of people is a *petition*.

require *verb*
1 *They require three runs to win.* be short of, lack, need, want.
2 *The official required her to show her passport.* command, compel, direct, force, instruct, oblige, order, request.

required *adjective*
He didn't have the required documents. compulsory, essential, indispensable, necessary, needed, obligatory.
AN OPPOSITE IS optional.

rescue *verb*
1 *The police rescued the hostages.* free, liberate, release, save, set free.
To rescue someone by paying money is to *ransom* them.
2 *The passengers had no time to rescue their belongings from the sinking ship.* recover, retrieve, salvage.

research *noun*
Their research showed that many cars carry only one person. analysis, inquiry, investigation, probe, study.

resemblance *noun*
It's easy to see the resemblance between the two sisters. closeness, likeness, similarity.
AN OPPOSITE IS difference.

resemble *verb*
He resembled his father. be similar to, look like, [*informal*] take after.

resent *verb*
He resented her success. be angry about, begrudge, be resentful about, envy, grudge, object to, take exception to.

resentful *adjective*
She felt resentful about his interference. angry, annoyed, bitter, envious, grudging, indignant, jealous, offended, spiteful, upset, vexed.

resentment *noun*
They felt a lot of resentment about the way they had been treated. anger, annoyance, bitterness, hatred, indignation, spite, unfriendliness, vexation.

reservation *noun*
1 *They visited a wildlife reservation.* game park, reserve, safari park, sanctuary.

2 *She had reservations about whether the plan would work.* doubt, hesitation.
If you have reservations about something, you are *sceptical* about it.

reserve *verb*
1 *She decided to reserve some food for later.* hoard, hold back, keep, preserve, put aside, retain, save, set aside, stockpile, store up.
2 *They had to reserve their seats on the train.* bag, book, order, pay for, secure.

reserve *noun*
1 *The climbers kept a reserve of food in their base camp.* hoard, stock, stockpile, store, supply.
A reserve of money is a *fund* or *savings*.
2 *They put him down as a reserve for Saturday's game.* replacement, standby, substitute.
Someone who can take the place of an actor is an *understudy*.
Someone who can take the place of a person in charge of something is a *deputy*.
Soldiers brought in to help other soldiers are *reinforcements*.
3 *She saw many kinds of animal at the wildlife reserve.* game park, reservation, safari park, sanctuary.

reserved *adjective*
1 *These seats are reserved.* bagged, booked, ordered, paid for.
2 *She is too reserved to speak up for herself.* bashful, coy, modest, quiet, retiring, secretive, self-conscious, shy, timid.

reside *verb*
to reside in *Most of the students reside in college.* dwell in, inhabit, live in, occupy.

residence *noun*
The palace was the official residence of the head of state. [*old use*] abode, dwelling, home.

resident *noun*
The local residents got together to set up a neighbourhood watch scheme. citizen, inhabitant.
A temporary resident in a hotel, apartment, etc., is a *guest*, *lodger*, *occupant*, *tenant*, or *visitor*.

resign *verb*
> **to resign from something** *She's just resigned from the committee.* give up, leave, pull out of, [*informal*] quit, withdraw from.
> When a monarch resigns from the throne, he or she *abdicates*.
> **to resign yourself to something** *When the bus broke down, I had to resign myself to being late.* accept, be patient about, put up with, tolerate.

resist *verb*
> **1** *They were too weak to resist an enemy attack.* defend yourself against, defy, oppose, stand up to, try to stop, withstand.
> **2** *Sometimes it's hard to resist temptation.* avoid, deal with, fight.
> AN OPPOSITE IS surrender to.

resistance *noun*
> *Their resistance crumbled when they ran out of ammunition.* defence, fighting, opposition.

resolute *adjective*
> *Her voice sounded calm but resolute.* bold, confident, courageous, decisive, determined, firm, strong-minded.
> If you are resolute in a selfish or unhelpful way, you are *obstinate* or *stubborn*.
> AN OPPOSITE IS hesitant.

resolution *noun*
> **1** *They showed great resolution in the face of danger.* boldness, courage, firmness, perseverance, will-power.
> **2** *We made a resolution to work harder.* commitment, decision, promise.

resolve *verb*
> **1** *We resolved to work harder.* agree, decide, determine, make a firm decision, promise, undertake.
> **2** *They hoped the crisis could be resolved.* end, overcome, settle, sort out.

resort *noun*
> **1** *We stayed in a resort on the coast.* holiday town.
> **2** *As a last resort, we could always walk.* alternative, course of action, option.

resort *verb*
> *If negotiations fail they may resort to strike action.* adopt, fall back on, make use of, rely on, start using, turn to, use.

resound *verb*
> *Our voices resounded in the cave.* boom, echo.

resources *plural noun*
> **1** *We should all try to use natural resources wisely.* materials, raw materials, reserves.
> **2** *He started a business with his own resources.* assets, capital, funds, money, riches, wealth.

respect *noun*
> **1** *His colleagues had the deepest respect for him.* admiration, honour, love, regard, reverence.
> **2** *Have some respect for other people's feelings.* concern, consideration, sympathy, thought.
> **3** *In some respects, she's a better player than I am.* aspect, characteristic, detail, feature, particular, point, way.

respect *verb*
> *Everyone respects her for her courage.* admire, esteem, honour, revere, think well of, value.
> AN OPPOSITE IS scorn.

respectable *adjective*
> **1** *He came from a very respectable family.* decent, honest, honourable, upright, worthy.
> **2** *Could you change into something a bit more respectable?* clean, proper, suitable.
> **3** *He earns a respectable income.* adequate, considerable, reasonable, satisfactory, sizeable, substantial, tolerable.

respectful *adjective*
> **1** *He gave us a respectful greeting.* civil, courteous, polite.
> AN OPPOSITE IS rude.
> **2** *People expect respectful behaviour in a place of worship.* considerate, humble, proper, reverent.
> AN OPPOSITE IS disrespectful.

respective *adjective*
> *We all returned to our respective homes.* individual, own, particular, personal, separate, specific.

respond *verb*
>**to respond to** *He didn't respond to my question.* acknowledge, answer, react to, reply to.

response *noun*
>*Did you get a response to your letter?* acknowledgement, answer, reaction, reply.
>An angry response is a ***retort***.
>A response you may get to something you do for people is ***feedback***.

responsible *adjective*
>**1** *Parents are legally responsible for their children.* in charge (of).
>AN OPPOSITE IS not responsible.
>**2** *He's a very responsible sort of person.* careful, conscientious, dependable, dutiful, honest, law-abiding, reliable, sensible, trustworthy.
>AN OPPOSITE IS irresponsible.
>**3** *Looking after people's money is a responsible job.* important, serious.
>**4** *I was responsible for the damage.* guilty (of), to blame.

rest *noun*
>**1** *Let's have a rest.* break, breather, breathing-space, holiday, interlude, intermission, interval, lie-down, lull, nap, pause.
>**2** *The doctor said the patient needed complete rest.* ease, idleness, leisure, quiet, relaxation, time off.
>**3** *I made a rest for my telescope.* base, prop, stand, support.
>**the rest** *Take a few sweets now, but leave the rest for later.* the others, the remains, the remnants, the remainder, the surplus.

rest *verb*
>**1** *I think we should stop and rest for a while.* doze, have a rest, lie down, relax, sleep.
>**2** *Rest the ladder against the wall.* lean, place, prop, stand, support.

restaurant *noun*

> VARIOUS PLACES WHERE YOU CAN BUY A MEAL AND EAT IT: buffet, burger bar, café, cafeteria, canteen, carvery, diner, dining room, grill, pizzeria, pub, snack bar, steakhouse. ➡

> A French-style restaurant is a ***bistro***.
> A Greek-style restaurant is a ***taverna***.
> An Italian-style restaurant is a ***trattoria***.

restful *adjective*
>*They spent a restful Sunday morning reading the papers.* calm, comfortable, leisurely, peaceful, quiet, relaxing, soothing, tranquil, undisturbed, untroubled.
>AN OPPOSITE IS exhausting.

restless *adjective*
>**1** *The animals became restless during the storm.* agitated, anxious, edgy, excitable, fidgety, impatient, jumpy, nervous.
>AN OPPOSITE IS relaxed.
>**2** *I'm tired—I had a restless night.* disturbed, interrupted, sleepless, troubled, uncomfortable, unsettled.
>AN OPPOSITE IS restful.

restore *verb*
>**1** *Please restore the book to its proper place on the shelf.* put back, replace, return.
>**2** *My uncle loves to restore old cars.* clean up, [*informal*] fix, mend, rebuild, renew, repair, touch up.
>**3** *The council is going to restore our local train service.* bring back.
>To restore someone to health is to ***cure*** them.

restrain *verb*
>**1** *Some members of the crowd had to be restrained by police.* control, keep back, keep under control, repress, restrict, subdue, tie up.

> THINGS USED TO RESTRAIN PEOPLE OR ANIMALS: bridle, chains, fetters, handcuffs, harness, irons, lead or leash, muzzle, reins, ropes.

>**2** *She tried to restrain her anger.* control, curb, govern, stifle, suppress.

restrict verb
1 *The new law restricts the sale of fireworks.* control, limit, regulate.
2 *The warders were ordered to restrict the prisoners to their cells.* confine, enclose (in), imprison (in), keep (in), restrain (in), shut (in).

restriction noun
1 *There are certain restrictions we must all obey.* check, control, curb, limitation, regulation, restraint, rule.
2 *They imposed a speed restriction through the village.* ban, limit.

result noun
1 *The water shortage is a result of the long drought.* consequence, effect, outcome, sequel (to), upshot.
The result of a game is the **score**.
The result of a trial is the **verdict**.
2 *If you multiply 9 by 12, what is the result?* answer, product.

result verb
The road was closed to traffic, and chaos resulted. come about, develop, emerge, ensue, follow, happen, occur, take place, turn out.
to result in *The accident resulted in the death of two pedestrians.* bring about, cause, develop into, give rise to, lead to, provoke.

resume verb
We'll resume work after lunch. begin again, carry on, continue, proceed with, recommence, restart, start again.

resuscitate verb
The doctors tried to resuscitate him. bring back to life, restore, revive.

retain verb
1 *Please retain your ticket.* [informal] hang on to, hold on to, keep, preserve, reserve, save.
AN OPPOSITE IS surrender.
2 *They built a dam to retain the water.* hold back, keep in.
AN OPPOSITE IS release.

retire verb
1 *He's hoping to retire next year.* finish working, give up work, leave your job, stop working.

To leave your job voluntarily is to **resign**.
2 *The attack failed and the soldiers had to retire.* give up, leave, quit, withdraw.

retiring adjective
As a child, he was very retiring. bashful, coy, quiet, reserved, shy, timid.

retort verb
'There's no need to be rude!' she retorted angrily. answer, react, reply, respond.

retort noun
His sharp retort upset her. answer, reaction, reply, response.

retrace verb
to retrace your steps *The bridge had collapsed, so we had to retrace our steps.* go back, return.

retreat verb
1 *The army retreated.* back away, go away, leave, move back, retire, withdraw.
To retreat in a shameful way is to **run away**.
2 *The flood began to retreat when the rains stopped.* disappear, go down, recede, shrink.
When the tide retreats, it **ebbs**.

retrieve verb
I was sent to retrieve the ball from next door's garden. fetch back, find, get back, recover, rescue, track down.

return verb
1 *I'll see you when you return.* come back, get back, reappear.
2 *You'll have to return the way you came.* go back, retrace your steps.
3 *Return the books to the shelf.* put back, replace, restore.
4 *Faulty goods may be returned to the shop.* send back, take back.
5 *Please return the money I lent you.* give back, refund, repay.
6 *The illness may return.* happen again, recur.

return noun
1 *We look forward to your return.* arrival, reappearance.
2 *He's hoping for a good return from his investment.* gain, income, interest, profit.

reveal *verb*
1 *He decided to reveal the truth.*
announce, communicate, confess,
declare, disclose, make known,
proclaim, publish, tell.
To reveal secret information in a sly
way is to **leak** it.
2 *Next week the manufacturer will
reveal a new design.* display, exhibit,
show, unveil.
3 *The nurse took off the bandage to
reveal the wound.* expose, uncover.
AN OPPOSITE IS hide.

revenge *noun*
*The assassination was an act of
revenge.* reprisal, vengeance.
to take revenge on someone *He
declared that he would take revenge on
them all.* get even with, [*informal*] get
your own back on, repay.

revere *verb*
*He was greatly revered by his fellow
poets.* admire, adore, honour, idolize,
respect, value, worship.
AN OPPOSITE IS despise.

reverence *noun*
*He had a deep reverence for the
traditions of the church.* admiration,
devotion, respect.

reverent *adjective*
*The worshippers knelt in reverent
silence.* adoring, pious, respectful,
solemn.
AN OPPOSITE IS irreverent.

reverse *noun*
He says one thing and does the reverse.
contrary, converse, opposite.

reverse *verb*
1 *We decided to reverse the order in
which we did things.* change, invert,
turn round.
2 *The driver tried to reverse into the
parking space.* back, drive backwards,
go backwards.

review *noun*
1 *The council undertook a review of the
town's traffic problems.* examination,
inspection, study, survey.
2 *We had to write reviews of our
favourite books.* appraisal, criticism.

review *verb*
1 *The judge began to review the
evidence.* appraise, assess, consider,
evaluate, examine, go over, scrutinize,
study, survey, weigh up.
2 *He reviewed the play for the Sunday
paper.* criticize, write a review of.

revise *verb*
1 *We revised the work we did last term.*
go over, learn, review, study.
2 *The new evidence forced me to revise
my opinion.* alter, change, modify,
reconsider, update.
3 *The articles were revised before being
published.* correct, edit, improve,
rewrite.

revive *verb*
1 *Many songs from the seventies have
been revived.* bring back.
2 *He soon revived after the anaesthetic.*
awaken, come back to life, come round,
come to, rally, recover, wake.
3 *A cold drink will revive you.* bring
back to life, freshen up, invigorate,
refresh, restore, wake up.

revolt *verb*
1 *The people revolted against the
military dictatorship.* rebel, riot, rise
up.
To revolt on a ship is to **mutiny**.
2 *Cruelty to animals revolted her.*
appal, disgust, horrify, repel, sicken.

revolting *adjective*
What is that revolting smell? appalling,
disgusting, foul, horrible, loathsome,
nasty, offensive, repulsive, sickening,
unpleasant.
AN OPPOSITE IS attractive or pleasant.

revolution *noun*
1 *The revolution brought in a new
government.* civil war, rebellion, revolt,
uprising.
2 *Computers brought about a
revolution in the way we do things.*
change, transformation, [*informal*] U-
turn.
3 *One revolution of the earth takes 24
hours.* rotation, turn.

revolutionary *adjective*
He's full of revolutionary and exciting ideas. innovative, new, radical, [informal] unheard of.
AN OPPOSITE IS conservative.

revolutionize *verb*
Computers have revolutionized the way people do business. change completely, transform.

revolve *verb*
The earth revolves once every 24 hours. rotate, turn.
To revolve quickly is to *spin* or *whirl*.
To move round something is to *circle* or *orbit* it.

reward *noun*
A reward for hard work is a *bonus* on top of your wages.
A reward for bravery is a *decoration* or *medal*.
A reward for winning something is an *award* or *prize*.
AN OPPOSITE IS punishment.

reward *verb*
She was generously rewarded for her work. compensate, repay.
AN OPPOSITE IS punish.

rewarding *adjective*
They say that nursing is a rewarding job. pleasing, satisfying, worthwhile.
AN OPPOSITE IS thankless.

rhyme *noun*
She sang her sister little rhymes. poem, verse.

rhythm *noun*
She could hear the rhythm of his heartbeat. beat, pulse.
The speed or type of rhythm of a piece of music is the *tempo*.
The type of rhythm of a piece of poetry is its *metre*.

rhythmic *adjective*
The rhythmic beat of the music makes you want to dance. rhythmical, regular, repeated, steady, throbbing.

ribbon *noun*
She tied a red velvet ribbon in her hair. band, braid, strip.

rich *adjective*
1 They must be rich to live in a huge house like that. affluent, prosperous, wealthy, well-off.
AN OPPOSITE IS poor.
2 The rooms were full of rich furnishings. costly, elaborate, expensive, lavish, luxurious, splendid, valuable.
3 She wore a dress of a rich red colour. deep, intense, strong, vivid.
4 This cake is a bit too rich for me. creamy, fat, fattening, fatty.

riches *plural noun*
They acquired riches beyond their wildest dreams. affluence, fortune, prosperity, wealth.

richly *adverb*
1 The palace was richly furnished. elaborately, expensively, lavishly, luxuriously.
2 They richly deserved their punishment. absolutely, completely, thoroughly.

rickety *adjective*
Take care—that ladder looks rickety. decrepit, flimsy, shaky, unsteady, wobbly.
AN OPPOSITE IS solid.

ricochet *verb*
The bullet ricocheted off the wall. bounce, rebound.

rid *verb*
The new vaccine may rid the world of this disease. clear, empty, free, purge.
to get rid of 1 I managed to get rid of him at last. eject, evict, expel, remove, throw out.
2 He decided to get rid of his old car. dispose of, dump, scrap, throw away.

riddle *noun*
The police have not yet solved the riddle of her death. conundrum, mystery, problem, puzzle, question.

ride *verb*
Can you ride a horse? control, handle, manage, sit on.

ride *noun*
He took us for a ride in his new car. drive, journey, outing, trip.

ridicule *verb*
Everyone ridiculed me because of my novel ideas. be sarcastic or satirical about, deride, jeer at, joke about, laugh at, make fun of, make jokes about, mock, scoff at, [*informal*] send up, sneer at, taunt, tease.

ridiculous *adjective*
1 *He looks ridiculous in that hat.* absurd, daft, funny, foolish, laughable, silly, stupid.
2 *It was ridiculous to go out in that weather.* absurd, [*informal*] crazy, [*informal*] daft, foolish, ludicrous, senseless, silly, stupid, unreasonable.
AN OPPOSITE IS sensible.

right *adjective*
1 *Most people write with their right hand.*
AN OPPOSITE IS left.
The right side of a ship when you face the bow is the **starboard** side.
2 *Put up your hand if you got the right answer.* correct, exact, true.
3 *She was waiting for the right moment to tell him.* appropriate, fitting, proper, suitable.
4 *It's not right to steal.* decent, fair, honest, honourable, just, lawful, legal, moral, upright, virtuous.
5 *Have we come the right way?* best, convenient, normal, sensible, usual.
AN OPPOSITE IS wrong.

right *adverb*
1 *Turn right at the corner.*
AN OPPOSITE IS left.
2 *Turn right round.* all the way, completely.
3 *She stood right in the middle.* exactly, precisely.
4 *Go right ahead.* directly, straight.

right *noun*
1 *The post office is on the right along the High Street.*
AN OPPOSITE IS left.
2 *People have the right to walk across the common.* freedom, liberty.
3 *You don't have the right to tell me what to do.* authority, power.

righteous *adjective*
He was a devout and righteous man. blameless, good, guiltless, just, law-abiding, moral, pure, upright, virtuous.
AN OPPOSITE IS sinful.

rigid *adjective*
1 *The tent was supported by a rigid framework.* firm, hard, solid, stiff.
2 *The referee was rigid in applying the rules.* harsh, inflexible, stern, strict, uncompromising.
AN OPPOSITE IS flexible.

rim *noun*
She looked at him over the rim of her glass. brim, brink, edge, lip.

ring *noun*
The wooden barrel had metal rings round it. band, circle, hoop.

ring *verb*
1 *The police ringed the whole area.* circle, encircle, enclose, surround.
2 *The bell rang.* chime, clang, clink, jangle, peal, resound, tinkle, toll.
3 *Ring me tomorrow evening.* call, phone, ring up, telephone.

rinse *verb*
Rinse the plates in clean water. clean, swill, wash.
To rinse out the lavatory is to **flush** it.

riot *noun*
The police moved in to stop the riot. commotion, disorder, disturbance, rioting, turmoil, uproar, violence.
Unruly behaviour by sailors on a ship is a **mutiny**.

riot *verb*
The crowds were rioting in the streets. go wild, rampage, rebel, revolt, rise up, run wild.

riotous *adjective*
Their riotous behaviour led to their arrest. boisterous, disorderly, lawless, mutinous, noisy, rebellious, rowdy, unruly, violent, wild.
AN OPPOSITE IS orderly.

rip *verb*
The barbed wire ripped my jeans. tear.

ripe *adjective*
Choose a nice ripe peach. mature, mellow, ready to eat.

ripen *verb*
The pears need to ripen. become riper, develop, mature.

ripple *verb*
The wind rippled the surface of the pond. disturb, make waves on, ruffle, stir.

rise *verb*
1 The lark rose into the air. ascend, climb, fly up, mount, soar.
When a plane rises into the air, it **takes off**.
When a rocket rises into the air, it **lifts off**.
AN OPPOSITE IS descend.
2 A high cliff rose above us. loom, stand out, stick up, tower.
3 They say that prices may rise soon. go up, increase.
AN OPPOSITE IS fall.
4 He rose and shook her hand. get up, stand up.
AN OPPOSITE IS sit.
to rise up The people rose up against the military dictatorship. rebel, revolt, riot.

rise *noun*
1 The bad weather resulted in a rise in the price of vegetables. increase, jump.
AN OPPOSITE IS fall.
2 At the top of the rise they paused for a break. ascent, bank, hill, incline, ramp, slope.

risk *verb*
He risked his life to save them. gamble, venture.

risk *noun*
1 All outdoor activities carry an element of risk. danger, hazard, peril.
2 Starting a business involves risk. a gamble, uncertainty.
3 The forecast says there's a risk of frost. chance, likelihood, possibility.

risky *adjective*
Cycling on icy roads is risky. dangerous, hazardous, perilous, unsafe.
AN OPPOSITE IS safe.

ritual *noun*
Most religions have rituals, performed on special occasions. ceremony, rite, tradition.

rival *noun*
He has no serious rival for the championship. adversary, competitor, contender, contestant, enemy, opponent.

rival *verb*
Few countries can rival Scotland for mountainous scenery. compete with, contend with.

rivalry *noun*
There was fierce rivalry between the two teams. competition, competitiveness, opposition.
AN OPPOSITE IS cooperation.

river *noun*
A small river is a **stream** or **rivulet**.
A small river which flows into a larger river is a **tributary**.
The place where a river begins is its **source**.
The place where a river goes into the sea is its **mouth**.
A wide river mouth is an **estuary**.
The place where the mouth of a river splits into several channels before going into the sea is a **delta**.
A river of ice is a **glacier**.

road *noun*

KINDS OF ROAD FOR TRAFFIC:
bypass, dual carriageway, [*American*] freeway, highway, lane, main road, motorway, one-way street, ring road, trunk road.
A road on which a toll was collected at a toll gate in former times was a **turnpike**.
A private road up to a house is a **drive**.
A firm road across marshy land is a **causeway**.

KINDS OF ROAD IN TOWNS: alley, avenue, boulevard, crescent, cul-de-sac, side street, shopping street, street.

THINGS WHICH MAY BE PART OF A ROAD SYSTEM: bridge, flyover or overpass, footbridge, ford, hairpin bend, junction, lay-by, level crossing, motorway interchange, pedestrian crossing, roundabout, service area or service station, signpost, slip road, traffic lights, underpass, viaduct. ➡

WAYS LIKE ROADS BUT NOT MADE FOR MOTOR VEHICLES: bridle path or bridleway, cart track, footpath, pedestrian precinct or pedestrianized street, track, trail, walkway.
A way along the side of a river or canal is a **tow-path**.
A way for people to walk on along the sea front in a seaside town is an **esplanade** or **promenade**.

SURFACES USED TO MAKE ROADS AND PATHS: asphalt, cobbles, concrete, gravel, paving blocks or stones, sets or setts, [*trademark*] tarmac.

roam *verb*
1 *We roamed about town aimlessly.* meander, ramble, walk, wander.
2 *Herds of wild deer roamed over the hills.* prowl, range, rove.

roar *noun, verb*
FOR VARIOUS WAYS TO MAKE SOUNDS, SEE **sound** *verb*.

rob *verb*
Make sure no one robs you when you're taking money to the bank. mug, pick your pocket, steal from.
SEE ALSO **steal, stealing**.

robber *noun* SEE **thief**

robbery *noun* SEE **stealing**

robe *noun*
A kind of robe you might wear in your bedroom is a **dressing gown** or **bathrobe**.
Robes worn by a priest are **vestments**.
The robe worn by a monk is a **habit**.
A robe certain officials might wear at a ceremony is a **gown**.
Robe is also a formal word for a woman's **dress**.

robust *adjective*
1 *A mountaineer needs a robust constitution.* athletic, fit, hardy, healthy, muscular, powerful, strong, vigorous.
AN OPPOSITE IS weak.

2 *She wore a pair of robust leather shoes.* durable, hard-wearing, solid, sturdy, tough.
AN OPPOSITE IS flimsy.

rock *noun*
1 *We clambered over the rocks.* boulder, stone.
2 *The rocks towered above them.* cliff, crag, precipice.

Igneous rocks have solidified from molten rock.
Metamorphic rocks have been transformed by heat, or high pressure, or both.
Sedimentary rocks were formed from layers of particles deposited by winds or water.
Rock from which metal or other valuable minerals can be extracted is **ore**.

SOME KINDS OF ROCK: agglomerate, basalt, chalk, conglomerate, flint, granite, gypsum, lava, limestone, marble, quartz, sandstone, shale, slate, tufa.

rock *verb*
1 *I rocked the baby's cradle to and fro.* move gently, sway, swing.
2 *The ship rocked in the storm.* lurch, pitch, reel, roll, shake, toss.

rocky *adjective*
1 *Nothing was growing in the rocky ground.* barren, pebbly, stony.
2 *Take care—that chair's a bit rocky.* rickety, shaky, unsafe, unsteady, wobbly.

rod *noun*
VARIOUS KINDS OF ROD: bar, baton, cane, curtain rail, fishing rod, pole, rail, shaft, spoke, staff, stick, strut, wand.

rogue *noun*
Don't trust him—he's a rogue. cheat, [*slang*] conman, fraud, rascal, scoundrel, swindler, villain.

roguish *adjective*
He gave me a roguish smile. impish, mischievous, naughty, playful, wicked.

role *noun*
    1 *He plays the role of a journalist in his new film.* character, part.
    2 *Both sides have important roles to play in the discussions.* contribution, function, job, position, task.

roll *verb*
    1 *The wheels began to roll.* move round, revolve, rotate, spin, turn, twirl, whirl.
    2 *I rolled up my beach-mat and carried it home.* coil, curl, twist, wind.
    To roll up a sail on a yacht is to **furl** it.
    3 *Roll out the pastry on a flat surface.* flatten, level out, smooth.
    4 *The ship rolled in the storm.* pitch, rock, sway, toss, wallow.
    5 *He rolled along the street as if he were drunk.* lumber, lurch, reel, stagger, totter.

romance *noun*
    1 *The moonlight gave the scene a touch of romance.* excitement, glamour.
    2 *She had a holiday romance during the summer.* affair, love affair, relationship.

romantic *adjective*
    1 *Her boyfriend is very romantic.* emotional, sentimental, tender.
    2 *A holiday on a desert island sounds very romantic.* exotic, glamorous.

romp *verb*
    The children romped around the playground. caper, dance about, frisk, frolic, leap about, play, prance, run about, skip about.

roof *noun*

> MATERIALS USED TO MAKE ROOFS: corrugated iron, roofing felt, slates, thatch, tiles.
> A sloping roof is a **pitched roof**.
> The sloping beams in the framework of a roof are **rafters**.
> The overhanging edge of a roof is the **eaves**.

room *noun*
    1 *How many rooms are there in your house?*

> ROOMS YOU MIGHT FIND IN A HOUSE: bathroom, bedroom, conservatory, dining room, drawing room or living room or lounge or sitting room, hall, kitchen or kitchenette, landing, larder or pantry, lavatory or toilet or WC, nursery, parlour, scullery, spare room or guest room, study, utility room.
>
> ROOMS YOU MIGHT FIND IN A SCHOOL: assembly hall, classroom, cloakroom, corridor, laboratory, library, music room, office, staff room, storeroom, workshop.
> A small room in a monastery or prison is a **cell**.
> An underground room is a **basement** or **cellar** or **vault**.
> The space in the roof of a house is the **attic** or **loft**.
> A room where an artist works is a **studio**.
> A room where you wait to see a dentist, etc., is a **waiting room**.
> A room in a boarding school where pupils sleep is a **dormitory**.
> A room in a hospital for patients is a **ward**.

    2 *I need more room to spread my things out.* freedom, scope, space.

roomy *adjective*
    It's a surprisingly roomy car. big, large, sizeable, spacious.

root *noun*
    We need to get to the root of the problem. basis, origin, source, starting point.

rope *noun*
    The sailors threw a rope to the men in the water. cable, cord, line.
    The ropes that support a ship's mast and sails are the **rigging**.
    A rope for raising and lowering a sail is a **halyard**.
    A thick rope for mooring a ship is a **hawser**.
    A rope with a loop at one end used for catching cattle is a **lasso**.

rot *verb*
  The wooden fence had begun to rot. become rotten, crumble, decay, decompose, disintegrate.
  If metal rots it is said to **corrode**.
  If rubber rots it is said to **perish**.
  If food rots it is said to **go bad** or **putrefy**.

rotate *verb*
  The globe rotates on its axis. pivot, revolve, spin, swivel, turn, twirl, twist, wheel, whirl.

rotten *adjective*
  1 The window frame is rotten. crumbling, decayed, decaying, decomposed, disintegrating, unsound.
  Rotten metal is **corroded** or **rusty** metal.
  AN OPPOSITE IS sound.
  2 The fridge smelled of rotten eggs. bad, decomposing, foul, mouldy, perished, smelly.
  AN OPPOSITE IS fresh.
  3 [informal] We had rotten weather. [informal] abysmal, awful, bad, dreadful, nasty, poor, unpleasant.
  AN OPPOSITE IS good.

rough *adjective*
  1 A rough track led to the farm. bumpy, craggy, irregular, jagged, rocky, rugged, stony, uneven.
  AN OPPOSITE IS even or smooth.
  2 The sea was rough, and I was seasick. choppy, heaving, stormy, tempestuous, turbulent.
  AN OPPOSITE IS calm.
  3 The blanket felt rough against my skin. bristly, coarse, harsh, scratchy.
  AN OPPOSITE IS soft.
  4 He's been hanging around with some rough company. badly behaved, boisterous, disorderly, noisy, riotous, rowdy, unruly, violent, wild.
  AN OPPOSITE IS well behaved.
  5 At a rough guess there were a hundred people present. approximate, imprecise, inexact, vague.
  AN OPPOSITE IS exact.
  6 He carved a rough figure out of wood. amateurish, careless, clumsy, crude, hasty, unskilful.
  AN OPPOSITE IS skilful.

roughly *adverb*
  There were roughly a hundred people present. about, approximately, around, close to, nearly.

round *adjective*
  The plant has small round berries. rounded, spherical.
  A flat round shape is **circular**.

round *noun*
  We were knocked out in the first round of the competition. bout, contest, game, heat, stage.

round *verb*
  The car rounded the corner at top speed. go round, travel round, turn.
  to round something off They rounded the evening off with some songs. bring to an end, complete, conclude, end, finish.
  to round up people or **things** The captain rounded up his players. assemble, bring together, collect, gather, muster, rally.

roundabout *adjective*
  We went home by a roundabout route to avoid the traffic. devious, indirect, long, meandering, twisting, winding.
  AN OPPOSITE IS direct.

rouse *verb*
  1 She was roused by the sound of the telephone ringing. arouse, awaken, call, wake up.
  2 He was a quiet man, not easily roused to anger or jealousy. agitate, excite, provoke, stimulate, stir up.

rout *verb*
  We routed the opposition. conquer, crush, defeat, overwhelm, thrash.

route *noun*
  We drove home by the quickest route. course, direction, journey, path, road, way.

routine *noun*
  1 His departure had upset her daily routine. method, pattern, procedure, system, way.
  2 The skaters performed a new routine. act, performance, programme.

row *noun*
1 *They arranged the chairs in a row.*
[Rhymes with *go*.] column, line,
sequence, series, string.
A row of people waiting for something
is a **queue**.
A row of people walking behind each
other is a **file**.
A row of soldiers standing side by side
on parade is a **rank**.
A row of police, etc., is a **cordon**.
2 *The class next door was making a
terrible row.* [Rhymes with *cow*.]
commotion, din, disturbance,
hullabaloo, noise, racket, tumult,
uproar.
3 *They had a terrible row.* [Rhymes
with *cow*.] argument, disagreement,
dispute, fight, quarrel, squabble.

rowdy *adjective*
The crowd became rowdy. badly
behaved, boisterous, disorderly, noisy,
riotous, rough, unruly, violent, wild.
AN OPPOSITE IS quiet.

royalty *noun*

WORDS FOR MEMBERS OF A ROYAL
FAMILY: Her or His Majesty, Her or
His Royal Highness, king, monarch,
prince, princess, queen, queen
mother, sovereign.
The husband or wife of a royal
person is a **consort**.
A person who rules while a monarch
is too young or too ill to rule is a
regent.
SEE ALSO **ruler**.

rub *verb*
1 *She rubbed her stiff arms and legs.*
knead, massage, stroke.
2 *The heel of his shoe was rubbing his
foot.* graze, scrape.
3 *I rubbed the plate until it gleamed.*
polish, scour, scrub, wipe.
to rub something out *He rubbed out
the pencil marks.* delete, erase, remove,
wipe out.

rubbish *noun*
1 *She took the rubbish out to the bin.*
garbage, junk, litter, refuse, scrap,
trash, waste.
2 *Don't talk rubbish!* [*slang*] bilge,
nonsense, [*informal*] rot, [*informal*]
tripe.

rubble *noun*
*The building collapsed into a pile of
rubble.* broken bricks, debris,
fragments, remains, wreckage.

ruddy *adjective*
*He has a ruddy face because he spends
so much time out of doors.* fresh,
glowing, healthy looking, red,
sunburnt.

rude *adjective*
1 *That was a very rude remark.* abrupt,
abusive, bad-mannered, blunt, cheeky,
disrespectful, ill-mannered,
impertinent, impolite, impudent,
inconsiderate, insolent, insulting,
saucy, tactless, uncivil,
uncomplimentary, uncouth, unfriendly.
To be rude to someone is to **insult**
them or **snub** them.
AN OPPOSITE IS polite.
2 *He kept telling rather rude jokes.*
coarse, crude, dirty, foul, improper,
indecent, naughty, obscene, offensive,
smutty, vulgar.
Words which are rude about sacred
things are **blasphemous** or
irreverent.
AN OPPOSITE IS decent.

rudeness *noun*
I'm sick of her rudeness. abuse, bad
manners, cheek, impertinence,
impudence, insolence, insults,
tactlessness, vulgarity.
AN OPPOSITE IS politeness.

ruffian *noun*
He was attacked by a gang of ruffians.
bully, gangster, hooligan, lout, mugger,
scoundrel, thug, villain.

ruffle *verb*
1 *A breeze ruffled the water.* agitate,
disturb, ripple, stir.
AN OPPOSITE IS smooth.

2 *Some of the audience booed, and the speaker began to get ruffled.* annoy, fluster, irritate, [*informal*] rattle, unsettle, upset, worry.
AN OPPOSITE IS calm.

rug *noun*
A rug to go on the floor is a ***mat***.
A rug to wrap yourself in is a ***blanket***.

rugged *adjective*
1 *He was tall and dark with rugged features.* irregular, rough, uneven.
2 *It was difficult for boats to land on the rugged coast.* bumpy, craggy, jagged, rocky.

ruin *verb*
The storm had ruined the flowers in the garden. damage, demolish, destroy, devastate, flatten, shatter, spoil, wreck.

ruin *noun*
1 *The ruin was covered in ivy.* ruined building.
2 *The ruin of his business meant that he had to sell his house.* breakdown, collapse, failure.
Financial ruin is ***bankruptcy***.
ruins *After the earthquake, people wandered hopelessly through the ruins.* debris, remains, rubble, wreckage.

ruined *adjective*
A notice near the ruined building told people to keep out. crumbling, derelict, uninhabitable, unsafe, wrecked.

ruinous *adjective*
Pollution is having a ruinous effect on the environment. calamitous, catastrophic, destructive, devastating, disastrous.

rule *noun*
1 *Stick to the rules of the game.* law, principle, regulation.
A set of rules is a ***code***.
2 *The country was formerly under French rule.* administration, authority, command, control, domination, government, management, power, reign.

rule *verb*
1 *The judge rules the court.* administer, command, control, direct, dominate, govern, lead, manage, run.
2 *The queen ruled for many years.* be ruler, reign.
3 *The umpire ruled that the batsman was out.* decide, decree, determine, judge, pronounce.

ruler *noun*

VARIOUS RULERS: caesar, dictator, emir, emperor, empress, governor, kaiser, king, lord, monarch, president, prince, princess, queen, rajah, regent, satrap, sovereign, sultan, tyrant, tzar, viceroy.
SEE ALSO **chief** *noun*.

rummage *verb*
I rummaged through my bag looking for my purse. comb, hunt, scour, search.

rumour *noun*
The rumour began with an anonymous telephone call to a newspaper. gossip, scandal.

run *verb*
1 *We ran as fast as our legs could carry us.* bolt, career, dash, hurry, race, rush, scamper, scurry, scuttle, speed, sprint, tear.
To run at a gentle pace is to ***jog***.
When a horse runs, it ***gallops*** or ***trots***.
2 *Water ran down the wall.* dribble, flow, gush, leak, pour, spill, stream, trickle.
3 *The bus doesn't run on Sundays.* go, operate, provide a service, travel.
4 *The car runs well.* behave, function, operate, perform, work.
5 *The government runs the country's affairs.* administer, conduct, control, direct, govern, look after, manage, rule, supervise.
to run away *They ran away when they saw the policeman.* bolt, escape, flee, make off.
to run into 1 *I didn't expect to run into you!* [*informal*] bump into, come across, encounter, meet.
2 *A car ran into our bus.* collide with, hit.

run *noun*
1 *We went for a run in the park.*
A fast run is a **dash**, **gallop**, **race**, or
sprint.
A gentle run is a **canter**, **jog**, or **trot**.
2 *We went for a run in the car.* drive,
journey, ride.
3 *She's had a run of good luck recently.*
sequence, series, stretch.
4 *The animals lived in a run
surrounded by wire netting.* compound,
coop, enclosure, pen.

runaway *noun*
A person who has run away from the
army is a **deserter**.
A person who is running away from the
law is a **fugitive** or **outlaw**.

runner *noun*
*The runners were ready to start the
race.* athlete, competitor.
Someone who runs fast over short
distances is a **sprinter**.
Someone who runs to keep fit is a
jogger.

runny *adjective*
This gravy is too runny. fluid, liquid,
thin, watery.
AN OPPOSITE IS thick.

rural *adjective*
They live in a peaceful rural area.
agricultural, pastoral, rustic.

rush *verb*
I rushed home with the good news. bolt,
career, charge, dash, fly, gallop, hasten,
hurry, race, run, scamper, scurry,
scuttle, shoot, speed, sprint, tear, zoom.
When cattle rush along together they
stampede.

rush *noun*
1 *We've got plenty of time, so what's the
rush?* haste, hurry, urgency.
2 *There was a sudden rush of water.*
cataract, flood, gush.

rust *verb*
*Iron rusts if you leave it exposed to the
weather.* become rusty, corrode,
crumble away, oxidize, rot.

rustic *adjective*
The village had a rustic charm.
agricultural, pastoral, rural.

rusty *adjective*
*I found a rusty knife buried in the
garden.* corroded, oxidized, rotten.

rut *noun*
The tractor left ruts along the track.
channel, furrow, groove, indentation,
pothole.

ruthless *adjective*
*Many people were killed in the ruthless
attack.* barbaric, bloodthirsty, brutal,
callous, cruel, ferocious, fierce,
heartless, pitiless, sadistic, savage,
vicious, violent.
AN OPPOSITE IS merciful.

Ss

sabotage *noun*
The sabotage was blamed on terrorists.
damage, destruction, disruption,
vandalism, wrecking.

sabotage *verb*
The machinery has been sabotaged.
cripple, damage, destroy, put out of
action, vandalize, wreck.

sack *noun*
He bought a sack of potatoes. bag.
SEE ALSO **container**.
to get the sack [*informal*] *She got the
sack because of her laziness.* be sacked,
lose your job.
to give someone the sack SEE **sack**
verb.

sack *verb*
The boss threatened to sack him.
dismiss, [*informal*] fire, [*informal*] give
you the sack, make you redundant.
To **lay off** employees is to tell them
there is no work for them at present.

sacred *adjective*
The Koran is a sacred book. blessed,
divine, holy, religious, revered.

sacrifice *verb*
1 *She sacrificed her weekend to finish the job.* give up, surrender.
2 *They sacrificed animals to please the gods.* kill, offer up, slaughter.

sad *adjective*
1 *He was looking a bit sad.* broken-hearted, dejected, depressed, desolate, despairing, dismal, distressed, downcast, downhearted, forlorn, gloomy, glum, grave, heartbroken, in low spirits, [*informal*] low, miserable, regretful, sorrowful, sorry, tearful, troubled, unhappy, upset, wistful, woeful, wretched.
If you are sad because you are away from home, you are **homesick**.
AN OPPOSITE IS happy.
2 *It was sad to see how badly the animals were treated.* depressing, distressing, heartbreaking, pathetic, pitiful, upsetting.
AN OPPOSITE IS cheering.
3 *They sang a sad song.* melancholy, mournful, moving, plaintive, touching, wistful.
AN OPPOSITE IS cheerful.
4 *She has had some sad news.* grim, painful, regrettable, serious, tragic, unfortunate, unpleasant.
AN OPPOSITE IS pleasant.

sadden *verb*
The bad news saddened her. [*informal*] break your heart, depress, disappoint, distress, grieve, upset.
AN OPPOSITE IS cheer up.

sadistic *adjective*
He takes a sadistic pleasure in hurting people. brutal, callous, cruel, heartless, inhuman.
AN OPPOSITE IS kind.

sadness *noun* SEE **sorrow**

safe *adjective*
1 *They got home safe in spite of the storm.* [*informal*] in one piece, intact, sound, undamaged, unharmed, unhurt, uninjured.
AN OPPOSITE IS damaged or hurt.
2 *They made their house safe from intruders.* defended, guarded, protected, secure.
AN OPPOSITE IS vulnerable.

3 *She's a safe driver.* cautious, dependable, reliable, trustworthy.
4 *The dog's quite safe.* docile, friendly, gentle, harmless, tame.
5 *This drinking water is safe.* drinkable, pure, uncontaminated.
6 *The food is safe to eat.* eatable, good, wholesome.
A safe car is **roadworthy**.
A safe aircraft is **airworthy**.
A safe ship is **seaworthy**.
AN OPPOSITE IS dangerous.

safeguard *noun*
She made a copy of the computer disk as a safeguard. protection, security.

safety *noun*
1 *You must wear a seat belt for your own safety.* protection, security.
2 *The nurse assured him of the safety of the drug.* harmlessness, reliability.

safety belt *noun*
It's against the law to drive without a safety belt on. safety harness, seat belt.

sag *verb*
The clothes line sagged in the middle. dip, droop, slump.

sail *verb*
1 *She sailed to France rather than going by air.* travel by ship.
To have a holiday sailing on a ship is to **cruise**.
2 *It needs a lot of experience to sail a boat.* navigate, pilot, steer.

sailor *noun*

VARIOUS PEOPLE WHO WORK ON BOATS OR HELP TO SAIL THEM: able seaman, bargee, boatman, boatswain or bosun, captain, cox or coxswain, helmsman, mariner, mate, midshipman, navigator, pilot, rating, rower, seaman, yachtsman.
The team of sailors who sail a boat is the **crew**.
FOR RANKS IN THE NAVY, SEE **rank**.

saintly *adjective*
He had such a saintly expression on his face. angelic, holy, innocent, pure, religious, virtuous.
AN OPPOSITE IS devilish.

sake *noun*
for my sake *He did it for my sake.* on my behalf, for my benefit, to help me.

salad *noun*

> VEGETABLES OFTEN EATEN IN SALADS: beetroot, carrot, celery, chicory, cress, cucumber, lettuce, mustard and cress, onion, peppers, potato, radish, spring onion, watercress.
> FOR OTHER VEGETABLES, SEE **vegetable**.

salary *noun*
He gets a salary of £15,000 a year. earnings, income, pay.
If your pay is calculated week by week, it is called **wages**.

sale *noun*

> KINDS OF SALE: auction, bazaar, car-boot sale, closing-down sale, fair, jumble sale, market.

salty *adjective*
The water tasted salty. saline, salted.
AN OPPOSITE IS fresh.
Salty water is **brine**.
Water which is slightly salty is **brackish**.
Food with a salty taste is said to have a **savoury** taste.

salvage *verb*
They were able to salvage a few possessions from the wreck. reclaim, recover, rescue, retrieve, save.

same *adjective*
the same 1 *Each person will get the same amount.* equal, equivalent, identical.
2 *Everyone in the choir wore the same clothes.* matching, similar, uniform.
3 *She hadn't seen him since last year, but he looks the same.* unaltered, unchanged.
Lines which go in the same direction are **parallel**.
Words which mean the same are **synonymous**.
AN OPPOSITE IS different.

sample *noun*
He showed the visitor a sample of his work. example, illustration, instance, selection, specimen.

sample *verb*
She let him sample the home-made fudge. taste, test, try.

sanctuary *noun*
The hunted fox found sanctuary in a wood. a haven, protection, refuge, safety, shelter.

sand *noun*
He got some sand in his shoes. grit.
sands *They played on the sands until the tide came in.* beach, shore.
Hills of sand along the coast are **dunes**.

sane *adjective*
A sane person would not do something like that. rational, reasonable, sensible.
AN OPPOSITE IS insane.

sanitary *adjective*
It's important to have sanitary conditions in a hospital. clean, disinfected, germ free, healthy, hygienic, pure, sterilized, uncontaminated, unpolluted.
AN OPPOSITE IS insanitary.

sanitation *noun*
Has the camp site got proper sanitation? drainage, drains, lavatories, sewage disposal, sewers.

sarcasm *noun*
He found her constant sarcasm very irritating. derision, irony, mockery, ridicule, satire.

sarcastic *adjective*
She made some sarcastic remarks about politicians. ironical, mocking, satirical, sneering, taunting.

satirical *adjective*
There was a satirical article about him in the paper. ironic, irreverent, mocking, sarcastic.

> DEVICES USED IN SATIRE TO MAKE PEOPLE LAUGH: caricature, exaggeration, irony, mimicry, mockery, parody, ridicule.

satisfaction *noun*
She gets a lot of satisfaction from her hobby. contentment, enjoyment, fulfilment, happiness, pleasure, pride, sense of achievement.
AN OPPOSITE IS dissatisfaction.

satisfactory *adjective*
She said his work was not satisfactory. acceptable, adequate, all right, competent, good enough, passable, tolerable.
AN OPPOSITE IS unsatisfactory.

satisfy *verb*
Nothing satisfies him—he's always complaining. make you happy, meet your needs, please.
To satisfy your thirst is to **quench** or **slake** it.
AN OPPOSITE IS frustrate.

saturate *verb*
Their clothes were saturated when they got caught in the storm. drench, soak.
If something is saturated, it is said to be **wringing wet**.

sauce *noun*

SOME KINDS OF SAUCE YOU EAT WITH VARIOUS FOODS: bread sauce, cheese sauce, cranberry sauce, curry sauce, custard, gravy, horseradish sauce, ketchup, mayonnaise, mint sauce, salad cream, sauce tartare.

saucepan *noun*
FOR THINGS YOU COOK WITH, SEE **cook** *verb*.

saucy *adjective*
He was told off for making saucy remarks. cheeky, disrespectful, facetious, impertinent, impudent, insolent, rude.
AN OPPOSITE IS respectful.

saunter *verb*
They sauntered through the park. amble, stroll, walk slowly.
SEE ALSO **walk** *verb*.

savage *adjective*
1 *The soldiers launched a savage attack against the enemy.* barbarous, bloodthirsty, brutal, cold-blooded, cruel, diabolical, merciless, murderous, pitiless, ruthless, sadistic, vicious, violent.
AN OPPOSITE IS humane.
2 *At one time Britain was the home of savage tribes.* barbaric, primitive, uncivilized.
AN OPPOSITE IS civilized.
3 *Savage beasts roam the plain in search of prey.* ferocious, fierce, untamed, wild.
AN OPPOSITE IS domesticated.

save *verb*
1 *They tried to save their belongings from the fire.* recover, retrieve, salvage.
2 *Most animals have an instinct to save their young from danger.* defend, guard, preserve, protect, shield.
3 *She saved him from making a fool of himself.* deter, prevent, stop.
4 *He saves £50 a month.* hoard, invest.
5 *They saved some food for him.* hold on to, keep, reserve, set aside.
6 *They discussed ways to save our natural resources.* be sparing with, conserve, economize on, use wisely.

savings *plural noun*
She kept her savings in the bank. investments, reserves, resources, riches, wealth.

savoury *adjective*
They had a savoury stew for dinner. appetizing, delicious, tasty.
Savoury food usually tastes **salty**.
AN OPPOSITE IS sweet.

saw *noun*

SOME KINDS OF SAW: chainsaw, circular saw, cross-cut saw, fretsaw, hacksaw, jigsaw, ripsaw, tenon saw.
FOR OTHER TOOLS, SEE **tool**.

say *verb*
He sometimes finds it hard to say what he means. communicate, convey, express, put into words.

> VARIOUS WAYS WE SAY THINGS:
> announce, answer, ask, assert,
> comment, declare, exclaim,
> maintain, mention, query, recite,
> remark, repeat, reply, report,
> respond, retort, shout, state,
> suggest, utter, whisper.
> SEE ALSO **talk**.

saying *noun*
'Many hands make light work' is a common saying. catchphrase, cliché, expression, motto, phrase, proverb, quotation, remark, slogan, statement.

scales *plural noun*
He weighed himself on the bathroom scales. balance, weighing machine.

scamper *verb*
The rabbits scampered away to safety. dash, hasten, hurry, run, rush, scuttle.

scan *verb*
1 He scanned the horizon, hoping to see a ship. examine, eye, gaze at, look at, scrutinize, search, study, survey, view, watch.
2 She scanned the newspaper looking for interesting news. glance through, read quickly, skim.

scandal *noun*
1 The waste of food was a scandal. disgrace, embarrassment, outrage, shame.
2 Newspapers shouldn't print scandal about people's private lives. gossip, rumours.

scandalous *adjective*
It was a scandalous waste of money. disgraceful, outrageous, shameful, shocking, wicked.

scanty *adjective*
They had only a scanty supply of water. inadequate, insufficient, meagre, mean, [informal] measly, scarce, small, sparse.
AN OPPOSITE IS plentiful.

scar *noun*
The cut left a scar on his face. blemish, mark.
A scar which still has a clot of dried blood on it is a **scab**.

scar *verb*
The injuries he received scarred him for life. deface, leave a scar on, mark.

scarce *adjective*
Fresh vegetables have been scarce during the drought. hard to find, in short supply, insufficient, lacking, scanty, sparse, [informal] thin on the ground, uncommon.
AN OPPOSITE IS plentiful.

scarcely *adverb*
She was so tired that she could scarcely walk. barely, hardly, only just.

scarcity *noun* SEE **shortage**

scare *noun*
The explosion gave them a nasty scare. alarm, fright, shock.

scare *verb*
The sudden noise scared us. alarm, frighten, petrify, shock, startle, terrify.
AN OPPOSITE IS reassure.

scatter *verb*
1 She scattered the seeds on the ground. shower, sow, spread, sprinkle, strew, throw about.
AN OPPOSITE IS collect.
2 The crowd scattered when the gun went off. break up, disintegrate, disperse, split up.
AN OPPOSITE IS gather.

scene *noun*
1 The police arrived quickly at the scene of the crime. location, place, position, site, situation, spot.
2 They were rehearsing a scene from the play. act, episode, part, section.
3 He gazed at the beautiful scene. landscape, outlook, panorama, prospect, scenery, setting, sight, spectacle, view.
4 He created a scene because he didn't win the argument. commotion, disturbance, fuss, quarrel, row.

scenery *noun*
1 *They admired the scenery from the top of the hill.* landscape, outlook, panorama, prospect, scene, view.
2 *He built the scenery for the play.* set.

scent *noun*
1 *She loves the scent of roses.* fragrance, perfume.
A word often used for pleasant food smells is **aroma**.
A word usually used for unpleasant smells is **odour**.
SEE ALSO **smell**.
2 *He gave her a bottle of scent for her birthday.* perfume.
3 *The dogs followed the scent of the fox.* trail.

scented *adjective*
He wrote the letter on scented notepaper. aromatic, fragrant, perfumed, sweet smelling.
SEE ALSO **smell** *noun*.

sceptical *adjective*
She was a bit sceptical about the plan. cynical, disbelieving, distrustful, doubting, incredulous, suspicious, uncertain, unconvinced, unsure.
AN OPPOSITE IS trustful.

schedule *noun*
According to the schedule, it's his turn to wash up. list, plan, programme, timetable.
A schedule of topics to be discussed at a meeting is an **agenda**.
A schedule of places to be visited on a journey is an **itinerary**.

scheme *noun*
1 *They worked out a scheme to raise some money.* method, plan, procedure, project, proposal, system.
2 *The men involved in the dishonest scheme were arrested.* conspiracy, plot, [*informal*] racket.

scheme *verb*
They were scheming against her. conspire, intrigue, plan, plot.

scholar *noun*
The professor is a real scholar. intellectual.

scholarly *adjective*
The professor is a very scholarly woman. academic, [*informal*] brainy, intellectual, studious.

scholarship *noun*
1 *She got a scholarship to study at university.* award, grant.
2 *The professor is a woman of great scholarship.* academic achievement, education, knowledge, learning, wisdom.

school *noun*

VARIOUS KINDS OF SCHOOL: academy, boarding school, coeducational school, college, comprehensive school, grammar school, high school, infant school, junior school, kindergarten, nursery school, playgroup, preparatory or prep school, primary school, public school, secondary school.

PARTS OF A SCHOOL: assembly hall, cafeteria or refectory, classroom, cloakroom, dormitory, foyer, gymnasium, hall, laboratory, library, office, playground, playing field, reception, staffroom, stockroom.

PEOPLE WHO HELP RUN A SCHOOL: caretaker, groundsman, head teacher, librarian, monitor, prefect, principal, secretary, teacher, technician, tutor.
The people who are paid to help run a school or teach the children are the **staff**.

schoolchild *noun*
pupil, scholar, schoolboy or schoolgirl, student.

science *noun*

BRANCHES OF SCIENCE AND TECHNOLOGY INCLUDE: anatomy, anthropology, astronomy, biology, botany, chemistry, computer science, ecology, electronics, engineering, environmental science, ➡

food science, forensic science, genetics, geology, information technology, mechanics, medical science, meteorology, physics, psychology, telecommunications, veterinary science, zoology.

scientific *adjective*
They are very scientific in their approach. analytical, methodical, organized, systematic.

scoff *verb*
to scoff at *They scoffed at the idea.* deride, jeer at, laugh at, make fun of, mock, ridicule, sneer at.

scold *verb*
She scolded us for being late. criticize, find fault with, [*informal*] nag, reprimand, reproach, tell off, [*informal*] tick off.

scoop *verb*
Rabbits had scooped out holes in the turf. dig, excavate, gouge, hollow, scrape.

scope *noun*
1 *They had plenty of scope to do what they wanted.* freedom, liberty, opportunity, room, space.
2 *The coroner said the question of who was to blame was outside the scope of his inquiry.* capacity, competence, extent, limit, range.

scorch *verb*
The bonfire scorched the hedge. blacken, char, singe.
SEE ALSO **burn**.

score *noun*
She added up the score. marks, points, total.
The final score is the **result**.

score *verb*
1 *How many did he score yesterday?* earn, gain, get, make.
2 *The knife scored a line on the polished table.* cut, gouge, mark, scrape, scratch.

scorn *noun*
She dismissed his suggestion with scorn. contempt, derision, disgust, dislike, disrespect, mockery, ridicule.
AN OPPOSITE IS admiration.

scorn *verb*
They scorned his pathetic efforts. be scornful about, deride, despise, insult, jeer at, laugh at, look down on, make fun of, mock, ridicule, scoff at, sneer at.
AN OPPOSITE IS admire.

scoundrel *noun*
He'd like to catch the scoundrel who damaged his car! [*old use*] knave, rascal, rogue, ruffian, villain.

scour *verb*
1 *He scoured the pan till it was shiny.* clean, polish, rub, scrape, scrub.
2 *She scoured the house looking for her purse.* comb, hunt through, ransack, rummage through, search.

scout *noun*
They sent out scouts to find the enemy. lookout, spy.

scowl *verb*
He scowled when he saw her. frown, glower.

scramble *verb*
1 *He scrambled over the rocks to safety.* clamber, climb, crawl, move awkwardly.
2 *The starving people scrambled to get at the food.* compete, fight, jostle, push, scuffle, struggle.

scrap *noun*
1 *They fed the scraps of food to the birds.* bit, crumb, fragment, morsel, particle, piece, speck.
2 *He took a pile of scrap to the tip.* junk, litter, odds and ends, refuse, rubbish, waste.
Scraps of cloth are **rags** or **shreds**.
3 [*informal*] *There was a scrap between the two gangs.* brawl, fight, scuffle, squabble.

scrap *verb*
1 *The car had to be scrapped after the accident.* discard, throw away, write off.
2 *The plans for the new road have been scrapped.* abandon, abort, cancel, drop, give up.
3 [*informal*] *They're always scrapping.* fight, quarrel, scuffle, squabble.

scrape *verb*
She scraped her knee when she fell over.
graze, scratch.
to scrape something clean *It took him ages to scrape the frying pan clean.* rub, scour, scrub.

scrape *noun*
He's always getting into scrapes.
[*informal*] jam, [*informal*] pickle.
Getting into scrapes is also getting into *mischief* or into *trouble*.

scrappy *adjective*
She complained that my work was scrappy. careless, fragmentary, hurried, imperfect, incomplete, sketchy, slipshod, unfinished, unsatisfactory, untidy.
AN OPPOSITE IS perfect.

scratch *verb*
1 *Someone scratched the side of the car.*
gouge, graze, mark, score, scrape.
2 *The cat tried to scratch her.* claw.

scratch *noun*
Who made this scratch on the side of the car? gash, groove, line, mark, scrape.

scrawl *verb*
She scrawled his phone number on a scrap of paper. jot, scribble, write untidily.

scream *noun, verb*
All these synonyms can be used both as nouns and verbs
bawl, cry, howl, roar, screech, shout, shriek, squeal, wail, yell.
FOR VARIOUS WAYS TO MAKE OTHER SOUNDS, SEE **sound** *verb*.

screen *noun*
The room was divided into two by a screen. curtain, partition.

screen *verb*
1 *The farmer put up a fence to screen the manure heap.* camouflage, conceal, cover, disguise, hide, mask, veil.
2 *A line of trees screened them from the sun.* protect, safeguard, shade, shelter, shield.
3 *All employees are screened before being appointed.* examine, investigate, test.

scribble *verb*
He scribbled his phone number on a scrap of paper. jot, scrawl, write untidily.
To scribble a rough drawing or pattern, especially when you are bored, is to *doodle*.

script *noun*
The script for a broadcast or a speech, etc., is the *text*.
The script for a film is a *screenplay*.
A handwritten or typed script is a *manuscript*.

scrounge *verb* [*informal*]
He scrounged some money from friends.
beg for, cadge.

scrub *verb*
She scrubbed the floor clean. brush, clean, rub, scour, wash.

scruffy *adjective*
Her clothes looked a bit scruffy.
bedraggled, dirty, messy, ragged, shabby, slovenly, tatty, untidy.
AN OPPOSITE IS smart.

scrutinize *verb*
He scrutinized the timetable to find the time of the next bus. examine, inspect, investigate, look at, search, study.

scrutiny *noun*
His work was subjected to close scrutiny. examination, inspection, investigation, study.

scuffle *noun*
Scuffles broke out between police and demonstrators. brawl, fight, [*informal*] scrap, [*informal*] squabble, struggle.

sculpture *noun*
The ancient church was full of interesting sculptures. carving, figure, statue.

scum *noun*
There was a nasty scum on the pond.
dirt, film, foam, froth.

sea *noun*

The very large seas of the world are called *oceans*.
An area of sea partly enclosed by land is a *bay* or *gulf*.
A wide inlet of the sea is a *sound*. ➡

A wide inlet where a river joins the sea is an *estuary*, or in Scotland a *firth*.
A narrow stretch of water linking two seas is a *strait*.
The bottom of the sea is the *seabed*.
The land near the sea is the *coast* or the *seashore*.
Ships that travel long distances at sea are *ocean-going* or *seagoing* ships.
People who work on ships at sea are *nautical* or *seafaring* people.
Creatures that live in the sea are *marine* or *saltwater* creatures.
SEE ALSO **seaside**.

seal *verb*
To seal an envelope is to *stick it down*.
To seal a box or container is to *close*, *fasten*, *lock*, *secure*, or *shut* it.
To seal a leak is to *plug* it or *stop* it.

seam *noun*
1 *The seam on his trousers split.* join.
2 *Geologists discovered a seam of coal.* layer, stratum.

search *verb*
1 *He was searching for the book he had lost.* hunt, look, poke about, seek.
To search for gold or some other mineral is to *prospect*.
2 *The police searched the house but didn't find anything.* comb, explore, ransack, rummage through, scour.
3 *Security staff searched all the passengers.* check, examine, [*informal*] frisk, inspect, scrutinize.

search *noun*
After a quick search, she found her purse. check, hunt, look.
A long journey searching for something is a *quest*.

searching *adjective*
The police asked some searching questions. deep, detailed, penetrating, probing, thorough.
AN OPPOSITE IS superficial.

seaside *noun*

The land near the sea is the *coast*.

VARIOUS TYPES OF LAND ALONG THE COAST: cliffs, dunes, mudflats, rocks, sandy beach, shingle beach.
A town where you go to have fun by the sea is a *seaside resort*.

PLACES YOU OFTEN FIND IN A SEASIDE RESORT: amusement arcade, bed and breakfast place, bingo hall, café, guesthouse, hotel, nightclub, restaurant, shop, souvenir shop, theatre, tourist information office.
The area next to the sea where you play and sunbathe is the *beach* or *seashore*.

THINGS YOU MIGHT SEE ON OR NEAR THE BEACH: aquarium, beach huts, breakwater, cave, cliff, funfair, harbour, lifeboat station, lighthouse, marina, pier, promenade or esplanade, Punch and Judy, rock pool, rocks, seagulls and various sea birds.

THINGS YOU MIGHT TAKE TO THE SEASIDE: bat and ball, beach ball, bucket and spade, deckchair or folding chair, fishing line or net, inflatable dinghy, snorkel, sunglasses, sunhat, sunshade, suntan cream or oil, swimming costume, towel, windbreak.

THINGS YOU MIGHT DO AT THE SEASIDE: ball games, beachcombing, boat trip, building sandcastles, donkey ride, fishing, paddling, scuba diving, snorkelling, sunbathing, surfing, swimming, water-skiing, windsurfing.

THINGS YOU MIGHT FIND LYING ON THE BEACH: driftwood, flotsam and jetsam, pebble, seashell, seaweed.

WILDLIFE YOU MIGHT SEE ON OR NEAR THE BEACH: barnacle, cockle, cormorant, crab, cuttlefish, dolphin, fish, jellyfish, limpet, mussel, octopus, porpoise, sandhopper, sea anemone, seagull, seal, sea urchin, shrimp, squid, starfish, whelk.
SEE ALSO **sea**.

season *noun*
The hotels are full during the holiday season. period, time.

seat *noun*

FURNITURE DESIGNED FOR PEOPLE
TO SIT ON: armchair, bench, chair,
chaise longue, couch, deckchair,
dining chair, pew, pouffe, reclining
chair, rocking chair, settee, settle,
sofa, stool, throne, window seat.
A seat on a cycle or horse is a
saddle.
A seat for a passenger on a motor
cycle is a *pillion*.

secluded *adjective*
They found a secluded beach for their picnic. cut off, isolated, lonely, private, quiet, remote, sheltered, unfrequented.
AN OPPOSITE IS crowded.

second *adjective*
She was given a second chance. additional, alternative, another, extra, further.

second *noun*
1 He was second in the race. runner-up.
2 Between rounds the second gave the boxer some advice. assistant, helper, supporter.
3 The pain only lasted a second. flash, instant, [*informal*] jiffy, moment, [*informal*] tick.

second *verb*
1 The boxer needed a reliable man to second him in his fight. assist, encourage, help, side with.
2 She seconded the proposal. back, support.

secondary *adjective*
When human lives are in danger, money is of secondary importance. inferior, lesser, lower, minor, subordinate.

second-hand *adjective*
She bought a second-hand car. used.
AN OPPOSITE IS new.

secret *adjective*
1 The spy was trying to get hold of secret information. classified, [*informal*] hushed up, hush-hush.

2 The things he writes in his diary are secret. confidential, intimate, personal, private.
3 They say there is a secret passageway into the castle. concealed, disguised, hidden, underground.
AN OPPOSITE IS well known.

secretary *noun*
A secretary who handles business for an important member of a firm is a *personal assistant*.
FOR OTHER PEOPLE WHO WORK IN
OFFICES, SEE **office**.

secrete *verb*
1 He secreted his money in a drawer. conceal, hide, put out of sight.
2 The pores of your body secrete sweat. discharge, give out, let out, produce.

secretive *adjective*
Why is he so secretive about his private life? furtive, mysterious, quiet, reserved, uncommunicative.
AN OPPOSITE IS communicative.

section *noun*
If it is too long, divide it into sections. bit, division, fraction, fragment, part, portion, sector, segment.
A section of a book is a *chapter*.
A section from a piece of classical music is a *movement*.
A section taken from a book or from a long piece of music is a *passage*.
A section of a journey is a *stage*.
A section of business is a *branch* or *department*.

sector *noun*
Soldiers occupied one sector of the town. area, district, part, region, section, zone.

secure *adjective*
1 The ladder was not very secure. fast, firm, fixed, immovable, solid, steady.
2 She needs a secure job. permanent, regular, steady.
3 Is the house secure against burglars? defended, guarded, protected, safe.
4 They felt secure indoors. snug, unharmed, unhurt.
AN OPPOSITE IS insecure or unsafe.

secure *verb*
1 *The door wasn't properly secured.* fasten, lock, make safe.
2 *He managed to secure two tickets for the concert.* buy, get hold of, order, reserve.

security *noun*
You must wear a seat belt for your own security. protection, safety.

sedate *adjective*
The procession moved at a sedate pace. calm, cool, deliberate, dignified, grave, quiet, sensible, serene, serious, slow, sober, solemn, tranquil.
AN OPPOSITE IS lively.

sediment *noun*
They dredged a lot of sediment from the bottom of the canal. deposit, mud, sludge.

see *verb*
The verb *to see* can be used in many senses. These are some of the common ones
1 *Did you see the film on TV last night?* look at, view, watch.
2 *They saw a kingfisher.* catch sight of, distinguish, make out, note, notice, observe, perceive, recognize, sight, spot, spy.
To see something briefly is to **glimpse** it.
To see an accident or some unusual event is to **witness** it.
3 *He asked her to see him in his office.* go to, report to, visit.
4 *I didn't expect to see you here!* [*informal*] bump into, encounter, meet, run into.
5 *She went to see her friend.* call on, drop in, visit.
6 *I see what you mean.* appreciate, comprehend, follow, grasp, realize, take in, understand.
7 *She found it hard to see herself in the role.* imagine, picture, visualize.
8 *Please see that the windows are shut.* ensure, make certain, make sure.
9 *I'll see what I can do.* consider, investigate, reflect on, think about, weigh up.

10 *He saw them to the door.* accompany, conduct, escort, guide, lead, take.
to see to something *He said he would see to the dinner.* attend to, deal with, look after, make arrangements for, take care of.

seed *noun*
The seed in an orange, etc., is a **pip**.
The seed in a plum, etc., is a **stone**.

seek *verb*
1 *For many years he sought his long-lost brother.* hunt for, inquire after, look for, search for.
2 *Most people seek happiness.* ask for, desire, pursue, strive after, want, wish for.

seem *verb*
1 *Everything seems to be all right.* appear, look.
2 *She isn't the nice person she seems to be.* give the impression (of), pretend.

seep *verb*
Oil began to seep through the crack. dribble, drip, flow, leak, ooze, run, soak, trickle.

seethe *verb*
The water in the pan began to seethe. boil, bubble, foam, froth up.
to be seething *She was seething when someone crashed into her car.* be angry, be agitated, be in a temper, rage, storm.

segment *noun*
He ate a few segments of an orange. bit, division, fragment, part, portion, section, slice.

segregate *verb*
They segregated the visitors from the home supporters. cut off, isolate, keep apart, separate, set apart.

seize *verb*
1 *He stretched out to seize the rope.* catch, clutch, grab, grasp, grip, hold, pluck, snatch, take.
2 *The police seized him in the act of committing the crime.* arrest, capture, detain, [*informal*] nab, take prisoner.

To seize someone's property as a punishment is to **confiscate** it.
To seize someone's power or position is to **usurp** it.
To seize an aircraft or vehicle during a journey is to **hijack** it.

seldom *adverb*
It seldom rains in the desert.
infrequently, rarely.
AN OPPOSITE IS often.

select *verb*
They had to select a new captain.
appoint, choose, decide on, elect, nominate, opt for, pick, settle on, vote for.

select *adjective*
Only a select few were invited. carefully chosen, privileged, selected, special.

selection *noun*
There's a wide selection to choose from.
assortment, choice, range, variety.

self-centred *adjective*
She's very self-centred—she never thinks of other people. demanding, grasping, greedy, inconsiderate, selfish, thoughtless.
AN OPPOSITE IS selfless.

self-confident *adjective*
He tried to look self-confident at the interview. assertive, bold, confident, cool, decisive, fearless, forceful, positive, sure of yourself.
AN OPPOSITE IS insecure.

self-conscious *adjective*
She always feels self-conscious in front of an audience. awkward, bashful, coy, embarrassed, insecure, nervous, sheepish, shy, uncomfortable, unnatural.
AN OPPOSITE IS confident.

self-control *noun*
He showed a lot of self-control by not answering back. calmness, coolness, patience, restraint, will-power.

self-evident *adjective*
She had the stolen goods on her, so her guilt was self-evident. clear, evident, obvious, plain, unmistakable.

self-important *adjective*
He acted in a very self-important way.
arrogant, haughty, pompous, snobbish, [*informal*] stuck-up.
AN OPPOSITE IS modest.

selfish *adjective*
She's too selfish to even think of sharing her sweets. demanding, grasping, greedy, mean, miserly, self-centred, thoughtless.
AN OPPOSITE IS selfless.

selfless *adjective*
He's so selfless—he'll do anything to help you. caring, considerate, generous, helpful, kind, thoughtful, unselfish.
AN OPPOSITE IS selfish.

self-respect *noun*
Losing his job made him lose a lot of self-respect. dignity, pride.

self-righteous *adjective*
He acted with self-righteous indignation. haughty, pious, pompous, priggish, proud, self-satisfied, superior.
AN OPPOSITE IS humble.

self-sufficient *adjective*
The village used to be a self-sufficient community. independent, self-contained, self-supporting.

sell *verb*
The shop on the corner sells newspapers and sweets. deal in, offer for sale, retail, stock, trade in.
To sell things such as drugs illegally is to **traffic** in them.

VARIOUS WAYS TO BUY AND SELL THINGS: auction, barter, cash sale, hire purchase, on credit, part-exchange, trade-in.

PEOPLE WHO SELL THINGS INCLUDE: dealer, [*old use*] hawker, market trader, merchant, pedlar, representative or [*informal*] rep, retailer, salesman or saleswoman, shopkeeper or storekeeper, stockist, street trader, supplier, trader, vendor, wholesaler.
FOR PARTICULAR SHOPS, SEE **shop**.

send *verb*
  1 *She sent him a letter.* dispatch, post.
  2 *They plan to send a rocket to Mars.*
  direct, fire, launch, propel, shoot.
  to send something out *The chimney
  was sending out evil-smelling fumes.*
  belch, discharge, emit, give off, issue.

senior *adjective*
  1 *She's the senior member of the team.*
  chief, oldest, principal.
  2 *He is a senior officer in the navy.* high-
  ranking, important.
  AN OPPOSITE IS junior.

sensation *noun*
  1 *She had a tingling sensation in her
  fingers.* feeling, sense.
  2 *The unexpected news caused a
  sensation.* excitement, thrill.
  A sensation caused by something bad
  is an *outrage* or a *scandal*.

sensational *adjective*
  1 *The new roller coaster is a sensational
  experience!* exciting, hair-raising,
  spectacular, stimulating, stupendous,
  thrilling.
  2 *The newspaper contained a
  sensational account of a murder.*
  shocking, startling, violent.
  3 [*informal*] *Did you hear the
  sensational result of yesterday's match?*
  amazing, extraordinary, fantastic,
  remarkable, surprising, unexpected.

sense *noun*
  1 *A baby learns about the world
  through its senses.*
  Your five senses are **hearing**, **sight**,
  smell, **taste**, and **touch**.
  2 *He has no sense of shame.* awareness,
  consciousness, feeling, perception.
  3 *If you had any sense you'd stay at
  home.* brains, cleverness, intelligence,
  judgement, wisdom.
  4 *The sense of the word is not clear.*
  gist, meaning, significance.
  to make sense *When she explained it,
  it began to make sense.* be intelligible,
  have a meaning, mean something.

to make sense of something *She
couldn't make sense of the message.*
explain, follow, interpret, understand.
out of your senses [*informal*] *You're
out of your senses to go swimming in
this weather!* crazy, daft, foolish,
insane, mad, [*informal*] out of your
mind, stupid.

sense *verb*
  1 *He sensed that she didn't like him.* be
  aware, feel, guess, notice, perceive,
  realize, suspect.
  2 *The machine senses any change of
  temperature.* detect, respond to.

senseless *adjective*
  1 *It was a senseless action.* crazy, daft,
  foolish, illogical, insane, irrational,
  mad, silly, stupid, unreasonable.
  AN OPPOSITE IS sensible.
  2 *The blow on the head left him
  senseless.* knocked out, unconscious.
  AN OPPOSITE IS conscious.

sensible *adjective*
  1 *He made a sensible decision not to set
  sail until the weather improved.*
  careful, intelligent, logical, prudent,
  rational, reasonable, sane, sound,
  thoughtful, wise.
  AN OPPOSITE IS stupid.
  2 *Wear sensible shoes to go walking.*
  comfortable, practical.
  AN OPPOSITE IS impractical.

sensitive *adjective*
  1 *She stays out of the sun because she
  has sensitive skin.* delicate, fine, soft,
  tender.
  2 *Take care what you say—he's very
  sensitive.* easily offended, quickly
  upset, touchy.
  3 *She's very sensitive towards other
  people.* considerate, sympathetic,
  tactful, thoughtful, understanding.
  AN OPPOSITE IS insensitive.

sentence *verb*
  The judge sentenced the convicted man.
  condemn, pass judgement on,
  pronounce sentence on.

sentiment *noun*
1 *What are your sentiments about experiments on animals?* attitude, belief, idea, judgement, opinion, thought, view.
2 *There's no room for sentiment in this business.* emotion, feeling.

sentimental *adjective*
1 *He gets sentimental when he looks at old family photographs.* emotional, nostalgic, tearful.
2 *She hates sentimental messages on birthday cards.* insincere, romantic, [*informal*] sloppy, [*informal*] soppy.
AN OPPOSITE IS cynical.

sentinel, sentry *nouns*
He gave the password to the sentry at the gate. guard, lookout, watchman.

separate *adjective*
1 *She keeps her books separate from his.* apart, distinct, independent, separated.
2 *They slept in separate rooms.* detached, different.
3 *The visiting supporters were kept separate from ours.* cut off, divided, fenced off, isolated, segregated.
AN OPPOSITE IS combined.

separate *verb*
1 *The farmer wanted to separate the sheep from the lambs.* cut off, divide, fence off, isolate, keep apart, remove, segregate, set apart, take away.
AN OPPOSITE IS combine or mix.
To separate something which is connected to something else is to **detach** or **disconnect** it.
To separate things which are tangled together is to **disentangle** them.
2 *They walked along together until their paths separated.* branch, fork, split.
AN OPPOSITE IS merge.
3 *Her friend's parents have separated.* part company, split up.
To end a marriage legally is to **divorce**.

septic *adjective*
The cut became septic. infected, inflamed, poisoned.

sequel *noun*
1 *They looked forward to hearing the sequel to the story.* continuation.
2 *The taxi broke down, and the sequel was that she missed her train.* consequence, outcome, result, upshot.

sequence *noun*
1 *They learned about the sequence of events which led to the First World War.* chain, course, series, string, succession, train.
2 *He arranged the cards in a logical sequence.* order, progression.

serene *adjective*
She had a serene smile on her face. calm, contented, peaceful, placid, quiet, tranquil, untroubled.
AN OPPOSITE IS agitated.

series *noun*
1 *We learned about the series of events that led to the First World War.* chain, course, progression, sequence, set, succession, train.
2 *The parade consisted of a series of floats depicting life in Victorian times.* line, procession, row, set, string.
3 *Are you watching the new series on TV?* mini-series, serial.
A kind of TV drama series is a **soap** or **soap opera**.
A kind of TV comedy series is a **sitcom** or **situation comedy**.

serious *adjective*
1 *They had a serious debate about conservation.* deep, earnest, intellectual, profound, sincere.
AN OPPOSITE IS frivolous.
2 *Global warming is a serious problem.* important, significant, weighty.
AN OPPOSITE IS unimportant.
3 *Her serious expression told them something was wrong.* grave, grim, solemn, stern, thoughtful, unsmiling.
AN OPPOSITE IS cheerful.
4 *There has been a serious accident on the motorway.* appalling, awful, dreadful, frightful, ghastly, hideous, horrible, nasty, shocking, terrible.
AN OPPOSITE IS trivial.
5 *His illness wasn't serious.* critical, dangerous, life-threatening, major, severe.
AN OPPOSITE IS minor.

servant *noun*

> Many of the words given below are not often used. They apply to a past time when it was common for some people to be served by others.
>
> PEOPLE WHO WORK OR USED TO WORK IN SOMEONE ELSE'S HOUSE: butler, chambermaid, char or charwoman, chauffeur, cook, errand boy, footman, groom, home help, housekeeper, housemaid, kitchenmaid, maid, manservant, page, parlourmaid, retainer, valet. A young person from another country who works for a time in someone's home is an *au pair*. The servant of an army officer is a *batman*.
>
> PEOPLE WHO HELP US IN HOTELS, ETC.: attendant, barmaid or barman, doorman, steward or stewardess, waiter or waitress.

serve *verb*
1 *He wanted to serve the community.* aid, assist, help, work for.
2 *How long did he serve in the army?* be employed, do your duty.
3 *She serves in a shop at weekends.* be an assistant, sell things.
4 *When everyone had sat down they served the first course.* dish up, distribute, give out, pass round.
To serve food at table is to *wait*.
5 *This room will serve as a study.* be suitable.

service *noun*
1 *He was able to do her a small service.* favour, help, kindness.
2 *Their marriage service was held in the local church.* ceremony.
A service in church is a meeting for *worship*.
3 *Mum says her car needs a service.* a check-over, maintenance, servicing.
the services SEE **armed services**.

service *verb*
The garage serviced her car. maintain, mend, overhaul, repair.

session *noun*
1 *They have a training session on Thursday evenings.* period, time.
2 *The Queen will open the next session of Parliament.* meeting, sitting.

set *verb*
The verb *to set* has many meanings. We give just some of the important ones here
1 *He set the vase on the sideboard.* place, position, put, stand.
2 *She set the table.* arrange, lay, set out.
3 *He set the clock to the correct time.* adjust, correct, put right, regulate.
4 *The jelly will set quicker in the fridge.* become firm, harden, stiffen.
5 *They decided to set the fence posts in concrete.* fasten, fix.
6 *The teacher didn't set any homework.* prescribe, specify, suggest.
7 *They set a date for the Christmas party.* allot, appoint, choose, decide, determine, establish, identify, name, settle.
to set about something *He set about the job immediately.* begin, commence, start.
to set someone free *The prisoners were set free.* free, let out, liberate, release, rescue.
to set off 1 *They set off on their journey.* depart, get going, leave, set out, start out.
2 *They set off a bomb.* detonate, explode.
to set something out *Her work is always very well set out.* display, exhibit, present.
to set something up *She wanted to set up a playgroup.* bring into existence, create, found, initiate, introduce, launch.

set *noun*
1 *He bought a set of spanners.* batch, collection.
2 *She bought a new TV set.* apparatus, receiver.
3 *They painted the set for the play.* scenery, setting.

setting *noun*
The house stood in a rural setting. background, environment, location, place, position, site, surroundings.

settle *verb*
1 *They have settled what to do.* agree, choose, decide, determine.
2 *They tried to settle their differences.* deal with, end, solve, sort out.
3 *She settled in the chair.* make yourself comfortable, relax, rest, sit down.
4 *They are planning to settle in Canada.* emigrate (to), go and live, make your home, move (to), set up home.
5 *You can see lots of fish when the mud settles.* clear, sink to the bottom, subside.
6 *She settled the bill.* pay.

settlement *noun*
They established a settlement on the bank of the river. colony, community, encampment.

settler *noun*
The early European settlers in America looked forward to beginning a new life. colonist, immigrant, newcomer, pioneer.

sever *verb*
The partners eventually decided to sever their relationship. break off, end, terminate.
To sever a branch of a tree is to *cut it off* or *remove* it.
To sever a limb is to *amputate* it.

severe *adjective*
1 *He was very severe with the children.* hard, harsh, stern, strict.
AN OPPOSITE IS lenient.
2 *The traffic warden gave him a severe look.* disapproving, grim, unkind, unsmiling, unsympathetic.
AN OPPOSITE IS kind.
3 *She had a severe bout of flu.* acute, bad, serious, troublesome.
AN OPPOSITE IS mild.
4 *The explorers experienced severe conditions.* dangerous, difficult, extreme, tough.
A severe frost is a *sharp* frost.
Severe cold is *intense* cold.
A severe storm is a *violent* storm.

sew *verb*
He sewed up the tear in his jeans. darn, mend, repair, stitch, tack.
To sew pictures or designs is to do *embroidery* or *tapestry*.

sewers *plural noun*
We expect modern cities to have efficient sewers. drainage, drains, sanitation.

sex *noun*
What sex is the hamster? gender.

sexist *adjective*
She hates it when people make sexist remarks. male chauvinist, prejudiced.

sexy *adjective* [*informal*]
She looked very sexy. attractive, desirable, glamorous.

shabby *adjective*
1 *She'd like to throw away those shabby clothes and get new ones.* drab, dreary, faded, frayed, ragged, scruffy, tattered, tatty, threadbare, unattractive, worn, worn out.
AN OPPOSITE IS smart.
2 *That was a shabby trick!* dishonest, mean, nasty, shameful, unfair, unfriendly, unkind.

shade *noun*
1 *They sat in the shade of a tree.* shadow.
2 *She put up a shade to keep the sun off.* blind, canopy, parasol, screen.
3 *They painted the room a pale shade of blue.* colour, hue, tinge, tint, tone.

shade *verb*
1 *She used her hand to shade her eyes from the sun.* hide, mask, protect, screen, shield.
2 *He shaded the background of the picture with a pencil.* darken, fill in, make darker.

shadow *noun*
Her face was deep in shadow. gloom, shade.

shadow *verb*
The detective was shadowing the suspect. follow, keep watch on, pursue, stalk, tail, track, trail.

shadowy *adjective*
1 *They walked along a shadowy path through the woods.* dark, dim, gloomy, shady, sunless.
AN OPPOSITE IS bright.
2 *She saw a shadowy figure in the mist.* faint, ghostly, hazy, indistinct, obscure, unclear, unrecognizable, vague.
AN OPPOSITE IS clear.

shady *adjective*
1 *They found a shady spot under a tree.* cool, dark, shaded, shadowy, sheltered, sunless.
AN OPPOSITE IS sunny.
2 *He's involved in some shady business.* corrupt, [*informal*] crooked, dishonest, disreputable, doubtful, [*informal*] fishy, suspicious, untrustworthy.
AN OPPOSITE IS honest.

shaft *noun*
1 *The horse was harnessed between the shafts of the cart.* pole, rod.
An upright shaft is a **column** or **pillar** or **post**.
A shaft that you shoot is an **arrow**.
The shaft on a broom, etc., is the **handle**.
2 *He nearly fell into an old shaft.* hole, mine, pit.
3 *A shaft of light shone through the window.* beam, ray.

shaggy *adjective*
You could hardly see his face behind his shaggy beard. bushy, hairy, rough, untidy, woolly.

shake *verb*
1 *An explosion made the ground shake.* quake, quiver, rattle, rock, shiver, shudder, sway, totter, vibrate, wobble.
2 *She shook her umbrella.* brandish, flourish, twirl, wag, waggle, wave, wiggle.
3 *They were shaken by the terrible news.* alarm, distress, disturb, frighten, shock, startle, surprise, upset.
4 *He was so upset that his voice was shaking.* quaver, tremble.

shaky *adjective*
1 *Be careful—the table is rather shaky.* decrepit, flimsy, frail, insecure, precarious, rickety, unsteady, weak, wobbly.

2 *He was so nervous that his hands were shaky.* quivering, shaking, trembling.
3 *He spoke in a shaky voice.* faltering, nervous, quavering, tremulous.
AN OPPOSITE IS steady.

shallow *adjective*
1 *They paddled about in the shallow water.*
Surprisingly, there are no convenient synonyms for this common sense of *shallow.*
AN OPPOSITE IS deep.
2 *She thought that the discussion was rather shallow.* foolish, frivolous, silly, superficial, trivial.
AN OPPOSITE IS profound.

sham *noun*
It was all a sham. deception, pretence.

shambles *noun*
a shambles [*informal*] *It was so badly organized it turned into a shambles.* chaos, confusion, disorder, a mess, a muddle.

shame *noun*
He was overcome with feelings of shame when he was caught stealing. disgrace, dishonour, embarrassment, guilt, humiliation.

shameful *adjective*
1 *Losing 10–0 was a shameful defeat.* embarrassing, humiliating.
2 *They showed a shameful lack of concern.* contemptible, despicable, disgraceful, outrageous, scandalous, wicked.
AN OPPOSITE IS honourable.

shameless *adjective*
1 *He's quite shameless about having cheated in the test.* brazen, unashamed, unrepentant.
AN OPPOSITE IS ashamed.
2 *Her shameless behaviour shocked everyone.* bold, improper, impudent, indecent, insolent, outrageous, rude.
AN OPPOSITE IS modest.

shape *noun*
> The badge was in the shape of a star. form.
> The shape of your body is your *figure*.
> A line showing the shape of a thing is the *outline*.
> A dark outline seen against a light background is a *silhouette*.
> A container for making things in a special shape is a *mould*.

> FLAT SHAPES: circle, diamond, ellipse, heptagon, hexagon, oblong, octagon, oval, parallelogram, pentagon, polygon, quadrilateral, rectangle, rhombus, ring, semicircle, square, trapezium, triangle.
>
> THREE-DIMENSIONAL SHAPES: cone, cube, cylinder, hemisphere, polyhedron, prism, pyramid, sphere.

shape *verb*
> The sculptor shaped the stone into a human figure. carve, cut, fashion, form, mould.
> To shape something in a mould is to *cast* it.

share *noun*
> Everyone got a share of the food. allowance, bit, [informal] cut, division, fraction, helping, part, piece, portion, quota, ration.

share *verb*
> They shared the money equally. allot, deal out, distribute, divide, ration out, share out, split, subdivide.

sharp *adjective*
> **1** *The carving knife has a sharp edge.* keen, razor-sharp, sharpened.
> AN OPPOSITE IS blunt.
> **2** *The barbed wire has sharp points all along it.* jagged, pointed, spiky.
> AN OPPOSITE IS smooth.
> **3** *If you can see that, you must have sharp eyes!* alert, observant, perceptive, quick.
> AN OPPOSITE IS unobservant.
> **4** *She's very sharp.* bright, clever, intelligent, quick-witted, shrewd, smart.
> AN OPPOSITE IS stupid.
> **5** *We slowed down for a sharp bend in the road.* abrupt, sudden, unexpected.

A bend that doubles back on itself, such as you might find on a mountain road, is a *hairpin* bend.
AN OPPOSITE IS gradual.
> **6** *The sharp frost killed mum's geraniums.* extreme, intense, serious, severe.
> AN OPPOSITE IS slight.
> **7** *Focus the projector so that we get a sharp picture.* clear, distinct, focused, well defined.
> AN OPPOSITE IS blurred.
> **8** *He felt a sharp pain in his side.* acute, stabbing, stinging.
> AN OPPOSITE IS dull.
> **9** *This lemonade is a bit sharp.* acid, bitter, sour, tart.
> AN OPPOSITE IS sweet or tasteless.

sharpen *verb*
> He sharpened the carving knife. grind, make sharp.

shatter *verb*
> **1** *The ball shattered a window.* break, destroy, smash, wreck.
> **2** *The windscreen shattered when a stone hit it.* break, disintegrate, splinter.
> **shattered** *She was shattered by the bad news.* distressed, horrified, shaken, shocked, stunned, upset.

sheaf *noun*
> She had a sheaf of papers in her hand. bunch, bundle.

sheath *noun*
> He put his sword back in its sheath. casing, covering, scabbard, sleeve.

shed *noun*
> They kept their lawnmower in the garden shed. hut, outhouse, shack.

shed *verb*
> A lorry shed its load on the motorway. drop, let fall, scatter, spill.

sheen *noun*
> He polished the car until it had a nice sheen. brightness, gleam, gloss, lustre, polish, shine.

sheep *noun*
> A female sheep is a *ewe*.
> A young sheep is a *lamb*.
> A male sheep is a *ram*.
> Meat from sheep is *mutton* or *lamb*.

sheepish *adjective*
When she caught him out, he gave her a sheepish look. ashamed, bashful, coy, embarrassed, self-conscious, shy, timid.
AN OPPOSITE IS shameless.

sheer *adjective*
1 *The story he told was sheer nonsense.* absolute, complete, pure, total, utter.
2 *Don't try to climb that sheer cliff.* perpendicular, vertical.
3 *Her blouse was made of sheer silk.* fine, flimsy, see-through, thin, transparent.

sheet *noun*
A sheet of paper is a *leaf* or *page*.
A sheet of glass is a *pane* or *plate* of glass.
A sheet of ice is a *covering* or *layer* of ice.
A sheet of water is an *area* or *expanse* of water.

shelf *noun*
She put the vase of flowers on the shelf. ledge.

shell *noun*
A tortoise has a hard shell. case, casing, covering, exterior, outside.

shell *verb*
They shelled the town until it was in ruins. attack, bomb, bombard, fire at, shoot at.

shellfish *noun*

SOME SPECIES OF SHELLFISH:
barnacle, clam, cockle, conch, crab, crayfish, cuttlefish, limpet, lobster, mussel, oyster, prawn, scallop, shrimp, whelk, winkle.
Invertebrate creatures with a soft body and a shell are *molluscs*.
Molluscs like oysters and mussels with two hinged shells are *bivalves*.
Shellfish with legs like crabs, lobsters, and shrimps are *crustaceans*.

---

shelter *noun*
They reached shelter just before the storm broke. cover, protection, refuge, sanctuary, safety.

shelter *verb*
1 *The wall sheltered them from the wind.* defend, guard, protect, safeguard, screen, shield.
2 *He sheltered from the rain under the trees.* hide, take refuge.

shelve *verb*
1 *The plans had to be shelved.* abandon, cancel, postpone, put off, reject.
2 *The beach shelves steeply.* drop away, fall away, slope.

shield *noun*
They erected a wind shield. barrier, defence, guard, protection, screen, shelter.
The part of a helmet that shields your face is the *visor*.

shield *verb*
The bird tried to shield her chicks from danger. defend, guard, keep safe, protect, safeguard, shelter.

shift *verb*
1 *He asked his neighbour if she could shift her car.* move, remove.
2 *He shoved the wardrobe but it wouldn't shift.* budge, change position, move.

shine *verb*
1 *A light shone in the window.* be visible, show up.

DIFFERENT WAYS IN WHICH VARIOUS THINGS GIVE OUT OR REFLECT LIGHT: beam, blaze, burn, dazzle, flame, flash, flicker, glare, gleam, glimmer, glint, glisten, glitter, glow, radiate, shimmer, spark, sparkle, twinkle.
To shine in the dark is to be *luminous* or *phosphorescent*.

---

2 *He shines his shoes every morning.* clean, polish, rub.
3 *She's good at all sports, but she shines at tennis.* do best, excel, stand out.

shingle *noun*
The beach was shingle, not sand. gravel, pebbles, stones.

shiny *adjective*
> *She polished the silver until it was shiny.* bright, dazzling, gleaming, glistening, glossy, lustrous, polished, reflective, shining, sleek.
> AN OPPOSITE IS dull.
> Shiny paint is *gloss* paint.
> The opposite is *matt* paint.

ship *noun*
> FOR VARIOUS SHIPS, SEE **vessel**.

ship *verb*
> *The firm ships goods all over the world.* convey, export, move, send, shift, take, transport.

shirk *verb*
> *He always shirks the unpleasant tasks.* avoid, evade, get out of, ignore, neglect.

shiver *verb*
> *She began to shiver with cold.* quake, quaver, quiver, shake, shudder, tremble.

shock *noun*
> **1** *His sudden death was a great shock.* blow, surprise, [*informal*] upset.
> **2** *People felt the shock of the explosion miles away.* bang, impact, jolt.
> **3** *The driver involved in the accident was in a state of shock.* collapse, dismay, distress, fright.
> A formal word for a state of shock is *trauma*.

shock *verb*
> **1** *They were shocked by the news.* alarm, amaze, astonish, astound, dismay, distress, frighten, [*informal*] give you a turn, scare, shake, stagger, startle, stun, surprise, upset.
> A formal synonym is *traumatize*.
> **2** *The bad language in the play shocked them.* appal, disgust, horrify, offend, outrage, repel, revolt.

shoddy *adjective*
> **1** *Their work was rather shoddy.* careless, messy, negligent, slipshod, sloppy, slovenly, untidy.
> AN OPPOSITE IS careful.
> **2** *That shop sells shoddy goods.* cheap, inferior, poor quality, [*informal*] tacky, trashy, worthless.
> AN OPPOSITE IS superior.

shoe *noun*

> KINDS OF SHOE: ankle boot, boot, bootee, brogue, clog, court shoe, espadrille, flip-flop, galosh, gumboot, gymshoe, moccasin, mule, plimsoll, pump, sandal, slip-on, slipper, sneaker, trainer, wader, wellington.

shoot *verb*
> **1** *He prepared to shoot at the target.* aim, fire.
> **2** *They were told to shoot the dangerous animal if necessary.* fire at, gun down, hit, open fire on, snipe at.
> **3** *They watched the racing cars shoot past.* [*informal*] dash, hurtle, rush, speed, streak, [*informal*] zoom.
> **4** *They are going to shoot a TV series in the town.* film, photograph.

shoot *noun*
> *Young shoots grow in the spring.* bud, new growth, sprout.

shop *noun*

> VARIOUS PLACES WHERE YOU CAN BUY THINGS: boutique, cash and carry, corner shop, department store, hypermarket, market, retailer's, shopping arcade, shopping centre, shopping mall, shopping precinct, supermarket, wholesaler's.
>
> PEOPLE INVOLVED IN SELLING THINGS TO US: dealer, market trader, merchant, retailer, salesman or saleswoman, shop assistant, shopkeeper, shop manager, stockist, storekeeper, supplier, trader, tradesman.
>
> SHOPS AND BUSINESSES DEALING IN DIFFERENT KINDS OF GOODS OR SERVICES: antique shop, baker, bank, barber, betting shop, bookmaker, bookshop, building society, butcher, chemist, clothes shop, confectioner, dairy, delicatessen, DIY or do-it-yourself shop, draper, electrician, estate agent, fish and chip shop, fishmonger, florist, furniture store, garden centre, greengrocer, grocer, haberdasher, hairdresser, hardware store, health-food shop, ➡

ironmonger, jeweller, launderette, newsagent, off-licence, pawnbroker, pharmacy, post office, shoemaker, stationer, tailor, tobacconist, toyshop, video shop, watchmaker.

shop verb
She was shopping for Christmas presents. buy things, go shopping.

shopper noun
The market is crowded with shoppers on Saturdays. buyer, customer.

shopping noun
He put the shopping in a carrier bag. goods, purchases.

shore noun
They walked along the shore looking for seashells. beach, edge of the water, sands, seashore, seaside, shingle.

short adjective
1 They live a short distance from the shops.
There is no obvious synonym for short in this sense
AN OPPOSITE IS long.
2 It was a very short visit. brief, fleeting, hasty, quick, temporary.
AN OPPOSITE IS long.
3 He's very short. dumpy, little, small, tiny.
AN OPPOSITE IS tall.
4 During the drought water was in short supply. inadequate, insufficient, limited, meagre, scanty, scarce.
AN OPPOSITE IS plentiful.
5 He was short with her when she asked for a loan. abrupt, bad-tempered, cross, grumpy, impolite, irritable, rude, sharp, unfriendly, unsympathetic.
AN OPPOSITE IS friendly.

shortage noun
The shortage of water is worrying. inadequacy, lack, scarcity.
A shortage of water is a **drought**.
A shortage of food is a **famine**.

shortcoming noun
He has many shortcomings. defect, failing, fault, flaw, imperfection, weakness.

shorten verb
She had to shorten the speech because it was too long. abbreviate, compress, condense, curtail, cut down, prune, reduce, summarize, trim.
AN OPPOSITE IS lengthen.

shortly adverb
The post will arrive shortly. before long, presently, soon.

shot noun
1 They heard a shot. bang, blast, crack.
2 He's a good shot!
A person who is good at shooting with a gun is a **marksman**.
3 He had a shot at goal. hit, kick, strike.
4 The photographer took some unusual shots. photograph, picture, snap, snapshot.
5 She had a shot at solving the problem. attempt, effort, go, try.

shout verb
You'll deafen me if you shout like that! bawl, bellow, call, cry out, exclaim, rant, roar, scream, screech, shriek, yell, yelp.
AN OPPOSITE IS whisper.

shove verb
They shoved her out of the way. barge, drive, elbow, hustle, jostle, propel, push.

shovel verb
He shovelled the snow off the path. clear, dig, move, scoop, shift.

show verb
1 He showed the garden to the visitors. display, exhibit, present, reveal.
2 The photo shows them on holiday. depict, illustrate, picture, portray, represent.
3 She showed them how to do it. explain to, instruct, make clear to, teach, tell.
4 The evidence shows that he was right. demonstrate, prove.
5 She showed him to the manager's office. conduct, direct, guide.
6 The signpost shows the way. indicate, point out.

7 *His vest showed through his shirt.*
appear, be seen, be visible.
to show off *He's always showing off.*
bluster, boast, brag, crow, gloat,
swagger, [*informal*] swank.

show *noun*
1 *They put up a show of his paintings.*
display, exhibition, presentation.
2 *There's a good show on at the theatre.*
entertainment, performance,
production.
SEE ALSO **entertainment**.

shower *noun*
FOR KINDS OF RAIN, SEE **rain**.

shower *verb*
*A passing bus showered mud over
them.* spatter, splash, spray, sprinkle.

showy *adjective*
She was wearing very showy jewellery.
bright, conspicuous, flashy, gaudy,
loud, striking.
AN OPPOSITE IS plain.

shred *noun*
*The accused man said they didn't have
a shred of evidence against him.* bit,
piece, scrap, trace.
shreds *The barbed wire tore his shirt to
shreds.* rags, ribbons, strips, tatters.

shred *verb*
*She shredded the lettuce and put it in a
salad bowl.* cut into shreds, cut up, tear
up.
To shred something hard like cheese is
to **grate** it.

shrewd *adjective*
He's too shrewd to be fooled like that.
artful, bright, clever, crafty, cunning,
ingenious, intelligent, quick-witted,
sharp, smart, wily, wise.
AN OPPOSITE IS stupid.

shriek *noun, verb*
All these synonyms can be used both as
nouns and verbs. bawl, cry, howl,
scream, screech, shout, squeal, wail,
yell.
FOR VARIOUS WAYS TO MAKE SOUNDS,
SEE **sound** *verb*.

shrill *adjective*
She heard the shrill sound of a whistle.
high, high-pitched, penetrating,
piercing, sharp.
AN OPPOSITE IS gentle or low.

shrink *verb*
His clothes shrank in the wash. become
smaller, contract.
AN OPPOSITE IS expand.
to shrink from *He shrinks from
meeting strangers.* avoid, keep or stay
away from.

shrivel *verb*
The plants shrivelled in the heat.
become dehydrated, droop, dry out, dry
up, shrink, wilt, wither, wrinkle.

shroud *verb*
The mountain was shrouded in mist.
conceal, cover, envelop, hide, mask,
screen, veil, wrap.

shrub *noun*
*She bought some shrubs at the garden
centre.* bush.

SOME POPULAR GARDEN SHRUBS:
azalea, berberis, broom, buddleia,
camellia, daphne, forsythia, heather,
hydrangea, jasmine, lavender, lilac,
privet, rhododendron, rosemary, rue,
viburnum.

shudder *verb*
*He shuddered when he heard the gory
details.* quake, quiver, shake, shiver,
tremble.

shuffle *verb*
1 *She shuffled upstairs in her slippers.*
FOR VARIOUS WAYS TO WALK, SEE
walk *verb*.
2 *Shuffle the cards before you deal
them.* jumble, mix, mix up.

shut *verb*
Please shut the door. bolt, close, fasten,
latch, lock, push to, seal, secure.
To shut a door with a bang is to **slam**
it.
to shut down *The chip shop is going to
shut down.* cease trading, close.

to shut someone up *They shut him up in a dark room.* confine, detain, imprison.
Shut up! Be quiet! Be silent! [*informal*] Hold your tongue! Hush! Keep quiet! [*informal*] Pipe down! Silence! Stop talking!

shy *adjective*
He was too shy to say anything. bashful, cautious, coy, hesitant, inhibited, modest, nervous, reserved, self-conscious, timid, wary.
AN OPPOSITE IS bold.

sick *adjective*
1 *She can't work because she's sick.* ailing, bedridden, diseased, ill, infirm, poorly, sickly, suffering, unhealthy, unwell.
AN OPPOSITE IS healthy.
2 *The sea was rough and he felt sick.* likely to vomit, queasy.
to be sick *I think I'm going to be sick.* vomit.
sick of 1 *They're sick of his rude behaviour.* annoyed by, disgusted by, upset by.
2 *I'm sick of that tune.* bored with, [*informal*] fed up with, tired of.

sicken *verb*
She is sickened by cruelty to animals. appal, disgust, distress, offend, repel, revolt, shock, [*informal*] turn your stomach.

sickly *adjective*
He's a sickly child. ailing, delicate, frail, unhealthy, weak.
AN OPPOSITE IS healthy.

sickness *noun*
FOR VARIOUS ILLNESSES, SEE **illness**.

side *noun*
1 *Each side of the dice has a different number on it.* face, surface.
2 *The path runs along the side of the field.* border, boundary, edge, fringe, limit, perimeter.
The side of a page is the ***margin***.
The side of a road is the ***verge***.
3 *She could see both sides of the argument.* angle, aspect, point of view, view.
4 *The football club has a strong side this year.* team.

side *verb*
to side with someone *She sided with him against the others.* agree with, back, give support to, stand up for, support.

siege *noun*
The town held out against the siege for months. blockade.

sieve *noun*
A device for straining liquid from food is a ***colander*** or ***strainer***.
A device for sifting things in the garden is a ***riddle***.

sift *verb*
1 *He sifted the flour through a sieve.* filter, separate, strain.
2 *They began to sift the evidence they had collected.* analyse, examine, review, scrutinize, select, sort out.

sigh *noun, verb*
FOR VARIOUS WAYS TO MAKE SOUNDS, SEE **sound** *verb*.

sight *noun*
1 *He has good sight.* eyesight, vision.
2 *The woods in autumn are a lovely sight.* display, scene, show, spectacle.
3 *They live within sight of the power station.* range, view.
4 *She went to London to see the sights.* attraction, tourist attraction.

sight *verb*
The lookout sighted a ship on the horizon. distinguish, glimpse, make out, notice, observe, perceive, recognize, see, spot, spy.

sightseer *noun*
London was full of sightseers. holidaymaker, tourist, visitor.

sign *noun*
1 *A sign pointed to the exit.* notice, placard, poster, signpost.
The sign belonging to a particular business or organization is a ***logo***.
The sign on a particular brand of goods is a ***trademark***.
2 *She gave no sign that she was angry.* clue, hint, indication, warning.
3 *She gave them a sign to begin.* cue, gesture, reminder, signal.

sign *verb*

1 *She signed her name on the form.* inscribe, write.
2 *He signed that he was turning left.* communicate, gesticulate, give or send a signal, indicate, signal.
3 *The club signed a new player last week.* engage, enrol, recruit, take on.

signal *noun*

She gave a clear signal. indication, sign, warning.

SIGNALS USED IN VARIOUS SITUATIONS: alarm bell, beacon, bell, bugle call, burglar alarm, buzzer, flag, flare, gesture, gong, green light, hooter, indicator, lights, red light, rocket, semaphore signal, siren, smoke signal, traffic lights, warning light, whistle.
SEE ALSO **gesture**.

signal *verb*

He signalled that he was ready. gesticulate, give a sign or signal, indicate.

signature *noun*

The author wrote his signature in the book. autograph.

significance *noun*

What's the significance of that remark? importance, meaning, message, point, relevance.

significant *adjective*

1 *They made a note of the significant facts.* important, meaningful, telling, valuable, vital.
2 *He's made significant progress in maths.* considerable, noticeable, perceptible, striking.
3 *He made a significant profit on the sale of his business.* biggish, largish, sizeable, substantial, worthwhile.
AN OPPOSITE IS negligible.

signify *verb*

1 *A red light signifies danger.* be a sign of, denote, mean, represent, stand for, symbolize.
2 *They signified their agreement by raising their hands.* communicate, convey, express, indicate, make known, signal.

silence *noun*

There was silence while we sat the exam. calm, hush, peace, quiet, quietness, stillness.
AN OPPOSITE IS noise.

silence *verb*

He tried to silence the noise of the engine. deaden, muffle, quieten, suppress.
To silence someone by putting something in or over their mouth is to *gag* them.
Silence! Be quiet! Be silent! [*informal*] Hold your tongue! Hush! Keep quiet! [*informal*] Pipe down! Shut up! Stop talking!

silent *adjective*

1 *It was a silent night.* hushed, noiseless, quiet, soundless, still. Something you can't hear is *inaudible*.
2 *He remained silent throughout the meeting.* dumb, mute, speechless, tongue-tied, uncommunicative.
AN OPPOSITE IS talkative.

silky *adjective*

A cat has silky fur. fine, sleek, smooth, soft, velvety.

silly *adjective*

1 *It was silly of him to waste all his money.* brainless, crazy, foolish, idiotic, illogical, irrational, misguided, naïve, pointless, rash, reckless, senseless, stupid, thoughtless, unintelligent, unreasonable, unwise.
AN OPPOSITE IS sensible.
2 *She laughed at their silly games.* absurd, amusing, comic, frivolous, light-hearted, ludicrous, playful, ridiculous.
AN OPPOSITE IS serious.

similar *adjective*

1 *Twin brothers are similar in appearance.* alike, identical, indistinguishable, matching, the same.
2 *She tried to find a similar dress to the one she had lost.* comparable.
AN OPPOSITE IS different.

similarity *noun*

It's easy to see the similarity between the twins. likeness, resemblance.
AN OPPOSITE IS difference.

simple *adjective*
  1 *Can you answer this simple question?*
  easy, elementary.
  AN OPPOSITE IS difficult.
  2 *This computer program is simple to use.* clear, foolproof, intelligible, lucid, straightforward, uncomplicated, understandable, user-friendly.
  AN OPPOSITE IS complicated.
  3 *She wore a simple dress.* austere, plain, undecorated.
  AN OPPOSITE IS elaborate.
  4 *He enjoys simple pleasures like walking and gardening.* homely, honest, humble, modest, ordinary, unsophisticated.
  AN OPPOSITE IS sophisticated.
  5 *He seems a bit simple.* brainless, foolish, idiotic, naïve, senseless, silly, stupid, unintelligent.
  AN OPPOSITE IS wise.

simplify *verb*
  They simplified the rules so that they are easier to understand. clarify, make simpler.
  AN OPPOSITE IS elaborate.

simulate *verb*
  The machine simulates space flight. counterfeit, imitate, reproduce.

sin *noun*
  The preacher said that everyone is guilty of sin. evil, immorality, sinfulness, vice, wickedness, wrongdoing.

sin *verb*
  He said that he had sinned. do wrong, misbehave, offend.

sincere *adjective*
  He sent her his sincere good wishes. frank, genuine, honest, open, real, straightforward, true, truthful.
  AN OPPOSITE IS insincere.

sincerity *noun*
  They doubted the sincerity of his welcome. frankness, genuineness, honesty, integrity, openness, straightforwardness, truthfulness.

sinful *adjective*
  He asked forgiveness for his sinful behaviour. bad, corrupt, evil, guilty, immoral, perverted, unholy, unrighteous, villainous, wicked, wrong.
  AN OPPOSITE IS righteous.

sing *verb*

VARIOUS WAYS TO SING: chant, croon, descant, hum, trill, warble, yodel.

DIFFERENT SINGING VOICES: alto, baritone, bass, contralto, soprano, tenor, treble.

VARIOUS KINDS OF SINGER: choirboy or choirgirl, chorister, crooner, folk singer, [*old use*] minstrel, opera singer, pop singer, prima donna, vocalist.
A group of singers is a ***choir*** or ***chorus***.
FOR KINDS OF MUSIC FOR SINGING, SEE **song**.

---

singe *verb*
  The hot iron singed his T-shirt. blacken, burn, char, scorch.

single *adjective*
  1 *We saw a single house high on the moors.* isolated, solitary.
  When only a single example of something exists, it is ***unique***.
  2 *She says she'll never marry: she wants to stay single.* unmarried.
  An unmarried man is a ***bachelor***.
  An unmarried woman is a ***spinster***.

single *verb*
  to single someone out *He singled me out as the best player in the team.* choose, identify, pick out, select.

single-handed *adverb*
  You can't shift the piano single-handed. alone, independently, on your own, unaided, without help.

singular *adjective*
  1 [*in grammar*] *You use the singular form of a word when you refer to only one person or thing.*
  AN OPPOSITE IS plural.

2 *It was a singular event.* abnormal, curious, extraordinary, odd, peculiar, remarkable, uncommon, unusual.
AN OPPOSITE IS common.

sinister *adjective*
1 *He had a sinister smile on his face.* disturbing, evil, forbidding, frightening, menacing, threatening, upsetting, villainous.
2 *There was something sinister about his behaviour.* bad, corrupt, criminal, dishonest, illegal, questionable, shady, suspicious.

sink *verb*
1 *The ship hit the rocks and sank.* become submerged, founder, go down.
To let water into a ship to sink it deliberately is to **scuttle** it.
2 *He fainted and sank to the ground.* drop, fall, slip down, subside.
When the sun sinks to the horizon it **sets**.

sit *verb*
1 *Please sit on the bench.* be seated, perch, rest, seat yourself, settle down.
To sit on your heels is to **squat**.
To sit to have your portrait painted is to **pose**.
2 *My cousin has to sit important exams this year.* [informal] go in for, take.

site *noun*
This is the site for a new sports centre. location, place, plot, position, setting, situation.

site *verb*
They decided to site the shopping centre in the middle of the town. establish, locate, place, position, situate.

sitting room *noun*
They were watching TV in the sitting room. drawing room, living room, lounge.
FOR NAMES OF OTHER ROOMS, SEE **room**.

situated *adjective*
The house is situated next to the park. located, positioned.

situation *noun*
1 *The house is in a pleasant situation.* locality, location, place, position, setting, site, spot.

2 *He was in an awkward situation.* circumstances, condition, plight.
3 *She applied for a situation in the new firm.* appointment, employment, job, post.

size *noun*
They were amazed by the sheer size of the building. dimensions, magnitude, proportions, scale.
Size can be measured in many ways. Other synonyms we might use depend on how we would measure the thing we are talking about
OTHER SYNONYMS MIGHT INCLUDE: amount, area, breadth, bulk, capacity, depth, extent, gauge, height, length, volume, width.
FOR UNITS OF SIZE, SEE **measurement**.

sizeable *adjective*
She gave them sizeable helpings of pudding. biggish, considerable, decent, generous, largish, significant, worthwhile.
AN OPPOSITE IS small.

skeleton *noun*
1 *They dug up a human skeleton.* bones.
2 *So far they've only put up the skeleton of the building.* frame, framework, shell.

sketch *noun*
1 *He drew a quick sketch of her.* drawing, outline, picture.
A sketch you do while you think of other things is a **doodle**.
2 *They performed a comic sketch.* scene, skit, turn.

sketch *verb*
He sketched the man the police were looking for. depict, draw, portray, represent.

sketchy *adjective*
She has a rather sketchy knowledge of the subject. fragmentary, imperfect, incomplete, rough, scrappy.
AN OPPOSITE IS perfect.

skid *verb*
He skidded on the ice. go out of control, slide, slip.

skilful *adjective*
She's a skilful driver. able,
accomplished, brilliant, capable, clever,
deft, expert, gifted, talented.
If you are skilful at a lot of things, you
are **versatile**.
If you are skilful at deceiving people,
you are **artful** or **crafty** or **cunning**.
AN OPPOSITE IS unskilful.
SEE ALSO **skilled**.

skill *noun*
1 *She showed great skill at the game.*
ability, accomplishment, aptitude,
capability, cleverness, competence,
deftness, expertise, gift, ingenuity,
proficiency, talent, versatility,
workmanship.
2 *He wanted to learn new skills.* art,
craft, knack, technique.

skilled *adjective*
*You need a skilled electrician to replace
the wiring.* competent, experienced,
professional, proficient, qualified,
trained.
AN OPPOSITE IS amateur.

skim *verb*
1 *The stone skimmed across the surface
of the pond.* glide, skid, slide, slip.
2 *He skimmed through the book.* glance
through, look through, scan, skip
through.

skin *noun*
People used to dress in animal skins.
coat, fur, hide, pelt.
The type of skin you have on your face
is your **complexion**.
A scientific word for your skin is
epidermis.
Skin on fruit, vegetables, etc., is **peel**
or **rind**.
Skin that might form on top of a liquid,
etc., is a **coating**, **film**, or **membrane**.

skinny *adjective*
He's very skinny—he should eat more.
bony, gaunt, lanky, spare, thin.
AN OPPOSITE IS plump.
SEE ALSO **thin**.

skip *verb*
1 *They skipped about the room.* bound,
caper, dance, frisk, frolic, hop, jump,
leap, prance, romp, spring.

2 *He skipped the boring bits in the book.*
ignore, leave out, miss out, pass over,
skim through.
3 *She was told off for skipping lessons.*
be absent from, miss, play truant from.

skirt *verb*
The path skirts the playing field. circle,
go round, pass round.

skittish *adjective*
*They were in a skittish mood and
couldn't get any work done.* excitable,
frisky, impish, lively, playful, sprightly.
AN OPPOSITE IS sedate.

sky *noun*
Clouds moved across the sky. air,
heavens.

slab *noun*
*She took a slab of chocolate in case she
got hungry.* block, chunk, hunk, lump,
piece.

slack *adjective*
1 *She had to tighten any guy-ropes that
were slack.* limp, loose.
AN OPPOSITE IS tight.
2 *He's too slack in his approach to
work.* casual, idle, lazy, negligent,
relaxed, unbusinesslike.
AN OPPOSITE IS businesslike.
3 *Business has been slack this year.*
quiet, slow.
AN OPPOSITE IS busy.

slacken *verb*
1 *He slackened the ropes.* ease off,
loosen, relax, release.
AN OPPOSITE IS tighten.
2 *The pace of the game slackened after
half-time.* decrease, lessen, reduce,
slow down.
AN OPPOSITE IS increase.

slam *verb*
Don't slam the door! bang, shut loudly.

slant *verb*
1 *Her handwriting slants backwards.*
be at an angle, incline, lean, slope, tilt.
2 *He slanted the evidence in her favour.*
distort, twist.

slant *noun*
1 *The floor of the caravan was at a slant.* angle, gradient, incline, slope, tilt.
A slant on a damaged ship is a **list**.
A slanting line joining opposite corners of a square, etc., is a **diagonal**.
A surface slanting up to a higher level is a **ramp**.
2 *He didn't like the slant they gave to the news.* bias, distortion, emphasis, point of view.

slap *verb*
She was so angry she slapped him. smack, spank.
FOR OTHER WAYS TO HIT THINGS, SEE **hit** *verb*.

slash *verb*
FOR VARIOUS WAYS TO CUT THINGS, SEE **cut** *verb*.

slaughter *verb*
They had to slaughter the cattle. kill, massacre, slay.

slaughter *noun*
The battle ended in terrible slaughter. bloodshed, butchery, killing, massacre.

slaughterhouse *noun*
A formal word is **abattoir**.

slave *verb*
They slaved all day to get the job done. exert yourself, labour, toil, work hard.

slavery *noun*
Thousands of Africans were taken away into slavery. bondage, captivity.
AN OPPOSITE IS freedom.

slay *verb*
[*old use*] *Many men were slain in the battle.* exterminate, kill, massacre, put to death, slaughter.

sledge *noun*
The sledge sped down the snowy slope. sled, toboggan.
A large sledge pulled by horses is a **sleigh**.
A sledge with steering and brakes used in winter sports is a **bobsleigh**.

sleek *adjective*
The cat has a sleek coat. glossy, shiny, silky, smooth, soft, velvety.
AN OPPOSITE IS coarse.

sleep *verb*

To sleep peacefully is to **be asleep** or **slumber**.
To sleep for a time during the day is to **snooze** or **take a nap**.
To be half-asleep is to **doze** or **drowse**.
To go to sleep is to **drop off** or **nod off**.

INFORMAL WORDS FOR A SHORT SLEEP: catnap, forty winks, kip, nap, shut-eye, snooze.
An afternoon sleep is a **siesta**.
A deep sleep caused by an injury, etc., is a **coma**.
The long sleep some animals have through the winter is **hibernation**.

sleepless *adjective*
She had a sleepless night. restless, wide awake.
The formal name for sleeplessness is **insomnia**.

sleepy *adjective*
He always feels sleepy after dinner. [*informal*] dopey, drowsy, heavy-eyed, lethargic, ready to sleep, tired, weary.
AN OPPOSITE IS wide awake.

slender *adjective*
1 *She has a slender figure.* graceful, lean, slim, spare, trim.
AN OPPOSITE IS fat.
2 *The spider dangled on a slender thread.* delicate, fine, fragile, thin.
AN OPPOSITE IS thick.
3 *He's only got a slender chance of winning.* insignificant, negligible, poor, slight.
AN OPPOSITE IS good.
4 *He won by a slender margin.* narrow, small.
AN OPPOSITE IS large.

slice *verb*
To slice meat is to **carve** it.
SEE ALSO **cut** *verb*.

slick *adjective*
The conjuror's slick movements deceived them all. artful, clever, cunning, deft, quick, smart.
AN OPPOSITE IS clumsy.

slide *verb*
He began to slide down the icy slope.
glide, skid, slip, slither.
To enjoy yourself sliding over ice or
snow is to **skate** or **ski** or **toboggan**.

slight *adjective*
1 There is a slight problem with the
system. insignificant, minor, negligible,
superficial, trifling, trivial,
unimportant.
AN OPPOSITE IS important.
2 In spite of his slight build he's a good
runner. delicate, fragile, frail, slender,
slim, small, spare, thin, tiny.
AN OPPOSITE IS stout.

slightly *adverb*
She was slightly hurt in the accident. a
little, hardly, only just, scarcely.
AN OPPOSITE IS seriously.

slim *adjective*
1 He stays slim by taking exercise.
graceful, lean, slender, spare, thin,
trim.
AN OPPOSITE IS fat.
2 Her chances of winning are slim.
insignificant, negligible, poor, slight.
AN OPPOSITE IS good.
3 They won by a slim margin. fine,
narrow, small.
AN OPPOSITE IS large.

slim *verb*
He's been trying to slim for years.
become slimmer, diet, lose weight,
reduce.

slimy *adjective*
She slipped in the slimy mud. mucky,
slippery, squashy, sticky.

sling *verb*
He slung the rubbish into the skip. cast,
[informal] chuck, fling, [informal]
heave, hurl, lob, pitch, throw, toss.

slink *verb*
They tried to slink away without being
seen. creep, move guiltily, slip, sneak,
steal.

slip *verb*
1 He slipped on the ice. move out of
control, skate, skid, slither.
2 The lifeboat slipped into the water.
glide, slide.

3 She slipped out of the room. creep,
edge, move quietly, slink, sneak, steal,
tiptoe.
to slip up The burglar slipped up when
he left his fingerprints on the window.
go wrong, make a mistake.

slip *noun*
He made a silly slip. blunder, error,
fault, lapse, mistake, oversight,
[informal] slip-up.
to give someone the slip The robber
gave them the slip. escape, get away,
run away.

slippery *adjective*
Take care—the floor is slippery. glassy,
slithery, smooth.
A surface slippery with frost is **icy**.
A surface slippery with grease is
greasy or **oily**.
To put oil on something to make it
slippery is to **lubricate** it.

slipshod *adjective*
His work was rather slipshod. careless,
hasty, messy, shoddy, sloppy, slovenly,
untidy.
AN OPPOSITE IS careful.

slit *noun*
He made slits in his jeans with a pair of
scissors. cut, gash, hole, opening, split,
tear.

slit *verb*
FOR VARIOUS WAYS TO CUT THINGS,
SEE **cut** *verb*.

slither *verb*
The snake slithered away. glide, slide,
slip.

slog *verb*
He slogged the ball over the boundary.
[informal] bash, [informal] belt, clout,
drive, hammer, hit, [slang] slosh,
swipe, thump, [informal] wallop.

slogan *noun*
They were trying to think up a new
advertising slogan. catchphrase, motto,
saying.

slop *verb*
He slopped tea into the saucer. slosh,
spill, splash, upset.

slope *verb*
The beach slopes gently down to the sea.
fall, rise, shelve.

slope *noun*
1 *It was hard work pushing the cart up the slope.* bank, gradient, hill, incline, ramp, rise.
An upward slope is an ***ascent***.
A downward slope is a ***descent***.
2 *There was a slope in the floor of the caravan.* slant, tilt.

sloppy *adjective*
1 *He stirred the sloppy mixture of flour, eggs, and milk.* liquid, messy, runny, watery, wet.
2 *Her work was very sloppy.* careless, hasty, shoddy, slipshod, slovenly, untidy.
3 [*informal*] *He hates sloppy love stories.* romantic, sentimental, [*informal*] soppy, weak.

slosh *verb*
1 *He sloshed water on to the dirty floor.* slop, spill, splash.
2 [*slang*] *He sloshed the man on the chin.* [*informal*] bash, [*informal*] belt, clout, hit, thump, [*informal*] wallop.

slot *noun*
1 *She put a coin into the slot.* chink, hole, opening, slit.
2 *TV has a regular slot for local news.* place, space, time.

slouch *verb*
She told him to stop slouching. droop, lounge, shamble, slump, stoop.

slovenly *adjective*
She told him off for his slovenly work.
careless, hasty, messy, shoddy, sloppy, thoughtless, untidy.
AN OPPOSITE IS careful.

slow *adjective*
1 *They made slow progress.* careful, cautious, deliberate, gradual, leisurely, plodding, tedious, unhurried.
2 *She told them to hurry up—they were being too slow.* dawdling, idle, late, lazy, loitering, straggling.
3 *He was slow to answer.* hesitant, reluctant.
AN OPPOSITE IS quick.

slow *verb*
to slow down *Slow down—you're driving too fast.* brake, go slower, reduce speed.
AN OPPOSITE IS accelerate.

sludge *noun*
They cleared a lot of sludge out of the pond. muck, mud, ooze, slime.

slump *verb*
He slumped in his chair. collapse, flop, loll, sag, slouch.

slump *noun*
There was a slump in trade after Christmas. collapse, decline, drop, fall.
A general slump in trade is a ***depression*** or ***recession***.
AN OPPOSITE IS boom.

sly *adjective*
She thought he was a bit sly. artful, crafty, cunning, deceitful, devious, furtive, scheming, secretive, [*informal*] sneaky, stealthy, tricky, underhand, wily.
AN OPPOSITE IS straightforward.

smack *verb*
His mother threatened to smack him. slap, spank.
FOR WAYS OF HITTING, SEE **hit** *verb*.

small *adjective*
1 *The model village showed everything on a small scale.* compact, little, microscopic, miniature, minute, tiny.
AN OPPOSITE IS big.
2 *He complained that his helping of stew was rather small.* inadequate, insufficient, meagre, [*informal*] measly, scanty, stingy.
AN OPPOSITE IS generous.
3 *She had a small problem.* insignificant, minor, negligible, trifling, trivial, unimportant.
AN OPPOSITE IS important.

smart *adjective*
1 *Everyone looked smart at the wedding.* chic, elegant, fashionable, neat, [*informal*] posh, spruce, stylish, tidy, trim, well-dressed.
AN OPPOSITE IS scruffy.

2 *It was smart of him to think of that.*
acute, artful, bright, clever, crafty,
ingenious, intelligent, shrewd.
AN OPPOSITE IS stupid.
3 *They set off at a smart pace.* brisk,
fast, quick, rapid, speedy, swift.
AN OPPOSITE IS slow.

smart *verb*
*The cut will smart when she puts
antiseptic on it.* be painful, hurt, sting.

smarten *verb*
*He smartened himself up before the
visitors arrived.* clean, tidy.

smash *verb*
1 *He dropped a plate and smashed it.*
break, crush, squash.
When glass smashes it **shatters**.
When wood smashes it **splinters**.
To smash something completely is to
demolish or **destroy** or **wreck** it.
2 *She thought the lorry was going to
smash into them.* bang, bump, collide,
crash, knock, ram, slam.

smear *verb*
*The chef smeared butter over the
cooking dish.* dab, rub, smudge, spread,
wipe.

smear *noun*
There was a smear of paint on his face.
mark, smudge, streak, trace.

smell *noun*

> PLEASANT SMELLS: aroma,
> fragrance, perfume, scent.
> The smell of wine is its **bouquet**.
>
> ADJECTIVES USED TO DESCRIBE
> THINGS WITH A PLEASANT SMELL:
> aromatic, fragrant, perfumed,
> savoury, scented, spicy, sweet, sweet-
> smelling.
>
> UNPLEASANT SMELLS: odour,
> [*informal*] pong, reek, stench, stink,
> whiff.
>
> ADJECTIVES USED TO DESCRIBE
> THINGS WITH AN UNPLEASANT
> SMELL: foul, musty, odorous,
> reeking, rotten, sharp, smelly, sour,
> stinking, [*informal*] whiffy.

smell *verb*
1 *She smelled the roses.* scent, sniff.
2 *Those onions smell.* reek, stink.

smelly *adjective* SEE **smell** *noun*
AN OPPOSITE IS fragrant or odourless.

smile *verb*
*He smiled because he was pleased to see
her.* beam, grin.
To smile in a silly way is to **smirk**.
To smile in an insulting way is to
sneer.
All these words can be used both as
nouns and as verbs

smoke *noun*
The chimney sent out clouds of smoke.
fumes, gases, steam, vapour.
The smoke given out by a car is
exhaust.
Poisonous fumes which hang in the air
like fog are **smog**.

smoke *verb*
1 *The bonfire was still smoking next
morning.* smoulder.
2 *He likes smoking cigars.* puff at.
To breath in tobacco smoke is to
inhale.

smoky *adjective*
*The smoky air near the factory affected
people's health.* dirty, foggy, grimy,
hazy, murky, sooty.

smooth *adjective*
1 *The road was smooth, with no bumps.*
even, flat, level.
AN OPPOSITE IS uneven.
2 *They sailed across a smooth sea.*
calm, glassy, peaceful, placid, quiet,
unruffled.
AN OPPOSITE IS rough.
3 *The cat's fur was shiny and smooth.*
silky, sleek, soft, velvety.
AN OPPOSITE IS coarse.
4 *The new trains give you a smooth
ride.* comfortable, steady.
AN OPPOSITE IS bumpy.
5 *Whisk the ingredients to make a
smooth mixture.* creamy, flowing,
runny.
AN OPPOSITE IS lumpy.

smooth *verb*
> He smoothed down the wood with sandpaper. even out, flatten, level, level off.
> To smooth metal you can *file* or *polish* it.
> To smooth wood you can *plane* or *sandpaper* it.
> To smooth cloth you can *iron* or *press* it.

smother *verb*
> 1 She was smothered with a pillow. choke, stifle, suffocate.
> 2 The pudding was smothered with cream. cover.

smoulder *verb*
> A bonfire can smoulder for days. burn slowly, smoke.

smudge *noun*
> There was a smudge on the painting. blot, mark, smear, stain, streak.
> All these words can be used both as nouns and as verbs.

snack *noun*
> She eats a lot of snacks between meals. bite, [informal] nibble, refreshments.
> A snack in the middle of the morning is sometimes called *elevenses*.

snag *noun*
> An unexpected snag delayed the plan. complication, difficulty, hindrance, hitch, obstacle, problem.

snake *noun*
> serpent.

> SOME KINDS OF SNAKE: adder, anaconda, boa constrictor, cobra, grass snake, mamba, puff adder, python, rattlesnake, sand snake, sea snake, sidewinder, tree snake, viper.

snap *verb*
> 1 She heard a twig snap. break, crack.
> 2 The dog is always snapping at people. bite, nip.
> 3 She was in a bad mood and snapped at him. speak angrily, speak irritably.

snare *noun*
> The rabbit was caught in a snare. booby trap, noose, trap.

snare *verb*
> The poacher was trying to snare some game. catch, net, trap.

snarl *verb*
> 1 The dog snarled at her. bare the teeth, growl.
> 2 'Go away!' he snarled.
> FOR DIFFERENT WAYS TO SAY THINGS, SEE **talk** *verb*.
> **snarled up** The motorway was completely snarled up. at a standstill, blocked, congested, jammed, obstructed.

snatch *verb*
> The thief snatched her bag and ran off. grab, grasp, pluck, seize, wrench away.

sneak *verb*
> I managed to sneak in without anyone seeing. creep, move stealthily, slink, slip, steal, tiptoe.
> **to sneak on someone** [informal] She sneaked on her sister. inform against, report, [informal] split on, tell tales about.

sneaky *adjective*
> [informal] That was a really sneaky trick. cheating, crafty, deceitful, devious, furtive, sly, underhand, untrustworthy.
> AN OPPOSITE IS honest.

sneer *verb*
> **to sneer at** They sneered at her ideas. be scornful of, deride, jeer at, make fun of, mock, ridicule, scoff at.

sniff *verb*
> FOR VARIOUS WAYS TO MAKE SOUNDS, SEE **sound** *verb*.

snip *verb*
> She snipped off a lock of her hair. chop, clip, cut, trim.

snippet *noun*
> She could hear snippets of conversation from the next room. fragment, piece, scrap, snatch.

snivel *verb*
> For goodness' sake, stop snivelling! cry, sniff, sob, weep, whimper, whine.

snobbish *adjective*
She's too snobbish to mix with us.
arrogant, haughty, pompous,
[informal] posh, [informal] stuck-up,
superior.
AN OPPOSITE IS humble.

snoop *verb*
She caught him snooping round her
office. look furtively, poke, pry,
rummage, spy.

snooper *noun*
A person who snoops is a **busybody** or
a **spy**.

snore, snort *verbs*
FOR VARIOUS WAYS WE MAKE SOUNDS,
SEE **sound** verb.

snout *noun*
The crocodile's snout was visible above
the water. face, muzzle, nose.

snub *verb*
She deliberately ignored you in order to
snub you. be rude or unfriendly to,
humiliate, insult, offend, [informal]
put you down.

snug *adjective*
I was tucked up snug in bed.
comfortable, cosy, relaxed, safe, secure,
warm.
AN OPPOSITE IS uncomfortable.

soak *verb*
The rain had soaked his jacket and
trousers. drench, saturate, wet
thoroughly.
To put something into a liquid is to
immerse or **submerge** it.
to soak up A sponge soaks up water.
absorb, take in, take up.

soaked, soaking *adjectives*
My jacket is soaked. drenched,
dripping, saturated, soggy, sopping,
waterlogged, wet through.

soar *verb*
1 The bird spread its wings and soared
into the air. ascend, climb, fly, glide,
rise.
2 The cost of living continued to soar. go
up, increase, rise, shoot up.

sob *verb*
She threw herself on the bed, sobbing
loudly. cry, shed tears, weep.

sober *adjective*
1 He drank a little wine, but he stayed
sober.
A person who drinks very little alcohol
is **abstemious** or **temperate**.
AN OPPOSITE IS drunk.
2 We'll discuss the problem when you
are in a sober mood. calm, composed,
logical, lucid, rational, sensible,
serious.
AN OPPOSITE IS frivolous or irrational.
3 The funeral was a sober occasion.
dignified, grave, plain, sedate, solemn,
sombre.
AN OPPOSITE IS bright or showy.

sociable *adjective*
They are a pleasant, sociable couple.
amiable, friendly, hospitable,
neighbourly, welcoming.
AN OPPOSITE IS unfriendly.

social *adjective*
1 Elephants are social animals.
People and creatures who like to be in
groups or communities are said to be
gregarious.
AN OPPOSITE IS solitary.
2 They organized several social
activities. communal, community,
group, public.

society *noun*
1 Britain is a multi-racial society.
civilization, community.
2 He's a member of a secret society.
association, club, group, organization.
3 She enjoyed the society of others.
companionship, company, fellowship,
friendship.

soft *adjective*
1 The baby can only eat soft food.
crumbly, pulpy, spongy, squashy.
AN OPPOSITE IS hard.
2 The gloves are made of soft leather.
elastic, flexible, pliable, springy,
supple.
AN OPPOSITE IS rigid.
3 I sank into a soft chair. comfortable,
cosy, padded.
AN OPPOSITE IS uncomfortable.
4 The cat's fur felt very soft. downy,
feathery, fleecy, furry, silky, sleek,
smooth, velvety.
AN OPPOSITE IS coarse.
5 A soft breeze stirred the leaves.

delicate, gentle, light, mild.
AN OPPOSITE IS rough.
6 *They spoke in soft whispers.* faint,
muted, quiet.
AN OPPOSITE IS loud.
7 *Soft light created a romantic
atmosphere.* diffused, dim, low, shaded,
subdued.
AN OPPOSITE IS bright or dazzling.

soggy *adjective*
1 *The ground was soggy after so much
rain.* drenched, saturated, soaked,
sopping, wet through.
AN OPPOSITE IS dry.
2 *The cake was rather soggy.* heavy,
moist, stodgy.
AN OPPOSITE IS light.

soil *noun*
*The plants grow best in well-drained
soil.* earth, ground, land.
Good fertile soil is ***loam***.
Decayed plant material which enriches
the soil is ***humus***.
The fertile top layer of soil is ***topsoil***.
Soil under the topsoil is ***subsoil***.

soil *verb*
*Their clothes were soiled with mud and
grass stains.* defile, dirty, make dirty.

soldier *noun*

A soldier in a regular army is a
serviceman or ***servicewoman***.
Soldiers are also called ***troops***.
A person who is compelled to become
a soldier is a ***conscript***.
A new soldier is a ***recruit***.
A young person training to be a
soldier is a ***cadet***.
A soldier who makes a career in the
army is a ***regular*** soldier.
A soldier who makes money fighting
for a foreign army is a ***mercenary***.
An old word for a soldier is ***warrior***.
Soldiers who use big guns are the
artillery.
Soldiers who fight on foot are the
infantry.

VARIOUS KINDS OF SOLDIER:
cavalryman, commando, guardsman,
gunner, infantryman, marine,
paratrooper, rifleman, sapper,
sentry, trooper. ➡

POSITIONS SOLDIERS MAY HOLD IN
THE ARMY: officer, non-
commissioned officer or NCO,
private.
FOR RANKS IN THE ARMY, SEE **rank**.

sole *adjective*
He is the sole survivor of the accident.
lone, one, only, single, solitary, unique.

solemn *adjective*
1 *She sat down, a solemn expression on
her face.* earnest, grave, serious, sober,
sombre, thoughtful, unsmiling.
AN OPPOSITE IS cheerful.
2 *The coronation was a solemn
occasion.* dignified, formal, grand,
important, impressive, pompous,
stately.
AN OPPOSITE IS frivolous.

solid *adjective*
1 *A cricket ball is solid.*
There are no convenient synonyms for
this sense of *solid*
AN OPPOSITE IS hollow.
2 *The water turned into solid ice.* dense,
hard, rigid, unyielding.
AN OPPOSITE IS soft.
3 *The hut has a solid framework.* firm,
robust, sound, stable, steady, strong,
sturdy, tough.
AN OPPOSITE IS weak.
4 *He got solid support from his team-
mates.* dependable, reliable,
unanimous, undivided, united.
AN OPPOSITE IS variable.

solidify *verb*
*The lava from the volcano solidifies as
it cools.* become solid, harden, set,
stiffen.
AN OPPOSITE IS soften.

solitary *adjective*
1 *He was a solitary man and rarely
spoke to others.* isolated, lonely,
secluded, unsociable.
To be solitary is to be ***alone***.
AN OPPOSITE IS sociable.
2 *There was a solitary tree in the
middle of the field.* one, only, single,
sole.

solitude *noun*
She enjoyed her few hours of solitude.
isolation, loneliness, privacy, seclusion.

solve *verb*
He tried to solve the riddle his friend had set him. answer, decipher, explain, find the solution to, interpret, unravel, work out.

sombre *adjective*
1 The room was decorated in sombre brown and grey. cheerless, dark, depressing, dim, dingy, dismal, drab, dull.
AN OPPOSITE IS bright.
2 He had a sombre expression. gloomy, grave, melancholy, mournful, sad, serious, sober.
AN OPPOSITE IS cheerful.

song *noun*

VARIOUS KINDS OF MUSIC FOR SINGING: anthem, ballad, calypso, carol, chant, ditty, folk song, hymn, jingle, lament, love song, lullaby, nursery rhyme, pop song, psalm, shanty, spiritual.

LONG COMPOSITIONS FOR SINGERS: anthem, cantata, chant, musical, opera, oratorio.
A song from a musical is a ***number***.
A song from an opera or oratorio is an ***aria***.
The words for a song are the ***lyrics***.
FOR OTHER MUSICAL TERMS, SEE **music**.

soon *adverb*
I'll be ready soon. before long, in a short time, presently, quickly, shortly.

soothe *verb*
1 The quiet music soothed her nerves. calm, comfort, pacify, relax.
2 This cream will soothe the pain. ease, lessen, relieve.

soothing *adjective*
They played soothing music. calming, gentle, peaceful, pleasant, relaxing, restful.

sophisticated *adjective*
1 It's a play that will only appeal to a sophisticated audience. adult, cultivated, cultured, grown-up, mature.
AN OPPOSITE IS naïve.

2 They like going to sophisticated restaurants. fashionable, [informal] posh, stylish.
AN OPPOSITE IS unfashionable.
3 This is a sophisticated computer. advanced, complex, complicated, elaborate.
AN OPPOSITE IS primitive or simple.

sorcerer, sorceress *nouns*
The sorcerer waved a magic wand. conjuror, magician, wizard.

sore *adjective*
1 My feet are still sore from the walk. aching, hurting, inflamed, painful, raw, red, sensitive, smarting, tender.
2 [informal] He's still sore because I forgot to phone him back. angry, annoyed, bitter, resentful, upset.

sore *noun*
I put ointment on the sore.

VARIOUS KINDS OF SORE PLACE: abscess, boil, carbuncle, graze, inflammation, laceration, pimple, rawness, scab, spot, ulcer, wound.

sorrow *noun*
1 It was a time of great sorrow. anguish, dejection, depression, desolation, despair, distress, gloom, glumness, grief, heartache, heartbreak, melancholy, misery, sadness, tearfulness, unhappiness, woe, wretchedness.
Sorrow because of someone's death is ***mourning***.
Sorrow at being away from home is ***homesickness***.
AN OPPOSITE IS happiness.
2 She expressed her sorrow for what she had done. apologies, guilt, penitence, regret, remorse, repentance.

sorrowful *adjective*
Her face looked sorrowful. broken-hearted, dejected, distressed, grief-stricken, heartbroken, long-faced, melancholy, miserable, mournful, regretful, sad, sombre, sorry, tearful, unhappy, upset, woeful, wretched.
AN OPPOSITE IS happy.

sorry *adjective*
  1 *He's sorry for what he did.* apologetic, ashamed, penitent, regretful, remorseful, repentant.
  AN OPPOSITE IS unrepentant.
  2 *He felt sorry for her—she seemed so unhappy.* compassionate, pitying, sympathetic, understanding.
  AN OPPOSITE IS unsympathetic.

sort *noun*
  What sort of music do you like? category, class, description, form, kind, type, variety.
  A particular sort of goods is a **brand** or **make**.
  A sort of animal is a **breed** or **species**.
  sort of [*informal*] *'Do you see what I mean?' 'Sort of'.* a bit, a little, in a way, somewhat, to some extent.

sort *verb*
  The books are sorted according to their subjects. arrange, catalogue, categorize, classify, divide, file, grade, group, organize.
  AN OPPOSITE IS mix.
  to sort something out 1 *Sort out the things you need.* choose, select, separate, set aside.
  2 *The problem has been sorted out.* attend to, clear up, cope with, deal with, solve.

soul *noun*
  Many people believe that a person's soul is immortal. spirit.

sound *noun*
  I heard the sound of people talking. noise.
  For other words, see the next entry.
  SEE ALSO **noise**.

sound *verb*
  1 *A loud buzzer sounded.* become audible, be heard, make a noise, resound.

Many of these words can be used either as verbs or as nouns.

VARIOUS WAYS PEOPLE MAKE SOUNDS: boo, clap, croak, cry, groan, ➡

hiccup, hum, jeer, lisp, moan, murmur, scream, shout, shriek, sigh, sing, sniff, snore, sob, splutter, wail, whimper, whisper, whistle, yell, yodel.
SEE ALSO **talk**.

WAYS VARIOUS ANIMALS MAKE SOUNDS: bark, bay, bellow, bleat, bray, buzz, croak, growl, grunt, hiss, howl, jabber, low, miaow, moo, neigh, purr, roar, snarl, snort, squeak, squeal, trumpet, whine, whinny, yap, yelp.

WAYS VARIOUS BIRDS MAKE SOUNDS: cackle, caw, chirp, chirrup, cluck, coo, crow, honk, hoot, quack, screech, squawk, tweet, twitter, warble.

WAYS VARIOUS THINGS MAKE SOUNDS: bang, blare, bleep, boom, chime, chink, clang, clank, clash, clatter, click, clink, crack, crackle, crash, creak, fizz, grate, gurgle, jangle, jingle, patter, peal, ping, plop, pop, rattle, ring, rumble, rustle, sizzle, slam, snap, swish, throb, thud, thunder, tick, ting, tinkle, twang, whir, whistle, whiz.

  2 *They sounded the depth of the river.* measure, plumb.
  to sound out *They did a survey to sound out public opinion.* examine, find out about, investigate, probe, test.

sound *adjective*
  1 *The car engine seemed sound.* in good condition, undamaged, whole, working.
  AN OPPOSITE IS damaged.
  2 *They returned safe and sound.* fit, healthy, strong, well.
  AN OPPOSITE IS ill.
  3 *His ideas are sound.* convincing, logical, rational, reasonable, sensible, wise.
  AN OPPOSITE IS silly.
  4 *Savings certificates are usually a sound investment.* dependable, reliable, safe, secure, trustworthy.
  AN OPPOSITE IS unreliable.

soup *noun*

> SOME KINDS OF SOUP: broth, chowder, consommé, minestrone, mulligatawny, Scotch broth.
> There are many other kinds of soup. Often they are named after the main ingredient: *chicken soup*, *tomato soup*, etc
> The liquid in which you stew fish, meat, or vegetables is *stock*.

sour *adjective*
1 *These apples are a bit sour.* acid, bitter, sharp, tart.
AN OPPOSITE IS sweet.
2 *She gave him a sour look.* cross, disagreeable, grumpy, ill-natured, irritable, unpleasant.

source *noun*
The source of the river is in the hills. beginning, head, origin, start, starting point.
The source of a river or stream is usually a *spring*.

south *noun, adjective, adverb*
The parts of a continent or country in the south are the *southern* parts.
To travel towards the south is to travel *southward* or *southwards* or *in a southerly direction*.
A wind from the south is a *southerly* wind.
A person who lives in the south of Britain is a *southerner*.

souvenir *noun*
He brought home some souvenirs of his trip to Paris. reminder.

sow *verb*
To sow seeds in the ground is to *plant* them.
To sow an area of ground with seeds is to *seed* it.

space *noun*
1 *The six astronauts on board the shuttle will spend ten days in space.*

> Everything that exists in space is the *universe*.
> Distances in space stretch to *infinity*.
> Travel to other stars is *interstellar* travel. ➡

> Travel to other planets is *interplanetary* travel.
> A traveller in space is an *astronaut*.
> A Russian traveller in space is a *cosmonaut*.
> In stories, an astronaut is often called a *spaceman* or *spacewoman*.
> In stories, beings from other planets are *alien* or *extraterrestrial* beings.
>
> WORDS TO DO WITH TRAVEL IN SPACE: blast-off, booster rocket, capsule, countdown, docking bay, heat shield, life-support system, module, orbit, probe, re-entry, retrorocket, rocket, satellite, solar panel, spacecraft, spaceship, space shuttle, space station, spacesuit, spacewalk, splashdown, sputnik.
> FOR ASTRONOMICAL TERMS, SEE **astronomy**.

2 *There wasn't much space to move about.* freedom, room, scope.
3 *He peered through the tiny space in the curtains.* blank, break, gap, hole, opening.
A space without any air in it is a *vacuum*.
A space of time is an *interval* or *period*.

spacious *adjective*
The living room is spacious and comfortably furnished. big, large, roomy, sizeable.
AN OPPOSITE IS small.

span *noun*
The arch had a span of 60 metres. breadth, distance, extent, length, width.
A span of time is a *period* or *stretch*.

span *verb*
A narrow bridge spanned the river. arch over, cross, extend across, pass over, reach over, straddle, stretch over.

spare *verb*
1 *Can you spare any money for the homeless?* afford, do without, part with, provide, sacrifice.
2 *She begged him to spare her.* be merciful to, forgive, free, [*informal*] let off, pardon, release, reprieve, save.

spare *adjective*
1 *The spare tyre is in the boot.*
additional, extra, standby.
2 *Have you any spare boxes I could have?* leftover, odd, remaining, surplus, unnecessary, unneeded, unused, unwanted.
3 *He was tall and spare.* lean, slender, slim, thin, trim.

sparing *adjective*
He's sparing with his money. careful, economical, frugal, prudent, thrifty.
Insulting synonyms are mean, miserly, stingy.
AN OPPOSITE IS generous or wasteful.

spark *noun*
There was a spark of light as he struck the match. flash, flicker, gleam, glint, sparkle.

sparkle *verb*
The diamond ring sparkled in the sunlight. flash, glint, glitter, spark, twinkle.
FOR VARIOUS EFFECTS OF LIGHT, SEE **light** *noun*.

sparse *adjective*
In the desert, vegetation is very sparse. inadequate, light, meagre, scanty, scarce, scattered, thin.
AN OPPOSITE IS plentiful.

spatter *verb*
The bus spattered water over us. scatter, shower, slop, splash, spray, sprinkle.

speak *verb*
He was so shocked he couldn't speak. communicate, express yourself, say something, talk, utter your thoughts.
SEE ALSO **talk**.

speaker *noun*
A person who gives a talk is a ***lecturer***.
A person who makes formal speeches is an ***orator***.
A person who speaks on behalf of an organization is a ***spokesperson***.

spear *noun*
A spear used in whaling is a ***harpoon***.
A spear thrown as a sport is a ***javelin***.
A spear carried by a knight fighting on horseback was a ***lance***.

special *adjective*
1 *They were keeping the champagne for a special occasion.* exceptional, extraordinary, important, memorable, momentous, notable, out-of-the-ordinary, significant, uncommon, unusual.
AN OPPOSITE IS ordinary.
2 *She had her own special way of doing things.* characteristic, different, distinctive, individual, recognizable, unique, unmistakable.
3 *You need special tools for this job.* particular, proper, specialized, specific.

specialist *noun*
She's a specialist in military history. authority, consultant, expert, professional.
FOR SPECIALISTS WHO LOOK AFTER YOUR HEALTH, SEE **medicine**.

speciality *noun*
What's your speciality? expertise, special knowledge or skill, strength, strong point.

specialize *verb*
to specialize in 1 *She decided to specialize in chemistry.* be a specialist in, concentrate on.
2 *The restaurant specializes in seafood.* be best at, have a reputation for.

species *noun*
Many species of animals and birds are facing extinction. breed, class, kind, race, sort, type, variety.

specific *adjective*
1 *The instructions he gave were very specific.* detailed, exact, precise.
AN OPPOSITE IS general.
2 *There are several specific problems that need to be dealt with.* definite, particular, special, specified.
AN OPPOSITE IS unspecified.

specify *verb*
He did not specify what action he would like them to take. be specific about, define, identify, name.

specimen *noun*
The police asked for a specimen of his handwriting. example, illustration, instance, sample.

speck *noun*
She brushed a speck of dust from her shoes. bit, dot, fleck, grain, mark, particle, spot, trace.

speckled *adjective*
A brown, speckled egg lay on the nest. dotted, flecked, mottled, spotted, spotty.
If you have a lot of brown spots on your skin you are *freckled*.
Something with patches of colour is *dappled* or *patchy*.

spectacle *noun*
The military parade was a magnificent spectacle. display, exhibition, extravaganza, show.

spectacles *plural noun* SEE **glass**

spectacular *adjective*
1 *The flying display at the air show was really spectacular.* dramatic, exciting, impressive, magnificent, sensational, thrilling.
2 *The flowers are spectacular at this time of year.* beautiful, breathtaking, colourful, eye-catching, showy, splendid.

spectator *noun*
The spectators at a show are the *audience*.
The spectators at a football match are the *crowd*.
A person watching TV is a *viewer*.
If you see an accident or a crime you are an *eyewitness* or *witness*.
If you just happen to see something going on you are a *bystander* or *onlooker*.

spectrum *noun*
The library caters for a wide spectrum of interests. range, variety.

speech *noun*
1 *His speech was slurred and he looked tired.* articulation, elocution, pronunciation, speaking, talking.
2 *She gave a speech lasting for more than an hour.* address, lecture, oration, presentation, talk.
A talk in church is a *sermon*.
Speech between actors in a play is *dialogue*.
A speech delivered by a single actor is a *monologue*.

speechless *adjective*
She was speechless with surprise. dumb, mute, silent, tongue-tied.
AN OPPOSITE IS communicative.

speed *noun*
She worked with amazing speed. pace, quickness, rapidity, rate, swiftness.
A formal synonym is *velocity*.
The speed of a piece of music is its *tempo*.

speed *verb*
1 *They sped down the road.* career, dart, dash, [informal] fly, gallop, hasten, hurry, hurtle, move quickly, race, run, rush, shoot, sprint, streak, tear, [informal] zoom.
2 *She was caught speeding on the motorway.* break the speed limit, go too fast.
to speed up *The train began to speed up.* accelerate, go faster, increase speed, quicken, spurt ahead.

speedy *adjective*
They sent their best wishes for a speedy recovery. fast, immediate, prompt, quick, swift.
AN OPPOSITE IS slow.

spell *noun*
1 *After a brief spell in the navy, he decided to become a teacher.* period, session, stretch, time.
2 *A magic spell put the princess to sleep for a thousand years.* charm, magic formula.
Making magic spells is *sorcery* or *witchcraft* or *wizardry*.

spend *verb*
1 *I spent all my money.* exhaust, [informal] fork out, get through, [informal] lash out, pay out, use up.
To spend money unwisely is to *fritter* or *squander* it.
2 *She seems to spend all her time gossiping.* fill, occupy, pass.
To spend time doing something useless is to *waste* it.

sphere *noun*
1 *The earth has the shape of a sphere.* ball, globe.
2 *He's an expert in his own sphere.* area, department, field, subject.

spherical *adjective*
The earth is spherical. ball-shaped, round.

spice *noun*

SOME SPICES USED IN COOKING: allspice, aniseed, bayleaf, capsicum, cardamom, cayenne, chilli, cinnamon, cloves, coriander, cumin, curry powder, ginger, juniper, mace, nutmeg, paprika, pepper, pimento, saffron, sesame, turmeric.

spike *noun*
The wall was topped with iron spikes. barb, nail, point, projection, prong.

spill *verb*
1 *You'll spill that tea if you're not careful.* overturn, tip over, upset.
2 *Milk spilled onto the floor.* overflow, pour, run out, slop, slosh, splash.
3 *The bag fell off the table, spilling its contents on to the floor.* drop, scatter, shed, tip.

spin *verb*
The rear wheels of the car spun round. revolve, rotate, twirl, whirl.

spine *noun*
1 *Your spine runs down the middle of your back.* backbone, spinal column. The bones in your spine are your **vertebrae**.
2 *A hedgehog has sharp spines.* bristle, needle, point, spike.

spine-chilling *adjective*
The ghost story was spine-chilling. creepy, exciting, frightening, [*informal*] scary.

spirit *noun*
1 *Although he is dead, his spirit lives on.* soul.
2 *The charm was meant to keep evil spirits away.*

VARIOUS SPIRITS YOU READ ABOUT IN STORIES: bogeyman, demon, devil, genie, ghost, ghoul, gremlin, hobgoblin, imp, incubus, nymph, phantom, poltergeist, spectre, sprite, sylph, wraith, zombie.

3 *Everyone who knew her admired her spirit.* bravery, cheerfulness, confidence, courage, daring, determination, energy, enthusiasm, heroism, morale, optimism, pluck, valour.
4 *It took a while to get into the spirit of the party.* atmosphere, feeling, mood.

spiritual *adjective*
The Dalai Lama is the spiritual leader of Tibet. holy, religious, sacred.
AN OPPOSITE IS worldly.

spite *noun*
She's only saying it out of spite. [*informal*] bitchiness, bitterness, hate, hostility, ill-feeling, malevolence, malice.

spiteful *adjective*
He made some really spiteful comments. [*informal*] bitchy, bitter, cruel, hostile, ill-natured, malevolent, malicious, nasty, unkind, venomous, vicious.
AN OPPOSITE IS kind.

splash *verb*
1 *The bus splashed water over us.* shower, slop, slosh, spatter, spill, spray, sprinkle.
2 *The children splashed about in the water.* bathe, dabble, paddle, wade.

splendid *adjective*
1 *The celebrations ended with a splendid banquet.* beautiful, brilliant, costly, dazzling, elegant, glorious, gorgeous, grand, great, imposing, impressive, lavish, luxurious, magnificent, majestic, marvellous, noble, [*informal*] posh, rich, stately, superb, wonderful.
2 *That's a splendid idea!* admirable, excellent, first-class.

splendour *noun*
They admired the splendour of the cathedral. brilliance, ceremony, colourfulness, display, glory, grandeur, magnificence, majesty, pageantry, pomp, show, spectacle.

splinter *noun*
There were splinters of glass all over the floor. chip, flake, fragment, sliver.

splinter *verb*
> The glass splintered into pieces. chip, crack, fracture, shatter, smash, split.

split *verb*
> **1** *He split the log in two.* chop, crack open, cut up, splinter.
> **2** *He split his trousers climbing over the fence.* rip open, tear.
> **3** *They split the profits.* distribute, share out.
> **4** *The path splits here.* branch, fork, separate.
> **to split up** *The search party decided to split up.* break up, divide, go different ways, part, separate.
> If a married couple splits up, they may **divorce**.

split *noun*
> He had a split in the seat of his trousers. slash, slit, tear.

spoil *verb*
> **1** *Bad weather spoiled the holiday.* mar, mess up, ruin, wreck.
> There are many different ways you can spoil things. Here are just a few examples
> You can **burn** or **overdo** or **undercook** things you are cooking.
> You can **blot** or **smudge** your handwriting.
> You can **crease** or **crumple** a clean shirt.
> Vandals may **deface** or **disfigure** a public place.
> You can **interrupt** someone's enjoyment of something.
> **2** *The strawberries will spoil in this wet weather.* go bad, go off, perish, rot.
> AN OPPOSITE IS improve.
> **3** *His parents have spoiled him since he was a baby.* indulge, make a fuss of, pamper.

spoken *adjective*
> Her spoken French is excellent. oral.
> AN OPPOSITE IS written.

sponge *verb*
> **1** *The nurse gently sponged the wound.* clean, mop, wash, wipe.
> **2** *[informal] He's been sponging off his friends for months.* cadge (from), *[informal]* scrounge (from).

spongy *adjective*
> The spongy material quickly soaked up the water. absorbent, porous, soft, springy.

sponsor *noun*
> The money for the pantomime came from local sponsors. backer, benefactor, patron, promoter.

sponsor *verb*
> The event was sponsored by several local firms. back, be a sponsor of, finance, help, promote, subsidize, support.

spontaneous *adjective*
> The audience broke into spontaneous applause. impromptu, impulsive, instinctive, involuntary, natural, unconscious, unplanned, unrehearsed, voluntary.
> An action done without any conscious thought is a **reflex** action.

spoon *noun* SEE **cutlery**

sport *noun*
> I'm not very good at sport. exercise, games, pastime, play, recreation.

> OUTDOOR SPORTS INCLUDE: American football, archery, Association football or soccer, baseball, bowls, canoeing, climbing, cricket, croquet, cross-country running, diving, gliding, golf, hockey, horse racing, jogging, lacrosse, motor racing, mountaineering, netball, orienteering, polo, potholing, rock-climbing, roller skating, rounders, rowing, rugby, sailing or yachting, showjumping, skydiving, surfing or surfriding, swimming, tennis, volleyball, water polo, water-skiing, windsurfing.
> SEE ALSO **athletics**.
>
> INDOOR SPORTS INCLUDE: badminton, basketball, billiards, boxing, darts, gymnastics, martial arts, pool, snooker, squash, table tennis or *[informal]* ping-pong, trampolining, wrestling. ➡

> WINTER SPORTS INCLUDE:
> bobsleigh, ice hockey, skating,
> skiing, tobogganing.
>
> BLOOD SPORTS INCLUDE: beagling,
> fishing, deer hunting, fox hunting,
> shooting.

sporting *adjective*
*It was sporting of him to admit the ball
was out.* fair, generous, honourable.

sportsman, sportswoman *nouns*
contestant, participant, player.

spot *noun*
1 *There were several spots of paint on
the carpet.* blot, blotch, dot, fleck, mark,
smudge, speck, stain.
Small brown spots on your skin are
freckles.
A small dark spot on your skin is a
mole.
A mark you have had on your skin
since you were born is a ***birthmark***.
A small round swelling on your skin is
a ***pimple***.
A lot of spots is a ***rash***.
A disease which gives you a lot of spots
is ***impetigo***.
2 *She felt a few spots of rain.* bead, blob,
drop.
3 *Here's a nice spot for a picnic.* locality,
location, place, position, site, situation.

spot *verb*
1 *She spotted her friend in the crowd.*
catch sight of, distinguish, make out,
note, notice, observe, recognize, see,
sight, spy.
2 *The floor was spotted with paint.* blot,
fleck, mark, mottle, spatter, speckle,
stain.

spotless *adjective*
*He polished his shoes until they were
spotless.* clean, shiny, unmarked.
AN OPPOSITE IS dirty.

spotty *adjective*
She had a pale, spotty complexion.
blotchy, pimply.

spout *noun*
The teapot has a chipped spout. lip,
nozzle, outlet.
A spout carved like an ugly face
sticking out from a church roof is a
gargoyle.

spout *verb*
The volcano spouted ash and lava.
erupt, flow, gush, pour, spurt, squirt,
stream.

sprawl *verb*
1 *We sprawled on the lawn.* flop,
lean back, lie, loll, lounge, recline,
relax, slouch, slump, spread out,
stretch out.
2 *The housing estate had sprawled out
into the countryside.* spread.

spray *verb*
A passing bus sprayed mud over us.
scatter, shower, spatter, splash,
sprinkle.

spray *noun*
1 *The dog shook itself briskly, sending
a spray of water over the floor.*
fountain, mist, shower, splash,
sprinkling.
2 *She arranged a spray of freesias in a
small glass vase.* arrangement,
bouquet, bunch, posy.

spread *verb*
1 *I spread the map on the table.*
arrange, display, lay out, open out,
unfold.
2 *Water leaked out and was spreading
over the floor.* broaden, enlarge,
expand, extend, get bigger or longer or
wider, lengthen.
3 *She's always spreading rumours
about other people.* advertise, circulate,
give out, make known, pass on, pass
round, publicize, transmit.
4 *She spread jam on a piece of toast.*
smear.
5 *He spread the seeds over the ground.*
distribute, scatter.

sprightly *adjective*
She's quite sprightly for her age. active,
agile, brisk, energetic, frisky, lively,
nimble, quick.
AN OPPOSITE IS inactive.

spring *verb*
He sprang over the gate. bound, hop,
jump, leap, vault.
When a cat springs at a mouse, it
pounces.

to spring up 1 *Fast food restaurants have sprung up all over the country.* appear, arise, develop, emerge.
2 *Weeds spring up quickly in damp weather.* germinate, grow, shoot up, sprout.

springy *adjective*
The bed felt soft and springy. bouncy, elastic, flexible, pliable, stretchy.
AN OPPOSITE IS rigid.

sprinkle *verb*
1 *He sprinkled vinegar on his chips.* drip, shower, spatter, splash, spray.
2 *Sprinkle some cheese over the bread and grill for five minutes.* scatter.

sprout *verb*
The seeds will sprout if they are warm and damp. develop, emerge, germinate, grow, shoot up, spring up.

spruce *adjective*
He looked very spruce in a cream linen jacket. clean, elegant, neat, [*informal*] posh, smart, tidy, trim, well-dressed.
AN OPPOSITE IS scruffy.

spur *verb*
The cheers of the crowd spurred them on to greater efforts. egg on, encourage, inspire, prompt, stimulate, urge.

spurt *verb*
1 *Water spurted from the hole.* erupt, flow, gush, shoot out, spout, spray, squirt.
2 *She spurted ahead.* accelerate, go faster, increase speed, quicken, speed up.

spy *noun*
He was accused of being a spy. agent, informer, secret agent.

spy *verb*
She spied a figure in the distance. catch sight of, distinguish, make out, notice, recognize, see, sight, spot.
to spy on someone or **something** *She was sure her neighbours were spying on her.* keep an eye on, keep under surveillance, watch.

squabble *verb*
They were still squabbling about whose turn it was to wash up. argue, fall out, fight, quarrel.

squalid *adjective*
The refugees lived in squalid conditions. degrading, dingy, dirty, filthy, foul, mucky, nasty, unpleasant.
AN OPPOSITE IS clean.

squander *verb*
He squandered his money on an expensive sports car. fritter, misuse, spend unwisely, waste.
AN OPPOSITE IS save.

square *adjective*
All the tiles have square corners. right-angled.
A pattern of squares is a **chequered** pattern.

squarely *adverb*
The ball hit him squarely in the face. directly, exactly, head on, straight.
AN OPPOSITE IS obliquely.

squash *verb*
1 *Don't put tomatoes at the bottom of the bag—they'll get squashed.* crush, flatten, smash.
To squash food, etc., deliberately is to **mash** or **pound** or **pulp** it.
2 *She squashed down her clothes and zipped up the suitcase.* compress, press.
3 *We all squashed into the car.* cram, crowd, pack, squeeze.

squat *verb*
She told us to squat on the ground. crouch, sit.

squat *adjective*
It's hard to look elegant if you have a squat figure like me. dumpy, plump, podgy, portly, stocky.
AN OPPOSITE IS graceful.

squawk, squeak, squeal *nouns, verbs*
FOR VARIOUS WAYS TO MAKE SOUNDS, SEE **sound** *verb*.

squeeze *verb*
1 *She squeezed the water out of the sponge.* compress, press, wring.
2 *The three fat men squeezed into the back seat of the car.* cram, crowd, push, shove, squash, stuff, wedge.
3 *He squeezed her affectionately.* clasp, embrace, hug.
To squeeze something between your thumb and finger is to **pinch** it.

squirm *verb*
She managed to squirm out of his grasp. twist, wriggle, writhe.

squirt *verb*
He dropped the hosepipe, and water squirted all over him. gush, shoot, spout, spray, spurt.

stab *verb*
1 He stabbed the sausage with his fork. impale, jab, pierce, spear.
2 She stabbed a finger at him. push, stick, thrust.

stab *noun*
He felt a sudden stab of pain. pang, prick, sting.

stabilize *verb*
They had to move the cargo to stabilize the ship. balance, keep upright, make stable, steady.
AN OPPOSITE IS upset.

stable *adjective*
1 That ladder isn't very stable. balanced, firm, fixed, solid, steady.
AN OPPOSITE IS wobbly.
2 He's been in a stable relationship for years. durable, established, lasting, permanent, secure, steady.
AN OPPOSITE IS temporary.

stack *noun*
There were stacks of books all over the floor. heap, mound, pile, quantity.
Another word for a stack of hay is a **rick** or **hayrick**.

stack *verb*
Stack the books on the table. assemble, collect, gather, heap up, pile up.

staff *noun*
There was a party at the hospital for the staff. assistants, employees, personnel, team, workers, workforce.
The staff of a school are the **teachers**.
The staff on a ship are the **crew**.

stage *noun*
1 They went up on the stage to collect their prizes. platform.
2 The final stage of the journey was made by coach. leg, period, phase.
3 At this stage of his life, he had been very unhappy. moment, point, step, time.

stage *verb*
1 The show is being staged at the local theatre. perform, present, produce, put on.
2 They decided to stage a protest. arrange, organize.

stagger *verb*
1 He staggered and fell. falter, lurch, reel, stumble, sway, totter, walk unsteadily, waver, wobble.
2 Everyone was staggered at the jury's verdict. amaze, astonish, astound, shake, shock, startle, stun, surprise.

stagnant *adjective*
The water was stagnant and smelt unpleasant. motionless, static, still.
AN OPPOSITE IS flowing.

stain *noun*
He had a large stain on his shirt. blemish, blot, blotch, fleck, mark, smudge, spot.

stain *verb*
1 Her trousers were stained with mud. blacken, dirty, make dirty, mark, soil, tarnish.
2 The wood can be stained a darker shade. colour, dye, paint, tint, varnish.

stair *noun*
She sat down on the bottom stair. step.
A set of stairs taking you from one floor to another is a **flight** of stairs, or a **staircase** or **stairway**.
A moving staircase is an **escalator**.

stake *noun*
The sapling was supported by a stake. pile, pole, post, stave, stick.

stale *adjective*
The bread had gone stale. dry, hard, mouldy, old.
AN OPPOSITE IS fresh.

stalk *noun*
He was chewing a stalk of grass. shoot, stem, twig.

stalk *verb*
1 The lion stalked its prey. follow, hunt, pursue, shadow, tail, track, trail.
2 She turned and stalked out of the room. stride, strut.
FOR VARIOUS WAYS WE WALK, SEE **walk** *verb*.

stall *verb*
> *Don't stall—tell us where he's gone.*
> delay, hang back, hesitate, hold things
> up, pause, put it off.

stammer *verb*
> *He went red and started stammering.*
> falter, splutter, stumble, stutter.

stamp *verb*
> **1** *He stamped on the tent peg to get it in.*
> step, tread.
> **2** *The librarian stamped his library
> book.* mark, print.
> To stamp a postmark on a letter is to
> ***frank*** it.
> To stamp a mark on cattle with a hot
> iron is to ***brand*** them.

stampede *noun*
> *When the alarm went, there was a
> stampede towards the exit.* charge,
> dash, rout, rush.

stand *verb*
> **1** *He was too weak to stand.* get to your
> feet, get up, rise.
> **2** *They stood the ladder against the
> wall.* erect, put up, set up, situate,
> station.
> **3** *The offer still stands.* be unchanged,
> continue, remain valid.
> **4** *She couldn't stand the heat.* abide,
> bear, endure, put up with, suffer,
> tolerate.
> **to stand for something 1** *She won't
> stand for any nonsense.* accept, allow,
> endure, permit, put up with, tolerate.
> **2** *What do these initials stand for?*
> indicate, mean, represent, signify.
> **to stand in for someone** *She stood in
> for the regular teacher.* be a substitute
> for, deputize for, replace, take over
> from.
> **to stand out** *Her clothes made her
> stand out in a crowd.* be obvious, catch
> the eye, show, stick out.
> **to stand up for someone** *He always
> stands up for his friends.* defend, fight
> for, help, look after, protect, shield, side
> with, speak up for, [*informal*] stick up
> for, support.

stand *noun*
> A three-legged stand for a camera, etc.,
> is a ***tripod***.
> A stand for a Bible or other large book
> is a ***lectern***.
> A stand to put a statue on is a
> ***pedestal***.

standard *noun*
> **1** *She praised the high standard of
> their work.* achievement, grade, level.
> **2** *He considered the book good by any
> standard.* guidelines, ideal,
> measurement, model.
> **3** *The soldiers carried their standard
> proudly.* colours, flag.

standard *adjective*
> *He did it according to the standard
> procedure.* accepted, approved, basic,
> common, conventional, customary,
> established, familiar, habitual, normal,
> official, ordinary, orthodox, recognized,
> regular, routine, traditional, typical,
> usual.
> AN OPPOSITE IS abnormal.

standby *noun*
> *They need a standby in case someone
> drops out.* replacement, reserve,
> substitute.

standstill *noun*
> **to come to a standstill** *The traffic
> came to a standstill.* draw up, halt, pull
> up, stop.

staple *adjective*
> *Rice is the staple diet in many
> countries.* chief, main, principal,
> standard.

star *noun*
> **1** *Astronomers study the stars.*
> FOR ASTRONOMICAL TERMS, SEE
> **astronomy**.
> FOR SIGNS OF THE ZODIAC, SEE
> **Zodiac**.
> A mark in the shape of a star in a piece
> of writing is an ***asterisk***.
> **2** *Many stars attended the premiere of
> the film.* celebrity, idol, personality.

stare *verb*
What are you staring at? contemplate, examine, gape at, gaze at, keep your eyes on, look at, peer at, scrutinize, study, watch.
To stare angrily at someone is to *glare* at them.

start *verb*
1 *They were ready to start work.* begin, commence, [*informal*] get cracking on, get going on.
AN OPPOSITE IS finish.
2 *He plans to start a new business.* create, establish, found, initiate, institute, introduce, launch, open, originate, set up.
AN OPPOSITE IS close.
3 *She started when the gun went off.* flinch, jerk, jump, recoil, spring up, twitch, wince.

start *noun*
1 *The start of something new is always exciting.* beginning, birth, commencement, creation, dawn, establishment, initiation, introduction, launch, opening.
AN OPPOSITE IS finish.
2 *His father gave him a start in business.* advantage, opportunity.
3 *The explosion gave him a nasty start.* jolt, jump, shock, surprise.

startle *verb*
The sudden noise startled them. agitate, alarm, frighten, make you jump, make you start, scare, shock, surprise, take you by surprise, upset.

starvation *noun*
The refugees were dying of starvation. famine, hunger, malnutrition.

starve *verb*
Many animals will starve if the drought continues. die of starvation, go hungry, go without, perish.
To choose to go without food is to *fast*.
If prisoners protest by starving themselves, they are **on hunger strike**.

starving *adjective* [*informal*]
What's for dinner? I'm starving! famished, hungry, [*informal*] peckish, ravenous.

state *noun*
1 *The building was in a bad state.* condition, shape.
The state of a person or animal is their *fitness* or *health*.
2 *He was in a terrible state!* [*informal*] flap, panic, plight, situation.
3 *The queen is the head of state.* country, nation.
SEE ALSO **country**.

state *verb*
The prime minister stated that the election would be held in May. announce, communicate, declare, proclaim, pronounce, put into words, report, say.

stately *adjective*
They admired the stately way she walked into the room. dignified, elegant, formal, grand, imposing, impressive, majestic, noble, solemn, splendid.
AN OPPOSITE IS informal.

statement *noun*
The minister made a statement about the new policy. announcement, bulletin, communication, declaration, explanation, message, notice, proclamation, pronouncement.

station *noun*
1 *The train stopped at the station.*
The station at the end of a line is the *terminus*.
A small platform without any station buildings is a *halt*.
FOR OTHER WORDS TO DO WITH RAILWAYS, SEE ALSO **railway**.
2 *They were taken to the police station.* depot, headquarters.
3 *She enjoyed listening to the local radio station.* channel.

station *verb*
They stationed a lookout on the roof. locate, place, position, put, situate, stand.

stationary *adjective*
The car was stationary at the traffic lights. at a standstill, at rest, halted, immobile, motionless, parked, standing, static, still, unmoving.
AN OPPOSITE IS moving.

stationery noun

KINDS OF STATIONERY: cards,
computer paper, copier paper,
envelopes, exercise books, jotters,
postcards, writing paper.

statistics plural noun
The newspaper reported the latest crime
statistics. data, figures, numbers.

statue noun
There a statue of Lord Nelson in
Trafalgar Square. carving, figure,
sculpture.

status noun
They discussed the changing status of
women in society. grade, importance,
level, position, prestige, rank.

staunch adjective
He's a staunch supporter of the team.
constant, dependable, faithful, firm,
loyal, reliable, sound, strong.
AN OPPOSITE IS unreliable.

stave verb
to stave something off They did all
they could to stave off disaster. avert,
avoid, fend off, prevent, ward off.

stay verb
1 She stayed late at the office. continue,
hang about, remain, wait.
AN OPPOSITE IS depart.
2 He planned to stay in the town for the
rest of his life. carry on, live, reside,
settle, stop.
3 They are going to stay in a hotel. be
accommodated, board, lodge.

stay noun
She came for a short stay. holiday, stop,
visit.

steady adjective
1 Is the ladder steady? balanced, fast,
firm, safe, secure, settled, solid, stable.
AN OPPOSITE IS wobbly.
2 They need a steady supply of water.
ceaseless, continuous, dependable,
non-stop, reliable, uninterrupted.
AN OPPOSITE IS unreliable.
3 They kept up a steady pace. constant,
even, regular, rhythmic, unchanging,
unvarying.
AN OPPOSITE IS irregular.

steady verb
She tried to steady the boat. balance,
stabilize.

steal verb
1 He stole some money from her. rob,
take.
INFORMAL OR SLANG SYNONYMS:
knock off, lift, make off with, nick,
pinch, swipe, whip.
SEE ALSO **stealing**.
2 She stole quietly upstairs. creep,
move stealthily, slink, slip, sneak,
tiptoe.

stealing noun
The police accused him of stealing.
robbery, theft.

VARIOUS KINDS OF STEALING:
Stealing from someone's home is
burglary or **housebreaking**.
Stealing from someone in the street
is **mugging** or **picking someone's
pocket**.
Stealing from a shop is **shoplifting**.
Stealing from homes or shops during
a riot is **looting**.
Stealing small things is **pilfering**.
Stealing fruit from people's gardens
is **scrumping**.
Stealing fish or game on someone
else's land is **poaching**.
Stealing from ships at sea is **piracy**.
Stealing from the funds of a business
is **embezzlement**.

stealthy adjective
Why did you sneak out in that stealthy
manner? cautious, furtive,
inconspicuous, quiet, secret, secretive,
sly, [informal] sneaky, underhand.
AN OPPOSITE IS conspicuous.

steam noun
She couldn't see through the steam.
haze, mist, smoke, vapour.
Steam on a cold window is
condensation.

steamy adjective
1 The bathroom gets steamy when he
has a hot shower. close, damp, humid,
moist, muggy.
2 She wiped the steamy mirror. cloudy,
hazy, misty.

steep *adjective*
Climbing up the steep slope exhausted them. abrupt, sharp, sudden, uphill.
Something such as a cliff which goes straight up is **sheer** or **vertical**.
AN OPPOSITE IS gradual.

steer *verb*
He steered the car into the garage. direct, guide.
To steer a car is to **drive** it.
To steer a boat is to **navigate** or **pilot** it.

stem *noun*
The gardener pulled out the dead stems. branch, shoot, stalk, twig.
The main stem of a tree is its **trunk**.

step *noun*
1 *The baby took her first steps yesterday.* footstep, pace, stride.
2 *She stood on the bottom step.* doorstep, stair.
A set of steps going from one floor of a building to another is a **staircase**.
A folding set of steps is a **stepladder**.
The steps of a ladder are the **rungs**.
3 *Just take it one step at a time.* action, phase, stage.

step *verb*
Don't step in the mud! put your foot, stamp, trample, tread, walk.
to step something up *They stepped up the pressure.* boost, increase, intensify, strengthen.

sterile *adjective*
1 *Very little grows in the sterile soil of the desert.* arid, barren, dry, infertile, lifeless.
AN OPPOSITE IS fertile.
2 *The nurse put a sterile bandage on the wound.* antiseptic, clean, disinfected, germ-free, hygienic, sterilized.
AN OPPOSITE IS infected.

sterilize *verb*
1 *He sterilized the equipment before conducting the experiment.* clean, decontaminate, disinfect, make sterile.
Milk is partially sterilized by **pasteurizing** it.
AN OPPOSITE IS infect.

2 *The vet is going to sterilize the cat.* neuter.
To sterilize a male horse is to **geld** it.
To sterilize a female animal is to **spay** it.

stern *adjective*
He gave them a stern look. disapproving, grim, hard, harsh, severe, strict, unsmiling.
AN OPPOSITE IS lenient.

stew *verb*
FOR VARIOUS WAYS TO COOK FOOD, SEE **cook** *verb*.

steward, stewardess *nouns*
A steward on a ship, etc., is an **attendant** or a **waiter** or **waitress**.
A steward at a football ground, etc., is an **official**.

stick *noun*
They collected sticks to make a fire. branch, stalk, twig.

KINDS OF STICK MADE FOR VARIOUS PURPOSES: bar, bat, baton, cane, club, hockey stick, pole, rod, staff, stilt, walking stick, wand.

stick *verb*
1 *He stuck his fork into the potato.* dig, jab, poke, prod, stab, thrust.
To stick something into a tyre, etc., is to **puncture** it.
2 *She tried to stick the pieces of the broken vase together.* cement, fasten, glue, join.
To stick pieces of metal together using heat is to **fuse** or **weld** them.
3 *The stamp wouldn't stick to the envelope.* adhere, cling.
4 *The door was always sticking.* become jammed, become wedged.
5 *He can't stick people who are always complaining.* abide, bear, endure, put up with, stand, tolerate.
to stick out *The shelf sticks out too far.* jut, overhang, poke out, project, protrude.
to stick up for [*informal*] *She stuck up for him when he was in trouble.* defend, fight for, help, look after, protect, shield, side with, speak up for, stand up for, support.

sticky *adjective*
1 *She secured the parcel with sticky tape.* adhesive, glued, gummed.
AN OPPOSITE IS non-adhesive.
Paint that is still wet is said to be *tacky*.
2 *They didn't like the hot sticky weather.* clammy, damp, humid, moist, muggy, steamy, sweaty.
AN OPPOSITE IS dry.
3 [*informal*] *The criminal came to a sticky end.* dreadful, grisly, gruesome, horrible, nasty, unpleasant.

stiff *adjective*
1 *Stir the flour and water to a stiff paste.* firm, hard, solid.
AN OPPOSITE IS soft.
2 *He mounted the picture on stiff card.* inflexible, rigid, thick.
AN OPPOSITE IS pliable.
3 *Her muscles were stiff after the long walk.* aching, painful, taut, tight.
AN OPPOSITE IS supple.
4 *It was a stiff exam.* difficult, hard, severe, tough.
AN OPPOSITE IS easy.
5 *His stiff manner made him hard to talk to.* awkward, cold, formal, tense, unfriendly, unnatural, wooden.
AN OPPOSITE IS relaxed.
6 *The judge imposed a stiff penalty.* harsh, severe, strict.
AN OPPOSITE IS lenient.
7 *A stiff wind was blowing.* brisk, fresh, strong.
AN OPPOSITE IS gentle.

stifle *verb*
1 *He was almost stifled by the fumes.* choke, suffocate.
To kill someone by stopping their breathing is to *strangle* or *throttle* them.
2 *She stifled a yawn.* check, cover up, curb, hold back, repress, restrain, suppress.

still *adjective*
1 *He sat still and said nothing.* motionless, unmoving.
2 *It was a beautiful still evening.* calm, hushed, noiseless, peaceful, placid, quiet, restful, serene, silent, tranquil, untroubled, windless.

still *verb*
She tried to still my fears. calm, lull, quieten, settle, soothe.
AN OPPOSITE IS agitate.

stimulate *verb*
1 *His experiences stimulated him to write a book on the subject.* encourage, inspire, spur.
2 *The exhibition stimulated her interest in painting.* arouse, excite, provoke, rouse, stir up, whip up.
AN OPPOSITE IS discourage.

stimulus *noun*
The prize acted as a stimulus to the competitors. encouragement, incentive, inducement, inspiration.

sting *verb*
1 *He was stung by a bee.* bite, nip.
2 *The smoke made her eyes sting.* hurt, smart, tingle.

stingy *adjective*
He's too stingy to give money to charity. mean, [*informal*] mingy, miserly, selfish, tight, uncharitable, ungenerous.
AN OPPOSITE IS generous.

stink *noun*
The stink from the rubbish tip was overpowering. odour, smell, stench.
SEE ALSO **smell** *noun*.

stink *verb*
The room stank of rotting food. reek, smell.

stir *verb*
1 *Pour in the cream and stir the mixture well.* agitate, beat, blend, mix, whisk.
2 *He stirred in his sleep.* begin to move, change position, move, shift, toss, turn.
to stir something up *She's always stirring up trouble.* arouse, cause, encourage, excite, provoke, set off, stimulate, whip up.

stir *noun*
The news caused quite a stir. commotion, excitement, fuss, hullabaloo.

stock *noun*
  1 *Stocks of food were running low.*
  hoard, reserve, stockpile, store, supply.
  2 *The shopkeeper arranged his new stock.* goods, merchandise, wares.
  3 *The farmer took some of his stock to market.* animals, beasts, cattle, flocks, herds, livestock.
  4 *The duke is descended from royal stock.* ancestors, ancestry, family, line.

stock *verb*
  Most supermarkets now stock organic fruit and vegetables. deal in, handle, keep in stock, sell, trade in.

stocky *adjective*
  He had a strong stocky body. compact, dumpy, solid, squat, sturdy.
  AN OPPOSITE IS thin.

stodgy *adjective*
  1 *The food was extremely stodgy.* filling, heavy, indigestible, solid, starchy.
  AN OPPOSITE IS light.
  2 *He thought the book was a bit stodgy.* boring, dull, slow, tedious, unexciting, uninteresting.
  AN OPPOSITE IS lively.

stoke *verb*
  She stoked the fire to warm up the room. keep burning, put fuel on, tend.

stomach *noun*
  The part of the body that contains the stomach is the **abdomen**.
  Informal or slang synonyms are belly, guts, insides, paunch, tummy.

stomach *verb* [*informal*]
  I can't stomach any more of his rudeness! bear, put up with, take, tolerate.

stone *noun*

STONES USED BY BUILDERS: block, flagstone, sett, slab, slate.
A large lump of stone is a **rock**.
A large rounded stone is a **boulder**.
Small rounded stones are **pebbles**.
Small pieces of broken stone are **chippings**.
A mixture of sand and small stones is **gravel**.
Pebbles on the beach are **shingle**.
Round stones used to pave a path, etc., are **cobbles**. ➡

SEE ALSO **rock** *noun*.

STONES USED TO MAKE JEWELLERY, ETC.: gem, jewel, semi-precious stone.
SEE ALSO **jewel**.

stony *adjective*
  1 *The waves broke over the stony beach.* pebbly, rocky, rough, shingly.
  AN OPPOSITE IS sandy.
  2 *He gave me a stony look and said nothing.* cold, expressionless, hard, hostile, indifferent, uncaring, unemotional, unfriendly.
  AN OPPOSITE IS friendly.

stoop *verb*
  The doorway was so low that he had to stoop to go in. bend, bow, duck, hunch your shoulders, lean forward.

stop *verb*
  1 *Stop what you are doing.* break off, cease, conclude, end, finish, [*informal*] knock off, leave off, quit, suspend, terminate.
  AN OPPOSITE IS start.
  2 *The manager stopped the thief before he could escape.* arrest, capture, catch, detain, grab, hold, seize.
  3 *You can't stop me from going.* prevent.
  4 *How do you stop this machine?* immobilize, turn off.
  5 *Wait for the bus to stop.* come to rest, draw up, halt, pull up.
  6 *He tried to stop the leak in the pipe.* block up, bung up, close, plug, seal.
  7 *They planned to stop in London for a few days.* spend some time, stay.

stop *noun*
  1 *Everything suddenly came to a stop.* conclusion, end, finish, halt, standstill.
  2 *They drove down through France, with a short stop in Paris.* break, interval, pause.
  3 *This is my stop.* destination, station.

store *verb*
  Squirrels need to store food for the winter. hoard, put away, reserve, save, set aside, stock up, stow away.

store *noun*
  1 *The building is now used as a grain store.*

VARIOUS PLACES WHERE PEOPLE
STORE THINGS: armoury, arsenal,
barn, cache, cellar, cold storage,
depot, granary, larder, pantry,
repository, safe, silo, stockroom,
storage, storehouse, storeroom,
strongroom, treasury, vault,
warehouse.

---

  2 *He kept a large store of wine in the cellar.* accumulation, hoard, quantity, reserve, stock, stockpile, supply.
  3 *He's the manager of the local grocery store.* SEE **shop** *noun.*

storey *noun*
  The new building has six storeys. floor, level.

storm *noun*
  1 *Crops were damaged in the heavy storms.* tempest.

VARIOUS KINDS OF STORM: blizzard,
cyclone, deluge, dust-storm, gale,
hurricane, rainstorm, sandstorm,
squall, thunderstorm, tornado,
typhoon, whirlwind.
The effect of a storm when you are in
an aircraft is *turbulence*.
An old word for storm is *tempest*.

---

  2 *Plans to close the library caused a storm of protest.* eruption, outburst, tumult.

storm *verb*
  The soldiers stormed the castle. charge at, rush at.

stormy *adjective*
  1 *It was a dark, stormy night.* blustery, choppy, gusty, raging, rough, squally, tempestuous, wild, windy.
  AN OPPOSITE IS calm.
  2 *Several arguments broke out at the stormy meeting.* angry, bad-tempered, disorderly, ill-tempered, quarrelsome, turbulent.
  AN OPPOSITE IS orderly.

story *noun*
  1 *Tell me a story.* tale, [*informal*] yarn.

VARIOUS KINDS OF STORY: crime
story, detective story, fable, fairy
tale, fantasy, folk tale, legend,
mystery, myth, novel, parable,
romance, saga, science fiction or SF,
thriller.
Invented stories are all kinds of
fiction.

---

  2 *The book tells the story of her childhood in New York.* account, history, narrative.
  A story of a person's life is a *biography*.
  The story of your life told by yourself is your *autobiography*.
  3 *It was the front-page story in all the papers.* article, feature, news item, report.
  4 [*informal*] *She's been telling stories again.* fib, lie.

stout *adjective*
  1 *He was a stout man with grey hair.* chubby, dumpy, fat, heavy, overweight, plump, portly, stocky, well-built.
  AN OPPOSITE IS thin.
  2 *They wore stout walking boots.* robust, sound, strong, sturdy, substantial, thick, tough.
  AN OPPOSITE IS weak.
  3 *They put up a stout resistance.* bold, brave, courageous, determined, fearless, gallant, heroic, intrepid, plucky, resolute, valiant.
  AN OPPOSITE IS cowardly.

stove *noun*
  A stove used for heating is a *boiler* or *furnace*.
  A stove used for cooking is a *cooker* or an *oven*.
  An old-fashioned cooking stove is a *range*.

stow *verb*
  1 *He stowed the luggage in the boot.* pack, pile, load.
  2 *They stowed the books in the attic.* put away, store.

straggle *verb*
  1 *Brambles straggled across the path.* grow untidily, spread out, trail.
  2 *The children straggled behind her.* dawdle, fall behind, lag, loiter, ramble about, stray, wander.

straight *adjective*
1 *They walked in a straight line.* direct, unswerving.
AN OPPOSITE IS crooked.
2 *It took a long time to get the room straight.* neat, orderly, tidy.
AN OPPOSITE IS untidy.
3 *She found it difficult to get a straight answer from him.* blunt, frank, honest, outspoken, plain, sincere, straightforward.
AN OPPOSITE IS dishonest.

straightforward *adjective*
He's a very straightforward man. blunt, direct, frank, genuine, honest, open, plain, simple, sincere, straight, truthful, uncomplicated.
AN OPPOSITE IS devious.

strain *verb*
1 *The dog was straining at its lead, eager to be off.* haul, pull, stretch, tug.
2 *People were straining to see what was going on.* attempt, endeavour, exert yourself, make an effort, struggle, try.
3 *Take it easy and don't strain yourself.* exhaust, tire out, weaken, wear out, weary.

strain *noun*
The strain of his job was too much for him. anxiety, difficulty, hardship, pressure, stress, tension, worry.

strand *noun*
The strands of the rope began to come apart. fibre, filament, thread.

stranded *adjective*
1 *A ship was stranded on the beach.* aground, [*informal*] high and dry, stuck.
2 *He was stranded in London without any money.* abandoned, alone, deserted, helpless, in difficulties, lost, marooned, without help.

strange *adjective*
1 *A strange thing happened this morning.* abnormal, curious, exceptional, extraordinary, funny, odd, out of the ordinary, queer, remarkable, singular, surprising, uncommon, unexpected, unfamiliar, unnatural, unusual.
If something is like nothing else, it is ***unique***.

2 *He's a very strange man.* eccentric, peculiar, unconventional, weird, zany.
3 *I heard strange noises in the night.* baffling, bewildering, eerie, inexplicable, mysterious, mystifying, perplexing, puzzling, sinister, uncanny.
AN OPPOSITE IS familiar or ordinary.

stranger *noun*
Please help me find the way—I'm a stranger here. alien, foreigner, guest, newcomer, outsider, visitor.

strangle *verb*
The victim had been strangled. throttle.

OTHER WAYS TO KILL PEOPLE BY STOPPING THEIR BREATHING: choke, smother, stifle, suffocate.

strap *noun*
He fastened a leather strap around his case. band, belt.

strategy *noun*
The government are developing a new strategy for dealing with unemployment. approach, method, plan, policy, procedure, programme, scheme, tactics.

stratum *noun*
You can see different strata of rock in the cliff. layer, seam, thickness, vein.

stray *verb*
Tourists sometimes stray into dangerous areas. get lost, go astray, meander, ramble, range, roam, rove, straggle, wander.

streak *noun*
1 *He had a streak of red paint on his face.* band, line, smear, stain, strip, stripe.
2 *There's a streak of selfishness in her character.* element, trace.

streak *verb*
1 *Rain had begun to streak the window panes.* smear, smudge, stain.
2 *Cars streaked past.* dash, flash, fly, hurtle, move at speed, rush, speed, tear, zoom.

streaky *adjective*
The kitchen wallpaper was old and streaky with grease. smeary, smudged, streaked.

stream *noun*
1 *A stream flowed down the valley.*
brook, small river.
In northern England, a stream is a
beck.
In Scotland, a stream is a ***burn***.
2 *The dinghy was carried along with
the stream.* current, flow, tide.
3 *A stream of water poured through the
hole.* cataract, flood, gush, jet, rush,
torrent.
4 *There was a steady stream of visitors.*
line, series, string, succession.

stream *verb*
Water streamed through the hole. flood,
flow, gush, issue, pour, run, spill, spout,
spurt, squirt.

streamlined *adjective*
The new trains are streamlined.
A formal word is ***aerodynamic***.
AN OPPOSITE IS air resistant.

street *noun* SEE **road**

strength *noun*
1 *Despite being a small woman she still
had great strength.* fitness, might,
muscle, power, sturdiness, toughness.
2 *Patience is her greatest strength.*
advantage, asset, virtue.
AN OPPOSITE IS weakness.

strengthen *verb*
1 *Regular exercise strengthens the
muscles.* build up, harden, make
stronger, toughen.
2 *They need to strengthen their defence.*
back up, bolster, fortify, prop up,
reinforce.
AN OPPOSITE IS weaken.

strenuous *adjective*
1 *They made strenuous efforts to
improve security after the break-in.*
determined, energetic, resolute,
strong, tireless, vigorous.
AN OPPOSITE IS feeble.
2 *He was advised to avoid strenuous
exercise.* demanding, difficult,
exhausting, hard, laborious, tiring,
tough, uphill.
AN OPPOSITE IS easy.

stress *noun*
1 *High winds put great stress on the
structure of the building.* force,
pressure.
2 *Stress made him ill.* anxiety, strain,
tension, worry.
3 *He puts great stress on the need for
discipline.* emphasis, importance.

stress *verb*
*She stressed the importance of a
healthy diet.* draw attention to,
emphasize, show clearly, underline.

stretch *verb*
1 *She stretched the piece of elastic until
it snapped.* draw out, elongate, expand,
extend, lengthen, pull out.
2 *She stretched her arms wide.* extend,
open out, spread out.
3 *The road stretched into the distance.*
continue, disappear, go on and on.

stretch *noun*
1 *He had a 2-year stretch in the army.*
period, spell, time.
2 *There are often accidents on this
stretch of road.* length, piece, section.
3 *It's a beautiful stretch of countryside.*
area, expanse, tract.

strict *adjective*
1 *The club has strict rules about
smoking.* [*informal*] hard and fast,
inflexible, rigid.
AN OPPOSITE IS flexible.
2 *His father was very strict.* firm,
harsh, severe, stern.
AN OPPOSITE IS lenient.
3 *He used the word in its strict scientific
sense.* complete, exact, precise.
AN OPPOSITE IS approximate.

stride *noun*
He took two strides forward. pace, step.

strife *noun*
*There has been a great deal of strife
within the company.* arguments,
conflict, disagreements, fighting,
friction, hostility, quarrelling.

strike *verb*
1 *She fell, and struck her head on the floor.* bang, bump, crack, hit, knock, [*informal*] wallop, whack.
SEE ALSO **hit** *verb*.
2 *The enemy struck for the second time in a week.* attack.
3 *The clock struck one.* chime, ring.
4 *Workers threatened to strike over the proposed job losses.* stop work, take industrial action, withdraw labour.

strike *noun*
During the strike, no buses were running. industrial action, stoppage, withdrawal of labour.

striking *adjective*
Her most striking feature was her long, curly red hair. conspicuous, distinctive, effective, interesting, noticeable, obvious, outstanding, prominent, remarkable.
AN OPPOSITE IS inconspicuous.

string *noun*
1 *She tied some string round the box.* cord, line, rope, twine.
FOR MUSICAL INSTRUMENTS WITH STRINGS, SEE **music**.
2 *The incident was the latest in a string of burglaries.* chain, sequence, series, succession.

string *verb*
She strung the beads together. connect, join, link, thread.

stringy *adjective*
This meat is very stringy. chewy, fibrous, tough.
AN OPPOSITE IS tender.

strip *verb*
1 *He stripped the paper off the parcel.* peel, remove.
AN OPPOSITE IS wrap.
2 *He stripped and got into the bath.* get undressed, undress.
AN OPPOSITE IS dress.

strip *noun*
A strip of carpet covered the hall floor. band, bit, piece, ribbon.

stripe *noun*
The tablecloth was white with blue stripes. band, bar, line, strip.

strive *verb*
They were striving to finish the decorations in time for the party. aim, attempt, make an effort, try hard.

stroke *noun*
1 *He split the log with a single stroke.* action, blow, effort, hit, movement.
2 *She added a few quick pencil strokes to her drawing.* line, mark.

stroke *verb*
She was curled up on the sofa, stroking the cat. caress, pat, rub, touch.

stroll *verb*
They strolled quietly home. amble, saunter, walk slowly.
SEE ALSO **walk**.

strong *adjective*
The adjective *strong* can be used in many senses. Here are some of the most important ones
1 *He became very strong after taking up weightlifting.* [*informal*] beefy, brawny, burly, fit, hefty, mighty, muscular, powerful, robust, sturdy, tough, well-built, wiry.
2 *The chair wasn't strong enough and broke when he sat on it.* durable, hard-wearing, stout, substantial.
3 *He made a strong effort to improve.* determined, forceful, resolute, vigorous.
4 *The lights were too strong.* bright, brilliant, clear, dazzling, glaring.
5 *The cheese had a strong taste.* definite, highly-flavoured, hot, obvious, overpowering, pronounced, spicy, unmistakable.
6 *The drink was too strong for her.* alcoholic, intoxicating.
7 *The police have strong evidence that she's guilty.* convincing, persuasive, solid, sound, valid.
8 *He's a strong supporter of the team.* avid, enthusiastic, fervent, genuine, keen, passionate, zealous.
AN OPPOSITE IS weak or feeble or flimsy.

stronghold *noun*
They besieged the enemy stronghold for months. castle, fort, fortress, garrison.

structure *noun*
1 *The cathedral is a magnificent structure.* building, construction, framework.
FOR VARIOUS KINDS OF STRUCTURE, SEE **building**.
2 *She explained the structure of the poem.* arrangement, composition, design, organization, plan, shape.

struggle *verb*
1 *He was struggling to get free.* endeavour, fight, make an effort, strain, strive, try hard, tussle, wrestle, wriggle about, writhe about.
2 *She had to struggle through deep mud.* flounder, stagger, stumble, wallow.

struggle *noun*
After a long struggle she got what she wanted. battle, contest, fight, match, [*informal*] scrap, tussle.

stubborn *adjective*
He's too stubborn to give in now. defiant, difficult, disobedient, inflexible, obstinate, pig-headed, uncooperative, wilful.
AN OPPOSITE IS docile.

stuck-up *adjective* [*informal*]
Nobody likes her—she's so stuck-up. arrogant, [*informal*] cocky, conceited, haughty, pompous, [*informal*] posh, proud, self-important, snobbish, superior.
AN OPPOSITE IS humble.

student *noun*
A student at school is a ***pupil***.
A old word for a pupil is ***scholar***.
A student at university is an ***undergraduate***.

studious *adjective*
She's a quiet, studious girl. academic, [*informal*] brainy, clever, intellectual, scholarly, thoughtful.

study *verb*
1 *He went to university to study medicine.* learn about, research into.
2 *They studied the evidence carefully.* analyse, consider, contemplate, enquire into, examine, investigate, look closely at, read carefully, scrutinize, survey, think about.
3 *She has to study for her exams.* cram, revise, [*informal*] swot.

stuff *noun*
1 *What's this stuff in the saucepan?* matter, substance.
2 *That's his stuff on the table.* articles, belongings, gear, possessions, things.

stuff *verb*
1 *She managed to stuff everything in the suitcase.* compress, cram, force, jam, pack, push, ram, shove, squeeze, stow.
2 *The cushions are stuffed with foam rubber.* fill, pad.

stuffy *adjective*
1 *Open a window—it's stuffy in here.* airless, close, [*informal*] fuggy, humid, muggy, musty, stale, unventilated.
AN OPPOSITE IS airy.
2 *She found the lecture a bit stuffy.* boring, dreary, dull, formal, humourless, pompous, stodgy.
AN OPPOSITE IS informal or lively.

stumble *verb*
1 *He stumbled on a tree root.* flounder, lurch, stagger, totter, trip.
2 *She stumbled over her words.* falter, hesitate, stammer, stutter.
to stumble across something *He stumbled across some old photos.* come across, dig up, discover, encounter, find, unearth.

stump *verb*
They were all stumped by the problem. baffle, bewilder, defeat, fox, mystify, outwit, perplex, puzzle.

stun *verb*
1 *The blow stunned him.* daze, knock out, knock senseless, make unconscious.
2 *She was stunned by the news.* amaze, astonish, astound, bewilder, confuse, shake, shock, stagger, surprise.

stunt *noun*
We watched the daredevils performing their stunts. exploit, feat, trick.

stupendous *adjective*
Everyone congratulated her on her stupendous achievement. amazing, colossal, enormous, exceptional, extraordinary, huge, incredible, marvellous, miraculous, notable, phenomenal, remarkable, sensational, singular, special, staggering, tremendous, unbelievable, wonderful.
AN OPPOSITE IS ordinary.

stupid *adjective*
1 He's such a stupid man.
All these words can be insulting, and some can be more insulting than others. Many are informal. Therefore you need to think carefully how you use them brainless, dense, dim, dopey, dull, dumb, feeble-minded, foolish, half-witted, idiotic, ignorant, mindless, moronic, naïve, silly, simple, slow, thick, unintelligent, unwise.
2 It was a stupid thing to do. absurd, crazy, daft, irrational, laughable, ludicrous, [informal] mad, pointless, rash, reckless, ridiculous, senseless, thoughtless.
AN OPPOSITE IS intelligent.

sturdy *adjective*
1 She is short and sturdy. athletic, brawny, burly, healthy, hefty, husky, muscular, powerful, robust, stocky, strong, vigorous, well-built.
AN OPPOSITE IS weak.
2 She bought some sturdy walking boots. durable, solid, sound, substantial, tough, well made.
AN OPPOSITE IS flimsy.

stutter *verb*
She tends to stutter when she's nervous. stammer, stumble.

style *noun*
1 He doesn't like the new styles of clothes. design, fashion, pattern.
2 The book is written in an informal style. manner, tone, way, wording.
3 He dresses with great style. elegance, sophistication, stylishness, taste.

stylish *adjective*
She always wears stylish clothes. chic, elegant, fashionable, modern, smart, sophisticated, [informal] trendy, up to date.
AN OPPOSITE IS old-fashioned.

subdue *verb*
1 The army managed to subdue the rebels. beat, conquer, control, crush, defeat, overcome, overpower, vanquish.
2 He tried to subdue his anger. check, curb, hold back, quieten, repress, restrain, suppress.

subdued *adjective*
They were all in a subdued mood. depressed, grave, quiet, serious, silent, sober, solemn, thoughtful.
AN OPPOSITE IS excited.

subject *noun*
1 She had strong views on the subject. issue, matter, point, question, theme, topic.
2 Maths is his favourite subject.

SUBJECTS WHICH STUDENTS STUDY: agriculture, anatomy, anthropology, archaeology, architecture, art, astronomy, biology, botany, business studies, chemistry, classics, computing, domestic science, drama, economics, electronics, engineering, English, environmental science, foreign languages, geography, geology, history, law, mathematics, medicine, music, pharmacy, philosophy, physics, politics, psychology, religious studies, science, scripture, sociology, sport, surveying, technology, theology, zoology.

3 They are British subjects. citizen, passport-holder.

subject *verb*
They subjected him to a string of questions. expose, submit.

subjective *adjective*
1 Our reactions to music are bound to be subjective. emotional, in the mind, instinctive, intuitive.
2 It was a very subjective account of what had happened. biased, prejudiced.
AN OPPOSITE IS objective.

submerge *verb*
1 *He watched the submarine submerge.*
dive, go under.
2 *They feared that the flood would submerge the village.* cover, drown, engulf, immerse, inundate, overwhelm, swallow up, swamp.

submission *noun*
1 *They starved the town into submission.* giving in, surrender.
2 *The judge accepted counsel's submission.* claim, idea, presentation, proposal, suggestion.

submissive *adjective*
He's too submissive—he needs to stand up for himself. docile, gentle, humble, meek, obedient, passive, tame, uncomplaining.
AN OPPOSITE IS assertive.

submit *verb*
1 *They finally submitted to the enemy.* give in, surrender, yield.
2 *He submitted the plans to the council for approval.* give in, hand in, present.

subordinate *adjective*
1 *An officer can give orders to soldiers of subordinate rank.* inferior, junior, lesser, lower.
AN OPPOSITE IS higher or superior.
2 *The other issues are subordinate to that one.* minor, secondary, subsidiary.
AN OPPOSITE IS major.

subscribe *verb*
to subscribe to *She subscribes to several good causes.* contribute to, donate to, give to, pay a subscription to, support.

subscriber *noun*
The book club sent a letter to all its subscribers. patron, regular customer, supporter.

subscription *noun*
He couldn't afford the club subscription. contribution, fee, regular payment.

subside *verb*
1 *The wall cracked when the house subsided.* settle, sink.
2 *When the rain stopped the flood began to subside.* decline, ebb, fall, go down, recede, shrink.
3 *The pain eventually subsided.* decrease, diminish, dwindle, lessen, moderate, wear off.

subsidize *verb*
The project was subsidized by the government. back, finance, sponsor, support.

subsidy *noun*
Public transport gets a subsidy from taxes. backing, financial help or support, a grant.

substance *noun*
1 *The scientists couldn't identify the substance.* material, matter, stuff.
2 *What was the substance of the book?* essence, gist, subject matter, theme.

substantial *adjective*
1 *He gave them a substantial amount of money.* big, considerable, generous, large, significant, sizeable, worthwhile.
AN OPPOSITE IS small.
2 *He built a substantial fence to keep the cattle out.* durable, hefty, solid, sound, strong, sturdy, well made.
AN OPPOSITE IS flimsy.

substitute *verb*
1 *In most recipes you can substitute margarine for butter.* exchange, [*informal*] swap.
Other ways you can express the example sentence are: *Margarine can take the place of butter*, or *You can replace butter with margarine*.
2 *He substituted for the injured goalkeeper.* deputize, stand in, take the place (of).

substitute *noun*
They had to bring on a substitute during the match. deputy, replacement, reserve, standby.
A substitute for a regular teacher is a ***supply teacher***.
A substitute for a sick actor is an ***understudy***.
A substitute for a thing that isn't available is an ***alternative***.

subtle *adjective*
1 *There was a subtle smell of perfume in the room.* delicate, faint, mild, slight.
2 *His jokes are too subtle for them.* ingenious, sophisticated.
3 *He gave her a subtle hint.* gentle, indirect, tactful.
AN OPPOSITE IS obvious.

subtract *verb*
Subtract 5 from 20 and you have 15 left. deduct, remove, take away.
AN OPPOSITE IS add.

suburbs *plural noun*
They lived in the suburbs of the city. fringes, outer areas, outlying areas, outskirts.
The suburbs of large towns are also known as **suburbia**.

succeed *verb*
1 *You have to work hard if you want to succeed.* be successful, do well, flourish, [*informal*] make it, prosper, thrive.
2 *She hoped the plan would succeed.* be effective, [*informal*] catch on, produce results, work.
AN OPPOSITE IS fail.
3 *Elizabeth II succeeded George VI.* come after, follow, replace, take over from.

success *noun*
1 *She talked about her success as an actress.* achievement, attainment, fame.
2 *They congratulated the team on their success.* triumph, victory, win.
3 *The group's recent CD was a success.* hit, [*informal*] winner.
4 *The success of the plan depends on their cooperation.* completion, effectiveness, successful outcome.
AN OPPOSITE IS failure.

successful *adjective*
1 *She runs a successful business.* booming, flourishing, profitable, prosperous, rewarding, thriving.
2 *His final attempt to fix it was successful.* effective.
3 *The supporters cheered the successful team.* triumphant, victorious, winning.
AN OPPOSITE IS unsuccessful.

succession *noun*
They suffered a succession of disasters. run, sequence, series, string.

successive *adjective*
It rained on seven successive days. consecutive, in succession, uninterrupted.
You can also say: *It rained on several days in succession.*

suck *verb*
to suck something up *A sponge will suck up water.* absorb, draw up, soak up.

sudden *adjective*
1 *He made a sudden decision.* hasty, hurried, impulsive, quick, rash.
2 *The bus came to a sudden halt.* abrupt, swift.
3 *A sudden bang made her jump.* sharp, startling, unexpected.
AN OPPOSITE IS expected.

suffer *verb*
1 *He suffers terribly with his back.* feel pain, hurt.
2 *He will suffer for his crime.* be punished, pay.
3 *She had to suffer the disgrace of coming last.* bear, cope with, endure, experience, feel, go through, put up with, stand, tolerate, undergo.

suffering *noun*
The refugees experienced terrible suffering. deprivation, hardship, illness, misery, pain, torture.
SEE ALSO **pain**.

sufficient *adjective*
They had sufficient money to live on. adequate, enough, satisfactory.
AN OPPOSITE IS insufficient.

suffix *noun*
AN OPPOSITE IS prefix.

suffocate *verb*
He was suffocated by the fumes. choke, stifle.
To stop someone's breathing by squeezing their throat is to **strangle** or **throttle** them.
To stop someone's breathing by covering their nose and mouth is to **smother** them.

sugar *noun*

VARIOUS FORMS OF SUGAR: brown sugar, cane sugar, caster sugar, demerara, glucose, granulated sugar, icing sugar, lump sugar, molasses, sucrose, syrup, treacle.
Things you eat which are made mainly of sugar are *sweets*.

suggest *verb*
1 *She suggested going to the zoo.* advise, advocate, propose, recommend.
2 *Her yawn suggests that she's bored.* hint, imply, indicate, mean, signal.

suggestion *noun*
They didn't like his suggestion. advice, offer, plan, proposal, recommendation.

suit *verb*
1 *The ten o'clock train would suit them very well.* be acceptable or convenient to, fit in with, satisfy.
AN OPPOSITE IS displease.
2 *Her new haircut didn't suit her.* be appropriate to, become, look good on.

suitable *adjective*
1 *They wore clothes suitable for cold weather.* acceptable, appropriate, apt, fit, well chosen.
2 *Is this a suitable time to have a chat?* convenient, proper, satisfactory.
AN OPPOSITE IS unsuitable.

sulk *verb*
He sulked for days when he was dropped from the team. be resentful or sullen, brood, mope.

sullen *adjective*
1 *She became sullen when she lost.* bad-tempered, brooding, cross, gloomy, moody, morose, resentful, silent, sour, sulky.
AN OPPOSITE IS cheerful.
2 *The sullen sky promised rain.* cloudy, dark, dismal, dull, grey, overcast, sombre.
AN OPPOSITE IS bright.

sum *noun*
1 *The sum of 2 and 2 is 4.* result, total.
2 *He lost a large sum of money.* amount, quantity.
sums *She doesn't like doing sums.* adding up, arithmetic, [*informal*] maths, mathematical problems.
FOR OTHER MATHEMATICAL TERMS, SEE **mathematics**.

sum *verb*
to sum up SEE **summarize**.

summarize *verb*
1 *The judge began to summarize the evidence.* make a summary of, outline, [*informal*] recap, sum up.
2 *He had to summarize his story because of the lack of time.* abbreviate, condense, reduce, shorten.
AN OPPOSITE IS elaborate.

summary *noun*
She wrote a short summary of her story. condensation, outline, précis.

summit *noun*
The summit of the mountain was covered in snow. cap, peak, tip, top.
AN OPPOSITE IS base.

summon *verb*
The head will summon you when she's ready to see you. call, command you to come, order you to come, send for.
To ask someone politely to come is to *invite* them.

sun *noun*
They went out into the garden to sit in the sun. sunlight, sunshine.

sunbathe *verb*
She spent the whole holiday sunbathing on the beach. bask in the sun, get a tan, sun yourself.

sunburned *or* sunburnt *adjective*
If you are often in the sun you become *bronzed* or *tanned* or *weather-beaten*.
If your skin is damaged by the sun you may be *blistered* or *peeling*.

sunlight *noun*
Most plants can only grow in sunlight. daylight, sun, sunshine.
Rays of light from the sun are *sunbeams*.

sunny *adjective*
1 *It was a lovely sunny day.* clear, cloudless, fine.
AN OPPOSITE IS cloudy.
2 *She worked in a nice sunny office.* bright, cheerful, sunlit.
AN OPPOSITE IS gloomy.

sunrise *noun*
He always woke up at sunrise. dawn, daybreak.

sunset *noun*
They finished work at sunset. dusk, evening, nightfall, twilight.

sunshade *noun*
She sat under a sunshade. canopy, parasol.

superb *adjective*
It was a superb goal. excellent, exceptional, impressive, magnificent, marvellous, outstanding, remarkable, splendid, wonderful.
INFORMAL SYNONYMS ARE: brilliant, fabulous, fantastic, great, smashing, super.

superficial *adjective*
1 *It's only a superficial wound.* on the surface, shallow, slight, unimportant.
AN OPPOSITE IS deep.
2 *He gave the car a superficial examination.* careless, casual, hasty, hurried, quick.
AN OPPOSITE IS thorough.
3 *Her arguments seemed superficial.* frivolous, simple, trivial, unconvincing, unsophisticated.
AN OPPOSITE IS profound.

superfluous *adjective*
They put the superfluous cups back in the box. excess, redundant, spare, surplus, unnecessary, unwanted, waste.
AN OPPOSITE IS necessary.

superintend *verb*
The keeper superintends the park. be in charge of, control, direct, lead, look after, manage, organize, run, supervise, watch over.

superior *adjective*
1 *In the army, a major is superior in rank to a lieutenant.* greater, higher, more important, senior.
2 *You have to pay more to get superior quality.* better, first-class, first-rate, select, top.
3 *They didn't like her superior attitude.* arrogant, haughty, self-important, smug, snobbish, stuck-up.
AN OPPOSITE IS inferior.

supernatural *adjective*
She claimed to have supernatural powers. inexplicable, magical, miraculous, mysterious, spiritual, unearthly, unnatural.
AN OPPOSITE IS natural.

superstition *noun*
It's a superstition that 13 is an unlucky number. myth.

supervise *verb*
He supervised the men unloading the lorry. be in charge of, control, direct, lead, look after, manage, organize, preside over, run, superintend, watch over.
To supervise candidates in an exam is to ***invigilate***.

supervision *noun*
They worked under the supervision of the manager. administration, control, management.

supervisor *noun*
Her supervisor told her off for being late. administrator, controller, director, inspector, manager, organizer.
The person who supervises you in an exam is the ***invigilator***.

supple *adjective*
The shoes are made of nice supple leather. flexible, pliable, soft.
AN OPPOSITE IS brittle or rigid.

supplementary *adjective*
You have to pay a supplementary fare to travel first class. additional, extra.

supplier *noun*
The store ordered more goods from the suppliers. dealer, retailer, seller, shopkeeper, wholesaler.

supply *verb*
The supermarket supplies everything
you need. give, provide, sell.

supply *noun*
They have a good supply of food.
quantity, reserve, stock, store.
supplies He bought supplies for the
camping trip. equipment, food,
necessities, provisions.

support *noun*
1 She thanked them for their support.
aid, assistance, backing, cooperation,
encouragement, friendship, help,
interest, loyalty.
2 The support of a local business
enabled them to buy sports equipment.
contributions, donations, sponsorship.
3 The supports prevented the wall from
collapsing. prop.

A support for a shelf is a ***bracket***.
A support built against a wall is a
buttress.
A support for someone with an
injured leg is a ***crutch***.
A support for a roof is a ***pillar***.
A support for a broken arm is a
sling.
A bar of wood or metal supporting a
framework is a ***strut***.
A support put under a board to make
a table is a ***trestle***.

---

support *verb*
1 The rope couldn't support his weight.
bear, carry, hold up.
2 The beams support the roof. prop up,
reinforce, strengthen.
3 They supported him when he was in
trouble. aid, assist, back, comfort,
defend, encourage, give support to,
rally round, reassure, side with, speak
up for, stand by, stand up for.
4 They agreed to support her proposal.
advocate, agree with, argue for,
promote, uphold.
5 She had to work to support her
family. bring up, feed, keep, maintain,
provide for.
6 He supports OXFAM. contribute to,
donate to, give to.
7 He supports Nottingham Forest. be a
supporter of, follow.

supporter *noun*
1 The supporters cheered their team.
fan, follower.
2 The government's supporters
welcomed the new law. ally, backer,
collaborator, helper.
The supporter of the main speaker in a
debate is the ***seconder***.
A supporter of someone in a fight is
their ***second***.

suppose *verb*
1 I suppose you want to borrow some
money. assume, believe, expect, guess,
infer, presume, think.
2 Just suppose you had lots of money!
fancy, imagine, pretend.
to be supposed to do something She's
supposed to get up at 7.30. be due to, be
expected to, be meant to, have a duty
to, need to, ought to.

supposition *noun*
That's only a supposition—we don't
know if its really true. assumption,
guess, hypothesis, opinion, suggestion,
theory.

suppress *verb*
1 He managed to suppress his anger.
bottle up, conceal, cover up, hide,
repress, smother.
To suppress ideas for political or moral
reasons is to ***censor*** them.
2 The army suppressed the rebellion.
crush, overcome, put an end to, put
down, stamp out, stop, subdue.

supremacy *noun*
The country has achieved military
supremacy. dominance, lead,
predominance.

supreme *adjective*
Her supreme achievement was winning
a gold medal. best, greatest, highest,
outstanding, top.

sure *adjective*
1 I'm sure that I'm right. certain,
confident, convinced, definite, positive.
2 He's sure to come. bound, certain.
3 A high temperature is a sure sign of
illness. clear, guaranteed, true,
undeniable.

4 *He's a sure friend.* dependable, faithful, firm, loyal, reliable, trustworthy.
AN OPPOSITE IS uncertain.

surface *noun*
1 *Much of the surface of the earth is covered with sea.* exterior, outside.
The surface of something may be covered with a *crust* or *shell* or *skin*.
A thin surface of expensive wood on furniture is a *veneer*.
AN OPPOSITE IS centre.
2 *A dice has dots on each surface.* face, side.
AN OPPOSITE IS inside.
3 *Oil floated on the surface of the water.* top.
AN OPPOSITE IS bottom.

surface *verb*
1 *They surfaced the road with asphalt.* coat, cover.
To surface cheap wood with a thin layer of expensive wood is to *veneer* it.
2 *The submarine surfaced.* appear, come up, emerge, [*informal*] pop up, rise to the surface.

surge *verb*
1 *Water surged around them.* billow, heave, make waves, rise, roll, swirl.
2 *The crowd surged forward.* push, rush, sweep.

surgery *noun*
1 *She went to see the doctor at the surgery.* clinic, health centre, medical centre.
2 *She had surgery in the local hospital.* an operation.

surpass *verb*
It will be hard to surpass their score. beat, do better than, exceed, outdo.

surplus *noun*
Eat what you want and put the surplus in the fridge. excess, extra, [*informal*] leftovers, remainder.

surprise *noun*
She looked up in surprise when he walked in. alarm, amazement, astonishment, dismay, incredulity, shock, wonder.

surprise *verb*
1 *They were surprised by the news.* alarm, amaze, astonish, astound, shock, stagger, startle, stun, take aback, take by surprise.
2 *She surprised the burglars as they went through her cupboards.* catch, catch red-handed, come upon, detect, discover.

surprised *adjective*
He gave her a surprised look when she told him. alarmed, amazed, astonished, astounded, dismayed, dumbfounded, [*informal*] flabbergasted, shocked, speechless, startled, stunned, taken aback.

surprising *adjective*
It was a surprising decision. amazing, astonishing, astounding, extraordinary, incredible, shocking, staggering, startling, sudden, unexpected, unplanned, unpredictable.
AN OPPOSITE IS predictable.

surrender *verb*
1 *The soldiers refused to surrender.* admit defeat, give in, submit, yield.
2 *She surrendered her ticket to the driver.* give, hand over.

surround *verb*
1 *The courtyard was surrounded by buildings.* enclose, fence in, wall in.
2 *The police surrounded the suspects.* besiege, encircle, hem in.

surroundings *plural noun*
They lived in very pleasant surroundings. conditions, environment, location, setting.

survey *noun*
1 *They did a survey of local leisure facilities.* investigation, study.
A survey to count the number of people, cars, etc., is a *census*.
2 *The builders did a survey of the house.* examination, inspection.

survey *verb*
1 *From the hill you can survey the whole valley.* examine, inspect, look over, scrutinize, study, view.

2 *They surveyed the damage done by the storm.* appraise, assess, evaluate, investigate, weigh up.
3 *The contractors surveyed the building plot.* map out, measure, plan out.

survive *verb*
1 *You can't survive without water.* carry on, continue, keep going, last, live, remain alive, stay alive.
AN OPPOSITE IS die.
2 *She survived her husband by twenty years.* outlast.
3 *Will the birds survive this cold weather?* come through, endure, live through, weather, withstand.

suspect *verb*
1 *They suspected his motives.* doubt, have suspicions about, mistrust.
2 *I suspect that it will rain.* expect, guess, imagine, sense, think it likely.

suspend *verb*
1 *The chairman suspended the meeting.* adjourn, break off, interrupt.
2 *The head threatened to suspend the troublemakers from school.* bar, dismiss, exclude, expel.
3 *They suspended the rope from a branch.* dangle, hang, swing.

suspense *noun*
He could hardly bear the suspense of waiting to know what had happened. anxiety, drama, excitement, expectation, tension, uncertainty, waiting.

suspicion *noun*
He had a suspicion that she was lying. feeling, hunch, impression, inkling, intuition, uncertain feeling.

suspicious *adjective*
1 *There was something about his story which made her suspicious.* cautious, distrustful, doubtful, incredulous, sceptical, unconvinced, uneasy, wary.
AN OPPOSITE IS trusting.
2 *What do you make of her suspicious behaviour?* [*informal*] fishy, peculiar, questionable, shady.

sustain *verb*
1 *Is there enough food to sustain the animals through the winter?* keep alive, keep going, preserve.
2 *The runners couldn't sustain the high speed.* keep up, maintain.
3 *Will the branch sustain his weight?* bear, carry, stand, support.

swallow *verb*
Chew your food properly before swallowing it. consume.
To swallow food is to **eat**.
To swallow liquid is to **drink**.
to swallow something up *They were swallowed up in the fog.* cover, envelop, hide.

swamp *verb*
A huge wave swamped the ship. engulf, flood, inundate, overwhelm, sink, submerge, swallow up.

swamp *noun*
He began to sink into the swamp. bog, fen, marsh, mud, quicksands.

swampy *adjective*
She warned them not to go near the swampy ground. boggy, marshy, muddy, soft, soggy, unstable, waterlogged, wet.
AN OPPOSITE IS firm.

swan *noun*
A female swan is a **pen**.
A male swan is a **cob**.
A young swan is a **cygnet**.

swap or **swop** *verb* [*informal*]
She swapped the computer game for a CD. change, exchange, substitute.

swarm *verb*
The crowd swarmed around him. crowd, flock.
swarming with *The garden is swarming with ants.* alive with, full of, infested with, overrun by, teeming with.

sway *verb*
The trees swayed in the breeze. bend, lean from side to side, rock, swing, wave.

swear *verb*
1 *Do you swear to tell the truth?* give your word, pledge, promise, take an oath, vow.
2 *She swore when she hit her finger.* blaspheme, curse, use swear words.

swear word *noun*
He was told off for using swear words. curse, oath, obscenity.
Using swear words is **bad language**.
Using religious words when you swear is **blasphemy**.

sweat *verb*
He sweats a lot in hot weather. perspire.

sweaty *adjective*
Her hands were sweaty. clammy, damp, moist, perspiring, sticky, sweating.

sweep *verb*
1 *She swept the floor.* brush, clean, dust.
2 *The bus swept past.* shoot, speed, zoom.
to sweep something away 1 *He tried to sweep away the rubbish.* clear away, get rid of, remove.
2 *The flood swept away several houses.* destroy, flatten, level.

sweet *adjective*
1 *The pudding was too sweet for him.* sickly, sugary, sweetened, syrupy.
AN OPPOSITE IS acid or bitter or savoury.
2 *The sweet smell of roses filled the room.* fragrant.
AN OPPOSITE IS foul.
3 *I heard the sweet sound of a harp.* melodious, pleasant, soothing, tuneful.
AN OPPOSITE IS ugly.
4 *What a sweet little cottage!* attractive, charming, dear, lovely, pretty, quaint.
AN OPPOSITE IS unattractive.

sweet *noun*
1 *Would you like a sweet?*
An American word is **candy**.
A formal word for sweets is **confectionery**.

VARIOUS KINDS OF SWEET: acid drop, barley sugar, boiled sweet, bull's-eye, butterscotch, candyfloss, caramel, chewing gum, ➡

chocolate, fruit pastille, fudge, humbug, liquorice, lollipop, marshmallow, marzipan, mint or peppermint, nougat, rock, toffee, Turkish delight.

2 *They had apple crumble for sweet.* dessert, pudding.

swell *verb*
The balloon swelled as it filled with hot air. become bigger, billow, blow up, bulge, enlarge, expand, grow, inflate, puff up, rise.
AN OPPOSITE IS shrink.

swelling *noun*
He had a painful swelling on his foot. blister, bulge, bump, growth, inflammation, lump.
A **tumour** is a serious swelling on the body.

swelter *verb*
They sweltered in the heat. become hot, perspire, sweat.

swerve *verb*
The car swerved to avoid a hedgehog. change direction, dodge, swing, turn aside, veer.

swift *adjective*
1 *He set off at a swift pace.* brisk, fast, nimble, [*informal*] nippy, quick, rapid, speedy.
2 *She didn't expect such a swift reaction.* hasty, hurried, immediate, instantaneous, prompt, snappy, sudden, unhesitating.
AN OPPOSITE IS slow.

swill *verb*
He swilled the front steps with soapy water. clean, rinse, sponge down, wash.
To swill out the lavatory is to **flush** it.

swim *verb*
She loves to swim in the sea. bathe, go swimming, take a dip.

VARIOUS SWIMMING STROKES: backstroke, breaststroke, butterfly, crawl.

PLACES WHERE YOU CAN SWIM: baths, leisure pool, lido, swimming bath or swimming pool. ➡

CLOTHING YOU WEAR TO SWIM IN: bathing costume, bathing suit, bikini, swimming costume, swimsuit, swimwear, trunks.

swindle *verb*
She was arrested for trying to swindle an insurance company. cheat, [*slang*] con, deceive, [*informal*] diddle, double-cross, fool, hoax, [*slang*] rip off, trick.

swindle *noun*
They were victims of a swindle. deception, fraud, [*informal*] racket, [*slang*] rip-off, trick.

swing *verb*
1 *The bucket swung from the end of a rope* dangle, flap, hang, sway, wave about.
2 *He swung the car round to avoid the bus.* swerve, turn, twist.

swing *noun*
There was a swing in public opinion before the election. change, movement, shift, variation.

swirl *verb*
The water swirls as it goes down the plughole. churn, spin, twirl, whirl.

switch *verb*
1 *He switched off the light.* turn.
2 *She switched her attention to more important matters.* change, shift.
3 *They switched places.* exchange, [*informal*] swap.

swivel *verb*
He swivelled in his chair. pivot, revolve, rotate, spin, turn, twirl.

swoop *verb*
The owl swooped and caught the mouse. descend, dive, drop, fall, fly down, pounce.
to swoop on *The police swooped on the criminals' hideout.* attack, descend on, invade, pounce on, raid, rush, storm.

swop *verb* SEE **swap**

sword *noun*
FOR VARIOUS WEAPONS, SEE **weapon**.

syllabus *noun*
The teacher explained what was on the syllabus for next term. course, curriculum, programme of study.

symbol *noun*
The dove is a symbol of peace. emblem, image, sign.
The symbols we use in writing are **characters** or **letters**.
The symbols used in ancient Egyptian writing were **hieroglyphics**.
The symbol of a school, sports club, etc., is their **badge**.
The symbol of a firm or organization is their **logo**.
A religious symbol is an **icon**.

symbolize *verb*
The dove symbolizes peace. be a sign of, indicate, mean, represent, signify, stand for, suggest.

symmetrical *adjective*
The garden was designed in a symmetrical shape. balanced.
AN OPPOSITE IS asymmetrical.

sympathetic *adjective*
1 *She was sympathetic when my dog died.* caring, comforting, compassionate, concerned, kind, merciful, pitying, tender, understanding.
2 *He took a sympathetic interest in what they were doing.* benevolent, friendly, interested, open-minded, positive.
AN OPPOSITE IS unsympathetic.

sympathize *verb*
to sympathize with *He sympathized with the people who had lost their homes.* be sorry for, feel for, identify with, pity, show sympathy for, understand.

sympathy *noun*
She showed no sympathy for him. compassion, consideration, feeling, kindness, mercy, pity, tenderness, understanding.

symptom *noun*
A rash is one symptom of measles. indication, sign, warning.

synonym *noun*
AN OPPOSITE IS antonym.

synthetic *adjective*
Nylon is a synthetic material. artificial, man-made, manufactured, unnatural.
AN OPPOSITE IS natural.

system *noun*
1 *Large towns need an efficient railway system.* network, organization, [*informal*] set-up.
2 *She couldn't see any system in his work.* arrangement, logic, order, structure.
3 *They've introduced a new system for teaching people languages.* method, plan, procedure, process, routine, scheme, technique.

systematic *adjective*
He worked in a very systematic way. businesslike, logical, methodical, orderly, organized, scientific.
AN OPPOSITE IS unsystematic.

table *noun*

KINDS OF TABLE: coffee table, dining table, gate-leg table, kitchen table, trestle table.

SPECIAL TABLES FOR PLAYING GAMES ON: billiard table, card table, snooker table, table tennis table.
FOR OTHER ITEMS OF FURNITURE, SEE **furniture**.

tablet *noun*
1 *The doctor prescribed some tablets.* capsule, pellet, pill.
2 *She bought a tablet of scented soap.* bar, block, chunk, piece.

tack *verb*
1 *She tacked down the carpet.* nail, pin.
2 *She tacked up the hem of her skirt.* sew, stitch.

tackle *verb*
1 *They left him to tackle the washing-up.* attempt, attend to, cope with, deal with, do, face, grapple with, handle, manage, set about.
2 *Another player tackled him and got the ball.* attack, challenge, intercept.

tackle *noun*
1 *He kept his fishing tackle in a special case.* apparatus, equipment, gear, kit, paraphernalia.
2 *The referee said it was a fair tackle.* block, challenge, interception.

tact *noun*
He showed tact in discussing the problem. consideration, diplomacy, tactfulness, thoughtfulness, understanding.
AN OPPOSITE IS tactlessness.

tactful *adjective*
She gave him some tactful advice. considerate, diplomatic, discreet, judicious, polite, thoughtful.
AN OPPOSITE IS tactless.

tactics *plural noun*
They discussed their tactics for the next game. approach, course of action, plan, policy, procedure, scheme, strategy.

tactless *adjective*
She made a tactless remark about his illness. impolite, inappropriate, inconsiderate, insensitive, rude, thoughtless, undiplomatic, unkind, untimely.
AN OPPOSITE IS tactful.

tag *noun*
The price is marked on the tag. label, sticker, ticket.

tag *verb*
Every item is tagged with a price label. identify, label, mark.
to tag along with someone *She tagged along with them when they left.* accompany, follow, go with, join.
to tag something on *He tagged on a PS at the end of his letter.* add, attach, tack on.

tail *noun*
He joined the tail of the queue. back, end, rear.

tail *verb*
The police tailed the car for miles. follow, go after, pursue, track.
to tail off *The number of tourists tails off in October.* decline, decrease, diminish, dwindle, flag, lessen, reduce, subside, wane.

take *verb*
The verb *to take* has many meanings.
We give the commoner ones here
1 *He took her hand.* clutch, get hold of,
grab, grasp, hold, seize, snatch.
2 *The soldiers took many prisoners.*
capture, catch, detain, secure, trap.
3 *Someone took his pen.* move, pick up,
remove, steal.
4 *The caravan can take six people.*
accommodate, contain, have room for,
hold.
5 *He wanted to take her to the party.*
accompany, conduct, escort, lead.
6 *The bus will take you into the city.*
bring, carry, convey, drive, transport.
7 *They took a taxi to the station.* catch,
engage, hire, travel by.
8 *Do you take sugar?* have, make use of,
use.
9 *She can't take rich food.* abide, bear,
endure, put up with, stand, [*informal*]
stomach.
10 *He finds it hard to take criticism.*
accept, experience, receive, suffer,
tolerate, undergo.
11 *It'll take two people to lift that table.*
need, require.
12 *He took their names and addresses.*
make a note of, record, write down.
13 *She took a new name.* adopt, choose,
select.
14 *A new teacher took us today.* look
after, organize, supervise, teach.
15 *Take 2 from 8 and you get 6.* deduct,
subtract, take away.
to take someone in *They were taken in
by his lies.* cheat, deceive, delude, fool,
mislead, trick.
to take off *The plane took off on time.*
depart, leave the ground, lift off.
to take something off *Take off your
coat.* peel off, remove, strip off.
to take part in something *Would you
like to take part in a quiz?* be involved
in, join, share in, participate in.
to take place *When did the accident
take place?* come about, happen, occur.
to take something up *He's taken up a
new hobby.* begin, commence, embark
on, start.

takings *plural noun*
*The takings in auntie's shop were better
last week.* earnings, income, proceeds,
profits, revenue.

tale *noun*
She told a tale of adventure. account,
narrative, report, story, [*informal*]
yarn.
FOR VARIOUS KINDS OF STORY, SEE
story.

talent *noun*
She is a musician of great talent.
ability, aptitude, expertise, skill.
Unusually great talent is **genius**.

talented *adjective*
He's a very talented painter. able,
accomplished, brilliant, capable, clever,
expert, gifted, skilled.
If you are talented in many different
ways, you are **versatile**.

talk *verb*
He learned to talk at a very early age.
communicate, express yourself,
pronounce words, say things, speak,
use language.

DIFFERENT THINGS WE MAY DO
WHEN WE TALK: address people,
advise people, answer questions,
argue, ask for something, beg for
something, complain, confer,
converse, declare our intentions,
deliver a speech, discuss problems,
explain things, express opinions,
give information or orders, have a
conversation, negotiate, object to
something, plead for something,
pray, preach, read aloud, recite a
poem, tell each other things.

DIFFERENT WAYS TO TALK OR SAY
THINGS: babble, bawl, bellow, blurt
out, burble, call out, chat, chatter,
croak, cry, drawl, drone, exclaim,
gabble, gossip, grunt, howl, intone,
jabber, lisp, moan, mumble, murmur,
mutter, prattle, rant, rave, roar,
scream, screech, shout, shriek, slur,
snap, snarl, splutter, squeal,
stammer, stutter, wail, whimper,
whine, whinge, whisper, yell.

talk *noun*
1 *She had a long talk with him.* chat, conversation, discussion, gossip.
The talk in a novel or play is the *dialogue*.
2 *He gave a talk on his visit to China.* address, lecture, presentation, speech.
A talk in church is a *sermon*.

talkative *adjective*
She's a very talkative child. chatty, communicative, eloquent, fluent, vocal, wordy.
A talkative person is a *chatterbox* or a *gossip*.

tall *adjective*
1 *She is tall for her age.* big.
AN OPPOSITE IS short.
2 *The city is full of tall buildings.* giant, high, lofty, towering.
Buildings with many floors are *high-rise* or *multi-storey* buildings.
AN OPPOSITE IS low.

tally *verb*
to tally with *Her story didn't tally with her sister's.* agree with, correspond with, match.

tame *adjective*
1 *The animals are quite tame.* docile, domesticated, gentle, manageable, obedient, safe, submissive.
AN OPPOSITE IS wild.
2 *The film seemed very tame.* boring, dull, feeble, tedious, unadventurous, unexciting, uninteresting.
AN OPPOSITE IS exciting.

tame *verb*
They were trying to tame a wild horse. control, subdue, train.

tamper *verb*
to tamper with something *Someone has been tampering with the lock.* fiddle about with, interfere with, meddle with, tinker with.

tan *verb*
She tans quickly in the sun. get a tan, go brown.
If your skin goes red in the sun, you get *sunburn*.

tang *noun*
The drink has a tang of lemon. sharp flavour or smell, sharpness.

tangle *verb*
1 *He tangled all the ropes together.* confuse, muddle, twist.
Tangled hair is **dishevelled** or **matted** hair.
2 *A fish tangled itself in the net.* catch, entangle, trap.

tangle *noun*
She sorted out a tangle of wires. confusion, jumble, knot, muddle.

tank *noun*
A water tank is a *cistern*.
A tank to keep fish in is an *aquarium*.
FOR OTHER CONTAINERS, SEE **container**.

tantalize *verb*
They were tantalized by the smell of food. taunt, tease, tempt, torment.

tantrum *noun*
He had a tantrum when he didn't get his own way. fit of anger, fit of temper, rage.

tap *verb*
Someone tapped on the door. knock, rap, strike.

tape *noun*
1 *The parcel was tied with tape.* braid, ribbon.
2 *She bought a tape of her favourite pop group.* tape recording.
A tape for listening to is an *audiotape*.
A tape for watching on TV is a *videotape*.
You usually buy tapes in a *cassette*.

tape *verb*
He taped the film so he could watch it later. record, video.

target *noun*
1 *Their target was to raise £100.* aim, ambition, goal, hope, intention, objective, purpose.
2 *She was the target of his insults.* object, victim.

tarnish *verb*
1 *Most metals tarnish in the open air.* corrode, discolour.
When iron corrodes it *rusts*.
2 *The scandal tarnished his reputation.* blot, mar, spoil, stain.

tart *adjective*
Lemons have a tart taste. acid, sharp,
sour.
AN OPPOSITE IS sweet.

task *noun*
1 He was given a number of tasks to do.
chore, errand, job, work.
2 The soldiers' task was to capture the
hill. assignment, duty, mission,
operation, undertaking.

taste *verb*
She tasted the soup to see if it needed
some more salt. sample, try.

WORDS TO DESCRIBE HOW THINGS
TASTE: acid, bitter, creamy, fresh,
fruity, hot, juicy, meaty, mellow,
mild, peppery, rancid, refreshing,
salty, savoury, sharp, sour, spicy,
stale, strong, sugary, sweet, syrupy,
tangy, tart, tasteless, tasty, watery.

taste *noun*
1 I love the taste of strawberries.
flavour.
2 He gave her a taste of the cheese. bit,
bite, morsel, mouthful, nibble, piece,
sample.
3 Her taste in clothes is a bit odd.
choice, discrimination, judgement,
preference.

tasteful *adjective*
He usually wears tasteful colours.
artistic, attractive, elegant,
fashionable, in good taste, smart,
stylish.
AN OPPOSITE IS tasteless.

tasteless *adjective*
1 The decorations seemed rather
tasteless. crude, gaudy, showy, ugly,
unattractive, unfashionable.
2 He keeps making tasteless jokes.
improper, in bad taste, unpleasant,
vulgar.
AN OPPOSITE IS tasteful.

tasty *adjective*
That pie was very tasty. appetizing,
delicious.

tattered *adjective*
Why does she wear tattered clothes?
frayed, ragged, ripped, tatty, torn,
worn out.
AN OPPOSITE IS smart.

tatters *plural noun*
His jeans were in tatters. rags, ribbons,
shreds.

tatty *adjective*
He was wearing tatty old clothes.
frayed, old, patched, ragged, ripped,
scruffy, shabby, tattered, torn,
threadbare, untidy, worn out.
AN OPPOSITE IS smart.

taunt *verb*
They taunted the losers. barrack,
insult, jeer at, laugh at, make fun of,
mock, ridicule, sneer at.
AN OPPOSITE IS flatter or praise.

taut *adjective*
Make sure the rope is taut. stretched,
tense, tight.
AN OPPOSITE IS slack.

tax *noun*

SOME TAXES PEOPLE HAVE TO PAY:
airport tax, council tax or [old use]
rates, customs duty, death duty,
income tax, road tax, [old use] tithes,
VAT or value-added tax.

teach *verb*
If you want to learn about computers,
you need an expert to teach you.
educate, inform, instruct.
To teach people to play a sport is to
coach or **train** them.
To teach one person at a time or a
small group is to **tutor** them.
To teach a large group of people is to
lecture to them.
To try to fill people's minds with your
ideas is to **brainwash** or
indoctrinate them.

teacher *noun*

VARIOUS PEOPLE WHO MIGHT
TEACH US: coach, counsellor, [old
use] governess, guru, headteacher or
principal, instructor, lecturer,
preacher, professor, schoolteacher or
schoolmaster or schoolmistress,
trainer, tutor.

team *noun*
He was left out of the team. side.
FOR VARIOUS KINDS OF GROUP, SEE
group.

tear *verb*
1 *The barbed wire tore his clothes.*
gash, rip, shred, slit, split.
2 *He tore home to watch TV.* career,
dash, hurry, race, run, rush, zoom.

tear *noun*
There was a tear in his shirt. cut, gap,
gash, hole, opening, rip, slit, split.

tearful *adjective*
*She was tearful when they said
goodbye.* crying, emotional, sad,
sobbing, weeping.

tease *verb*
They teased him about his new haircut.
annoy, bait, irritate, laugh at, make
fun of, mock, pester, provoke, ridicule,
tantalize, taunt, torment, vex, worry.

technical *adjective*
*You need someone with technical
knowledge to mend this equipment.*
expert, professional, scientific,
specialized, technological.

technique *noun*
1 *The musician's technique was
flawless.* art, craft, expertise, know-
how, skill.
2 *They use modern techniques.* method,
procedure, way.

technological *adjective*
*Modern aircraft are full of
technological equipment.* advanced,
automated, computerized, electronic,
scientific.

tedious *adjective*
It was a tedious journey. boring, dreary,
dull, long, monotonous, slow, tiresome,
tiring, unexciting, uninteresting.
AN OPPOSITE IS exciting.

tedium *noun*
*She complained about the tedium of the
meeting.* boredom, dullness, monotony,
slowness, tediousness.
AN OPPOSITE IS excitement.

teem *verb*
to teem with *The pond teemed with
tadpoles.* abound in, [*informal*] be
crawling with, be full of, be infested by,
be overrun by, swarm with.

teenager *noun*
*The film was designed to appeal to
teenagers.* adolescent, youngster.
A word for a teenage boy is **youth**.

telephone *verb*
*He telephoned her to say he couldn't
come.* call, dial, phone, ring.

televise *verb*
The match is being televised. broadcast,
relay, send out, transmit.

television *noun*
She bought a new television. receiver,
set, [*informal*] telly, [*short form*] TV.
The part of a computer system with a
screen is the **monitor**.

VARIOUS TYPES OF TELEVISION
PROGRAMMES: cartoon, chat show,
comedy, documentary, drama or play,
film or movie, interview, mini series,
news, panel game, quiz, serial,
series, [*informal*] sitcom or situation
comedy, [*informal*] soap or soap
opera.
TV programmes recorded on tape
are **videos**.
SEE ALSO **entertainment**.

tell *verb*
The verb *to tell* can be used in many
ways. We give some of the more
important ways here
1 *Tell us what you can see.* describe,
explain, reveal, say.
2 *Tell me when you are ready.*
announce, communicate, inform.
3 *He told them what they ought to do.*
advise, recommend, suggest.
4 *Tell them to stop.* command, direct,
instruct, order.
5 *She told them a story.* narrate, relate.
6 *He told her she could trust him.*
assure, promise.
7 *She couldn't tell who it was in the
dark.* discover, identify, make out,
perceive, recognize, see.
8 *Can you tell one from the other?*
distinguish, separate.
to tell someone off *She told them off
for being late.* reprimand, reproach,
scold, [*informal*] tick off.
to tell tales about someone *She didn't
like him because he was always telling
tales.* betray, inform against, report,
[*informal*] sneak on.

telling *adjective*
She made a *telling* contribution to the discussion. effective, important, impressive, meaningful, significant, striking.
AN OPPOSITE IS unimportant.

temper *noun*
1 He couldn't put up with her bad *temper*. humour, mood, state of mind.
2 He flew into a *temper*. fit of anger, fury, rage, tantrum.
to keep your temper Try to keep your *temper*. calm down, control yourself, stay calm, stay cool.
to lose your temper She lost her *temper* with him. become angry, flare up, get annoyed, rage.

tempestuous *adjective*
It was a *tempestuous* night. rough, stormy, turbulent, violent, wild, windy.
AN OPPOSITE IS calm.

temple *noun*
FOR PLACES OF WORSHIP, SEE
worship *verb*.

temporary *adjective*
It's just a *temporary* arrangement until they can find something better. makeshift, provisional.
AN OPPOSITE IS permanent.

tempt *verb*
Can I *tempt* you to have more pudding? coax, persuade.
To tempt someone by offering them money is to **bribe** them.
Something used to tempt an animal into a trap is **bait** or a **decoy**.

tempting *adjective*
The shop has some *tempting* special offers. appealing, attractive, desirable, irresistible.

tend *verb*
1 The shepherd was *tending* the sheep. keep, mind, protect, watch over.
2 He spends a lot of time *tending* his garden. cultivate, manage.
3 Nurses *tend* the sick. attend to, care for, look after, nurse, treat.
to tend to do something She *tends* to eat too much. be inclined to, be liable to, have a tendency to.

tendency *noun*
He has a *tendency* to be lazy. bias, inclination.

tender *adjective*
1 Frost may damage *tender* plants. delicate, soft.
AN OPPOSITE IS hardy or strong.
The opposite of tender meat is **tough** meat.
2 The bruise is still *tender*. aching, painful, sensitive, sore.
AN OPPOSITE IS numb.
3 She gave him a *tender* smile. affectionate, caring, compassionate, fond, gentle, kind, loving, merciful, soft-hearted, sympathetic.
AN OPPOSITE IS cruel.

tense *adjective*
1 He tried to relax his *tense* muscles. strained, stretched, taut, tight.
2 Everyone was *tense* as they waited for the game to start. anxious, apprehensive, edgy, excited, fidgety, jumpy, nervous, touchy, [*informal*] uptight, worried.
3 It was a *tense* moment. exciting, nerve-racking, stressful, worrying.
AN OPPOSITE IS relaxed.

tension *noun*
1 He checked the *tension* on the guy ropes. strain, tautness, tightness.
2 They felt the *tension* as the spacecraft lifted off. anxiety, excitement, nervousness, stress, suspense, worry.

tent *noun*

KINDS OF TENT: bell tent, big top, frame tent, marquee, ridge tent, tepee, trailer tent, wigwam.

tepid *adjective*
By the time he got into the bath, the water was *tepid*. lukewarm, slightly warm.

term *noun*
1 He was sentenced to a *term* in prison. period, spell, stretch, time.
2 He didn't understand the technical *terms*. expression, phrase, saying, word.
terms The others wouldn't agree to the *terms*. conditions.

terminal *noun*
> She spends all day working at a
> *terminal.* computer screen, VDU or
> visual display unit.
> A desk with a terminal where you work
> on a computer is a **workstation**.

terminate *verb*
> The company terminated his contract.
> end, finish, put an end to, stop.

terminus *noun*
> They stayed on the bus until it reached
> the terminus. destination, terminal.

terrible *adjective*
> They saw a terrible accident. appalling,
> awful, distressing, dreadful, [*informal*]
> fearful, frightful, ghastly, horrible,
> horrific, horrifying, revolting,
> shocking.
> The adjective *terrible* is most
> commonly used informally to mean
> *very bad*. See *bad* for the many other
> synonyms you could use

terrific *adjective* [*informal*]
> **1** *The fish he caught was a terrific size.*
> big, colossal, enormous, giant, gigantic,
> great, huge, immense, impressive,
> large, massive, mighty, monstrous,
> monumental, stupendous, tremendous,
> vast.
> **2** *She's a terrific tennis player.*
> excellent, exceptional, first-class, good,
> marvellous, outstanding, phenomenal,
> remarkable, sensational, superb,
> supreme, unequalled, wonderful.
>
> INFORMAL SYNONYMS ARE: brilliant,
> fabulous, fantastic, great, incredible,
> smashing.
> The adjective *terrific* is used informally
> to describe anything which is extreme
> in some way, and synonyms you might
> use depend on what you are talking
> about. Here are some examples of
> words you could use as synonyms in
> particular senses.
> A terrific noise is a **loud** or **deafening**
> noise.
> A terrific storm is a **violent** storm.
> Terrific food is **delicious** food.
> A terrific speed is a very **fast** speed.

terrify *verb*
> The dog was terrified by thunder.
> alarm, dismay, frighten, horrify, make
> afraid, petrify, scare.

territory *noun*
> They entered the enemy's territory. area,
> country, district, land, region, sector,
> zone.
> A territory which is part of a country is
> a **province**.

terror *noun*
> They were filled with terror when the
> volcano erupted. alarm, dread, fear,
> fright, horror, panic.

terrorist *noun*
> A terrorist may be a **gunman** or a
> **bomber**.
> A terrorist who kills someone is an
> **assassin**.
> A terrorist who takes over an aircraft
> or vehicle is a **hijacker**.

terrorize *verb*
> The local people were terrorized by a
> gang. bully, frighten, intimidate,
> menace, persecute, scare, terrify,
> threaten.

test *noun*
> She did very well in the test. appraisal,
> assessment, evaluation, examination.
> A set of questions you answer for fun is
> a **quiz**.
> A test for a job as an actor or singer is
> an **audition**.
> A test to find the truth about
> something is an **experiment** or **trial**.

test *verb*
> **1** *They were tested on all that they had
> learned.* examine, question.
> **2** *They test a new medicine before they
> let people use it.* appraise, assess,
> check, evaluate, experiment with,
> investigate, try out.

testify *verb*
> He testified that he had seen the
> robbery take place. declare, give
> evidence, state on oath, swear.

testimonial *noun*
> Her boss gave her a testimonial when
> she applied for a new job.
> commendation, recommendation,
> reference.

tether *verb*
He tethered the goat to a post. chain up, fasten, secure, tie up.

text *noun*
1 *She studied the text of the document.* contents, wording, words.
2 *He quoted a text from the Bible.* extract, passage, sentence, verse.

textiles *plural noun*
FOR VARIOUS KINDS OF TEXTILES, SEE **cloth**.

texture *noun*
Silk has a smooth texture. feel, quality, touch.

thankful *adjective*
He was thankful for her help. appreciative, grateful, happy, pleased, relieved.
AN OPPOSITE IS ungrateful.

thanks *plural noun*
She sent him a card to show her thanks. appreciation, gratefulness, gratitude.

thaw *verb*
1 *The snow began to thaw when the sun came out.* melt.
2 *Leave frozen food to thaw before cooking it.* defrost, soften, unfreeze.
AN OPPOSITE IS freeze.

theatre *noun*

PARTS OF A THEATRE: auditorium, balcony, bar, boxes, box office, circle, dress circle, dressing rooms, foyer, gallery, orchestra pit, stage, stalls.

PEOPLE WHO PERFORM OR WORK IN A THEATRE: actor, actress, ballerina, dancer, director, dresser, make-up artist, musician, producer, prompter, scene shifter, stage manager, understudy, usher or usherette.

VARIOUS THINGS YOU MIGHT GO TO SEE AT A THEATRE: ballet, comedy, drama, farce, mime, music hall, opera, operetta, pantomime, play.
FOR OTHER ENTERTAINMENTS, SEE **entertainment**.

theft *noun*
He was found guilty of theft. robbery, stealing.
FOR VARIOUS KINDS OF THEFT, SEE **stealing**.

theme *noun*
1 *What was the theme of the lecture?* argument, idea, subject, topic.
2 *The band played themes from well-known films.* air, melody, tune.

theoretical *adjective*
The book is too theoretical. abstract, hypothetical.

theory *noun*
1 *He has a theory about what happened.* belief, explanation, hypothesis, idea, notion, suggestion, view.
2 *She began to study musical theory.* laws, principles, rules.

therapy *noun*
He needs therapy after his accident. treatment.

SOME KINDS OF THERAPY:
acupuncture, aromatherapy, chemotherapy, homeopathy, hydrotherapy, hypnotherapy, occupational therapy, osteopathy, physiotherapy, psychotherapy, radiotherapy.
FOR OTHER KINDS OF MEDICAL TREATMENT, SEE **medicine**.

thick *adjective*
The shed was made from thick planks of wood. chunky, stout, substantial.
The adjective *thick* is used in many other ways, and synonyms you might use often depend on what you are talking about. We give some common examples here
A thick line is a **broad** or **wide** line.
A thick book is a **bulky** or **chunky** book.
Thick snow is **deep** snow.
Thick cloth is **heavy** cloth.
Thick rope is **stout** or **substantial** rope.
Thick fog is **dense** fog.
Thick mud is **sticky** or **stiff** mud.
AN OPPOSITE IS thin.
Thick is also an informal word for **stupid**.

thief *noun*

The police managed to catch the thief. robber.
Someone who steals from people's homes is a **burglar** or **housebreaker**.
Someone who steals from people in the street is a **mugger** or **pickpocket**.
Someone who steals from shops is a **shoplifter**.
Someone who steals by cheating people is a **con man** or **swindler**.
A person who steals fish or game on someone else's land is a **poacher**.
Someone who steals from homes or shops during a riot is a **looter**.
Someone who used to steal from travellers was a **highwayman**.
Sailors who steal from other ships at sea are **pirates**.

thin *adjective*

The refugees were dreadfully thin. bony, gaunt, lean, skinny, spare, underweight.
Someone who is thin and tall is **lanky**.
Someone who is thin but strong is **wiry**.
Someone who is thin but attractive is **slim** or **slender**.
The adjective *thin* is used in many other ways, and synonyms you might use often depend on what you are talking about. We give some common examples here.
A thin line is a **fine** or **narrow** line.
A thin book is a **slim** book.
A thin covering of snow is a **light** covering.
Thin cloth is **delicate** or **flimsy** cloth.
Thin fog is **slight** or **wispy** fog.
Thin gravy is **runny** or **watery** gravy.
AN OPPOSITE IS fat or thick.

thin *verb*

He thinned the paint. dilute, water down, weaken.
to thin out *The crowd thinned out later in the day.* become less dense, diminish, disperse.

thing *noun*

The word *thing* can be used instead of almost any other noun, apart from nouns which refer to people. The list of synonyms, therefore, could be virtually endless. We give just some of the more general synonyms here.

WORDS FOR A THING YOU CAN TOUCH AND HOLD: article, device, implement, item, object.

WORDS FOR A THING THAT HAPPENS: affair, event, happening, incident, occurrence, phenomenon.

WORDS FOR A THING YOU TALK OR THINK ABOUT: concept, detail, fact, factor, idea, point, statement, thought.

WORDS FOR A THING YOU HAVE TO DO: act, action, job, task.

things *Put your things on the table.*
baggage, belongings, equipment, gear, luggage, possessions, stuff.

think *verb*

1 *Think before you do anything rash.*
consider, deliberate, reason, reflect, use your intelligence, work things out.
To think hard about something is to **concentrate** on it or **contemplate** it.
To think quietly and deeply about something is to **meditate**.
To keep thinking anxiously about something is to **brood** on it.
2 *Do you think this is a good idea?*
accept, admit, be convinced, believe, conclude, judge.
3 *What do you think this is worth?*
assume, estimate, feel, guess, imagine, presume, reckon, suppose.
to think something out *She thought out a solution to the problem.* analyse, calculate, puzzle out, work out.
to think something up *They thought up a plan.* conceive, create, design, devise, invent, make up.

thirsty *adjective*

She was thirsty after her long walk. parched.
If someone is ill through lack of fluids, they are **dehydrated**.

thorn *noun*

Don't scratch yourself on the thorns.
needle, prickle, spike, spine.

thorny *adjective*

1 *He fell into a thorny gorse bush.*
bristly, prickly, scratchy, sharp, spiky, spiny.
2 *They discussed the thorny problem for hours.* baffling, complex, complicated, difficult, formidable, hard, involved, perplexing, ticklish, tricky.

thorough *adjective*
1 *The mechanic made a thorough examination of the car.* attentive, careful, comprehensive, conscientious, full, methodical, meticulous, observant, orderly, organized, painstaking, systematic, thoughtful.
AN OPPOSITE IS superficial.
2 *He's made a thorough mess of it!* absolute, complete, downright, perfect, total, utter.

thought *noun*
1 *She gave a lot of thought to the problem.* attention, consideration, deliberation, study.
2 *He spent much time in thought.* brooding, contemplation, meditation, reflection, thinking.
3 *He explained his thoughts about the issue.* belief, conclusion, idea, notion, opinion.

thoughtful *adjective*
1 *She had a thoughtful expression on her face.* absorbed, attentive, brooding, reflective, serious, solemn, studious, wary.
AN OPPOSITE IS carefree.
2 *It was a thoughtful piece of work.* careful, conscientious, methodical, meticulous, systematic, thorough.
AN OPPOSITE IS careless.
3 *It was very thoughtful of her to visit him in hospital.* caring, considerate, friendly, good-natured, helpful, kind, unselfish.
AN OPPOSITE IS thoughtless.

thoughtless *adjective*
He acted in a thoughtless way. careless, forgetful, inconsiderate, irresponsible, negligent, rash, reckless, selfish, uncaring, unthinking.
AN OPPOSITE IS thoughtful.

thrash *verb*
1 *She hated seeing him thrash that donkey.* hit, thump, [*informal*] wallop, whack, whip.
2 *We thrashed them 6–0.* beat, defeat, win against.

thread *noun*
There was a loose thread hanging from her dress. fibre, strand.

SOME KINDS OF THREAD: cotton, nylon, silk, string, twine, wool, yarn.

threadbare *adjective*
The beggar wore threadbare clothes. frayed, old, shabby, tattered, tatty, worn, worn out.

threat *noun*
1 *The terrorists issued a threat against his life.* warning.
2 *They lived under constant threat of famine.* danger, menace, risk.

threaten *verb*
1 *A gang of hooligans threatened them.* intimidate, make threats against, menace, terrorize.
2 *The forecast threatened rain.* warn of.
3 *The species is threatened with extinction.* endanger, put at risk.

three *noun*
A group of three musicians is a ***trio***.
Three babies born at the same time are ***triplets***.
A shape with three sides is a ***triangle***.
To multiply a number by three is to ***triple*** it.

thrifty *adjective*
She's very thrifty and manages to save a lot of money. careful, economical, frugal, prudent, sparing.
AN OPPOSITE IS extravagant.

thrill *noun*
He loves the thrill of rock climbing. adventure, [*slang*] buzz, excitement, [*informal*] kick, sensation, tingle.

thrill *verb*
The music thrilled them. delight, electrify, excite, rouse, stimulate, stir.
AN OPPOSITE IS bore.

thriller *noun*
She was reading an exciting thriller. crime story, detective story, murder story, mystery story.

thrive *verb*
Tomato plants thrive in the greenhouse. do well, flourish, grow, prosper, succeed.

thriving *adjective*
He runs a thriving business. booming, expanding, healthy, profitable, prosperous, successful.
AN OPPOSITE IS unsuccessful.

throb *noun*
He felt the throb of the ship's engine. beat, pulse, rhythm, vibration.

throb *verb*
She could feel the blood throbbing through her veins. beat, pound.

throng *noun*
There were throngs of people on the street. crowd, horde, swarm.
SEE ALSO **group**.

throttle *verb*
The mugger tried to throttle him. choke, strangle, suffocate.

throw *verb*
1 *I threw a stone into the pool.* [*slang*] bung, cast, [*informal*] chuck, fling, pitch, sling, toss.
To deliver the ball in cricket is to ***bowl***.
To throw the shot in athletics is to ***put*** the shot.
To throw something high in the air is to ***lob*** it.
To throw something heavy is to ***heave*** it.
To throw something with great force is to ***hurl*** it.
If someone throws a lot of things at you, they ***pelt*** you.
2 *The horse threw its rider.* dislodge, shake off, throw off.
to throw away *She threw away her old clothes.* discard, dispose of, [*informal*] dump, get rid of, scrap.

thrust *verb*
1 *He thrust his hands into his pockets.* force, push, shove.
2 *They saw the murderer thrust with a dagger.* jab, lunge, poke, prod, stab.

thump *verb*
Someone thumped him and left him with a black eye. [*informal*] bash, hit, punch, slog, [*informal*] slosh, wallop.
SEE ALSO **hit** *verb*.

thunder *noun, verb*
They could hear the thunder.
You can also speak of a ***clap***, ***crack***, ***peal***, or ***roll*** of thunder.

thunderous *adjective*
The audience greeted the actors with thunderous applause. deafening, loud, noisy, resounding.
AN OPPOSITE IS quiet.

tick *verb*
A clock was ticking in the background.
FOR VARIOUS WAYS TO MAKE SOUNDS, SEE **sound** *verb*.
to tick someone off [*informal*] *She ticked him off for talking in class.* reprimand, reproach, scold, tell off.

ticket *noun*
1 *They got free tickets for the concert.* coupon, pass, permit, token, voucher.
2 *What does it say on the price ticket?* label, tab, tag.

tickle *verb*
1 *She giggled when he tickled her feet.*
FOR VARIOUS WAYS TO TOUCH SOMEONE, SEE **touch** *verb*.
2 *This idea will tickle you.* amuse, cheer you up, make you laugh, please.

ticklish *adjective*
1 *He's very ticklish.* sensitive.
2 *It was a ticklish problem.* awkward, complex, complicated, difficult, hard, involved, perplexing, thorny, tricky.

tide *noun*
The moon determines the sea's tides. current, movement, rise and fall.
When the tide is coming in it is ***flowing***.
When the tide is going out it is ***ebbing***.
Tides when there is the biggest difference between high and low water are ***spring tides***.
Tides when there is the least difference between high and low water are ***neap tides***.

tidy *adjective*
He always kept his room tidy. neat, orderly, smart, spruce, straight, trim, uncluttered.
AN OPPOSITE IS untidy.

tie *verb*
1 *She tied the rope around the tree.*
bind, fasten, hitch, knot, loop, secure.
AN OPPOSITE IS untie.
To tie up a boat is to ***moor*** it.
To tie up an animal is to ***tether*** it.
2 *The two teams tied.* be equal, be level,
draw, score the same.

tight *adjective*
1 *The lid was too tight for him to
unscrew.* close, firm, secure, snug.
If it is so tight that air cannot get
through, it is ***airtight***.
If it is so tight that water cannot get
through, it is ***watertight***.
AN OPPOSITE IS loose.
2 *They squeezed into the tight space.*
cramped, crowded, packed, small.
AN OPPOSITE IS spacious.
3 *The ropes were too tight.* rigid,
stretched, taut, tense.
AN OPPOSITE IS slack.
4 *She's tight with her money.* mean,
[*informal*] mingy, miserly, stingy.
AN OPPOSITE IS extravagant or
generous.

tighten *verb*
1 *She tightened her grip on his hand.*
hold tighter, squeeze.
2 *You need to tighten the guy ropes.*
make taut, pull tighter, stretch.
3 *He tried to tighten the screw.* make
tighter, screw up.
AN OPPOSITE IS loosen.

till *verb*
Farmers use tractors to till the land.
cultivate, dig, plough, prepare.

tilt *verb*
The caravan tilted to one side. incline,
keel over, lean, slant, slope, tip.
When a ship tilts to one side, it ***lists***.

timber *noun*
He bought some timber to build a shed.
wood.

VARIOUS FORMS OF TIMBER: beams,
boards or boarding, deal, hardwood,
laths, logs, lumber, planks or
planking, posts, softwood, stakes,
tree trunks.

MANUFACTURED KINDS OF BOARD:
blockboard, chipboard, hardboard,
plywood.

time *noun*
1 *Is this a convenient time to phone?*
moment, occasion, opportunity.
2 *Spring is her favourite time of the
year.* phase, season.
3 *He spent a time in prison.* session,
spell, stretch, term, while.
4 *Shakespeare lived in the time of
Elizabeth I.* age, days, epoch, era,
period.
5 *Please try to keep time with the music.*
beat, rhythm, tempo.
in good time, **on time** *Please try to be
on time.* prompt, punctual.

UNITS WE USE TO MEASURE TIME:
second, minute, hour, day, week,
fortnight, month, year, decade,
century, millennium, eternity.

DEVICES FOR MEASURING TIME:
calendar, chronometer, clock, digital
clock, digital watch, hourglass,
stopwatch, sundial, timer, watch,
wristwatch.

timetable *noun*
*They worked out a timetable for sports
day.* programme, rota, schedule.

timid *adjective*
She was too timid to say anything.
afraid, anxious, apprehensive, bashful,
cowardly, coy, fearful, nervous,
sheepish, shy, unadventurous.
AN OPPOSITE IS brave or confident.

tin *noun*
He opened a tin of beans. can.
FOR OTHER CONTAINERS, SEE
container.

tingle *verb*
Her fingers were tingling with the cold.
itch, prickle, sting, tickle.

tingle *noun*
1 *She felt a tingle in her foot.* itch,
itching, pins and needles, prickling,
stinging, tickle, tickling.
2 *He felt a tingle of excitement.* quiver,
sensation, shiver, thrill.

tinker *verb*
*He tinkered with the TV, trying to get it
to work.* fiddle, interfere, meddle, mess
about, play about, tamper.

tinny *adjective*
> *The car seemed rather tinny.* cheap, inferior, poor quality, trashy.

tint *noun*
> *The paint she chose had a nice blue tint.* colour, hue, shade, tone.
> FOR NAMES OF COLOURS, SEE **colour**.

tiny *adjective*
> *You can hardly see it—it's so tiny.* little, microscopic, midget, miniature, minute.
> AN OPPOSITE IS big.

tip *noun*
> **1** *The tip of his nose felt cold.* end, point, sharp end.
> The tip of an ink pen is a **nib**.
> **2** *The tip of the mountain was covered in snow.* cap, head, peak, summit, top, [*formal*] vertex.
> **3** *He gave them some useful tips on first aid.* clue, hint, piece of advice, suggestion, warning.
> **4** *They took a load of rubbish to the tip.* dump, recycling centre, rubbish heap.

tip *verb*
> **1** *She tipped the waiter.* give a tip to, reward.
> **2** *The caravan tipped to one side.* incline, keel over, lean, slant, slope, tilt.
> When a ship tips slightly to one side, it **lists**.
> When a ship tips right over, it **capsizes**.
> **3** *He tipped his stuff on to the table.* dump, empty, turn out, unload.
> **to tip over** *He tipped the milk bottle over.* knock over, overturn, topple, upset.

tiptoe *verb*
> FOR VARIOUS WAYS WE WALK, SEE **walk** *verb*.

tire *verb*
> *The long game tired them.* exhaust, wear out.
> AN OPPOSITE IS refresh or rest.

tired *adjective*
> *Have a lie down if you're tired.* [*informal*] all in, drowsy, exhausted, fatigued, flagging, listless, sleepy, weary, worn out.
> **to be tired of something** *I'm tired of watching TV.* bored with, [*informal*] fed up with, sick of.
> If you are not interested in anything, you are **apathetic**.

tireless *adjective*
> *She's a tireless worker.* determined, energetic, persistent, unflagging, untiring.
> AN OPPOSITE IS lazy.

tiresome *adjective*
> *The children were being rather tiresome.* [*informal*] aggravating, annoying, exasperating, irritating, troublesome, trying, unwelcome, vexing.
> AN OPPOSITE IS welcome.

tiring *adjective*
> *Digging the garden is tiring work.* demanding, difficult, exhausting, fatiguing, hard, laborious, tough.
> AN OPPOSITE IS refreshing.

title *noun*
> *She couldn't think of a title for the story.* heading, name.
> The title above a newspaper story is a **headline**.
> A title or brief description next to a picture is a **caption**.

A person's title shows their **position**, **rank**, or **status** in society.

TITLES USED BEFORE THE NAMES OF MOST ORDINARY PEOPLE: Miss, Mr, Mrs, Ms.
The full forms of these words no longer exist, although you can use *mister* informally for *Mr*, and *missis* or *missus* informally for *Mrs*

OTHER TITLES USED BEFORE A PERSON'S NAME: Doctor or [*short form*] Dr, Professor, Reverend or [*short form*] Rev. ➡

TITLES OF NOBLES OR KNIGHTS: Baron, Baroness, Count, Countess, Dame, Duchess, Duke, Earl, Lady, Lord, Marchioness, Marquis, Sir, Viscount, Viscountess.

TITLES YOU MIGHT USE WHEN SPEAKING TO PEOPLE: madam, my lady, my lord, sir, sire, your grace, your honour, your majesty.
A person's rank in the armed services may also be used as a title before their name.
SEE ALSO **rank**.

toast verb
1 *He toasted the stale bread.* brown, grill.
2 *They toasted the bride and groom.* drink a toast to, drink the health of, raise your glass to.

together adverb
1 *They walked to school together.* hand in hand, shoulder to shoulder, side by side.
2 *The men all shouted together.* all at once, at the same time, in chorus, in unison, simultaneously.
AN OPPOSITE IS independently or separately.

toil verb
He's been toiling all day. exert yourself, labour, slave, struggle, work hard.

toilet noun
Can you tell me where the toilet is? cloakroom, conveniences, lavatory, WC.

token noun
1 *You can exchange this token for a free drink.* counter, coupon, voucher.
2 *They gave her the flowers as a token of their affection.* evidence, expression, indication, reminder, sign, signal, symbol.

tolerable adjective
1 *The heat was tolerable.* acceptable, bearable, endurable.
2 *The food was tolerable.* adequate, all right, fair, mediocre, [*informal*] OK, passable, satisfactory.
AN OPPOSITE IS intolerable.

tolerant adjective
She's very tolerant towards other people. broad-minded, easygoing, forgiving, generous, indulgent, lenient, liberal, open-minded, permissive, sympathetic, understanding, unprejudiced, willing to forgive.
AN OPPOSITE IS intolerant.

tolerate verb
1 *He won't tolerate bad language.* accept, forgive, make allowances for, permit, put up with.
2 *She can't tolerate pain.* abide, bear, endure, [*informal*] stand, stick, [*informal*] stomach, suffer.

tomb noun

PLACES WHERE DEAD PEOPLE ARE BURIED: catacomb, crypt, grave, mausoleum, sarcophagus, sepulchre, vault.

THINGS WHICH MARK PLACES WHERE PEOPLE ARE BURIED: gravestone, headstone, memorial, monument, plaque, tombstone.

tone noun
1 *There was an angry tone to her voice.* inflection, intonation, manner, note, quality, sound.
2 *The house was painted in subtle tones.* colour, hue, shade, tint.
3 *Eerie music created the right tone for the film.* atmosphere, effect, feeling, mood, spirit.

tone verb
to tone something down *He asked them to tone down the noise.* lessen, quieten, reduce, soften, turn down.
to tone in with *The new curtains tone in with the background.* blend with, fit in with, match, merge into.

tongue-tied adjective
He gets tongue-tied when he's embarrassed. dumb, mute, silent, speechless.

tool *noun*
 He keeps his tools in the garage.
 apparatus, appliance, device, gadget,
 implement, instrument, utensil.

TOOLS YOU MIGHT USE DOING
WOODWORK: auger, awl, brace and
bit, bradawl, chisel, clamp, drill,
gimlet, hammer, jigsaw, mallet,
pincers, plane, power drill, rasp,
sander, saw, set square, spokeshave,
T-square, vice.
SEE ALSO **saw.**

TOOLS YOU MIGHT USE IN THE
HOME: brush, cooking utensil,
needle, penknife, scales, scissors,
tape measure, tweezers.
FOR VARIOUS COOKING UTENSILS,
SEE **cook** *verb.*

TOOLS YOU MIGHT USE IF YOU HAVE
A COAL FIRE: bellows, poker, tongs.

TOOLS YOU MIGHT USE IN
GARDENING, ETC.: axe, chain saw,
chopper, crowbar, dibber, fork, grass
rake, hoe, ladder, lawnmower,
mattock, pick, pickaxe, pitchfork,
rake, roller, scythe, secateurs,
shears, shovel, sickle,
sledgehammer, spade, strimmer,
trowel.

TOOLS YOU MIGHT USE ON A BIKE
OR CAR, ETC.: Allen key, box spanner,
file, jack, lever, pliers, pump, ring
spanner, screwdriver, wrench.

---

tooth *noun*

VARIOUS TEETH IN A PERSON'S
MOUTH: canine tooth, eyetooth,
incisor, molar, wisdom tooth.
A dog's or wolf's canine tooth is a
fang.
A long tooth that sticks out of an
animal's mouth is a ***tusk***.

FALSE TEETH: bridge or bridgework,
dentures, plate.

SOME PROBLEMS PEOPLE HAVE
WITH THEIR TEETH: caries, cavity,
decay, plaque, toothache.
SEE ALSO **dentist.**

---

top *noun*
 1 They climbed to the top of the hill.
 crest, crown, head, peak, summit, tip,
 [*formal*] vertex.
 AN OPPOSITE IS bottom.
 2 The table top was covered with
 newspapers. surface.
 3 He couldn't get the top off the jar. cap,
 cover, covering, lid.

top *adjective*
 1 She got top marks in the exam. best,
 highest, most, winning.
 2 They set off at top speed. greatest,
 high, maximum.
 AN OPPOSITE IS low.
 3 She's the top executive in her firm.
 most important, senior, supreme.
 AN OPPOSITE IS junior.

top *verb*
 1 She topped the cake with chopped
 nuts. cover, decorate, finish off.
 2 Their new record topped the charts.
 be at the top of, dominate.

topic *noun*
 They discussed several topics. issue,
 matter, question, subject, talking-
 point.

topical *adjective*
 He asked what the topical issues were.
 current, up to date.

topple *verb*
 1 He toppled off the wall. fall, tumble.
 2 The gale toppled their TV aerial.
 knock down, overturn, tip over, upset.
 3 They managed to topple the prime
 minister. get rid of, overthrow, remove.

torment *verb*
 1 Toothache tormented her. afflict, hurt,
 inflict pain on, torture.
 2 He told them to stop tormenting the
 other children. annoy, bother, bully,
 distress, harass, pester, tease, vex,
 worry.
 To torment people continually is to
 plague or ***victimize*** them.
 To torment people because of their
 beliefs is to ***persecute*** them.

torment *noun*
 She was in great torment. affliction,
 agony, anguish, distress, misery, pain,
 persecution, plague, purgatory,
 scourge, suffering, torture.

torrent *noun*
A torrent of water flowed down the hill.
cascade, flood, gush, rush, stream.

torrential *adjective*
They got caught in a torrential rainstorm. heavy, soaking, violent.
Torrential rain is sometimes called a **cloudburst** or **deluge** or **downpour**.

torture *noun*
1 *He died under torture.* cruel treatment, persecution.
2 *She was suffering the torture of a bad toothache.* affliction, agony, anguish, pain, suffering, torment.

torture *verb*
They tortured prisoners who refused to cooperate. be cruel to, cause pain to, hurt, inflict pain on, persecute, torment.

toss *verb*
1 *He tossed a coin into the wishing-well.* cast, [*informal*] chuck, fling, lob, pitch, sling, throw.
2 *They tossed a coin to see who would go first.* flick, flip, spin.
to toss about 1 *The little boat tossed about on the waves.* bob up and down, lurch, pitch, rock, roll.
2 *She tossed about in the uncomfortable bed.* move restlessly, twist and turn, writhe.

total *noun*
Add the figures and tell me the total. amount, answer, sum.

total *adjective*
1 *The bill shows the total amount due.* complete, entire, full, whole.
2 *The party was a total disaster.* absolute, downright, perfect, sheer, thorough, utter.

total *verb*
1 *He totalled the figures.* add up, calculate, count, find the total of, reckon up, work out.
2 *The collection totalled £37.* add up to, amount to, come to, make, reach.

totter *verb*
The child tottered across the floor. reel, stagger, stumble, wobble.
FOR VARIOUS WAYS TO WALK, SEE **walk** *verb*.

touch *verb*
1 *He doesn't like people touching him.* caress, feel, finger, fondle, handle, nuzzle, pat, paw, pet, rub, stroke, tickle.
2 *The car just touched the gatepost.* brush, contact, graze, hit, knock.
3 *Their speed touched 100 m.p.h.* reach, rise to.
4 *She was touched by the sad music.* affect, move, stir.
to touch down *They expect the plane to touch down on time.* arrive, get in, land.
to touch something up *She touched up the paintwork on her car.* improve, repair.

touch *noun*
1 *I felt a touch on my arm.* caress, contact, pat, stroke, tap.
2 *Working with animals requires a special touch.* ability, knack, manner, sensitivity, skill, technique, understanding, way.
3 *There's a touch of frost in the air.* hint, suggestion, trace.

touchy *adjective*
Be careful what you say because he's very touchy. easily offended, irritable, quick-tempered.

tough *adjective*
1 *You'll need tough shoes for the climb.* durable, hard wearing, robust, stout, strong, sturdy, substantial, well made.
AN OPPOSITE IS flimsy.
2 *The meat was very tough.* chewy, gristly, leathery, rubbery.
AN OPPOSITE IS tender.
3 *They played against tough opposition.* determined, powerful, resistant, resolute, ruthless, stiff, strong, stubborn.
AN OPPOSITE IS weak.
4 *The police deal with some tough criminals.* brutal, disorderly, rough, unruly, violent.
AN OPPOSITE IS feeble.
5 *It was a tough climb.* demanding, exhausting, gruelling, laborious, strenuous, tiring.
AN OPPOSITE IS gentle.

6 *The problem was too tough for him.*
baffling, difficult, hard, knotty,
puzzling, thorny.
AN OPPOSITE IS easy.

toughen *verb*
Joining the army will toughen him up.
harden, make tougher, strengthen.

tour *noun*
They went on a sightseeing tour. drive,
excursion, expedition, jaunt, journey,
outing, ride, trip.

tourist *noun*
The cathedral was full of tourists.
holidaymaker, sightseer, traveller,
visitor.

tournament *noun*
*He reached the semi-final of the tennis
tournament.* championship,
competition, contest, series.

tow *verb*
They towed the car to the garage. drag,
draw, haul, pull, tug along.

tower *noun*

VARIOUS KINDS OF TOWER: belfry,
castle, fort, fortress, keep, minaret,
silo, skyscraper, steeple, turret.
The pointed structure on a church
tower is a **spire**.

tower *verb*
   to tower above something *The castle
   towers above the village.* dominate,
   loom over, rise above, stand above,
   stick up above.

town *noun*

A town with its own local council is a
borough.
An important town, often with a
cathedral, is a **city**.
Several towns that merge into each
other are a **conurbation**.

PLACES OR THINGS YOU MAY FIND
IN TOWNS: bank, bus station, café,
car park, cinema, college, concert
hall, council offices, factory, filling
station, flats, garage, hotel, housing
estate, industrial estate, leisure
centre, library, market, ➡

market place, museum, office block,
park, police station, post office, pub,
railway station, recreation ground,
residential area, restaurant, roads,
school, shopping centre, shops, snack
bar, sports centre, square, suburb,
supermarket, theatre, university,
warehouse.

toxic *adjective*
The toxic fumes made him ill.
dangerous, deadly, harmful, poisonous.
AN OPPOSITE IS harmless.

toy *noun*

SOME TOYS CHILDREN PLAY WITH:
ball, balloon, board game, building
bricks, card game, computer game,
construction kit, doll, doll's house,
frisbee, hoop, kaleidoscope, kite,
marbles, puppet, puzzle, rattle,
rocking horse, rollerblades, roller
skates, skateboard, skipping rope,
teddy bear, top, tricycle, water pistol,
yo-yo.
The names of some toys are simply
names of real things with the word
toy or *model* before them. For
example, *toy car, toy theatre, model
aeroplane*, etc. Many toys have
names which are trademarks, which
we don't give here

trace *noun*
   1 *He left no trace of his presence.* clue,
   evidence, hint, indication, mark, sign,
   track, trail.
   A trace left by an animal might be its
   footprint or **scent** or **spoor**.
   2 *They found traces of poison in the
   food.* tiny amount.

trace *verb*
   1 *She was trying to trace her lost
   relatives.* seek out, track down.
   2 *They managed to trace the cause of
   the fire.* discover, find.

track *noun*
   1 *He walked along a track past the
   farm.* bridle path or bridleway, cart
   track, footpath, path, way.
   2 *They followed the fox's tracks for
   miles.* footmark or footprint, scent,
   trail.

3 *They laid the track for a tram system.* line, rails.
4 *They ran round the track.* circuit, course, racetrack.

track *verb*
The hunters were tracking a fox. chase, follow, hound, hunt, pursue, stalk, tail, trail.
to track someone or **something down**
They tracked down the owner of the car. discover, find, trace.

tract *noun*
They had to cross a tract of desert. area, expanse, stretch.

trade *noun*
1 *The shopkeeper says that trade is good at present.* business, buying and selling, commerce, dealing, the market, trading.
2 *He wanted to learn a trade.* craft, occupation, profession.
FOR VARIOUS KINDS OF EMPLOYMENT, SEE **job**.

trade *verb*
to trade in something *The company trades in second-hand computers.* buy and sell, deal in, do business in, retail, sell.
FOR VARIOUS PEOPLE WHO SELL THINGS, SEE **sell**.
To trade in something illegally is to *traffic* in it.
to trade something in *She wants to trade her old car in.* exchange, offer in part exchange, [*informal*] swap.

tradition *noun*
It's a tradition to sing 'Auld Lang Syne' on New Year's Eve. convention, custom, fashion, habit, routine.

traditional *adjective*
They wore traditional costumes. conventional, customary, familiar, habitual, historic, normal, regular, typical, usual.

traffic *noun*
FOR VARIOUS KINDS OF VEHICLE, SEE **vehicle**.

traffic *verb*
He was accused of trafficking in drugs. trade illegally.

tragedy *noun*
1 *'Romeo and Juliet' is a tragedy.* AN OPPOSITE IS comedy.
2 *His death was a tragedy.* calamity, catastrophe, disaster, misfortune.

tragic *adjective*
1 *He died in a tragic accident.* awful, calamitous, catastrophic, disastrous, distressing, dreadful, fatal, terrible, unfortunate, unlucky.
2 *She had a tragic expression on her face.* distressed, hurt, mournful, pathetic, pitiful, sad, sorrowful, woeful, wretched.
AN OPPOSITE IS comic or happy.

trail *noun*
1 *They walked along a trail through the woods.* path, pathway, route, track.
2 *The hounds followed the fox's trail.* footprints, scent, signs, spoor, traces.
The trail left in the water by a ship is its *wake*.

trail *verb*
1 *The hounds trailed the fox for miles.* chase, follow, hunt, pursue, shadow, stalk, tail, track.
2 *He trailed a cart behind him.* drag, draw, haul, pull, tow.
3 *They told him to stop trailing behind.* dawdle, hang about, lag, loiter, straggle.

train *noun*
1 *They went to London by train.* FOR WORDS CONNECTED WITH TRAVEL BY TRAIN, SEE **railway**.
2 *It was a strange train of events.* chain, sequence, series, string, succession.

train *verb*
1 *He trains the football team every Saturday.* coach, instruct, prepare, teach.
2 *She needs to train harder.* do exercises, exercise, get fit, practise, prepare yourself.
3 *He trained his rifle on the target.* aim (at), line up, point (at).

trainer *noun*
1 *Their trainer makes them work hard.* coach, instructor, teacher.
2 *Where are my trainers?* FOR THINGS YOU WEAR ON YOUR FEET, SEE **shoe**.

traitor noun
> The traitor betrayed his country.
> collaborator, defector, deserter, double-crosser, spy, turncoat.

tramp verb
> They tramped across the hills. hike, march, plod, stride, trek, trudge.
> FOR VARIOUS WAYS WE WALK, SEE **walk** verb.

trample verb
> They trampled on the flowers. crush, flatten, squash, stamp on, tread on, walk over.

trance noun
> He was lost in a trance. daydream, daze, dream.
> One way to be in a trance is to be **hypnotized**.
> Unconsciousness caused by an illness or accident is a **coma**.

tranquil adjective
> They led a tranquil life in the country. calm, peaceful, placid, quiet, restful, serene, still, undisturbed.
> AN OPPOSITE IS exciting or stormy.

transact verb
> He has some business to transact. attend to, carry out, deal with, do, execute, perform, undertake.

transfer verb
> 1 They transferred some of the books to another classroom. carry, convey, move, remove, take.
> 2 He transferred all the money to her. give, hand over.

transform verb
> He transformed the attic into a bedroom. adapt, alter, change, convert, modify, turn.

transformation noun
> They were amazed by the transformation in her appearance. alteration, change, difference, improvement.

transition noun
> The transition from child to adult is a gradual process. alteration, change, change-over, evolution, movement, progression, shift, transformation.

translate verb
> She translated the visitor's remarks into English. interpret.

translator noun
> A person who translates a foreign language is an **interpreter**.
> An expert in languages is a **linguist**.

transmission noun
> A transmission on radio or TV is a **broadcast**.

transmit verb
> 1 The ship's radio began to transmit a distress signal. broadcast, emit, relay, send out.
> 2 He transmitted the information through the computer network. communicate, convey, dispatch, pass on, send.
> AN OPPOSITE IS receive.

transparent adjective
> The box had a transparent lid. clear, [informal] see-through.
> Something which is not fully transparent, but allows light to shine through, is **translucent**.

transplant verb
> She transplanted the seedlings into the flower bed. move, shift, transfer.

transport verb
> They have to transport goods from the factory to the shops. bring, carry, convey, fetch, haul, move, shift, ship, take, transfer.

> TRANSPORT BY AIR: airship, helicopter, plane.
> SEE ALSO **aircraft**.
>
> TRANSPORT BY ROAD: bus, car, coach, cycle, horse, lorry, minibus, taxi, tram, van.
> SEE ALSO **vehicle**.
>
> TRANSPORT BY RAIL: Metro, monorail, train, tram.
> SEE ALSO **railway**.
>
> TRANSPORT BY WATER: barge, boat, ferry, ship.
> SEE ALSO **vessel**.
>
> FOR VARIOUS WAYS TO TRAVEL, SEE **travel**.

trap *noun*
The animal was caught in a trap. booby trap, net, noose, snare.
Something used to tempt something into a trap is **bait** or a **decoy**.

trap *verb*
They tried to trap the mouse. capture, catch, corner, snare.

trash *noun*
1 He put the trash into the bin. garbage, junk, litter, refuse, rubbish, waste.
2 Don't listen to that trash! nonsense.

travel *verb*
She likes to travel at a leisurely speed. go, journey, move along, proceed, progress.

VARIOUS WAYS TO TRAVEL:
commute, cruise, cycle, drive, fly, go by rail, hike, hitch-hike, motor, pedal, ramble, ride, roam, row, sail, tour, trek, voyage, walk, wander.
When birds travel from one country to another they **migrate**.
When people travel to another country to live there they **emigrate**.
FOR VARIOUS METHODS OF TRANSPORT, SEE ALSO **transport**.

PEOPLE WHO TRAVEL AS A WAY OF LIFE: gypsy, itinerant or tramp, nomad, traveller.

PEOPLE WHO TRAVEL FOR VARIOUS REASONS: astronaut or cosmonaut, commuter, cyclist, driver or motorist, explorer, flyer or aviator, hitch-hiker, holidaymaker, motorcyclist, passenger, pedestrian, rambler or walker, sailor, tourist.
A person who travels to a religious place is a **pilgrim**.
A person who travels illegally on a ship or plane is a **stowaway**.
A person who likes travelling round the world is a **globetrotter**.

treacherous *adjective*
1 A treacherous member of the team revealed our plan to the other side. cheating, deceitful, disloyal, double-crossing, faithless, false, [informal] sneaky, unfaithful, untrustworthy.
AN OPPOSITE IS loyal.
A treacherous person is a **traitor**.

2 The roads are often treacherous in winter. dangerous, hazardous, perilous, risky, unpredictable, unreliable, unsafe.
AN OPPOSITE IS safe.

treachery *noun*
They were appalled by his treachery. betrayal, disloyalty, treason, untrustworthiness.
AN OPPOSITE IS loyalty.

tread *verb*
Please tread carefully. put your foot down, step, walk.
to tread on He asked them not to tread on the flowers. crush, flatten, squash, stamp on, step on, trample, walk on.

treason *noun*
He was executed for treason. betrayal (of), disloyalty (to), rebellion, treachery.
AN OPPOSITE IS loyalty.

treasure *noun*
The treasure was buried somewhere on the island. fortune, hoard, riches, wealth.
Treasure which someone has found hidden is **treasure trove**.

TREASURE MIGHT CONSIST OF:
bullion, coins, gems or precious stones, gold or other precious metals, jewellery, valuables.

treasure *verb*
He treasures the letter she sent him. cherish, prize, value.

treat *verb*
1 She always treated him kindly. behave towards, deal with.
2 The doctor treated her for flu. give treatment to, prescribe medicine for.
To treat a wound is to **dress** it.
To treat an illness or wound successfully is to **cure** or **heal** it.
3 He didn't have any money so she treated him. give you a treat, pay for.

treat *noun*
They took him to the zoo as a birthday treat. special event, surprise.

treatment *noun*
1 *She was angry at the poor treatment of the animals.* attention, care.
2 *His rough treatment of the equipment led to some breakages.* handling, management, use.
3 *He went to the hospital for treatment.* cure, nursing, remedy, therapy.
Treatment you give someone before a medical person arrives is *first aid*.
FOR KINDS OF MEDICAL TREATMENT, SEE **medicine, therapy**.

treaty *noun*
The two sides signed a peace treaty. agreement, armistice, ceasefire, truce.

tree *noun*

> Trees which lose their leaves in winter are *deciduous*.
> Trees which have leaves all year round are *evergreen*.
> Trees which grow cones are *conifers*.
> A young tree is a *sapling*.
> Small, low trees are *bushes* or *shrubs*.
> Miniature trees grown in small containers are *bonsai* trees.
>
> SOME VARIETIES OF TREE: ash, bay, beech, birch, cedar, chestnut, cypress, elder, elm, eucalyptus, fir, hawthorn, hazel, holly, horse chestnut, larch, lime, maple, oak, olive, palm, pine, plane, poplar, rowan, spruce, sweet chestnut, sycamore, tamarisk, willow, yew.
> FOR NAMES OF FRUIT TREES, SEE **fruit**.

tremble *verb*
She was trembling with cold. quake, quiver, shake, shiver, shudder.

tremendous *adjective*
1 *They heard a tremendous bang.* awful, big, enormous, fearful, frightful, great, huge, massive, mighty, [*informal*] terrific.
2 *Winning first prize was a tremendous achievement.* excellent, exceptional, impressive, magnificent, marvellous, outstanding, remarkable, superb, wonderful.

tremor *noun*
A tremor in her voice showed she was nervous. hesitation, quavering, quivering, shaking, trembling, vibration, wobble.

trend *noun*
1 *The general trend is for prices to go up.* bias, direction, movement, shift, tendency.
2 *What's the latest trend in clothes?* craze, fad, fashion, style.

trendy *adjective* [*informal*]
His clothes weren't very trendy. contemporary, fashionable, modern, stylish, up to date.
AN OPPOSITE IS old-fashioned.

trial *noun*
1 *Scientists conducted trials on the new drug.* experiment, test.
2 *The judge predicted that the trial would last a long time.* case, hearing.
A military trial is a *court martial*.

triangular *adjective*
A triangular shape is *three-cornered* or *three-sided*.

tribe *noun*
A group of people who are closely related is a *family*.
A group of related Scottish families is a *clan*.
A succession of people from the same powerful family is a *dynasty*.

tribute *noun*
They heard a moving tribute to the dead woman's courage. appreciation, commendation, compliment.
If you pay tribute to someone, you *praise* them.

trick *noun*
1 *She played a trick on him.* joke, practical joke, prank.
Tricks which are supposed to look like magic are *conjuring tricks*.
2 *The so-called special offer was just a trick.* cheat, [*informal*] con, deception, fraud, hoax, pretence, swindle.
3 *He learnt the tricks of the trade.* art, dodge, knack, secret, skill, technique.

trick *verb*
He tricked them into buying worthless rubbish. cheat, [*slang*] con, deceive, [*slang*] diddle, fool, hoax, swindle.

trickle *verb*
Water trickled from the tap. dribble, drip, flow slowly, leak, ooze, seep.
AN OPPOSITE IS gush.

tricky *adjective*
1 It was a very tricky job. awkward, complicated, difficult, intricate, involved, ticklish.
AN OPPOSITE IS straightforward.
2 He's a tricky person to deal with. crafty, cunning, deceitful, dishonest, sly, [*informal*] sneaky, untrustworthy, wily.
AN OPPOSITE IS trustworthy.

trifle *verb*
She told him not to trifle with her. behave frivolously, fool about, play about.

trifling *adjective*
It was a trifling sum of money. insignificant, minor, negligible, paltry, petty, small, tiny, trivial, unimportant.
AN OPPOSITE IS important or large.

trigger *verb*
to trigger something off The burnt toast triggered off the smoke alarm. activate, set off, start, switch on.

trim *adjective*
He keeps his garden trim. neat, orderly, smart, spruce, tidy, well kept.
AN OPPOSITE IS untidy.

trim *verb*
1 He asked the hairdresser just to trim his hair. clip, cut, shorten.
2 She trimmed her blouse with lace. adorn, decorate.

trip *noun*
They went on a trip to the seaside. day out, excursion, expedition, jaunt, journey, outing, visit.

trip *verb*
1 He tripped on the loose carpet. catch your foot, fall, stagger, stumble, tumble.
2 She was tripping happily along. run, skip.

triumph *noun*
1 They celebrated their great triumph over their opponents. conquest, success, victory, win.
2 They returned in triumph. celebration.

triumphant *adjective*
1 They cheered the triumphant team. conquering, successful, victorious, winning.
AN OPPOSITE IS unsuccessful.
2 He could hear their triumphant laughter. elated, exultant, gleeful, joyful, jubilant.

trivial *adjective*
Don't bother him with trivial details. frivolous, insignificant, little, minor, negligible, paltry, petty, silly, slight, small, superficial, trifling, unimportant, worthless.
AN OPPOSITE IS important.

troop *noun*
A troop of soldiers marched past. company, force, group, platoon, squad.

troop *verb*
They trooped along the road. march, parade, proceed, walk.
To walk one behind the other is to **file** along.

troops *plural noun* SEE **armed services**

trophy *noun*
She won a trophy in swimming. award, cup, medal, prize.

trouble *noun*
1 He's had a lot of trouble recently. affliction, anxiety, burden, difficulty, distress, grief, hardship, illness, inconvenience, misery, misfortune, pain, problem, sadness, sorrow, suffering, unhappiness, vexation, worry.
2 The police dealt with trouble in the crowd. bother, commotion, disorder, disturbance, fighting, fuss, misbehaviour, quarrelling, turmoil, unrest, violence.
to take trouble He took trouble to get it right. take care, labour, make an effort, struggle, take pains, work hard.

trouble verb
 1 *Something is troubling her.* afflict,
concern, distress, grieve, hurt, pain,
torment, upset, vex.
 2 *He asked them not to trouble him just
now.* annoy, bother, disturb, interfere
with, interrupt, pester, worry.
To trouble people in an unfriendly way
is to *molest* or *threaten* them.
To trouble people over a long period is
to *plague* them.
 3 *Nobody troubled to tidy up the room.*
bother, take care, make an effort, take
pains, take trouble, work hard.

troublesome adjective
 1 *He found the heat troublesome.*
annoying, distressing, inconvenient,
irritating, tiresome, trying, upsetting,
vexing, worrying.
 2 *She told off the troublesome children.*
badly behaved, disobedient, disorderly,
naughty, rowdy, unruly.
AN OPPOSITE IS helpful.

trousers plural noun

GARMENTS WITH LEGS: breeches,
corduroys, [*informal*] drainpipes,
dungarees, [*informal*] flares, jeans,
jodhpurs, overalls, [*American*] pants,
shorts, ski pants, slacks, tights,
[*Scottish*] trews, trunks.
FOR OTHER GARMENTS, SEE
clothes.

truant noun
 to play truant
If you play truant from school you are
absent without permission.
To run away from the army is to
desert.

truce noun
 The two sides agreed on a truce.
armistice, ceasefire, end to hostilities,
peace.

true adjective
 1 *His story sounded true.* accurate,
authentic, correct, exact, factual,
genuine, real, right, undeniable.
AN OPPOSITE IS untrue or fictional.
 2 *The police asked him if he was the
true owner of the car.* authorized, legal,
legitimate, official, proper, rightful.
AN OPPOSITE IS false or illegal.

 3 *She's a true friend.* constant,
dependable, devoted, faithful, honest,
loyal, reliable, sincere, steady,
trustworthy, trusty.
AN OPPOSITE IS unreliable.

truncheon noun
 FOR VARIOUS WEAPONS, SEE **weapon**.

trundle verb
 A wagon trundled up the road. lumber,
lurch, move heavily.

trunk noun
 The trunk of a tree is its *main stem*.
A formal word for an elephant's trunk
is *proboscis*.
A trunk to keep things in is a *box* or
chest.
Another word for a person's trunk is
torso.

trust verb
 1 *They trusted him to do what he had
promised.* bank on, believe in, be sure
of, count on, depend on, have
confidence in, have faith in, rely on.
 2 *I trust you are well.* hope.

trust noun
 1 *He has trust in her ability.* belief,
confidence, faith.
 2 *She's in a position of trust.*
responsibility.

trustful adjective
 He's too trustful of other people.
trusting, unquestioning, unsuspecting,
unwary.
If you are trustful but easily deceived,
you are *gullible* or *naïve*.
AN OPPOSITE IS suspicious.

trustworthy adjective
 She's a trustworthy friend. dependable,
honest, loyal, reliable, responsible,
sensible, trusty, truthful, upright.
AN OPPOSITE IS deceitful or
untrustworthy.

truth noun
 1 *The police doubted the truth of her
story.* accuracy, authenticity,
correctness, genuineness, reliability,
truthfulness, validity.
AN OPPOSITE IS inaccuracy or
falseness.
 2 *He wasn't telling the truth.* facts.
AN OPPOSITE IS lies.

truthful *adjective*
1 *She's a truthful person.* frank, honest, reliable, sincere, straight, straightforward, trustworthy.
2 *He gave a truthful answer.* accurate, correct, credible, proper, right, true, valid.
AN OPPOSITE IS dishonest.

try *verb*
1 *He always tries to do his best.* aim, attempt, endeavour, make an effort, strive, struggle.
2 *She tried her new computer.* evaluate, examine, experiment with, test, try out.
3 *He tries them with his constant chatter.* annoy, bother, exasperate, irritate, provoke, trouble, upset, vex, worry.

try *noun*
1 *He may not succeed, but it's worth a try!* attempt, effort, go, shot.
2 *He had a try of her new pen.* experiment, test, trial.

tub *noun*
FOR VARIOUS CONTAINERS, SEE **container**.

tube *noun*
A flexible tube is a **hose**.
A rigid tube is a **pipe**.
A very narrow tube like a hair is a **capillary** tube.
A large tube carrying water or sewage underground is the **main**.
A tube which liquid pours out of is a **spout**.

tuck *verb*
He tucked the flap inside the envelope. hide, insert, push, stuff.

tuft *noun*
He had a tuft of hair sticking up. bunch, clump.

tug *verb*
1 *They tugged the rope.* jerk, pluck, twitch, wrench, yank.
2 *He tugged the cart up the hill.* drag, draw, haul, heave, lug, pull, tow.

tumble *verb*
He tumbled into the water. collapse, drop, fall, flop, pitch, stumble, topple, trip up.

tumult *noun*
He had to shout to be heard above the tumult. bedlam, chaos, commotion, confusion, disorder, noise, pandemonium, racket, turmoil, upheaval, uproar.

tumultuous *adjective*
Tumultuous applause greeted her winning shot. boisterous, excited, noisy, wild.
AN OPPOSITE IS gentle or restrained.

tune *noun*
They sang her favourite tune. air, melody, song, theme.

tune *verb*
He was trying to tune the TV. adjust, regulate.

tuneful *adjective*
It was a nice, tuneful song. catchy, melodious, pleasant, singable.
AN OPPOSITE IS tuneless.

tunnel *noun*
A tunnel dug by rabbits is a **burrow**.
A system of burrows is a **warren**.
A tunnel in a mine is a **gallery**.
A tunnel beneath a road is a **subway** or **underpass**.

tunnel *verb*
A rabbit tunnelled under the fence. burrow, dig a tunnel, excavate a tunnel.

turbulent *adjective*
1 *The turbulent sea made him feel sick.* agitated, boisterous, heaving, rough, stormy, tempestuous, violent, wild, windy.
AN OPPOSITE IS calm.
If the sea is turbulent with small waves it is said to be **choppy**.
A turbulent journey by air is said to be **bumpy**.
2 *The police were trying to control the turbulent crowd.* badly-behaved, disorderly, excited, restless, riotous, rowdy, unruly.
AN OPPOSITE IS well-behaved.

turmoil *noun*
The whole place was in turmoil.
bedlam, chaos, commotion, confusion,
disorder, disturbance, ferment,
pandemonium, tumult, upheaval,
uproar.
AN OPPOSITE IS calmness or order.

turn *verb*
1 *A wheel turns on its axle.* pivot,
revolve, roll, rotate, spin, swivel, twirl,
twist, whirl.
2 *He signalled before he turned.* change
direction, corner.
To turn unexpectedly is to **swerve** or
veer off course.
If you turn to go back in the direction
you came from, you **do a U-turn**.
If marching soldiers change direction,
they **wheel**.
3 *She turned quite pale.* become, go.
4 *They turned the basement into a
games room.* adapt, alter, change,
convert, make, modify, transform.
to turn something down *He turned the
invitation down.* decline, refuse, reject.
to turn into *The tadpoles will turn into
frogs.* become, be transformed into,
change into, develop into.
to turn something on or **off** *He turned
on the TV.* switch on or off.
to turn out *Everything turned out well
in the end.* happen, result.
to turn over *The boat turned over.*
capsize, flip over, keel over, overturn,
turn upside down.
to turn up *A friend turned up
unexpectedly.* appear, arrive, come,
drop in, visit.

turn *noun*
1 *She gave the handle a turn.* spin,
twirl, twist, whirl.
A single turn of wheel, etc., is a
revolution.
The process of turning is **rotation**.
2 *The house is just past the next turn in
the road.* angle, bend, corner, curve,
junction.
A sharp turn in a mountain road is a
hairpin bend.
3 *It was his turn to bat.* chance, duty,
go, job, opportunity, task.
4 *He did a comic turn in the concert.*
item, performance, scene, sketch, skit.

5 [*informal*] *He had a nasty turn.*
attack, bout, fit.
6 [*informal*] *Seeing that accident gave
her quite a turn.* fright, shock, surprise.

tussle *noun*
The argument led to a bit of a tussle.
contest, fight, [*informal*] scrap, scuffle,
struggle.

twiddle *verb*
He was twiddling a knob on the radio.
fiddle with, fidget with, turn, twirl,
twist.

twig *noun*
They gathered twigs to make a fire.
branch, shoot, stalk, stem, stick.

twin *noun*
*This statue is a twin of one they saw in
the antique shop.* clone, double,
duplicate, lookalike, match, one of a
pair.

twinkle *verb*
The stars twinkled in the sky. glint,
glitter, shine, sparkle.

twirl *verb*
1 *The dancers twirled faster and faster.*
revolve, rotate, spin, turn, whirl.
2 *He twirled his umbrella.* twiddle,
twist.

twist *verb*
1 *She twisted the rope round a post.*
coil, curl, loop.
2 *Twist the handle to open the door.*
revolve, rotate, turn.
3 *The road twists through the hills.*
curve, weave, wind, zigzag.
4 *The snake twisted and turned.*
wriggle, writhe.
5 *He tried to twist the lid off the jar.*
unscrew, wrench.
6 *Heat can twist metal out of shape.*
bend, buckle, crumple, distort, warp.

SHAPES THINGS MAKE IF YOU
TWIST THEM: coil, corkscrew, curl,
kink, knot, loop, screw, spiral,
tangle, zigzag.

twitch *verb*
The dog twitched in his sleep. fidget,
jerk, jump, start, tremble.

two *noun*
Two musicians playing or singing together is a ***duet***.
Two people or things who belong together are a ***couple*** or a ***pair***.
To multiply a number by two is to ***double*** it.

type *noun*
1 *She doesn't like that type of film.* category, class, description, kind, sort, variety.
2 *The book was printed in large type.* characters, lettering, letters, print.

typical *adjective*
He described a typical day at work. average, conventional, normal, ordinary, predictable, standard, unsurprising, usual.
AN OPPOSITE IS unusual.

tyrannical *adjective*
The tyrannical government was finally overthrown. cruel, dictatorial, hard, harsh, merciless, oppressive, ruthless, severe, unjust, unkind.
AN OPPOSITE IS liberal.

tyrant *noun*
The people rejoiced when the tyrant died. dictator, oppressor.
FOR OTHER KINDS OF RULER, SEE **ruler**.

Uu

ugly *adjective*
1 *The room was filled with ugly furniture.* horrid, nasty, plain, tasteless, unattractive, unpleasant.
AN OPPOSITE IS beautiful.
2 *It was a fat, ugly dog.* grotesque, hideous, repulsive, revolting, unattractive.
AN OPPOSITE IS beautiful.
3 *The crowd was in an ugly mood.* angry, dangerous, hostile, menacing, ominous, sinister, threatening, unfriendly.
AN OPPOSITE IS friendly.

ultimate *adjective*
Their ultimate aim was to force him to resign. eventual.

umpire *noun*

> OTHER OFFICIALS WHO MAKE SURE PLAYERS KEEP TO THE RULES:
> adjudicator, assistant referee, linesman, referee, touch judge.

un- *prefix*

> There are so many words beginning with the prefix *un-* that we can give synonyms for only a few of the more interesting ones. For some other words beginning with *un-*, we suggest another entry which you can look up to find synonyms.
> If you want synonyms for words which we do not include, look up the root word—that is, the word to which *un-* has been added. There you will often find words to which you can add the prefix *un-* or the word *not*. For example, if you look up *able*, you can work out that you could use *not allowed, unwilling*, etc. as synonyms for *unable*

unaided *adjective*
She can no longer walk unaided. on your own, single-handed, without help.

unanimous *adjective*
It was a unanimous decision. collective, joint, united.
A decision where most but not all people agree is a ***majority*** decision.

unattractive *adjective* SEE **ugly**

unavoidable *adjective*
The accident was unavoidable. bound to happen, certain, destined, inevitable, sure to happen.

unaware *adjective* SEE **ignorant**

unbearable *adjective*
The toothache was unbearable. impossible to bear, intolerable, unacceptable, unendurable.

unbelievable *adjective*
1 *Her excuse was unbelievable.* far-fetched, improbable, incredible, unconvincing, unlikely.
2 *He scored an unbelievable goal.* amazing, astonishing, extraordinary, [*informal*] fantastic, phenomenal, remarkable.

uncalled for *adjective* SEE **unnecessary**

uncanny *adjective* SEE **eerie**

uncertain *adjective*
1 *I was uncertain what to do next.* doubtful, in two minds, unconvinced, unsure, wavering.
2 *They are facing an uncertain future.* indefinite, undecided, unknown, unreliable.
3 *The weather will be uncertain.* changeable, erratic, inconsistent, unpredictable, unreliable, variable.
AN OPPOSITE IS certain.

unclean *adjective* SEE **dirty**

unclear *adjective* SEE **uncertain**

uncomfortable *adjective*
1 *The seats were extremely uncomfortable.* cramped, hard, lumpy.
2 *She complained that her shoes were uncomfortable.* restrictive, stiff, tight, tight-fitting.
3 *He spent an uncomfortable night, tossing and turning in the strange bed.* disagreeable, restless, troubled, uneasy.
AN OPPOSITE IS comfortable.

uncommon *adjective* SEE **unusual**

uncomplimentary *adjective* SEE **rude**

unconscious *adjective*
1 *He's been unconscious for two days.* If you are unconscious because of a hit on the head, you are ***knocked out***. If you are unconscious for an operation, you are ***anaesthetized***. If you are unconscious because of an accident or illness, you are ***in a coma***.
2 *She's unconscious of the effect she has on other people.* ignorant, unaware.
3 *They laughed at her unconscious slip of the tongue.* accidental, unintended, unintentional.
AN OPPOSITE IS conscious.

uncontrollable *adjective* SEE **unruly**

uncooperative *adjective* SEE **unhelpful**

uncover *verb*
1 *She uncovered the surprise gift her sister had bought for her.* disclose, expose, reveal, show, unveil, unwrap. To uncover your body is to ***bare*** yourself, or ***strip*** or ***undress***.
2 *Archaeologists have uncovered the ruins of a Roman fort.* come across, dig up, discover, expose, locate, unearth.
AN OPPOSITE IS cover.

undecided *adjective* SEE **uncertain**

undeniable *adjective* SEE **true**

underclothes *plural noun*
underclothing, undergarments, underwear, [*informal*] undies. Women's underclothes are ***lingerie***.

VARIOUS UNDERGARMENTS: bra or brassière, briefs, corset, drawers, garter, girdle, knickers, panties, pants, pantyhose, petticoat, slip, suspenders, tights, trunks, underpants, underskirt, vest.
FOR OTHER GARMENTS, SEE **clothes**.

undergo *verb*
She underwent a three-hour operation. be subjected to, endure, experience, go through, put up with, suffer.

undergrowth *noun*
They cleared a path through the undergrowth. bushes, ground cover, plants, vegetation.

underhand *adjective*
He had been involved in underhand financial deals. deceitful, devious, furtive, secret, secretive, sly, [*informal*] sneaky, unfair.

underline *verb*
The accident underlines the need to take care. draw attention to, emphasize, give emphasis to, show clearly, stress.

undermine *verb*
Her criticism undermined his confidence. destroy, lessen, reduce, ruin, weaken.
AN OPPOSITE IS support.

underprivileged *adjective*
He works for underprivileged children.
badly off, deprived, needy, poor.

understand *verb*
1 *Do you understand what I mean?*
appreciate, comprehend, fathom,
follow, grasp, interpret, make sense of,
realize, recognize, see, take in,
[*informal*] twig, work out.
2 *Can you understand this writing?*
decipher, make out, read.
To understand something in code is to
decode it.
3 *She understands animals.* know,
show understanding of, sympathize
with.
4 *I understand you've been ill?* believe,
hear.

understanding *noun*
1 *The tutor was amazed by his young
pupil's understanding.* cleverness,
insight, intellect, intelligence,
judgement, perceptiveness, sense,
wisdom.
2 *He has only a limited understanding
of the problem.* appreciation,
awareness, comprehension, grasp,
knowledge.
3 *The two sides reached an
understanding.* accord, agreement,
arrangement, bargain, contract, deal,
settlement, treaty.
4 *There was a great deal of
understanding between them.*
friendship, harmony, sympathy,
tolerance.

understanding *adjective*
She's an understanding person. broad-
minded, caring, friendly, helpful, kind,
open-minded, sympathetic, tolerant,
unprejudiced.

undertake *verb*
*He undertook to deliver the letter right
away.* agree, commit yourself, consent,
guarantee, promise.

undertaking *noun*
*Organizing the festival has been a
difficult undertaking.* enterprise, job,
mission, operation, project, task,
venture.

underwear *noun* SEE **underclothes**

undisguised *adjective* SEE **obvious**

undo *verb*
1 *Undo the ropes.*

> WORDS MEANING TO UNDO THINGS
> THAT ARE JOINED TOGETHER:
> detach, disconnect, loosen, part,
> separate, unclip, uncouple, unfasten,
> unhook, unravel, untether, untie.

2 *She undid the parcel carefully.*

> WORDS MEANING TO UNDO THINGS
> THAT ARE CLOSED OR SEALED OR
> WRAPPED UP: open, unbutton,
> unclasp, unfold, unlock, unpin,
> unroll, unscrew, unseal, unstick,
> unwind, unwrap, unzip.

3 *It was too late to undo the damage.*
cancel out, reverse, wipe out.

undoubtedly *adverb*
She is undoubtedly our best player.
certainly, definitely, doubtless, of
course, surely.

undress *verb*
She undressed quickly and got into bed.
get undressed, strip, take off your
clothes.
AN OPPOSITE IS dress.

unearth *verb*
1 *The dog unearthed an old bone.* dig
up, uncover.
2 *She unearthed some old diaries in the
attic.* come across, discover, find,
stumble upon, track down.

unearthly *adjective*
They heard an unearthly cry. eerie,
frightening, ghostly, [*informal*] scary,
sinister, [*informal*] spooky, strange,
supernatural, uncanny, unnatural,
weird.

uneasy *adjective*
1 *She had an uneasy feeling that
something was wrong.* anxious,
apprehensive, edgy, fearful, insecure,
nervous, tense, troubled, uncertain,
upsetting, worried.
AN OPPOSITE IS confident.
2 *She passed an uneasy night.*
disturbed, restless, uncomfortable,
unsettled.
AN OPPOSITE IS comfortable.

unemployed *adjective*
Since the factory closed, many people have been unemployed. jobless, [*informal*] on the dole, out of work.
To be unemployed because there is not enough work for you to do is to be **redundant**.
AN OPPOSITE IS employed or working.

uneven *adjective*
1 *The ground was very uneven in places.* broken, bumpy, jagged, rough, rutted.
AN OPPOSITE IS smooth.
2 *Their performance has been uneven this season.* erratic, fluctuating, inconsistent, irregular, unpredictable, variable, varying.
AN OPPOSITE IS consistent.
3 *It was a very uneven contest.* ill-matched, one-sided, unbalanced, unequal, unfair.
AN OPPOSITE IS balanced.

unexpected *adjective*
Her reaction was totally unexpected. sudden, surprising, unforeseen, unpredictable.
AN OPPOSITE IS expected.

unfair *adjective* SEE **unjust**

unfaithful *adjective* SEE **disloyal**

unfamiliar *adjective* SEE **strange**

unfashionable *adjective* SEE **old-fashioned**

unfasten *verb* SEE **undo**

unfavourable *adjective*
1 *The new television series received unfavourable reviews.* attacking, critical, disapproving, hostile, negative, uncomplimentary, unfriendly, unkind, unsympathetic.
2 *Unfavourable weather conditions prevented the journey.* adverse, bad, unhelpful.
AN OPPOSITE IS favourable.

unfinished *adjective*
Her last novel was unfinished. incomplete, uncompleted.
AN OPPOSITE IS complete.

unfit *adjective*
1 *He never gets any exercise and is really unfit.* out of condition, unhealthy.
AN OPPOSITE IS fit.
2 *She is unfit for the job.* unsatisfactory, unsuitable, useless.

unforgettable *adjective*
It was an unforgettable occasion. impressive, memorable, notable, outstanding, remarkable.
AN OPPOSITE IS ordinary.

unforgivable *adjective*
Losing your temper with him was unforgivable. shameful, unjustifiable, unpardonable.
AN OPPOSITE IS excusable.

unfortunate *adjective*
1 *It was an unfortunate mistake.* calamitous, dreadful, unlucky.
AN OPPOSITE IS fortunate or lucky.
2 *He was unfortunate enough to lose his job.* luckless, unlucky, unsuccessful.
AN OPPOSITE IS fortunate or lucky.
3 *His unfortunate remark silenced the whole room.* inappropriate, regrettable, tactless, unsuitable, untimely.

unfriendly *adjective*
He was abrupt and unfriendly. cold, cool, disagreeable, distant, hostile, impolite, inhospitable, uncivil, unhelpful, unkind, unsociable, unsympathetic, unwelcoming.
AN OPPOSITE IS friendly.

ungrateful *adjective*
Don't be so ungrateful. unappreciative, unthankful.
AN OPPOSITE IS grateful.

unhappy *adjective*
You look unhappy today—what's the matter? brokenhearted, dejected, depressed, desolate, despairing, dismal, distressed, [*informal*] down, downcast, downhearted, forlorn, gloomy, glum, grave, heartbroken, in low spirits, miserable, regretful, sad, sorrowful, sorry, tearful, troubled, upset, wistful, woeful, wretched.
AN OPPOSITE IS happy.

unhealthy *adjective*
1 *He looked extremely unhealthy.*
ailing, delicate, diseased, feeble, frail,
ill, infirm, poorly, sick, sickly, suffering,
[*informal*] under the weather, unwell,
weak.
2 *They were living in damp and
unhealthy conditions.* dirty, harmful,
insanitary, polluted, unclean,
unhygienic, unwholesome.
AN OPPOSITE IS healthy.

unheard-of *adjective* SEE **exceptional**

unhelpful *adjective*
The shop assistant was unhelpful.
inconsiderate, reluctant to help, slow,
uncooperative, unfriendly, unwilling to
help.
AN OPPOSITE IS helpful.

unidentified *adjective*
*An unidentified benefactor gave the
school a computer.* anonymous,
nameless, unknown, unnamed,
unrecognized, unspecified.
AN OPPOSITE IS named.

uniform *adjective*
The planks should be of uniform width.
consistent, identical, regular, the same,
similar, unvarying.
AN OPPOSITE IS different or
inconsistent.

unify *verb*
*His main aim was to unify the different
groups within the organization.*
amalgamate, bring together, combine,
integrate, join, merge, unite.
AN OPPOSITE IS separate.

unimportant *adjective*
Don't worry about unimportant details.
insignificant, irrelevant, minor,
negligible, petty, secondary, slight,
small, trifling, trivial, uninteresting,
worthless.
AN OPPOSITE IS important.

uninhabited *adjective* SEE **unoccupied**

unintelligent *adjective* SEE **stupid**

unintelligible *adjective* SEE
incomprehensible

unintentional *adjective*
*If he upset you, I'm sure it was
unintentional.* accidental, unconscious,
unintended, unplanned.
AN OPPOSITE IS deliberate.

uninterested *adjective* SEE **apathetic**

uninteresting *adjective* SEE **boring**

union *noun*
A union of two organizations or parties
is an **amalgamation** or **merger**.
A union of two groups is their
integration.
A union of two countries is their
unification.
A union of two substances is a
compound or **fusion** or **synthesis**.
A union of two people is a **marriage** or
partnership.

unique *adjective*
Strictly, *unique* means *being the only
one of its kind.* However, it is often
used informally to mean *very unusual*
1 *Your fingerprints are unique.*
different, distinctive, individual,
peculiar to you, special.
2 [*informal*] *She is a woman of unique
talent and determination.*
SEE **unusual**.

unit *noun*
*You can build up the units into a
complex system.* bit, component,
element, module, part, piece, section,
segment.
FOR UNITS OF MEASUREMENT, SEE
measurement *noun*.

unite *verb*
1 *The store manager decided to unite
the two departments.* amalgamate,
bring together, combine, integrate,
join, link, merge, unify.
AN OPPOSITE IS separate.
2 *The two groups united to demand
changes in the law.* become allies,
collaborate, cooperate, go into
partnership, join forces.
AN OPPOSITE IS compete.
To unite to do something bad is to
conspire.

universal *adjective*
It's an issue of universal interest.
general, global, international,
worldwide.

unjust *adjective*
The referee's decision was unjust.
biased, prejudiced, unfair,
unjustifiable, unjustified, unlawful,
unreasonable, wrong.
AN OPPOSITE IS just.

unkind *adjective*
That was an unkind thing to do!
callous, hard-hearted, harsh,
heartless, impolite, inconsiderate,
inhumane, malicious, mean, nasty,
ruthless, selfish, spiteful, tactless,
thoughtless, uncaring, unfriendly,
unpleasant, unsympathetic, vicious.
People can be unkind in many ways,
and there are many other words you
can use in addition to those listed here.
For example, SEE **angry, cruel, rude,
unjust**, etc
AN OPPOSITE IS kind.

unknown *adjective*
1 The man was unknown to her.
unidentified, unrecognized.
AN OPPOSITE IS known.
2 The author of the story is unknown.
anonymous, nameless, unnamed,
unspecified.
AN OPPOSITE IS named.
3 The explorers entered unknown
territory. alien, foreign, strange,
undiscovered, unexplored, unfamiliar.
AN OPPOSITE IS familiar.
4 The part was played by an unknown
actor. little-known, obscure,
undistinguished, unheard of.
AN OPPOSITE IS famous.

unlike *adjective*
Surprisingly, the twins are unlike each
other. different from, distinct from,
distinguishable from.
AN OPPOSITE IS similar.

unlikely *adjective*
It seemed an unlikely explanation of the
events. far-fetched, improbable,
incredible, suspicious, unbelievable,
unconvincing.
AN OPPOSITE IS likely.

unload *verb*
1 The driver unloaded the boxes from
the back of the van. drop off, [*informal*]
dump, take off.
2 We unloaded the van. clear, empty.
AN OPPOSITE IS load.

unlucky *adjective*
They were unlucky not to win. luckless,
unfortunate.
AN OPPOSITE IS lucky.

unmarried *adjective*
If you are unmarried, you are **single**.
If your marriage has been legally
ended, you are **divorced**.
An unmarried man is a **bachelor**.
An unmarried woman is a **spinster**.
A man whose wife is dead is a
widower.
A woman whose husband is dead is a
widow.

unmistakable *adjective* SEE **obvious**

unnatural *adjective*
1 It's unnatural for the weather to be so
warm in March. abnormal,
extraordinary, odd, queer, strange,
unusual.
2 They thought the acting in the film
was unnatural. insincere, self-
conscious, stiff, theatrical, unrealistic,
unspontaneous.
3 Her hair was an unnatural orange
colour. artificial, manufactured,
simulated, synthetic.
AN OPPOSITE IS natural.

unnecessary *adjective*
All this food is unnecessary. excessive,
extra, non-essential, redundant,
superfluous, surplus, uncalled for,
unneeded, unwanted, useless.
AN OPPOSITE IS necessary.

unoccupied *adjective*
1 Since the fire, the flats have been
unoccupied. abandoned, deserted,
empty, uninhabited, unused, vacant.
AN OPPOSITE IS occupied.
2 The bathroom is unoccupied.
available, vacant.
AN OPPOSITE IS engaged.

unofficial *adjective*
The police gave him an unofficial
warning. informal.
AN OPPOSITE IS official.

unplanned *adjective* SEE **spontaneous**

unpleasant *adjective*
Unpleasant can refer to almost anything you don't like, so there are many synonyms you could use. We give some of the common ones here.
1 *He's a thoroughly unpleasant man.* bad-tempered, disagreeable, malicious, nasty, spiteful, unfriendly, unkind.
2 *Her visit to the dentist had been an unpleasant experience.* awful, disagreeable, nasty, uncomfortable.
3 *The smell from the drain was very unpleasant.* dirty, disgusting, filthy, foul, horrible, horrid, objectionable, repulsive, revolting.
AN OPPOSITE IS pleasant.

unpopular *adjective*
He was unpopular at work. despised, disliked, hated, unloved.
AN OPPOSITE IS popular.

unreal *adjective*
It seemed as unreal as a dream. fanciful, fictional, imaginary, unrecognizable.
AN OPPOSITE IS real.

unrealistic *adjective*
1 *The film gives an unrealistic picture of everyday life.* false, unconvincing, unlifelike, unnatural, unrecognizable.
2 *His ideas were unrealistic.* impracticable, impractical, too ambitious, unworkable.
AN OPPOSITE IS realistic.

unreasonable *adjective*
It's unreasonable to expect him to pay. absurd, crazy, illogical, irrational, nonsensical, senseless, silly, unfair, unjustifiable.
AN OPPOSITE IS reasonable.

unreliable *adjective*
1 *The prosecution claimed the evidence was unreliable.* inaccurate, misleading, unsound.
2 *He's lazy and unreliable.* changeable, inconsistent, irresponsible, unpredictable, untrustworthy.
AN OPPOSITE IS reliable.

unrest *noun*
The delay caused unrest in the crowd. commotion, discontent, disorder, disturbance, rioting, trouble.

unruly *adjective*
The police found it hard to control the unruly mob. badly behaved, disobedient, disorderly, naughty, rebellious, troublesome, uncontrollable, unmanageable.
AN OPPOSITE IS well behaved.

unsafe *adjective* SEE **dangerous**

unsatisfactory *adjective*
Her work was unsatisfactory. disappointing, inadequate, incompetent, inefficient, insufficient, poor, unacceptable.
AN OPPOSITE IS satisfactory.

unseemly *adjective*
It's unseemly to tell rude jokes in church. improper, inappropriate, offensive, out of place, unsuitable, untimely.
AN OPPOSITE IS suitable.

unseen *adjective* SEE **invisible**

unselfish *adjective*
She's loyal and unselfish. caring, charitable, considerate, generous, humane, humanitarian, kind, selfless, thoughtful.
AN OPPOSITE IS selfish.

unsound *adjective* SEE **unreliable, weak**

unstable *adjective* SEE **unsteady**

unsteady *adjective*
1 *The table was a bit unsteady.* insecure, precarious, rickety, shaky, unbalanced, unsafe, unstable, wobbly.
2 *The unsteady candlelight flickered.* changeable, erratic, inconstant, intermittent, irregular, quavering, quivering, trembling, variable, wavering.
AN OPPOSITE IS steady.

unsuccessful *adjective*
He made several unsuccessful attempts to see her. fruitless, futile, ineffective, ineffectual, unlucky, unproductive, unsatisfactory, useless, vain.

unsuitable *adjective*
The remarks she made were unsuitable at a funeral. inappropriate, incongruous, out of place, unsatisfactory, unseemly, untimely, wrong.
AN OPPOSITE IS suitable.

unsure *adjective* SEE **uncertain**

unsympathetic *adjective*
She complained to the authorities but they were unsympathetic. indifferent, uncaring, unhelpful, uninterested, unmoved.
AN OPPOSITE IS sympathetic.

untidy *adjective*
1 *The room wasn't dirty, but it was dreadfully untidy.* chaotic, cluttered, disorderly, [*informal*] higgledy-piggledy, jumbled, littered, messy, [*informal*] topsy-turvy, [*informal*] upside down.
2 *His work was untidy and full of mistakes.* careless, confused, disorganized, haphazard, muddled, slapdash, [*informal*] sloppy.
3 *He looked very untidy.* rumpled, scruffy, slovenly.
4 *She smoothed her untidy hair.* dishevelled, tangled, uncombed, ungroomed.
AN OPPOSITE IS tidy.

untie *verb*
She quickly untied the knots. free, loosen, undo, unfasten.
To untie a boat is to **cast off**.
To untie an animal is to **release** or **untether** it.

untimely *adjective* SEE **unsuitable**

untrue *adjective* SEE **false**

untrustworthy, untruthful
adjectives SEE **dishonest**

unused *adjective*
Any unused goods may be returned or exchanged. new, unopened.
An unused recording tape is a **blank** tape.
Unused paper is **clean** paper.
Unused clothes are **unworn**.
Unused coins are **in mint condition**.
AN OPPOSITE IS used.

unusual *adjective*
1 *The weather was unusual for the time of year.* abnormal, exceptional, extraordinary, irregular, odd, out of the ordinary, peculiar, remarkable, singular, strange, surprising, unconventional, unexpected, unheard-of, [*informal*] unique, unnatural, untypical.
AN OPPOSITE IS ordinary.
2 *She has a very unusual name.* rare, uncommon, unfamiliar.
AN OPPOSITE IS common.

unwanted *adjective* SEE **unnecessary**

unwelcome *adjective*
He had attracted a lot of unwelcome attention. disagreeable, objectionable, unacceptable, undesirable, unwanted.
AN OPPOSITE IS welcome.

unwell *adjective* SEE **ill**

unwilling *adjective* SEE **reluctant**

unwise *adjective* SEE **silly**

update *verb*
The files are updated every week. amend, bring up to date, correct, revise.

upgrade *verb*
They plan to upgrade their computer. enhance, expand, improve, make better.

upheaval *noun*
Moving to a new house causes such an upheaval. commotion, disturbance, fuss, turmoil, upset.

uphill *adjective*
1 *The last part of the road is uphill all the way.* ascending, rising, steep, upward.
2 *It was an uphill struggle, but eventually she achieved her objectives.* arduous, difficult, exhausting, gruelling, hard, laborious, never-ending, stiff, strenuous, taxing, tough.

upkeep *noun*
The upkeep of a car can be expensive. care, maintenance, running.

upper *adjective*
My bedroom is on the upper floor. higher, upstairs.

upright *adjective*
1 *The builder made sure the scaffolding poles were upright.* erect, perpendicular, standing straight up, vertical.
AN OPPOSITE IS horizontal.
2 *He's an upright member of society.* conscientious, fair, good, honest, honourable, just, moral, righteous, trustworthy, virtuous.
AN OPPOSITE IS corrupt.

uproar *noun*
The meeting ended in uproar. bedlam, chaos, commotion, confusion, din, disorder, disturbance, hullabaloo, noise, pandemonium, riot, row, turmoil.

upset *verb*
1 *The accusation upset her.* dismay, displease, distress, disturb, grieve, irritate, offend, ruffle.
2 *Bad weather upset the train timetable.* affect, disrupt, interfere with, interrupt, spoil.
3 *She upset the bottle of milk.* knock over, spill, tip over, topple.
4 *A large wave upset the boat.* capsize, overturn.

upset *noun*
1 *He's got a stomach upset.* ailment, [*informal*] bug, illness, infection.
2 *They caused a major upset by winning 7–0.* shock, surprise.

upside-down *adjective*
1 *I can't read it if it's upside-down.* inverted, wrong way up.
2 [*informal*] *They'd left the room upside-down as usual.* chaotic, cluttered, disorderly, [*informal*] higgledy-piggledy, jumbled, littered, messy, [*informal*] topsy-turvy, untidy.

uptight *adjective* [*informal*]
She's really uptight about the interview. anxious, apprehensive, edgy, fearful, jumpy, on edge, tense, upset, worried.
AN OPPOSITE IS relaxed.

up to date *adjective*
You write it as *up-to-date* if it goes immediately before a noun.
1 *The spacecraft uses up-to-date technology.* advanced, current, the latest, modern, new, present-day, recent.
AN OPPOSITE IS out of date or out-of-date.
2 *Her clothes are always up to date.* contemporary, fashionable, stylish, [*informal*] trendy.
AN OPPOSITE IS old-fashioned.

upward *adjective*
He started on the steep, upward climb. ascending, rising, uphill.

urban *adjective*
Most of the population live in urban areas. built-up, densely populated.

urge *verb*
He urged her to reconsider her decision. advise, appeal to, beg, counsel, entreat, implore, plead with, press.
To urge someone to do something is also to **advocate** or **recommend** it.
to urge someone on *The fans urged their team on.* egg on, encourage, spur on.
AN OPPOSITE IS discourage.

urge *noun*
I had an urge to buy sweets. desire, eagerness, impulse, itch, longing, wish, yearning, [*informal*] yen.

urgent *adjective*
1 *He had urgent business in Paris.* essential, important, necessary, pressing, top priority, unavoidable.
AN OPPOSITE IS unimportant.
2 *If it's an urgent problem, deal with it immediately.* acute, immediate, severe.
3 *She spoke in an urgent whisper.* anxious, earnest, insistent.

usable *adjective*
1 *The lift is not usable today.* fit for use, functional, functioning, operating, working.
AN OPPOSITE IS unusable.
2 *This ticket is usable only on certain trains.* acceptable, valid.
AN OPPOSITE IS invalid.

use *verb*
1 *She used a calculator to add the figures up.* employ, make use of, utilize. There are many other synonyms for the verb *to use*, depending on what you are talking about. These are a few examples.
To use your knowledge is to **apply** it.
To use your muscles is to **exercise** them.
To use a musical instrument is to **play** it.
To use an axe, sword, etc., is to **wield** it.
To use people or things selfishly is to **exploit** them.
2 *Show me how to use this machine.* deal with, handle, manage, operate, work.
3 *You've used all the hot water.* consume, exhaust, spend, use up.

use *noun*
1 *Are these things any use to you?* advantage, profit, value.
2 *This tool has many uses.* point, purpose.

useful *adjective*
1 *A microwave is useful for preparing meals quickly.* convenient, effective, efficient, handy, practical.
2 *He gave me some useful advice.* beneficial, constructive, good, helpful, invaluable, positive, profitable, valuable, worthwhile.
3 *He's a very useful player.* able, capable, competent, gifted, proficient, skilful, successful, talented.
AN OPPOSITE IS useless.

useless *adjective*
1 *This old vacuum cleaner is useless.* broken down, [slang] duff, ineffective, inefficient, impractical, unusable.
2 *Her advice was completely useless.* fruitless, futile, pointless, unhelpful, unprofitable, worthless.
3 *He's useless at football.* incapable, incompetent, ineffectual, unskilful, unsuccessful.
AN OPPOSITE IS useful.

user-friendly *adjective*
Computers should be as user-friendly as possible. easy to use, straightforward, uncomplicated, understandable.

usual *adjective*
1 *I'll meet you at the usual place.* accustomed, customary, familiar, habitual, normal, regular, standard.
2 *It's usual to tip the waiter or waitress if the service has been good.* accepted, common, conventional, traditional.
AN OPPOSITE IS unusual.

utensil *noun*
The shelves were loaded with cooking utensils. appliance, device, gadget, implement, instrument, machine, tool.
FOR VARIOUS TOOLS, SEE **tool**.

utilize *verb* SEE **use**

utter *adjective*
He stared at her in utter amazement. absolute, complete, extreme, perfect, total.

utter *verb*
He didn't dare to utter his thoughts. communicate, express, pronounce, put into words, say, speak.
SEE ALSO **talk** *verb*.

vacancy *noun*
They have vacancies for secretaries with word processing experience. job, opening, position, post, situation.

vacant *adjective*
1 *The house over the road is still vacant.* deserted, uninhabited, unoccupied.
AN OPPOSITE IS occupied.
2 *He gave her a vacant stare.* absent-minded, blank, expressionless, inattentive, mindless, vague.
AN OPPOSITE IS alert.

vacate *verb*
Guests must vacate their rooms by midday. evacuate, leave, quit, withdraw from.

vacation *noun*
[*mainly American use*] *She spent her vacation in Europe.* holiday, leave, time off.

vaccinate *verb*
The children were vaccinated against measles. immunize, inoculate.

vacuum *noun*
A trade name used as a synonym for a vacuum cleaner is **Hoover**.
A trade name used as a synonym for a vacuum flask is **Thermos**.

vague *adjective*
1 *His description was rather vague.* ambiguous, broad, general, generalized, indefinite, uncertain, unclear, woolly.
AN OPPOSITE IS exact.
2 *A vague shape could be seen through the mist.* blurred, dim, hazy, indistinct, shadowy, unrecognizable.
AN OPPOSITE IS definite.
3 *She's always been a bit vague.* absent-minded, careless, forgetful, inattentive.
AN OPPOSITE IS attentive.

vain *adjective*
1 *He's vain about his appearance.* arrogant, boastful, [*informal*] cocky, conceited, haughty, proud, self-satisfied, [*informal*] stuck-up.
AN OPPOSITE IS modest.
2 *She made a vain attempt to tidy the room.* fruitless, futile, ineffective, pointless, unsuccessful, useless, worthless.
AN OPPOSITE IS successful.

valiant *adjective*
He made a valiant attempt to break the world record. bold, brave, courageous, daring, fearless, gallant, heroic, plucky.
AN OPPOSITE IS cowardly or feeble.

valid *adjective*
1 *The ticket is valid for three months.* approved, authentic, authorized, current, legal, official, permitted, proper, suitable, usable.
2 *He made several valid points.* acceptable, convincing, genuine, legitimate, reasonable, sound.
AN OPPOSITE IS invalid.

valley *noun*

VARIOUS KINDS OF VALLEY: canyon, chasm, dale, defile, dell, glen, gorge, gulch, gully, hollow, pass, ravine, vale.

valour *noun*
He was decorated for valour in battle. bravery, courage, daring, gallantry, heroism, pluck.
AN OPPOSITE IS cowardice.

valuable *adjective*
1 *Apparently the painting is very valuable.* costly, dear, expensive, precious, priceless.
2 *He gave her some valuable advice.* beneficial, constructive, good, helpful, invaluable, positive, useful, valued, worthwhile.
AN OPPOSITE IS worthless.
Notice that *invaluable* is not the opposite of *valuable*

value *noun*
1 *The alterations greatly increased the value of the house.* cost, price, worth.
2 *He stressed the value of taking regular exercise.* advantage, benefit, importance, merit, significance, use, usefulness.

value *verb*
1 *He had always valued her advice.* appreciate, esteem, have a high opinion of, prize, respect, treasure.
2 *A surveyor was sent to value the house.* assess, estimate the value of, evaluate, price.

van *noun*
FOR VARIOUS VEHICLES, SEE **vehicle**.

vandal *noun*
The windows of the shop were smashed by vandals. delinquent, hooligan, lout, ruffian, troublemaker.

vanish *verb*
By the time she came back he had vanished. disappear, go away, melt away.
AN OPPOSITE IS appear.

vanity *noun*
He spoke without a trace of vanity.
arrogance, [*informal*] cockiness,
conceit, pride, self-esteem, self-
importance.

vanquish *verb*
He successfully vanquished his
opponent. beat, conquer, crush, defeat,
overcome, overwhelm, [*informal*]
thrash.

vaporize *verb*
Water vaporizes when it boils. dry up,
evaporate, turn to vapour.
AN OPPOSITE IS condense.

vapour *noun*
Smelly vapour hung in the air. fumes,
gas, smoke, steam.
Vapour hanging in the air is **haze**, **fog**,
mist, or **smog**.

variable *adjective*
The temperature is variable at this time
of year. changeable, erratic,
fluctuating, inconsistent, uncertain,
unpredictable, unreliable, unstable,
unsteady, [*informal*] up-and-down,
varying, wavering.
If your loyalty to friends is variable,
you are **fickle**.
AN OPPOSITE IS constant.

variation *noun*
There are wide regional variations in
house prices. alteration, change,
difference, fluctuation, shift.

variety *noun*
1 The centre offers a variety of leisure
activities. array, assortment,
miscellany, mixture.
2 The supermarket has over thirty
varieties of pasta. brand, kind, make,
sort, type.
A variety of animal is a **breed** or
species.
3 Her job lacked variety. change,
difference, diversity, variation.

various *adjective*
The shirts are available in various
colours. assorted, contrasting,
different, differing, diverse,
miscellaneous, mixed, several, varying.

vary *verb*
1 The price of fruit and vegetables
varies with the seasons. alter, change,
differ, fluctuate, go up and down.
2 He tried to vary his diet. adjust, alter,
change, modify.

vast *adjective*
1 The miser accumulated a vast
fortune. enormous, great, huge,
immense, large, massive.
2 A vast expanse of water stretched
ahead of them. big, broad, extensive,
wide.
AN OPPOSITE IS small.

vault *verb*
to vault over something He vaulted
over the fence. bound over, clear,
hurdle, jump over, leap over, spring
over.

vault *noun*
The gold was stored in the vaults of the
bank. strongroom, treasury.
An underground part of a house is a
cellar.
An underground part of a church is a
crypt or **undercroft**.

veer *verb*
The car veered across the road. change
direction, dodge, swerve, turn.

vegetable *noun*

GREEN VEGETABLES: broccoli,
Brussels sprout, cabbage,
cauliflower, Chinese cabbage, kale,
spinach.

ROOT VEGETABLES: beetroot, carrot,
parsnip, swede, turnip.
Sugar beet is a root vegetable used
to make sugar.
A **mangel** or **mangel-wurzel** is a
root vegetable used for cattle.

LEGUMES OR PULSES: beans,
chickpeas, dhal, lentils, mangetout
or sugar pea, peas.
FOR VARIOUS BEANS, SEE **bean**.

OTHER VEGETABLES: artichoke,
asparagus, aubergine, celeriac,
celery, courgette, garlic, leek,
marrow, mushroom, okra, onion, ➡

pepper, potato, pumpkin, shallot, sweet corn, sweet potato, water chestnut, yam.
FOR VEGETABLES EATEN IN SALADS, SEE **salad**.

vegetarian *noun*
A person who doesn't eat any products that come from animals is a **vegan**. An animal that feeds only on plants is a **herbivore**.
The opposite—a person or animal that eats flesh—is a **carnivore**.

vegetation *noun*
The gardens were filled with lush vegetation. foliage, greenery, growing things, growth, plants, undergrowth, weeds.

vehicle *noun*

VEHICLES WHICH CARRY PEOPLE: ambulance, bus, cab, camper, car or motor car, caravan, [*old use*] charabanc, coach, double-decker, go-kart, jeep, minibus, minicab, [*old use*] omnibus, police car, rickshaw, single-decker, taxi, tram, trolleybus. SEE ALSO **bicycle, car.**

VEHICLES USED TO TRANSPORT THINGS: articulated lorry, breakdown vehicle, dump truck, HGV or heavy goods vehicle, horsebox, juggernaut, lorry, milk float, pantechnicon or removal van, pick-up truck, tanker, traction engine, tractor, trailer, transporter, truck, van.

OTHER MECHANICAL VEHICLES: bulldozer, dustcart, fire engine, hearse, roadroller or [*old use*] steamroller, snowplough, tank.

OLD HORSE-DRAWN VEHICLES: carriage, cart, chariot, coach, gig, hackney carriage, omnibus, phaeton, stagecoach, trap, wagon.

veil *verb*
Her face was veiled with a silk scarf. conceal, cover, hide, mask, shroud.

vein *noun*
A tube in the body that carries blood away from the heart is an **artery**. Veins and arteries are **blood vessels**. Delicate hairlike blood vessels are **capillaries**.

velocity *noun*
The rocket has to reach a great velocity before it can leave the earth's atmosphere. rate, speed, swiftness.

venerable *adjective*
The Bank of England is a venerable institution. aged, ancient, dignified, old, respected, revered, worthy of respect.

vengeance *noun*
His cruel heart was set on vengeance. reprisal, revenge.

venomous *adjective*
The adder is Britain's only venomous snake. poisonous.

vent *noun*
A vent in the roof lets the smoke out. gap, hole, opening, outlet, slit.
to give vent to *She gave vent to her anger.* express, let go, release.

ventilate *verb*
Ventilate the greenhouse properly. air, freshen, let fresh air in.

venture *noun*
He became involved in one business venture after another. enterprise, project, undertaking.

venture *verb*
They ventured out into the snow. dare to go, have an expedition, risk going.

verdict *noun*
What was the jury's verdict? conclusion, decision, judgement, opinion.

verge *noun*
Don't park on the verge of the road. edge, margin, side.
A stone or concrete edging beside a road is a **kerb**.
The flat strip of tarmac or concrete beside a motorway is the **hard shoulder**.

verify *verb*
Several witnesses verified his statement. [*informal*] check out, confirm, prove, show the truth of, support.

vermin *noun*
The barn was infested with vermin. pests.
Vermin such as fleas that live on other animals are *parasites*.

versatile *adjective*
He's one of the game's most versatile players. adaptable, all-round, gifted, talented.

verse *noun*
1 *Most of the play is written in verse.* lines, rhyme.
The rhythm of a line of verse is its *metre*.
Something written in verse is *poetry* or a *poem*.
SEE ALSO **poem**.
2 *She'd managed to learn the first two verses of the poem by heart.* stanza.

version *noun*
1 *The two newspapers gave different versions of the accident.* account, description, report, story.
2 *It's an English version of a French play.* adaptation, interpretation, paraphrase.
A version of something which was originally in another language is a *translation*.
3 *They brought out a new version of the car last summer.* design, form, model, variation.

vertical *adjective*
The fence posts must be vertical. erect, perpendicular, upright.
A vertical drop is a *sheer* drop.
AN OPPOSITE IS horizontal.

very *adverb*
Her work is always very good. enormously, especially, exceedingly, extremely, greatly, highly, intensely, [*informal*] jolly, outstandingly, particularly, really, remarkably, [*informal*] terribly, [*informal*] terrifically, truly, uncommonly, unusually.
AN OPPOSITE IS slightly.

vessel *noun*
1 *Their fishing vessel collided with a tanker in rough seas.* boat, craft, ship.

VESSELS USED TO TRANSPORT PEOPLE OR GOODS: barge, coaster, collier, cruise liner, dhow, ferry, freighter, gondola, hovercraft, hydrofoil, junk, lighter, liner, merchant ship, narrow boat, oil tanker, steamship, supertanker, tanker, tramp steamer.

OTHER WORKING VESSELS: dredger, ice-breaker, lifeboat, lightship, trawler, tug, whaler.

MILITARY VESSELS: aircraft carrier, battleship, corvette, cruiser, destroyer, frigate, gunboat, landing craft, minesweeper, submarine, torpedo boat, troop ship, warship.

VESSELS USED MAINLY FOR LEISURE: cabin cruiser, canoe, catamaran, dinghy, houseboat, launch, motor boat, powerboat, punt, raft, rowing boat, sailing boat, speed boat, yacht.

SOME VESSELS USED IN FORMER TIMES: brigantine, clipper, coracle, cutter, dugout, galleon, galley, man-of-war, packet boat, paddle steamer, schooner, trireme, windjammer.

WORDS FOR PARTS OF A VESSEL: boom, bow, bowsprit, bridge, bulwark, cabin, conning tower, crow's nest, deck, engine room, fo'c'sle or forecastle, funnel, galley, helm, hull, keel, mast, poop, porthole, propeller, prow, quarterdeck, rigging, rudder, sail, stern, tiller.

2 *Archaeologists discovered gold and silver vessels at the site.*
FOR VARIOUS CONTAINERS, SEE **container**.
blood vessels Blood vessels are your *arteries*, *capillaries*, and *veins*.

veteran *noun*
He is a veteran of the Second World War. old soldier, survivor.

veto *noun*
> They couldn't have a party because of the head's veto. ban, prohibition, refusal, rejection.
> AN OPPOSITE IS approval.

veto *verb*
> The boss vetoed the proposed holiday. ban, forbid, prohibit, refuse, reject, rule out, say no to, turn down.
> AN OPPOSITE IS approve.

vex *verb*
> It vexed her that he had forgotten her birthday. anger, annoy, exasperate, irritate, make you cross, upset, worry.

vibrate *verb*
> You can feel the engine vibrate. quake, quiver, rattle, shake, shudder, throb, tremble.

vibration *noun*
> The vibrations from the earthquake could be felt for miles around. pulse, quivering, rattling, shaking, shuddering, throbbing, trembling, tremor.

vicar *noun* SEE **clergyman**

vice *noun*
> **1** The police wage war on crime and vice. corruption, evil, immorality, sin, wickedness, wrongdoing.
> **2** Vanity is not one of his vices. bad habit, blemish, defect, failing, fault, imperfection, shortcoming, weakness.
> AN OPPOSITE IS virtue.

vicinity *noun*
> The car was found in the vicinity of the station. district, locality, neighbourhood, surrounding area.

vicious *adjective*
> **1** He suffered a vicious attack. atrocious, barbaric, barbarous, beastly, bloodthirsty, brutal, callous, cruel, diabolical, fiendish, inhuman, merciless, murderous, pitiless, ruthless, sadistic, savage, violent.
> **2** He's not a vicious person. evil, heartless, immoral, malicious, perverted, spiteful, villainous, wicked.

> **3** Take care—that dog's vicious. aggressive, bad-tempered, dangerous, ferocious, fierce.
> **4** A vicious wind was blowing. nasty, severe, sharp, unpleasant.
> AN OPPOSITE IS gentle.

victim *noun*
> **1** Ambulances took the victims to hospital. casualty.
> Victims of an accident are also **the injured** or **the wounded**.
> A person who dies in an accident is a **fatality**.
> **2** The hawk seized its victim. prey.
> People who are attacked and killed because of their beliefs are **martyrs**.

victimize *verb*
> He was victimized at school because he hated sport. bully, intimidate, oppress, persecute, pick on, terrorize, torment, treat unfairly.
> To victimize people who work for you is to **exploit** them.
> To victimize people because of their race, religion, etc., is to **discriminate against** them.

victor *noun*
> After the match, the victors returned in triumph. champion, conqueror, winner.

victorious *adjective*
> A trophy was presented to the victorious team. conquering, leading, successful, top, top-scoring, triumphant, unbeaten, undefeated, winning
> AN OPPOSITE IS defeated.

victory *noun*
> The streets were full of people celebrating the team's victory in the world cup. success, triumph, win.
> AN OPPOSITE IS defeat.

view *noun*
> **1** There's a good view from the top of the hill. outlook, panorama, prospect, scene, scenery.
> **2** He has strong views about politics. attitude, belief, conviction, idea, notion, opinion, thought.
> **in view of something** In view of his recent conduct, the club has decided to suspend him. as a result of, because of, considering, taking account of.

view *verb*
1 *Thousand of tourists come to view the cathedral each year.* contemplate, examine, eye, gaze at, inspect, look at, observe, see, stare at, survey.
2 *She viewed the prospect of an interview with dread.* consider, regard, think of.

viewer *noun*
People who view a performance are the **audience** or **spectators**.
People who view something as they happen to pass by are **bystanders** or **onlookers** or **witnesses**.

vigilant *adjective*
He warned the public to be vigilant and report anything suspicious. alert, attentive, careful, observant, on the lookout, on your guard, wary, watchful.
AN OPPOSITE IS negligent.

vigorous *adjective*
1 *Vigorous exercise does you good.* active, brisk, energetic, enthusiastic, lively, strenuous.
2 *I gave the door a vigorous push.* forceful, mighty, powerful.
3 *He was a vigorous man in the prime of life.* healthy, strong.
AN OPPOSITE IS feeble.

vigour *noun*
1 *He tackled the job with vigour.* energy, enthusiasm, keenness, liveliness, spirit, vitality, zeal, zest.
2 *I banged on the door with vigour.* force, might, power, strength.

vile *adjective*
1 *What a vile smell!* disgusting, filthy, foul, horrible, loathsome, nasty, offensive, repellent, repulsive, revolting, sickening, unpleasant.
AN OPPOSITE IS pleasant.
2 *Murder is a vile crime.* contemptible, dreadful, evil, ugly, vicious, wicked.

villain *noun*
The police have caught the villains who broke into the shop. criminal, delinquent, offender, rogue, wretch, wrongdoer.
SEE ALSO **criminal** *noun*.
An informal word for the villain in a story is **baddy**.
AN OPPOSITE IS hero.

villainous *adjective*
People were appalled by his villainous behaviour. corrupt, cruel, diabolical, dreadful, evil, immoral, perverted, sinful, terrible, vicious, vile, wicked.
AN OPPOSITE IS virtuous.

violate *verb*
1 *He was penalized for violating the rules.* break, disobey, ignore.
2 *It's rude to violate someone's privacy.* abuse, interfere with, invade, show disrespect for.

violation *noun*
He's guilty of a violation of the rules. breach, breaking, offence (against).
A violation of the rules of a game is a **foul** or an **infringement**.

violence *noun*
1 *The violence of the attack horrified us.* barbarity, brutality, cruelty, ferocity, fierceness, fury, savagery, viciousness.
AN OPPOSITE IS gentleness.
2 *The violence of the storm uprooted trees.* destructiveness, intensity, power, rage, severity, strength.
AN OPPOSITE IS feebleness.
3 *The terrorists are prepared to use violence to achieve their objectives.* fighting, force, might, war.
AN OPPOSITE IS non-violence or pacifism.

violent *adjective*
1 *There were violent clashes between demonstrators and police.* brutal, cruel, ferocious, fierce, frenzied, furious, savage, vicious, wild.
AN OPPOSITE IS gentle.
2 *The bridge was washed away in a violent storm.* destructive, devastating, forceful, intense, powerful, raging, rough, serious, severe, strong, tempestuous, [*informal*] terrific, turbulent, wild.
AN OPPOSITE IS feeble.

virtual *adjective*
virtual reality Virtual reality is an **imitation** or **simulation** of the real world

virtually *adverb*
I've virtually finished. almost, as good as, in effect, more or less, nearly, practically.

virtue *noun*
1 *She has the virtue of a saint!* decency,
goodness, honesty, honour, integrity,
morality, nobility, righteousness,
sincerity, uprightness, worthiness.
2 *Our car's main virtue is that it's
cheap to run.* advantage, asset, good
point, merit, strength.
AN OPPOSITE IS vice.

virtuous *adjective*
She's always led a virtuous life. good,
honest, honourable, innocent, just,
law-abiding, moral, praiseworthy,
pure, righteous, trustworthy, upright,
worthy.
AN OPPOSITE IS wicked.

visible *adjective*
*The spire of the church is visible from
miles away.* apparent, clear,
conspicuous, distinct, evident,
noticeable, obvious, perceptible, plain,
recognizable, unconcealed.
AN OPPOSITE IS invisible.

vision *noun*
1 *He had perfect vision.* eyesight, sight.
2 *He claimed he saw his future in a
vision.* dream, hallucination.
Something travellers in the desert
think they see is a *mirage*.
3 *He is a man of great political vision.*
foresight, imagination, insight,
understanding.

visit *verb*
She's visiting friends in London. call
on, come to see, drop in on, go to see,
pay a call on, stay with.

visit *noun*
1 *My grandmother came for a visit.* call,
stay.
2 *We went to London for a visit.* day
out, excursion, outing, trip.

visitor *noun*
1 *They've got some visitors from Ireland
staying with them.* caller, guest.
2 *Rome welcomes millions of visitors
every year.* holidaymaker, sightseer,
tourist, traveller.

visual aids *plural noun*
FOR AUDIO-VISUAL EQUIPMENT USED
IN SCHOOLS, SEE **audio-visual**.

visualize *verb*
I can't visualize you with long hair.
conceive, imagine, picture.

vital *adjective*
*This leaflet contains vital information
for travellers.* crucial, essential,
imperative, important, indispensable,
necessary, relevant.
AN OPPOSITE IS unimportant.

vitality *noun*
*Although she's quite old, she's still full
of vitality.* animation, energy,
exuberance, life, liveliness, spirit,
sprightliness, vigour, zest.

vivid *adjective*
1 *She loved to dress in vivid colours.*
bright, brilliant, colourful, dazzling,
[*uncomplimentary*] gaudy, glowing,
intense, showy, striking, strong.
2 *He gave a vivid description of the
scene.* clear, graphic, imaginative,
lifelike, lively, memorable, powerful,
realistic.
AN OPPOSITE IS dull.

vocal *adjective*
*Usually she's quiet, but today she's
quite vocal.* chatty, communicative,
outspoken, talkative.
AN OPPOSITE IS uncommunicative.

vocalist *noun*
FOR OTHER KINDS OF SINGER, SEE
sing.

voice *noun*
I recognized her voice. accent,
speaking, speech, tone.

voice *verb*
He voiced several objections to the plan.
communicate, express, give vent to,
put into words, speak.

volcano *noun*
Lava, ash, etc., pouring from a volcano
is an *eruption*.

volley *noun*
A volley of shots rang out. barrage,
bombardment.

volume *noun*
1 *What is the volume of the container?*
capacity, dimensions, size.
2 *The firm couldn't deal with the volume of orders it received.* amount, bulk, mass, quantity.
3 *He turned down the volume.* loudness.
4 *She published two volumes of poetry.* book.

voluntary *adjective*
She does voluntary work for a charity. optional, unpaid.
AN OPPOSITE IS compulsory.

volunteer *verb*
She volunteered to wash up. be willing, offer, put yourself forward.

vomit *verb*
The smell made him want to vomit. be sick, bring up your food.

vote *verb*
Everyone has a right to vote in the election. cast your vote.
to vote for someone or **something**
Who did you vote for? choose, elect, nominate, opt for, pick, select, settle on.

vote *noun*
The results of the vote were printed in the newspaper. ballot, election, poll, referendum, show of hands.

voucher *noun*
Exchange this voucher for a free drink. coupon, ticket, token.

vow *noun*
She made a vow never to tell anyone what she'd heard. pledge, promise.

vow *verb*
He vowed that one day he would return. give an assurance, give your word, guarantee, pledge, promise, swear, take an oath.

voyage *noun*
A holiday voyage is a **cruise**.
A voyage across a channel or sea is a **crossing**.
A long voyage is a **sea passage**.
A short voyage in a yacht is a **sail**.
FOR OTHER WAYS TO TRAVEL, SEE **travel**.

vulgar *adjective*
1 *The jokes were rather vulgar.* coarse, foul, impolite, improper, indecent, obscene, offensive, rude, smutty.
AN OPPOSITE IS polite.
2 *Those gaudy colours look vulgar.* common, crude, in bad taste, tasteless, unsophisticated.
AN OPPOSITE IS tasteful.

vulnerable *adjective*
1 *The soldiers were in a vulnerable position.* at risk, defenceless, exposed, open, unguarded, unprotected, weak.
AN OPPOSITE IS safe.
2 *He's a kind and vulnerable man.* easily hurt, sensitive, thin-skinned.
AN OPPOSITE IS insensitive or robust.

wad *noun*
He took a wad of banknotes from his pocket. bundle, mass, pad, roll.

wag *verb*
The dog wagged its tail. move to and fro, shake, waggle, wave, wiggle.

wage *noun*
Her weekly wage is £150. earnings, income, pay, pay packet.
A fixed regular amount an employer agrees to pay you is a **salary**.

wage *verb*
The government waged a war against crime. carry on, conduct, fight.

wager *noun*
He had a wager that she would win. bet.

wail *verb*
Upstairs, the baby began to wail. cry, howl, moan, shriek.

wait *verb*
Wait here until I get back. [*informal*] hang about or around, [*informal*] hold on, linger, pause, remain where you are, stay, stop.
to wait on someone *The owner of the restaurant waits on his customers from time to time.* serve.

wait *noun*
There was a long wait before the bus came. delay, hold-up, interval, pause.

wake, waken *verbs*
1 *I usually wake at about 8.* become conscious, [*informal*] come to life, get up, rise, stir, wake up.
2 *She woke me at 7.* arouse, awaken, call, disturb, rouse.

walk *verb*

VARIOUS WAYS PEOPLE OR ANIMALS WALK: amble, crawl, creep, dodder, hike, hobble, limp, lope, lurch, march, mince, pace, pad, paddle, parade, plod, prowl, ramble, saunter, scuttle, shamble, shuffle, slink, stagger, stalk, steal, step, [*informal*] stomp, stride, stroll, strut, stumble, swagger, tiptoe, [*informal*] toddle, totter, traipse, tramp, trek, troop, trot, trudge, waddle, wade.

walk *noun*
1 *We went for a walk in the country.* hike, ramble, saunter, stroll, tramp, trek, trudge.
2 *There are some lovely walks in the surrounding countryside.* path, route.

walker *noun*
When you walk along the street, you are a *pedestrian*.
If you go for long walks, you are a *hiker* or *rambler*.

wall *noun*

VARIOUS KINDS OF WALL: barricade, barrier, dam, dike, dividing wall, embankment, fence, fortification, hedge, obstacle, paling, palisade, parapet, partition, rampart, screen, sea wall, stockade.

wallow *verb*
1 *Hippos like to wallow in mud.* flounder, lie, roll about, wade.
2 *She was wallowing in a hot bath.* indulge yourself, take delight.

wander *verb*
1 *The sheep wander about the hills.* go aimlessly, meander, ramble, range, roam, rove, stray, travel, walk.
2 *They'd wandered off the path.* stray, swerve, turn, veer.

wane *verb*
1 *At sunset, the light began to wane.* become dimmer, disappear, fade, fail.
AN OPPOSITE IS brighten.
2 *Her enthusiasm waned after a while.* decline, decrease, diminish, dwindle, lessen, subside, weaken.
AN OPPOSITE IS strengthen.

want *verb*
1 *You can't always have what you want.* crave, desire, fancy, hanker after, [*informal*] have a yen for, hunger after, itch to have, long for, pine for, [*informal*] set your heart on, wish for, yearn for.
If we want something, we can say that we *would like* it, or we *wish* it would happen.
2 *My hair wants cutting.* need, require.

want *noun*
1 *The hotel staff saw to all their wants.* demand, desire, need, requirement, wish.
2 *The plants died from want of water.* absence, lack, need, scarcity, shortage.

war *noun*
The incident led to war between the two countries. conflict, fighting, hostilities, military action, strife, warfare.
A war fought in the Middle Ages for religious reasons was a *crusade*.

VARIOUS THINGS THAT HAPPEN IN WAR: ambush, assault, attack or counter-attack, battle, blitz, blockade, bombardment, campaign, espionage, guerrilla warfare, invasion, manoeuvres, negotiations, operation, resistance, retreat, siege, skirmish, surrender, withdrawal.

SEE ALSO **fight** *noun*.

ward *verb*
to ward off someone or **something**
1 *He turned to ward off his attackers.*
beat off, fend off, keep away, push
away.
2 *The ritual was intended to ward off
evil spirits.* avert, block, check, deflect,
repel, stave off, turn aside.

warder *noun*
*He was handcuffed to a warder and
taken to prison.* gaoler or jailer, guard,
keeper, prison officer.

warehouse *noun*
The goods were stored in a warehouse.
depot, store, storehouse.

wares *plural noun*
*The market traders displayed their
wares.* commodities, goods,
merchandise, produce, stock.

warlike *adjective*
*The Picts were a notoriously warlike
people.* aggressive, fierce, hostile,
militant, quarrelsome, violent.
AN OPPOSITE IS peaceful.

warm *adjective*
1 *It was a warm September evening.*
pleasantly hot.
Weather which is unpleasantly warm
is *close* or *sultry*.
Water or food which is only just warm
is *lukewarm* or *tepid*.
AN OPPOSITE IS cold.
2 *She changed into her warm clothes.*
cosy, thick, woolly.
Underwear specially made to keep you
warm is *thermal* underwear.
AN OPPOSITE IS thin.
3 *They gave us a warm welcome.*
affectionate, enthusiastic, friendly,
genial, kind, loving, sympathetic,
warm-hearted.
AN OPPOSITE IS unfriendly.

warm *verb*
*She sat by the fire, warming her hands
and feet.* heat, make warmer, raise the
temperature (of), thaw, thaw out.
AN OPPOSITE IS chill.

warn *verb*
He warned her not to walk home alone.
advise, alert, caution, remind.
To warn people of a disaster is to *raise
the alarm*.

warning *noun*
1 *There was no warning of the danger
ahead.* advance notice, indication, sign,
signal.
FOR VARIOUS SIGNALS, SEE **signal**
noun.
2 *The police let him off with a warning.*
caution, reprimand, [*informal*] ticking
off.

warp *verb*
The girders warped in the heat. become
deformed, bend, buckle, curl, curve,
distort, twist.

warrant *verb*
*The allegations are serious enough to
warrant investigation.* deserve, justify,
merit.

warrior *noun* SEE **fighter**

wary *adjective*
*I had a wary look round before I went
in.* apprehensive, attentive, careful,
cautious, distrustful, suspicious,
vigilant, watchful.
AN OPPOSITE IS reckless.

wash *verb*
1 *If it's dirty, you'd better wash it.* clean.
To wash something with a cloth, etc., is
to *mop*, *sponge*, or *wipe* it.
To wash something with a brush is to
scrub it.
To wash something in clean water is to
rinse, *sluice*, or *swill* it.
To wash your hair is to *shampoo* it.
To wash yourself all over is to *bath* or
shower.
To wash and iron clothes is to *launder*
them.
2 *Waves washed over the beach.* flow,
splash.

waste *verb*
*Don't waste money on things you don't
really need.* fritter away, misuse,
squander, throw away.
AN OPPOSITE IS save.
to waste away *She was visibly wasting
away.* become thinner, lose weight.

waste *adjective*
1 *Ensure that waste materials are
carefully disposed of.* discarded, left
over, spare, superfluous, unnecessary,
unwanted.

2 *There was a patch of waste ground behind the factory.* derelict, empty, overgrown, uncultivated, undeveloped, unused, wild.

waste *noun*
1 *The organization was keen to avoid any waste of resources.* unnecessary use, wastage.
2 *A lot of household waste can be recycled.* garbage, junk, litter, refuse, rubbish, trash.
Waste food is *leftovers*.
Waste timber is *offcuts*.
Waste fabrics are *remnants*.
Waste metal is *scrap*.
Waste from our bodies is *sewage*.

wasteful *adjective*
It's wasteful to cook more food than is necessary. extravagant, needless, prodigal, reckless, thriftless, uneconomical.
AN OPPOSITE IS economical.

watch *verb*
1 *She sat and watched the children playing in the garden.* contemplate, gaze at, look at, see, stare at, view.
2 *Watch how I do it.* attend to, concentrate on, heed, keep your eyes on, note, observe, pay attention to, take notice of.
3 *Could you watch my bag for a few minutes?* care for, defend, guard, keep an eye on, keep watch over, look after, mind, protect, safeguard, shield, supervise, tend.
to watch out *Watch out—there's a car coming!* be careful, beware, pay attention, take care, take heed.

watch *noun*

INSTRUMENTS USED TO MEASURE TIME: chronometer, clock, digital watch, hourglass, stopwatch, sundial, timepiece, timer, wristwatch.

watchful *adjective*
She kept a watchful eye on the time. alert, attentive, observant, perceptive, sharp-eyed, vigilant.

watchman *noun*
He found a job as a watchman in a local factory. caretaker, guard, lookout, nightwatchman, security guard.

water *noun*

VARIOUS KINDS OF WATER:
bathwater, bottled water, brine, distilled water, drinking water, rainwater, seawater, spa water, spring water, tap water.

VARIOUS STRETCHES OF WATER:
brook, canal, lake, lido, [Scottish] loch, ocean, pond, pool, reservoir, river, sea, stream.

water *verb*
She went out to water the plants. dampen, drench, irrigate, moisten, soak, sprinkle, wet.
to water something down *The milk had been watered down.* dilute, thin, weaken.

waterlogged *adjective*
The match had to be abandoned because the pitch was waterlogged. full of water, saturated, soaked.

waterproof *adjective*
These shoes aren't waterproof. showerproof, water-resistant, weatherproof.
Joints or containers that do not let water through are *watertight*.

watery *adjective*
1 *The soup was watery and tasteless.* diluted, runny, thin, watered down.
2 *The smoky air made her eyes watery.* damp, moist, tear filled, tearful, wet.

wave *verb*
1 *The flags waved in the breeze.* flap, flutter, move to and fro, sway, swing.
2 *Demonstrators waved banners and placards as they marched through the town.* brandish, flourish, shake, twirl, wag, waggle, wiggle.

wave *noun*
1 *I watched the waves break on the shore.* billow, breaker, roller.
A very small wave is a *ripple*.
A huge wave caused by an earthquake, etc., is a *tidal wave*.

A number of white waves following each other is **surf**.
The top of a wave is the **crest** or **ridge**.
2 *A wave of anger spread through the crowd.* outbreak, surge.
3 *With a wave of his hand he walked off.* flourish, gesture, shake.

waveband *noun*
The radio isn't tuned to the right waveband. channel, station, wavelength.

waver *verb*
1 *She wavered, uncertain whether to accept his offer or not.* be uncertain, dither, falter, hesitate, pause, think twice.
2 *The candle flame wavered in the draught.* flicker, shake, sway, tremble.

wavy *adjective*
The paper was decorated with wavy gold lines. curling, curly, curving, rippling, winding, zigzag.
AN OPPOSITE IS straight.

way *noun*
1 *He walked along the covered way between the two buildings.* path, road, street.
2 *Show me the way to your house.* direction, route.
3 *Is it a long way from here?* distance, journey.
4 *I'll show you the way to make a pancake.* knack, method, procedure, process, system, technique.
5 *She behaved in a mature way.* fashion, manner, style.
6 *They are very alike in some ways.* aspect, detail, feature, particular, respect.
7 *Things are in a bad way.* condition, state.

weak *adjective*
1 *The bridge was too weak to carry heavy traffic.* decrepit, flimsy, fragile, rickety, shaky, unsafe, unsound, unsteady.
2 *He was too weak to walk very far.* delicate, exhausted, feeble, frail, helpless, infirm, sickly.
3 *Weak leadership was blamed for the current crisis.* ineffective, ineffectual, powerless, useless.

4 *The soldiers were in a weak position.* defenceless, exposed, unguarded, unprotected, vulnerable.
5 *The play was quite entertaining but the plot was a bit weak.* feeble, lame, unconvincing, unsatisfactory.
6 *She gave me a cup of weak tea.* diluted, tasteless, thin, watery.
AN OPPOSITE IS strong.

weaken *verb*
1 *Hunger weakened their resistance.* diminish, lessen, lower, make weaker, reduce, sap, undermine.
2 *Our resolve weakened.* become weaker, decline, decrease, dwindle, ebb away, fade, flag, give way, wane.
AN OPPOSITE IS strengthen.

weakness *noun*
1 *Engineers discovered a structural weakness in the aircraft.* defect, fault, flaw, imperfection, mistake, shortcoming.
2 *Most people saw her sensitivity as a sign of weakness.* fragility, inadequacy, incompetence, ineffectiveness, uselessness.
AN OPPOSITE IS strength.

wealth *noun*
No one knew how she had acquired her wealth. affluence, assets, capital, fortune, money, opulence, possessions, property, prosperity, riches.
AN OPPOSITE IS poverty.
a wealth of *There's a wealth of information in this book.* an abundance of, [*informal*] heaps of, lots of, much, plenty of, a profusion of.

wealthy *adjective*
He must be wealthy to live in a house like that. affluent, opulent, prosperous, rich, well-off, well-to-do.
AN OPPOSITE IS poor.

weapon *noun*

VARIOUS KINDS OF GUN: airgun, automatic pistol or rifle, bazooka, [*old use*] blunderbuss, Bren gun, cannon, Gatling gun, handgun, howitzer, machine-gun, mortar, [*old use*] musket, pistol, revolver, rifle, shotgun, Sten gun, sub-machine gun, tommy-gun, water-cannon.
Heavy guns are **artillery**. ➡

A set of heavy guns on a warship, etc., is a *battery*.
Hand-held guns are *firearms* or *small arms*.

VARIOUS MODERN BOMBS AND MISSILES: atom bomb, ballistic missile, depth charge, grenade, H-bomb, incendiary bomb, landmine, mine, napalm bomb, nuclear weapons, rocket, time bomb, torpedo, warhead.

OTHER MODERN WEAPONS: biological weapons, chemical weapons, CS gas, flame-thrower, tear gas.

OLD WEAPONS OR WEAPONS WHICH DO NOT USE MODERN TECHNOLOGY: baton, battering ram, battleaxe, bayonet, blowpipe, boomerang, bow and arrow, broadsword, catapult, club, cosh, crossbow, cudgel, cutlass, dagger, dart, harpoon, javelin, lance, longbow, machete, pike, pole-axe, quarterstaff, rapier, sabre, scimitar, sling, spear, staff, sword, tomahawk, trident, truncheon.
Weapons in general are *armaments*, *munitions*, or *weaponry*.
A collection or store of weapons is an *armoury* or *arsenal* or *magazine*.

wear *verb*
1 *She was wearing a short, black dress.* be dressed in, clothe yourself in, dress in, have on.
2 *The carpets were starting to wear.* fray, wear away, wear out.
3 *The boots haven't worn well.* endure, last, survive.
to wear off *The pain soon wore off.* die down, disappear, ease, fade, lessen, moderate, subside, weaken.

weary *adjective*
She looked pale and weary. [*informal*] all in, exhausted, fatigued, flagging, sleepy, tired, worn out.

weather *noun*

The prevalent weather conditions in a particular area is the *climate*.
The study of weather is *meteorology*. ➡

VARIOUS ASPECTS OF WEATHER WHICH PEOPLE NOTICE: blizzard, breeze, cloud, cyclone, deluge, dew, downpour, drizzle, drought, fog, frost, gale, hail, haze, heatwave, high or low temperatures, hoar frost, hurricane, ice, lightning, mist, rain, rainbow, shower, sleet, slush, snow, snowstorm, squall, storm, sunshine, tempest, thaw, thunder, tornado, typhoon, whirlwind, wind.

WORDS USED TO DESCRIBE DIFFERENT KINDS OF WEATHER: autumnal, blustery, breezy, bright, chilly, clear, close, cloudless, cloudy, cold, drizzly, dry, dull, fair, fine, foggy, freezing, frosty, grey, hazy, hot, humid, icy, inclement, misty, overcast, pouring, rainy, rough, showery, slushy, snowy, springlike, squally, stormy, sultry, summery, sunless, sunny, sweltering, thundery, torrential, turbulent, wet, wild, windy, wintry.

weather *verb*
The ship weathered the storm. come through, endure, live through, survive, withstand.

weave *verb*
He managed to weave his way through the crowd. twist and turn, wind, wriggle, zigzag.

web *noun*
The map was a web of criss-cross lines. mesh, net, network.

wedding *noun*
She was a bridesmaid at her cousin's wedding. marriage.

PEOPLE INVOLVED IN A WEDDING: best man, bride, bridegroom, bridesmaid, groom, maid or matron of honour, page, registrar, usher, wedding guests. ➡

OTHER WORDS TO DO WITH
WEDDINGS: bouquet, ceremony,
church service, confetti, honeymoon,
reception or wedding breakfast,
registry office, signing the register,
trousseau, vows, wedding bells,
wedding dress, wedding march,
wedding ring.

wedge *verb*
Wedge the door open. jam, stick.

weedy *adjective*
1 *A weedy path led to the front door.*
overgrown, untidy, unweeded, wild.
2 [*insulting*] *A weedy little man opened
the front door.* feeble, puny, thin.

weep *verb*
*She buried her face in her hands and
began to weep.* cry, shed tears, sob.
To weep or cry in an annoying way is to
snivel or *whimper*.

weigh *verb*
to weigh someone down 1 *Her
troubles weighed her down.* afflict,
depress, sadden, worry.
2 *She was weighed down with
shopping.* load.
to weigh something up *They weighed
up the evidence.* assess, consider,
evaluate, examine, give thought to,
meditate on, ponder, study, think
about.

weight *noun*
Take care when lifting heavy weights.
burden, load, mass.
FOR UNITS OF WEIGHT, SEE
measurement.

weighty *adjective*
1 *He lifted a weighty volume off the
shelf.* heavy, massive, ponderous.
AN OPPOSITE IS light.
2 *They had weighty matters to discuss.*
important, major, pressing, serious,
urgent.
AN OPPOSITE IS unimportant.

weird *adjective*
1 *Weird shrieks were heard in the
darkness.* creepy, eerie, ghostly,
mysterious, [*informal*] scary, [*informal*]
spooky, supernatural, uncanny,
unearthly, unnatural.
AN OPPOSITE IS natural.
2 *Some of her clothes were a bit weird.*
curious, extraordinary, [*informal*]
funny, grotesque, odd, peculiar, queer,
quirky, strange, unconventional,
unusual.
AN OPPOSITE IS ordinary.

welcome *noun*
She gave us a friendly welcome.
greeting, reception.

welcome *adjective*
1 *A cup of tea would be very welcome.*
acceptable, agreeable, pleasant,
pleasing.
AN OPPOSITE IS unacceptable.
2 *You're welcome to use my bike.*
allowed, free, permitted.
AN OPPOSITE IS forbidden.

welcome *verb*
1 *She welcomed us at the door.* greet,
receive, say hello to.
2 *The company welcomes customers'
comments.* accept, appreciate, approve
of, like, want.

weld *verb*
*Panels of steel are welded together to
form the body of the car.* fix, fuse, join,
solder.

welfare *noun*
*Her only concern was the welfare of her
children.* happiness, health, interests,
well-being.

well *noun*

PLACES WHERE YOU GET WATER OR
OIL OUT OF THE GROUND: artesian
well, borehole, geyser, gusher, oasis,
oil well, shaft, spring, waterhole,
wishing-well.

well *adverb*
1 *The whole team played well.*
admirably, effectively, efficiently,
expertly, marvellously, satisfactorily,
skilfully, successfully, wonderfully.
AN OPPOSITE IS badly.
2 *It was a difficult job but they paid
him well.* fairly, generously, properly,
reasonably, suitably.
3 *I know her well.* closely, intimately,
personally.

well *adjective*
You look well. fit, healthy, hearty, in
good health, lively, robust, sound,
strong, thriving, vigorous.
AN OPPOSITE IS ill.

well-known *adjective*
*A well-known television personality
opened the new shop.* celebrated,
distinguished, eminent, famous,
notable, outstanding, prominent,
renowned.
AN OPPOSITE IS unknown.

well-mannered *adjective*
*They were well-mannered and eager to
please.* civil, considerate, courteous,
polite, respectful, tactful.
AN OPPOSITE IS rude.

west *noun, adjective, adverb*
The parts of a continent or country in
the west are the **western** parts.
People from countries west of the
oriental countries—especially from
Europe and N America—are called
westerners.
To travel towards the west is to travel
westward or **westwards**.
A wind from the west is a **westerly**
wind.

wet *adjective*
1 *She took off her wet clothes and had a
hot bath.* clammy, damp, drenched,
dripping, moist, soaked, sopping,
wringing wet.
2 *The field's wet, so we can't play.* dewy,
muddy, saturated, soaking, soggy,
submerged, waterlogged, watery.
3 *Take care—the paint is still wet.*
runny, sticky, tacky.
4 *It was a miserable, wet day.* drizzly,
misty, pouring, rainy, showery.
AN OPPOSITE IS dry.

wet *verb*
Wet the clay before you start to mould it.
dampen, moisten, soak, water.
AN OPPOSITE IS dry.

wheel *noun*
A small wheel under a piece of
furniture is a **caster**.
A set of wheels under one end of a
railway carriage is a **bogie**.
The centre of a wheel is the **hub**.
The outer edge of a wheel is the **rim**.

wheel *verb*
1 *Gulls wheeled overhead.* circle, move
in circles.
2 *The column of soldiers wheeled to the
right.* change direction, swerve, swing
round, turn, veer.

wheeze *verb*
*He was coughing and wheezing all
night.* breathe noisily, cough, gasp,
pant, puff.

whiff *noun*
*As she walked by, he caught a whiff of
her perfume.* hint, puff, smell.

while *noun*
I waited for a while. period, spell, time.

whimper, whine *verbs*
*The dog whimpered in the corner of the
room.* cry, moan.

whip *verb*
1 *They whipped the horse with a leather
belt.* beat, cane, flog, hit, lash, thrash.

VARIOUS INSTRUMENTS USED FOR
WHIPPING: birch, cane, cat, cat-o'-
nine-tails, crop, horsewhip, lash,
riding crop, scourge, switch, whip.

2 *Whip the cream until it is thick.* beat,
stir vigorously, whisk.

whirl *verb*
The snowflakes whirled in the icy wind.
circle, reel, revolve, rotate, spin, turn,
twirl, twist.

whisk *verb*
Whisk the egg yolks together in a bowl.
beat, mix, stir, whip.

whiskers *plural noun*
He had long whiskers on his face.
bristles, hairs, a moustache.

whisper *verb*
What are you two whispering about?
murmur, speak softly.

whistle *verb*
FOR VARIOUS WAYS TO MAKE SOUNDS,
SEE **sound** *verb*.

white *adjective, noun*

SHADES OF WHITE: cream, ivory, off-
white, platinum, silvery, snow-white,
whitish.
When coloured things become whiter
they become **bleached** or **faded** or
pale.

whole *adjective*
1 *She told us the whole story.* complete,
entire, full, total, unabbreviated.
AN OPPOSITE IS incomplete.
2 *Much of the building was damaged,
but the front wall remained whole.* in
one piece, intact, perfect, sound,
unbroken, undamaged, unharmed.
AN OPPOSITE IS broken or in pieces.

wholesale *adjective*
*The storm caused wholesale
destruction.* complete, comprehensive,
extensive, general, total, universal,
widespread.
Something which affects the whole
world is **global** or **worldwide**.

wholesome *adjective*
The food was plentiful and wholesome.
good, healthy, nourishing, nutritious.
AN OPPOSITE IS unhealthy.

wicked *adjective*
1 *He is a wicked, cruel man.* corrupt,
evil, immoral, perverted, sinful,
vicious, villainous.
People who are not seriously wicked
are **mischievous** or **naughty**.
2 *It was a wicked attack on a
defenceless woman.* bad, cruel,
diabolical, dreadful, fiendish, foul,
malevolent, malicious, scandalous,
shameful, spiteful, terrible, vile,
wrong.
AN OPPOSITE IS virtuous.

wide *adjective*
1 *The cottage was not far from the wide
sandy beach.* broad, expansive,
extensive, large.
AN OPPOSITE IS narrow.
2 *She has a wide knowledge of classical
music.* comprehensive, encyclopedic,
vast, wide-ranging.
AN OPPOSITE IS limited.

widely *adverb*
*The story of Cinderella is widely
known.* commonly, everywhere, far and
wide.

widespread *adjective*
*After the drought famine was
widespread.* common, extensive,
general, prevalent, universal.
Something which spreads over the
whole world is **global** or **worldwide**.
AN OPPOSITE IS uncommon.

width *noun*
The room is about eight feet in width.
breadth.
The distance across a circle is its
diameter.

wield *verb*
The lumberjack was wielding his axe.
brandish, flourish, hold, use.

wild *adjective*
1 *She didn't like seeing wild animals in
captivity.* undomesticated, untamed.
AN OPPOSITE IS tame.
2 *The hedgerow was full of wild
flowers.* natural, uncultivated.
AN OPPOSITE IS cultivated.
3 *It's a wild, mountainous region.*
deserted, desolate, rough, rugged,
uncultivated, waste.
AN OPPOSITE IS cultivated.

VARIOUS AREAS OF WILD COUNTRY:
[*informal*] barren wastes, the bush,
desert, heath, jungle, marsh,
moorland, wasteland, wilderness,
[*informal*] the wilds.

4 *The crowd were wild with excitement.*
aggressive, boisterous, disorderly,
excited, hysterical, noisy, out of control,
rash, reckless, riotous, rowdy,
uncontrollable, uncontrolled, unruly,
violent.
AN OPPOSITE IS gentle or restrained.

5 *Outside, a wild wind was blowing.*
blustery, stormy, tempestuous,
turbulent, windy.
AN OPPOSITE IS calm.

wilful *adjective*
1 *He's a very wilful child.* determined,
obstinate, stubborn.
2 *She told him off for wilful
disobedience.* conscious, deliberate,
intentional, planned.

will *noun*
He seemed to have lost the will to win.
aim, desire, determination, intention,
purpose, resolution, will-power, wish.

willing *adjective*
1 *I'm willing to help.* eager, happy,
pleased, prepared, ready.
2 *The task will be a lot easier if you can
find a couple of willing helpers.*
cooperative, enthusiastic, helpful,
obliging.
AN OPPOSITE IS unwilling.

wilt *verb*
The plants wilted in the heat. become
limp, droop, fade, flop, shrivel, wither.
AN OPPOSITE IS flourish.

wily *adjective*
*He was constantly outwitted by his wily
opponents.* artful, clever, crafty,
cunning, deceitful, devious, furtive,
scheming, sly, [*informal*] sneaky,
tricky.

win *verb*
1 *Who do you think will win?* be
successful or victorious, come first,
prevail, succeed, triumph.
To win against someone is also to *beat*,
conquer, *defeat* or *overcome* them.
AN OPPOSITE IS lose.
2 *She won first prize in the poetry
competition.* gain, get, obtain,
[*informal*] pick up, receive, secure.

wind *noun*
A gentle wind is a *breath*, *breeze*, or
draught.
A violent wind is a *cyclone*, *gale*,
hurricane, or *tornado*.
A sudden unexpected wind is a *blast*,
gust, *puff*, or *squall*.
wind instruments FOR MUSICAL
INSTRUMENTS PLAYED BY BLOWING,
SEE **music**.

wind *verb*
1 *He wound the line on to a reel.* coil,
curl, curve, loop, roll, turn.
2 *The road winds up the hill.* bend,
curve, meander, ramble, twist and
turn, zigzag.

window *noun*

KINDS OF WINDOW: casement,
dormer, double-glazed window,
fanlight, French window, pane, sash
window, shop window, skylight,
stained-glass window, windscreen.

windy *adjective*
1 *It was a cold, windy day.* blustery,
breezy, gusty, squally, stormy.
AN OPPOSITE IS calm.
2 *This spot is too windy for a picnic.*
bare, bleak, exposed.
AN OPPOSITE IS sheltered.

wine *noun*
FOR VARIOUS DRINKS, SEE **drink**.

wink *verb*
1 *He winked at me.*
To shut and open both eyes quickly is
to *blink*.
2 *The lights winked on and off.* flash,
flicker, sparkle, twinkle.

winner *noun*
*The winner was presented with a silver
trophy.* champion, conqueror,
medallist, victor.
AN OPPOSITE IS loser.

winning *adjective*
*The winning team went up to receive
their medals.* champion, conquering,
first, leading, successful, top,
triumphant, unbeaten, undefeated,
victorious.
AN OPPOSITE IS losing.

wintry *adjective*
It was a grey, wintry day. arctic, bitter,
cold, freezing, frosty, icy, snowy.

wipe *verb*
I wiped the table with a cloth. dry, dust,
mop, polish, rub.
to wipe something out *Whole villages
were wiped out by the plague in the
Middle Ages.* annihilate, destroy,
exterminate, get rid of, kill.

wire *noun*
A wire to carry electric current is **cable** or **flex** or **a lead**.
The system of electric wires in a building is the **wiring**.

wiry *adjective*
His body was wiry and athletic. lean, strong, thin, tough.
AN OPPOSITE IS flabby.

wisdom *noun*
She's a woman of great wisdom. cleverness, common sense, good sense, insight, intelligence, judgement, prudence, reason, sense, understanding.

wise *adjective*
1 He's a very wise man. clever, intelligent, knowledgeable, perceptive, prudent, rational, reasonable, sensible, shrewd, thoughtful, well-informed.
2 I think you made a wise decision. appropriate, fair, just, proper, right, sound.
AN OPPOSITE IS foolish.

wish *noun*
Her dearest wish was to have a family of her own one day. ambition, craving, desire, fancy, hope, longing, request, urge, want, yearning, [*informal*] yen.

wish *verb*
I wish they'd be quiet.
If we wish something would happen, we can say that we **would like** it, or we **want** it to happen.
to wish for It's no use wishing for things you can't have. crave, desire, fancy, hanker after, long for, want, yearn for.

wisp *noun*
She brushed a wisp of hair away from her eyes. shred, strand.

wispy *adjective*
The moon was partly hidden behind some wispy clouds. feathery, fluffy, light, soft, woolly.

wistful *adjective*
Her voice trailed off and she looked wistful. nostalgic, sad.

wit *noun*
1 He didn't have the wit to realize what she meant. brains, cleverness, intelligence, quickness, sharpness, understanding.
2 His sharp wit had them all laughing. comedy, humour, jokes, puns.
3 He was a great wit and an entertaining storyteller. comedian, comic, joker.

witchcraft *noun*
She didn't believe in the power of witchcraft. black magic, charms, sorcery, spells, wizardry.

withdraw *verb*
1 The general withdrew his troops. call back, pull out, recall.
AN OPPOSITE IS send in.
2 She withdrew her offer. cancel, take back.
AN OPPOSITE IS make or present.
3 The attackers withdrew. back away, draw back, fall back, leave, move back, retire, retreat, run away.
AN OPPOSITE IS advance.
4 Some competitors withdrew at the last minute. back out, drop out, pull out.
AN OPPOSITE IS enter.

wither *verb*
The flowers had withered and died. become dry or limp, droop, dry up, flag, flop, shrink, shrivel, waste away, wilt.
AN OPPOSITE IS flourish.

withhold *verb*
He was accused of withholding information from the police. hold back, keep back, refuse.
AN OPPOSITE IS grant.

withstand *verb*
These desert plants are able to withstand extremes of temperature. bear, cope with, endure, hold out against, resist, stand up to, survive, tolerate, weather.

witness *noun*
A witness said that the car was going too fast. bystander, eyewitness, looker-on, observer, onlooker, spectator.

witty *adjective*
He made several witty remarks about the situation. amusing, clever, comic, funny, humorous, quick-witted.
AN OPPOSITE IS dull.

wizard *noun*
1 Suddenly everyone froze, as if a wizard had cast a spell over them. magician, sorcerer.
2 He's a wizard with computers. clever person, expert, specialist.

wobble *verb*
1 The cyclist wobbled all over the road. move unsteadily, sway, totter, waver.
2 The pile of bricks wobbled and fell over. quake, quiver, rock, shake, tremble.

wobbly *adjective*
1 She's still a bit wobbly on her legs after her illness. insecure, shaky, unsafe, unsteady.
2 This table is a bit wobbly. loose, rickety, unstable.
AN OPPOSITE IS steady.

woeful *adjective*
He had such a woeful look on his face. dejected, gloomy, melancholy, miserable, mournful, sad, sorrowful, sorry, unhappy, wretched.
AN OPPOSITE IS cheerful.

woman *noun*

A polite word for a woman is *lady*.
A married woman is a *wife*.
A woman who has children is a *mother*.
A woman who stays at home to look after the house is a *housewife*.
An unmarried woman is a *spinster*.
A woman whose husband has died is a *widow*.
A woman on her wedding day is a *bride*.
A woman who is engaged to be married is a *fiancée*.
A woman who is going out with a man is his *girlfriend*.
A man who plays the part of a woman in a pantomime is the *dame*.
Words for a young woman are *girl*, *lass*.
Old words for a young woman are *maid*, *maiden*.

wonder *noun*
1 The sight of the Taj Mahal filled them with wonder. admiration, amazement, astonishment, awe, reverence, surprise.
2 It's a wonder that she recovered. marvel, miracle.

wonder *verb*
I wonder why she left in such a hurry. ask yourself, be curious about, ponder, question yourself, think.
to wonder at People wondered at his bravery. admire, be amazed or astonished by, marvel at.

wonderful *adjective*
1 It's wonderful what doctors can do these days. amazing, astonishing, astounding, extraordinary, incredible, marvellous, miraculous, phenomenal, remarkable, surprising, unexpected.
2 It was a wonderful party. excellent, exceptional, magnificent, splendid, superb.
INFORMAL SYNONYMS ARE: brilliant, fabulous, fantastic, great, terrific, tremendous.
AN OPPOSITE IS ordinary.

wood *noun*
1 The garden shed was made of wood. timber.

VARIOUS FORMS OF TIMBER: beams, boards or boarding, deal, hardwood, laths, logs, lumber, planks or planking, posts, softwood, stakes, tree trunks.

KINDS OF WOOD OFTEN USED TO MAKE THINGS: balsa, beech, cedar, chestnut, ebony, elm, mahogany, oak, pine, rosewood, sandalwood, teak, walnut.

MANUFACTURED KINDS OF WOOD: blockboard, chipboard, hardboard, plywood.

2 We walked through the wood. trees, woodland, woods.
Planting an area with trees is *afforestation*.

wooded *adjective*
Many birds prefer to live in wooded areas. tree-covered, woody.

DIFFERENT KINDS OF WOODED AREA: coppice, copse, covert, forest, grove, jungle, orchard, plantation, spinney, thicket, wood.

wooden *adjective*
1 *They sat down on a wooden bench.* timber, wood.
2 *The acting was a bit wooden.* awkward, emotionless, expressionless, lifeless, stiff, unemotional, unnatural.

woodwind *noun*
FOR MUSICAL INSTRUMENTS, SEE **music**.

woodwork *noun*
He went to evening classes to learn how to do woodwork. carpentry, joinery.

woolly *adjective*
1 *She wore a thick woolly jumper.* wool, woollen.
2 *The animal had a woolly coat.* cuddly, downy, fleecy, furry, fuzzy, hairy, soft.
3 *His ideas were rather woolly.* confused, hazy, indefinite, uncertain, unclear, unfocused, vague.

word *noun*
1 *What's the Spanish word for 'table'?* expression, term.
All the words we know are our *vocabulary*.

IN DICTIONARIES, WORDS ARE CLASSIFIED ACCORDING TO THE JOB THEY DO: adjective, adverb, conjunction, exclamation or interjection, noun, preposition, pronoun, verb.
A word or part of a word that has one separate sound when you say it is a *syllable*.
Syllables that you add to the beginning of a word to change its meaning are *prefixes*. ➡

Syllables that you add to the end of a word to change its meaning or function are *suffixes*.
The main part of a word to which endings like -ing or -ed can be added is the *stem*.

2 *You gave me your word.* assurance, guarantee, pledge, promise, vow.
3 *There has been no word from him for several weeks.* information, message, news.

word *verb*
She spent ages thinking how to word the letter. express, phrase, put into words.

wording *noun*
The wording of the question was not precise. choice of words, language, phrasing, style.

work *noun*
1 *Digging the garden involves a lot of hard work.* effort, exertion, labour, toil.
2 *He set the class some work.* an assignment, a chore, homework, housework, a job, a project, a task, an undertaking.
3 *What kind of work does he do?* business, employment, job, occupation, profession, trade, vocation.
FOR VARIOUS KINDS OF WORK, SEE **job**.

work *verb*
1 *He'd been working in the garden all morning.* be busy, exert yourself, make efforts, slave, toil.
2 *She works in the local department store.* be employed, earn your living, go to work, have a job.
3 *My watch isn't working.* be effective, function, go, operate.
4 *This video recorder is easy to work.* deal with, manage, operate, run, use.
to work something out *I can't work this problem out.* answer, calculate, explain, find the solution to, solve.

workable *adjective*
Her plan isn't workable. feasible, possible, practicable, practical, realistic.
AN OPPOSITE IS impracticable.

worker *noun*
> *Local government workers went on strike.* employee.
> All the workers in a business or factory are the **staff** or **workforce**.

> PEOPLE WHO DO VARIOUS TYPES OF WORK: businessman or businesswoman, craftsman, executive, labourer, manager, operative, operator, servant, skilled worker, tradesman, unskilled worker, workman.
> FOR WORKERS DOING SPECIFIC JOBS, SEE **job**.

workmanship *noun*
> *The car is a wonderful example of British workmanship.* art, competence, craft, craftsmanship, expertise, handicraft, handiwork, skill, technique.

world *noun*
> **1** *Scotland is a very beautiful part of the world.* earth, globe.
> **2** *Scientists are still not certain if there's life on other worlds.* planet.

worldly *adjective*
> *He had no interest in worldly success or power.* earthly, materialistic, mundane, physical.
> AN OPPOSITE IS spiritual.

worm *verb*
> *He wormed through the undergrowth.* crawl, creep, slither, squirm, wriggle, writhe.

worried *adjective*
> *He had a worried expression.* agitated, anxious, apprehensive, bewildered, bothered, concerned, distressed, disturbed, edgy, fearful, nervous, perplexed, puzzled, tense, troubled, uneasy, unhappy, upset.
> AN OPPOSITE IS relaxed.

worry *verb*
> **1** *There's no need to worry.* be anxious or worried, brood, fret.
> **2** *It worried her that he hadn't replied to her letter.* bewilder, disturb, mystify, perplex, puzzle, trouble, upset.
> **3** *Don't worry her now—she's busy.* annoy, [*informal*] badger, bother, harass, irritate, nag, pester, tease, torment, vex.

worry *noun*
> **1** *He's been a constant source of worry to her.* anxiety, distress, fear, tension, uneasiness, vexation.
> **2** *She has a lot of financial worries at the moment.* burden, care, concern, problem, trouble.

worsen *verb*
> **1** *Complaining may only worsen the situation.* aggravate, make worse.
> **2** *The patient's condition worsened during the night.* become worse, degenerate, deteriorate, get worse.
> AN OPPOSITE IS improve.

worship *verb*
> **1** *People go to church to worship God.* glorify, praise, pray to.

> VARIOUS PLACES WHERE PEOPLE WORSHIP: abbey, basilica, cathedral, chapel, church, meeting house, minster, mosque, oratory, pagoda, sanctuary, synagogue, tabernacle, temple.

> **2** *She adores her sons and they worship her.* adore, be devoted to, idolize, look up to, love, revere.

worship *noun*
> *The priests led the congregation.* adoration, devotion, glorification, praise, prayer.
> Your worship of God or gods is your **faith** or **religion**.
> The worship of idols is **idolatry**.

worth *noun*
> *This artist's paintings are of lasting worth.* importance, merit, quality, significance, value.
> **to be worth something** *How much is the ring worth?* be priced at, cost, have a value of.

worthless *adjective*
> *It's nothing but a worthless piece of junk.* [*informal*] trashy, unusable, useless, valueless.
> AN OPPOSITE IS valuable.

worthwhile *adjective*
> *It might be worthwhile to get a second opinion.* beneficial, helpful, important, profitable, useful, valuable.
> AN OPPOSITE IS useless.

worthy *adjective*
> They gave the money to a worthy cause.
> admirable, commendable, deserving,
> good, honest, praiseworthy,
> respectable, worthwhile.
> AN OPPOSITE IS unworthy.

wound *noun*
> Soldiers returned from the war with
> dreadful wounds. injury.

> KINDS OF WOUND: amputation, bite,
> bruise, burn, cut, fracture, gash,
> graze, laceration, scab, scald, scar,
> scratch, sore, sprain, sting, strain.

wound *verb*
> Seven people were seriously wounded in
> the attack. harm, hurt, injure.

> WAYS PEOPLE, THINGS, OR ANIMALS
> CAN WOUND YOU: bite, blow up,
> bruise, burn, claw, crush, cut,
> fracture bones, gash, gore, graze, hit,
> impale, knife, lacerate, maim,
> mangle, maul, mutilate, scald,
> scratch, shoot, sprain, stab, sting,
> strain, torture.

wrap *verb*
> **1** She wrapped the presents in shiny
> gold paper. bind up, cover, pack.
> To wrap water pipes, etc., is to
> **insulate** or **lag** them.
> **2** The mountain was wrapped in mist.
> cloak, conceal, envelop, hide, shroud,
> surround.

wreathe *verb*
> The altar was wreathed in flowers.
> adorn, decorate, encircle, festoon,
> surround.

wreck *verb*
> **1** His car was wrecked in the accident.
> break up, crumple, crush, demolish,
> destroy, shatter, smash, write off.
> **2** The injury wrecked his chances of a
> professional football career. ruin, spoil.

wreckage *noun*
> Investigators sifted through the
> wreckage of the aircraft. bits, debris,
> fragments, pieces, remains.
> The wreckage of a building is **rubble**
> or **ruins**.

wrench *verb*
> He wrenched the door open. force, jerk,
> prise, pull, strain, tug, twist, [*informal*]
> yank.

wrestle *verb*
> **1** He wrestled with the intruders.
> grapple, struggle, tussle.
> SEE ALSO **fight** *verb*.
> **2** I wrestled with my maths for hours.
> try to solve, worry over.

wretched *adjective*
> **1** She lay in bed with a migraine feeling
> absolutely wretched. dejected,
> depressed, miserable, pitiful,
> unfortunate, unhappy, woeful.
> **2** The wretched car won't start!
> annoying, exasperating, maddening,
> tiresome, useless.

wriggle *verb*
> The snake wriggled away. squirm,
> twist, worm, writhe, zigzag.

wring *verb*
> **1** He wrung the water out of his shirt.
> press, squeeze, twist.
> **2** He wrung her hand enthusiastically.
> clasp, grip, shake, wrench.
> **wringing wet** My towel is wringing
> wet. drenched, dripping, saturated,
> soaked, sopping.

wrinkle *noun*
> His face was covered in wrinkles.
> crease, crinkle, fold, furrow, line, ridge.
> A small hollow on someone's skin is a
> **dimple**.

wrinkle *verb*
> Someone will trip over if you wrinkle
> the rug. crease, crinkle, crumple, fold,
> make wrinkles in, pucker up.
> AN OPPOSITE IS smooth.

write *verb*
> **1** I'll write a shopping list. compile,
> compose, draw up, jot down, note,
> print, scrawl, scribble, set down, take
> down.
> To write letters to people is to
> **correspond** with them.
> To write a rough version of a story, etc.,
> is to **draft** it.

To write on a document or surface is to *inscribe* it.
2 *She decided at an early age that she wanted to write for a living.* be an author.

THINGS YOU WRITE WITH: ballpoint, chalk, crayon, felt tip, fountain pen, ink pen, pencil, typewriter, word processor.

THINGS YOU WRITE ON: blackboard or chalkboard, card, exercise book, form, jotter, notepaper, pad, paper, parchment, postcard, stationery, whiteboard, writing paper.

---

writer *noun*
A person who writes books is an *author*, *biographer*, or *novelist*.
A person who writes plays, films, etc., is a *dramatist*, *playwright*, or *scriptwriter*.
A person who writes for newspapers is a *correspondent*, *journalist*, or *reporter*.
A person who writes poetry is a *poet*.
A person who writes music is a *composer*.

writhe *verb*
He was writhing in agony. squirm, thrash about, twist, wriggle.

writing *noun*
1 *Can you read his writing?* handwriting.
Untidy writing is *scrawl* or *scribble*.
Neat writing is *copperplate*.
The art of beautiful handwriting is *calligraphy*.
2 *The writing on the stone was very faint.* inscription.
3 [*often plural*] *He introduced her to the writings of Charles Dickens.* literature, works.

KINDS OF LITERATURE: autobiography, biography, children's story, comedy, crime or detective story, diary, drama or play, essay, fable, fairy story or fairy tale, fantasy, fiction, film or TV script, folk tale, history, journalism, ➡

---

legend, letters or correspondence, lyrics, myth, newspaper article, non-fiction, novel, parody, philosophy, poetry or verse, prose, romance, satire, science fiction or SF, thriller, tragedy, travel writing.

---

wrong *adjective*
1 *It is wrong to steal.* corrupt, criminal, [*informal*] crooked, deceitful, dishonest, evil, illegal, immoral, irresponsible, naughty, sinful, unfair, unjust, unlawful, wicked.
2 *His calculations were wrong.* inaccurate, incorrect, mistaken, unacceptable.
3 *Did I say the wrong thing?* improper, inappropriate, unconventional, unsuitable.
4 *There's something wrong with the car.* defective, faulty, not working, out of order.
AN OPPOSITE IS right.

wrong *noun*
to do wrong *He has done wrong and must be punished.* behave badly, be naughty, break the law, misbehave, offend, sin.

wrong *verb*
He felt that he'd been wronged. harm, hurt, treat unfairly.

wry *adjective*
1 *He gave me a wry smile.* crooked, distorted, twisted.
2 *She has a wry sense of humour.* dry, ironic, mocking, sarcastic.

Xx

X-ray *noun*
Taking X-ray pictures is *radiography*.
Medical treatment using X-rays is *radiotherapy*.

yacht *noun*
FOR VARIOUS KINDS OF BOAT, SEE
vessel.

yard *noun*

> WORDS FOR PIECES OF GROUND
> BESIDE OR SURROUNDED BY
> BUILDINGS: cloister, court,
> courtyard, enclosure, farmyard,
> garden, parking space, patio,
> precinct, quadrangle or [*informal*]
> quad.

yearly *adjective*
The car is due for its yearly service.
annual.

yearn *verb*
to yearn for something *She yearned
for some peace and quiet!* [*informal*] be
dying for, desire, long for, pine for,
want, wish for.

yell *verb*
I yelled to attract her attention. bawl,
bellow, call out, cry out, shout.

yellow *adjective, noun*

> VARIOUS SHADES OF YELLOW:
> amber, chrome yellow, cream, gold,
> golden, lemon, orange, tawny.

yield *verb*
1 *The government refused to yield to the
hijackers' demands.* admit defeat, give
in, submit, surrender.
2 *Drivers must yield to vehicles on the
main road.* give way.
3 *The apple trees yielded a good crop of
fruit.* bear, grow, produce, supply.
4 *This savings account yields a high
interest.* earn, pay out, provide.

yield *noun*
1 *They got a good yield from the
orchard this year.* crop, harvest,
produce.
2 *Investors get an annual yield of 10%.*
earnings, income, interest, profit.

young *adjective*
1 *A lot of young people went to the
concert.* juvenile, youngish, youthful.
2 [*sometimes insulting*] *She's rather
young for her age.* babyish, childish,
immature, infantile.

> YOUNG PEOPLE: adolescent, baby,
> boy, child, girl, infant, juvenile,
> [*informal*] kid, lad, lass, teenager,
> toddler, youngster, youth.
>
> YOUNG ANIMALS:
> A young animal is a ***baby***.
> A young cow: ***calf***, ***heifer***.
> A young horse: ***colt***, ***foal***.
> A young fox, wolf, etc.: ***cub***.
> A young deer: ***fawn***.
> A young goat: ***kid***.
> A young cat: ***kitten***.
> A young sheep: ***lamb***.
> A young hare: ***leveret***.
> A young pig: ***piglet***.
> A young dog: ***pup*** or ***puppy***.
>
> YOUNG BIRDS:
> A young bird is a ***chick***, ***fledgling***,
> or ***nestling***.
> A young swan: ***cygnet***.
> A young duck: ***duckling***.
> A young goose: ***gosling***.
> A young farmyard hen: ***pullet***.
>
> YOUNG FISH:
> Young fish are ***fry***.
> A young eel: ***elver***.
> A young salmon: ***grilse***.
>
> YOUNG PLANTS:
> A young plant is a ***cutting*** or
> ***seedling***.
> A young tree: ***sapling***.

young *plural noun*
*The female bird feeds its young until
they are able to leave the nest.* children,
family, offspring, young ones.
A family of young birds is a ***brood***.
A family of young cats, dogs, etc., is a
litter.

youth *noun*
1 *In her youth, she had been a keen tennis player.* adolescence, childhood, teens.
2 *The fight had been started by a group of youths.*
When you use it like this, the noun *youth* usually refers to boys rather than girls adolescent, juvenile, [*informal*] kid, [*informal*] lad, teenager, young man, youngster.

youthful *adjective*
1 *It's a popular radio station with a big, youthful audience.* juvenile, young, youngish.
2 *She has a very youthful appearance.* fresh, lively, sprightly, vigorous, young-looking.

Zz

zany *adjective*
The audience laughed at his zany humour. absurd, crazy, daft, eccentric, funny, ludicrous, ridiculous, silly.

zealous *adjective*
The council was extremely zealous in enforcing the new regulations. conscientious, eager, enthusiastic, fervent, keen.
AN OPPOSITE IS apathetic.

zero *noun*
Four minus four makes zero. nothing, nought.
A score of zero in football is *nil*, in cricket it is a *duck*, in tennis it is *love*.

zest *noun*
She has a great zest for life. eagerness, enjoyment, enthusiasm.

zigzag *verb*
The road zigzags up the hill. bend, meander, twist, wind.
When a sailing boat zigzags to make use of the wind, it *tacks*.

zodiac *noun*

THE SIGNS OF THE ZODIAC:
Aquarius *the Water-Carrier*, Aries *the Ram*, Cancer *the Crab*, Capricorn *the Goat*, Gemini *the Twins*, Leo *the Lion*, Libra *the Scales*, Pisces *the Fish*, Sagittarius *the Archer*, Scorpio *the Scorpion*, Taurus *the Bull*, Virgo *the Virgin*.

zone *noun*
No one may enter the forbidden zone. area, district, locality, neighbourhood, region, sector, territory, vicinity.

zoo *noun*
Which is your favourite animal in the zoo? menagerie, safari park, zoological gardens.
FOR ANIMALS YOU MIGHT SEE IN A ZOO, SEE **animal**.

zoom *verb*
[*informal*] *Cars zoomed along the motorway.* dash, hurry, hurtle, race, rush, speed, tear, [*informal*] whiz, [*informal*] zip.

Notes

Notes

Notes

Notes

Notes

Notes

Notes

Notes

Notes

Notes

Notes

Notes

Notes